VIETNAM REMEMBERED

UGE · JOSEPH McCANTS Jr · RICHARD E MAY · LOWELL W MEYER · CHARLE
· DOUGLAS E LOHMEYER · JAMES B JOHNSON Sr · RONALD E PACE · GILBE
ER · DENNIS H RHEN · WILLIAM R SESSIONS · RICHARD E STAAB · VIRGIL
KENNETH E VAN HOY · DAVID W WILSON · RAYMOND C WOOD · WILLIA
A ARKOETTE · GREGORY G BECK · PAUL G BELLINO · MILTON J BUSH · LARF
ROBERT A BONEBRIGHT · STEVEN B CALHOUN · JAMES P CASEY · DAVID F
OFER · GREGORY D CORNETT · ROGER M COURVILLE · JAMES A COX · RALF
EN R CULPEPPER · THOMAS J DE MARINIS · JAMES A DIMOCK Jr · DOUGLA
NS · DAVID G FINNEGAN · JAMES R FIUME · JAMES O FOGLEMAN · ROBERT
ANUN · JOSE GARZA Jr · KITCHELL S GIBBS · DANIEL J GIORDANO III · PHILI
NEIL W HAYDEN · HAROLD C HEDDEN Jr · CARROLL F HERSEY · LEONARD N
OLMES · LEO J HUBER III · STEVEN R HUFFSTUTLER · RUSSELL L JETT · KENNE
N J LASKOWSKI · BIRDEN J LAWSON · THOMAS D LIPSCOMB · KENNETH E
NALD J MALICEK · CALVIN MEADOWS Jr · HANS L MILLS · MIGUEL ORTEGA
OVCHAN · GARY D McCRAY · BRIAN R McNEW · JOHN L NALLS · BOBBY GE
RED H PADDLEFORD · NORMAN P SINGER · RONNIE E PARKER · WILLIAM J
W PIGOTT · JORY J PITRE · EDMOND C POLENSKI · PATRICK L RICE · KERMIT
OLPH ROSSI · GARY J J SCHEULEN · JIMMY D SELLS · JOHN C PAPE · THOM
RIGGS Jr · DANA M SYKES · GEORGE E TACKETT · GARY R TROWER · GARRY L
M VOLLMERHAUSEN Jr · CARL J WANNER · JOSEPH J WILLIAMS · JOHN C W
AN · RICHARD CARBONE · JAMES C COCKERL · W K UTAH CREASON · WILI
HRISTOPHER C DONAHUE · WILEY B EARLEY · JOEL W FORRESTER · DAVID
NG Jr · BILLY RAY HEAD · THOMAS M HOFFMANN · JEREMIAH JUNE · DONA
OTHY K LE CLAIR · THOMAS C TREIBLE · EDDIE MONTGOMERY Jr · KENNET
ONALD F SCORSONE · DONALD A TURSO · ROBERT A THOMPSON · RANE
ON Jr · WILLIAM E WHALEY III · THOMAS F BARTH · DANIEL S BEHAR · SAMU
KS · ROBERT W BUCKLEY · JOE T CONKLE · LARRY F DODDS · DONOVAN R
· RAEFORD J GERALD Jr · ROY W GRAHAM · BENJAMIN W HAIRE · ANTHON
RUCE I LUTTRELL · WILLIAM L MARCY · TOMMY DEE WRIGHT · ROBERT J Mc
IMOTHY F ROBSON · JAMES B SHELBY · RAYMOND M SHINELDECKER · DAI
E · JON RAY SUMMERS · JOHN S TAYLOR · PASQUALE TORRE · DOUGLAS D
UADALUPE ESPARZA MONTOYA · HARRY D ASHCRAFT · JIMMIE V BOCK ·
ARK · ROBERT L COOPER · PATRICK R DIEHL · MICHAEL K L DIXON · CAREY
K W DWYER · CLYDE S EVANS · LOUIS E FENCEROY · GENE T GIETZEN · PET
ES R HASH · KENNETH D PETTIGREW · MARK J HAVERLAND Jr · CHARLES E F
THOMAS P JACKSON Jr · ALBERT JOHNSON Jr · JERRY J KOCANDA III · JOHN
IN · ENRIQUE MARTINEZ · ROY G MATTHEWS · PHILIP J MODDERMAN · LE
RLES H PEARCE Jr · MICHAEL M HATZELL · EDISON R PHILLIPS · THOMAS A
R PTACEK · JAMES T RALPH · KEITH N STARNES Jr · JOHN W RICHARD · PET
AMES S SCARMEAS Jr · LYNN D SHUGART · CLARENCE SIZEMORE · WILLIA

VIETNAM REMEMBERED

Editor
Gregory Pemberton

NEW HOLLAND

CONTENTS

Introduction 7

Australia's Road to Vietnam 13
1945–1965

Gregory Pemberton

Into Battle 45
Counter-Revolution

Greg Lockhart

Conscription and Dissent 69
The Genesis of Anti-War Protest

Ann Mari Jordens

Conflict and Withdrawal 93
1968–1972

Frank Frost

The War the Media Lost 121
Australian News Coverage
of Vietnam

Rodney Tiffen

Mobilising Dissent 151
The Later Stages of Protest

Ann Curthoys

At War At Home 177
Australian Attitudes
during the Vietnam Years

Peter Cochrane

Australia's Legacy 199
The Vietnam Veterans

Jane Ross

After the War Was Over 231
Vietnamese in Australia

Nancy Viviani

Conclusion 250

Notes 254

Roll of Honour 264

Those who Served 266

Acknowledgements 318

The Authors 319

INTRODUCTION

Few living Australians have been untouched by the Vietnam war and the conflict it represented, at home and abroad. This may seem like an odd statement, since proportionately very few – around 50 000 – Australians saw military service in Vietnam; far fewer visited there with a peaceful purpose. Even today, Australian travellers to Vietnam are rare. Few Vietnamese had been to Australia before 1975; just over 300 (mainly students) lived here.

Yet, Australia's involvement in Vietnam has come to be defined in a very wide sense: as a symbol for Australia's role in the period of Asian decolonisation. It also has come to be intimately associated in the public mind with many wider issues of that era: long hair, public protest, the explosion of rock music, drug use, distrust of authority, counter-cultures, sexual freedom, and numerous other aspects of our society, many persisting today long after the war has ended. Indeed, such developments were directly related to the war. Both our military involvement in Vietnam, and the resulting dissent, were the products of far more profound international and domestic processes, already at work long before the first Australian soldiers were involved.

In this book, for the first time, all aspects of Australia's Vietnam conflict, abroad and at home, are covered. Although a supposedly 'limited war' in a military and political sense, Australia's involvement in Vietnam and its aftermath touched all aspects of Australian society. Until now no book has attempted this ambitious task, because the basic groundwork of scholarship of the many and varied aspects of the complex story of Australia's Vietnam were still to be completed. This book is one of the results of that work.

Truth, it is often said, is the first casualty of war. The Vietnam war was no exception. Indeed, it has become a byword for official deceit and manipulation of information, providing us with the now-famous euphemism – the 'credibility gap'. Over the last five years or so, the authors in this book have led their respective fields of study, penetrating the fog of official deception and popular mythology to establish really what the Vietnam conflict, both at home and abroad, was about for Australia. Here, they draw upon their previous publications, plus more recently available information, to present the first comprehensive history of Australia's Vietnam. Special acknowledgement should be made to Professor Ken Maddock of Macquarie University, who drafted the detailed outline on which this book is based.

The book opens with 'Australia's Road to Vietnam', an examination of the interplay between international events, developments in Vietnam, and the Australian policies which combined to involve Australia in the Vietnam war. The story of the diplomatic and strategic policies which led Australia into Vietnam have been covered in detail in *All the Way: Australia's Road to Vietnam* (1987). This book was based on my doctoral thesis at Sydney University, completed after six years of Army service following my graduation from the Royal Military College, Duntroon, in 1976. The above work was essentially a study of Australian and American foreign policies. During my subsequent employment, research and writing on the strategic and diplomatic aspects of the official history of Australia's involvement in the Southeast Asian conflicts, I developed an appreciation of the vital need to weave the story of events in Vietnam itself, so often neglected, into this story of Western foreign policy. For the first time, I have done so here.

'Into Battle' examines the initial commitment of Australian troops to Vietnam, as training, and later as combat, personnel. Dr Greg Lockhart brings a unique background to the writing of this chapter. After graduation from the Royal Military College, Duntroon, in 1968, he served as an officer in the elite Army

Training Team in Vietnam during the closing stages of the war. He is fluent in Vietnamese and his doctoral thesis, published in 1989 as *Nation in Arms*, was about the Peoples' Army of Vietnam (PAVN), based on Vietnamese sources. The leading authority on the 'enemy' in Vietnam, Greg Lockhart was able to translate recent Vietnamese official histories on the war in Phước Tuy province; important selections from these works are published for the first time in English in his and Frank Frost's chapters. Greg Lockhart shows that after the Second World War. Australia developed its first professional army. Although small in size, it honed an expertise in jungle warfare tactics learnt during battles with the Japanese in the Pacific War and married it with a doctrine of counter-revolutionary warfare. After 1945, this force was committed along with its British and American allies to combat revolutionary Asian nationalism in Malaya, Borneo and Vietnam. In Vietnam, the Malayan and Borneo success could not be repeated. There, Australia was committed to opposing a revolutionary movement which had the support of the great majority of Vietnamese, and so the political conditions necessary for success in counter-revolutionary warfare were not present. Moreover, the Australians were inadequately prepared to fight simultaneously both village-based guerrillas and the well-armed conventional forces of the PAVN.

In the third essay, 'Conscription and Dissent', Ms Ann Mari Jordens examines the early opposition to Australia's involvement in Vietnam, as well as the supporters of the commitment. During the war she was representative of that large slice of the Australian population which had no clear stance on the conflict. She has previously published articles on anti-war movements in Australia, particularly the liberal middle-class and religious elements in these movements. From 1983, she researched and wrote on the 'home front' volumes of the official history of Australia's involvement in the Southeast Asian conflicts, including Vietnam, until the official decision in 1988 not to proceed with separate 'home front' volumes. Here, she corrects the popular myth that the early anti-war movement mainly comprised long-haired students bedecked in beads and flowers, and refutes the then government's claim that the movement was controlled by communists. Instead, she shows that the early anti-war movement was a loose coalition which included communists but was dominated by middle-aged, middle-class moderates; liberals rather than leftists; the Second World War generation rather than the 'baby-boomers'. She concedes that until the Tet Offensive, in which official optimism over the war was shattered, the anti-war movement was limited in its influence on the wider Australian community. She also provides the first detailed examination of the system of conscription. Unlike the American experience, the system here was socially equitable wherever it was under the control of bureaucrats. Only when lay persons were involved, such as magistrates and doctors, did inequities emerge, leading to criticism of the system. She shows that the majority of Australians consistently approved of conscription for home defence but not for overseas service, including Vietnam.

In the fourth essay, 'Conflict and Withdrawal', Dr Frank Frost outlines the experience of the Australian combat forces in the war during and after the crucial Tet Offensive of early 1968.

Frank Frost was present at the battlefront – in Phước Tuy province in Vietnam – during the war. As a young doctoral student he conducted his academic fieldwork at the front in Vietnam in early 1971 and 1972, not just in archives or libraries. He interviewed many Australian, American and Vietnamese commanders and soldiers, leading to the publication of his highly acclaimed *Australia's War in Vietnam* in 1987, accepted as the authoritative and comprehensive account of Australia's combat experience in that war.

In this essay, Frank Frost draws from material made available since the publication of that work, to develop further the arguments in his book. In particular, he examines the severe problems Australian forces faced. Ill-prepared by their government to meet these problems, the Australians nevertheless performed capably, although their limited impact on the overall campaign held no chance of affecting the final outcome. He adds to this a detailed outline of the war as the 'other' side fought it, enhanced by translations of Vietnamese sources provided by Greg Lockhart. He also takes care to place the Australian operations within the framework of the conduct of the war by the American-led allies.

In the fifth essay, Dr Rodney Tiffen, who has taught for many years on the media and politics in Australia and already published on the media and Vietnam, examines the controversial question of 'the War the Media Lost'. True, the media, particularly the American media, enjoyed greater political independence and logistical effectiveness than in any previous war, but he rejects the widely cited assertions that the media were critical and 'betrayed' the war for the Western allies by allegedly publishing false, biased or distorted accounts; or that the vividness and power of the coverage of the first 'television war' undermined popular support for it. These hypotheses, certainly not true even for America, are 'ludicrous' suggestions with respect to Australia. Rod Tiffen shows that the media played a much less significant role in Australia than has been assumed by those who rely too heavily on the American experience. Television coverage was limited in Australia and the media coverage in general was far less sophisticated. The commercial media had no permanent correspondents in Asia, let alone Vietnam. The ABC, the mainstay of the Australian media in Southeast Asia and Vietnam, did not enjoy the political independence that it does today. Finally, since Australia was a junior ally in the war, its media, like the government, did not concern themselves with the broader questions and doubts over involvement, because such matters were left to the United States. The war the media lost, then, was that of critically evaluating official statements and policies.

In the sixth essay, 'Mobilising Dissent', Dr Ann Curthoys, Professor of Social History at the New South Wales University of Technology, presents the story of the anti-war movement particularly after the Tet Offensive. Like Greg Lockhart, she was an active participant in the conflict, but at home and on the anti-war side. The daughter of communist parents, she was one of the first participants in early anti-war demonstrations from the age of 19. She has published widely on post-1945 Australian history, co-editing two collections of articles on the Cold War in history and the *Australians Since 1939* (1987) volume of the Australians and Historical Library series. Here she traces the emergence of a large radical student movement and the competition between groups, notably the ALP, the communists, more left-wing groups and even the students themselves, for leadership of this movement. She shows that following Labor's defeat in 1966, this part of the anti-war movement became more radicalised, openly supporting the 'enemy'. Wider support, however, was not won until the Tet Offensive convinced many Australians, like many Americans, of the futility if not the immorality of the war. By 1969, polls were showing a majority in favour of returning the troops, which was in fact done once the Americans decided to withdraw from the conflict. The influence of the anti-war movements on these decisions remains problematical.

The seventh essay, 'At War at Home', situates the anti-war movement in the broader protest and reform impulse of the period. Dr Peter Cochrane has published and taught on many fronts of Australian history. He was enthusiastically involved in campus and Moratorium politics in Melbourne, in the latter stages of the Vietnam war. His chapter pays particular attention to the flow on from the 'permissive consumerism' of post-war capitalism into dissatisfaction and protest, to the role of the new middle class in reform and anti-war politics, and to the phenomenon we now call 'youth culture'. Some of the generational tensions of the period are examined. So are the effects of the war on the gender order, notably the assault on traditional standards of masculinity. As Cochrane puts it: 'the Vietnam war would seriously discredit the style of aggressive masculinity that had been kept alive (and culturally dominant) by a succession of "just wars", and the Cold War, for decades.' The chapter illustrates how the politics and style of the protest movement fused with other currents, particularly within youth culture, to break up the strict standards of masculine conformity which had prevailed. The soldier's fall from grace, the demise of his once pre-eminent standing in Australian culture is considered at length. The chapter concludes with a Postscript on the legacy of the 'sixties'.

In the eighth essay, Dr Jane Ross takes the story beyond the war years to look at one of the most controversial legacies of the war – Australia's Vietnam veterans. As a doctoral student Jane Ross, like Frank Frost, visited Vietnam in early 1971, interviewing a number of national servicemen as research for several articles she subsequently published. Author of the well-respected *The Myth of the Digger* (1985), in which she analysed the nature and origins of that myth, Jane is currently researching oral history of the Vietnam veteran. In this essay, she stresses the extent to which Australian perceptions of the Vietnam veteran and, to a degree, their perception of themselves, have been shaped by the portrayal, not always accurate even there, of the Vietnam veteran in America. She records the fact that many Australian infantrymen and other troops participated in 'Welcome Home' marches, and that not all experienced the traumatic and alienating return from Vietnam so often portrayed. She assesses the image of the typical veteran as a disturbed, alienated and potentially dangerous loner in civilian society, and its relationship to Australian conditions. On the much debated question of Agent Orange. Jane carefully examines the Royal Commission's finding that there is insufficient evidence to support the claim that Vietnam veterans suffer from disabilities, physical or mental, above that of the civilian community, or that there is a link between exposure to Agent Orange and such disabilities. She records the claims of the Vietnam Veterans Association (VVA), their differences with the RSL, and their active promotion of their image of the Australian veteran. She notes also that what the veterans seek is reintegration into the ANZAC tradition.

In the ninth essay, 'After the War was Over', Dr Nancy Viviani complements this with a study of the other major Vietnam legacy in Australia – Vietnamese migration. Professor of Political Science at the Australian National University, with many years' experience teaching and writing on Australian foreign policy and Asian politics, Nancy Viviani published in 1984 the authoritative study of Vietnamese migration and settlement in Australia, entitled *The Long Journey*. In this essay she outlines the identity of the Vietnamese who came to Australia after 1975 and where and how they live here. They are a relatively small ethnic minority in this country, but their arrival has nonetheless provoked emotive responses. She argues that their presence has been, and will continue to be, a litmus test of Australia's commitment to a non-discriminatory society. In other words, although the formal superstructure of the White Australia policy was swept away in the maelstrom largely generated by the Vietnam war, Australia's response to the Vietnamese will expose whether the attitudinal foundations of that racially supremacist policy survive.

Finally, the conclusion places 'Vietnam' in the context of Australia's historical experience, drawing several conclusions about its significance for today's Australia. The Vietnam war, it is argued, represents one of the most significant events in Australian history, helping to change Australian society in a number of fundamental ways.

This book, then, tells the story of the Vietnam war – a story which is as complete as years of investigation, scholarly work and first-hand examination can make it. Deeply involved in the subject in their daily life, each of the authors also has a commitment to this particular publication – the first to attempt a full picture of what the Vietnam conflict meant to Australians at the time, and of its wide-ranging significance throughout past and present Australian society.

It provides not an abstract view of our history, but a look into the lives of those involved in the conflict, at home and abroad. Appropriately, it ends with a Roll of Honour of those who died as a result of the war in Vietnam, and with the lists, published here for the first time together and in full, of those who served in Vietnam. This is a valuable record of tens of thousands of Australians who experienced most drastically the consequences of those foreign policies which were then so hotly debated at home.

Note: Abbreviations used in the text are listed on page 263.

AUSTRALIA'S ROAD TO VIETNAM
1945–1965

Gregory Pemberton

> The United States of America is on our side. It is on the side of democracy, decency and right, and the forces of darkness opposed to it are very apparent and very powerful. The world may have a show-down at any time between our form of life and the forces of darkness.
> – R.G. Casey, 8 April 1954.

> It is therefore foolish, superficial, and dangerous to speak of the conflict in the world as a contest between two economic systems, capitalism and communism. Nor can the cynics dispose of it as an old-fashioned struggle for military or physical power, with territory and resources as the prizes of victory. It is desperately important that the world should see this as a moral contest, a battle for the spirit of man. There can be no easy or enduring compromise between peoples who affirm the existence of a divine authority and the compulsion of a spiritual law and those others who see nothing beyond an atheistic materialism.
> – R.G. Menzies, in Parliament, August 1954.

EAST WIND PREVAILS OVER WEST WIND

Vietnamese independence, defended tenaciously for centuries principally against China, ended in 1883 with full French colonisation, which ended unity by dividing Vietnam into Cochinchina (south), Annam (central), Tonkin (north). Traditional Vietnamese society, notably the monarchy and Mandarin class, was discredited. Underground political parties, influenced by modern European ideas, then emerged. The strongest was the Communist party, led eventually by Hồ Chí Minh. Later, some claimed that Hồ and his supporters were communists and thus not 'nationalists'. This was false. They were an integral part of revolutionary Vietnamese nationalism. In 1941 Japan shattered the European hold in Asia, including Vietnam. Hồ merged his Communist Party (renamed Vietnamese Workers Party [VWP] in 1951) into a broad coalition – the Việt Minh. They assumed power with Japan's surrender in August 1945, and Emperor Bảo Đại abdicated. Before 500 000 people in Hanoi, Hồ, as President, proclaimed the independence and unity of the Democratic Republic of Vietnam (DRV). With British help, however, the French seized power in the south, and after failing to divide Vietnam again into several regions, they provoked war with the DRV in December 1946. Next, they re-installed Bảo Đại over a central government.

Australia's Labor government, like America, supported Indonesian independence but said little initially on Vietnam. In February 1950, Britain and America led most Western powers, including the newly-elected Liberal government, in recognising Bảo Đại's government. Socialist countries recognised the DRV. By 1954, America had given $US1.1 billion to France's military campaign; over ten times what the DRV got from Peking and Moscow. From 1953, Australia gave small amounts of military and

Here, in June 1969, an Australian soldier blazes away with his M-60 machine-gun at an invisible enemy.

economic aid. France's military failure culminated in the surrender at Điện Biên Phủ in May 1954, the Western powers opposing America's call for intervention. On 21 July, at Geneva, the powers divided Vietnam temporarily along the seventeenth parallel; the DRV to the north, France-Bảo Đại the south. They clearly agreed on elections for reunification in July 1956. The Western powers, expecting Hồ to win, secretly resolved on maintaining partition permanently through the SEATO alliance.

The central feature of post-1945 history was the struggle between the forces of Western imperialism against anti-colonial nationalism. Neither were monolithic. The latter invariably comprised a wide spectrum of political forces, of which communist parties were an integral, often leading, part. Sometimes these forces were allied; sometimes they fought themselves, some even allying with European colonialism or its American replacement for control of their country. The fundamental political divide in the world was not between communists and non-communists as the rhetoric of Menzies and many others claimed it to be in order to exploit the demonic reputation of communism in the West and thus divide the anti-colonial movements.

In June 1954, the French paper *Le Figaro* observed with the sober and perceptive insight of the vanquished, that 'What is to be decided at Geneva, is not only the position of France in Indochina, nor the condemned fate of colonialism' it was, rather, whether the West would continue to hold its pre-eminent position east of Suez. Điện Biên Phủ and Geneva together, 'could well be a turning point of history, reversing a hegemony of almost five centuries' (some compared Điện Biên Phủ to the fall of Constantinople to the Turks in 1453). Indeed, in the following years. European imperialism appeared to be rolling back on all fronts in the face of the apparently irresistible wave of nationalism. Sometimes, nationalist movements were led by traditional rulers; but, often, these too were swept away by revolution as colonial collaborators and upholders of feudal rule.

From July 1954, Britain's plan to keep Cyprus as a Middle Eastern base, given the impending loss of Suez, was challenged by Greek Cypriots seeking unity with Greece. By March 1956, Britain was executing nationalists and exiling their leader, Archbishop Makarios. Following an agreement in February 1959, he returned as President in August 1960, Cyprus gaining independence after 82 years of British rule. In October 1954, 72 years of British occupation of the Suez Canal Zone was ended by a pact with Egypt. In March 1956, King Hussein of Jordan dismissed the British commander (since 1939) of the British-subsidised Arab legion for defying a royal decree to prepare the country's defence against Israel. Exactly one year later, the Anglo-Jordanian Treaty of 1948 was terminated, severing economic and military ties. Hussein, however, recalled British troops in July 1958 to protect him against republican nationalists following the overthrow of the pro-Western Iraqi monarch by similar elements. Similarly, the ruling sheikh of oil-rich Kuwait recalled British troops in view of Iraqi threats of annexation following the end of Britain's 62-year-old protectorate in June 1961. Nigeria gained independence from Britain in October 1960; Jamaica in August, Uganda in October and Tanganyika in December, 1962; and, Kenya in December 1963.

VIETNAM: AN ASIAN BATTLEFIELD

Although it included several significant ethnic minorities, Vietnam was dominated by the culturally homogeneous Vietnamese, who had long expressed a strong sense of national unity. The partition of the country in 1954 laid the basis for the subsequent conflict.

Australia's decision, in the late 1950s, to pursue closer cooperation with the United States in Southeast Asia, was to have a number of direct military results, one of them being Australia's eventual entry into the war in Vietnam. Here, in an inauguration parade to welcome the Australian Army Training Team, the Australian and US flags are unfurled together on Vietnamese soil.

Britain enjoyed mixed results in determining the final form of independence where it wanted to retain some control. In its oldest overseas colony, Ireland, the activities of Irish nationalists reminded the world that not all colonies would be surrendered willingly. In Malaya, the emergency ended in August 1960 with the British-backed rulers firmly in control, having gained formal independence in 1957. With independence in Singapore in 1959, Britain was less successful initially, with the mistakenly feared Lee Kwan Yew being elected Prime Minister against British wishes. In South Africa, the Afrikaans element, which politically had eclipsed the British element just after the war, took the new Republic out of the Commonwealth in May 1961.

France's experience was worse: they had learnt nothing from their Indochina nightmare. Uprisings in Algeria in November 1954 signalled the start of a bitter eight-year war against the National Liberation Front. Algeria finally gained independence in July 1962 only after France itself was brought to the brink of civil war. In August 1955, following anti-colonial violence in Morocco, France entered negotiations which led to the abdication of the pro-French sultan in October: France's 44-year-old protectorate ended in March 1956, the same month as its 75-year-old protectorate over Tunisia ended. French military bases remained in Morocco until a series of bloody clashes led to France's complete withdrawal in September

Hồ Chí Minh

THE 'MAN AS PURE AS LUCIFER'

The icy beams of the crystal moon struck in flashes through the window of our compartment, and amidst these flashes and dancing lights our train pushed on, drawing ever nearer to Moscow.

The Chinese intellectual Qu Quibai, 1921.

The most famous Vietnamese nationalist, who eventually took the name Hồ Chí Minh (the 'bringer of enlightenment'), was born in 1890 of scholar-gentry parents in Annam. He left Vietnam in 1911 as a stoker on a French freighter. For a time he worked as a chef in the Carlton Hotel in London and in a photographer's studio in Paris.

In 1919, he hired a bowler hat and suit, and sought admission to the Paris Peace Conference at Versailles, to petition the great powers to grant his country's independence. Unsurprisingly, he was refused admission: not for the last time liberal internationalism had failed him. Soon after, on reading Lenin's powerful critique of imperialism, Hồ cried out, 'Dear martyrs, compatriots! This is what we need, this is the path to our liberation!' Lenin had promised electricity to the Russian people; for Hồ, the Bolshevik Revolution illuminated, for the Vietnamese people, the path leading out of the darkness of colonialism.

A founding member of the French Communist Party in 1920, he next studied at the University of the Toilers of the East in Moscow, and published articles in France on Western imperialism, before travelling on Comintern duties to China and Siam where communist parties were being established and helping to found the Vietnamese Revolutionary Youth League among exiled Vietnamese students in southern China.

Hồ later became for the Vietnamese people the most highly regarded nationalist; far more than the ex-emperor. Graham Greene, on meeting 'the man as pure as Lucifer' in 1955, wrote:

Dressed in khaki drill, Hồ Chí Minh gave an impression of simplicity and candour, but overwhelmingly of leadership. There was nothing evasive about him: this was a man who gave orders and expected obedience and also love. The kind, remorseless face had no fanaticism about it. A man is a fanatic about a mystery – tablets of stone, a voice from a burning bush – but this was a man who had patiently solved an equation.

1961. Subsequent French criticism of America's Indochina policy was inspired by rivalry, not a progressive change of heart on colonialism.

The smaller European powers underwent similar experiences. The Indonesians took their claim to Dutch New Guinea to the UN three times in the mid-1950s. Frustrated by failure there, they expelled Dutch nationals and appropriated Dutch assets in 1957–58. In December 1961, inspired by India's seizure of the 400-year-old Portuguese possessions of Goa, Damao and Diu. Sukarno announced that Indonesia would 'reclaim' Dutch New Guinea by the end of 1962. Indonesia also harboured ambitions towards Portuguese Timor. The Belgian Congo became an independent republic in June 1960, its President expressing goodwill towards Belgium but Prime Minister Lumumba launching a fierce attack on colonialism. In July, British, French and Belgian financial interests conspired to have the mineral-rich province of Katanga secede and appeal for Belgian military aid. Lumumba appealed to the United Nations but was then deposed by a military coup and later murdered, allegedly at American instigation.

The Europeans certainly did not surrender their empires without a fight. In July 1956, Egypt's President Nasser nationalised the Suez Canal Company to finance construction of the Aswan dam following the withdrawal of Western financial backing. While Washington tried to negotiate a settlement, Britain and France moved forces into the area and conspired with Israel, Europe's last 'colony', to attack Egypt, giving them a pretext with which to intervene to 'protect' the canal. When Egypt refused to yield to an outrageous ultimatum, they began bombing; in November, they invaded. These actions were condemned jointly by the Soviet Union, America and virtually the whole UN; only Australia and New Zealand supported this aggression.

Suez was one of the last major attempts by the European powers to hold their empires by force. After their dismal failure, albeit political not military, these powers focussed more on European integration to make themselves competitive with the superpowers having lost their empires; consequently, the Treaty of Rome in 1957 formed the European Economic Community (EEC). Britain did not join immediately but Harold MacMillan and younger Tories took over the Conservative Party and directed it away from the policies of traditional imperialists like Churchill and Eden. The new defence policy announced in April 1957 confirmed the retreat from empire; colonial garrisons would be withdrawn, conventional forces reduced and greater reliance placed on nuclear deterrence.

This shift in British policy held profound implications for Australia, notwithstanding the tremendous reception given Queen Elizabeth in Australia in February 1954 when she unveiled the National Memorial to America. This could not mask the decline in economic, political and military links with Britain as its global power contracted. Accordingly, Australia's focus in all these areas was shifting from Western Europe-Middle East towards the Asian-Pacific region. Canberra announced a new defence policy in March 1957 providing for closer cooperation with America in Southeast Asia. Menzies told parliament, 'though this is a wholeheartedly British nation this is not a heresy. It merely recognises the facts of war.' In May, the biggest US naval fleet since the second world war visited Australia for Coral Sea Week.

Fortunately, American interest in Australia was growing at this time both in terms of economic value, as a 'suitable piece of real estate' for defence and space facilities, and as an ally in Southeast Asia. Under the cautious, relatively introspective Eisenhower administration, however, Australia could not forge links with Washington as closely as it desired. This required a more active American presence in Southeast Asia, something Eisenhower resisted. Casey thought of offering military bases, greater economic opportunities

Australian soldiers from an Assault Platoon with 7 RAR, during a 1967 operation in Vietnam.

Troops of 7th Battalion, The Royal Australian Regiment, prepare to board an American Iroquois helicopter near the Vietnamese village of Phước Hai during Operation Ulmarrah in 1967.

The Vietnam war would expose soldiers to jungle warfare, in which the Army was fully trained and experienced. To many observers at home, however, seeing the 'digger' in such conditions would be unexpected and disturbing.

and even chairs of American studies at Australian universities: but all to little avail. He was repeatedly frustrated in his attempts to realise meaningful joint planning in ANZUS and SEATO. The problem would only be resolved when the Americans pursued a more active policy in Southeast Asia.

The competition from an integrated Europe was one spur to a more active American policy: the signs of apparent success of the other blocs, socialist and non-aligned, inhibiting American hegemony, was another. In April 1955, 29 Afro-Asian nations met at Bandung, Indonesia, and called for an end to colonialism, for self-determination and UN membership for all; NATO was condemned as a protector of colonialism. In November 1956, the admission of three Arab nations to the UN gave the Afro-Asian bloc the numbers to veto a General Assembly resolution if they voted with the socialist bloc, ending the period of assured Western dominance. In December 1957 in Cairo, 40 Afro-Asian states attacked Western imperialism and the Eisenhower doctrine, while supporting the Soviet Union's call for peaceful co-existence. Among these powers regional political, economic and military blocs were emerging: the United Arab Republic (UAR) forming in February 1958; the UAR itself joining with Morocco, Ghana and Mali in January 1961; and Morocco, Algeria and Tunisia moving in April 1958 to form a North African federation. In May 1963, 30 African states at Addis Ababa formed the Organisation for African Unity. Divisions and rivalries soon fractured the non-aligned group but the foregoing trend was a source of anxiety in Washington.

The Soviet Union rode the crest of the anti-colonial surge. True, it had problems within its own sphere of interest: Polish workers rioted in June 1956, the biggest such disturbance since Berlin 1953. Polish leaders next defied Moscow by establishing a more independent government. Also in June 1956, a nation-wide revolt erupted in Hungary; Soviet troops, at first withdrawn, crushed the revolt and installed a more pliant government. In 1959, a major rift opened in Sino-Soviet relations. Yet, none of this fatally dimmed Soviet prestige in the third world and elsewhere which had been steadily improving since Stalin's death in March 1953 and Nikita Krushchev's consolidation of power in September. Relations with Yugoslavia were improved from May 1955 and the Warsaw Pact consolidated Soviet hegemony in Eastern Europe. Progress at the Big Four's Geneva meeting in July seemed to confirm the sincerity of 'peaceful co-existence' as did Krushchev's denunciation of Stalin in February 1956.

The third world nations responded to Soviet policies. At the Afro-Asian conference in Cairo, there was clear support for Moscow; Afghanistan, Egypt and Indonesia accepted Soviet aid; Iraq left the West's Middle East alliance. Even in the field of technology, hitherto an unchallenged American preserve, Moscow seemed a step ahead: its first inter-continental ballistic missile was launched in August 1957, its Sputnik in October; five and three months respectively ahead of the United States. China also improved the socialist bloc's image at Bandung by calling on Washington to discuss the Formosa issue. Although criticised for its suppression of Tibetan independence in 1959 and harshly blamed for its border clash with India in 1962, China was gaining wider international acceptance; the International Olympic Committee (IOC) withdrew Formosa's membership in 1959 and offered China its place.

America retaliated to the IOC's decision by withdrawing funds for the winter games; a defensive reaction typical of this period. America received orchestrated praise from the Commonwealth nations for its aid to the Colombo Plan; a ploy to counter Bandung. In January 1956, it promised to compete with the Soviet Union in giving aid to the third world; joining Britain the next month to warn countries against accepting Soviet aid. It persuaded Iran but this was an isolated success. Eisenhower promised to lift living standards in Latin America but when Fidel Castro's revolution began to do this, initial American favour turned sour once he accepted Soviet aid. Vice-President Nixon cut short his Central American tour in 1958 in the face of anti-American protests. Eisenhower had to do the same following leftist riots in Japan. Accordingly, more emphasis was placed on military assistance to resist revolution. Declarations were issued pledging the defence of Formosa and Lebanon against 'communist aggression'. So, by the end of the Eisenhower years, America needed a new initiative to recapture global leadership; it came with Kennedy's vision of the 'New Frontier'.

In the 1950s, in the light of its slackening industrial performance after the heady days of the Marshall Plan, the United States adopted a basically defensive posture. Anti-communist rhetoric retained its vitriol but apart from relatively minor interventions, using the CIA to overthrow unacceptable governments in Guatemala, Iran and Laos, and less successfully in northern Vietnam, Indonesia and China, military confrontation with the forces of revolution abroad was avoided. 'Strategically, it was a defensive age even if the tactics were often aggressive.' This posture did not outlast the decade. The slow economic growth and unimaginative policies of the later Eisenhower years were being challenged by acute social tensions, particularly the emerging civil rights movement in the South, which were coming to the surface and could no longer be ignored. 'Golf had long symbolised the Eisenhower years – played by soft, boring men with ample waistlines who went around rich men's country clubs in the company of wealthy businessmen and

The helicopter, a familiar symbol of the war, was to revolutionise counter-guerilla tactics by allowing the easy insertion and extraction of patrols deep in the jungle. Here, a helicopter of 9 Squadron, RAAF, returns an ARVN patrol to its base.

were tended by white-haired dutiful Negroes.' It is not surprising that today the United States hearkens back to the Eisenhower years as the great era of the American dream: a just, harmonious and prosperous time, which for many never existed.

Amongst those American liberals who had survived the McCarthy era with their ideals intact, there were still aspirations of realising that dream. They got their chance with the election of John Kennedy as President. Although originally a supporter of McCarthy, Kennedy built up strong liberal credentials prior to his election especially on civil rights, labour laws and social welfare. Internationalists could look to a Kennedy administration pursuing an offensive liberal program abroad against revolution. For in January 1961, Krushchev seemed to challenge the United States by promising to support liberation struggles. Earlier, in 1957, Walt Whitman Rostow, soon to be a key Kennedy adviser, had co-authored an influential report which concluded that: 'the United States is now within sight of solutions to the range of issues which have dominated political life since 1865.' In 'a chauvinist tone heralding the future excesses of the new leadership', Rostow urged American leaders to adopt a more activist international posture, because with so many accomplishments at home, 'we run the danger of becoming a bore to ourselves and the world'.

> Rostow himself was to play a crucial role in averting this danger. 'A classic example of the militarized liberal', Rostow was to become prominent among those 'New Mandarins' criticized by Noam Chomsky, whose 'high mood of confidence and self-righteousness' and keen sense of control over events' would lead the United States into the Vietnam War and keep it there until it came out on its knees.

Sustained by a half decade of exceptionally high domestic growth, the United States would undertake far more military action abroad between 1960 and 1965 than at any time since the end of the second world war.

An Australian soldier fumigates buildings in a village.

The Kennedy liberal offensive at times crossed, rather than complemented, European interests. Anxious to maintain good relations with Sukarno in Indonesia where American interests were extensive, Kennedy sacrificed the last vestige of the Netherlands' colonial empire, western New Guinea – which an ebullient White House aide dismissed as 'a few thousand square miles of cannibal land'. In 1962, Kennedy overcame support in the State Department and Pentagon for British, French and Belgian financial interests, reversing the Eisenhower position, and supported UN action which eventually enforced the return of Katanga to the Congo.

Not only Britain and France were disturbed by this new activism. Kennedy's active promotion of Indonesia's claim to Dutch New Guinea, over Australian protestations, gravely disturbed and surprised Australians. The ambivalence felt about the Americans and their liberal drive to supplant colonialism was captured by Australia's ambassador in Washington at this time. Howard Beale: 'they believed in power and thought they knew how to use it; they believed in military strength, in the weight of metal, in the efficacy of technology and in machines; and they were in a hurry.' Nevertheless, the virility of the Kennedy team and its extravagant rhetoric about the 'New Frontier' promised much to Australian leaders at a time when Britain's withdrawal 'East of Suez' was touching sensitive nerves deep within the Australian colonial psyche. Sukarno's survival of the 1958 CIA-backed rebellion in Indonesia disturbed Canberra, which felt increasingly isolated as Britain and America suddenly vied to supply arms to Indonesia in competition with Soviet aid and eventually supported his claim to Dutch New Guinea, both against Australian wishes. Then, in July 1961 came a bombshell; Britain announced it would seek to join the EEC, causing Menzies great distress. Anxiously, Canberra organised an ANZUS meeting for May 1962 (Washington had refused to hold them in 1960 and 1961 to avoid upsetting Indonesia) to forge even closer links with America to supplement fading British power and prevent the repetition of Australia's isolation over New Guinea. The American crusade in Vietnam would provide the opportunity to forge the close relations that Canberra had long desired.

Thus the key to the impending holocaust in Indochina was the new activist, indeed interventionist, turn in American foreign policy of the early 1960s. Unfortunately for the Vietnamese, Indochina was to be the crucible for the 1960s American liberal offensive against revolution. As the United States

In Phước Tuy province: the interior of a 'Viet Cong' camp.

reached out once again to make contact with pro-Western forces in the third world, some of Kennedy's program, such as the Peace Corps and the Alliance for Progress, appeared progressive. But there was more that was purely reactionary. Cuba was subjected to economic embargo in 1960 after Castro's popularly-supported forces seized power from the dictator Batista; in 1963 sanctions were threatened against other countries wanting trade with Cuba. Plans to overthrow Castro, including the plotting of his assassination, culminated in the disastrous Bay of Pigs fiasco in April 1961. In Indochina, attempts by the CIA to prevent an accommodation between political rivals in Laos brought that country to the point of civil war and the United States to the brink of intervention there. The attempt of Vietnamese, north and south of the seventeenth parallel, to reunify the country under the DRV was seized upon by the best and the brightest of the Kennedy administration as a symbolic struggle against revolution.

AGGRESSION FROM THE NORTH

'In Viet-Nam a Communist government has set out deliberately to conquer a sovereign people in a neighbouring state ... [by a] carefully planned program of concealed aggression ... as real as that of an invading army.'

'The war in Viet-Nam is *not* a spontaneous and local rebellion against the established government.'

State Department, 1965.

One of the most pressing concerns for US officials after Geneva had been to establish a strong, stable leadership in Saigon. They bemoaned the lack of an 'authentic Vietnamese nationalist government', unable to accept the one now in Hanoi. They were utterly unimpressed by the incumbent, 'valorous' Saigon government, having observed that most members of it, including Bảo Đại, were 'safely in Paris' throughout the crisis. Immediately after the fall of Điện Biên Phủ, the US embassy in Saigon recommended to Washington that these leaders be encouraged to depose Bảo Đại and establish a new government under a 'figurehead' Council of Regency with an American-drafted constitution. This intrusion into Vietnamese sovereignty was considered justified given the vast funds Washington had expended trying to save Bảo Đại and French rule: 'in case of bankruptcy ... bankers have right to organise a receivership.' A coup was impossible, however, without French agreement owing to the presence of French troops; and there was as yet no available substitute. So, Instead, Washington decided to support Bảo Đại for the moment. To make him lift his game, the American ambassador in Paris recommended that France be made to accept Washington's control of his income: 'nothing impresses him as much as gold.' Meanwhile, officials in Washington already had a successor under consideration – Ngô Đình Diệm.

Appalled by Diệm's apparent lack of political sophistication and administrative skill, most Americans harboured few illusions over his prospects. The US ambassador in Paris informed Washington that he was 'favourably impressed' by Diệm – 'but only in the realisation that we are prepared to accept the seemingly ridiculous prospect that this yogi-like mystic could assume the charge he is apparently about to undertake ... because the standard set by his predecessor is so low.' US officials in Saigon described Diệm as a 'messiah without a message', whose only policy was to ask for American assistance in every form. Nevertheless, even with his 'personal limitations', Diệm was seen as far better than the 'prototype of suave Europeanised money-seeking dilettante' which had 'failed so miserably' in the previous government.

Diệm, however surprised everyone. He consolidated and maintained his hold over Saigon by armed force. Soon, Western leaders from Washington to Canberra were singing his praises. He toured both capitals in 1957. In 1961, Vice-President Johnson hailed him as the 'Winston Churchill of Asia'. Privately, American officials characterised his rule as 'dictatorial, repressive and unpopular'. By the end of 1961, the repressiveness of the Diệm regime, due particularly to the growing influence of his brother and his brother's wife, was alienating even the most anti-communist Vietnamese. The noted Harvard economist, John Kenneth Galbraith reported to Kennedy from Saigon in November:

> It is certainly a can of snakes. I am reasonably accustomed to oriental government and politics, but I was not quite prepared for Diệm ... his surface travel through Saigon requires the taking in of all laundry along the route, the closing of all windows, an order to populace to keep their heads in, the clearing of all streets, and a vast bevy of motorcycle outriders to protect him on his dash ... if Diệm leaves town for a day, all members of his cabinet are required to see him off and welcome him back, although this involves less damage to efficiency than might be supposed. The political reality is the total stasis which arises from his greater need to protect himself from a coup than to protect the country from the Viet Cong ... The desire to prolong one's day in office has a certain consistency the world around and someday somebody should explain this to the State Department with pictures.

Galbraith's acidity had no impact on US policy which was 'sink or swim with Ngô Đình Diệm'. This was until 1963, when Diệm was disposed of coldly, another expendable pawn in the power politics of the Cold War.

In the 1960s, the American and Australian governments in particular, generally aided by their mainstream media, projected a simplistic, distorted and fundamentally false picture of the origins and nature of the conflict in Vietnam: this picture persists in some quarters today. Essentially, they asserted

A combat engineer of 1st Field Squadron removes the NLF flag from a pole in Hoa Long village during a cordon-and-search operation by 9 RAR, one day after the PLAF have been in the village. Many Australians, soldiers and civilians alike, could not grasp that in many cases it was not intruders from the 'North', but the villagers themselves, who were the PLAF.

that after Geneva there were now (exactly when was never made clear) two nation-states in Vietnam: one they dubbed 'south Vietnam', the other 'North Vietnam'. The former allegedly was stable, democratic, prosperous and an independent member of the free world: the latter totalitarian, repressive and a satellite of Moscow and/or (it varied) Peking. The military conflict which followed was between the 'non-communist' South and the 'communist' North, aided by 'communists' in the South. It supposedly started in 1959 when the North launched 'aggression' against the South by training, supplying and directing insurgents which it infiltrated into the South. These four assertions contain some truth but overall are deficient, factually and conceptually, in explaining the conflict.

First, Diệm's Republic of Vietnam (RVN) was far more the creation and the creature of foreign powers than the DRV. Both governments were integrated into respective foreign blocs: the RVN recognised by about 35 nations and the DRV by twelve. Both toured the key capitals of their respective blocs and received official visits in return. The DRV, however, had greater standing among the non-aligned powers, notably India, Indonesia and Burma. Both received foreign aid but the DRV's total between 1955 and 1960 of US$578.5 million was far less than the RVN's US$1393.1 million; it was also, by contrast, mainly economic not military aid and represented a decreasing percentage of the national budget. The DRV was certainly under pressure to conform to the policies of its two major allies but it was never the client government that the RVN was, With its domestic policies largely determined in Washington and leaders who reported, sometimes weekly, to the American ambassador (and on one occasion were berated by him like errant schoolboys), and ultimately disposed of, if they did not prove sufficiently compliant.

Second, by inclination and necessity, the RVN was far more repressive than the DRV: its popular support was limited because it owed its existence mainly to backing from foreign powers rather than Vietnamese society. Some degree of repression was inevitable in a revolutionary situation where new and competing structures of authority were seeking to impose themselves on a fractured society. The flight south of 900 000 people, mainly Catholics, after 1954, inspired partly by CIA propaganda, certainly

Ngô Đình Diệm

THE 'WINSTON CHURCHILL OF ASIA'

Born to Catholic Mandarin parents in Hue in 1901, Ngô Đình Diệm attended the French school of administration in 1921 before embarking on a career in the colonial administration. Appointed district chief at a young age, governor of a small province in 1929, he rose to secretary of the interior in Bảo Đại's court by 1933. Although he had so far pursued the career of a collaborator with colonial rule, he was a strong patriot and even resigned office over French refusal to accept reforms he proposed. During the Pacific war, he cooperated with the Japanese. After the August revolution, he was offered a place in the DRV by Hồ because of his reputation as a strong nationalist. He refused, however, blaming the Việt Minh for the death of a brother. He also refused a senior position in Bảo Đại's government in 1949 because he doubted the degree of independence granted to it by France.

In 1950, after having tried to form an anti-Việt Minh coalition outside the government, Diệm left Vietnam, eventually staying for two years at a seminary in New Jersey. American officials in Saigon reported to Washington: 'Hồ Chí Minh is the only Viet who enjoys any measure of national prestige ... [and] far after him would come Ngô Đình Diệm.' The Eisenhower administration, however, was at this stage firmly committed to the French and Bảo Đại, who both distrusted Diệm. In 1953, Diệm left for a seminary in Belgium. Although the exact details are not clear, it appears that during the Geneva conference in May 1954, American officials convinced Bảo Đại to accept the appointment of Diệm as Prime Minister, in order to bolster the Saigon government.

In 1955, novelist Graham Greene reflected sympathetically on Diệm:

> ... He is separated from the people by cardinals and police cars with wailing sirens and foreign advisers droning of global strategy, when he should be walking in the rice-fields unprotected, learning the hard way how to be loved and obeyed – the two cannot be separated.
> One pictured him there in the Norodom Palace, sitting with his blank, brown gaze, incorruptible, obstinate, ill-advised, going to his weekly confession, bolstered up by his belief that God is always on the Catholic side, waiting for a miracle. The name I would write under his portrait is the Patriot Ruined by the West.

made the DRV's task easier. But for many Vietnamese it was still the legitimate government of all Vietnam. A literacy campaign and land reforms had consolidated its support. Representatives on the National Assembly, elected on a nation-wide basis, continued to meet although they were only a rubber stamp to decisions made by the Central Committee of the VWP. There was some resistance from highland minorities, as the RVN experienced, and also dissatisfaction about lack of freedoms among intellectuals and the small middle class. Moreover, the land reform program of 1955–56 alienated landlords and rich peasants who lost land in the redistribution. There was a short-lived disturbance in Catholic Quynh Luu in late 1956, requiring PAVN forces to suppress it. Land reform was successful, however, in breaking the grip of the severely inequitable land ownership system. Peasant committees, more than the government, were guilty of grave excesses, imprisoning and executing people as national or revolutionary enemies. Nevertheless, in August 1956, Hồ apologised publicly for this, removed persons responsible, and took steps to prevent its continuation. Between 5000 and 15 000 people were killed in this revolutionary period, far less than the 500 000 'bloodbath' claimed in Western propaganda.

One of the first post-Geneva actions of the Diệm government was to fire on people publicly welcoming the peace. Its authority as the government of southern, as of all, Vietnam was largely illusory and depended upon American support. Diệm himself was not a southerner and, indeed, was part of the Catholic minority. First, he had to overcome the pro-French supporters of Bai Dai: having done this, he deposed Bảo Đại in October 1955. Next, he drove the Bình Xuyên bandits, erstwhile supporters of Bảo Đại, out of Saigon. Then, after virtual civil war, he crushed the private armies of the sects and next the Dai Viet party. Finally, he turned to the countryside and his main opponent, the revolutionary coalition which he misleadingly dubbed the 'Viet Cong' (Vietnamese communist). He launched major military operations, killing and arresting thousands, indeed, any suspected enemy of the regime. The Anti-Communist Denunciation Campaign begun in May 1956 involved reprisals against those actively involved in resistance to the French, proscription of strikes and communist' organisations – which meant virtually any organisation not set up by Diệm or his brother, Nhu. In June 1956, he replaced the traditional village administrations, because of the presence in them of anti-government leaders, with his chosen officials, usually Catholics from the centre and north. The estimate (which is accepted in the West) of the number of people killed under Diệm is 75 000.

Third, the explanation of the so-called 'second Indochina conflict' does not lie in 'aggression from the North' as claimed by Washington: 'aggression', at international law, requires two states; moreover, military conflict was not initiated by the 'North'; in fact it never stopped. True, most of the international community accepted by 1959 there were two de facto states in Vietnam. The Vietnamese, however, did not. Moreover, the Western-imposed 'two states' paradigm distorts the true nature of the Vietnam conflict. There was a nation-wide revolution in Vietnam after 1945 led by a nation-wide political organisation. The line drawn across the country at the seventeenth parallel, whatever American international lawyers argued, did not alter this. Significantly, Vietnamese both north and south, regardless of political allegiance, did not accept this division as permanent. Diệm made this clear in Washington in 1957, as did the RVN's 1967 constitution. Both governments always regarded themselves as the sole, legitimate government of a single, united Vietnam, regardless of what foreigners argued. Diệm's refusal in 1955–56 to hold the reunification talks required by Geneva brought protests in the south as well as from Hanoi. In the nation-wide struggle for a unified, essentially socialist Vietnam, Diệm's forces never put down their

A Vietnamese child is shown the camera equipment of an Australian Army film unit. Australian soldiers had an ambiguous relationship with Vietnamese villagers: on the one hand they sought to win their hearts and minds'; on the other, they confronted them in combat.

arms, attacking the rural population after 1956 to such an extent that the villages formed self-defence units to ward off the army (ARVN). This repression and Diệm's return of previously appropriated land to the landlords, ignited the rural insurgency in the south long before any decision in Hanoi. Indeed, the pressure for armed struggle came from the southern branch of the VWP through 1956–57. Hanoi relented partly in late 1956, allowing limited violence in self-defence to prevent the liquidation of the party. Only in early 1959, did Hanoi sanction greater armed struggle, after representations from the southern party official Le Duan, who was subsequently appointed Secretary-General. Complete PAVN units did not enter southern Vietnam until late in 1964: there were only 6500 PAVN troops there by May 1965 and never more than 80–90 000 in the 1960s. Local forces were around 250 000–300 000.

Fourth, the conflict was not simply one between 'communists' and 'non-communists'. The VWP, as the main nation-wide political force, was the brain and backbone of the DRV. Yet, it was supported in the north by a wide coalition of political forces. Nor was this merely a facade or 'front' manipulated by the party. The congress of the Lien Viet Front in September 1955, which formed the Fatherland Front for reunification, was the largest such meeting since 1951. In the south, the National Front for the Liberation of Southern Vietnam (NLF), formed on 20 December 1960 in response to Diệm's repression, was a very wide coalition, most of whose members (over 97%) were not in the VWP. True, the VWP enjoyed a dominant position through its southern branch (known as the People's Revolutionary Party) as an extension of the nation-wide revolutionary leadership. For tactical reasons, mainly to escape US retaliation, Hanoi played up the supposed independence of the NLF. In reality, the NLF was an integral part of the DRV just as the southern-based People's Liberation Armed Forces (PLAF) were an extension of the PAVN. Thus, while the 'aggression from the north' thesis was misleading, so was the left's counterclaim that the war was the product purely of a southern-based insurgency. Nevertheless, the view of the conflict as a civil war was correct.

Australian traditions were not to be forgotten in Vietnam: here the Australian Army Training Team in Da Nang participates in an ANZAC commemoration service in 1969.

CHANGING HORSES

> ... there is no country in the world more completely British than Australia, nor ... more devoted to the throne and person of Her Majesty the Queen. We are a proud member of a Crown Commonwealth, and will ever continue to be so. But we would be strangely blind if we did not see that ... the rise of the United States to supremacy in industrial power, her vast population, her intellectual and moral influence are all such that she has become ... vital to the existence of the free world ... [her] friendship and cooperation are vital to our own safety.
>
> R.G. Menzies, Parliament, April 1955.

> Our objective should be ... to achieve such an habitual closeness of relations ... and sense of mutual alliance that in our time of need ... the United States would have little option but to respond as we would want. The problem of Vietnam is one ... where we could without disproportionate expenditure pick up a lot of credit with the United States.
>
> Alan Renouf, Australian Minister in Washington, May 1964.

Australia's and America's final slide into Vietnam actually began in neighbouring Laos. In contravention of its own understanding of the Geneva Accords, America refused to respect the neutrality of Laos. Military advisers in disguise and military assistance were provided to help defeat the Pathet Lao insurgents; the CIA blatantly interfered in the Laotian political process to secure the government it favoured. In 1959 and again in 1960–61, these actions produced major crises within Laos which in turn produced international crises. Neither Eisenhower or Kennedy wished to intervene militarily. They made threatening moves: moving units of the 7th Fleet carrying Marines to the Gulf of Thailand, alerting other units in Okinawa, deploying more military advisers, combat aircraft and troops nearby in Thailand. Military advisers favoured the complete occupation of southern Laos but neither president wanted world war over distant Laos. Moreover, as in 1954, both were concerned to intervene only as part of a UN or SEATO action. This was unlikely. The UN would not accept the charge of outside aggression in Laos while Britain and France refused to sanction SEATO action (at this stage SEATO required a unanimous vote to act) because they had no vital interests at stake. Australia privately agreed with Britain initially but did not make this too obvious to Washington. It provided some token non-military assistance to signify its support for American policies but said little in public. It escaped an embarrassing test of its loyalties when on 3 May 1961 a ceasefire was negotiated in Laos.

The Laos crisis was not only a dress rehearsal for intervention in Vietnam; it added momentum to the final result. The psychological impact in Washington was profound: US officials believed they had suffered a great reverse because America's credibility as a defender of anti-communists was tarnished. Vice-President Johnson reported after a tour of Southeast Asia that the whole region could be lost – the Pacific becoming a 'Red Sea' – unless local leaders were given reason to take heart and not succumb to communism or neutralism. The brewing crisis over Berlin added weight to this argument. Kennedy's advisers counselled that 'Vietnam [is] a better place than Laos to achieve the desired result.' Compromise in Laos demanded a strong stand in Thailand and Vietnam (from where the US ambassador had been reporting for a year that Diệm was in serious trouble) to stop the spread of the 'Laos disease'. Kennedy deferred his military advisers' call for large combat units because, as his Secretary of State, Dean Rusk, said: 'Saving Southeast Asia would be worth a lot of money and doing it without US forces would be worth a lot more.' Instead, Kennedy deployed 100 military advisers and 400 Special Force personnel in Vietnam in mid-1961. He asked Britain, but not Australia, to help: it provided five police counterinsurgency advisers from Malaya.

When Diệm's position alarmingly deteriorated further in September 1961, Kennedy again considered and deferred (but did not exclude) the deployment of ground troops. He commented: 'the troops will march in, the band will play, the crowds will cheer, and in four days everyone will have forgotten. Then we will be told to send in more troops. It's like taking a drink. The effect wears off, and you have to take another.' Instead, on 15 November, he decided to deploy two American-piloted helicopter companies, transport aircraft and coastal vessels. The number of American advisers rose from 685 to 16 000 by the end of 1963. This time he sought wide allied support to soften criticism, domestic and international, that he was violating the Geneva Accords and international law. SEATO could not act as a body, so instead he sought to give the illusion of SEATO participation by involving willing members – the 'rump alliance' – and announcing SEATO did not require unanimous action. Australia's participation, as a 'white' nation, was an important part of the illusion, especially as Britain declined.

On 17 November. Australia's ambassador in Washington advised that meeting the American request for a handful of counterinsurgency advisers, small arms and ammunition would 'make Australia's mark'

OPPOSITE PAGE: The war in Vietnam was to be accompanied by widespread civic action: here at Dong Chau orphanage in Saigon, an Australian soldier holds a Vietnamese child, accompanied by the French-Canadian priest who is accepting one thousand jars of baby food, a gift from the Albury Apex club.

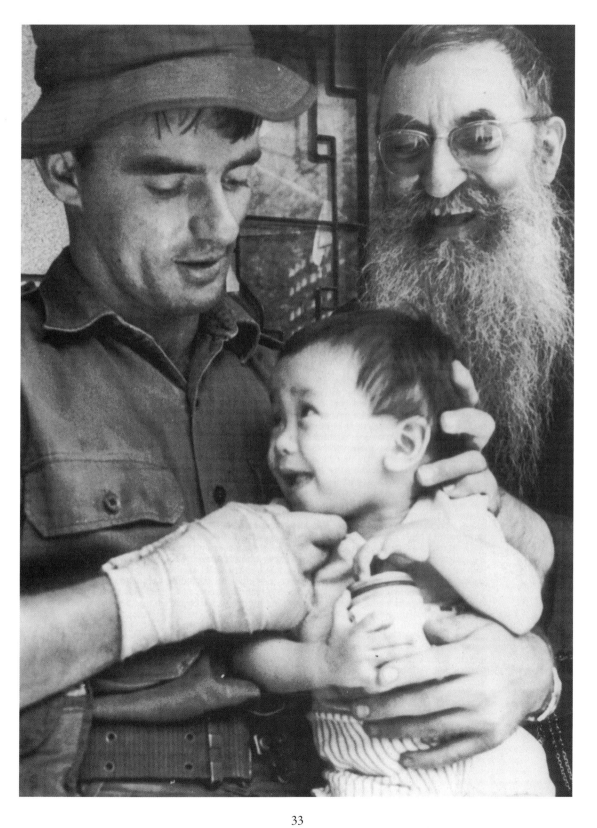

with the administration. Defence officials were reluctant for manpower reasons to give much, but Menzies and External Affairs Minister Garfield Barwick were sympathetic. They wished, however, to wait until after the December elections in which the government's one seat majority would be tested. Following Menzies's victory in the election, the situation in Southeast Asia became more urgent. Thailand threatened to quit SEATO unless the unanimity rule was changed and in early May civil war erupted yet again in Laos. Once again, Kennedy deferred intervention but threateningly moved 5000 troops to Thailand near the Laotian border to achieve the dual purpose of reassuring Bangkok and cautioning the Pathet Lao. (Meanwhile, the Soviet Union and Britain negotiated a new ceasefire in Laos, established a coalition government and supervised the agreement of 23 July 'neutralising' Laos.) Outside of SEATO, members were asked to provide non-combatant assistance to Thailand. Britain and New Zealand did so reluctantly. Australia, more willingly, deployed eight RAAF Sabres to Thailand and announced the following day that 30 'non-combatant' army instructors would be sent to Vietnam at the request of the RVN. In fact, there was no such request; nor was this, as implied, part of a SEATO action. Soon, some of these 'advisers' were operating with the CIA in combat roles.

The commitment of the first 30 combat advisers to Vietnam attracted little notice in the press. Even in parliament, the Opposition largely let the issue pass without comment, with the exception of Eddie Ward, 'the firebrand of East Sydney'. He kept at the government's heels, demanding more information on the nature of the war and Australia's commitment, also arguing that Vietnam was a local conflict in one country which should be settled by negotiation. But in response he only received obfuscation. It is likely that ministers did not expect their decision to become a major issue: eventually the advisers would return, or remain a minor commitment to a low-level counterinsurgency conflict which would eventually peter out, just as the Malayan Emergency had after 12 relatively uncontroversial years. In the meantime, American gratitude would have been won. Indeed, American officials were soon talking publicly about the success of the strategic hamlet program, the more effective performance of ARVN, the decline in NLF incidents and influence, and the likelihood that American advisers would soon be withdrawn. In fact, it did not pan out like that at all. In the 18 months after Australia's announcement, the government failed to appreciate or publicly acknowledge the stark signs of disintegration in southern Vietnam.

The influx of armoured vehicles and American-piloted helicopters only temporarily threw the PLAF onto the defensive. The bankruptcy of Kennedy's strategy of fighting the war by limited assistance and advice to the ARVN was exposed in January 1963 near the village of Ấp Bắc, 80 kilometres southwest of Saigon. A less than aggressive force of 2000 ARVN troops, supported by aircraft, helicopters, armoured vehicles and US advisers, suffered 165 casualties and lost five US helicopters in unsuccessfully trying to overcome 300–400 PLAF soldiers who escaped with less than twelve dead. Eddie Ward, attuned to extensive reports in the American press, called on Barwick to explain the defeat and its significance. Barwick, however, simply cited a US general, denying it was a defeat, when all knowledgeable commentators knew otherwise. Even ARVN generals admitted their army did not have its heart in the war. In the next few months, even while Barwick continued to espouse the merits of the strategic hamlets, the political fabric in Saigon was being rent apart.

Diệm's repression of all opposition, besides the NLF, further isolated his regime. On 8 May, a large crowd of Buddhists protested the banning of celebrations of the Buddha's birthday; police shot nine dead. Subsequently, other dissidents joined the Buddhists in almost daily protests seeking the removal

The self-immolation of seventy-three-year old Buddhist monk Venerable Thích Quảng Đức on 11 June 1963, in protest against the Diệm regime and its repressive policy towards Buddhists. The worldwide transmission of a series of photographs of the event by A.P. correspondent Malcolm Browne won him a World Press Photo Award.

of Diệm and American influence, and the reunification of the country under a coalition government. On 11 June, the world was rocked by pictures of a Buddhist monk calmly sitting in the lotus position while aflame, immolating himself in protest. Madame Nhu fuelled matters by referring contemptuously to 'Buddhist barbeques'. On 21 August, despite private expressions of concern by the Australian and American governments, Nhu unleashed his private police, disguised as ARVN, in brutal raids with mass arrests against Buddhist pagodas.

Earlier, in March, a special federal conference of the ALP had expressed concern at the report to Kennedy by four US senators visiting Vietnam that democracy was not flourishing under Diệm. When Gough Whitlam took up this point in parliament after the pagoda raids, Barwick conceded the government's concern should any religious persecution be involved, but identified himself with Diệm's hard line by implying that the events were related to the 'communist insurgency'. Claiming he had better sources than newspaper reports, he denied that the Diệm government had failed to win popular support. In the next few weeks Labor figures Tom Uren and Jim Cairns followed up Whitlam's attack, describing Diệm's government as a 'reactionary police state', only to be met by counter-claims from the government benches that Diệm's 'democratic republic' was facing a threat from 'communist infiltration' and Chinese expansionism. One government member, Leslie Bury, conceded Diệm's faults, but rhetorically asked what was the alternative: surely Labor was not making the 'shocking' suggestion that the United States should use its power to remove him – precisely what was already happening.

The State Department now believed Diệm must remove Nhu, otherwise Diệm himself had to go. Rumours that Nhu was trying to open negotiations with the NLF and Hanoi strengthened this conviction. A number of ARVN's leading generals agreed the war could not be won with Diệm. Though they formulated their plans without American advice, they sought Washington's approval. The new US ambassador, Henry Cabot Lodge, strongly supported them. Kennedy soon agreed, The United States now distanced itself from Diệm, publicly voiced displeasure with his rule, and on 5 October made certain aid cuts, knowing this would promote a coup. On the afternoon of 1 November, ARVN troops surrounded the presidential palace. In a pathetic telephone conversation recorded for all time, Diệm pleaded to Lodge, seeking the American attitude. Stonily, Lodge replied that he was not well enough informed to say: it was

LEFT: A Centurion tank of A Squadron, 1 Armoured Regiment, moves across a portable bridge during Operation Matilda, the biggest Australian armoured operation since the second world war.

OPPOSITE PAGE: Troops of the 1st Australian Task Force prepare to search the village of Đất Đỏ during Operation Burnside in 1967.

too early in the morning in Washington. Diệm persisted: surely Lodge had a general idea. 'After all, I am Chief of State. I have tried to do my duty. I want to do now what duty and good sense require. I believe in duty above all.' Lodge readily conceded that Diệm had done his duty, saying he admired his courage and great contributions to his country: no one, he added, could deny that. But, his immediate concern was Diệm's 'physical safety'. He informed Diệm he had heard that he had been offered safe conduct out of the country if he resigned. Diệm's closing words were that he was trying to establish order: 'You have my telephone number.' He and his brother escaped the palace that evening, seeking sanctuary in a nearby church they were promised safe conduct, seized and shot. The news was greeted by jubilant celebrations in the streets of Saigon. Although shocked by Diệm's end, Kennedy soon recognised the new military government under General Dương Văn Minh. Even the facade of democracy had now gone from Saigon.

Barwick, apparently unaware of the plotting, was disoriented by the rapid ebb of US endorsement of Diệm. Fortunately for him, parliament was not sitting. On 4 November, he said the government was following events in Vietnam closely and would only consider recognition of a new government when one was formed, 'saddened' by the recent internal troubles there, he now admitted that the government had hoped Diệm's regime would have found 'a wider basis of popular support'. Four days later, following the American lead, he announced Australia's recognition of the new government, claiming this was a well-considered

decision: the violence associated with the change of government and reports of Diệm's end having caused concern. In a remarkable understatement, he concluded about Diệm's death, 'a matter of regret,' that: some of his internal policies in recent times appeared to have lost him the popular support that was necessary to the continuance of his government.' But the 'primary objective' for Australia was to continue its support for the new government to resist the 'North Vietnamese threat.'

Within three weeks of Diệm's death, Kennedy too had fallen to an assassin's bullet. In a few months Johnson had strengthened the American commitment to Vietnam. Behind this was concern that Minh also wanted negotiations with the NLF and resisted greater American control over the war and its demands for bombing of DRV territory under ARVN cover. So on 30 January, the military junta was itself overthrown in a bloodless coup led by General Nguyễn Văn Khánh, possibly at the Pentagon's instigation. In February, with Khánh proving more amenable than Minh, Johnson commenced an extensive program of covert operations against the DRV, superseding the earlier limited program. ARVN saboteurs began parachuting into DRV territory. Contingency planning for open and direct military action, including airstrikes, was also approved, with the possibility this would commence once the situation in Saigon improved. There was also a presidential election pending and Johnson would run against the 'hawkish' Barry Goldwater as the candidate most likely to keep the country out of an Asian war. Nevertheless, by June there was almost universal agreement among Johnson's advisers that the DRV must be bombed, As part of this planning, a congressional resolution giving the President the legal power to undertake such action, was drafted.

Washington's plans were threatened by a growing international call for the 'neutralisation' of Vietnam, begun by De Gaulle in August 1963 and supported by Prince Sihanouk of Cambodia, the NLF and even

Australian soldiers probe the jungle of Vietnam in 1968.

US Senate Majority Leader Michael Mansfield. Johnson attacked neutralism in his New Year message but his administration's position was further weakened when the UN Secretary-General called for negotiations in July. De Gaulle supported him, as did the Soviet Union, China, Cambodia, the NLF and Hanoi in requesting the Geneva Conference be reconvened for both Laos and Vietnam. In Australia, Labor supported these proposals but the government strongly condemned neutralisation as being a formula for the eventual loss of southern Vietnam to communism.

Increasing international isolation over 'neutralism' prompted Washington to augment tangible signs of allied support for its Vietnam policies. In May, having failed to secure unanimous SEATO support at Manila the previous month, Washington approached 24 of its allies seeking more non-combat assistance for the RVN as part of a public campaign to have 'more flags' supporting US efforts in Vietnam. Australia was asked for more advisers, and for their use at battalion level where there was a real risk of casualties. Alan Renouf, the Chargé d'Affaires in the Washington embassy, recommended Australia's response be as 'positive and prompt' as possible. He added that this advice should be considered in the light of

Australian infantrymen on tactical patrol in Vietnam.

Washington's less than forthcoming attitude over support for Australia over confrontation. The new Minister for External Affairs. Paul Hasluck quickly replied that, 'We should like the United States to know that we are anxious to reply promptly and sympathetically; indeed, it was the first positive response. On 29 May, cabinet decided to offer an additional 30 advisers to be deployed at battalion level, a flight of six transport aircraft, an army dental team and a transport team, Despite the government's reference to 'joint consultations' including with the RVN, the latter was not informed until 8 June, the day the decision was publicly announced in Australia: embarrassing Australia's ambassador in Saigon, David Anderson. A month later a further 23 advisers were offered. Washington was extremely pleased and feted the decision publicly to try and sway more reluctant allies. To win additional gratitude, Hasluck strongly commended to other countries Khánh's July request for assistance which was prompted by Washington.

The explanation for Australia's more forthcoming response to America's request for support in Vietnam in 1964, as compared to previously, lay in Australia's growing concern over Indonesia. Britain's creation of 'Malaysia' would perpetuate the division of culturally-linked peoples divided by Anglo-Dutch imperialism. When Britain crushed an Indonesian-favoured popular revolt seeking democratic representation in Brunei in December 1962, Indonesia proclaimed its opposition – Konfrontasi – to Malaysia. When minor military incidents occurred from April 1963, Britain pressed Australia to provide combat forces for the defence of the Borneo territories not just the Malay peninsula. Anxious not to upset Indonesia, Australia only provided political support. When in September Malaysia formally came into being and the British embassy in Jakarta was burned down, Menzies proclaimed Australia's support for Malaysia, Barwick redoubled his efforts to have America publicly pledge that ANZUS covered Australian troops in Borneo. He received a very equivocal response. Kennedy supported Malaysia but, with important interests in Indonesia and his hands already full in Vietnam, preferred to keep in the background with the Commonwealth bearing the military burden of securing Malaysia and the brunt of Indonesian displeasure. Australian military assistance to Malaysia began in April 1964 with non-combatant units being sent to Borneo. So, Barwick again pressed the Americans for an ANZUS guarantee. He failed disastrously and left office. So, without a clear ANZUS guarantee the government finally succumbed to British pressure in February 1965 and committed an infantry battalion to Borneo. This decision made even more vital Australia's aim of securing an American military presence in Vietnam.

ALL THE WAY

> Our men stand together as they have stood before, to check aggression. And I want for every boy that stands there in the rice paddy on this warm summer's day to know that every American and LBJ is with Australia, all the way.
>
> You have already shown that your commitment is a matter of policy and action and not rhetoric. And when your Prime Minister said symbolically in Washington speaking on the crisis that faces our men on the far away battlefront at the moment, that he would go 'all the way with LBJ', there wasn't a single American that felt that was new information.
>
> There's not a boy wearing the uniform yonder today that hasn't always known that when freedom is at stake, and when honorable men stand in battle shoulder to shoulder, that Australians will go all the way, just as Americans will go all the way, not a third of the way, not part of the way … but all the way until liberty and freedom have won.
>
> Lyndon Baines Johnson, Canberra, October 1966.

The RVN's military position continued to deteriorate through 1964, as did the situation in Laos where CIA pilots began 'secret' bombing of the Pathet Lao and even PAVN forces using the Hồ Chí Minh trail into southern Vietnam. At the Honolulu conference in June, Johnson's advisers agreed on the necessity of direct military action – bombing – against the DRV to induce it to negotiate. There were two obstacles, The coming presidential election of 3 November and the constitutional requirement that only Congress, not the President, could authorise such open acts of war. Whatever the true facts of the Tonkin Gulf incident, it served Washington's purpose. Johnson's approval rating jumped from 42 to 72% and Congress passed the 'Tonkin Gulf Resolution' with only two dissenting votes. Johnson could now wage warlike measures without seeking a formal declaration of war which might expose the administration to various political difficulties in Congress and in public. The twin facts that the resolution had been drafted before the incident and that planning was already under way for this military action against the DRV has given rise to suspicions, still unconfirmed, that the administration deliberately provoked the incident for this very purpose. Johnson would still not act until after 3 November but planning for escalation continued secretly.

The Australian government anticipated, and now even welcomed, American escalation. The new External Affairs Minister, Paul Hasluck, instructed all Australia's overseas missions in September that a primary objective was to secure a firm American commitment to Vietnam. On 10 November Menzies announced the introduction of selective conscription for the expansion of the Army from 24 000 to 37 500 over three years. True, there was a need for troops to cover Indonesian actions in Malaysia and possibly

New Guinea, But new legislation being drafted, which would permit, for the first time in Australia's history, these conscripts and regulars to be sent to overseas operations beyond Malaya, showed clearly that the government was preparing to meet an expected American request for a ground commitment to Vietnam. Indeed, the increased forces gave the government the basis for actually encouraging escalation.

On 1 December, Johnson cautiously approved limited escalation in Vietnam. There were to be two phases: Phase 1 (Barrel Roll), which commenced on 14 December, involved only a slight intensification of current covert actions combined with open retaliation for any 'spectacular' PLAF or PAVN attacks against Americans; Phase 2 (Rolling Thunder) was a gradually expanding bombing campaign against military targets in the DRV and Laos. It was not to be implemented, however, until Saigon had demonstrated the stability needed to resist any DRV counteraction. The objective was psychological not military, to convince Hanoi to cease its support for the insurgency so that, supposedly, ARVN by itself would be able to defeat the PLAF. Western ground troops were not required at this stage, as Johnson explained to Menzies: 'Down the road in the future, if the situation in Saigon should require and justify it, there may be a need for combat units, but that is not the immediate problem.' Instead, Washington sought only more non-combatant assistance from its allies, including 200 more military advisers from Australia, to accompany this escalation.

Australian officials were utterly unimpressed by Johnson's cautious decisions. Australia's ambassador in Washington, Keith Waller, reported to Canberra that the 'somewhat irresolute American attitude gives cause for increasing uneasiness': US policy was in the 'doldrums', with the administration prepared to 'muddle along' with policies which had not succeeded in the past. Indeed, Australia's defence officials ignored the American request for more advisers and instead recommended the offer of an infantry battalion. They believed American troops were needed there now, and thus Australia should be willing, and would be expected, to provide its own ground forces. So Menzies replied to Johnson that although there were few advisers available, Australia was ready to hold staff talks with the Americans on deploying ground troops. Over the next few weeks, Australian officials waged a concerted campaign following Cabinet's direction of 16 January, to convince the Americans that Phase 1 was inadequate and to move onto Phase 2, deploy ground forces and reject any call for negotiations. Hasluck instructed Waller to take any opportunity 'to bring certainty to American policy and planning.' In the meantime, only a further 17 advisers were provided. Understandably, American officials were unimpressed: one snapped that if Australia was so concerned, why could it not provide 50 more instructors.

Johnson's hope for 'stability' in Saigon never looked like being realised. ARVN suffered major defeats in January – losing about a battalion a week, further Buddhist riots carried a distinctly anti-American flavor; on 27 January, Khánh's successor Hương was overthrown and eventually replaced by Phan Huy Quát. Johnson's most influential advisers, McGeorge Bundy and Robert McNamara, now pushed for the 'sustained reprisal' of Phase 2 without waiting for the unlikely prospect of stability in Saigon. Johnson still hesitated, but after the successful attacks on American bases at Pleiku and Tuy Hòa in early February, he accepted their advice. A few days later he sanctioned Phase 2; it began on 2 March. With this psychological barrier down, his advisers now pressed for some ground troops, though 'only' for base security. On 26 February Johnson agreed to the two Marine battalions which splashed ashore in Vietnam on 8 March, the first US ground combat units to be deployed operationally on the Asian mainland since Korea. The final taboo was now broken. Johnson's advisers soon called for a major troop deployment actually to fight the war. On 1 April he also agreed to this: approving the deployment of thirteen battalions (including three Korean and one Australian) for counterinsurgency operations up to fifty miles from their bases (virtually to Laos). Although described as an 'experiment' only, Washington was now moving towards taking up the major role in fighting the PLAF, restrained only by the desire to 'minimise the appearance of a sudden change in policy'.

During their deliberations over these crucial decisions, American officials spoke of 'favourable Australian sentiment and indeed some pressure' from them for the commitment of ground troops, and that the Australians, 'most anxious' to begin staff talks, 'had been urging us to take stronger action for at least two weeks prior.' Indeed, Renouf told his hosts that he 'could not overemphasise the degree to which Australia supported US policy'; of the Marines and Phase 2 he said, 'the more of this the better.' Australia's support was not the decisive factor behind the American decision but it was an important reassurance. Rusk explained: 'At the end of the trail in Vietnam, the American people are prepared to do whatever needs to be done, but it helps us a great deal to realise that we are not alone.'

Cabinet decided formally on 7 April to offer the Americans a battalion. It placed far greater concern on receiving a formal request for the battalion from Washington rather than Saigon, gaining the former verbally on 13 April. Saigon's approval was more difficult to secure. The American ambassador in Saigon, Maxwell Taylor, had earlier warned that Quát's government had 'no great enthusiasm' for foreign forces and was 'highly sensitive' to criticism that the country was being 'taken over': 'anti-American sentiment lies just under the surface'. Washington decided that although it was a 'tricky problem', Quát must be 'persuaded' to accept these forces so as to overcome a 'troublesome aspect' of its domestic and international presentation of the escalation: 'the implication that it is the US and not the GVN which is requesting help'. Australia's ambassador Anderson reinforced the doubts of his American colleague: foreign forces would only heighten Vietnamese xenophobia and encourage them to leave the fight to the Americans. These shared doubts were ignored by Washington which told Taylor on 7 April to secure the RVN's request for the troop deployments, including the Australian battalion.

Accepting this situation, Anderson now stressed the importance of arranging the 'request' with due respect to Quát. He should be consulted prior to Australia's announcement and not just presented with a *fait accompli* as Saigon's leaders were in 1962 and 1964. Otherwise, Anderson warned, it could imply that:

> ... our offer is prompted exclusively by dependence on American military advice and our relationship with the United States that we are indifferent or insensitive to their situation and special problems and that we take their eventual request for granted and do not consider them genuinely independent.

Unaware of the irony, Anderson had just described Canberra's exact approach to the issue. A few days later, he again warned: 'We failed last year to give them opportunity to make parallel announcement... Consultations with them on present project has been minimal.' Anderson's concerns were drowned in the last-minute scramble to extract Quát's consent so Australia's decision could be announced by Thursday 29 April when parliament recessed for a long weekend, so lessening the risk of a premature leak to the press.

As late as 23 April, however, Quát was reported as still 'noticeably reticent' about accepting the foreign troops: 'serious difficulties' were anticipated in persuading him otherwise. Under American pressure he began to relent the next day and on 27 April he finally acceded to the major escalation desired by Washington. With only a short time left, Menzies desired Quát's request in writing before his announcement. This proved impossible. Unsure whether to go ahead, Menzies did not warn the Opposition leadership of his impending announcement. So, Calwell and Whitlam travelled to Sydney for the state election and were not present in parliament when the momentous decision was announced. With his decision already the subject of press speculation, Menzies decided to go ahead once he received news from Saigon that Quát verbally accepted the battalion and would later forward a written request. So, Australia's commitment was announced at 8 pm on 29 April without any formal invitation from Saigon. Menzies' carefully worded speech – saying Australia was 'in receipt of a request' – disguised the fact that the battalion had been offered, not requested as implied.

In Calwell's and Whitlam's absence, there was no parliamentary debate until 4 May when Menzies tabled Johnson's request for the battalion but not Quát's, presumably because the wording betrayed the true circumstances of the 'request'. (It would be tabled reluctantly in August 1971.) At times, as on 29 April, Menzies justified the decision as a response to a direct threat from China. This was hyperbole. Indonesia, not China, was the real concern and only in a long-term sense. The immediate objective behind the commitment was to tighten the American alliance beyond the loose bonds of ANZUS. In a very temporary sense, this was achieved but the takeover of Indonesia by pro-American army officers on 1 October 1965 removed some of the incentive for Australia being in Vietnam.

Meanwhile, stability, of a sort, had finally been achieved in Saigon in terms of tenure of government when Quát was deposed and succeeded in June by General Nguyễn Văn Thiệu and Air Marshal Nguyễn Cao Kỳ. Washington privately regarded this new leadership as 'the bottom of the barrel, absolutely the Bottom of the barrel'. Ky, an avid admirer of Hitler who on one occasion inspired an American official to observe that 'a Hollywood central casting bureau would have grabbed him for a role as a sax player in a second-rate Manila nightclub,' was the model of a third world, tin-pot dictator. Nevertheless, the momentum in Washington was irreversible. On 27 July. Johnson made what has been seen as America's formal decision for a major war. He decided to increase American forces in Vietnam from 75 000 to 175 000 (he only announced half the increase). Australia was pressed to follow. It did: with only 250 more men. Although, Australia subsequently increased steadily its Vietnam commitment until a maximum of 8300 in late 1967, its overall contribution like its defence spending remained small in proportion to the American effort. Australia's primary contribution was extravagant, even promiscuous, rhetorical support – notably Harold Holt's famous 'All the way with LBJ' – but this was nothing more than political hyperbole.

INTO BATTLE

Counter-Revolution

Greg Lockhart

The main feature of the Australian military commitment to the Vietnam war between 1962 and 1972 was its small size: Australian forces peaked at around 8300 men. By contrast, the Thai commitment peaked at around 11 000 men, the Korean at around 48 000, and the American at around 500 000, Few American histories of the war have space for 'Australia' in their index. One recent Vietnamese regional history, which includes old Phước Tuy province where the Australians mainly operated, has little to say about them. Australian authors have noted that there was a marked discrepancy between the size of the force committed and the volume of the government's strident anticommunist rhetoric. Yet Australians could raise six divisions and speak of eleven when there was a real threat to Australia during the Second World War.

The key to this discrepancy is that from at least 1949, Australian governments opposed revolutionary Asian nationalism, but could not say so. This opposition was rooted in the fears of the Anglo-Australian elite – they believed that if the old imperial order ended, their interests would be undermined in both Asia and Australia. Asian revolutions had to be suppressed. But at the time it was not politically acceptable to oppose decolonisation in Asia: so opposition to revolutionary Asian nationalism was couched in exclusively anticommunist terms, even though communist parties never acted alone, invariably participating as they did in wider national fronts with other nationalists and anti-colonialists. By this emphasis, communism was wrongly portrayed as the *enemy* of nationalism and Asian communism was said to be a threat to Australia's interests in Asia. Anticommunist rhetoric was also useful in justifying Australia's increasing military dependence on the United States.

Although Asian communism threatened the West's Asian economic interests, there could be no serious suggestion that it represented a direct threat to Australia. Consequently, there was no convincing argument to put to the people for recruiting a large army. In any event, a larger Australian army by itself would still have been insufficient to achieve the desired goal: the establishment of a new kind of Western hegemony in Asia through the defeat of revolutionary Asian nationalism. So Australian governments began to shape a force that could be used primarily to support, and hence attract and maintain. American and British power into the region. This approach led to a new era in Australian military history: the emergence of a professional counter-revolutionary army.

Up to 1945 the Australian army was a citizens' army. Official historian of the Second World War, Paul Hasluck, accurately depicted 'the government and the people' confronting the Japanese threat between 1941 and 1945, However, with the formation of The Royal Australian Regiment in 1947, Australia had its first professional standing army. Given the absence of a popular base for recruiting and for large defence

OPPOSITE PAGE: The jungle conditions for which the Australian Army was being trained are shown here in a sticky operation known as Portsea, carried out by Alpha Company of 6th Battalion, Royal Australian Regiment, in Vietnam in 1967.

expenditure, this standing army was necessarily a small one, of around 30 000 men. Its first 'operation' was against other Australians, striking in the coal mines around Newcastle in 1949.

Increasingly the small standing army was then shaped to operate in Asia, in response to the appearance of people's armies in China, Vietnam, Malaya and Indonesia in the period of decolonization, In Australia, the absence of a popular base often necessitated shrouding the government's defence arrangements in great secrecy. Small-scale operations, professionalism and secrecy were the main elements of the counter-revolutionary 'forward defence' posture which led the Australian army to Vietnam.

DIRT BOYS' STUFF

On 19 May 1950, a leading Liberal cabinet minister, R.G. (later Lord) Casey, spoke in cabinet on the need for 'dirt boys' stuff' in handling the Malayan Emergency. Casey was not impressed with conventional British tactics in Malaya. He raised the need for 'cunning versus brute force', for 'bribery, deception, whispering, and underground methods generally'. Australia, he thought, could provide such expertise if not large forces. Accordingly, Prime Minister R.G. Menzies suggested to British officials that a group of Australian officers, experienced in jungle warfare from New Guinea, should be sent to Malaya. Five days later, a small informal subcommittee of cabinet decided on the establishment of an Australian Secret Intelligence Service (ASIS), modelled on Britain's SIS, for covert intelligence operations in Southeast Asia. Australia's small paramilitary secret service was thus established as part of the British imperial structure. A very important strand of Australian military thinking, post-1945, can be related to this decision.

At first, the small professional standing army was designed primarily as a core force that could be expanded rapidly for operations in the Middle East in the event of the world war that many were predicting would erupt in the mid- to late 1950s. Thus, the idea of a volunteer army for imperial service was not entirely dead. However, the world war proved illusory, and the memory of Japanese expansionism in the 1940s meanwhile strengthened a predisposition to think in terms of the yellow peril. Especially after 1954, Australian forces became primarily preoccupied in the struggle against anticolonial forces in Southeast Asia. This narrower role demanded a professional force, necessarily small, for deployment with larger British, and later, American forces. Once again, Australia saw itself as providing expertise rather than sizable forces. Accordingly, the Australian Army became very proficient at small-scale jungle warfare tactics.

This proficiency had initially developed during the Second World War. The army had learned to counter the Japanese in the New Guinea jungles: Japanese tactics were to hold Australian forces in front and then attack on a flank or the rear. By 1944 the Jungle Training Centre at Canungra in Queensland was turning out around 4000 men a month versed in ambush techniques and 'close encounter' drills which emphasised speed, fire power, and Japanese-style flanking movements. Small, mobile patrols with maximum fire power from Bren and Owen guns became entrenched in Australian military thinking, 'Cav Commando' units carrying out the traditional role of cavalry – sending out screens, gaining intelligence, and long-range reconnaissance behind enemy lines – were the forerunners of the British-style Special Air Service Regiment (SAS) formed at Swanbourne in Western Australia in July 1957.

Australia's proficiency in this type of unconventional warfare was not unique. Wingate's Special Forces

('Chindits') and the American-led Merrill's Marauders, operating like guerrilla units behind enemy lines in Burma, had a similar function to Australian Commando Units in New Guinea. In 1956 Sir William Slim, who commanded the Burma campaign, published his *Defeat Into Victory*, which immediately became an examinable text in Australian Army promotion exams. This book emphasised the importance of 'special forces' trained in jungle warfare for small-scale guerrilla action behind enemy lines. In 1950, Menzies urged the British to carry out the kind of operations that Britain's Far Eastern Special Operations Executive (SOE), based in India, had conducted in Southeast Asia during the Second World War. These had included deploying agents to gather intelligence and building indigenous guerrilla forces in Japanese-occupied territories. They had been most effective against the Japanese in Burma. Australia's interest and proficiency in such tactics dovetailed neatly into British plans for retaining its Asian empire after 1945.

The Anglo-Australian predisposition towards SOE-style operations was already well established before 1950. For example, to strengthen imperial links between India and Australia in 1944, SOE had generated a whispering campaign to popularise the appointment of Casey as Governor of Bengal. A number of SOE operations, including the *Krait's* famous raid on Singapore harbour in 1943, had been orchestrated from Australia. Another leading imperial figure, General Cawthorne, who helped to set up the British-style Joint Intelligence Bureau in Melbourne in the 1940s and became head of ASIS in the early 1960s, also had experience of earlier SOE operations. After leaving the Australian army in 1918, he served with the British for many years before becoming Director of Intelligence, India Command, between 1941 and 1945. In 1949, just before Menzies and Casey were suggesting the old-new methods for Malaya, F. Spencer Chapman published a popular book about his intrepid SOE guerrilla operations behind Japanese lines in Malaya, entitled *The Jungle is Neutral*. Casey was reading it at the time he proposed the dirt boys' stuff to Cabinet. He noted 'disturbing' news from Malaya: 'apparently the jungle is not neutral, it is red'. So, just as an Australian branch of the British Secret Service was established to help defend the declining empire, the Australian army with its jungle prowess, small size, and new professionalism, was being developed as an instrument of Anglo-Australian opposition to revolutionary Asian nationalism.

One key officer in this process (who later described the Australian Army Training Team Vietnam [AATTV] as the most highly decorated unit in the 'British Army') was Colonel (later Brigadier) Ted Serong. He too moved through the jungle of post-war imperial intelligence organisations. Eventually, he also moved in American intelligence circles as American power superseded Britain's pre-eminence in the region. In the late 1940s, he had been a military attaché to Burma, where the American Central Intelligence Agency (CIA) was working among the Nationalist Chinese divisions that General Stilwell and other American officers had commanded during the War. (These divisions had stayed in Burma even after Mao's popular forces came to power in China – the CIA apparently had ideas about using them to infiltrate that country!) Serong therefore became familiar with both SOE – and subsequent CIA-style activities. Later he brought this experience of small-scale clandestine operations to bear on Australian Army thinking. He became Commandant of the Jungle Training Centre (JTC) at Canungra when it reopened in 1955. It was to prepare Australian battalions for Malaya and later Vietnam.

At JTC, Serong's Burma experience was meshed with earlier Australian experience by people such as his Chief Instructor, 'Jungle George' Warf, a Lieutenant-Colonel who had been in the 2/3rd Commandos in New Guinea in the early 1940s. A younger generation of soldiers such as Ray Simpson VC, Peter Rothwell (who was later commissioned), and George Chinn also helped to cast the army's old tactical proficiency in a new mould. Such men had joined the army around the end of the Second World War, fought in the Korean War, held important instructional posts at JTC, the Infantry Centre, or other training institutions, and usually campaigned in Malaya. The Australian Army was on almost continual overseas service between 1945 and Vietnam, and constituted the first professional group of warriors to emerge in Australian history.

This warrior class was enriched by numerous soldiers of fortune set adrift by the crumbling of the old imperial world order. Major John Essex-Clark, Captain Peter Isaacs, and Sergeant Bob Buick were representative of numerous others from England and Africa. Buick was from South Africa, Isaacs was ex-British Army with service in Germany, and Essex-Clark was a former soldier and officer in the Rhodesian Army with wide operational experience in the Congo, Malawi, and Zambia. He had also been to British Staff College and served with a Gurkha division in Malaya. Fewer in number than the Africans, but still conspicuous in the Army at this time, were people of central European origin such as Captain Felix Fazekas. He was reputed to have fought his first battles against Russian tanks in the streets of Budapest in 1956. Such soldiers generally fitted well into the Australian Army class whose only real requirement for admission was fighting prowess. Nonetheless these professionals shared the government's commitment to opposing communism.

When the First, Second, and Third Battalions of The Royal Australian Regiment (1, 2, and 3 RAR), as well as SAS squadrons, were rotated through the jungles of Malaya and Borneo between 1955 and 1966, they conducted stealthy, small-unit patrols as SOE and the Commandos had before them. For example, in Malaya in 1959, 1 RAR operated from a forward operational base at Grik in Ipoh, with company bases dispersed in the jungle. From these bases, small groups of seven to ten men would patrol meticulously for up to forty days. Tracker teams held in reserve could be called forward to follow up the slightest hint of enemy presence. Operations were so meticulous that 1 RAR once placed a three-month ambush on one pair of spectacles found on a track.

Such was the outlook of the Australian Army when the first group of thirty jungle warfare advisers were committed to Vietnam in August 1962. Led by Serong, the AATTV included many Malayan veterans, such as Captain Barry Petersen, who had also undergone 'special forces' training which his memoirs say was sponsored by ASIS. His activities as a CIA operative among the Montagnards in the Southern Highlands of Vietnam were very similar to the old SOE-style operations. The surviving imperial ethos was reflected initially in the treatment by Army headquarters in Canberra of its advisory commitment to Vietnam as 'an offshoot' of Malaya – in 1962 Serong was still technically responsible to the headquarters of Far Eastern Land Forces (FARELF) in Singapore. Similarly, when the first Australian ground forces were committed to Vietnam in 1965, a very large number of officers and NCO, including most company commanders, were also veterans of the Malayan Borneo campaigns.

The commitment of advisers to Vietnam in 1962 led to attempts to take account of the specific conditions in Vietnam. Bernard Fall, a well-known commentator on French operations in Indochina, lectured at JTC. In association with British experts, Brigadier F.G. Hassett and a small study team visited Vietnam and other Southeast Asian countries and began to formulate a counter-insurgency doctrine that emphasised the political nature of revolutionary war. In 1965, the army finally published a training pamphlet candidly entitled *Counter Revolutionary Warfare*. This accurately depicted the Australian army's role in Vietnam. As Frank Frost has shown, however, it was flawed by several fundamental

A corporal with the Army Engineers emerges from a tunnel below a village, having searched it, along with infantrymen of the 6th Battalion, during operation Enoggera in 1966.

contradictions. Most important, while it acknowledged that in revolutionary war 'the main part of the struggle is political', it described the methods of revolutionary war supposedly employed by guerrillas as almost entirely coercive and violent.

This inability to conceptualise accurately the nature of the conflict was inherent in the development of the counter-revolutionary army. Its professionalism, organisation, and tactics in Vietnam had been shaped from the late 1940s by a reaction against fundamental changes in the world order generally, and in Asia, specifically. The battalions which went to Vietnam were very proficient in small-scale patrolling tactics. But the political conditions in Vietnam were completely different from those in Malaya which had shaped this tactical thinking. Following the success in Malaya, the Australian government simplistically projected its Malayan view onto Vietnam's affairs where they confronted the alarming success of Vietnam's nationalism. This placed the army in an unnecessarily perilous position.

YOU WILL TELL THE SOLDIERS NOTHING

The first sentence of the Chiefs of Staff Directive to the Commander, Australian Force Vietnam (COMAFV) is at best misleading. It stated that 'as a result of a request of the Republic of Vietnam' the Australian Government had 'agreed' to provide it military assistance to defeat 'Communist-inspired insurgency and aggression'. It is now well established that the Saigon government did not make the 'request' as Prime Minister Menzies claimed in Parliament on 29 April 1965. After weeks of pressure by the Americans on Australia's behalf, the Saigon government informed Menzies that it accepted the Australian 'offer' of combat troops. Menzies' careful wording hints of the government's paranoia and deceitfulness over its Vietnam commitment.

The fabricated request helped to obscure the fact that the Vietnamese conflict was a civil war, by suggesting Australia was responding to a plea for help against an external threat. Additionally, although the National Service Legislation of 1965 was absolutely necessary to maintain the Vietnam commitment, it had been passed without any public reference to Vietnam. Thus it was with 'great secrecy' that, two months before the 'request', on 24 February 1965, the Commanding Officer of 1 RAR, Lieutenant Colonel Brumfield, was warned that his unit would soon be deployed somewhere in Southeast Asia. He was told nothing more.

For the token combat force which the government began to send to Vietnam in 1965, the combination of secrecy and deliberately institutionalised ignorance was not edifying. After a stealthy drive in covered trucks to the Garden Island docks in Sydney, the first elements of 1 RAR to depart Holsworthy for Vietnam on 28 May 1965 slipped out of Port Jackson on HMAS *Sydney* in the dead of night. The soldiers were subdued. Many had left families that had been harassed by obscene telephone calls. The battalion's preparations for Vietnam had been hampered by ammunition shortages and insufficient time – only three months – to carry out more than one major training exercise.

Thus the main effect of official secrecy was to hamper the preparation of Australian forces for Vietnam (it is hard to imagine how it could have hampered the enemy). The situation did not improve over the next year. 105 Field Battery, Royal Australian Artillery, had no time for training because it was only given four weeks' notice before its departure in September. It was only through a prostitute, who was conducting parallel liaisons with a member of the battery and a sailor from the HMAS *Sydney,* that the

An Australian soldier digs in like the enemy, to improve the protection and camouflage of himself and his weapons.

battery finally found out its exact date of departure. In late January 1966, Lieutenant Colonel Warr, the Commanding Officer of 5 RAR, first heard from television that his battalion would be replacing 1 RAR in May. This meant that 5 RAR, like Lieutenant Colonel Townsend's 6 RAR which soon followed, was no better served with training time or stores than 1 RAR. Moreover, when Warr made special efforts to obtain information about the nature of the conflict so that his troops would have something to tell their families before they departed, Army intelligence channels replied. 'You will tell the soldiers nothing.'

This reply had a bizarre sequel. Warr, dissatisfied, requested information on the nature of the conflict from an academic at the Australian National University. Initially, the academic advised him not to seek such information. Eventually, however, he agreed to meet Warr on a street corner in Canberra and drove him to a quiet spot near Fairbairn airport where they had an unsatisfactory discussion. Finally, Captain Robert O'Neill, a Rhodes Scholar and later the battalion intelligence officer, prepared such lectures for the soldiers as he could under the circumstances.

The operational implications of the general lack of information were also reflected in the inability of the battalions to obtain suitable armaments and operational equipment. Before 1 RAR departed, Brumfield had made a logistics plan. This was thwarted because the supply authorities had not been informed the battalion was preparing to go to Vietnam. Similarly, Warr in 5 RAR could not put his plans into effect. He had not yet been officially informed that his battalion was to replace 1 RAR in May 1966 (although it was widely known). Nevertheless, he visited Biên Hòa in January 1966 where 1 RAR operated as a unit of the American 173rd Airborne Brigade. There Warr learned that, not only were 1 RAR's boots falling apart and its shirts disintegrating, but also that better communications equipment

ABOVE: The first Australian combat soldiers prepare to land in Vietnam in 1965.

OPPOSITE PAGE: Trucks and landrovers of the Australian Army on board HMAS *Sydney*, bound for Vietnam.

and more heavy weapons were required for operations under Vietnamese conditions. On his return to Australia, however, Warr's requests to Army Headquarters only elicited the response that his battalion would have to demonstrate the need for more radios and machine guns once it got to Vietnam; which in due course, it did.

Owing to the very different Australian and American operational styles, 1 RAR had felt uncomfortable operating with the Americans. Consequently, 5 RAR was given the responsibility of setting up an independent Australian Task Force Base at Núi Đất in Phước Tuy province. The battalion expected a regimental-size attack in the early phase of its occupation but lacked the necessary arms and equipment from Australian sources. So one of the battalion officers was sent to steal five .50 calibre machine-guns from an American depot at Vũng Tàu. Another went to Saigon with a load of slouch hats and shower buckets which he bartered for sixty field telephones. Meanwhile, 6 RAR, under Lieutenant Colonel Townsend, felt that his unit was not properly equipped to develop speedily the defences at Núi Đất. Initially, not even picks and shovels were available. The shortage of tents was exacerbated by their tendency to rot in the monsoon. One 5 RAR officer has described as 'criminal' the ignorance and negligence which this state of affairs reflected in the government and Army headquarters. This negligence, however, was endemic to the entire commitment, and it inevitably undermined from the start the Australian position in Phước Tuy province.

A major reason for choosing this province was the relative ease with which the anchorage and airfield at Vũng Tàu could be used to evacuate or reinforce the Task Force if the situation there suddenly deteriorated. Although this was a prudent command decision, it also indicated the general unease with which the Australian generals approached the war. The wisdom of the decision to locate the base at Núi Đất, in the centre of the province, has been questioned by at least two Task Force commanders, because

OPPOSITE PAGE: Better known as a pop star back in Australia, Trooper Normie Rowe is seen here in his M-113 armoured personnel carrier at fire support base Kerry, in Biên Hòa province.

RIGHT: Australian soldiers arriving in Vietnam in June 1965 are equipped with American-style camouflage helmets.

of the enormous strains it placed on the command system, the manpower, and the logistics necessary to maintain the security of the base. These strains could have been avoided by choosing the much more secure coastal area near Vũng Tàu, where the Australian Logistics Support Group was positioned. What overrode these considerations, however, was the Australian desire to go bush and operate independently.

This desire reflected the ethos of the small professional army. An American psychiatrist has observed that the 'token' Australian commitment to the war forced Australian soldiers to structure their perception of the environment through such intense identification with their unit that 'they have made it their sole reference group'. This intense unit identification arose partly from the official psychosis about secrecy that enveloped the involvement. It was also related to the greatest operational problem that commanders faced once their units scrounged enough equipment to 'go bush': their inability to get clear orders from the government.

The principal tasks which Canberra envisaged for the Task Force were to 'dominate' Phước Tuy province and to maintain the security of its main highway, Route 15. However, the recipient of this directive, the COMAFV (initially General Mackay in Saigon), did not really have operational control of the Task Force: this lay with the American II Field Force at Long Bình. The American commander, however, simply told the first Task Force Commander, Brigadier Jackson, to 'take over Phước Tuy'. Neither this instruction nor the tasks envisaged in Canberra were very meaningful. This was partly because the Task Force's relation to both the local allied Vietnamese authorities and the American advisory command structure in the province were largely unworkable. In addition, the government's refusal to acknowledge the nature of the war never permitted it to clarify the army's role.

When 5 RAR occupied the Task Force position at Núi Đất, it discovered that much of the enemy resistance in the province was coming from within the villages. This contradicted the government's simplistic rhetoric about 'communist aggression from the north'. In fact, Vietnamese histories show that the National Liberation Front's (NLF's) decision-making process was remarkably decentralised. For example, D445 Battalion, which would later become a familiar foe of the Australians in Phước Tuy, was formed in the Long Tan base area on 19 May 1965. Its formation was a local response to the growing

ABOVE: Australian soldiers of 8 RAR on the road to Núi Đất after their arrival in Vietnam.

LEFT: Australian troops en route for Vietnam.

momentum of the NLF whose forces were destroying approximately a battalion of the Saigon army each week. Furthermore, D445 was formed on instructions from the local province committee at Bà Rịa from the reorganisation of local units that had a genealogy going back to the 1940s.

Of course, the notion of some of the Australian government's opponents at the time, that the war was primarily the result of a local southern uprising in the early 1960s, was also over-simplified. Regular main force units of the People's Army of Vietnam (PAVN), with its high command in Hanoi, did enter Phước Tuy province. The main elements of the PAVN's 5th Division, 274 and 275 Regiments, frequently supported local units including D445 Battalion and the Châu Đức and Long Dat District Companies which had their roots in the villages of Phước Tuy. Australian commanders were also unaware that Phước Tuy had been the scene of divisional-size operations which PAVN launched around Bình Gia in late 1964 and early 1965 to mark their escalation of the anti-American phase of the war. The 'communist aggression from the north' or 'southern uprising' dichotomy was false. The Task Force had to discover for itself that the nature of the war was far more complex than it had been led to believe. This placed it in a very difficult position.

Despite government rhetoric about 'communist aggression', it had still armed the troops lightly for countering guerrillas. Yet, being a small force, it simply did not have the manpower to police all the villages. The Task Force was therefore confronted with the necessity of dealing with both main force units coming into the province and local guerrilla units supported by the villages. It was caught in multiple dilemmas while also lacking coherent command relationships and meaningful instructions from Canberra. One Australian Commander, General Pearson, said that the government's failure to develop a clear concept of the Task Force's functions was a serious problem: 'We weren't given a task, an aim…It's the first war we've gone into without a political aim that's expressed as an aim.'

The government had a clear political aim: to use the Task Force to encourage the Americans to suppress Vietnamese nationalism, principally by maintaining the division of the country and an unpopular client government in Saigon. But for political reasons this aim was inexpressible. Because the government's grounds for making a commitment and fabricating the 'request' were so politically dubious, it shrouded the involvement in obsessive secrecy. 1, 5, and 6 RAR therefore led the army into battle in Vietnam without adequate arms, equipment, and information. More importantly, they lacked a clear military rationale for being there in the first place. Yet, since the late 1940s, the Army had been shaped to operate in precisely those conditions. So as soon as the Army went into combat, its professionalism came to the fore to neutralise to some extent the dilemmas confronting it.

AIMLESS OPERATIONS

Five weeks into its tour with the 173rd Airborne Brigade, 12 platoon, D Company got 1 RAR's first kill. Three enemy soldiers had come up a track while the platoon was having a ten-minute break on one of its stealthy patrols. Machine-gunner, Private Bruno Jaudzemis, killed one of the enemy instantly at a range of 15 metres; another was wounded and the third crawled forward and dragged his wounded comrade away. This small-scale action, which caught both sides by surprise, was typical of many others fought by 1 RAR over the next twelve months. From time to time the pattern changed: Captain Rothwell surprised the village of Đức Thạnh and took it without casualties to his own force in November. Conversely, when the battalion attacked major NLF sanctuaries in the Hố Bò Woods in January 1966. D Company lost

two men killed and ten wounded in the first few days of the operation. In general, however, Australian operations relied on stealthy, well dispersed patrolling by small units. This makes a revealing contrast with American methods.

Initially, the Australians were in awe of American technology, 'the Yanks have a fantastic number of choppers. It's nothing to see 140 go past in a straggling line.' This was Second Lieutenant Clive Williams' first response to the American helicopter lift capacity. American artillery support was also far more lavish than anything the Australians had ever imagined (American gunners in fact accidentally bombarded 1 RAR's Headquarters area as the battalion embarked on the Hố Bò Woods operation in January 1966). Under the impact of the new technology, there were some ways in which Australian operations tended to break out of the old Malayan mould. In Vietnam, heliborne mobility, resupply, and rapid medical evacuation, as well as fire support from fixed-wing aircraft and helicopter gunships, all had an impact on Australian operational thinking. Yet, there were fundamental ways in which the Australians were unable to adapt to American methods. The Australian operational focus was still the thirty-man platoon: the American focus was the 900-man battalion.

The American army was a mass, largely conscripted army, totally committed to executing the war with a vast, demonic orchestration of technology, manpower, and fire power. The 173rd's operational methods consisted of saturation bombing with aircraft, artillery, and mortars. Infantry soldiers lined up for a 'partridge drive', advancing noisily. They were ambushed frequently. Yet they often broke out of these ambushes and inflicted heavy casualties on the enemy with sheer fire power and aggression. Typically, in a

OPPOSITE PAGE: Troops of the 1st Battalion, the Royal Australian Regiment, move through dry paddy fields after being landed by American helicopters.

RIGHT: Early in Australia's war in Vietnam, 1st Battalion drag out dead 'Viet Cong' at Chinh Duc.

one-hour contact in War Zone D on 6 July. Company B of the 2/503, 'the Bulls', had five killed and eight wounded, while Company C had six killed and thirty-one wounded when it broke out of an ambush on the same day. The entire Australian battalion lost some sixteen killed and 116 wounded during its twelve-month tour.

The Australian Army, being a very small force, depended on tactical proficiency for its survival. The American commander, General Westmoreland, observed that the Australian forces were:

> thoroughly professional ... small in numbers and well trained, particularly in antiguerrilla warfare ... the Australian Army was much like the post-Versailles German Army in which even men in the ranks might have been leaders in some less capable force.

Given their very different approaches to the war, however, there was inevitable friction between the Australians and the Americans.

Australian awe of American technology was mingled with strong professional criticism of the American 'partridge drive' approach. Sometimes, Australian officers found it hard to accept the mindless destruction caused by the American army. Villages were often destroyed, 'just leaving people squatting there in the fields'. On occasions the commando-style, antiguerrilla capability of the Australians irritated the Americans. One officer of the 173rd thought that Australian operations might have been suitable for Malaya but were 'far too detailed' for Vietnam. Dispersal and methodical patrolling tended to

The Big Picture

THE AMERICAN WAR IN VIETNAM 1965–68

1 RAR (First Battalion of the Royal Australian Regiment) was only one of the first thirteen allied battalions into Vietnam; it was planned soon to be only one out of forty-four. The strategy of the American commander, General Westmoreland, was in two phases: first, by the end of 1965, to establish forces in six coastal enclaves (Da Nang, Hue/ Phu Bai, Biên Hòa/Vũng Tàu, Chu Lai, Qui Nhon, Quảng Ngãi) as a logistical base for the larger force; second, to take the war to the PAVN and PLAF, especially main force units in the highlands who dominated the countryside, leaving a strengthened ARVN to deal with irregular forces in the lowlands. From fortified firebases they would patrol offensively – 'search and destroy' – seeking out the enemy and relying on artillery, airstrikes and heliborne reinforcements to devastate him with minimum cost in allied casualties. Westmoreland hoped for victory by late 1967.

    Seeking an early major victory, US forces attacked a PLAF base near Chu Lai in August 1965. Despite a considerable manpower – and overwhelming firepower – advantage, the bulk of the PLAF regiment escaped with heavy losses on both sides (600 PLAF dead and 122 captured; 200 American casualties). The area remained a PLAF stronghold. Meanwhile, in October, three PAVN regiments attacked ARVN outposts along the road link with Cambodia running through the Ia Drang valley to Pleiku. Fearing the enemy would try to cut southern Vietnam in two through the highlands, Westmoreland rushed the air-mobile US 1st Cavalry Division to the rescue. After a month. US forces claimed 1800 PAVN dead to 300 of their own casualties. This was a victory for air and fire power.

By the beginning of 1966, Westmoreland had established a foothold in the highlands, penetrating deeper into NLF-controlled territory than had any ARVN forces. Yet the PLAF and PAVN had driven the American-led special forces out of the A Shau valley and successfully attacked Da Nang airport and many other bases. Westmoreland now had 350 000 troops supporting 315 000 ARVN regulars and a similar number of irregulars. The revolutionary forces had just over a third of this strength: 68 000 PLAF and 46 000 PAVN regulars; 320 000 guerrillas. Although well supplied with small arms, the latter lacked heavy weapons, air power, armour and wheeled transport. Nevertheless, the DRV refused to go onto the defensive; main force attacks continued, along with guerrilla warfare, to convince Westmoreland he could not achieve a rapid decisive victory. When Buddhist protests revived in mid-1966 in Hue and Da Nang, PAVN forces seized the opportunity to try and seize Quảng Trị and Thua Thien provinces below the DMZ. The American response of building an anti-infiltration screen along the DMZ and a string of fire bases at Con Thien, Gio Linh, Camp Carroll, Rock Pile and Khe Sanh along route 9 to the Laotian border, led to fierce fighting and an American claim of another victory.

Further south, 2000 US and ARVN troops supported by extensive airstrikes, sought out the PLAF headquarters near the Cambodian border. Although another victory was claimed, supported by high enemy 'body counts', the region remained under NLF control. In January 1967, Westmoreland launched a major offensive against the Iron Triangle, a PLAF base area 35 kilometres northeast of Saigon, hoping to pre-empt an attack against RVN population centres. Using extensive helicopter support, massive infantry sweeps and extravagant artillery and air support, this led to the complete destruction of the large pro-NLF village of Ben Suc and to yet another victory claim: but the bulk of the PLAF forces again escaped. Almost immediately, Westmoreland returned to seek out again the PLAF head-quarters near Cambodia, with almost identical results.

By mid-1967, the war was in a new phase of stalemate. The Americans had inflicted heavy casualties, penetrated formerly secure PLAF base areas and even forced some PAVN support elements into Laos and Cambodia. ARVN had recovered significantly. An election was even held in September, making General Thiệu the president. It was now clear that the PAVN and PLAF could not defeat the Americans militarily. But they still controlled much of the countryside and villages, able to harass at will. Westmoreland returned to Washington in November to tell congressmen that although the enemy was not yet defeated, there was 'light at the end of the tunnel'. He did not realise that this was the light of a locomotive coming straight at him – the Tet Offensive.

minimise contact with the enemy and result in a lower kill ratio. American views of the Australians were thus ambiguous; they acknowledged Australian professionalism but questioned its effectiveness under Vietnamese conditions. This incompatibility in Australian and American methods had led to the establishment of the Núi Đất base from May-June 1966.

The Vietnamese enemy's perceptions of the Australian Task Force complemented the view which the Americans had already formed. References in recent Vietnamese accounts of Australian operations in 1966 and 1967 are relatively few and usually fleeting. For example, in a half-page reference to Operation *At Zi Hoc* (Hardihood), which cleared the Task Force base, one Vietnamese account dwells almost entirely on the American air, armoured, and airborne forces which assisted the Australians in their occupation, merely noting the presence of 'one Australian battalion' and a 'New Zealand artillery battery'. It indicates nothing of the small-scale contacts from late May in which 5 RAR began to suffer, and inflict, light casualties. Instead, it emphasises that D445 battalion and Châu Đức District Company, with a main force regiment, 'caused many losses for the *American Army*'.

The Vietnamese tended to have an ambiguous view of the Task Force. Although fleeting, their references usually suggest that it was having an impact in the region. The New Zealand artillery, which had operated with 1 RAR at Biên Hòa and then went on to support the Task Force, is singled out in a number of short, sharp references for its fierce effects. In operations in the Minh Dam base area in early June, for instance, the Vietnamese say 'the New Zealand Artillery fired into the base and demolished it violently'. There are other ways in which the Vietnamese sources confirm Australian assessments of the professionalism of the small Australian force in the second half of 1966. Australian accounts show that as the Task Force established itself under adverse conditions in Núi Đất, the soldiers had to mount pickets

OPPOSITE PAGE: A soldier of Charlie Company, 5th Battalion, is helped towards a helicopter after being injured by shrapnel from a booby-trap grenade, in 1966.

RIGHT: A prisoner is held by Delta Company, after an engagement.

and radio watches while also conducting a strenuous patrol program. The professionalism required to override the enormous strains inherent in this situation was soon revealed dramatically.

On 17 August, a heavy mortar barrage on the Task Force base killed one Australian soldier and wounded twenty-two others. The scale of this barrage indicated the presence of at least a main force regiment in the area. Patrols were sent out. Then in driving rain at 3.40 pm on the 18th, D Company 6 RAR under Major Harry Smith confirmed these indications when it came under sustained fire from strong elements of PAVN's 5th Division and D445 battalion in a rubber plantation near Long Tan.

The longest written Vietnamese reference to the action at Long Tan (which runs to thirteen lines), explains that there was 'a prearranged plan', which the Regional Military Committee and the Province Committee of Bà Rịa–Long Khánh ordered, 'to teach the Australian Army a lesson just after its new arrival'. It is almost certain that the mortar barrage was designed to draw Australian forces out of the Task Force base into what the Vietnamese saw as 'our ambush ground'. As D Company came under mass attacks, 11 Platoon, the right-hand forward platoon under Second Lieutenant Gordon Sharp, was cut off, sustaining heavy casualties, including Sharp, who inexplicably stood up and was fatally shot through the throat around 4 pm. By around 6.30 pm, when Colonel Townsend of 6 RAR broke through with infantry mounted in Armoured Personnel Carriers (APCs), D Company had been in very great danger of being overrun. Seventeen of its members were killed in the largest Australian action of the war. The Australians had learned a lesson about the dangers that a small force, trained in antiguerrilla tactics, faced against main-force regulars in Vietnam. Thereafter, it was standard procedure for a 'ready reaction company' to be constantly on stand-by at Núi Đất.

The Vietnamese history makes the grossly exaggerated claim that 500 Australians were killed at Long

Tan and ignores the very heavy casualties D Company inflicted on its attackers. Nevertheless, the unusual length of the reference suggests that the action had a considerable impact on the Vietnamese. D Company remained steady, and after a body count, claimed to have killed 245 of its enemy. The accurate defensive fire of three artillery batteries at Núi Đất also played a major role in saving D Company. Particular mention is also made in the Vietnamese history of how Townsend's APC-borne counter-attack from Núi Đất 'came through into our ambush ground in the pouring rain'.

In his own book, the Australian machine-gunner. Terry Burstall of 12 Platoon. D Company has most clearly illuminated the basic lesson which Long Tan had for all parties. The strong Vietnamese force had been unable to overrun D Company, before Townsend forced it to withdraw, because the Australians were so widely dispersed that their attackers could not fix the limits of their position. Part of the reason for this dispersal was fortuitous. The early isolation of the unlucky 11 Platoon had prevented the company from concentrating as it would otherwise have done, although the standard wide dispersal of Australian patrols was undoubtedly an additional factor.

Despite such professionalism, however, the Task Force could not escape the ambiguity of being an essentially small counterguerrilla force operating in a large war with both irregular and regular dimensions. As indicated, the Americans noted the professionalism of the Australians but doubted its effectiveness. The Vietnamese could see its effective side, but realised that this was ephemeral. Indeed by October, local resistance committees around Phước Tuy did what they had done on many occasions since the war began against the French in 1945. In the face of temporarily superior forces, they reverted from an emphasis on regular war to irregular guerrilla war. This change of strategy was part of a more generalised policy change in the Dong Nai region where a high level 'guerrilla conference' in October studied the American build-up around Biên Hòa, and decided that, to reduce casualties, small-scale guerrilla attacks on lines of communication was the appropriate course of action for the time being.

Meanwhile, the Australian commanders had come to recognise clearest of all the ambiguity of their new situation. While the Task Force had initially braced itself against the main-force threat, it had already become aware of the resistance that existed in the villages. 5 RAR became particularly skillful at cordon and search operations that were designed to destroy the enemy infrastructure in the villages and to encourage the villagers to support the Saigon government. Such operations required the Australian troops to move undetected to a village, cordon it, then search for enemy cadres and supplies. Australian troops also carried out civic aid where medical teams tended the villagers. Performances by the regimental band often heightened the tone of proceedings. In at least two cases, this more subtle approach was not maintained and villages were destroyed. One such incident occurred on Long Sơn Island involving 5 RAR, against the wishes of its officers. Another involved 6 RAR at Phước Long village in June, where Corporal Laurie Drinkwater commented, 'We've done the killing and burning, when does the raping start?'

The destruction of these villages draws attention to the limitations of the 'northern invasion' theory of the war. Indeed, the success which the Task Force generally enjoyed in its cordon and search operations was itself inherently limited in terms of winning the war. As soon as the Australians left the villages, their enemy returned. Moreover, while they continued to have many small-scale contacts with local guerrilla forces, the Australians could never ignore the main force threat. Despite the enemy emphasis on guerrilla operations after October, 274 and 275 Regiments were still located in the jungles of the far northeast and northwest of the province in December 1966, 275 Regiment attacked the small government post at

The battlefields of Long Tan.

Lò Gốm, Phước Tuy, in March 1967, but it failed badly.

The Task Force was thus caught in a web of strategic dilemmas. 5 RAR's intelligence officer, Robert O'Neill, has described how scarcely a week passed in which his commanding officer Colonel Warr 'did not ask me what our aim in Phước Tuy was and then proceed to debate the matter for half an hour or so.' Under the great pressure of these dilemmas, the second Task Force commander, Brigadier Graham, made an error in early 1967 that would cloud Australian operations until the Task Force withdrew from Vietnam in 1971. The decision was to build a barbed-wire fence and lay a minefield for eleven kilometres between Đất Đỏ and Phước Hai.

Mines and booby traps laid by the enemy had inflicted numerous casualties on Australian forces since 1 RAR's operations began in 1965. Both 5 RAR and 6 RAR had relatively minor incidents with mines in 1966. But on 21 February 1967, 5 RAR experienced an appalling incident in the Long Hải Hills. At 2.07 pm a tremendous explosion hurled an eleven-ton APC into the air and it landed on its side ten feet away. When help arrived for the wounded, antipersonnel mines seeded around the area were set off. As the Regimental Medical Officer, Captain Tony White, moved through the carnage without any consideration for his own safety, he treated some twenty-two casualties and organised their evacuation. Seven of these died. This was a mine ambush. The laying of the minefield provided the enemy with ammunition for many more.

Graham's decision had not necessarily been wrong in principle; because of his shortage of manpower, he simply did not have the necessary troops to cut off enemy forces in the east of the province from their main sources of supply in the southern and central areas of the province. In other wars including Malaya, and the Algerian-Tunisian frontier, barbed-wire fences had been used successfully to isolate guerrilla forces from their sources of supply. Furthermore, Vietnamese sources indicate the initial effectiveness of the minefield. They devote far more attention to it than to any other aspect of the Task Force's operations – one devotes half a chapter. They leave us in no doubt that it caused the guerrilla and main force units in the region serious problems once it was fully laid between March and July 1967.

> From the Minh Dam base to the south, the Australian fence and minefield had cut liaison between the three zones in [Long Dat] district. The Minh Dam base was isolated, Communications between the district and the province and vice versa were cut. Rice fields around Hoi My, Cầu Sa etc, had to be abandoned and the lack of production had a bad influence on the people's economy. Communications difficulties then created great food supply difficulties for the revolutionary forces outside (the villages). The cadres and soldiers of Long Dat had to eat bamboo shoots, dig for roots, and eat jungle vegetables in place of rice.

Nevertheless, the soldiers of Long Dat soon breached the minefield. More importantly, they soon learned how to lift the mines so that they could use them later against the Australians.

For minefields to be secure they must be patrolled or covered by fire. Graham had not neglected this vital necessity. With insufficient troops, however, he depended on the local Saigon government forces who failed to patrol his minefield properly.

The Vietnamese of Long Dat suffered perhaps thirty casualties trying to find a way to destroy the minefield. Nevertheless, in early September, one, Hung Manh, came across a mine with a damp detonator and lifted it. Once the mechanism of the mines was understood, courses on lifting them were conducted 'widely' for regular soldiers, guerrillas, and cadres. A mine-lifting 'emulation movement' swept through the villages. Hundreds of mines were soon being lifted and relaid to protect the Minh Dam base area.

From Da Che mountain running past Giếng Gạch temple to the fields at Bong we relaid over 200 mines. In the villages the guerrillas also used the Australian mines to create 'suicide zones' for the enemy, and to protect the base.

In some areas, the Australian minefield was also 'transformed into a base, a secure place for us to hide our supplies'. By late 1967, by which time 7 and 2 RAR had replaced 5 and 6 RAR, Graham's minefield strategies had clearly failed. In fact, the mines were being relaid by the Vietnamese with such effect that a later Task Force commander estimated that between September 1968 and May 1970. 50% of Australian casualties 'were from our own mines'.

The tragedy of the minefield thus brought into sharp focus the nature of Australia's commitment to the war. The Army had been sent to the war without a clear military aim. The dilemma of having to deal with both the main force and local guerrilla threats without being properly armed or manned for either role inevitably affected the Task Force. Most notably, this culminated in the decision to lay the minefield. Additionally, Australian commanders did not have a sufficiently clear understanding of their operational environment or the capacities of the Saigon government and its forces. This arose essentially because of the Australian government's failure to understand or acknowledge the nature of the war. Thus, if Graham had understood the nature of the Saigon regime, it is possible that he would not have taken the fatal decision to depend on its forces to patrol the minefield. But, then, if senior officers had understood the nature of

ABOVE LEFT: An Australian Army camp in Vietnam in 1967.

ABOVE RIGHT: Brigadier S.C. Graham. Commander of the Task Force, in 1967.

the war, they might have doubted the government's foundation for prosecuting it in the first place.

Indeed, by early 1967, the COMAFV in Saigon. General Mackay, held grave doubts about the outcome of the war. He communicated these privately to the Chairman of the Chiefs of Staff committee, General Wilton. Mackay had concluded from his own observations that the Saigon authorities...

> ... were chronically inefficient, corruption and graft were rife, there were no outstanding Vietnamese military or civilian leaders and there seemed to be no will to win.

About six months later, when Westmoreland offered the Australians the opportunity to take over from the Americans the full advisory as well as combat role in the province, the Australian response was negative. A colleague, General Vincent, believed that Wilton rejected this proposal because he was thinking of the consequences if the war was lost. The Australian commitment was therefore being kept as small, and as secret, as possible because of the government's and commanders' uncertainty over the war.

This secrecy would gradually lose its effect once the shock of the Tet Offensive in early 1968 began to alert the Australian public to the lies and deceptions which the government had used to commit the troops. Nevertheless, it would not entirely lose effect until basic changes in American policy forced the government to withdraw the Task Force in 1971. Once again, as a result of their professionalism, the succeeding units of the Task Force continued to fight as well as 1 RAR, 5 RAR, 6 RAR and their supporting units had done between 1965 and 1967.

CONSCRIPTION AND DISSENT

The Genesis of Anti-War Protest

Ann Mari Jordens

Most people today associate anti-war dissent with the intense controversy which erupted in Australia during the period of Australia's involvement in the Vietnam war. In fact, Australia has a long tradition of anti-war dissent. Since the time of the Boer War, anti-war organisations were formed which strove to influence both government decision making on foreign policy and defence, and the perceptions of these issues by the general public.

The influence of three overlapping ideological traditions can be detected among the people joining these organisations – religious, socialist, and liberal internationalist. Religious anti-war dissent generally came from those non-conformist Protestant churches, especially influential among the working and lower middle class, which stressed individual conscience more than the authority of the state, and looked back to the pacifist roots of early Christianity. Thus Quakers and Congregationalists were more likely to be found in anti-war organisations than were Anglicans or Catholics. Socialist anti-war dissent, prominent in such working-class bodies as trade unions, drew on a tradition of thinking which had its roots in the French Revolution. It accepted the legitimacy of class war, but saw most modern wars as the product of capitalist economic interests, conducted at the expense of a working class coerced into the army either by conscription or by economic necessity. Liberal anti-war dissent, often influenced by non-conformist Protestantism, rejected war as basically irrational. This tradition can be traced back to the Enlightenment, but derived largely from Rousseau. Kant and Bentham. Prominent in small but often influential sections of the middle and upper classes, including American tycoons such as Henry Ford and Andrew Carnegie, this liberalism sought to create an order in which international conflicts would be solved through the enforcement of international law by internationally accepted adjudicating bodies such as the Hague Court, the League of Nations or the United Nations. Its adherents looked forward to a future in which governments would be forced to seek such peaceful solutions to their problems by pressure from a public educated to reject war as an uneconomic and counterproductive way of achieving peace.

Before the First World War, religious and liberal dissenters collaborated in branches of the London Peace Society throughout Australia. They strove unsuccessfully to counteract what they saw as the growing militarisation of Australian society by lobbying politicians, attempting to influence the school curriculum and educating the public. They also attempted to have more liberal provisions for conscientious objectors incorporated into the compulsory military training scheme which was introduced in 1911. Social and legal sanctions during the war dissuaded many dissenters from anti-war activities. Those who persisted, however, amalgamated with socialist-based bodies. After the war liberal internationalism grew in popularity among the middle class and large numbers of often influential people joined the League of Nations Union. Socialists dissociated themselves from it, seeing the League as a device for perpetuating Western capitalism internationally, and for countering movements for political, social and economic reform.

OPPOSITE PAGE: The Anzac Day service at the Melbourne Shrine of Remembrance in 1967.

The perceived threat to world peace posed by the rise of fascism in Europe, prompted a new amalgamation between middle- and working-class dissent in the International Peace Campaign, founded in 1936. This body advocated war against fascism, and thus lost the support of pacifists, who joined the Peace Pledge Union, and of isolationists, who either advocated non-involvement in what they saw as 'Old World entanglements' or supported the British policy of appeasement and non-intervention. This 'popular front' against fascism dissolved in 1939 when the Soviet Union signed a non-aggression pact with Germany. After Hitler's invasion of the Soviet Union in June 1941, however, Australians of all political persuasions united in support of the war, with the exception of a handful of dedicated pacifists.

The use of the atomic bomb in the final days of the war against Japan introduced a new element into anti-war dissent. Although small in number, Australian pacifists campaigned to halt the manufacture of atomic bombs and their testing, particularly on Australian soil. Communists abandoned 'class collaboration' in the post-war years, and it was not until 1949 that Labor leftists and communists began drifting back into the peace movement.

The government of Robert Menzies, which came to power in 1949, mounted a concerted effort to discredit the left in Australia, Attempts to ban the communist party, the Petrov Royal Commission and attacks on public servants with liberal internationalist or socialist views, created a climate which discouraged liberal middle-class association with the left. Nevertheless, the peace movement had been revitalised in 1949 by the foundation in Melbourne of the Australian Peace Council by the Reverends Dickie, Hartley and James, an academic, Jim Cairns; a communist, John Rodgers; and a representative of the Student Christian Movement, Heather Wakefield. Branches were quickly established in other states and a peace conference was held in Melbourne in April 1950 which attracted 10 000 participants. Despite enormous public antipathy, created by a concerted government campaign to depict the peace movement as a subversive communist-front organisation, successful peace congresses were held at three-yearly intervals throughout the fifties, and the peace movement slowly grew and became more diversified. After the Labor Party split in 1955, with the largely Catholic right wing defecting to form what became eventually the Democratic Labour Party, its participation in peace movement activities gradually increased.

The Congress for International Cooperation and Disarmament, held in Melbourne in November 1959, attracted audiences of between three and four thousand. It established permanent organising committees in most Australian states which formed the nucleus of the peace movement in the 1960s. The issues with which anti-war dissenters were preoccupied in the early sixties were of little concern to most Australians. Little attention was paid to the commitment of 30 Australian 'advisers' to Vietnam in 1962. After the leadership of the peace movement shifted from Melbourne to Sydney in 1963, however, issues of more immediate concern such as Indonesian confrontation of Malaysia and events in Vietnam, were given more attention.

On 5 August 1964 the Minister for External Affairs and chief architect of Australia's involvement in Vietnam, Paul Hasluck, announced Australia's support for American actions in the Gulf of Tonkin. The following day, Hiroshima Day rallies in Sydney and Brisbane protested against this expression of support before the United Nations Security Council had discussed the incident. They expressed their fear of either a nuclear or a Korean-type war, and urged the immediate withdrawal of Australian troops.

The Congress for International Cooperation and Disarmament, held in Sydney from 25–30 of October 1964, revealed the principal preoccupations of the anti-war movement on the eve of its most

President Johnson expresses the initial optimism felt by the United States about its conflict in Vietnam, a war which was eventually to involve Australia. On the President's right is Australian Prime Minister, Harold Holt.

active period since the First World War. It devoted rather more attention to Indonesian confrontation of Malaysia than it did to Vietnam. There was however, one paper on Vietnam delivered by Mrs E.B. Gale, of the Women's International League for Peace and Freedom. She had visited Vietnam in January 1964 with a delegation which had interviewed the Australian Ambassador and Brigadier F.P. Serong. She described the war as unwinnable and advocated settlement by reconvening the Geneva Conference and the gradual reunification of the country under Hồ Chí Minh as an Asian Tito.

Although this conference was held less than a fortnight before the introduction of conscription was announced, the subject was barely mentioned. The youth section of the conference, representing that section of society whose interests were to be most affected by conscription, omitted to mention it when they first drew up their conference statement. Almost as an afterthought the last item in the amended statement contained the resolution – 'the re-introduction of national service is not a desirable policy on the part of the Australian Government.' Nine of the delegates opposed it.

CONSCRIPTION

The Commonwealth Defence Act of 1903 reflected the concern of liberals and the Labor Party, who exercised considerable influence over Barton's minority government, that Australians should not be obliged to serve in imperial wars. Thus it made no legislative provision for compulsory overseas service for either permanent or citizen soldiers. In short. Australia's defence forces could not be sent overseas: completely separate imperial forces had to be raised for the two world wars. This remained the position in Australia, despite frequently expressed British dissatisfaction that Australia could not support them with troops in the various military conflicts of the Cold War's 'peace'. Australia's defence forces remained exactly that, forces solely for Australia's defence, until 5 November 1964, when Cabinet decided to introduce new legislation which for the first time obliged conscripts as well as permanent soldiers to serve overseas.

CONSCRIPTION FOR OVERSEAS SERVICE – INITIAL ACCEPTANCE

Such a radical departure from Australia's traditional concept of military service was achieved with almost total secrecy. Menzies' decision to introduce conscription was known beforehand and discussed only by a small group within Cabinet. Even the service ministers were unaware that the Foreign Affairs and Defence Committee of Cabinet, from which they were normally excluded, was contemplating such a move. Less than two weeks before the decision was taken, the Minister for the Army, Dr J.A. Forbes, told the national congress of the Returned Services League in Hobart on 25 October that although the government did not have a closed mind on the matter, it accepted the clear and unmistakable advice of its military advisers that conscription was not the most effective way of meeting the current situation, and that an army composed entirely of long-term volunteers was preferred.

When Labor Prime Minister, William Morris Hughes, had attempted to introduce conscription for overseas service in 1916 he had lacked the majority in the Senate to pass the necessary amendment to the Defence Act, and so resorted to a referendum. The subsequent debate bitterly divided Australians and split his party. The proposal was narrowly defeated in referenda in 1916 and in 1917. In February 1943, at a time when there was a widely held apprehension that a Japanese invasion was imminent, Labor Prime Minister, John Curtin, risked splitting his party to introduce conscription for service in a limited area by the device of designating the 'south-Western Pacific Zone' in effect as part of Australia for the duration of the war only. Australian regular soldiers had to volunteer to serve in Korea and Malaya in the 1950s. In 1964, Menzies avoided seeking a mandate before introducing conscription for overseas service. Although conscription was strongly advocated by the Returned Services League and by several Liberal members of Parliament, the issue of compulsory overseas service was not widely debated outside military circles and such academic bodies as the Australian Institute of Political Science, and the intense secrecy with which the government enshrouded its plans, ensured that no widespread debate occurred before the scheme was firmly in place. It is unclear whether this extreme secrecy was the result of Menzies' supreme confidence in his power within his own party and his popularity with the electorate, or whether it demonstrated fear of provoking adverse public reaction until the decision was a *fait accompli*. Like Curtin in 1943. Menzies was acutely conscious of firstly British, and then. American criticism of the lack of conscription

ABOVE LEFT: The Australian Army's Senior District Officer at Nam Hua uses a sampan to travel to the remote parts of his district.

ABOVE RIGHT: An Australian soldier stands guard with his M-16 over the entrance to a tunnel complex created by the enemy. Below, a fellow soldier would ease along the tunnel, torch and pistol in hand.

for overseas military service in Australia and their pressure for Australia to play a more active military role in the region. Perhaps his fear of political dissension about conscription was overridden by his fear of the diplomatic repercussions which might follow if he did not introduce it. Given the radical nature of the decision, the initial public reaction was surprisingly positive.

Australians had become used to conscription for home defence, for between 1911 and 1964 only 16 years had passed when there had not been a scheme in operation of fairly universal compulsory military training. Such a scheme received strong popular support. Opinion polls on conscription from 1942 onwards reveal a consistently high rate of approval. The use of conscripts for overseas service even in the case of another world war, however, was firmly rejected when it was polled in 1950 and 1951. The National Service system in operation from 1951 to 1960 was solely for home defence. The initial public acceptance of the announcement on 10 November 1964 of a scheme which clearly indicated that conscripts would be required to serve overseas, therefore demonstrated the extent to which the authority of the federal government had become accepted by the Australian people. The reaction in 1964 revealed the success with which the government had managed, largely through the press, to alarm the Australian public by its vision of monolithic Chinese communism sweeping inexorably down to Australia.

Military institutions take their form from the societies which construct them. Conscription schemes, therefore, vary according to the country and the period in which they arise. The form and method of operation of the scheme which operated in Australia between 1965 and 1972 reveals a great deal about Australian aims and values at this time.

Although in 1950, 87% of those polled approved of the reintroduction of compulsory military

Australia's perception of America as a close ally influenced the public attitude right through the debate about conscription. The demonstrations of support in 1966, especially those by children, were carefully orchestrated by the government, which provided American flags and often transport for the schoolchildren who crowded the streets.

training, and approval of a universal scheme remained strong throughout the decade, the government decided in late 1959 to abolish the scheme which had operated from July 1951. The Army had become increasingly hostile to this form of conscription which it saw as diverting manpower and finance to produce large numbers of semi-trained youths who could not be deployed overseas in the conflicts in Korea or Malaya, where Australian troops served during the decade. Conscription for home defence was only seen as useless when the homeland was not threatened. The Army wanted to devote its resources to producing a skilled, mobile, professional force armed with the most modern equipment, compatible with that used by American forces in counter-revolutionary wars in Asia. This became the aim of the Army's reorganisation in late 1959, when compulsory military training was abandoned and a divisional structure adopted, modelled on the American system.

The decision to introduce conscription in 1964 was, therefore, a political one and derived primarily from the perceptions of the Prime Minister and the Minister for External Affairs, Paul Hasluck, of Australia's future role in Southeast Asia – the area they perceived to be our area of primary economic and strategic concern. As Menzies revealed in his radical rethinking of Australian defence presented to Parliament on 4 April 1957, he wanted to construct on a long-term basis a force which could be quickly mobilised for use in limited, periodic, excursionary, undeclared wars in Southeast Asia in a subsidiary role to America. The central problem since this date, highlighted by America's failure to consider Australia's interests in its dispute with Indonesia over West New Guinea, was how to have Australia's voice heard in decision making by the major powers in the region. As Hasluck explained to a largely American audience in October 1964, Australia's military involvement in Korea, Malaysia and Vietnam, its aid to Thailand and other countries in the region …

> … are the expression of our political, economic and strategic interests in the region. We believe that peace and stability cannot be achieved by neutralism but by combining with like-minded nations

Such a public protest as this, which occurred in 1966, was unthinkable only two years earlier.

to defeat aggression and, at this stage of events, to give a backing of strength and military resolution to diplomatic efforts to remove threats against the territorial integrity and political independence of the nations in this region.

Public acceptance of the introduction of conscription for overseas service was aided by the widespread assumption, evident in newspapers and journals at the time, that it had been introduced for deployment in a wider conflict against Indonesia, and was thus relevant to the immediate defence of Australia. Australian and Indonesian troops had engaged in combat for the first time in South Malacca on 29 October 1964. In fact, since 6 August 1964, when the US Congress had empowered the President to take whatever action he deemed necessary in Vietnam by passing the Gulf of Tonkin resolution, Menzies and Hasluck anticipated that Australia might be asked by the USA to make a major troop commitment in Vietnam. Although unsure of American policy until the results of the presidential election on 3 November, they timed the introduction of conscription so as to be in a position to be able to offer troops as soon as the new president made his intentions clear. Australian military support would, they hoped, encourage a substantial commitment of American troops to Southeast Asia. Because American intentions in Vietnam were still unclear when Menzies announced the introduction of conscription on 10 November 1964, he made only speculative references to the increased 'risks in this corner of the world' created by the current situation in Vietnam, Indonesia's confrontation of Malaysia, and by possible threats on the West New Guinea border. As so little public dissension was aroused in November 1964 by the announced intention to deploy conscripts in combat overseas, in times when neither war nor a defence emergency had been declared, the government went ahead with its intended legislative amendments to the Defence Act on 6 April 1965, the day before it decided to commit the first battalion to Vietnam.

The decision to use conscripts was not simply related to difficulties experienced in attracting the necessary number of volunteers in a time of full employment. The number of volunteers attracted to the army is always unpredictable, as it depends not only on economic and demographic factors, but also on the perceived importance and legitimacy of the conflict to which the government is currently committing troops. Menzies and Hasluck wanted a force of predictable size which could be deployed anywhere in the region. Compulsion was to replace individual commitment to military life, or to a particular conflict. It was also cheaper than offering the rates of pay necessary to attract volunteers in a time of full employment, and than advertising for recruits. Whereas 0.07% of the army's budget was spent on recruitment activities in 1960–61, this percentage fell to 0.04% in 1964–65, and to 0.01% in 1967–68. In times of high unemployment, reliance on a volunteer army is socially inequitable; in times of full employment, as was the case in Australia in 1964, the quality, in army terms, of those volunteering is low. In 1964–65 the army rejected 8088 volunteers, 70.5% of the 11 463 who applied.

Thus by introducing conscription, the government was able to draw upon a more educated and skilled section of the workforce than it was currently attracting. It expected no opposition to conscription from commerce and industry, as it was a time of full employment. Considerable support was expected, and obtained, from those sectors concerned to develop markets in Southeast Asia. As any Australian commitment was anticipated to form a subsidiary role within the framework of a wider American commitment, it was not anticipated that large numbers would be needed. Thus although the liability to serve was universal, a highly selective intake ensured that conscription drew so lightly and randomly from the workforce as not to affect productivity significantly. The Australian Chambers of Manufacturers advocated the introduction of conscription in 1962, and it was one of the first bodies to endorse the new scheme the day after it was announced.

Unlike America, Australia did not have a strong tradition of localism, individualism, and decentralised civilian control of the military. It thus produced a system of conscription which was entirely controlled by the federal government, relied on random selection by ballot instead of consideration of the individual conscript's value to the community, and was entirely administered by bureaucrats, instead of leaving the initial selection of conscripts to local civilian draft boards, as in America. Firmly established Australian traditions of egalitarianism ensured that a more socially equitable system was developed than in America. The first public criticisms of the system after it was announced focussed on its exclusion of Aboriginal people and non-naturalised migrants. A poll on the conscription of aliens in April 1966 found that an extraordinarily large 89% wanted them included.

HOW CONSCRIPTION WORKED

Registration: All twenty-year-olds in Australia were required to register, with the exception of those defined as Aboriginals, non-naturalised migrants, employees of a foreign government, and members of the permanent military forces. There were two registration periods a year, in January for those turning twenty in the first half of the year, and in July for those whose birthdays occurred in the second half.

The Department of Labour and National Service attempted to check on those failing to register through the records of the Department of Social Service and the Electoral Office, and demanded proof of registration from those using their own employment service and those seeking passports to travel overseas, except to New Zealand. Employers were expected to refuse employment to young men unable to produce evidence of registration.

In the absence of a system of identity cards, however, the government had no precise way of identifying those who failed to register. Apparently, almost 12 000 of the eligible population did not register between 1965 and 1972. Those found guilty of failing to register were fined and conscripted whether or not their birthdates were chosen in the ballot. The likelihood of being caught, however, was not great. An annual average of 202 young men was prosecuted for failure to register between 1965 and 1971, although efforts were stepped up in the final year of the scheme when 723 were prosecuted.

The Ballot: As 761 854 young men in the Australian population turned twenty from 1965 to 1972, the problem was to select the intake needed by the army while spreading the obligation evenly over all sections of the community. Very few were required: 4200 a year was the maximum set in 1965, and this was raised to only 8400 a year from 1966.

Although not provided for in the legislation, a ballot system of selection was decided on. Its legality and constitutionality were not finally determined until 1971, when it was challenged in the High Court. Draws were held twice a year following the registration period, usually in March and September. Each of the 184 marbles spun in a barrel represented two dates, one in the first half of the year and one in the second, so that men returning to Australia after the ballot for their age group could be included in the first ballot following their return. Each marble was drawn out singly, by a different individual each ballot.

The impression of random selection was maintained by varying the number of marbles drawn out at each ballot according to a statistical analysis of the information provided in the registration forms. The calculation took account of the numbers anticipated to be entitled to exemption, indefinite or temporary deferment, those who would not meet the standards of army fitness, and those who had been balloted in from previous registration but had not been available for call-up because they had been granted temporary deferment.

In fact this practice meant that those whose birthdates fell in the period of the first ballot had more chance of being conscripted than in any subsequent period, because there was no backlog of those who had received deferments. In this first ballot 96 marbles were drawn, thereafter the number decreased markedly: 38 were drawn in September 1966, and 30 in September 1969 and March 1970. By this means the numbers balloted in were reduced from 36 000 in 1965 to 22 056 in 1969–70.

As in 1957–58, when the government introduced selection by ballot in order to reduce the numbers of those eligible for the previously universal compulsory military training scheme to 15 000 a year, such selectivity was increasingly regarded as unfair. By 1971 when the chances were only 1 in 12, only 9.7% approved of this highly selective scheme. Approval dropped to 6.5% in October 1972 when the chances of being balloted fell to 1 in 20.

The results of 11 of the 16 ballots held were kept secret. On 28 September 1970 the government yielded to criticism in parliament and the press and announced it would make public the dates drawn in subsequent ballots. Refusal to disclose the dates drawn was principally to avoid the necessity of checking whether the birthdate given on the registration form was accurate, although it was publicly explained as an attempt to avoid embarrassing those who were eligible for call-up but had been rejected by the Army. It was not until 1973 when Labor minister Clyde Cameron tabled the full list of dates drawn that conscripts were able to verify that their birthdate had in fact been chosen.

Indefinite Deferments: On 26 November 1969 President Nixon prescribed random selection so as to determine the order in which conscripts were called up, until the required numbers were attained. This was the culmination of a series of a great number of lengthy studies revealing the social inequities resulting from the system of selection by classification administered by local civilian draft boards. This system was nothing like the lottery system operating in Australia, where it was used to select, once and for all, who was to be called up and who was to be for ever exempt. In Australia, there were no occupational exemptions, except for theological students and members of religious orders (of which a total of 530 were exempted over the period 1965–72), and no attempt to classify a conscript according to his value to the community, as in America. Any attempt to generalise from the American to the Australian experience is misleading.

There was, however, provision for what was described as 'indefinite deferments' – for those with medical and psychological disabilities (of which there were 1598 from 1965–72), men married before call-up action commenced for their age group (19 102 over the whole period), those who had volunteered for the Citizen Military Force (CMF) at the time of registration, or who had been accepted for it by the time the ballot for their age group came up and who undertook to serve in it for six years, and those found by State Courts of Petty Sessions to be conscientious objectors. Thus the system provided a legal outlet for those whose moral objections to the taking of human life were stronger than their sense of duty to the state. All attempts to require an alternative form of civilian service for those recognised as conscientious objectors, however, failed during this period.

The CMF provided a legal alternative for those who did not wish to risk interrupting their careers for two years, with the chance of being sent to Vietnam. It was also a place for those conscientious objectors awarded non-combatant status to serve. A loophole in the system, which was not closed until 1971, enabled men who joined the CMF a year before they registered, and who were subsequently balloted out, to leave the CMF immediately without further obligation. Far more men used the CMF as a means of avoiding active military service than used the provisions for conscientious objection. By 30 June 1971 1012 men had been determined by the courts to be conscientious objectors, whereas 34 970 had opted to join the CMF. 1967 was the peak year for CMF enrolments with 7.1% of all those registered for conscription opting to join the militia. Thereafter the rate fell steadily to 3.7% in 1970. At the same time, those defying the legislation and refusing to take advantage of the escape valves provided by the system, increased. By June 1972, 3286 men were under investigation for suspected breaches of the National Service Act and countless more were evading registration.

Limited Deferments: Limited deferments were granted to apprentices and full-time students at universities and similar institutions, until they had completed their primary qualifications. All young men remained liable for conscription until the age of twenty-six, except for post-graduate students for whom the age limit was extended to thirty. Limited deferments were also granted to those serving criminal sentences and those able to prove in a court of petty sessions that their conscription would cause 'exceptional hardship' to themselves, their parents or dependents.

In the period before the 1966 federal election the 'exceptional hardship' provision was used extensively by the rural community, which had never before been liable for conscription, to avoid call-up. Country Party representatives in parliament made numerous attempts to have exceptional hardship exemptions made easier for rural applicants. The most numerous and most successful applications for exemption on the grounds of exceptional hardship in this early period came from rural youth. However this pressure on the system was eased by a decision in May 1966 to provide special units of the CMF where rural youth could do their service in concentrated periods.

Culling by Medical and Other Examinations: Those to whom exemptions did not apply, or whose deferments had expired, were called up for medical examination. There were three medical examinations in all, the first being conducted by casually employed civilian doctors at various centres around Australia. Conscripts who had not reached the educational level of the New South Wales Intermediate Certificate, also had to sit for an aptitude test. The army considered their character and their civil and security records with the aid of ASIO and the Commonwealth Police.

It was at this stage of the selection process that the numbers of those called up were reduced most dramatically. Between 1965 and June 1972, while 59 548 had been called up, a total (including volunteers) of 90 782 had been rejected as not meeting the medical, psychological, educational or security standards of the Army.

The numbers excluded by these examinations grew each year. In 1965, 39.7% of conscripts examined did not meet the standards of army fitness. This grew steadily and reached 51.2% in 1967 and 1970. This was a reflection not of the increasing ill health or educational unsuitability of the young men drawn upon, for while those examined in the earlier intakes were almost all unskilled and semi-skilled workers, qualified tradesmen and clerical workers, the later intakes included many more university students and apprentices, who could be expected to have a high general standard of health and education.

The progressive increase in the numbers rejected at this stage of the selection process has been used as evidence to suggest that the medical examination was exploited, especially by 'men of greater intelligence and education', as a way of avoiding call-up. Such speculation seems to have been based on extrapolation from the supposed American experience, where a very different system operated. While some of those presenting themselves for medical examination probably did attempt to fake illness, there is no evidence to suggest that this was common enough to affect the statistics significantly. The numbers of those rejected as 'psychologically' unsuitable because they expressed anti-war or anti-conscription views when interviewed probably increased but, like the numbers of those rejected on security grounds for having been arrested at demonstrations or for belonging to 'subversive organisations', they were probably statistically insignificant. An average of 16 men a year between 1965–71 were prosecuted for not attending the medical, and 70 were prosecuted in 1971–72. More probably, the growing numbers of those rejected at the medical examination resulted from more stringent medical standards being applied as a result of the Army's Vietnam experience, but above all they reflected the administration's concern to diminish the growing pool of those who had been called up but who could not be absorbed by the Army.

So many conscripts were keen to go to Vietnam that, at the stage of allocation of units, the Army was able to stream all but the most enthusiastic away from areas where overseas service would be likely. This, of course, was vigorously denied by the government which always insisted that conscripts could not choose whether or not they would serve in Vietnam. When certain rather unsubtle attempts by sections of the Army to determine the level of enthusiasm of conscripts about to be posted came to the attention of the Opposition and were raised in Parliament, the government immediately moved to condemn and correct such practices.

The final result of this extensive culling process resulted in 63 735 conscripts serving in the Army between 1965 and 1972. Of these 19 450 went to Vietnam where they constituted no more than 50% of each army unit. In Vietnam 1479 became casualties and of these 200 died.

The conscription system which operated in Australia between 1965–72, therefore, was designed to eliminate social inequity and was operated impartially by the public servants in the Department of Labour and National Service, according to the guidelines laid down in government legislation. It was perceived by the general public as being fair, until its highly selective nature became increasingly apparent, late in the decade.

Elements of social inequity were, however, introduced at those points where the system relied on non-bureaucrats. It was inevitable that the decisions of some of the magistrates judging conscientious objection and exceptional hardship applications, and the medical practitioners who conducted the preliminary medical examination of conscripts were influenced by their own social, moral and political values. There was little the Department could do to check these biases. It was much easier for a magistrate to understand an articulate applicant for conscientious objector status, who was able to demonstrate his point from a wide range of religious or historical reading, and who had the support of an older person, preferably a lawyer. This gave an advantage to those educated middle-class youths whose parents were able to engage counsel, although this was not universally true, as the case of Sydney schoolteacher William White illustrates.

Only one magistrate was responsible for hearing all the conscientious objection cases in the Sydney metropolitan area, and by early 1966 analysis of the cases Australia-wide showed that it was more difficult to obtain exemption in New South Wales than it was in any other state. In February 1966 Mr E.L. Pollard of the Federal Pacifist Council told a National anti-conscription conference that only one objector in New South Wales had been granted total exemption and that was on an appeal from the magistrate's decision. In Melbourne, where these cases were heard by a pool of magistrates, it was much easier to gain total exemption. This imbalance between the states is evident in the statistics presented to Parliament in 1971. While 342 conscientious objectors had been granted total exemption in Victoria, only 119 had been totally exempted in New South Wales. While this discrepancy cannot be wholly attributed to the influence of individual magistrates, the different structure of these tribunals in the two states must have been a significant factor. The higher success rate of rural applicants for exceptional hardship exemption in the period before 1966 was also an indication of social, and perhaps also political, bias among magistrates hearing these cases.

Although civilian medical practitioners employed by the Department of Labour and National Service were issued with guidelines, they often introduced their own standards. Statistics of rejection varied from state to state. An enquiry conducted in Queensland of the medical rejection rates in the first and third registrations showed a higher than average rejection rate in that state. The *Sun Herald* of 15 May 1966 reported that a doctor in a country town passed as medically fit every conscript he examined, including one youth with one leg two inches shorter than another. Army doctors later rejected as medically unfit more than half those he had passed. The doctor's motive was to avoid causing resentment in his small community, 'the local doctor didn't want Mrs Smith accusing him of sending her son off to war, while leaving Mrs Jones' boy safe at home,' the paper reported. Publicity created by decisions made in individual cases which seemed unfair or sometimes ludicrous, had a cumulative effect on public opinion, and served to erode gradually the popular approval with which the scheme was initially greeted.

William White

CONSCIENTIOUS OBJECTOR

A twenty-one-year-old Sydney schoolteacher, William White was the first conscientious objector in the Vietnam era to refuse call-up after having been denied total exemption from military service. He believed in the absolute sanctity of human life and refused either to kill, or to play any part in an organisation whose purpose was killing, even in a medical or educational corps. His beliefs were not derived from religion, and he did not belong to any anti-war organisation. He believed that history demonstrated that war was ineffective in achieving peace.

The Sydney Court of Petty Sessions rejected White's application for total exemption on 20 December 1965. White appealed to the District Court, Sydney, but Judge Cameron-Smith rejected his appeal, stating that his ideas were 'the result of ignorance rather than good reasoning founded on learning and logic.'

White was removed from his class at Denistone East Primary School on 18 July 1966, the day he was due to be called up. This was the first time an employee had been dismissed under the National Service Act and it aroused considerable union concern. It also prompted a spate of protests and petitions. On 1 August the Bill White Defence Committee was formed. Save Our Sons widely disseminated his views through a pamphlet, and by selling a record of 'the Ballad of Bill White', composed and performed by popular Melbourne folk-singer, Glenn Tomasetti.

On 29 August 1966 White appealed to the High Court, which unanimously dismissed his application. Later, in the Court of Petty Sessions, he pleaded guilty of failing to comply with his call-up notice, and was committed to military custody. He submitted a second application for registration as a conscientious objector, and waited at home for the military police to arrest him.

Anti-war protesters kept vigil outside White's home until 22 November, when he was dragged away, passively resisting, in a blaze of publicity. By this time even the mainstream newspapers were sympathetic to his case. His arrest inspired demonstrations in Sydney and Melbourne, and the Prime Minister at his election meeting on 24 November was drowned out by chants of 'release Bill White!'

Court martialled to 21 days in a military gaol for disobeying orders, William White totally refused to co-operate. On the expiration of his sentence his second application for total exemption as a conscientious objector was granted by the Central Court of Petty Sessions on 23 December. He was formally discharged from the Army on 30 December 1966.

The Public Service Board deemed White unsuitable to teach in front of a class, and in January 1967 he was re-appointed as a correspondence teacher.

In 1966, such images as that of Prime Minister Harold Holt side by side with the President of the United States, had a powerful effect on the public mind.

THE BATTLE FOR THE PUBLIC MIND

In most societies, only a small minority of the population are politically active, organised, interested and well-informed. The great majority are usually none of these things, especially on matters of international affairs. In many cases where a government policy does not immediately affect or interest that majority it will support passively, or defer to, the government as the legitimate authority. Although the active minority provides most of the pressure groups which are the important domestic influences on government policies, it is valuable for both the government and its opponents to claim to have the support of what the Nixon Presidency dubbed 'the Silent Majority'. This support can be verified by publication of opinion polls. This passive support is often based on the public's lack of organisation, interest and, in particular, information. Governments and their opponents sometimes join battle over the 'public mind', bombarding it with competing information and views, in order to mobilise it behind their respective policies.

The government strove throughout the Vietnam period to maintain the level of public support which had been evident when the decisions to introduce conscription (71% in November 1964) and to send troops to Vietnam (52% in May 1965) were announced. It had a formidable advantage in relation to the media in that journalists usually sought, and often relied on, information from official sources. Editors also occasionally received visits from representatives of their regional office of the Department of Labour and National Service in order to explain to them the official viewpoint on a case and to provide them with material more favourable to the government's point of view.

In controlling the importation of information from overseas, the Australian government also had legal advantages not available to the United States government, where freedom of speech was guaranteed in the constitution. As Australia's involvement in the Vietnam war was neither a declared war nor a 'defence emergency', the government was unable to rely on the extensive censorship powers provided by the Defence Act. It did, however, have considerable powers under the Crimes Act, the Customs Act and the Broadcasting and Television Control Act. People could not be accused of treason under the Crimes Act for actions or words critical of the involvement in Vietnam or supportive of Hanoi and the National Liberation Front for Southern Vietnam because it required the 'enemy' to be proclaimed. To do this, however, would be admitting that Australia was a 'party principal' in the war rather than a country coming to the aid of the Republic of Vietnam. It would have been difficult for the government to justify military intervention on the grounds of self-defence, which would have led Australians to ask what threat Hanoi posed to Australia. Individuals could be charged with sedition under the Crimes Act. But for a variety of political and diplomatic reasons, the government chose not to rely on this legislation, rather to trust in the cooperation of the media to suppress material which did not support the view of the conflict it wished to project, and to publish material it wished to disseminate. Throughout the period it found such cooperation readily forthcoming

Both the Department of External Affairs and the Prime Minister's Department produced publications presenting the government's views on Vietnam in series such as *Select Documents on Australian Foreign Policy* and *Current Notes on International Affairs* beginning in early 1965 and continuing at six-monthly intervals. Such government pamphlets and information handbooks were widely circulated; 100 000 copies of the 1966 pamphlet *Vietnam: Questions and Answers* were produced and despatched unsolicited to people whom the government considered were 'community leaders'.

PRO-WAR ORGANISATIONS

The government also had the support of a number of organisations in the community, the largest, oldest and most politically powerful of which was the Returned Services League (RSL). It saw the government's conscription and Vietnam policies as a confirmation of the policies advocated by the League over the previous fifty years. One of the most practical ways in which it stimulated and publicised public support for Vietnam was through its Australian Forces Overseas Fund which it launched on 26 January 1966. The names of individuals and businesses contributing to the scheme were regularly published in the newspapers and much of the money was used to send entertainers to Vietnam. The scheme ultimately operated on an annual budget of $200 000. In September 1966 it launched its 'RSL Operation New Life in Vietnam' – an appeal for household utensils, clothing, carpentry and gardening tools for use by the Army in its civic action work in Vietnam. By the end of 1966 it had collected 50 tons of goods, a further demonstration of the public support for government activities in Vietnam it was capable of mustering. Rotary clubs also provided amenities for Australian troops in Vietnam.

More ephemeral and less influential pro-war organisations were created throughout the period. On 14 April 1966 the Australian Action Co-ordination Centre was formed in Sydney with the encouragement of right-wing Liberal back-bencher Sir Wilfrid Kent Hughes and Sir William Yeo of the RSL. On 22 April 1966 in Melbourne the Melbourne University ALP Club, the Young Country Party, the Young Democratic Labor Association and the Young Liberals joined forces to form the Joint Vietnam Rally Committee with the encouragement of J. Jess, Liberal member for La Trobe, Country Party Senator J. Webster, the State Secretary of the Democratic Labor Party, Frank Dowling and R. Evans, editor of the socialist journal *Partisan*.

A number of academics in Sydney, Canberra and Melbourne combined in 1968 to form the Friends of Vietnam (probably styled after the American Friends of Vietnam). The society's chairman was Professor David Armstrong of the Philosophy Department, University of Sydney and its secretary, Melbourne lawyer and former Communist Party member, Kenneth Gee. In an attempt to counter the information disseminated by anti-war bodies about the nature and effects of the war in Vietnam, they published a well illustrated journal containing locally written articles as well as reprints of articles sympathetic to American involvement from overseas. Known as *Vietnam Digest*, it appeared in seven numbers from December 1968 to July 1970 and was edited by Canberra journalist Peter Samuel. Among its local contributors were historian Geoffrey Fairbairn of Australian National University, B.A. Santamaria and Brigadier F.P. Serong.

THE EARLY ANTI-WAR AND ANTI-CONSCRIPTION MOVEMENT

Far more numerous were the anti-war and anti-conscription organisations. It is impossible to be certain how many operated in this period as some were fairly short-lived, others changed their names, and a number left little evidence of their existence. There were probably about 146 anti-war organisations (other than churches, trade unions and political parties) actively opposing the Vietnam commitment and conscription at some time or other throughout the period. Nine had branches in all or most states and are described as national. In addition to these organisations there were 24 in New South Wales, 44 in Victoria, 32 in Queensland, 8 in South Australia, 9 in Western Australia, 8 in Tasmania and 12 in the Australian Capital Territory.

Some were recently formed, others had a long history in Australian anti-war dissent. Only the Eureka Youth League had direct links with the Communist Party. Although the left-wing trade unions had sustained the peace movement both financially and organisationally throughout the fifties and early sixties, their contribution became less essential as the social basis of organised protest broadened from 1964 on. Anti-war and anti-conscription bodies quite deliberately formed a loose federation of groups, each maintaining their individual ideologies and styles of activities in order to provide a range of options for the diverse types of people who opposed the government's policies on Vietnam and conscription.

Despite popular mythology, which portrays the Vietnam protest movement in terms of flower-bedecked, long-haired student radicals in colourful 'hippy' clothes demonstrating in the streets, the protest movement, at least in its early stages, was overwhelmingly dominated by the middle-aged – that section of Australian society whose values and attitudes towards war had been formed by their experiences of the 1939–45 war as young adults.

The first meeting of students to protest against the introduction of conscription, held on 12 November 1964, at the University of Sydney, was organised by E.L. Wheelright, senior lecturer in economics and one of the sponsors of the October 1964 Congress for International Cooperation and Disarmament, and A. Roberts, lecturer in physics. The Youth Campaign Against Conscription (YCAC) was launched in Sydney on 29 November 1964, at a meeting addressed by a former academic and ex-serviceman, ALP politician Jim Cairns. Tom Uren, another prominent ALP anti-war spokesman throughout the Vietnam period, had reached his convictions after witnessing the results of the atomic blast on Nagasaki, where he was held as a prisoner of war. One of the few full-time workers in the anti-war movement was Geoffrey Anderson, the secretary of the largest anti-war organisation in New South Wales, the Association for International Cooperation and Disarmament (AICD). He had been awarded a DFC for his services in the Second World War. Formed on 16 March 1964, its foundation committee comprised educated middle-aged, middle-class, men – businessmen, clergy, academics and teachers – although it did include 3 women and 5 trade unionists. It had difficulty attracting young people. By May 1966 only 4% of its membership of 1000 were categorised as 'youth and students'.

The 'teach-ins', held at universities and other educational institutions from mid-1965, represent the determination of the Second World War generation to stimulate the interest of students in Australia's involvement in Vietnam. The teach-in format – long, sometimes all-night, public meetings, usually held on university campuses, during which large audiences were exposed to a range of viewpoints on a subject – originated at the University of Michigan on 24 March 1965. New York followed step the next night and more than 100 were held across America, culminating in a national teach-in in Washington on 15 May 1965. By June the movement had spread to Oxford University in England.

The first Australian meeting to follow this format was held at the Australian National University on 23 July 1965. It was organised by a committee of ANU scholars and chaired by one of Australia's few Chinese-speaking academics, Professor C.P. Fitzgerald, professor of Far Eastern History. Among the other anti-war speakers was popular Australian novelist Morris West, who had also served in the Second World War. Supporting the government were Liberal politician, T.E.F. Hughes; academics, T. B. Millar and Geoffrey Fairbairn; and *Canberra Times* journalist, Peter Samuel. This teach-in was reported in the ANU student newspaper under the caption 'Garbage, Mr West'. The article clearly illustrated the dominance of conservative students in student opinion making at this time. The second teach-in was held at Monash University on 29 July. It was organised by a committee comprising representatives of 5 student organisations and was sponsored by 21 professors. This teach-in was remarkable for the presence of the chief architect of Australia's Vietnam involvement, Minister for External Affairs, Paul Hasluck. He was clearly outshone by Labor's chief anti-war spokesman, Jim Cairns. Teach-ins followed in most Australian universities and some schools and technical colleges.

The youth of the sixties were remarkably conservative. Most middle-class children were raised according to the extremely rigid theories promulgated by, for example, New Zealand pediatrician Truby King, and the infant welfare nurses who instructed most urban middle-class mothers in his dogma in free government-run baby health clinics. Formed in the secure, authoritarian environment which prevailed in Australia during the 1950s, they could look forward to educational and employment opportunities enjoyed by few other generations before or since. Their faith in the benign nature of authority is clearly reflected in the opinion polls on conscription and Vietnam taken throughout the sixties. The early polls on Australian involvement in Vietnam showed that approval decreased with age. This pattern persisted until 1970 when, although approval of the commitment declined in all age-groups, the percentage of young still approving of the commitment, equalled that of their elders. The young also approved of conscription more than their elders, and were more approving than their elders of sending conscripts to Vietnam. This approval only began to decline as student and apprentice deferments expired and individuals became more aware of the likelihood of their own and their friends' call-up.

Despite the perceptions of ASIO and the government spokesmen, who obtained their information on the peace movement from ASIO, the leaders of dissenting organisations were not radicals or communists but largely middle-class moderates. According to Bob Gould, a leftist-radical member of the ALP who founded the militant Vietnam Action Campaign (VAC) on 10 August 1965, the peace movement by early 1966 was one in which the 'old leftists' were swamped by, in his words, 'a great number of the middle-class, the usual apoliticals ... A lot don't have a party political experience. A lot have humanist or religious backgrounds.' Of those members of the VAC and the YCAC involved in organising a demonstration on 15 April 1966 Gould commented, 'there would not be 30 communists among the 250 and they are not the best or most willing workers.' On the influence of communists in the peace movement at the time he concluded:

> A hunt for Communists in the peace movement now is too late. In a way it both overestimates and underestimates the party's role, overestimates it because they are no longer the leading or even significant moving force, underestimates the party's influence because it ignores the patient ground work of moulding opinion when the peace movement was still confined to the political fringe.

The leaders of the early anti-war movement were atypical of the sections of society to which they belonged. One clergyman most active in anti-war dissent throughout the Vietnam era was the Reverend Alan Walker of the Sydney Central Methodist Mission. On 22 November 1964 he became the first to organise a large public protest against conscription. Opinion polls, however, reveal that mainstream Methodist opinion in 1966 was more supportive of Australia's involvement in the war than any other denomination polled. The thirteen Anglican bishops who locked horns with Menzies in March 1965 when they advocated a negotiated peace in Vietnam while Menzies was secretly preparing to commit an Australian battalion there, were certainly not representative of opinion in their flock at the time. The Catholics who formed the anti-war organisations, Catholics for Peace in Sydney and Pax in Melbourne in early 1967, were decidedly out of step with the attitudes of their fellow Catholics.

The same applied to the black-veiled women who disturbed Menzies by standing silently while he was making his first public speech of the Senate campaign of November 1964, immediately after the introduction of conscription, and of those who joined the Save Our Sons (SOS) organisation from May 1965. Analysis of the opinions of women polled over the entire period of the operation of conscription showed that women in general showed no significant differences of opinion on the subject from men. The participation of women in Australian political life was rare throughout the sixties.

Not even the powerful RSL was immune to dissension. On 16 November 1966 the formation of a breakaway group of anti-war ex-servicemen was announced. Known as the Ex-services Human Rights Association (ESHRA) it destroyed the illusion that RSL pronouncements on conscription and Vietnam represented the views of all ex-servicemen. In early 1967 ESHRA amalgamated with a similar body in Melbourne – the Victorian Ex-Servicemen's Protest Committee. It eventually numbered among its

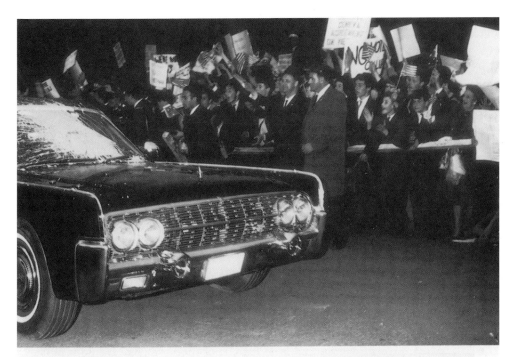

Although Australians were already in conflict over the official attitude to the war in Vietnam, demonstrations of protest during President Johnson's visit in 1966 were the exception rather than the rule. Here, two bags of red and green paint smear the Presidential limousine as it proceeds through Melbourne crowds. The President and Mrs Johnson were, reportedly, unconcerned by the incident: 'Isn't it an absolutely sparkling, beautiful morning!' Mrs Johnson tells her escort, Doug Anthony, Minister for the Interior, as she sightsees afterwards in Canberra.

members veterans of every war Australians had been involved in including the Boer War, and established branches in Brisbane and Perth as well as Sydney, Melbourne and Newcastle. Discrimination against its members on account of their political activities only served to draw attention to the body. On 29 November 1966, three days after the federal election, the Australian Broadcasting Commission dismissed ESHRA president, Allan Ashbolt, from his position as Acting Director of Talks, on the grounds that his political activity during the election campaign 'had limited his usefulness'. In June 1967 the New South Wales branch of the RSL expelled ESHRA's secretary, Les Waddington. An ex-prisoner of war, Ashley Pascoe, an ESHRA committee member, was suspended for five years. This decision was ultimately overridden by the RSL's National Executive but not before the League received considerable unfavourable publicity in the press.

Members of such dissenting organisations worked collectively and as individuals to erode the confidence with which members of their group initially accepted the government's decisions on conscription and Vietnam. Demonstrations were a small part of their activities, their principal role was educative – to arouse the interest of a compliant but largely uninformed and uninterested population in the issues raised by Australia's involvement in Vietnam. They did this by the traditional liberal techniques of circulating petitions, organising public meetings, writing letters to newspapers, producing their own journals and newsletters, collecting and disseminating information from overseas like antiwar books and periodicals (largely British and American), supporting conscientious objectors and other resisters and drawing public attention to perceived injustices and inconsistencies in the government's treatment of such individuals. They also strove to bring home to the Australian public the ghastly effects the war was having on the Vietnamese people.

Mass demonstrations were a new and increasingly effective way of attracting public attention to anti-war arguments. They were, however, something of a two-edged sword. Initially small, and highly controlled by wardens appointed by the anti-war bodies organising them, they quickly became more militant, less easily controlled, and were reported in the mainstream press in ways which drew opprobrium on the anti-war movement as a whole. Probably the first disruptive demonstration was that organised by the Vietnam Action Committee on 22 October 1965. This blocked Pitt Street, Sydney, during the Friday evening peak hour. Rowdy demonstrations such as that staged at Kew Town Hall on 28 March 1966, when Holt opened the Kooyong by-election, inspired increased organisers' efforts to control the behaviour of demonstrators. The action of only one person could be a public relations disaster for the movement, as Nadine Jenson proved by pouring red paint over herself and smearing it on the troops of 1 RAR during their welcome-home march in Sydney on 6 June 1966. Although she did not belong to any anti-war organisation, dramatic photographs of her action have served to perpetuate the conviction, particularly among Vietnam veterans, that anti-war protest was directed against them personally. Despite the numbers demonstrating during the visit of President Lyndon B. Johnson from 20–23 October 1966, the Project Vietnam Committee attempted to control them by distributing thousands of leaflets encouraging disciplined and non-violent behaviour. With few exceptions their efforts were successful, and editorial comment in mainstream newspapers was favourable. Allegations, however, that police behaved provocatively by deliberately driving cars and motorcycles into crowds, breaking banners, punching, pushing and abusing demonstrators (without any regard for age or sex) prompted a demand for a parliamentary enquiry in Victoria.

Save Our Sons

Save Our Sons was a non-party, non-sectarian organisation founded in Sydney on 13 May 1965 by Joyce Golgerth. Its aim was to oppose, on humanitarian, religious or pacifist grounds, the conscription of youth for service overseas. It did not have any official policy on the war in Vietnam, although it stated that war was an ineffectual means of settling international differences.

Although men were admitted as associates, its leaders and members were women, the majority of whom were middle-aged – women with sons of conscriptable age, ex-servicewomen, war widows and others who had lost relatives in the Second World War. Many of its male supporters were ex-servicemen. Between July and December 1965 autonomous branches were formed in Brisbane, Newcastle. Melbourne and Adelaide, and in Perth and Townsville by mid-1966.

SOS provided most of its members with their first experience of organised political activity, and they found acceptable its moderate policy on Vietnam and its peaceful, orderly style of protest. SOS demonstrations were characteristically Quaker-like silent vigils, held particularly outside Army barracks or at railway stations, when intakes of conscripts left for camp. They also conducted interviews with politicians, distributed leaflets, organised petitions, addressed public and private meetings, collaborated with other peace groups and attempted to get as much media exposure for their views as possible.

In most states SOS raised money to assist conscientious objectors to obtain legal aid for court challenges. By mid-1969, however, most preferred to defy the law rather than to utilise the legal safety valve provided by the government for conscientious objectors. SOS branches therefore terminated these funds.

Although mostly confined to urban protest, the Sydney branch succeeded in arousing considerable interest in rural New South Wales when it sent a Caravan Against Conscription to ten of the larger country towns in August 1968.

When Australian troops were withdrawn from Vietnam, the issue of conscription lost much of its urgency. Other concerns such as Aboriginal land rights and women's issues preoccupied SOS members. It is probable that the experience and confidence gained by women joining SOS encouraged them to engage in a wider range of political activity in the 1970s.

Although the Labor Party provided some of the most effective anti-war campaigners, most if not all of whom were ex-servicemen, the party as a whole could not provide reliable leadership for dissent. Before the 1966 elections, Labor supporters were equally divided on the merits of Australia's Vietnam commitment. They tended to be slightly more approving of conscription, but less so than supporters of other political groups. They strongly and consistently opposed, however, the sending of conscripts to Vietnam.

This mirrored the division within the party's parliamentary leadership. Calwell, who had campaigned strongly against the introduction of conscription during the First World War, strongly condemned both conscription and the Vietnam commitment. He believed that the commitment of Australian troops to Vietnam would not promote national security, would harm the fight against communism and would prolong and deepen the suffering of the Vietnamese people. He believed that America was supporting the wrong cause in Vietnam and would become interminably bogged down there, as France had been. He realised this was not the view of the majority of the electorate, but was prepared to suffer unpopularity 'in the sure and certain knowledge that we will be vindicated'.

Whitlam, who was locked in a leadership struggle with Calwell, most certainly was not prepared to alienate an electorate so obviously supportive of conscription and the Vietnam commitment. He strongly defended America's right to conduct military action in Vietnam and saw its presence in Asia as a necessary counterweight to China. 'America has now undertaken hostilities in a wider field,' he told parliament in early 1965, 'she has undertaken them in order to bring home to the North Vietnamese and their Chinese Allies that she will not be ousted, that she cannot be defeated.' Although he acknowledged that Australia was intervening in a civil war, he approved of it as the product of Australia's 'fraternal feeling for our great allies or our dependence on support from our great allies to whom we are related.' After the enormous Labor losses in the 1966 election, during which both parties campaigned strongly on conscription and Vietnam, Whitlam replaced Calwell as leader and attempted to downplay the issues of Vietnam and conscription until declining popular support indicated that it was politically expedient to revive them.

THE EFFECTIVENESS OF EARLY ANTI-WAR AND ANTI-CONSCRIPTION PROTEST

Opinion polls conducted throughout this period clearly show a steady erosion in the support for conscription and the Vietnam involvement. This erosion can be attributed to organised dissent only in part. Awareness of the casualties and deaths which inevitably resulted, had a cumulative effect on public thinking on the war. Unpopular government decisions, however, probably did more to arouse public resentment. Most notable of these were the 'pimping provisions' which it attempted to introduce in May 1968. Its proposal to legislate to oblige educational and other institutions to provide the names, dates and places of birth and addresses of present and past students, drew the public's attention to the already wide powers the government had been given over parents, doctors, employers, friends, neighbours and youth leaders by the National Service Act. All sections of the Federal Labor Caucus united behind Whitlam, who led the opposition against these proposals as a dangerous attack on civil liberties.

Editorial opinion in the mainstream newspapers was extremely critical of the government on this question. The *Sydney Morning Herald* on 17 May 1968 observed that, 'For the sake of making it easier for the Department of Labour and National Service to catch a small number of draft-dodgers, the Government is prepared to make informers of the general public.' It was attempting to get powers which it would be difficult to justify even if a state of emergency were declared, and attempting to achieve by administrative action what people would not tolerate from the police and the courts, the paper added.

After the Democratic Labor Party threatened to oppose the legislation unless the government exempted parents, close family members, guardians, doctors and lawyers from the obligation of pimping on suspected defaulters, the legislation was modified. Opposition from university administrators, academics and students was also mobilised, and even very conservative Vice-Chancellors spoke out against it. The Minister for Labour and National Service finally dropped the proposed amendment. It was a humiliating defeat for the government, entirely of its own making, which Western Australian Labor parliamentarian, Kim Beazley, predicted would enable 'a violent minority of a university ... [to] get the whole student body on its side.' Reports in the newspapers at the same time that conscientious objector, Simon Townsend, was being awakened half-hourly by his gaolers in Holsworthy Military Corrective Establishment did not improve the public image of conscription. Public opinion polls show that since the time of William White the general attitude towards resisters was easing, and gaoling, the current penalty, was the least favoured option.

CONCLUSION

On 17 December 1967, Harold Holt, the Prime Minister who had confidently asserted that the Australian people would go 'all the way with LBJ' in Vietnam, waded into the surf off Portsea, Victoria and was never seen again. Within a year the turbulence created in Australian society largely by events in Vietnam had eroded much of the uncritical confidence with which the greater part of the society had greeted the early commitment of troops to Vietnam.

In December 1968, 49% of the adult population believed that Australia should continue to fight in Vietnam; more significantly, 37.2% wanted our soldiers withdrawn. The Tet Offensive of 1–10 February 1968 had shaken the belief of many Australians in the inevitability of an American victory. Photographs published in Australian newspapers in early March 1968 of Australian soldiers torturing a beautiful young Vietnamese woman with water, damaged the traditional image of the Digger cherished by so many Australians. On 24 November 1968, news of the fate of the villagers of My Lai brought home to many Australians for the first time the horror being created by the Western intervention in Vietnam and the dehumanising effect the pursuit of the military goals was exercising on those whose task it was to realise those goals.

Although the young were still more approving of conscription and the war than were their elders, the ranks of the dissenters were being rapidly augmented by highly educated middle-class youth from universities and technical colleges. They brought with them more radical ideas and more effective techniques of protest with which to challenge the faith of Australians in the judgement of their government.

CONFLICT AND WITHDRAWAL 1968–1972

Frank Frost

The years between 1968 and 1972 were some of the most climactic and complex in the entire Vietnam war. In America the Tet Offensive of February 1968 had a shattering impact on the image of America's ability to prevail in Vietnam. Tet also produced a decisive shift in American approaches to the war. Within Vietnam, however, the offensive resulted in severe damage to the southern revolutionary forces and seemed for a time to have shifted the balance overall in favour of the Saigon regime. For several years after the Tet Offensive, the RVN achieved a much stronger position which seemed to give credibility to the prospects for America's revised strategy – a phased withdrawal coupled with continuing support to a reorganised RVN whose forces would replace the departing allies. However, while the revolutionary forces were weakened in the south, the Communist Party and the People's Army on a national level retained enough strength, flexibility and international support to maintain sufficient pressure (reinforced by further offensives in 1972) to force the United States to withdraw from the conflict without having defeated the revolutionary forces and without having secured the future of the RVN. The United States obtained its 'peace with honour' in a manner which in fact paved the way for the ultimate defeat of the RVN in 1975.

The Australian Task Force in this period continued its ill-defined and ambiguous role, fighting both main force units in set piece battles and attempting to confront the entrenched guerrilla forces and their bases of support in Phước Tuy. The Australians continued to operate with cohesion and tactical skill, and their approach to the military conflict in Vietnam was particularly relevant in the period after the Tet Offensive when the scale of the conflict subsided for several years and when MACV emphasised smaller-scale operations and the pursuit of territorial security. However, the emphasis on pacification after 1968 also served to highlight for the Australians the limitations of their involvement as a foreign military force in a complex war in support of an inefficient government and with ill-defined allied relationships. The failure of the process of 'Vietnamisation' in Phước Tuy revealed starkly the flaws in the role which the Australian government had expected its armed forces to fulfil.

By 1968 all three Australian services were now involved extensively in the war. The RAN had deployed a guided missile destroyer to operate with the US 7th Fleet in the South China Sea and in the Gulf of Tonkin and several vessels served in succession, pursuing tasks including coastal bombardment and interdiction of enemy coastal craft. A RAN clearance diving team served with US forces, as did a number of naval airmen. The RAAF operated Caribou and Hercules transports and helicopters in support of the Army's operations: from 1969, the helicopters included 'gunships' providing close fire support to Australian troops. Canberra bombers of No. 2 Squadron based at Phan Rang, north-east of Saigon, operated widely over southern Vietnam. The focus of the Australian involvement as a distinct national force in Vietnam, however, remained the Task Force, and it was the troops of the Task Force who encountered most directly the dilemmas of the Australian role in the changing Vietnam conflict from 1968.

An infantryman armed with a light antitank weapon and self-loading rifle.

A war scene in 1968: a helicopter lift of Australian troops.

TET – AMBIGUOUS OFFENSIVE

The Tet Offensive, as the American historian Gabriel Kolko has aptly suggested, was 'the most important and complicated event of the Vietnam war'. The offensive was seen widely as a climactic development in the war, yet it involved only about a quarter of the total available revolutionary forces. The offensive is usually seen as having decisively altered the course of US involvement, yet for some time afterwards many US military and civilian officials believed that Tet had cleared the way for ultimate success for the Saigon regime. The Communist Party has always claimed Tet to have been a famous victory, yet it imposed lasting damage on the revolutionary forces' strength in the south and the Party's strategies in the offensive have been subject to heavy internal criticism.

In 1967 the Vietnam war seemed to be in a condition of stalemate. With 425 000 troops and an enormous logistical base, the United States was clearly not going to be evicted from Vietnam. The Saigon regime, while fragile, had stabilised with the advent of Nguyễn Văn Thiệu as President and the ARVN was now no longer on the edge of collapse. On the revolutionary side, the NLF's guerrilla and regional forces retained their numerical strength and could attack outposts and ambush convoys in most areas at will, while the PAVN dominated the mountains and heavily influenced the areas south of the DMZ. Both local and main forces were supplied by the steadily improving Hồ Chí Minh Trail. US Secretary of Defense Robert S. McNamara had concluded in late 1966 that the USA could not destroy the enemy's forces at a rate which matched their replacement capacities; by mid-1967, the DRV had deployed less than 2% of its male labour force into combat. At the same time, the American public was turning against the continuing American involvement; by mid-1967 the proportion of people in polls supporting the American presence dropped for the first time below 50%. In this context, the Communist Party clearly saw a major offensive as a way of convincing the USA that the war was indeed stalemated and that the USA could not substantially alter this.

In June 1967, the Party's chief official in the south, Nguyễn Chí Thanh, went to Hanoi to present a draft plan to the Politburo for an attack on the Saigon regime and its allies. From the Party's perspective, American leaders still appeared to believe in the possibility of military victory, and rural struggle by itself

An Australian, an American, and a Vietnamese, combine in this patrol of Vũng Tàu, a leave and rest centre on the coast.

seemed unlikely to cause them to believe differently. It was essential to ward off any further American escalation of its involvement and instead to induce the USA to accept negotiations. The Politburo decided that a major blow should be struck against the United States and RVN but there seem to have been significant internal differences over strategy. Thanh proposed an all-out effort against the enemy, but General Giáp, while believing that the southern guerrilla forces could not achieve this task by themselves, was reluctant to place the main forces of the PAVN at risk. There also appear to have been divisions in Hanoi over whether the goal should be to terminate American involvement immediately or, less ambitiously, to forestall any further American escalation. At this critical time, Thanh was killed in a US air attack (on 6 July 1967) and his plans may have been scaled down as a result. Orders were given to the southern command in September: it was clear that while the PAVN would create diversions and stand in reserve, the burden of the attacks would fall on the southern guerrilla forces of the NLF. The strategy adopted sought a 'general offensive and general uprising'; simultaneous armed attacks would be accompanied by popular uprisings. Even if the strategy did not achieve its optimum goals the attacks, it was hoped, would destroy the Americans' illusions about their prospects for success in the war.

As the revolutionary forces prepared in late 1967 for a massive assault, the United States and RVN picked up considerable intelligence information on the preparations. By early December. MACV was aware that an 'all-out' attack was planned, and the US mission in Saigon actually issued a press release on 5 January 1968 which predicted an attack on the city, but not the time of its occurrence. The US Command did move substantial numbers of troops away from border areas into the Saigon region, but its attentions were to an extent diverted by a major assault initiated by the PAVN at the remote Khe Sanh base near the DMZ. The PAVN laid siege to the base for a number of weeks from 21 January 1968 and the USA responded with massive reinforcements and intense bombardment. The news of a major siege of a remote base immediately raised the spectre of the French defeat at Điện Biên Phủ, but the US forces were far stronger, the Khe Sanh base was much closer to US centres of strength, and the PAVN, in any case, committed only about half the number of troops to this confrontation that they had in the famous engagement of 1954. As the American historian William S. Turley has written, the level of effort by the

A 105 mm. M-101 field gun in action in Vietnam.

PAVN 'was sufficient to sustain a credible diversion, but not to mount a realistic attempt to overrun the base as long as the US was determined to hold it.'

On the night of 31 January, a few days after the onset of the Khe Sanh 'diversion', 80 000 guerrilla and local forces with limited PAVN support struck over 100 cities and towns. A small group attacked the US embassy, and although they did not penetrate the whole complex, the psychological impact was devastating. Four thousand guerrillas attacked a range of targets in Saigon including Tân Sơn Nhất Airport ARVN headquarters, government ministries and Independence palace. In Saigon and elsewhere the attackers were defeated within a few days and with great destruction. Only in Hue did the assault forces hold out for longer. There, the attack forces were, atypically, main force PAVN units, which held the citadel until their defeat on 24 February: the PAVN lost two-thirds of their 7500 troops, ARVN and US forces lost 500 dead, 100 000 people became refugees, 'the enemy's Tet offensive,' the editors of the Pentagon Papers wrote shortly after the event, 'although it had been predicted, took the US command, and the US public by surprise, and its strength, length and intensity prolonged this shock.'

While the guerrilla attacks achieved surprise and temporary military success, their losses were very heavy and the 'general uprising', which had clearly been a maximum goal of the offensive, did not

An M-60 machine-gunner on the perimeter of a fire support base, protecting the howitzers of a field battery north of Núi Đất.

eventuate. The US and Saigon commands claimed a military victory soon after the Tet attacks, but the impact in Washington was profound. General Westmoreland now proposed a plan to capitalise on the NLF and PAVN's military vulnerability; his plans for attacks around the DMZ, assaults on sanctuaries in Cambodia and Laos and further bombing of the DRV would require an extra 206 000 troops. When this request for more troops was reported by the *New York Times* on 10 March, internal criticism in America intensified. The success of anti-war presidential candidate Eugene McCarthy in gaining 42% of the vote in the presidential primary in New Hampshire on 12 March increased political pressures on President Johnson. The administration refused further escalation. On 31 March Johnson announced his decision not to recontest the Presidency, declared a bombing halt over most of the DRV and announced his support for negotiations with Hanoi. Speaking on national television, Johnson declared:

> Accordingly, I shall not seek, and I will not accept, the nomination of my party for another term as your President. But let men everywhere know, however, that a strong and a confident and a vigilant America, stands ready tonight to seek an honourable peace; and stands ready tonight to defend an honoured cause whatever the price, whatever the burden, whatever the sacrifice.

While the USA remained in a relatively strong position in Vietnam, the administration now took a decisive step to contain US involvement.

The Communist Party's official history claims the Tet Offensive to be a great victory: and in its ultimate strategic impact on Washington's will to pursue the war, it was. But the outcome for the revolutionary forces was heavily qualified by their severe losses amongst the cream of the southern guerrilla units and experienced political cadres. These very heavy losses, as Gabriel Kolko has observed, 'knocked the breath out of the Communist military and political organisation, a fact which only greater American and RVN failures obscured.' Many southern cadres were disturbed that the sacrifices had not decisively altered the course of the struggle within southern Vietnam. Many felt the outcome might have been different had the gifted leader Nguyễn Chí Thanh lived to help lead the attacks. A leading southern NLF leader. General Trần Văn Trà, gave a sober and critical account of the offensive in his memoirs published in 1982:

> In Tet 1968, we did not correctly assess the concrete balance of forces between ourselves and the enemy. Nor did we fully realise that the enemy still had considerable capabilities while ours were limited. Consequently, we set requirements that exceeded our actual strength. That is, we based our action not on scientific calculations or careful weighing of all factors but, in part, on an illusion which arose from subjective desire. Although the decision was wise, ingenious and timely ... and created a significant strategic turning point in Vietnam and Indochina, we suffered heavy losses of manpower and material, especially of cadres at various echelons, which caused a distinct decline in our strength. Subsequently, we not only were unable to preserve all the gains we had made but also had to endure myriad difficulties in 1969–70 so that the revolution could stand firm in the storm. While it is obvious that the road to revolution is never a primrose path ... in Tet, 1968, had we considered things more carefully and set forth correct requirements in conformity with the balance of forces between the two sides, our victory would have been even greater, our cadres, troops and people would have spilled less blood, and the subsequent development of the revolution would have been much different.

The Tet Offensive, and the two less intense offensives which followed in May and August, had a major impact on the role of Australia's forces. The Australian Task Force, in its first eighteen months in Vietnam, had concentrated essentially on operations in Phước Tuy. In October 1967, however, the force had gained a third battalion and the Australians now had the capacity to operate more widely. Between the beginning of 1968 and May 1969, the Task Force in fact spent an extensive amount of time out of the province. This period saw some of the most intensive actions of the entire Australian involvement, notably during Tet and the subsequent May offensive.

The Australians experienced the intensity of the Tet Offensive both within Phước Tuy and in the adjacent province of Biên Hòa to the northwest. Australian units were in fact assigned to help protect the US positions in Long Bình and the Saigon area generally, against an expected attack three weeks before the offensive actually began. On 10 January, the Task Force Commander, Brigadier Ron Hughes, was called to a conference at Long Bình by the commander of II Field Force (the US formation which had 'operational control' of the Australian force), General Fred Weyand. US units were to be deployed to meet an expected offensive. Weyand gave his own unit commanders precise instructions and then,

Following a successful fire fight in a PLAF bunker complex in northern Phước Tuy in 1968, soldiers of 4 RAR/NZ search enemy equipment, ever wary of booby traps.

pointing vaguely at the map of the Biên Hòa area, said: 'Say, Ron, would you mind bringing your Task Force up to this area here?' (at Hughes' request Weyand went on to clarify the suggestion). On 23 January, the Task Force headquarters and two battalions (2 RAR and 7 RAR) moved into the Biên Hòa area, leaving 3 RAR at Núi Đất to cover Phước Tuy. The Task Force units undertook operations aimed at denying an area east of the huge American Biên Hòa/Long Bình base complex to the NLF/PAVN as a rocket-launching base. The Australians conducted their customary extensive patrols and ambushes, but they also moved in to defend a fire support base called Andersen, which was near a rubber plantation on National Route 1 and which the NLF could easily observe by day. NLF/PAVN forces launched three attacks on the fire base; assault troops attacked in waves supported by machine-guns and rocket-propelled grenades (RPGs). The Australians, with American support, withstood the heavy fighting which resulted.

As Tet approached, the Task Force base in Phước Tuy was protected by its third battalion, 3 RAR; its commander, Lieutenant Colonel Jim Shelton, recalled that, 'It wasn't really expected that anything dramatic would happen in Phước Tuy. That's why two-thirds of the Task Force were away helping out around Biên Hòa.' The NLF command in the Phước Tuy and Long Khánh area, however, had ambitious plans (Long Khánh was the province immediately to the north of Phước Tuy; both RVN provinces came

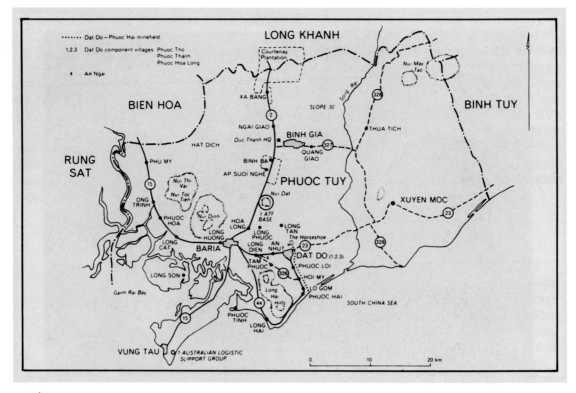

PHƯỚC TUY PROVINCE: AUSTRALIA'S MAIN AREA OF OPERATIONS

The Australian Task Force, desiring to operate independently, assumed responsibility for Phước Tuy province. Its main contacts with the enemy occurred there, although Australian units did operate outside the province. The Training Team, by contrast, operated widely throughout Vietnam. The position of Phước Tuy province is noted in the map of Vietnam which appears in the first essay, Australia's Road to Vietnam.

under the same NLF local command). A Party history states that, 'the essential responsibility was to attack and become masters of the two towns of Baria and Long Khánh ... by regional forces surrounding sub-sector installations and posts and forcing them to withdraw or surrender [and] by activating the people in the towns and villages to rise, destroy their cruel oppression, seize power and become masters.' These plans were duly implemented. 'In Baria township at sunrise on 1 February 1968 D445 battalion ... attacked and entered the Province Security Forces Compound, occupied the police offices and the American advisers' compound. The enemy resisted with drastic measures.'

The NLF had deployed about 600 local force guerrillas into the province capital; the Task Force in response sent A Company, 3 RAR, in nine armoured vehicles to assist the beleaguered RVN and US forces. Intense fighting followed in which the Australians battled to clear key buildings. The Australians were supported by American airstrikes and two ARVN battalions. In the afternoon. D445 attempted to counter-attack and 'at that time, the streets of the town kept changing hands.' After nightfall, the NLF forces withdrew from Baria to the nearby village of Long Điền.

While there was no evidence of any uprising to support D445 in Baria, the NLF did attract some active support in Long Điền according to the reports of the US province advisory team. An ARVN battalion

Examining a wounded enemy.

was sent to dislodge the guerrilla forces, but it failed badly. Elements of 3 RAR then cleared the NLF elements from the village in heavy fighting which is recalled by the province history: '… one Australian battalion with the Third Puppet [i.e. ARVN] Battalion … continuously counter-attacked and pressed us in the Long Điền township. Enemy aircraft bombed the hamlets … destroying property and killing many of our comrades.' The ejection of the NLF forces from Long Điền ended the Tet campaign in Phước Tuy. As elsewhere, the guerrillas had demonstrated dramatically the RVN's vulnerability and the poor quality of some of its forces, but paid a heavy price in doing so.

The Australians were also involved in heavy fighting in May during the second of the three offensives of 1968. In the early morning of 5 May, NLF and PAVN forces attacked 119 cities, towns and military targets across the RVN; 13 battalions entered Saigon and a week's fighting ensued. The US command immediately planned operations to block the withdrawal of the forces from Saigon. As part of this effort, Task Force units were deployed in Bình Duong province northeast of Saigon and about 32 kilometres north of Biên Hòa. Five PLAF/PAVN regiments were thought to be in the area and the Australians were assigned to attempt to block withdrawal and resupply routes.

A fire support base named Coral was established to support the infantry battalions. The operation

Australians survey the dead.

proved to be difficult from the start. Senior Task Force officers who flew over the areas selected for setting up a fire support base were unable to do a full reconnaissance because the helicopters had to remain at a substantial altitude to avoid possible ground fire. The major Task Force elements involved – the New Zealand 161 Field Battery, the 102nd Field Battery and elements of 1 RAR and 3 RAR – were deployed on 12 May, but the helicopter transport took much longer than expected, and the Task Force units did not have time to fully establish their base and its defences.

While the Task Force units were attempting to establish Coral a PAVN battalion had observed the artillery units' arrival and planned an attack. In the early morning of 13 May, Coral was bombarded by rockets and mortar rounds and then assaulted by the PAVN infantry. An Australian mortar platoon and one gun position were overrun and suffered heavy casualties. The Task Force fought a pitched battle, firing the artillery at point-blank range. Extensive US air support was soon provided. The PAVN ultimately withdrew having undoubtedly suffered very heavy casualties; the Task Force lost 9 killed and 28 wounded. Coral was attacked again on 16 May but despite heavy fighting the PAVN this time did not penetrate the defence perimeter.

The Task Force decided to bring up Centurion tanks from Núi Đất, 140 kilometres away, to reinforce its fire support bases; the tanks proved highly effective in the fighting which followed. Two further fire support bases. Coogee and Balmoral, were established near Coral. On 26 May, Balmoral, five kilometres

An Australian and an ARVN officer coordinate operations in northeast Phước Tuy, in June 1969. Often such cooperation could not be depended upon, and Australians blamed the ARVN for their lack of commitment. In this case, however, the operations were highly successful.

from Coral, was assaulted; the tanks helped defeat the attack. The tanks were then used to attack nearby PAVN bunker complexes. Balmoral was assaulted again on 28 May; further intense fighting and heavy PAVN losses followed. This proved to be the last major episode of this series of essentially conventional battles between the Task Force and the PAVN; twenty-six Australians died and 110 were wounded in these actions.

PACIFICATION AND PHƯỚC TUY

In the aftermath of the Tet Offensive, while many observers in Washington and elsewhere were concluding that the USA had suffered a major reverse, some American and allied officials in Vietnam itself were convinced that the United States and RVN now had a major opportunity to turn the tide in their favour. The Tet attacks had been tactically effective and dramatic, but they had generally failed to arouse popular support and the revolutionary forces were now substantially weaker. One figure who sought to seize on these opportunities was the influential American 'pacification' official, John Paul Vann. In the third week of February 1968 he sent out a memo to his fellow American advisers in the III Corps region and urged:

> Get your counterparts and their troops out from behind their barbed wire and aggressively on the offensive, both day and night. The enemy has never been more vulnerable to effective military action than he is today.

The Tet losses forced the PLAF/PAVN to change tactics. In 1969, the role of large units was temporarily de-emphasised; a number of PAVN units in the south split up into smaller groups to evade detection. The southern guerrilla forces were now much weakened; they suffered a high desertion rate in 1969 and they did not effectively recover their strength. US intelligence estimates indicated that the PLAF/PAVN armed strength in the south declined from 250 300 in 1968 to 197 700 in 1971; since the number of PAVN troops in the south remained steady at 80–90 000, the decline in strength had come mainly from depletion of the southern guerrilla ranks. By December 1969, PAVN leaders were effectively acknowledging that the southern revolution was temporarily in a defensive posture.

ABOVE LEFT: Examining an enemy ammunition box for booby traps.

ABOVE RIGHT: In March 1969, troops of C Company, 2nd Battalion, Royal Australian Regiment, jump for cover when their vehicle is ambushed during an exercise. The truck hit an anti-personnel mine simulator on the track.

The United States and the RVN responded to the post-Tet shift in the balance of forces by revising their own strategies. General Creighton Abrams, who replaced Westmoreland as US Commander in June 1968, abandoned the former 'search and destroy' tactics and ordered a greater emphasis on small-unit patrolling and territorial security and increased emphasis on pacification. An 'accelerated pacification program' was initiated in late 1968 and a number of policies were emphasised. The RVN stepped up efforts initiated in 1967 to establish elected and more active hamlet and village administrations. RVN decrees expanded the authority of village chiefs and village administrations were given increased powers and financial resources. Rural investment was promoted and in 1970 President Thiệu adopted a land reform measure which effectively recognised the extensive land distribution which the revolutionary forces had already effected and which placated landlords by offering compensation for lands they had often already lost.

The pacification programs also sought to increase military pressure on the local forces and political cadres of the NLF. The Americans established the notorious Phoenix Program to coordinate the numerous RVN intelligence bodies attempting to isolate and 'neutralise' the NLF's political structure. At the village and province level, the RVN's locally recruited 'territorial forces', which were intended to secure their local communities from NLF activity, were re-armed and given upgraded training. These local units (organised as Popular Force platoons and Regional Force companies) were crucial if the RVN was to hope to be able to defeat the decentralised and flexible NLF. The RVN also attempted to mobilise the population in local defence by establishing a militia, the People's Self Defence Force (PSDF).

For several years there was considerable optimism in Saigon at the prospects for these programs and for the RVN itself. The Australian counterinsurgency specialist, Brigadier Ted Serong, who worked as a consultant to the Americans, was now quite sanguine about the regime's prospects; he wrote that 'We entered 1969 balanced, with a proper understanding of the real strategic nature of our commitment, and an enemy who had played himself out.' John Paul Vann wrote in January 1970, 'We are now on the right road.'

However, there were severe limits to the RVN's capacities to change the rural balance of power decisively. Many programs and local forces were plagued by disorganisation, corruption and infiltration by the NLF. A further fundamental problem was that an increase in the armed strength of the government in the rural areas did not necessarily translate into a real increase in effective, organised popular support for the Saigon regime. Robert Komer, the US pacification chief, acknowledged in 1974 that however much the USA and RVN damaged the NLF at the local level, 'We were never able to translate this into positive and active rural popular support for the government of Vietnam … We were never able, ourselves, to generate a counter attraction in Saigon that ever had the charisma, the capability, the administrative effectiveness.'

The focus of activity of the Australian Task Force after 1968 was affected directly by these developments in the Vietnam conflict. In May 1969, after a period when a considerable number of operations had been conducted outside Phước Tuy, the Task Force again turned its full attention to the NLF's ongoing presence in the province. As an allied formation supporting the RVN the Task Force attempted to support the US/RVN pacification program. The Australians, however, continued to face a series of severe problems; they were operating in an area of substantial long-term support for the NLF, they had complex and difficult relationships with their US and Vietnamese allies and their presence in Vietnam as a relatively small Australian force in a controversial war meant that their activities were always a politically sensitive matter for Defence authorities and the government. The Australians conducted a wide range of operations in the post-1968 period and the dangers and dilemmas they faced are well illustrated by two of these; the attempt to isolate the NLF in Đất Đỏ in 1969, and the assault on the nearby Long Hải hills in early 1970.

The area in and near Long Điền and Đất Đỏ villages (which were included in the NLF's 'Long Dat' district) was the main centre of support for the NLF in Phước Tuy. The villages supplied recruits for the Front's local and main forces; the village of Phước Hoa Long in Đất Đỏ district was known as 'the home of D445' (the NLF's local battalion in Phước Tuy). The villages were able to supply large amounts of rice and fish for local and main force units. As well as the villages, the NLF's guerrillas could use the nearby Long Hải hills as an ideal base area. The hills, which had extensive cave systems, had been a centre of resistance to the French in the First Indochina War and were used often by the NLF forces.

The NLF's village-based cadres and the guerrilla forces which arose from those villages were the base of the NLF's structure of political and military strength. The Front also supported district and province local units and the province organisation gave extensive support to the main forces, which by 1969 were increasingly dominated by the PAVN. Cadres were essential as organisers and motivators at all levels. The Party saw the various levels of its movement and military forces as dynamically interrelated. Even though the southern-based NLF cadres and guerrilla forces were relatively weaker after 1968, they were never seen as being irrelevant to the struggle overall. They were, to the contrary, seen as playing a vital role in tying down a substantial part of the RVN's forces in local defence tasks. The NLF's strength in the Đất Đỏ area and areas like it was thus a highly significant element in the revolutionary struggle.

The first major Task Force attempt to confront NLF influence in this area was the ill-fated Đất Đỏ-Phước Hai minefield. After its return to a concentration on activity in the province in mid-1969, the Task Force made a second major attempt to confront NLF influence in the Đất Đỏ area. Between May and August 1969, the Australians conducted a series of operations intended to 'deny VC access from the surrounding countryside, including the Long Hải hills immediately to the south, to supplies and supporters in [Đất Đỏ] village, and to prevent movement of supplies, particularly fish, rice and salt, from

ABOVE LEFT: Tracker dogs were often used during operations in Vietnam: here, they accompany troops from 2 RAR in Western Phước Tuy province.

ABOVE RIGHT: Army engineers search for mines before an M-113 personnel carrier is brought forward. Mines, often lifted from the Australian positions and relocated, caused grave losses amongst troops in Vietnam.

the village.' This goal was to be achieved by a large number of ambushes by Australian forces, land-clearing operations near the villages (to reduce jungle cover), and artillery bombardment of NLF bases outside the populated areas. To assist the RVN's local forces (the RF and PF) 'protect' the villages more effectively, the Task Force erected a barbed-wire fence around Đất Đỏ and a series of defensive installations for the local forces to patrol from. The Task Force and RVN forces, it was planned, would control access by checkpoints.

The Task Force Commander at the time (Brigadier C.M.I. Pearson) regarded these operations as 'certainly the most ambitious' effort the Army had yet made to combat the NLF at the district and village level in the province. The NLF also saw it as a major challenge.

> The system of pill boxes surrounding the three villages in the Đất Đỏ area was a new tactical plan of the Australians. It replaced the M16-E3 minefield which the army and people of Long Dat rendered ineffective ... A situation fraught with new difficulties developed: lines of communication and liaison from the district to the three villages in the Đất Đỏ area were cut; food and supplies from inside could not be transported outside to the base. From the middle of 1969, the cadres and soldiers of Long Dat outside [in the bases] did not have rice to eat, but had to gather jungle vegetables ...

In addition, the Long Dat local history recalls, the Australians came into the villages 'prodding to find secret hides, and to find and eliminate our cadres hiding inside.'

While these operations clearly did have the potential to pressure the NLF in the area substantially, the Australians faced a number of serious problems in pursuing them. A major purpose of the operations was to try to improve the capacities of the RVN's local forces but the Task Force had few resources to provide special training and its efforts had little impact. The heavy involvement of the Australians also aroused some opposition from the US advisory authorities who seem to have felt that the Task Force was treading too much on their 'turf'. The most serious problems, however, were posed by the NLF's response. Because the 'pill boxes' built by the Australians were to be manned by government forces, one NLF response was to conduct a political propaganda campaign to undermine these units; the NLF felt that these efforts were very successful in the Đất Đỏ area, where the RVN local force units 'completely dissolved'. The major NLF response was mine warfare – using Australian mines. 'Regular soldiers and guerrillas used their acquired skill with Australian E3 mines to kill the Australians once more …

The NLF used the mines extensively and Task Force units suffered heavy casualties. 5 RAR, in its unit history of its tour in this period, recalled the mine problem vividly during Operation Esso in the Đất Đỏ area in June-July 1969:

> Operation Esso is remembered because of mines. Throughout the length and breadth of AO [Area of Operation] Aldgate the enemy used M16 mines taken from the Barrier minefield laid between the Horseshoe Hill and Long Phước Hai on the coast. The Vietcong used mines offensively in that, in most cases, they were placed not as an obstacle to protect his bases, but to slow down, disrupt and discourage allied operations in the district. The mines were placed in tracks, in likely ambush positions, in likely harbour positions, around houses in the villages, in short, anywhere where our troops were likely to move.

The high rate of Australian casualties from the mines attracted comment in Australian newspapers and federal parliament. The costs of the Đất Đỏ operations became of concern to senior Defence officials in Canberra. General Hay, the Australian commander in Vietnam, later recalled that he was under no political direction to reduce casualties, 'but rather there was a general understanding among Australian commanders that the loss of lives needed to be balanced carefully against military gains.' Nonetheless, the Secretary of the Department of the Army, Bruce White, informed Hay of attitudes in Australia and General Hay wrote to the Task Force Commander, Brigadier Pearson, on 24 July 1969:

> I enclose a signal from Sec Army which I have just received. You can see the Australian reaction to our recent casualties from mines … There is no doubt we should both take full account of Bruce White's comment.

The next month, in late August, the operations around Đất Đỏ were terminated. After the Task Force withdrew, the NLF rapidly destroyed at least half of the newly constructed defence positions and met no effective resistance from the RVN forces in doing so. The NLF was in no doubt as to why their resistance had been successful. The Long Dat history notes:

> In 1969 the army and people of Long Dat completely defeated the Australian pill box strategy at Đất Đỏ … using Australian mines (lifted from the minefield) to protect the base, and strike the enemy.

After the Australians concluded their period of intensive operations focussing on the villages of the Đất Đỏ area in August 1969, the Task Force concentrated on operations to combat the NLF's local force

ABOVE LEFT: Army and Navy get together in the Enlisted Men's Mess at Bear Cat in Biên Hòa province. Major-General R.A. Hay, the Commander of Australian Forces in Vietnam, talks to naval airmen from Cairns, Port Pirie and Brisbane, in May 1969.

ABOVE RIGHT: The headquarters of the Australian Task Force Vietnam, in Saigon.

OPPOSITE PAGE: Walking beside an armoured personnel carrier, soldiers leave the jungle for open paddy fields during a search-and-destroy mission near the Australian Task Force base.

units, particularly the local battalion, the experienced and often elusive D445. As we have noted, one of the strengths of the NLF in Phước Tuy was, its ability both to draw on popular, organised support from the villages and also to use the several groups of hills in the province as military bases. The Long Hải hills were consistently used as a base by the NLF and the Task Force's operational commanders, the American II Field Force, were well aware of this. A letter from the Australian commander in Vietnam to the Chief of the General Staff on 1 March 1970 said, 'there has been constant pressure from both CG [Commanding General] III Corps and CG II FFV over a long period to put Australian troops into the Long Hảis. This has always been resisted by IATF.' The Australians were well aware that operations to try to combat the NLF in their Long Hải hills bases ran heavy risks because of the NLF's use of M-16 mines from the Australian minefield and that the results of such operations were likely to be ephemeral, given that there would be nothing to stop the NLF moving back in once an allied operation was over.

The Task Force conducted a major operation in the Long Hải hills in February-March 1970 and it provided a further illustration of some of the dangers and cross-pressures the Australians faced. 8 RAR troops pursued operations in the area from 10 February and the Australians were encouraged by a major contact by C Company on 15 February in which 34 members of D445 were killed and which the Task Force Commander felt 'provided the opportunity for exploitation.' 8 RAR troops then patrolled and ambushed egress routes from the hills; the whole of D445 was now in the area. It appeared to 8 RAR that 'the elusive D445 Battalion would be forced to fight or to accept heavy casualties during any attempt to escape.' By 18 February, 8 RAR was poised to attack D445, but it was decided to call in an airstrike by US B52s.

As the Task Force Commander, Brigadier S.P. Weir, later explained, this saved the day for D445. To arrange a B52 strike relatively near populated areas, it was necessary to get a clearance from the RVN authorities.

Soldiers of the 1st Australian Task Force patrol the waterways and mangrove swamps of the Saigon River delta in Phước Tuy province.

One of the penalties that you pay for a B52 strike is that you've got to withdraw 3000 metres. Well of course we withdrew 3000 metres and the VC ... [has] got his own intelligence network and because we were having a B52 strike so close to a populated area you've got to get clearance right down to District level. The Province Chief has got to agree, the District Chief has got to agree; that means if the District Chief knows everybody knows ...

... We got the B52 strike and hit the target but the enemy had gone, and of course so had we: we'd gone back 3000 metres and we didn't have enough fellows to cover all the gaps and the VC battalion just melted through.

After the B52 strike, 8 RAR was deployed along with two RF companies to search the hills and assess the bomb damage to NLF camps and base areas; 'during the following ten days,' 8 RAR's history recalled, 'numerous caches were discovered and more than 200 enemy bunkers destroyed.' Australian casualties were light. On 28 February, however, an engineer party waiting to detonate a grenade booby trap triggered an M-16 mine. While a medical evacuation – dust-off – was being conducted, another M-16 mine detonated; nine Australians died and sixteen were wounded. These casualties produced an immediate reaction from Canberra. The Chief of the General Staff signalled to COMAFV:

Most distressed and concerned at casualties being suffered by 8 RAR in Long Hải area. In view of our experience I am at a loss to understand IATF undertaking operations in an area in which they have always been costly and of doubtful value. Please let me have a report urgently including the aims of the operation and the responsibility for its initiation.

COMAFV replied that until the incidents on 28 February he considered that 8 RAR had achieved significant results for minimum casualties and that the operation was having a considerable effect on the enemy. He also indicated that he had taken action the same day 'to prevent further offensive operations.' As the Australian military historian David Homer has observed, 'the incident shows Canberra's sensitivity

Two Army privates search an enemy shelter in the north of Phước Tuy.

to casualties and the operational pressures faced by commanders in Vietnam.'

Later in the year, the Americans suggested again that the Australians should operate in the Long Hảis; the US Deputy Commander in Vietnam, General William B. Rosson, writing on 23 July, included such operations in a list of suggested tasks for the Task Force. The Australian commander in Vietnam, General Fraser, agreed but expressed clear reservations. He replied on 1 August, 'I am obliged to invite attention to the fact that the 1st Australian Task Force has mounted a series of operations against the Long Hảis in the past, which have been costly in life and productive of limited military gains.' While recognising the importance of the area, Fraser thought 'the base area should not be subject to direct assault until such time as there are reasonable assurances of long term denial.' In fact, there were no further Australian operations in the Long Hải hills. The NLF returned to the area and continued to use it up until the Australians withdrew. The RVN's forces were unable and unwilling to challenge this presence. The Australian operation thus could not be of any lasting significance.

While they did not return to the Long Hảis, the Australians continued to harass the NLF, constantly patrolling and ambushing, and inflicting substantial losses on local units. In one single operation on 18 August 1970, an 8 RAR ambush outside the village of Hoa Long near the Australian base at Núi Đất, eighteen local NLF on a re-supply mission were killed. The fact that the survivors of the ambush were able to re-enter Hoa Long, and hide undetected for two days and then move out, illustrated the inability of local RVN forces to follow up Australian operational successes. Such operations, however, clearly did heavily pressure the NLF, and both sides indicated that the NLF in the 1969–1970 period was in considerable difficulties from allied operations. The Dong Nai history recalls that the period in the second half of 1969 was a severe one for the NLF in the Phước Tuy and Biên Hòa areas:

> Information and liaison were interrupted. Battalions lost contact with companies. District [headquarters] were not able to keep a grip on village [affairs] ... Important lines of communication from War Zone D to Baria and Biên Hòa were cut. National Routes 1 and 15 and Route 2 became the 'iron triangle'.

Contact with Vietnamese villagers: soldiers and civilians in dramatic contrast, in the rural setting of Vietnam.

While the Australians were exerting military pressure on the NLF in the post-1968 period, they also intensified their efforts to extend direct socioeconomic assistance to the villagers of Phước Tuy through the 'civic action' program. Civic action, which the Army had begun in Vietnam in a small way in 1965, had by 1970 come to involve about 300 men working full-time; a number of units supplied the personnel and the efforts were led and coordinated by a 55-man Civil Affairs Unit. The range of 'civic action' activities was extensive. Assistance was given to province authorities and villagers in public works and construction (including 104 school classrooms), medical care, agriculture, and youth and sports. Much of the activity involved construction; the Civil Affairs Unit was usually commanded by an engineer. Major efforts were made to improve village markets and water supplies. From 1969, much of the effort focussed on support for the RVN's village self-development plan, which granted villages funds for locally selected projects. These projects included community centres, maternity dispensaries, schools, water supply, electrification, markets and village roads. Liaison officers from the Unit assessed projects and kept in touch with the villages. Regular visits by medical and dental teams also fostered contacts.

The Civil Affairs Unit had as its mission, 'to win the support of the people for the RVN with the secondary aim of establishing goodwill towards the Australian forces in general.' Speaking in 1987, the Unit's commander in 1969–70, General Peter Gration (Chief of the Defence Force), commented of this mission. 'It was wrong to imagine that the efforts of Australian soldiers in a foreign country could win the support of the people for their own government which was the task we were given.' He felt, however, that civic action had performed useful functions; it helped develop contacts, understanding and respect between the local people and the Australians. 'It helped to create a climate in which the Vietnamese authorities had a better chance of winning the support of their own people – with better roads, commerce thriving, schools functioning, decent medical services and so on.' The civic action projects did seem to have wide acceptability; during 1969–1971 Australians could work widely in the province with virtually no risk of attack.

While the civic action programs had become extensive by 1970, they began to be wound back in 1971 as the short period of the Australian presence in Phước Tuy was clearly coming to a close. The withdrawal

A patrol from 8 RAR moves through a rubber plantation in southern Long Khánh province.

of American forces was already under way and Australian withdrawals began in 1970. A key question now was whether the RVN in Phước Tuy could take over successfully the roles which had been performed by the Australians.

WITHDRAWAL

When President Nixon came to office in early 1969 he began to develop, with his key adviser Henry Kissinger, a new set of policies for the US in Vietnam in the wake of the Tet Offensive. One strand of the policies involved phased withdrawals of US forces, the first of which were announced in June 1969. Washington also sought actively to develop a process of 'triangular diplomacy' with the Soviet Union and China, to try to pursue discussions which could redefine the international significance for the USA of the Vietnam conflict and increase international pressures on Hanoi. The USA sought simultaneously to bolster the position of the RVN, partly through the enhanced pacification program already discussed and partly by expanding the RVN's forces and giving them more resources and increased combat responsibilities; the catch phrase was 'Vietnamisation'. The size of the RVN's armed forces had been increased sharply with a 'general mobilisation' after Tet; in 1968 its forces were raised to 800 000 and in 1970 they reached 1 million, with half the numbers in the local or 'territorial forces'. As American forces withdrew, many of their arms and lavish base facilities were transferred to the RVN, providing them with more resources but creating severe training, logistics and maintenance problems. The United States also took the fateful step of widening the war by invading Cambodia along with the ARVN in March 1970 to destroy PLAF/PAVN bases and logistic systems. A further invasion was mounted by ARVN forces into Laos in February 1971; the well equipped but badly led ARVN forces encountered major difficulties and withdrew in disarray.

Senior Australian officers in Vietnam were sceptical about the prospects for Vietnamisation from the start. The Australian Commander in 1969, General Hay, in his discussions with General Abrams and the Vietnamese, 'thought they were being over-optimistic about the ability of the Vietnamese Army to survive if the allied forces were withdrawn.' This view was shared by his deputy, Colonel Alan Stretton, who wrote later that 'everybody realised the futility of the whole war' and that Vietnamisation was a 'face saving device'. The Commander of the New Zealand forces was not convinced that Phước Tuy could be secured if allied and 'North Vietnamese' forces were both withdrawn.

The Australian forces, however, which had been committed to Vietnam as a contribution to the Australian government's pursuit of security through the US alliance, were clearly going to follow along with American withdrawal programs. Prime Minister Gorton announced on 22 April 1970 that one of the Task Force's three battalions (8 RAR) would not be replaced when its year of duty ended in November; Gorton claimed that the process of Vietnamisation made this force reduction 'desirable and feasible'. Four months after 8 RAR left, 'Vietnamisation' began in earnest in Phước Tuy. In February 1971, large areas of the province were handed over (in terms of operational responsibility) to the territorial forces. This development, said Defence Minister Malcolm Fraser, 'is the very objective of the whole enterprise – so that the South Vietnamese can maintain security on their own in certain areas and ultimately over the whole of the Territory.'

The process of Vietnamisation in Phước Tuy in fact served to highlight some of the basic contradictions and problems underlying the whole Australian involvement. The Task Force was an efficient, well equipped and highly mobile military formation. It faced, as we have seen, great difficulties in combating the well established NLF but its capacities to defeat NLF units in tactical engagements were demonstrated regularly. However, for the presence of the Task Force to have had any lasting influence and relevance it would have needed to be able to cooperate closely and successfully with the local RVN forces and its own tactical operations would have needed to be accompanied by a concerted effort to combat the NLF's political structure in the province.

The RVN's local forces in the province were drawn from the same communities which provided support and recruits for the NLF. They were, not surprisingly, often infiltrated by the NLF, who therefore had an excellent capacity to evade their activities or confront them if necessary. Although it was part of Australian Army doctrine that an allied force involved in a 'counter-revolutionary' war would need to establish close contacts with the local forces of the government being assisted, the Army faced two major problems. The major responsibility for advising the RVN administration and local forces was assumed by the Americans, since Australia had not been willing to take on this role. Secondly, in its first three years of involvement the Task Force was heavily pressed by its operational requirements and had not been equipped with sufficient men and resources to be able to work extensively with the local forces. In 1970, the Australians finally made a greater effort to work with the local forces, when a major part of the elite Australian Army Training Team (AATTV) was transferred to Phước Tuy to work with the RF companies. But the Australians found that in the relatively short time available, when the withdrawal of the Australian forces was already in sight, they could make little headway. As Ian McNeill in his history of the Training Team notes succinctly:

> ... The Territorial Forces in Phước Tuy ... seemed to the advisers to be poorly led by officers who lacked interest and drive, to consist of troops without motivation and to be inadequately administered and supplied. Operations were badly conceived and planned and rarely produced results other than in statistical summaries ... It was a disappointment to the [Australian] Training

Team that the concentration of advisers in Phước Tuy through the MATTs had resulted in little improvement in the Territorial Forces.

When the RF companies were given wider areas of responsibility to cover in Phước Tuy in 1971, they proved unwilling and unable to fill the gap being left by the Task Force. The American advisory support to the local forces was disorganised and subject to frequent personnel changes. The net result was that, 'territorial Force operations were launched without a target or even a general aim … The operations of the territorial forces became fragmented and futile.'

Similar disarray characterised the RVN's efforts to combat the NLF's political structure. The USA and the RVN had developed from 1968 an elaborate program (Phoenix) to identify, locate and 'eliminate' (i.e. kill or capture) the NLF's cadre structure – the basis of the whole NLF political/military campaign. The program in Phước Tuy, however, was ineffective: intelligence data was not collected and used in a carefully planned way and the various RVN agencies involved never operated as a cohesive team. The Task Force sometimes acted to locate and capture cadres but these efforts ran the risk of arousing the ire of the US officials responsible for running the advisory effort. The net result was that while the NLF certainly was under pressure in the province in the post-Tet period (as recent local histories frankly admit) and while it did lose a number of cadres in military engagements, the NLF was able to maintain its political structure in the provinces up to the time of withdrawal of Australia's forces. Senior Australian Army officers were well aware of this fact and realised its significance. The Chief of the General Staff, General Daly, noted in October 1970 that the need to confront the NLF's organisation was 'the main problem' in Phước Tuy.

The result of these problems was that while the Australian forces operated in Phước Tuy with tactical proficiency in pressing the NLF, the Front retained its political structure in the villages and its cadres and local forces retained the capacity to maintain contacts with the villages because the RVN's local forces lacked the capacity to decisively prevent this.

The significance of these issues was heightened in 1971 by clear indications that the PLAF and PAVN retained substantial capacities to back up their weakened local forces with main force support. In March and April main force units re-entered Phước Tuy and were engaged by the Task Force. Between June and September a PAVN main force unit, the 33rd Regiment, extended its operations to the Phước Tuy area. In June and July elements of this unit and of the 27 4th Regiment (PLAF and PAVN) were contacted. In August and early September, the Task Force continued to operate in northern Phước Tuy, a major NLF resupply and communications area, searching for main force units and contacting some NLF from Phước Tuy. In late September, a major battle was fought between the 3 3rd regiment and 4 RAR. The PAVN had evidently sought to lure the Australians into an ambush by attacking an RF post on Route 2. On 21 September, 4 RAR contacted one of the regiment's battalions in a bunker system: in the intense fighting (later described vividly by one of the participants, Gary McKay) six Australians died.

These casualties, coming close to the planned withdrawal of the Task Force, caused some concern about the safety of the Australian forces in this period but the withdrawal went smoothly, being completed between late October and early December. The last battalion (4 RAR) departed on 8 December. The base at Núi Đất was not subsequently utilised by the ARVN – after the Australians left, it fell into disuse.

OPPOSITE PAGE: An Australian sergeant on guard with an M-60 machine-gun during a cordon-and-search of Ấp Bắc, a hamlet in Hoa Long province.

RIGHT: In 1971, the Chief of General Staff, Lieutenant-General M.F. Brogan, discusses the Đất Đỏ high school project with a captain and a lieutenant-colonel of the Civil Affairs Unit in Phước Tuy. Đất Đỏ was the scene of a fierce engagement in the following year.

Brigadier Ian Geddes, who commanded the residual Australian force in Vietnam in 1972, visited the base after the withdrawal.

> It was eerie. I had been there back in 1966 when it was crowded with thousands of young soldiers with a purpose. Now there was no-one. Just the empty husks of corrugated iron buildings, often half stripped by local scavengers ratting for timber and iron. The weeds were coming back everywhere. It was a military ghost town.

The Army felt that a complete Australian withdrawal was desirable with the departure of the Task Force, but the government considered that there were military and political advantages in retaining a presence. On 9 December 1971, the government announced that an Australian Army Assistance Group Vietnam (AAAGV) would remain, composed mainly of AATTV members and conducting training in Phước Tuy. A small group remained until after the elections in December 1972, after which the incoming Whitlam Government withdrew the remaining forty men.

After the Task Force withdrew, the Baria Party committee set about 'restoring the area to what it was before Tet 1968'. A major national offensive was launched across wide areas of southern Vietnam at the end of March 1972 when PAVN units struck across the DMZ, in the central highlands and in Bình Long on the Cambodian border. The 'Easter offensive' was conducted primarily by PAVN forces with the aim of inflicting defeats on ARVN and exposing the fragility of Vietnamisation, a goal which was substantially achieved. Although the PAVN conducted most of the fighting, NLF activity also rose across much of the south. In Phước Tuy, main force units and D445 were present in substantial strength and operated extensively throughout the province. In April and May, Baria and district capitals were isolated, Route 15 was cut for the first time since 1968 and a major battle occurred in Đất Đỏ between ARVN units and elements of the 33rd PAVN regiment.

In late 1972 the Americans and the DRV negotiated the basis for America's withdrawal from Vietnam, an agreement formalised by the Paris Agreements of January 1973. While the USA was withdrawing its forces, the agreements contained no provision for the withdrawal of PAVN forces from the south. The allied military effort to assure the future for the RVN had failed.

The officers' lines at Headquarters in Núi Đất, as they used to look during the occupation by the Australian Task Force.

Australia's Vietnam involvement illustrated starkly the dilemmas in Australia's approach to revolutionary conflict in Southeast Asia after the Second World War. Australia had developed a skilled and professional army well versed in the tactical challenges of jungle and small unit warfare. The government, however, deployed that force to Vietnam without adequate knowledge either of the character of the conflict or the locality (Phước Tuy) where it was placed, and without sufficient planning and preparation. As General Peter Gration, who had gained extensive experience of the situation in Phước Tuy in 1969–70, said in a speech in July 1987:

> The truth is that we knew very little about the province when we went in – of its long history of struggle against the French, of its history as a Việt Minh stronghold in the war against the French ... of the almost complete control of the province by the VC in 1966, based on a strongly entrenched political and military organisation and extensive popular support, or of the numerous local accommodations between both villages and government forces (the regional and popular forces or RF and PF) and the VC. Some of our own official perceptions of the war as an invasion from the north did not fit this local situation where there was a locally supported revolutionary war in an advanced stage, albeit with support and direction from the north. Many of the people of Phước Tuy *were* the VC and despite our nearly six years of operations in which we had continual and considerable military success, we weakened the local units but never destroyed them or prevented them from recruiting and continuing to regenerate and fight.

When the Australian Army arrived in Phước Tuy in 1966, the revolutionary forces had had twenty years of experience of organising for revolutionary conflict in that province and nationally. The NLF's integrated political and military strategy and its structure of mutually supporting forces at village, district

Soldiers from 4 RAR/NZ rush to board a helicopter which will fly them to HMAS *Sydney* in December 1971, as part of the withdrawal of Australian troops from Vietnam.

and province and main force level posed, as intended, a severe challenge to the RVN and to the foreign allies supporting it. The village level forces intimidated and contained the RVN locally while supporting the armed struggle more widely: the local and main force units ensured that the RVN and allied forces were prevented from consistently focussing on the village level forces. By placing the Task Force in the middle of Phước Tuy, the Australian government confronted it unavoidably with both major aspects of the NLF's structure of power.

The Task Force was consistently able to pressure severely the NLF's local forces and it acquitted itself well in its combat with main force units, for example at Coral and Balmoral in 1968 and in northern Phước Tuy in June-September 1971. However, in its efforts to contribute to the struggle against the village-based NLF forces, the Task Force encountered three sets of problems. Firstly, it was never able to establish an integrated working relationship with the RVN administration, partly because in its early years it lacked the personnel to try to pursue this, but also because US advisers and officials – with their own goals and priorities – worked directly with the RVN province authorities. Secondly, the RVN administration and forces were inefficient, lacking in motivation and widely penetrated by the NLF. These problems particularly affected the two most important RVN security programs: the village security supposed to be provided by the territorial forces, and the effort to counter the RVN's cadres. Thirdly, the military and organisational skills of the Australian forces were not readily transferable to the RVN; the belated effort to work extensively with the RVN's local forces in 1970–71, pursued by the highly experienced AATTV, did not achieve a major improvement in the time available as the failures of Vietnamisation in 1971 showed. These problems combined made the involvement of the Task Force – pursued with skill by a well organised and cohesive force – an interesting and distinctive but ultimately futile part of the allied effort to support the RVN.

THE WAR THE MEDIA LOST

Australian News Coverage of Vietnam

Rodney Tiffen

'Who betrayed those who died in Vietnam? Was it our own media?' asks a poster for the conservative American group, Accuracy in Media. Since the American defeat in Vietnam, many commentators have blamed the media as an important cause for the failure, asserting either that the vividness and power of TV coverage caused American disillusion with the war, or that the adversarial and oppositional attitudes of the press to the government made prosecution of the war impossible.

The basis for this charge is that news coverage of the Vietnam war departed from the tightly circumscribed and politically controlled norms of war reporting in several fundamental ways. Most importantly, for the United States, Vietnam was a 'limited war'. The nation was not fully mobilised. National survival was not at stake. The upper limits of American involvement were determined by the balance of global strategic priorities – the desire to avoid a nuclear war and direct conflict with China, and the international sensitivity about the 'Goliath against David' war with the DRV. Whereas in previous major wars, official censorship was in force, in a limited war like Vietnam it was all but impossible to implement. Even beyond formal censorship powers, the military in most wars have controlled journalists' movement in the war zone and communication channels between the military front and home base. In the Vietnam war, the Western media enjoyed considerable freedom of movement within Vietnam, and almost complete independence in transmitting material out of the country. (It should be stressed that with few exceptions the prime military rationale for censorship, the protection of troops in battle through not disclosing immediate battle plans, was scrupulously observed by the media. Similarly, they refrained from publishing the identities of killed or wounded Americans before their families were notified.)

A second distinctive feature was that the Vietnam war always involved extensive political controversy. Normally, when societies have been totally mobilised for war, political debate occurs within tight parameters, with all mainstream groups agreed on the war aims and the main strategies, and most opposition politically marginalised. In the United States, every move in the escalation of this limited war was a matter of contention, and subject to criticism from both sides. Its wisdom and its prospects, and whether there were alternatives, were weighed by various groups in Washington. President Johnson was faced with juggling an impossible political mandate: maintain their favoured government in Saigon but not go to war. On the one hand, the spectre of Korea, a protracted, stalemated and increasingly unpopular, land war in Asia hung over his decision making. But even more compellingly, Johnson feared the charge of being the first President to lose a war. As the fighting escalated, the controversy also increased, and although not often openly supportive of the war's critics, news reporting was sensitive to the constellation of political conflicts among Washington policy makers and to the strength of domestic dissent.

A third fundamental difference between Vietnam and earlier war reporting came simply through the media's improved capacities. Their communications were faster and more extensive than in any previous

OPPOSITE PAGE: War orphans: visible, through the media, to Australians at home.

war and, of course, television was for the first time a central medium of war reporting. Claims about the impact of TV usually cite one or two vivid pieces of news film – most famously the summary execution by General Loan of a captured 'Viet Cong' in a Saigon street during the Tet Offensive in 1968. Such powerful film was far from typical. The 'living room war' was not often an intensely emotional or violent experience: 'While half of all the TV reports filed from Vietnam were about battles and military action ... only about three per cent of all the evening news film reports from Vietnam showed "heavy battle"... A sample of Vietnam-related news stories from 1968 to 1973 found that ... only two per cent showed any dead or wounded.' Nor do studies of TV news suggest any idea of political bias against the war: in the most systematic research, Lichty found that in documentaries and news interview programs, there were always more administrative spokesmen and supporters than critics, at least until 1970. Before 1966, "hawks" outnumbered "doves" by about nine to one; between 1966 and 1970 about two-thirds of those discussing Vietnam policy on such programs were "hawks".

It is clear that, by the special standards of war reporting, the news media enjoyed a much greater political independence and logistical effectiveness than in any earlier war. The priorities, content and tone of American news coverage often departed from the short-term propaganda aims of the American government. It is not valid, however, to slide from this conclusion into the emerging conventional wisdom in conservative politics that the war effort was undermined by unduly critical news coverage, resulting from an adversarial mind set in the media. As the preceding paragraph suggests, the thesis of an oppositional media is very misleading about the patterns of American news content. It is only accurate for a small proportion of news content, although that content was more important than its percentage alone would suggest.

As a description of media motivations, the emerging conservative conventional wisdom, emphasising the alleged ideological hostility and adversarial mind sets of the journalists, is equally misleading. The primary influence upon news was the many-layered influence of the allied governments. Certainly, the American government did not get the news coverage it would have desired. However, it was US government policy aims which always provided the context for evaluating developments, and it was when the allied governments were divided or pessimistic or bewildered, that critical reporting most often emerged. This is illustrated clearly even in the two periods where news reporting has been most under attack, in the months preceding the coup against President Diệm in 1963 and following the Tet Offensive in 1968. In both, the reporting reflected very much the influence of important sources within the government – their doubts and disillusion, and their measures of success and failure. They will be examined briefly in turn, below.

From 1955 to 1962, the Western press image of Vietnamese President, Ngô Đình Diệm, was overwhelmingly positive. Politicians and editorialists vied with each other for extravagant epithets: Vice President Johnson called him 'the Winston Churchill of Southeast Asia': to *Time,* he was 'doughty little Diệm' and *Newsweek* called him 'one of Asia's ablest leaders'. In 1963, the image changed sharply, especially under the influence of the small corps of resident Western correspondents in Saigon. However, the change was not sudden or capricious. Rather the contrast of official optimism at the highest levels with the pessimism of officials in the field triggered reporters' scepticism. In October 1962, David Halberstam of *The New York Times* wrote, 'the closer one gets to the actual contact level of this war, the further one

Australian Soldiers of 7 RAR, on the beach at the fishing village of Phước Hai during Operation Ulmarrah in 1967. They had just searched the area for enemy activity, but found only twenty suspects, draft dodgers and sympathisers amongst the villagers.

Australian troops using a mortar in action, in 1968.

OPPOSITE PAGE: A soldier of 6 RAR/NZ instructs ARVN soldiers on loading an M-60 machine-gun, as part of a retraining program for four ARVN battalions in 1969.

RIGHT: The shooting of this 'Viet Cong' prisoner, shown on television worldwide, was to be one of the most enduring images of the war.

gets from official optimism.' When several reporters witnessed a military setback – the battle of Ấp Bắc in January 1963 – official reports afterwards portrayed it as a victory. The official US Army historian on public affairs in the war judged that Ấp Bắc 'marked a divide in the history of US relations with the news media in South Vietnam ... (Before they] were still relatively agreeable. After it, correspondents became convinced that they were being lied to and withdrew, embittered, into their own community.' Harassment of correspondents, including even assassination threats, hardly helped change their disposition. During 1963, the mounting clashes between the Diệm regime, dominated in its highest levels by Catholics, and various groups representing the Buddhist majority, provided many news stories. Most spectacularly, the self-immolation of Buddhist monks during large rallies in protest against official measures dramatised their grievances, as did government raids on pagodas. The essential point, however, is that it was dissident American sources, and the divisions within American officialdom, which fuelled their views, and their primary desire was for America to adopt more effective policies.

The Tet Offensive, often seen as one of the turning points of the war, was the one occasion in which there is some merit in the charge that the dominant impression was inaccurate in a dovish direction. The shock caused by the scale and suddenness of the attacks was reflected in early news reports. The fighting was intense in Saigon itself, including a suicide mission against the American embassy, as well as in the second largest city, Hue, where it lasted a month. The most prolonged battle occurred at Khe Sanh, where the Americans finally prevailed. More than in earlier episodes, the news reports showed the physical destructiveness of the war: 'We had to destroy the town in order to save it'. This unintentionally poignant observation of the American commander at Bến Tre epitomised the sense of futility many felt. By the end of the fighting, the revolutionary forces had suffered enormous losses and had not provoked the desired mass uprising. In that sense Tet was a military defeat for them. In other ways, in showing their capacity to mount such enormous attacks, and dispelling any American illusions about a quick victory, it was a political victory for them in both Vietnam and in America.

Reports on Vietnam

For the first time in modern history, the outcome of a war was determined not on the battlefield, but ... on the television screen.
- **Robert Elegant, US commentator**

Television's unique requirements contributed to a distorted view of the war ... The news had to be compressed and visually dramatic ... (and so) the war that Americans saw was almost exclusively violent, miserable, or controversial.
- **General William Westmoreland**

The Vietnam war was complicated by factors that had never before occurred in America's conduct of a war ... The American news media had come to dominate domestic opinion about its purpose and conduct ... In each night's TV news and each morning's paper the war was reported battle by battle, but little or no sense of the underlying purpose of the fighting was conveyed. Eventually this contributed to the impression that we were fighting in military and moral quicksand, rather than toward an important and worthwhile objective. More than ever before, television showed the terrible human suffering and sacrifice of war. Whatever the intention behind such relentless and literal reporting of the war, the result was a serious demoralisation of the home front, raising the question whether America would ever again be able to fight an enemy abroad with unity and strength of purpose at home.
- **Richard Nixon**

Maybe the historians will agree that the reporters and the cameras were decisive in the end. They brought the issue of the war to the people, before the Congress or the courts, and forced the withdrawal of American power from Vietnam.
- **James Reston, columnist, *New York Times***

Recognising that in a democracy, leaders are necessarily responsive to the will of the people, [the communists] bombarded our domestic opinion with continuing propaganda from Paris and Hanoi, often using for that purpose the 'free world' media ... The conclusion is inescapable that our adherence to traditional democratic practice appropriate for times of peace made it very difficult for our side to compete on an equal footing with our totalitarian adversaries 'in the settlement of an undeclared limited war.'
- **General Maxwell Taylor**

The press – not all, but the vast majority – was opposed to our Vietnam policy and very vocal. The television also. Allowing television on the battlefield after our troops got there created an impossible situation at home. Even in World War II I think we would probably have left Britain, or France, or Germany to come home if the bloody pictures which were available on those battlefields had been flashed into the American living-room as was the case in Vietnam.
– General Maxwell Taylor

At one time in Vietnam we had 700 accredited reporters – all practising, seeking and reporting news as they were accustomed to in the United States, all looking for the sensational stories. If we get involved again and we hope we won't, but we have to assume that we will, and if the enemy controls the information on his side and we continue the practice of reporting only the off-beat, the unusual or the bizarre in any future war, well then the American public are going to be influenced as they were during Vietnam. I think the bottom line in this subject is how an open society, and how our political democracy, are vulnerable to manipulation by an autocratic ... society. This is a lesson to be learned.
– General William Westmoreland

If, God forbid, we ever got into this sort of situation again, then when the Congress passes a resolution of involvement it must address itself to the censorship problem at the same time.
– Dean Rusk

This was the first struggle fought on television in everybody's living-room every day. What would have happened in World War II if Guadalcanal and the Anzio beach-head and the Battle of the Bulge or the Dieppe raid were on television and the other side was not doing the same thing? War is an obscene blot on the face of the human race. But whether ordinary people, who prefer peace to war in any country, whether ordinary people can sustain a war effort under that kind of daily hammering is a very large question.
– Dean Rusk

The self immolation of Thích Quảng Đức on 11 June 1963.

During Tet, the immediate influence on the tone of reports was the shock at the ferocity and scale of the fighting. The impact of the Tet Offensive was all the greater because it followed so soon after an American propaganda campaign stressing America's progress and optimism about the prospects for victory. The reaction to the offensive was shaped secondly by the official bewilderment at the time. This was apparent both in official divisions and from the widespread pessimism both in Saigon and Washington, an impression heightened when it was revealed that General Westmoreland had requested a further 206 000 troops to add to his over 500 000 already in Vietnam. Tet was perhaps also the culmination of a long period of frustration amongst American journalists concerning the manipulative news management by the Johnson administration, epitomised by the term 'credibility gap'. Indeed, perhaps the very constancy of official optimism made the rhetoric wear thin when confronted by negative events.

The critical reporting preceding the fall of Diệm and following the Tet Offensive should not be taken as typical. Any claims about an oppositional media must also take account of other episodes, such as the Gulf of Tonkin incident of 1964, when the government successfully manipulated the media, or when, as in President Nixon's introduction of 'Vietnamisation', the political strategy succeeded partly because it played upon media proclivities (in this case, including the media's perception of public war weariness and a movement away from coverage of Vietnam itself, and their inability to cover the air war with the same penetration as American ground combat operations).

'Winning' the War

We are going to win in Vietnam. We will remain here until we do win.
- Robert F. Kennedy, US Attorney-General, 1962

I feel that we shall achieve victory in 1964.
- General Tran Van Don, South Vietnamese Army, 1963

I can safely say that the end of the war is in sight.
- General Paul D. Harkins, U.S. Commander in Vietnam, 1963

It will take two or three more years of intensive activity to win military victory over the Viet Cong.
- Richard M. Nixon, former US Vice President, 1965

In two or three years, or even before, the Communists will accept defeat.
- Nguyễn Cao Kỳ, Premier of South Vietnam, 1966

The war is not a stalemate. We are winning it slowly but steadily.
- General William C. Westmoreland, Commander US Forces in South Vietnam, 1967

The enemy has been defeated at every turn.
- General William C. Westmoreland, Commander US Forces, in South Vietnam, 1968

They have been in a war for years and years and they are quite debilitated and decimated, and I don't think they are capable with any kind of resistance of continuing this fight.
- Spiro Agnew, US Vice-President, 1970

Peace is at hand.
- Dr Henry Kissinger, US National Security Adviser, 1972

We have achieved peace with honour.
- President Richard M. Nixon, 1973

Finally, as a hypothesis about media impacts upon policy direction, the oppositional media thesis is seriously incomplete. It is important to distinguish what was due to the media themselves and what to the events and developments they were reporting upon.

The disillusion of successive US Secretaries of Defense, McNamara and Clifford, and other high officials, for example, was not caused by the media but by the American inability to conclude the war successfully. In fact the extent of that disillusion did not emerge clearly in the news. The course of American public opinion during the Vietnam war showed closely parallel trends to the Korean war, before television was prevalent and when there was much less critical comment. The American media cannot be blamed for declining support over Korea. Nevertheless they did have some independent inputs into the political process during the Vietnam war and many organisations and individuals increased public disclosure and the range of debate by their activities.

LIMITED AUSTRALIAN MEDIA CAPACITIES

It is a fundamental mistake, however, to think the debate about American media coverage of the war can be simply translated to Australia. There are two key differences. The first is in the sophistication and capacities of the media organisations involved, especially in TV. The second derives from the contrasting politics given Australia's role as a junior ally in the war's prosecution. Each will be explored in turn.

In considering media coverage of the war, it is necessary to recall just how primitive Australian TV news was in the 1960s. Transmission had only begun in 1956. None of the commercial channels had any continuing independent capacity to gather overseas news. Similarly the syndication arrangements and technology now used for overseas news were not then in place – daily satellite feeds from Visnews only began in the mid 1970s and satellite feeds from other sources, such as the US networks, began later still. Indeed, even within Australia, networking was much less well developed than later. For much of the period of Australia's military involvement in Vietnam, TV news was barely capable of giving timely and pertinent coverage from Canberra, let alone Saigon.

> For many years the principal TV news supplied by the Gallery was filmed material which was despatched by plane to Sydney or Melbourne for processing and transmission. Very often, interviews or commentaries had to be filmed at Parliament House before 11 am to catch the midday planes out of Canberra, and this largely restricted political news to overnight follow-ups ... The problems were sufficiently daunting to frustrate the. Channel 9 network, which appointed a TV news journalist in 1962 but withdrew him after less than a year...
>
> Commercial television relied on improvisation for Canberra coverage until the late 1960s. Sydney's Channel 7 was represented by a freelance journalist, Mayo Hunter, who would set up his camera in front of Parliament House, stand a politician in front of it, trigger the lens by a delayed-action device, run hastily to his subject and conduct the interview ... Relays and studio links caused so many technical problems that even in the early 1970s much material was still filmed and sent to Sydney and Melbourne by plane. The great breakthrough for television came with the installation of studios within Parliament House, directly linked to metropolitan headquarters. Channel 9 established the practice ... early in 1972.

An Army Public Relations photographer captures a picture in Long Điền, which will show provincial health officials carrying out their duties with Army assistance.

The technologies for gathering and processing news were also more limited. Electronic News Gathering (ENG), which gives greater speed in processing and editing film and allows reports to integrate a variety of material, was not then available. In short, TV news was a much more parochial, less mobile product, less flexible and timely in its processing and editing capacities. There was necessarily less reportorial input and presence, with much less actual news film. American TV reporting of Vietnam was rarely the searing picture that is often asserted, but in Australia its presence on the TV screen was even more marginal, and less visual.

The Australian Broadcasting Commission (ABC) was the only broadcasting organisation with correspondents stationed permanently in Asia. As with TV news in general, however, the mid 1960s ABC should not be viewed through 1980s assumptions. It lacked the range of programs and styles, and the independence from government, that it took for granted later. ABC correspondents mainly covered the war by travelling from their base in Singapore. They filed for both radio and television regularly, although the use of voice reports from reporters was much rarer then. Film processing was often done back in Australia, and so the possibilities for sophisticated editing and the integration of material from different sources were far more limited. The transporting of the film back from Asian countries was slow and cumbersome. Current affairs programs, with their more penetrating capabilities for examining the backgrounds to events and the bases of policies, were still in their infancy. The duration of Australia's military involvement in Vietnam coincided with the growth of current affairs formats on the ABC. By the end of the war, programs such as *Four Corners* and *This Day Tonight*, *AM* and *PM*, were well-established, but when the first commitment of military aid was made they were still non-existent.

Similarly, the emergence of the ABC as strongly independent from the government of the day, was a more tenuous and protracted process than is often recognised. Indeed, the establishment of the ABC's bureau in Singapore actually followed an initiative from External Affairs Minister Casey. Cabinet approved the move in 1955 under a package of measures with the general title, 'Australian Activities in the Cold War'. In 1956, the Department of External Affairs dropped its previous insistence that if the

War correspondents sent out images from Vietnam, large numbers of which were used by the media. Here the two soldiers preceding a vehicle through the dense jungle are concentrating on the camera rather than hidden enemies – a situation not without its dangers.

ABC go ahead with a Singapore bureau. ABC staff should work under their direction, accepting instead a general injunction that they should work closely with Australian diplomats,

In the 1960s, the government could still veto funds for overseas trips and sometimes exercised humiliating control over ABC decisions. When the ABC, as part of a four nation program making venture called Intertel, sought to make a film on US-Canadian relations, the Menzies government stopped it, using the argument that because the Prime Minister would not consider making a statement on such a sensitive subject about our allies, neither should the ABC. At the prompting of the French Ambassador, in 1963 the government forbade the ABC from showing a BBC interview, already shown in Britain, with a French opposition figure, Georges Bidault. In justifying the government's stand, Deputy Prime Minister McEwen asserted a sweeping prerogative for government control:

> The truth of the matter is that the government of the country, whatever party forms it, should have the right and should exercise the right to control anything which in its judgement will impair friendly relations with any ally.

The government's penchant for heavy-handed intervention in such harmless areas suggests the ABC's willingness to probe sensitive areas in the Vietnam war would also be constrained. Naturally, with such a long-entrenched government having such direct capacities for influence, senior ABC management had become well attuned to their views. The long-serving Editor-in-Chief, W.S. Hamilton, had earned strong support in the news room for his professionalism and high standards, and for often asserting the independence of the ABC and of ABC news. Yet his conservative views, and those of other senior executives, doubtless had their impact on the journalists and on the news. Although there were many examples of independence and professionalism, there was an underlying ethos that stories conforming to the government's views were more welcome than ones casting doubt upon them. Occasionally there were pressures to do stories favourable to government policy.

> One correspondent was directly asked by General Manager. Talbot Duckmanton, in 1968 to make a TV news feature on the Australian Army's pacification program, 'the good work of the hearts and minds program', in order to balance 'the war story'. At Núi Đất he found this program to be so small-scale and unimportant that it was 'pathetic'. Nevertheless he felt an obligation to produce a story along the lines suggested, even though privately he felt he should have put the 'boot through it'. His impression was that the story had been suggested to the ABC 'by some area of government'.

More commonly, there were complaints about the difficulty of getting controversial and sensitive material to air.

> In 1968, during the battles in Hue following the Tet Offensive. Neil Davis filming for Visnews captured in sound and vision an ugly incident. A Vietnamese was trying to advance frantically waving a white flag. Davis caught an American voice saying 'he's got a white flag,' followed by his superior, yelling 'bullshit, bullshit, cut him down,' followed by automatic weapon fire. According to an ABC radio producer 'Wally (Hamilton) was very cross', saying 'Neil Davis is not a journalist, he's a photographer. He can't go reporting – unqualified people like that.' The tape therefore was banned from use in news bulletins, although the producer was bold enough to use it in the weekly round-up. *The Week in Asia,* without seeking permission. (The film went mysteriously missing from Visnews, and never appeared on TV.)
> Although no directive was issued about anti-war demonstrations, 'there was continuous pressure to scale down our coverage of (them)' (ABC executive)... When a news camera crew and reporter were assigned to do a story on the conscientious objector Simon Townsend, 'a former member of senior management saw the camera crew ... and put in a strong complaint, a very strong complaint, demanding to know what an ABC camera crew was doing outside the court where this fellow was appearing. There was this kind of pressure that continued throughout the war.'

THE PATHOLOGIES OF BEING A JUNIOR ALLY

Beyond the differing capacities of the media organisations, there is a more far-reaching reason for the different news coverage of the war in Australia and America, the political-cum-journalistic pathologies of being a junior ally. As many commentators have observed, the primary determinant of Australia's

The Communist Threat

Should the forces of communism prevail, and Vietnam come under the heel of Communist China. Malaya is in danger of being outflanked and it, together with Thailand and Indonesia, will become the next target for further Communist activities.
– Sir Percy Spender, Minister for External Affairs, 1950

[The conflict in Indo-China is] part of a world struggle ... The French are defending liberty.
– Sir Paul Hasluck, 1954

The courageous people of Vietnam [are in the] front line struggle against communist aggression, . . Recruits are obtained by kidnapping and other coercive measures, and sent to North Vietnam for training and indoctrination. Later they come back to form new Viet Cong units.
– Sir Garfield Barwick, Minister for External Affairs, 1962

The takeover of South Vietnam ... must be seen as part of a thrust by Communist China between the Indian and Pacific oceans.
– Sir Robert Menzies, 29-4-65

There is not the slightest doubt that the North Vietnamese are the puppets of the Chinese and that the whole conduct of the war, down to the last jot and tittle of it, comes out of the philosophy of Mao Tse-tung ... It is perhaps only the first round of an attack by the Chinese Communists in an effort to dominate the world.
– Alan Fairhall, Minister for Defence, 15-3-1966

What is happening in South-East Asia today is not a local, temporary or isolated situation. It is part of the rivalry of power and the ideological contest which is taking place throughout the world. It is part of the stream of events continuing into the future. In both of those contests the most significant factor in Asia is China.
– Sir Paul Hasluck, Minister for External Affairs, 1965

Behind Vietnam lies a wider conflict that extends from the northern frontiers of India to the dividing line in Korea: that engages the world wide diplomacy of the United States: and that casts the shadow of fear over millions of people in all lands of southern Asia no less than the shadow of terror over the villagers of the Mekong delta. This is a war that affects the fate of all countries of South-East Asia – a war that throws into sharp relief the aim of Communist China to dominate them by force.
– Sir Paul Hasluck, 1966

Getting the News Through

What Australian viewers saw of the Vietnam war on their television screens – and Neil Davis estimated that about 50% of the film coming in would have been his coverage – was governed by a rather arbitrary system of censorship. In order for newsfilm to be allowed to come in quickly without going through the usual formalities of Customs and a censorship board, the news editors of each of the television networks and the Australian Broadcasting Commission were designated as official censors. It was Davis' view that censorship was applied more rigidly under this scheme than if the film had been reviewed by the Commonwealth's Censorship Board. Jack Gulley, the ABC's newly-appointed Director of Television News in 1967, remembers his incredulity when called into the office of the controller of news and told, 'Forget about objectivity, we are at war!'

Davis believed his Vietnam footage was cut much more drastically in Australia than anywhere else in the world. 'You'd think it was a war without violence, that it was all sweetness and light. Just our Australian boys patrolling and keeping the dreaded Communists in check.

'The hierarchy of the ABC's news department believed that news programmes were a family affair, and they didn't want the wife and kids watching blood and guts over seven o'clock dinner – even in black and white. Therefore Australian viewers were deprived of the right to see exactly what was happening in Vietnam, and many other parts of the world, for that matter.'

Some of the censorship was crude. In 1966, ABC correspondent Tony Ferguson and an ABC film crew managed to get to Cambodia, then closed to the Western media. Ferguson was being driven along a Phnom Penh street by an Australian embassy diplomat when he did a double take. He had seen Australian journalist Wilfred Burchett, *persona non grata* with the Australian government, as he had reported the Korean and Vietnam wars from the Communist side. Often travelling in Communist countries closed to other Western journalists and denied a passport to return to his native land, Burchett was hated, admired, and he had extraordinary information.

Ferguson knew that Burchett had been in South Vietnam with the Viet Cong, hiding in their tunnel complexes while being strafed and bombed by American and South Vietnamese firepower. An exclusive interview with this enigmatic man would be of great interest in Australia … Burchett agreed to an interview … [which] went well and a delighted Ferguson cabled the ABC in Sydney that his Burchett footage had been despatched, and gave the usual flight and waybill details.

Meanwhile in Sydney, all hell broke loose. Burchett was regarded by many in Australia as a traitor – a view shared by the ABC's controller of news. He ordered the Burchett film to be destroyed on arrival. It never even made the processing lab.

– From Tim Bowden, *One Crowded Hour*, p. 186–187

Evacuating the wounded: a scene recalling the popular television programme, *M.A.S.H.* Although it was set in Korea, the US program really portrayed many aspects of the Vietnam experience. The 'medevac' or 'dustoff' was a vital part of the campaign in Vietnam, reducing to a minimum the time between injury and treatment.

actions in Asia was the self-perception that we were 'on a side', that the basic reality which overrode all else was the struggle between international communism and the West, and that the major importance of Asia was as a battleground in that struggle. Australian actions alone could not sway the balance in any major Asian arena. The important thing was to involve America. This permitted a mismatch between the government's open-ended rhetorical commitment to pursuing the Cold War, and its rather small substantive commitment. Australia took its cue from American positions, and conformity with America was the primary political test of a policy. The role of junior ally permitted the luxury of embracing alliance policies without the need to evaluate independently their costs and prospects. This had a pervasive and pernicious effect on the government's policy making, and by extension, had a debilitating impact on news coverage and commentary.

Certainly, there was no lack of sincerity in this – the Australian government totally accepted the Cold War views. Indeed the junior ally's insecurity made it more hawkish than the senior power. It feared that any departure from Cold War perceptions would weaken American resolve, and invalidate Australia's insurance policy. The twin fears of offending the ally and of being left alone to face an overwhelming enemy paralysed any independent questioning of perceptions about Vietnam. For America. Vietnam was part of global geopolitical manoeuvring, but for Australia it was portrayed as a direct threat. Whatever more sophisticated defences of the commitment are now made, the public language (and, as far as can be seen, the private thoughts) of the government painted the war and its threat to Australia in stunningly simple terms: China was bent on world domination and/or Asian conquest: 'Hanoi was its puppet'; 'the NLF was the creature of Hanoi': and if 'south Vietnam' fell, the inexorable fall of further dominoes would inevitably engulf an increasingly isolated and beleaguered Australia.

Such sweeping simplicities dominated political discourse so easily because the particularities and doubts about Vietnam itself figured much less in the junior ally's policy making. The United States government, assuming primary responsibility, had to face the uncertainties and dangers of Vietnam:

This is Cambodia

Tony Ferguson made a ... film on [Cambodia] for the innocuous program, *Weekend Magazine*. A sub-editor, Barry Toomey, cut the film and scripted it. Then an executive told him. 'Foreign Affairs want to look at the film and your script.'

'No way' said Toomey. 'Tell them to get stuffed.'

'We can't do that,' said the executive, 'they have a say in whether we can make overseas trips and things. They can be very difficult. You'll have to replace the film.'

'So ... I had to dig out some harmless piece of film with which to replace the Cambodian story.' ... The film came back from Foreign Affairs three weeks later... Toomey says, 'the alterations were puerile. For instance, the film opened with a long shot of water buffalo in a rice paddy and the words, 'this is Cambodia.' Then it panned to an enormous factory on the edge of the paddy and the words. 'And so is this. This factory built by Communist China for Cambodia produces 90 per cent of the country's cement needs.' Foreign Affairs had taken out the words, 'built by Communist China.'

(Toomey refused to rewrite it in accordance with the wishes of Foreign Affairs, and instead decided to resign, 'their cowardice convinced me I had no future at the ABC.' He went on to a successful law career.)

– From Pat Burgess, *Warco*, p. 124–5

---

would war with China result? Could any regime in Saigon be sufficiently stable and viable to wage the war? Would America find itself in an endless, expensive and unpopular military adventure? But the Australian government could deflect such doubts by invoking the certainty of the American alliance. The difference in the governments' responsibilities was well illustrated by their differing attitudes to the problems of the Diệm regime. The American government, both in Washington and Saigon, was internally divided over the prospects and effectiveness of Diệm. Official frustrations and debates often found their way into the news columns. Australian public statements, by contrast, never betrayed any doubts. Indeed, in dismissing Opposition Leader Evatt's criticisms of the Vietnamese elections in 1956 as unfair to Diệm's opponents. External Affairs Minister Casey suggested it was improper even to raise such questions. 'I do not think anyone ... should cast doubt on the conduct of affairs in a country with which Australia has friendly relations.' There is no evidence that the American doubts and debates were reproduced in the Australian government. The only occasion when official statements wavered from uncritical support was a formal note in June 1963 expressing repugnance at religious persecution, the culmination of a series of dramatic clashes between the Catholic-dominated regime and the Buddhists. Even after Diệm's overthrow. External Affairs Minister Barwick simply said, 'He had been a sincere patriot, although some of his internal policies in recent times appeared to have lost him the popular support that was necessary to the continuance of his government.' For the junior ally, simple reiteration of ideological themes could take precedence over an accurate appraisal of the Saigon government's performance and prospects.

LEFT: Besides the unprecedented media access to the war, another novel feature of Australia's conflict in Vietnam was the presence of performers from home, sent to entertain the troops. Here, Joan McInnes sings to members of 4 RAR and A Squadron of the 3rd Cavalry Regiment, in 1971.

OPPOSITE PAGE: Soldiers at play in Núi Đất, as depicted by Army Public Relations.

The political pathologies sketched above involve informational failures, so it is not surprising that they extended also to news media performance. Throughout, the Australian media were more a dependent than an independent variable in the political process. They were primarily creatures of the Australian political environment and shared the failures of Australian officialdom for similar reasons. The news media failed in their most basic political role – as an agent of disclosure. Rather than an independent input into the political process, their news columns overwhelmingly reflected the stances of the government. The news media failed also in their other main political role – as a forum for diverse commentary and analysis. Dissenting views on Vietnam, even where based on considerable expertise, were more often than not either ignored or denigrated.

The media's failure is evidenced first of all in the largely passive approach they took to gathering news from Vietnam. Just as Australia's military commitment was disproportionately smaller than America's, so was Australia's journalistic commitment. Australian news organisations never employed any resident correspondents in Saigon (although the ABC for some years essentially had one there permanently on rotation from Singapore]. The number of Australian correspondents in Vietnam at any one time never numbered more than a handful, while during peaks of newsworthiness there were several hundred from the United States.

The failure to commit resources was paralleled by a cognitive failure among media managements. When Australia committed troops on 29 April 1965, and again when Prime Minister Holt trebled the commitment in March 1966, the decisions received overwhelming editorial support. (Only two of the newspapers studied, *The Australian* and the *Daily Mirror*, both owned by Rupert Murdoch, were at all critical.) There was a striking coincidence between government rhetoric and most editorial comment. This was graphically illustrated in the *Courier-Mail* editorial (10–3–1966), where the first three paragraphs were simply direct quotes from Prime Minister Holt's speech. There were no outbursts of jingoism in the supportive editorials, no illusions about the glory of war, but the same images recur – there is talk of a heavy, grave decision, but inevitable and correct, and of sacrifices and costs that must be borne. The

1965 – Editorials

AUSTRALIA FACES UP TO REALITY

The Federal government has made a grave decision in committing 800 Australian troops to fight in South Vietnam. Yet, however much Australians might abhor the prospect of becoming physically embroiled in the conflict in Vietnam, the government could not shirk its responsibilities there. The decision gives expression to the fundamentals of our policy in South-East Asia. For the United States, the task of halting Communist aggression involves mainly the principles of freedom and peace. For Australia, in Borneo and Vietnam, our own security also is at stake, both now and in the future … The United States wants a negotiated settlement in Vietnam. Its stepped-up campaign is designed only to convince the Communists that they cannot take what they want by force. If the Americans lose militarily or diplomatically, so do we.
- *The West Australian,* 1-5-65

WE ARE AT WAR

This is a grim week-end for every Australian. We are now at war, a war which will touch every one of us far more directly than most people, even today, will realise. Australia is to fight on the Asian mainland to aid the United States in stopping the advance of Communism, which threatens us directly.

We are going with a token, but nonetheless committed and lethal, force to support the South Vietnamese Government against the aggression of North Vietnam, backed by Communist China.

Our Government has made the decision in our name, and that is its duty. The nation now has to support that …

For us, the cost will not be light. Brave men will die in jungles without even seeing the other side's soldiers; many others will be wounded.

At home we will have to commit a great deal of our manpower and our economy to the fight. The easy days ended with the Prime Minister's announcement on Thursday.
- *The Courier-Mail,* 1-5-65

NEW TASKS IN VIETNAM

The decision by the Australian Government to send a battalion to South Vietnam is a grave one and commits Australia to a more direct role in this cockpit of war where the conflict for power between Communist China and the West in South-East Asia has been joined … These are inescapable obligations which fall on us because of our geographical position, our treaty commitments and our friendships … There is clearly a United States call to share, even in a small way, more of the burdens … There was no alternative but to respond as we have.
- *The Age,* 30-4-65

AUSTRALIAN HELP TO SOUTH VIETNAM

The decision announced by the Prime Minister last night to send Australian troops to fight in Vietnam is a grave and heavy one. It commits Australia, in a much more positive way than the presence of a few Army instructors and a handful of planes, to a hard and bitter struggle which could easily develop into a wider war. Yet no Australian who is conscious of the dangerous position in which his country stands, and the crucial importance to it of the war in Vietnam, can doubt that this is a right and indeed inevitable decision.

... The war against aggression in Vietnam is in a very real and direct sense Australia's war. For what is being defended there is not just one small country's right to decide its own destinies free from armed aggression; it is, as Sir Robert Menzies pointed out, the security of all South-East Asia. It cannot be too often or too strongly emphasised that if South Vietnam is allowed to fall to Communism, then the extension of Communist influence down through the Malay Peninsula to the shores of Australia is inevitable.

From Australia's point of view the definitive battle against Chinese Communist expansionism is being fought in Vietnam, and it is a battle in which national honour and national interest dictate that Australia should play a positive part ... The dispatch of an Australian infantry battalion has greater importance than the numbers actually involved would suggest. Its real importance lies in the ranging of Australia beside the United States in a demonstration that resistance to Communist aggression is not the concern of any one country but of all free countries.
– *The Sydney Morning Herald,* 30-4-1965

THE WAR THAT CAN'T BE WON

The Menzies Government has made a reckless decision on Vietnam which this nation may live to regret. It has decided to send Australian soldiers into a savage, revolutionary war in which the Americans are grievously involved – so that America may shelve a tiny part of her embarrassment ...

Their decision is wrong, at this time, whichever way we look at it. It is wrong because Australia's contingent can have only insignificant military value, because it will be purely a political pawn in a situation for which Australia has no responsibility whatsoever ... It is wrong because it deliberately and coldly runs counter to the mounting wave of international anxiety about the shape of the Vietnam war and the justification and perils of America's military escalation ... Neither of the Pacific defence treaties to which Australia subscribes can honestly be invoked to justify the Menzies Government's decision. ANZUS cannot apply, because the United States is not under attack, Seato, more worthless than ever, certainly doesn't apply ...

But Australia has lined up her generations against the hatred and contempt of resurgent Asian peoples – without adding one iota of confidence or strength to the tragically embroiled American nation. It could be that our historians will recall this day with tears.
– *The Australian,* 30-4-65

AUSTRALIANS IN VIETNAM

The Prime Minister will undoubtedly carry the country with him in his deeply considered announcement that an Australian battalion is to be sent to Vietnam. It is the strongest possible reminder that the alliances contracted by this country impose demands as well as affording security ... If we needed finally to convince ourselves that our own security is involved in this war, we have now done it. We have made the necessary commitment ... The Prime Minister's assertion that we too regard the war in Vietnam as part of a Communist Chinese thrust against the whole region of South-East Asia may be an over-simplification. But essentially it is true that this is the greater danger that we face.
- *The Advertiser, 30-4-1965*

TROOPS FOR VIETNAM

The decision of the Menzies Government to dispatch troops to South Vietnam is opposed by many Australians.

— To send troops at this time is wrong because it flies deliberately in the face of increasing international pressure for negotiation.

— It is wrong because it is not justified under either of our two Pacific pacts, SEATO and ANZUS.

— It is wrong because our future is in South-East Asia, and further commitment in Vietnam could irreparably poison our relations with our neighbours.
- *The Daily Mirror, 5-5-65*

The Moratorium symbol

certainties – treaty obligations, the US alliance, communist aggression, the threat from China, the desire to protect democracy in 'south' Vietnam, the domino theory and its inevitable threat to Australia – were all accepted. The cumulative impact of these seemed to preclude the further questioning of any one.

Within the overall acceptance of the government's position, there were occasional undercurrents of questioning, usually made *sotto voce* in later paragraphs. The most insistent was the need for the government to spend more on defence, especially because we were also committed in Malaysia and feared Indonesia. Some yearned vaguely for more active diplomacy. Questions about Vietnam itself were almost never raised, at least not in any sustained way. The *Courier-Mail* (1–5–65) once asked. 'Just which of South Vietnam's repeatedly changing governments are we aiding?' But, as with the other editorials, it immediately passed over such a potentially subversive question.

The extent to which the editorialists took their lead from the government, rather than independently canvassing policy alternatives, is brought out, for example, in their attitudes to troop numbers. The editorials in April 1965, when the government sent 800 troops, and in March 1966, when they increased the number to 4500, sounded almost identical rhetorical themes. But in neither case was there any questioning of the size of the contingent. The great majority of editorials immediately endorsed the trebling of the numbers as a necessary and wise decision, even though, to my knowledge, none had recommended the increase before the decision was made.

Editorial acceptance of the government's world view – the basic reality of an imminent threat from Communist China, and the necessity of securing US protection against it – dwarfed all other considerations. The result was a lack of curiosity about the multitude of other questions related to the war. In retrospect, the lack of media scepticism about key questions is astounding. Three are examined below.

1. The lack of curiosity about Vietnam: Questions about the Saigon government – its representativeness and its effectiveness, its relationship to the internal bases of Vietnamese factions and the range of Vietnamese opinions were barely canvassed. Needless to add, there was little attention to Vietnamese social structure, culture or history. Just as any realities about Vietnam itself were secondary in the government's reasons for being there, they also remained secondary, almost to the point of absence, in news coverage.

2. Lack of curiosity about the enemy: The press saw us as fighting a faceless international communism, and was disinclined to explore how the insurgency might work at a local level, or relations between Hanoi and the NLF or the relations between China, the DRV and the USSR. (The development of the Sino-Soviet split, for example, one of the most significant international developments in this era, received scant attention and less analysis in the Australian media and, when it was mentioned, the USSR were the 'good guys'.)

3. Lack of curiosity about the international politics of the Vietnam war: There was little recognition of the coolness of West European governments towards the American commitment, little care about the distaste shown by neutralist Third World opinion (such as India), and even little probing of the private reservations of Southeast Asian allies. The Australian public was largely insulated from knowing too much about how isolated we were internationally in our zeal for the war. There was not even probing of one of the alleged pillars of our commitment – the SEATO alliance – why so few of its members were involved, how it worked (or failed to work) collectively, why other Asian nations chose not to join it.

The horror of the war, brought directly into Australian homes.

In sum, escalation brought stark differences between senior and junior allies in their domestic politics and news coverage. In America, each step was politically agonising, and the cumulative effect did great political damage to the Johnson administration. In contrast, for the first years after the commitment of Australian troops, the war was a great political success for the Menzies and Holt governments, where the Liberal Party made themselves the embodiment of the American alliance. Strong editorial support was paralleled by successful news management, climaxing in the visit by President Johnson and the Liberals' sweeping victory in the 1966 election.

BETWEEN TWO VICTORIES

The 1966 election was the high point of the Liberal-Country Government's electoral fortunes during the Vietnam war. Nine years later, the coalition parties under Malcolm Fraser won an equally resounding victory. In between, the most basic plank of Australia's Vietnam policy – the fear of an expansionist Communist China – was reversed, but without a clear re-evaluation of policies on the war itself. It was a decade of rapidly changing assumptions, both domestically and internationally, which in the years up to 1972 found the previously dominant conservatism in Australian politics brittle and crumbling. The rapid changes in domestic politics were liberating for the quality of journalism, although editorial attitudes typically lagged behind.

From 1967, the coalition's political fortunes went into a precipitate decline. After the Tet Offensive of 1968, and especially after the proclamation of President Nixon's Vietnamisation policies, the coalition government's foreign policy clearly added to its electoral liabilities. Simple reiteration of unqualified anticommunism was not well attuned to the more calculating ethos of the Nixon doctrine. The limits of American involvement presented dilemmas for Australia – more hawkish stands seemed 'out of step' with the senior ally, and so were ineffectual and reactionary; moving towards withdrawal seemed to confirm the criticisms of the Opposition, and be inconsistent with the Government's own rhetoric. In the face of a more adept ALP, a more probing Canberra press gallery, and increasing divisions within its own ranks, the Government's news management skills crumbled. The Vietnam involvement was not central in its electoral defeat in 1972, but it was a contributing factor. However, while there was obvious war weariness, and while the conservatives were floundering to reconcile their earlier rhetoric with the new realities, no far-reaching re-evaluation of the Vietnam commitment had occurred. Thus, the final defeat revived many of the old assumptions.

By 1975, the Australian press was disenchanted with the Whitlam Labor Government, and the events surrounding the end of the war brought it markedly unfavourable coverage. The communist victory rekindled the sense of threat. Prime Minister Whitlam's assertion that the communist victory presented no immediate threat to Australia was strongly overshadowed by contrary viewpoints: the *Herald* made a front-page headline of Country Party leader. Doug Anthony's, statement: 'We're so alone/Anthony warns on red threat' (3–5–1975), quoting him at length on how regional instability gave many Australians a sense of uncertainty and loneliness. No other views were quoted. The *Sydney Morning Herald* editorialised. 'We are witnessing a cataclysm that is already driving Thailand into the arms of Peking.' (26–4–1975.)

Two issues, both unfavourable to the Whitlam Government, were prominent in news reports, and were the main concern of editorials. Editorialists were outraged firstly by the government's behaviour in not taking more refugees and in having sent cables of somewhat discrepant tone to Hanoi and Saigon, when hostilities intensified. Both issues – the cables and the refugees – raised important questions about government policy, although the government contended that its behaviour in both cases had been subject to misrepresentation. (In the saturation coverage of the war's end between 1 April and 9 May 1975, around one in four stories focussed upon the plight of refugees and orphans, a strong contrast to their neglect in earlier coverage.)

What is damning to the press, however, is the disproportion in attention, the refusal to reflect upon the larger questions posed by the war's end. Why had so many years of massive allied intervention ended in defeat? The *Daily Telegraph* devoted a sixty-eight line editorial to the cables affair, but managed to dispose of the whole war in merely fourteen lines. When one of the great epics of contemporary history – and one of the great failures of Australian policy – was closing, the great majority of the Australian press could only indulge in their vendettas against the Whitlam Government. The *Age* was the only newspaper to write with dignity, compassion and a sense of history. Others failed to varying degrees, with the *Sydney Morning Herald* passing through a stage of particular apoplexy with the Whitlam Government.

Western intervention in Vietnam was by almost any policy measure a disaster. The perceptions that guided that intervention have proved to be fallacious, not only by the massive, immovable fact of defeat, but by the refutation of what were alleged to be the inevitable consequences of that defeat. Since the fall of Saigon, Vietnam has actually fought a war against its alleged puppet-master, China: closer relations have developed for a period between China and most Western nations, including Australia; and no Southeast Asian country outside Indochina has either become communist or had to face a major insurgency. The whole rationale of the intervention has proved to be based upon massive misperceptions. The futility and the failure, and the reasons for it, have been very unevenly absorbed. The dominant response has been one of expedient amnesia, Disapproval of the DRV seems to substitute for any reappraisal of our involvement.

News is concerned with ephemera – with what are seen as the most newsworthy events of any one news cycle. In the mid 1960s, most major Australian news organisations were deeply mediocre institutions, conservative and complacent, their journalistic capacities dulled by years of editorial support for the Menzies government. They proved themselves incapable of rising beyond the daily rush of newsworthy events to probe the policy's assumptions and rationale. The debates about an oppositional media are greatly overdrawn in America, but in Australia it would be ludicrous even to raise the issue. The Australian news media lost the war of trying to cover Vietnam. The political irresponsibility of being a junior ally combined with the majority of the Australian press' whole hearted support for the government produced an acquiescent, unquestioning media, which failed to challenge the assumptions which led to tragedy and failure.

1975 – Editorials

LET'S NOT BE HORRID TO HANOI

There was a nice contrast between two photographs published yesterday morning. One of them showed a smiling, shirt-sleeved Mr Whitlam and his wife taking their holiday ease in the Peruvian Andes; the other showed the result of a communist rocket attack on Saigon. The connection between the two pictures is that it is carefree Mr Whitlam who has condemned Vietnamese with claims on Australian asylum to remain in Saigon to face the very real threats of imprisonment, torture and death. Why has he done so? ... The answer can only be that, the Government of Hanoi having intimated that it does not approve of having its potential victims snatched away from its vengeance, the Prime Minister of Australia is prepared to risk an Inca-style human sacrifice to placate the red gods.
- *The Sydney Morning Herald,* 29-4-75

The Prime Minister has lied to Parliament. He has deceived the Australian people. He has abused their trust in him ... His duplicity has been damningly exposed by the publication (unauthorised) of secret cabled instructions sent by Mr Whitlam to our ambassadors in Hanoi and Saigon. Their publication brings into the open the gravest political scandal since Federation.
- *The Sydney Morning Herald,* 30-4-1975

ONE-SIDED, NOT EVEN-HANDED

The charge the Prime Minister [Mr Whitlam] must answer over his cable to Hanoi and Saigon earlier this month is – to put it kindly – that he misled the Australian people and their Parliament.
   If the Government's policy was in favour of Hanoi and against the Thiệu Government in Saigon, then he should have said so ...
   It was not even-handed.
   The cables were complementary, not similar. Both were directed against the Thiệu Government in South Vietnam ...
   This was one-sided. It was a pro-Hanoi and 'dump Thiệu' policy. He should have told Parliament this.
- *The Courier-Mail,* 30-4-75

THE END OF THE VIETNAM ERA

The final verdict on the Vietnam war and the commitment by America and its allies will be given by history – and perhaps that verdict will be kinder than contemporary opinion ...

The Whitlam Government, which has shown marked good will towards the Vietnam Communists, must use all the influence it possesses to try to prevent any slaughter ...

Australia, like America, has an obligation to help the Vietnamese people.
- *The Courier-Mail,* 2-5-1975

BUNGLE OVER REFUGEES

Misjudgement or callousness, or both, seem to have caused the premature closure of the Australian Embassy in Saigon and the withdrawal of Australian staff ...

An Australian presence needed to be maintained to deal with the claims for help ...

Two weeks ago there was supposed to be an urgent need to bring orphans out of Vietnam. Now the orphans are barely heard of, and the clamour has swung to adult refugees. Is the clamour justified?

The Government has bungled the adult refugee problem ... The Government in all conscience should have investigated what Vietnamese were owed sanctuary in Australia, and then have made arrangements to honour the obligation.
- *The Courier-Mail,* 29-4-1975

THE END TO A 30-YEAR WAR

The Vietnam war is over. It did not end in peace with honour. It ended in unconditional surrender by the South, in ignominious retreat by the United States, and in triumphant victory by the North and the Viet Cong. 'This closes a chapter in the American experience' said President Ford, in a monumental understatement. It closes much more, and not only in the bitter experience of the Americans and their allies. It marks the conclusion of one of the most tragic, brutal, costly and protracted human struggles in modem history.

To dismiss the war as a terrible exercise in futility is to see it from one side only, that of the losers. The conflict was not futile for the victors. Its culmination after a 30-year-long struggle means to them the achievement of their aims from which they never wavered. These were the liberation of their homeland from colonial rule and foreign intervention, and the establishment of an independent and indigenous communist society. They did not win the hearts and minds of all their fellow-countrymen, but their spirit, discipline, resourcefulness – yes, and ruthlessness – endured and ultimately triumphed over what were until recently superior numbers, firepower and technology.

The cost of this relentless struggle, this human tragedy, is almost beyond understanding. Total casualties from January 1961, to January 1975, have been estimated at 5,773,190. Excluding American casualties, this was more than 10 per cent of the whole population of Indo-China.

The dead numbered 2,122,244 including 56,231 Americans and 423 Australians. Before the final collapse, the South Vietnamese authorities estimated that 55 per cent of the population, about 10 million, were refugees, including some 900,000 orphans. The United States flew 1,899,668 sorties and dropped 6,727,084 tons of bombs on Indo-China, compared with the 2,700,000 tons of bombs dropped by the combined American and British air forces on Germany in the second world war. As well, 3,500,000 acres of Vietnam were sprayed with 19 million gallons of defoliants, the effects of which could last 100 years ...

In human terms, we should be thankful that the war has ended, and exert whatever influence we have to persuade the victors to be merciful and magnanimous towards the losers who could not withdraw or flee.
- *The Age,* 1-5-1975

END OF A TRAGEDY

A long and dreadful chapter of Asian history has ended ... another, unknown chapter is about to begin.

And suddenly there is nothing left to say.

The tears have been shed. A million words have described the agony and the horror and the bloodshed. It's over. Thank God.

Now we can only pray that the people of Vietnam will be shown the mercy they have, for so long, been denied.
- *The Daily Telegraph,* 1-5-1975

ARROGANT DECEIT

Australians today have the right to some straight answers from the Prime Minister over the astonishing affair of his cable to Hanoi ...

Mr Whitlam has a tremendous ego. He would like the world to see him as the statesman who took the diplomatic initiative that cut short the suffering of the Vietnamese ...

Mr Whitlam could argue that a total communist victory in Vietnam is inevitable, that his initiative was designed to hasten that victory by a political, rather than a military solution ...

But the fact is that Mr Whitlam went beyond the bounds of diplomacy and he then attempted to hide from Parliament the extent of his bias towards the communists ...

Most Australians view a communist victory in Vietnam with sadness, with anger, and with disgust. That it is inevitable cannot change the way we feel about it. We will not forget easily that Mr Whitlam did not share these emotions. Nor will we be able to forget that he has committed the unpardonable sin of misleading Parliament.
- *The Daily Telegraph,* 30-4-1975

MOBILISING DISSENT

The Later Stages of Protest

Ann Curthoys

During 1965 Prime Minister Menzies told an Australian Club audience in London that peace rallies in Australia were organised by communists. This was a frequent charge levelled against those in Australia who opposed their country's involvement in the war or the use of conscripts there. The charge was highly misleading. Ann Mart Jordens has shown in her essay that the backbone of the early anti-war movement was middle-aged and middle-class – the Second World War generation. These anti-war activists were moderates, mainly non-communists, liberals rather than leftists, and sometimes characterised more by religious than political beliefs. The Communist Party and its youth organisation, the Eureka Youth League, as well as the few left-wing unions, were, nevertheless, important organising forces in the anti-war movement. This did not mean the relationship was one of hardened party cadres manipulating well-meaning but naive idealists: instead, a loose coalition was being forged between very different groups which shared a broadly similar attitude to the war and conscription. For many of these people communists were genuine political allies, not political outlaws. Even together, however, these political forces were still very much a minority and clearly unable to threaten the government's policies or win over large segments of an essentially conservative Australian population. This would change in the following years as the politicization, even radicalisation, of Australian youth – the maturing 'baby boom' generation – particularly those in tertiary education, mobilised against conscription and the war.

Soon after the initial commitment of Australian troops to Vietnam in April 1965, the war and conscription became important issues on the campuses around Australia. An anti-war stance was far from being dominant at this early stage and the majority of students were still relatively conservative. Teach-ins were held from July, designed more as forums for information dissemination rather than the statement of any particular view of the war. Student newspapers, such as *Honi Soit* at the University of Sydney and *Tharunka* at the University of New South Wales, featured in July and August articles on Vietnam including reprints of debates in America and speeches by such anti-war figures in Australia as Jim Cairns and C.P. Fitzgerald, reports on Australian teach-ins and pro-government pieces such as that by Peter Manning, President of the DLP Club. At the University of Sydney, the Fabian journal *New Basis* carried articles by Peter King and Eric Myers attacking American and Australian policy in Vietnam. The Melbourne radical journal *Partisan* carried an article in its October/November issue by Cairns attacking the government's portrayal of events in Asia and Vietnam and calling for understanding of, and support for, Asia and the revolutions there. Critical of Stalinism and repression in Hungary and Tibet. Cairns said communism must be countered by 'basic political and economic progress' not military force.

OPPOSITE PAGE: The peak of protest: a Moratorium march in Adelaide, 1971.

> I first became aware of Vietnam at a demonstration in late 1964, protesting against the American bombing of the DRV, I was 19. Demonstrations against the war were to be a regular part of my political experience until after the Moratoriums of 1970. During the same period, I was involved also in pro-Aboriginal politics, an educational experiment called the 'Free University', and the establishment of Women's Liberation in Sydney. Mine was a middle-class baby boom generation experience, not uncommon, but not typical either.
>
> The demonstration in Sydney was outside the American consulate, then in Barrack Street. Organised by the Eureka Youth League, it was obedient and moderate in the extreme, moving on whenever the police said to, so that we walked around and around the city block in which the consulate stood. I'd say there were about 100 to 200 people, nearly all young, nearly all in the Eureka Youth League. This was the youth organisation of the Communist Party of Australia (CPA). Having been brought up the daughter of communist parents, I was a member. Our emphasis at this point was against American intervention in Vietnam.
>
> At the Australian Student Labor Federation's annual conference in Canberra in June 1965, 14 men and one woman were arrested during a demonstration against the war, I was the woman. We sat on the road in the busiest intersection we could find in Canberra – to our Sydney and Melbourne eyes, not very busy. We held up our banners, and the traffic. Cars honked, and one edged very close, as if to run us over. We sat there, and eventually were carried or walked to the police van. As the only woman, I was put in a separate cell. I could hear the others singing in another part of the lock-up. I was there for about two hours. It was actually quite boring. The policewomen were friendly. When we eventually got out, we didn't get any support. The conference was strongly divided between Right and Left, and the hostility around our (Left) action led to a hostile reception on our return. I was interviewed by Julie Rigg for the *Australian*. We went to court the next day, pleaded guilty (only later did it emerge you could actually get away with actions of civil disobedience), and paid our £5 fines. When we got back to Sydney, we organised some support for ourselves, to pay our fines, but it wasn't much. Some of us were in the Communist Party, others more Trotskyist in political orientation, or in the Labor Party.

The anti-war 'movement', if such a term can be used accurately, on the campuses as well as beyond, was far from monolithic. A variety of left groups emerged to contest the leadership of the anti-war movement, particularly on the campuses. The Sydney-based Vietnam Action Committee (later 'Campaign') which organised a demonstration in Martin Place in September 1965 under the strong influence of Trotskyist and ALP member Bob Gould, represented just one of a variety of competing stances including pacifism, purely anti-conscriptionism, or opposition to either or both Australian and American government policies. John Powles of the Sydney University Humanists Society carried a banner reading 'Land Reform not Scorched Earth'; that of the well-known identity Jack the Anarchist, 'As usual the bourgeoisie has god on its side'. Others, probably of libertarian persuasion, mocked the demonstration.

A less peaceful demonstration occurred in Sydney on 22 October, in Pitt Street during Friday late afternoon peak hour. The demonstration started peacefully enough, with hundreds of students, trade unionists and others parading outside the Commonwealth Bank building in Martin Place, housing the Commonwealth Parliamentary members' offices. Signalling the beginning of a more confrontationist

From left to right, Keith Holyoake of New Zealand, Paul Hasluck of Australia, and Dean Rusk of America, confer. This powerful group of political allies from the 1960s would help to steer their countries into war in Vietnam.

style, a breakaway group moved off down Pitt Street, and a sit-down began. Police began taking the demonstrators away in police vans; altogether 45 men and two women were arrested. The demonstration disrupted city traffic for more than an hour.

> I was there, sat down as part of the demonstration, but got up again when it was clear that arrest would follow. I can't remember why; perhaps I'd had my fill of arrests with the June demonstration in Canberra, perhaps I was just a little scared, or perhaps I just had an essay to complete.

From then on major demonstrations were held in the major capital cities about every three months. In Sydney, the anti-war movement continued to grow, holding an unusually large rally for this period in Sydney Town Hall in early December 1965, with 3000 present. Its size may have resulted partly from the fact that it was organised jointly by the Vietnam Action Campaign and Association for International Cooperation and Disarmament, thus bringing the various and competing anti-war groupings together. The emphasis, however, was still very much on argument and debate.

These voices in the traditional peace movement, the student movement, and the left of the ALP against Australian involvement in the war in Vietnam received in November 1965 a boost from an unexpected source when Gregory Clark, who had two months earlier left the Department of External Affairs where he was one of the very few Asian linguists, wrote an article, 'Australia and the Lost War' for the *Australian*. Clark began with the then astounding sentence, 'the West is losing the war in Vietnam' and went on to say that the war cannot be won unless the West is prepared to decimate the Vietnamese population.' He referred to the unpopularity of the government in Saigon with its own people, the growth in the numbers and fighting ability of the PLAF, the ineffectiveness of the ARVN, and the shrinkage of the area it controlled. He stressed the fact that the NLF was not simply a puppet of Hanoi and Peking but, rather, a force with popular support in southern Vietnam: 'the Viet Cong have succeeded in gaining this support ... because they can represent themselves as the successors to the popular nationalist struggle against the

ABOVE LEFT: In 1965. American and Australian administrators were united on the question of Vietnam: despite official demonstrations of unity, however, public protest was building up in both countries.

ABOVE RIGHT: In June 1965, Air Vice Marshal Nguyễn Cao Kỳ became the head of the military regime in southern Vietnam. Here, he expounds to an approving Australian audience, including, on the left. Harold Holt, and on the right. Ambassador David Anderson.

French ...' He argued also that it was no use supporting America in order to oblige it to defend Australia at some later time; US defence decisions would be based on other considerations. Clark was thus one of the first, if not the first, to argue publicly that America and Australia were engaged in an unwinnable war; his intervention gave the anti-war movement's armoury of arguments a pragmatic edge it previously lacked.

1966

On 8 March 1966, Prime Minister Harold Holt, who had succeeded Menzies in January, announced that the number of Australian troops in Vietnam would be increased from 1400 to 4500, and would include 500 conscripts. A wave of activity against conscription followed. In Sydney on Wednesday 16 March, 2000 demonstrators marched in the centre of Sydney. Women from *Save Our Sons* distributed leaflets, and a truck carrying half a dozen women dressed in the fashions of 1912 swept past, bearing the banner 'today's Suffragettes Demand Withdrawal from Vietnam'. A small counter-demonstration distributed 'red rat' leaflets, which said, 'Don't let the red rats stab diggers in the back, Fight in Vietnam or your backyard.' The anti-war marchers went on to Hyde Park, where Barry Robinson, secretary of the Youth Campaign Against Conscription, called for young men with National Service cards to come forward The demonstrators 'cheered, shouted and waved a forest of placards in Hyde Park, as a dozen young men burnt their National Service registration cards in protests against the Vietnam war.'

The campaign gained momentum. Over the weekend of April 15, 16 and 17 there were anti-war and

Prime Minister Harold Holt, contemplating the statements of American Vice President Hubert Humphrey, during the latter's visit in 1966.

anti-conscription protests in Sydney, Brisbane, Canberra, Adelaide and Perth, attracting wide publicity. The Seamen's Union refused to provide crews for the *Boonaroo*, chartered in May 1966 by the government to carry stores to Vietnam. It found, however, little support from the ACTU, which opposed strike action or stoppages staged as a protest against Australian involvement in the war. Nor was it supported by the other unions; six maritime unions, wishing not to jeopardise the position 'of our lads' in Vietnam, agreed to crew any ships carrying supplies to Vietnam. Faced with concerted opposition, the Seamen's Union, recognising its isolation, relented and manned the *Boonaroo,* which left for Vietnam on 26 May.

On 25 May 1966 the first conscript, Errol Wayne Noack, was killed. He had been in Vietnam for only ten days. From this point there was a concerted campaign by the antiwar movement to oust the Liberal government in the November elections. The aim was to make the Vietnam war as unpopular as possible and to mobilise that unpopularity on behalf of the ALP. The focus shifted to conscription, a simpler issue for ALP supporters than opposition to Australian involvement in the war itself.

The desire to encourage a Labor Party victory in the elections held the more militant sections of anti-war opinion back, and demonstrations appear to have remained largely peaceful during the rest of 1966. The major exception was to be the demonstration against the visit to Australia of President Johnson, the architect of American interventionist foreign policy. Holt's slogan, 'All the way with LBJ', seemed to the anti-war movement to summarise the wilful lack of independence in policy and an embarrassing subservience to a foreign power. On Friday 21 October, the population of Melbourne – half a million or more – took to the streets, to greet this first American president ever to visit Australia. The anti-war movement turned up too. Demonstrators splashed his car with red and green paint bombs, and the motorcade made an unscheduled detour to avoid a 1000-strong crowd of student demonstrators. Later, the Monash University Students' Representative Council published a pamphlet. *Facts about the Anti LBJ Demonstration,* which suggested a high level of police violence in keeping the demonstrators under control.

LEFT: Casualty evacuation after an engagement in Vietnam in 1967.

ABOVE: A massive twin-rotor Chinook helicopter airlifts supplies and guns to Fire Support Base Picton, in 1969.

BELOW LEFT: Army action continues side by side with village life in Vietnam, in this 1967 scene from the war.

BELOW RIGHT: An instructor from the Australian Army Training Team supervises parachute training for Vietnamese Montagnards.

LEFT: More than 500 000 well-wishers in Melbourne greet President Johnson with ticker-tape, flowers, balloons, flags and streamers. Despite the overwhelming success of the visit as a symbol of support for the alliance between Australia and the USA, crowds would gather in Melbourne again four years later, this time to attack the war.

BELOW LEFT: Villagers stack produce before enforced resettlement in a new location near 1 Task Force, Núi Đất. These people at Xà Bang were supplying the 'VC', and Australian troops destroyed the village after the relocation.

BELOW RIGHT: Troops help to install a windmill for a village, as part of Australia's civic action program in Vietnam.

While one million Sydney-siders turned out the next day, outdoing Melbournians in their welcome to the President, the anti-war movement had a major success in obstructing the motorcade and making their protest known. Five thousand demonstrators massed near the intersection of Liverpool and College Streets, with demonstrators standing ten and fifteen deep. Just as the motorcade appeared, students broke through the police barricades. It took thirty seconds for the police to drag them away and for the procession to move on. The protesters walked from Hyde Park to join the crowd gathering outside the Art Gallery.

> We hadn't expected actually to stop the motorcade. I was on the other side of the road from the one where the break was made. I wasn't out to get arrested, indeed I had moved away from communist politics and was with a rather conservative friend, Louise, who wouldn't have got arrested for anything. We stood there, shouting, but just slightly away from the real action. To my amazement, the demonstrators got past the police and filled the roadway. One of those who made it onto the roadway was my sister, whose photo went around the world. It was all over in a minute, but we had made our protest. Then we walked up to the Art Gallery to have another try at making Johnson know we were there. We chanted slogans, and jeered the speeches by Holt and Askin. When LBJ left the Gallery, we booed again.

The photographs in the afternoon paper were everything the struggling anti-war movement could have wished for. The images were graphic – young women and men lying in front of huge black official cars, stopping the progress of the President of the United States. Everyone now knew there was an anti-war movement in Australia.

The anti-war demonstrators were thrilled with the success of their protest. But a million people had turned up in Sydney and half a million in Melbourne to welcome LBJ: the total number of demonstrators throughout the country was only about 20 000. The LBJ visit had given a clear signal: the 1966 election a month later, on 26 November, was an overwhelming victory for the government, and a massive disaster for the ALP. While the election involved many issues, and a victory for the government was no new thing in Australian politics, it was clear that the majority of people supported Australian intervention in Vietnam. The anti-war movement represented an active and angry minority; it had not swayed the electorate.

Anti-war activists took some time to take stock of this situation, to adjust to the popularity of intervention, and to rethink their strategies for achieving an Australian withdrawal of troops.

1967

Reassessment went on both within the ALP and in the anti-war organisations. Australian involvement in the war had risen to 6300 troops, and was to rise again in October to 8300. Not wishing to be seen as undermining the position of 'our boys' in Vietnam, and mindful of the electoral liability opposition to the war had become, the Labor Party modified its policy. Gough Whitlam, having replaced Arthur Calwell on 8 February as leader of the ALP, headed the party's withdrawal from the issue. The party was internally divided, as became clear at the series of state conferences over the Queen's birthday weekend

Demonstrators in Sydney come up against a police cordon as President Johnson's cavalcade arrives.

in June, when the NSW branch abandoned the commitment to withdraw troops while the Victorian branch maintained it. At the federal conference in Adelaide on 31 July, however, a compromise emerged: a Labor Government would withdraw troops if the US and its other allies did not attempt to end the war through actions such as the cessation of bombing of the DRV, recognition of the NLF, and so on. It was a small shift, rather than a massive swing, to the right.

The anti-war movement outside the ALP also underwent a change. There was a mood of disillusionment, as the anti-war activists recognised they had just lost their best chance to have Australian troops withdrawn. This was especially true amongst the left political groupings on campus. *Lot's Wife*, the student newspaper at Monash University in Melbourne, expressed the current mood in its first issue for 1967:

> No matter whose interpretation one accepts of the election result, it was a shocking defeat for those who oppose the Australian and American commitments in Vietnam – a defeat also for those anti-conscription bodies and supporters ... In a sense the elections seemed the last hope for the anti-war groups. After the LCP victory the feeling was one of utter helplessness.

In this atmosphere, the foundations were laid for a marked move to the left and to militant action. There was a widening split between those who continued to seek a change in government policy through the traditional methods of campaigning and those who questioned the effectiveness of parliamentary politics for radical social change generally. In Sydney, an Anti-Vietnam-War Anti-Conscription Activists Conference, held from 27 to 30 January to assess the election results and plan for the future, revealed a split between moderates and militants. In both Sydney and Melbourne, the two main centres of antiwar politics, there emerged a strong political grouping to the left of both the ALP and the Communist Party. In Melbourne, the extreme left was dominated by Maoism, with its stress on the power of ideas to achieve revolutionary change, while in Sydney it was dominated by the Trotskyists, who placed greater emphasis on achieving a revolution through entering and influencing the Labor Party to a revolutionary left position. In Sydney, the influence of the far left was consolidated with the beginning of regular publication by the Vietnam Action Campaign of the journal, *Vietnam Action,* from May 1967.

On the campuses, in the Labor and other similar clubs, an increasingly 'revolutionary' style of politics emerged. The Monash Labor Club provides an example. As Julie Ockenden so neatly puts it, issues like Vietnam and conscription were now seen not just as policy mistakes, or abnormalities, but as the product of the value systems and economic demands of advanced Western capitalism. The Vietnam war was seen as a war between National Liberation and socialism on the one hand and American imperialism on the other. Further, this increasingly radical ideology was to go along with a belief in the necessity for militant confrontationist tactics. Since liberal democratic tactics had not worked, it was important to challenge the authority of the state and its instruments such as university administrations, police, courts, and so on.

> I was there, at Monash, for a while. I'd finished my honours degree at the end of 1966 and taken up a PhD scholarship at Monash. I only lasted five weeks. I didn't know anyone, and couldn't even decide on a thesis topic. I was aware of the Labor Club, but it all seemed very male and very unwelcoming. Certainly I pored over my copies of *Lot's Wife* trying to understand this university I'd tried to become a part of. The Labor Club seemed very prominent, very confident. I went back to Sydney in April, abandoning my PhD, and started a Diploma of Education at Sydney Teachers' College. The Vietnam war was not much of an issue there.

On the basis of this belief in the need for confrontationist tactics, the Monash Labor Club's own newsletter, *Print,* announced on 30 March the Club's solidarity with the NLF and published its official program. The war was seen as a war of national liberation waged by the NLF against foreign intervention from the USA and Australia. This was a radical departure for the Australian anti-war movement, which had always (and this included those parts of it influenced by the Communist Party of Australia), refrained from supporting the NLF, instead stressing the people's right to self determination. The Monash Labor Club then went a step further, establishing a fund to aid the NLF.

> I was back in Sydney, still attending meetings of anti-war activists at Sydney University. One member of the Sydney Uni Labor Club suggested we should do the same, send money to the NLF. I felt a little shocked by this; it seemed to move us away from the position of non-interference. But then I wondered if my doubts were based more on fear of public outrage.

On 21 July the Monash Labor Club set up an action committee to collect medical and unspecified aid for the NLF. The news broke on 24 July and for several weeks the students' action became front-page news. The DLP Club led the attacks on campus. Many students were shocked and outraged at the desertion of Australian conscripts, the people they had thought the Labor Club was fighting for. Some opposed collecting funds for the NLF on the grounds that it would prolong the war; others feared repercussions against the anti-war movement, which could now be identified as treasonous. The Labor Club set up a table to collect money, collecting about $60 before the Vice Chancellor announced on 23 August that all collections were banned. Largely as a result of these events, the federal government quickly pushed through parliament in early September the Defence Forces Protection Act, which made it illegal to send aid to the DRV, the VWP, and the NLF.

The debate continued on other fronts. A 'teach-in' called the 'National Forum on Vietnam' was held at Monash University on 2 October, and televised live by the ABC. Aiming to cover both sides of the debate, the teach-in included speakers such as Whitlam. Defence minister Malcolm Fraser, Cairns, Malcolm Salmon from the Communist Party newspaper *Tribune,* and academic specialists such as Professor John Legge. One sign that the anti-war movement was recovering its impetus came with the 'Vietnam Day' mobilisation on 22 October, when 10 000 marched, the most to date.

Those who supported the government were getting a little more organised. An organisation called 'Peace with Freedom' had been started in Melbourne in 1966, its Chairman, Catholic convert, *Quadrant* editor, and prominent member of the Congress for Cultural Freedom, James McAuley. Consisting of academics and students, it had strong links with the Democratic Labor Party.

In Sydney a combination of pro-intervention professors, led by philosophy Professor D.C. Stove, organised on 28 November 1967 an 'Appeal for Civic Aid for South Vietnam'. Other significant members of the group calling the appeal were Professors Spann, Armstrong, McCallum, and Mansfield. The appeal sought to raise from members of the teaching staff of Sydney's three universities the sum of $30 000 for reconstruction in Vietnam. Alex Carey, lecturer in psychology at the University of NSW, in a reply published in January 1968, argued that since this money was to be used by the Australian Army, to support the Appeal was to support the war; it could not be interpreted as a neutral humanitarian gesture.

> Professor McCallum was my uncle, my mother's brother. Our politically heterogeneous family found itself divided on the Vietnam issue, like most others. I assume we all embarrassed each other equally.

1968

The character of the anti-war movement was to change significantly from the beginning of 1968, not for reasons to do with the nature of Australian politics, but as a result of changes within Vietnam itself. Following the Tet Offensive, in public debate, the issue of the morality of the war was now joined, more strongly than before, by the question of its apparent futility.

Prime Minister John Grey Gorton, who had replaced Harold Holt after the latter drowned at Portsea in December 1967, agreed in March 1968 to place a ceiling, for the first time, on the commitment of combat forces in Vietnam. To add to the sense that a turning point was being reached, President Johnson announced his intention not to rerun for the presidency, a decision widely taken to indicate that he believed the war in Vietnam could not be won.

> I remember the shock that accompanied Johnson's announcement. We felt that the American anti-war movement had succeeded in making the war so unpopular that Johnson could not run for President again. It seemed that while the anti-war movement had not been able overtly to shift American policy, it had been significant in helping American determination to win the war

In a protest in Hyde Park, Sydney, in 1968, demonstrators 'Wash the Australian flag free of blood'

> crumble from within. The Vietnamese people, we felt, were bringing the most powerful nation on earth to its knees. Pictures of Johnson flashed around the world, showing him as a heavily lined, worried, broken man. So different from the Johnson who had met a million people on the streets of Sydney only eighteen months before. From the evidence of Johnson's ravaged features, we started to think the war might actually end.

Early in 1968 the Draft Resisters Movement was established. More militant than its organisational predecessors, it did not merely oppose conscription, but sought to make the system unworkable. Militant student groups throughout 1968 and 1969 mounted extensive resistance, in the form of sit-ins and raids on government offices. The tactic of non-cooperation was spreading among twenty-year-old draftees. The first man sent to a civilian gaol for non-compliance with the National Service Act was John Zarb, who spent over a year in Pentridge Prison in Melbourne. The resulting painted signs on railway walls and other public places were so extensive, and so daringly located, that 'Free John Zarb' signs lasted for many years afterwards.

The talk of ending the war now began in earnest. The Paris Peace Talks between the US and the DRV started in May 1968. Yet there did not seem much hope of an Australian withdrawal of troops, and anti-war demonstrations during the winter and spring of 1968 were sometimes marked by demonstrators' confrontationism and police violence. The anti-war movement had made little real headway.

If 1968 saw the growth of a feeling that the war was unwinnable, and the strengthening of resistance by potential conscripts, it saw also a growth in student radical politics generally. Attention often focussed inward, onto student issues and concerns. This was especially true at Monash University, in Melbourne, but was repeated around the country, with the media paying much attention to student leaders. The phrase 'student power' caught on, taken from student revolts in the US, Paris, West Germany, and elsewhere. It was taken to mean that students could act as a vanguard to a revolution, could ignite the spirit of revolt in workers, as in Paris in May 1968. As Rowan Cahill wrote in an article about 'student power' in *Outlook* in August 1968, the events in Paris had made the world's press take notice of student movements. In Australia the *Australian* and the *Sydney Morning Herald* carried major front page stories and editorials on the student movement in Australia, and wondered whether it was comparable to that in Paris. June and July saw a rash of student demonstrations on a variety of issues, especially those to do with university administrations. The Melbourne left intellectual journals. *Arena* and *Dissent*, began to carry articles which attempted to articulate the politics and philosophy of a new left and of student power. Particularly important were Denis Altmann and Warren Osmond, each of whom outlined a coherent new left or counter-cultural position.

1969

The small radical journal *International: A Revolutionary Socialist Magazine,* predicted in its January/February issue that 1969 would be the greatest year for the Australian Left since the war. The Communist Party, it argued, was rejecting its previous unswerving support for the Soviet Union, the students were restive, and there were major working-class actions against the penal powers and the arbitration system. It noted that during the summer vacation there had been intensive discussions of the tactic of 'occupations' in universities, taken from overseas examples. The revolution, it seemed, was just around the corner.

While this may be taken with a grain of salt, as the usual virtually unquenchable left optimism, it was true that 1969 saw a rapid upsurge in anti-conscription and anti-war activity. In the anti-conscription movement, the campaign to urge young men not to register for National Service was accelerating. The first intensive 'Don't Register' campaign was launched during the 1969 January/February registration period. By the beginning of March over 100 people, including Jim Cairns, had been arrested for inciting young men not to register. In Melbourne, Sydney, Canberra and Brisbane, students held large demonstrations in support of those arrested and handed out Don't Register leaflets. Actions such as these worried the Gorton government, and the first full debate on student demonstrations was held in federal parliament in May 1969.

The anti-war movement received a boost with the announcement by President Nixon in June 1969 that 25 000 American troops were to be withdrawn from Vietnam. The process of Vietnamisation of the war, the replacement of American, Australian, and other foreign troops with Vietnamese troops, had begun. For the Australian anti-war movement, the end was in sight. And yet Australia did not immediately follow America's example. Not only were troops to stay, but conscription was to be maintained and enforced. As the American withdrawal commenced, the Australian government began to crack down on its student dissidents, especially those resisting the National Service Act. The opposition to conscription became

increasingly organised. In June, civil disobedience spread from students to academics to the broader community. By the end of June more than 500 academics across the country had signed 'incitement statements', urging young men not to register under the Act. Early in July a Committee in Defiance of the National Service Act was formed, and its declaration of defiance received a wave of support. By late November over 8000 had signed, and the government backed away from disciplinary action against resisters.

Up until mid-1969 the government had had majority support for its intervention in Vietnam, though conscription for overseas service had been less popular. The year 1969 seems to have been a turning point in public opinion about the war to date. The government began to lose the moral and political authority it had so comfortably enjoyed to date. A Gallup Poll in August showed 55% in favour of bringing Australian troops home, and 40% in favour of them staying. This was the first poll to show less than 50% approval rate for the government's policy, and all polls after this date were to show a majority in favour of bringing the troops home.

Sensing a change in the public mood, the Federal ALP Conference in Melbourne in July adopted a firmer policy on the withdrawal of Australian troops. In October, during his policy speech for the 1969 federal elections. Whitlam declared that under a Labor government there would be no Australian troops in Vietnam after June 1970. The Labor Party lost the 25 October election, but a strong swing against the Gorton coalition government brought the Labor Party eighteen additional seats. Democratic Labor Party preferences, yet again, had kept Labor out of office. Nevertheless, the ALP's support for withdrawal of troops did not have the catastrophic effects it had had in 1966; indeed it might have contributed to the swing to Labor.

In the US, too, the anti-war movement was making headway. A Moratorium on 15 October on the war attracted 250 000 in New York and 100 000 in Washington. The idea was to put a moratorium on business as usual, thus drawing attention to the extent of protest against the war. The following month, in November, news of the My Lai massacre of March 1968, startling proof that American troops had engaged in massacres of civilians in Vietnam, hit world headlines. America's moral authority was at a low ebb. The American moratorium, the My Lai massacre, and the changing political climate, combined to galvanise the Australian anti-war movement into action. By the end of the year, there was a growing desire to put internal differences aside in the interests of developing mass demonstrations against continued military involvement in Vietnam. On 25 November, a national conference was held in Canberra to plan a US-style moratorium in Australia. Coordinating organisations emerged in most capital cities. In Sydney, for example, the various anti-war groups formed the December Mobilisation Committee, a coalition of antiwar organisations including Resistance (a combination of earlier left youth groups). High School Students against the War in Vietnam, Students for a Democratic Society, the Vietnam Action Campaign, and the Labor clubs at the universities of Sydney and New South Wales. Demonstrations were organised for 15 December, to coincide with those in America.

Resistance Bulletin No. 6, December 1969 carried an advertisement that was to have far reaching implications.

The Women's Liberation Group will be marching under their own banner on the Dec 15 mobilisation.

The Moratorium movement in Australia was so wide that it came to embrace trade unionists, veterans of previous wars, and people of all ages.

We have printed some pamphlets, some of which include: The Status of Women in Canada 5c; The Myth of the Vaginal Orgasm 15c; Only the Chains Have Changed free; Women's Liberation and Revolution 15c; Families 5c.

> I was at this demonstration. It was the most optimistic of success in years, possibly since the days of 1966, before the massive defeat of the elections that year. It was large, and it seemed the moderate and militant parts of the anti-war movement were acting in concert again. I was given a leaflet about the Women's Liberation Group, and thought this was rather trivial, people are dying in Vietnam. I stayed with my boyfriend and did not join the women. But this leaflet was to lead to a major change in perspective, for me, and many others in the anti-war movement.

The day after this demonstration. President Nixon announced the third stage of the withdrawal of US troops from Vietnam. For the first time, the Australian government also committed itself to withdrawal. Prime Minister Gorton announced that one battalion would be brought back by April 1970, to coincide with the fourth stage of the US withdrawal.

1970

In 1970 the anti-war movement briefly moved out of its minority status. It could see the end in sight. Public opinion polls continued to move against the war. Nixon instituted a phased American withdrawal. Gorton had announced the first step in Australia's withdrawal, the Labor Party began to press for a stronger commitment to the withdrawal of troops than the government was prepared to make. That the Labor Party to this point had been equivocal about the issue was remembered only by the more committed of

In the major cities, the size of the Moratorium marches prompted a massive police presence in the streets. Here, police line Collins Street in Melbourne during a march in 1970.

the antiwar activists. One sign of change in labour circles was that the ACTU and trade union movement began to oppose the war more strongly. A meeting of 300 union officials representing 32 unions had met in Fitzroy Town Hall in Melbourne in mid-December and called on national servicemen to lay down their arms in Vietnam.

Organisation for the May Moratorium got under way. Individuals and organisations affiliated to the Moratorium campaign, lending moral, financial, and organisational support. On 27 February, the ACTU narrowly endorsed the Moratorium, on a vote so close that the casting vote of the President, R.J. Hawke, was needed.

The universities became major centres of organisation of the Moratorium. A meeting on 22 February at Monash, for example, formed a central steering committee, to which all clubs were affiliated, except the Liberals and the DLP, to coordinate university activity. *Lot's Wife* joined forces with *Farrago* at the University of Melbourne and *Rabelais* at La Trobe, to bring out a special edition on the Moratorium on 6 May. For the first time, large numbers of students from Monash were involved in organising anti-war activities. It was seen as something concrete and effective, as against the Labor Club's empty revolutionary rhetoric. A similar level of organisation occurred on most campuses, affecting the academics as much as the students. The student newspaper at the University of New South Wales, *Tharunka,* reported on 21 April: 'In an attempt to decentralise the activities of the UNSW Moratorium Committee, departmental groups have so far been formed within faculties. So far, there are groups in Commerce, Engineering, Science and Arts.'

The Moratorium was to be one demonstration, however, which reached far beyond the universities. This was especially the case in Victoria, where it had significant ALP support. On 25 March. Jim Cairns, at a press conference in Melbourne, called for workers, students, and others to stop work and occupy the streets of Melbourne and Victorian provincial towns on 8 May. He wanted commercial and industrial life brought to a halt to show the depth of opposition to continuing Australia's involvement in the war. In the major cities, large press advertisements, with long lists of signatories who had become sponsors to the Moratorium, were organised during April, as a prelude to the 8 May actions. Sponsors' meetings were held regularly to organise the campaign, and Moratorium action groups sprang up all over the country. The Moratorium was to consist not only of the main marches in the capital cities, but also of local activities, such as public meetings in suburban town halls, film nights, dances, barbecues, debates,

Here, a Moratorium slogan has been painted over the names of the dead from previous wars, on the cenotaph in Brisbane. Anti-war protest, like this particular action, challenged the whole Anzac tradition, a sensitive and ideologically important aspect of Australian political culture.

teach-ins, concerts, luncheons, rallies, poetry competitions, music competitions … Occupational groups organised their own campaigns.

The government was clearly worried by the strength of the Moratorium campaign, having lost as never before, the moral ascendancy in the debate. On 14 April. Attorney General Tom Hughes, in a ministerial statement in the House of Representatives, attacked the Moratorium as a threat to law and order. Leading Liberal parliamentarian Billy Snedden, took up the attack on 7 May, the day before the mass demonstrations were to occur, when he called the organisers of the Moratorium campaign 'political bikies pack-raping democracy'. Attacks on the lawlessness of anti-war demonstrators had been a common part of government parliamentarians' rhetoric for as long as militant tactics had been evident in the peace movement, especially since the violent demonstrations of the middle of 1968. Contradictorily, though, it was during the almost entirely peaceful Moratorium demonstrations of May 1970 that 'law and order' rhetoric reached it height. Cairns' involvement meant that the Law and Order issue could be turned against the Labor Opposition, and the government saw this as its best hope of discrediting the Moratorium movement as a whole. Government attempts to counter the Moratorium were taken up in the schools, where students were frequently suspended for wearing Moratorium badges.

If Prime Minister Gorton's announcement on 21 April, that 900 Australian troops would be withdrawn by December, was meant to defuse the Moratorium, it had the opposite effect. Anti-war activists concluded that if the pressure were maintained, victory might be possible. On 8 May over 200 000 people from all over Australia took part in the Moratorium. It was successful beyond the wildest dreams of its organisers.

Outlook ran an editorial on the Moratorium in its June issue, called 'What Went Right?', examining why the Moratorium was a success. For this was success on a scale the anti-war movement had forgotten even how to dream about.

There were two more Moratorium campaigns, one in September, and another in June 1971. Neither

During the September 1970 Moratorium march, young people staged a sit-down demonstration at the intersection of Swanston and Flinders Streets in Melbourne.

was as successful as the first. The September 18 Moratorium in Sydney saw permission to march through the streets refused. The authorities actively sought confrontation with the demonstrators, and there was a huge police turnout, with over 200 demonstrators being arrested. Violent clashes occurred in other capital cities also.

> We marched down from Sydney University, down Parramatta Road, Broadway, and on to Town Hall. Gradually we realised this demonstration, like no other, was huge. The papers said 25 000, and Melbourne 75 000, but even the Sydney one felt as big as it could be. We sat down on the road outside the steps of the Town Hall and listened to speeches. It was our day. We felt legitimate and legitimated. We had the numbers to force the government to end the war. That's how we felt.

The strength of radicalism in the universities was revealed in a different way by the Socialist Scholars Conference at the University of Sydney from 21 to 24 May 1970. There were papers on Vietnam, Aboriginal people, and every radical issue on the agenda. The audience was a mixture of academics, students, and political activists. The idea that the Vietnam war movement had led to a need to rethink the whole of Australian society, and its history, was fully evident. A strong left presence in university and intellectual circles was beginning to emerge. It would get stronger during the seventies, and decline in the eighties.

> It was one of the most unpleasant demonstrations in the whole anti-war period. The police were organised and violent, forcing us off the road and into Hyde Park. It was nasty and demoralising. I felt that I never wanted to demonstrate again.

Warren Osmond, in *Old Mole,* a radical newspaper based at the University of Sydney, saw the future as requiring less reliance on issue-based politics, and the development of a broader political movement. 'New Left' politics had grown to the point where it could be criticised from within:

> ... there is an urgent need to break down distinctions between an atomistic set of groups called the 'abortion' movement, 'anti-censorship' movement, the 'civil liberties' movement, and so on. There is an obvious nexus, for instance, between our role in SE Asia and our domestic treatment of ethnic minorities, but especially the aboriginals.

In other words, the only long-term future for the movement was to attempt to change the nature of Australian society, so that such foreign policies were never adopted and supported again.

One of the key events at the first Moratorium had not been directly about Vietnam at all. This was a speech made by Kate Jennings on the front lawn of the University of Sydney, announcing the philosophy of Women's Liberation to a startled and often angry student audience, preparing to march downtown to the Moratorium. This speech was regarded as shocking by many who heard it, and has since become firmly fixed in the annals of Sydney feminism. It revealed just how angry the women had become at their male comrades in the anti-war movement:

> Watch out! You may meet a real castrating female or you'll say I'm a man-hating, bra-burning lesbian member of the castration penis envy brigade, which I am. I would like to speak.
>
> It's the Moratorium. I would say, oh yes, the war is bad, a pig bosses' war, may the NLF win. I also say VICTORY TO THE VIETNAMESE WOMEN. Now, our brothers on the left in the peace movement will think that what I am about to say is not justified, this is a moratorium ...

> That year, the Glebe Women's Liberation Group got going, and I went along. We went through our consciousness-raising period. We read avidly, especially roneoed material from the US. Part of our analysis was in opposition to Left men – their sexism and chauvinism (lovely to have words to describe them), the second place we'd been assigned in the anti-war movement. Of course, the attractions of feminism were much wider than that, but it was a relief to escape the factionalism and procedural motions of left groupings. We believed in collective discussion, and in not having leaders, or indeed much formal organisation at all. We were attacked for splitting the movement. We said it was already split. The men were outraged when we kept them out of our meetings. We had to, it was our only way of defining our own movement. We incorporated, however, the analysis of American imperialism which had been made so prominent by the anti-war movement into our analysis: capitalism, we said required women's cheap labour in the family: imperialism, then, was built on women's oppression. As time went on the connections faded, but in 1970 they were a powerful part of the development of a left feminist position.

On 12 October, the US President announced the withdrawal of an additional 40 000 American troops from Vietnam.

ABOVE LEFT: Before a Moratorium march in Brisbane, notices went up to warn protesters of police mobilisation. During these marches, many people showed themselves willing to risk arrest and injury for a political cause.

ABOVE RIGHT: Dr Benjamin Spock addresses thousands of Australian protesters in 1971.

1971

Scenting victory, yet also a loss of momentum, the anti-war movement held a National Anti-War Conference in February 1971.

The third and last Moratorium was held on 30 June 1971. The government ignored it, but on 18 August announced that all Australian troops would be withdrawn from Vietnam by the end of the year. Whitlam accused the government of withdrawing only because the US was, a little ironic and hardly a serious charge in view of his own pro-American policies. This announcement virtually spelt the end of the anti-war movement, which had now only to claim victory. Whitlam was the first of many to argue that Australia would have withdrawn, following America's lead, whether there had been an antiwar movement or not. Tom Hughes did, however, suggest in a speech on 23 August that the anti-war movement had indeed had some influence on the government's decision to withdraw troops.

During the second half of 1971, attention shifted to conscription, for on the same day as the withdrawal of troops was announced, the Gorton government indicated that conscription would remain. This was no

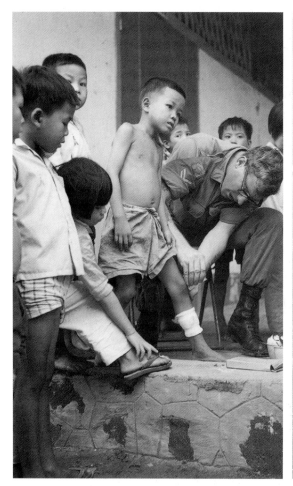

ABOVE LEFT: An Australian medical assistant dresses the leg of a Vietnamese boy in the village of An Nhut, near Núi Đất. A medical team regularly visited the villages in the province.

ABOVE: Vietnamese villagers harvest a crop of corn and other vegetables from a garden hidden amongst the jungle of northern Phước Tuy province. They were transported to this 'enemy' garden by troops of the 1st Australian Task Force.

LEFT: An Australian soldier and a Vietnamese mother confront each other during an identity check carried out by the Army.

LEFT: A wounded soldier is visited by senior army medical staff at a hospital in the War Zone, in 1969.

BELOW LEFT: Christmas Dinner, 1968, for those serving in Vietnam.

BELOW: Soldiers from 5 RAR man a road block set up to detect 'VC infiltration'.

doubt in order to maintain a strong military force for defence purposes, but it was, in retrospect, a serious political mistake. Without any clear ideological or defence reason for conscription, the government found it increasingly difficult to defend. The number of draft resisters was rising. The idea of underground resistance, where a draft resister would hide from government arrest, and make embarrassing public appearances whenever possible, took hold. The first major action was at the Melbourne Moratorium on 30 June 1971, when four resisters addressed the huge crowd which then marched from the city square to Parliament House. In the remainder of 1971, and throughout 1972, these 'underground resistance' actions were performed frequently and with considerable success. In November 1972. Michael Matteson, one of the four who had eluded police at Melbourne University, appeared live on an ABC TV *This Day*

Tonight program simultaneously with Attorney General Senator Ivor Greenwood, speaking on line from another state. Other public appearances followed, serving to embarrass the government.

On 8 December 1971 the last Australian troops left Vietnam.

1972

The government continued to lose popularity during 1972. For the first time in over twenty years, there seemed to be a real chance that the Labor Party would win the federal elections. The conscription issue, and especially the underground draft resisters, remained an embarrassment for the beleaguered government, now headed by Prime Minister William McMahon. In April, a crowd of several hundred Sydney University students spontaneously gathered on campus when it became known that two Commonwealth police had arrested Michael Matteson. The students found some bolt-cutters, released Matteson, and guided him to safety. Matteson's was the most well publicised case: altogether there were twenty-three underground resisters by the end of 1972. In an interview in *Nation Review* Michael Matteson announced that he would give himself up just before the elections, to embarrass the government.

> Michael Matteson stayed at our house for a few days in 1972. This was a communal house that we lived in only briefly. Michael stayed a couple of days and then moved on. He didn't seem very healthy. I think he'd hardly been out in the sun for a year. It didn't seem much of a way to live, but he was committed.

In an interview in the *Sydney Morning Herald* on 11 May 1989, on the nineteenth anniversary of the first Moratorium march. Matteson said:

> For me, it's still a live thing. I think about that kind of stuff once or twice a week. It's a very emotional thing ... I saw how things could be changed.

The question of conscription became an issue in the December 1972 election campaign, and helped Whitlam and the Labor Party to win. Compulsory national service was immediately abolished.

Yet if Australia's role in the war was over, the war itself was not. In mid-December 1972, the US government resumed the bombing of northern Vietnam. This time it was the Seamen's Union which led the protest, voting to ban US ships. The bombing stopped on 30 December, and on 27 January 1973 a ceasefire agreement was signed by the US and the DRV. The war within Vietnam lasted two more years, ending with the entry of PAVN troops into Saigon in April 1975.

CONCLUSION

The political movement which between 1965 and 1971 fought for the withdrawal of Australian troops from Vietnam can be interpreted in many ways. It can be seen as a product of the cultural and social changes of the period: the example par excellence of the emergence of a radical youth culture and counter-culture, and the questioning by the young middle class of an older, homogeneous, suburban Australia. It can be seen as indicating that there was a profound move to issue-based politics in the second half of the sixties: the traditional parties lost their appeal for radical youth, and broad political credos and perspectives were abandoned in favour of specific issues and campaigns. Or it can be seen as the last sign of the old Australia, rather than a first sign of the new: the last radical political movement before the emergence of a strong and independent Aboriginal political movement, of modern feminism, and of some kind of multicultural policy and politics. By and large, and especially in the student movement, the publicly visible leadership of the anti-war movement was Anglo-Australian, white, and male. The later anti-nuclear and ecological movements, with which it might be compared in terms of political style and tactics, saw a much stronger role for women, and a greater awareness of Aboriginal demands and politics. How, then, do we now interpret the anti-war movement? What kind of Australia produced it, and how does it differ from the Australia we live in now?

The anti-war movement was a product of its place and time. It challenged the government view of the world which saw China as the puppeteer behind the DRV, and developed alternative accounts of Southeast Asian politics. Lasting a mere seven years, it was often divided and confused. Few in the movement knew much about Vietnam in detail. Yet it had a lasting impact on Australian politics and society. A great many students and other young people learned to oppose government policy, not only on this issue but also generally. A section of the movement dived off into radical and revolutionary politics: a larger section saw the opposition to the war as a clear case of defending principles of freedom and self-determination. Various political cross currents, old and new, can be detected. We can see the important role of the Communist Party early on, based on an opposition to American policies in Southeast Asia, and a support for communist-led movements of national liberation. There is also, we can see, the emergence of a non-communist far left, outmanoeuvring the communists for leadership of the movement. And there is the emergence of a student movement, affected by these external political forces, and yet in the end larger than and independent of them. Middle-class radicalism, of both young and old, provided the core of the movement, a radicalism based on typically new left demands for self-expression, participatory politics, and new forms of collectivism and solidarity. In the end, the anti-war movement tells us less about Vietnam than it does about a changing Australian society and politics.

> My memories of this period are contradictory. On the one hand there was the deep moral commitment, and the exhilaration of feeling that you were right, that you had taken a stand. There was the sense of standing up before history, of trying to have an effect on that history. On the other hand, there was the factional infighting of the left of the movement, the astounding levels of sexism amongst the young student men, the moral ambiguities surrounding 'our boys', the sense of being out of step with the society, especially in the early phases of the movement. It was a hard movement, and a tough training ground. It brought many of us to political life; and yet within a few years there was the evidence, in the flow of refugees out or Vietnam, that the ending of the war had by no means ended the sorrows and struggles and travails of the Vietnamese people. We grew up with the war in our consciousness. If we were the lucky generation, spared economic depression and the Second World War, we nevertheless felt the world to be a serious, and seriously ill, place.

AT WAR AT HOME

Australian Attitudes During the Vietnam Years

Peter Cochrane

Popular memory has cast the 1950s as a decade of private life in the suburbs and the 1960s as a decade of public drama in the streets, 'the sixties' conjures up images of challenge and change, of retreating certainties, of disorder and fragmentation, of tradition counting for less and 'alternatives' for more. We remember this past through the mediations of journalists, historians and other writers who have not argued much about the contrast – their legacy has been a widely shared stereotype of one decade opposed to another. But history does not conform to tidy ten-year blocks: rock-and-roll took off in 1956, the term 'teenager' became popular about the same time: a peace movement was established before rock-and-roll or the 'teenager'. And if our memory *has* been sliced into these blocks then it is just as easy to overlook the abiding conformity that persisted in the sixties, alongside fashions and values that were taking sharp new directions. This conformity kept conservatives in power until 1972, and backed the sending of troops to Vietnam. Gradually it gave ground, politically and culturally. There were many threads unravelling; the process was highly uneven. Only in the latter part of the decade does 'the sixties' earn its reputation, 'the sixties' was at its best in 1970 and 1971.

 A lot of people were shocked by the widespread questioning and protest of the late sixties. The social order of the early post-war period had not prepared them for what was to come. Many had snapped up the opportunities offered by post-war economic stability and suburban living. Decades of depression, war and postponed expectations made home and family highly desirable goals. Household consumer goods further encouraged an inward-looking, privatised orientation. Community participation fell to low levels as people immersed themselves in the domestic scene. Their choice was idealised in the notion of an 'Australian way of life': the images associated with this suggested an absence of extremes such as poverty or great wealth: they suggested that all shared, or could share, in the 'affluence' of the middle order.

 A conservatism of apparent contentment followed from this. Its uniformity was encouraged by the politics of the Cold War which stressed how communism was out to destroy the Australian way of life, how the battle was centred on maintaining 'decent' values: how it would be won or lost in the homes of ordinary people. The behavioural constraints that followed from the Cold War atmosphere were strict. Middle-class men uniformly wore grey suits with short-back-and-sides haircuts, their women dressed cautiously with hat and gloves. There was great stress on discipline and hard work, on respectability and appearances, on knuckling down. It was widely believed that the Australian way of life could not survive without a passionate determination to preserve and defend it. There could be no wealth without work, no security without defence, no freedom without self-discipline, no liberty without restraint, no justice without sacrifice. To think otherwise was pure romanticism according to the standard bearers of the time.

 But increasingly there was room for romanticism in post-war Australia; for idealism too. These years

The music and fashions of the sixties, reaching the troops in Vietnam.

In the streets of an Australian town in 1966, a polarisation begins: well-wishers and protesters alike crowd the pavements as President Johnson's cavalcade goes by.

brought an easier life, greater security and higher hopes to many people. For their children it brought many more options and a shot at some of the life chances their parents had missed. Politically, the black and white certainties of the Cold War turned out to be less important than the reaction against them. There was decolonisation and national independence struggles in Africa and Asia. There was American intervention and saturation bombing of Vietnam from 1965. The Good versus Evil perspective of the 'Free World' began to crack.

Controversy around the Vietnam war was part of a wider, multi-pronged questioning of Australian society. Yet the war was to become central to the public drama of the period. It probably ripened, perhaps somewhat synchronised, the other calls for change, the social restlessness and the permissiveness of the time. It helped to connect issues, to broaden and deepen the assault on business-as-usual in many spheres. A lot of energy went into grasping the dynamics of a system that could produce a war like the one in Vietnam. Some analysis tied the war to foreign investment and colonialism, which in turn was related to poverty in the third world, and then linked back to affluence and consumer excess in advanced countries. Affluence got a good bit of the blame for pollution and other forms of environmental destruction: pollution was tied into the emerging critique of agri-business and herbicides. Chemical companies made herbicides, they might also make napalm. So problems in the food chain and ecology could lead back to third-world poverty, resistance and war. It was a circular, reinforcing thing once it got going. Thinking about the war underpinned the resurgence of political economy in the universities, in particular the spread of Marxian thought in the social sciences, and the idea that the point of philosophy was not to contemplate the world but to change it.

THE SOURCES OF DISCONTENT

Apologists for the war and opponents of change at home were fond of pointing to 'troublemakers'. They spoke of 'deviance' and delinquency'. They pointed the finger at 'adult moral cowardice' and bemoaned the breakdown of authority in the home. They saw the disorder around them as a failure of will and posed solutions in terms of discipline and leadership in the family, law and order in the streets. Such analysis was superficial. It failed to see that the stability of social life and politics in the 1950s was more apparent than real, being based on a temporary alignment of forces. It ignored the deeper currents of economic and demographic change that underpinned dissent – currents that got under way virtually as soon as the Second World War ended. The post-war period (1945–75) was one of continuous transition.

Underlying this transition were the vast productive powers of Western capitalism, magnified and sharpened by world war. With the decline of production for war, marketing solutions were sought in the consumer sector. Factories retooled to make the family car, household electrical goods, motor mowers, modem furniture, LP records, cosmetics and new fashions. The politics of the war had ensured this orientation. The welfare state, postwar reconstruction policy, and talk of a new social order, were guarantees of national unity for the duration of the fighting. The war was fought on a promise and labour shared with capital the promise of improved living standards and greater material security with the coming of the peace.

Capitalism itself signalled that the time for deviations was approaching. Its marketing strategists promoted acquisitiveness as it had never been promoted before; possessions, it said, would make people happy – the more possessions the happier the person. The sober bourgeois virtue of earlier times no longer prevailed, at least not in the shopping towns, malls and arcades of the cities. Thrift was slipping out of fashion: indulgence and leisure were on their way in. And their appeal was great. After decades of depression, war and rationing, the consumerism of the post-war period was embraced with great enthusiasm. The economic boom led away from pre-war austerity into an ideology of permissive consumerism. It was increasingly difficult to endorse puritan self-restraint in an economic system which promoted acquisitive individualism and indulgence at every turn.

Advertising agencies oozed with this perspective. They sponsored 'anti-drudgery' exhibitions and said the citizen's duty was to consume. There was no thought of diminishing natural resources, no talk about their careful husbanding. And the state, it seemed, had power to burn. Electricity is a good example: in the 1950s advertisements made it synonymous with chic. It was magic stuff: clean, modern, limitless. In the smartest new homes electricity was abundant and consumption was meant to be conspicuous. The slogan 'living better with less' was unheard of and would have seemed preposterous had it been suggested. Hardly anyone talked about conservation: that was something practised by crusty old people in dusty old museums. Thus the foundations of permissiveness were laid in the marketplace as a quest for independence and self-fulfilment. But why should such a quest be confined to the marketplace? That is what some began to ask as the consumer boom wore on.

The connection between permissive consumerism and change in other spheres, such as morals and sexuality, was quite visible in some respects. Modern advertising, for example, aims to create dissatisfaction with the way things are, it offers the promise of transformation. As John Berger has shown in *Ways of Seeing*, advertising was always talking about unrealised possibilities which could come true if only you bought this or that: 'Follow the Freedom-Lovers into the beautiful world of Berlei.' It was never a celebration of the here and now but a promise of thrills that might be. Market relations' experts emerged to identify and target the prejudices, anxieties and deeper psychological needs of consumers. 'We are the advanced guard,' one of them announced, 'that is going forward into the unknown and uncharted fields of human desires and happiness.' They were enormously successful. But they also fostered resentment, anti-consumerism and resistance: for example, the increasing use of women in advertising as objects of sexual desire would upset the settled, monogamous, house-centred imagery of the 1950s and lead into new constructions of femininity the following decade, some simply permissive in a sexual sense, others genuinely radical. And from the use of sex to sell other things it was only a short step – albeit a huge cultural leap – to the selling of sex itself. As Donald Home suggested in *Time of Hope,* the new sexuality was an extension of consumer self-indulgence.

The basic point here, again connecting economic transformation to cultural change, is that permissive consumerism was an ideology asserting the importance of, perhaps even the right to, self-fulfilment. It was an ideology with a commitment to subjectivity at its core. Market researchers and advertising men posed the answer to self-fulfilment in terms of lifestyles constructed around consumer goods. They wanted to make pleasure a marketable commodity. No doubt this satisfied many, but for others it was a very shallow answer. The new left began to call mass society 'dehumanised' and empty; Herbert Marcuse spoke of 'one-dimensional man'. The logic of permissiveness was a Pandora's Box that held many options. And in the sixties people began to seek some of these, beyond or away from consumerism. Here again, it was capitalism, or more accurately its creative helmsmen, who were laying foundations for the discontent of the Vietnam era.

A second irony, also related to the one above, is that public concern and protest had their foundation in the economic optimism associated with affluence. The Western economies were booming: Keynes had given economics a good name: governments spoke of 'fine-tuning', suggesting economic management could now be handled with precision: new heights in consumer spending were reached and migrants were slotting in at the bottom of the work pyramid, ensuring vocational mobility for greater numbers of established Australians. There was confidence that progress was here to stay; that economics looked after itself: that there was room for largesse, for plans to improve the quality of life and the human condition. This sort of disposition was to be found most commonly amongst the new middle class, youth and students.

Whereas the growth centre of the economic system had formerly been manufacturing, the post-war period saw capitalism transformed by a disproportionate expansion of the tertiary or service sector. Manufacturing continued to thrive, but the hub of the system was now in information – and people-processing; employment growth was fastest in the bureaucracies of government and business, in professional and technical occupations, and in the army of white-collar workers. Sociologists dubbed this highly varied group 'the new middle class', and studies of affluence focussed on their lifestyles. Many of them were content; many were fearful of protest and change. But a significant fragment of the new middle class was articulate and opinionated: it had a sense of responsibility: it asserted the lightness of sharing in the decision-making process; it was altruistic and public spirited, believing people could and should be part of changes for the better. And it was quite open-minded by contemporary standards: 'Dissenting from the view that beards, suede shoes and duffel coats were signs of degeneracy ... [it] did not share the fears that modem art, dirty books, "wogs" and their smelly food were undermining the

Australian Way of Life.' The new middle class played a leading part in late sixties protest. From its ranks came political leaders, conservationists, anti-censorship activists, women's liberation groups, abortion law and education reformers. ZPG advocates, sex therapists, consumer protection people, ecology 'freaks' and resident action movements. Frequently they worked in alliance with concerned sections of the working class. In anti-Vietnam protest and matters of the urban environment, certain trade unions were especially prominent. Support from the union movement overall was meagre; some of the largest unions wholeheartedly supported the war. But a select few, with radical traditions and high levels of solidarity (the Seamen's Union and the Waterside Workers' Federation, for example), were consistently at the forefront.

These points make it clear that the dissent and protest of the sixties was not simply a youth rebellion, as is often suggested. Don Chipp, for example, a reformer in the Liberal Party, a leader of the move to liberalise censorship laws, was forty years old in 1965. Gordon Barton, founder of the Liberal Reform Group, was thirty. Most of the women in 'Save Our Sons' were in their forties or older. Germaine Greer was somewhere in between – she was twenty-seven in 1965. Jim Cairns, the leading figure in the Moratorium movement was fifty-one. It was A.D. Hope, a poet in his mid sixties who adopted the voice of youth to challenge the right of one generation to conscript another.

> *Linger not, stranger, shed no tear;*
> *Go back to those who sent us here.*
> *We are the young they drafted out*
> *To wars their folly brought about.*
> *Go tell those old men, safe in bed.*
> *We took their orders and are dead.*

The fact that an older generation, whose politics had been shaped by depression, war and the Soviet model, rather than post-war prosperity, led the way on many of the burning issues. Indeed, it had laid a foundation for the protest era in the peace movement of the fifties, led by communists, radical sections of the dissenting churches and left-wing trade unionists – brave people who stood against the pressures of the Cold War.

Yet the public drama of the late sixties was heavily coloured by the presence, the style and the ideas of youth culture. It has become commonplace to talk about a 'Vietnam generation', meaning those who grew up during the period in which conscription for Vietnam was in force (1965–71), or those whose teenage years more or less corresponded with this period. These youngsters were an unusually large cohort, due to the post-war baby boom, which led to a proportionately greater number in the 10–19 age bracket. For example, between the census of 1954 and 1966 the numbers in that age group grew by 74% compared with a rate of growth for the total population of just 28.5%. It was 14.3% of the total population in 1954 and 18.5% in 1966.

Young people were likely to stay at school longer, thus putting off the responsibilities of work and marriage, and greater numbers amongst them were going on to tertiary education with the rapid growth of the university system. Numbers at universities grew from 15 586 to 83 320 between 1945 and 1965. The content and substance of university education was changing, with new subjects such as sociology and new challenges in old subjects such as the rise of left-wing Keynesianism in economics. Student life broke the swift transition to dutiful bread-winning and home making. It was this period of extended adolescence and education that would provide the space for questions of identity and meaning to arise, making students into possibly the most energetic, idealistic and visible political force of the era. But student activism was not simply a matter of political dissent, because student rebels came out of a distinctive youth culture, a movement which had its own fashions and tastes and, most importantly, its own music.

The marketing intuition of manufacturers and retailers rapidly became attuned to the surge of teenagers in their midst. The spending power of the young became a topic of fascination for the media. A teen market was nurtured by merchandisers and advertisers, and youth culture was heavily commercialised by the late fifties. It gave new and distinctive identities to young people, emphasising individualism, 'doing your own thing', breaking free. Difference was marketable. Rock-and-roll and blue jeans, folk and cheesecloth, cars, surf boards and transistor radios were new sources of profit as well as identity. The new term, 'teenager', disguised a variety of subcultural groupings – mods, rockers, sharpies, hippies and surfers, for example – each with its own stylistic mode of dissent from the dominant culture. We can overestimate the unity of 'youth culture' – the term itself encourages that – but collectively these groupings still made for a generation gap that was unusually wide. Perhaps more than any other age group, teenagers would take the search for self-fulfilment to heart, and a significant number would take it beyond the marketplace into alternative culture and political action. For many, Vietnam would be the catalyst.

The rebellious, iconoclastic spirit was exemplified at La Trobe University in 1969 when Malcolm Muggeridge, a distinguished conservative intellectual from England, arrived to speak on the topic 'What I Hate About Universities'. Muggeridge's religious faith, his assertion of obedience to a supreme authority, coupled with his aristocratic Oxbridge style and opposition to the new permissiveness, provoked juvenile interjections and giggles from the audience. The effect of such disrespect on Muggerdige was devastating. Tears trickled down the esteemed gentleman's cheeks as the derision persisted. At the evening's conclusion, he declared: 'All I can say is that if you are the product of Australian university education, then I feel really sorry for you.' Boos and jeers rained up on him as he continued: the old man had not just attacked the student Left, but all those who were questioning, or estranged from, the customs of his generation.

'ALMOST CUT MY HAIR...

For those like Muggeridge who identified with the old values, the problem was the infectious appeal of the new ones – the explosion in taste and style, the rejection of conservative drabness and of what Muggeridge might have called 'civilised restraint'; the desire to challenge, question, even to outrage, the yearning for experimentation, the appeal of alternative philosophies. If conservatism is essentially a disposition to settle for the way things are, then the spirit of the age was profoundly anti-conservative. It was a spirit shared by many different kinds of people going in many different directions, but all in one way or another critical of society as it was, and prepared to speak or act in defiance – at least some of the time.

This was especially so for the Vietnam generation. Not every member of that generation carried a sharp sense of separate identity or alienation from the parent culture: not all teenagers were moved by the public drama and sensationalism around youth. Those who were moved sometimes had the support of

These youths welcoming the American President to their harbour reflect one aspect of youth culture – surfing – but not the growing spirit of defiance towards political authority.

their parents. Draft dodgers, for example, often did. There were studies of student rebels which showed many of them were acting consistently with values handed down by liberally minded parents. But this made the pervasive values and practices associated with youth culture no less threatening to the more traditional sections of society. Youth *culture* sharply separated the tastes of youth from their elders. It was self-consciously alienated, as the youth magazine *Go-Set* made clear in its first edition of February 1966: 'Every one of you cats has felt the lash of the Oldies kicking back ... Now's the time to really break loose ... *Go-Set* is *your* paper.'

Hairstyles dramatised the rift. Consider them: they are a way into the tensions generated by youth culture and protest. The social meaning of long hair has never been fixed but rather, determined historically and culturally, taking on quite different meanings in different contexts. The dramatic associations of hair go back a very long way, as biblical mythology attests. The links between hair and order, order and authority, are fairly obvious. In the sixties the top of one's head was a site (and a sight) of great tension for young men and women. We could just as easily discuss clothes or music, but hair had a great symbolic importance for the identity of a young man at a time when conscription was a major public issue. Long hair, unkempt hair, was a defiant gesture, a way of stepping outside the circle which encompassed short-back-and-sides, soldiering, patriotism and more. Long hair was an assertion of individual freedom. It was demonstrative, emblematic. It carried with it a multiplicity of meanings. There was no doubt that some got sheer joy from projecting these meanings even when they did not practise all of them. Long hair was an important part of youth solidarity. It was absorbed into fashion and lifestyle: it figured prominently in the musical lyrics of the Vietnam generation.

The cover for the RCA album of the rock musical *Hair* said its actors-authors and 'sundry short-haired observers' considered it 'a pagan ritual, a theatrical be-in, a demonstration, a riot, a happening and a scandal'. The musical was pro-love, pro-drugs and pro-sex. Its participants were an 'anti-establishment tribe who, in the course of the action, attend be-ins, scare tourists, protest at [Army] induction centres, re-create a war or two, smoke pot, take off their clothes, sing in the streets, make love and otherwise amuse themselves.'

Almost cut my Hair
It happened just the other day,
It's gettin' kinda long
I coulda said it was in my way.
But I didn't and I wonder why
I feel like lettin' my freak flag fly
Yes I feel like I owe it to someone.

Long hair was an affront to the strict standards of masculine conformity. Donald Home spoke of the 'short-back-and-sides sober-suited puritanism that had been an essential expression of masculinity, and of a general upholding of a social order.' For three generations short hair had been ·a symbol of manliness, virility and national virtue in a country where long hair symbolised the evils of an impractical but arrogant intellectuality, or of a boozy and morally lax bohemian artiness, or a plain cissiness and poofterism'. In July 1971, after police attacked anti-war demonstrations in Melbourne, *Go-Set* responded with a classic generational interpretation:

> The police and other officials made it clear they saw this battle as them versus the Long-hairs ... all those old men in power think long hair means rock music, freewheeling, sex, dope, and socialism. The symbol of everything that threatens their scene, They're right! Keep on growin' that hair everyone.

This was an overly simple interpretation, but it was a perspective with a mass following. It had a lot of older people worried. Authorities commonly connected long and ungroomed hair with uncleanliness,

In 1968, a soldier in Núi Đất tacks images of Vietnam over those from 'home'.

rampant sexuality and traitorous values. On young males it was understood in gender terms, as a lack of manliness. Police frequently expressed concern about 'long-haired young men' in conjunction with fears of agitators trained to incite people to oppose authority; they attacked and pulled the hair of protesters on many occasions. In 1967, a spokesman for the New South Wales Police Department alleged 'natural prejudices' against long-haired men because they looked effeminate or dirty. And the national secretary of the RSL took an optimistic line, in 1968, when he expressed the view that there was nothing wrong with some students that could not be corrected by a 'wash, a haircut and two years in the Army'.

For the Army, hair of non-regulation shape or length could readily suggest unwelcome associations. Gary McKay's *In Good Company* tells the story of a new cadet officer (Brian O'Sullivan) who arrives with long hair at Scheyville officer training camp (New South Wales) in 1968:

> His hair was so long the drillies were licking their lips as they moved in for the kill. One of the drillies used an old favourite line by standing behind O'Sullivan and asking him if it was hurting him. When O'Sullivan answered 'No,' the drillie roared 'Well I bloody well oughta be, because I'm standing on your bloody hair!'

There is no doubt that conscientious objectors who were in the Army, and in trouble, found their hair was an object of attention and part of a ritual of harassment. When William White went into the Army, he immediately requested a crew-cut hairstyle 'just to have the satisfaction of beating them to it." As military prisoners, conscientious objectors were subjected to various assaults including verbal abuse, solitary confinement, constantly broken sleep, bread and water diet, naked dousing with buckets of water, as well as assaults on their hair. When Desmond Phillipson, 21, applied for exemption from any form of further Army training he was sent to Holsworthy military prison in New South Wales, where he was mistreated by guards. Phillipson was dragged seventy-five yards along a road after refusing to march to his cell. The guards held him up by the hair, twisted his arms and wrists, and dragged him along the bitumen on his knees. A pin was stuck into his shoulder when he was lying on the ground, but in the court case that followed the Army disputed this saying the pin was only held between Phillipson and a wall to stop him slumping to the ground. We know little more about these events because at that point the presiding magistrate said the case was not an inquiry into the methods of the Australian Army.

This sort of treatment and its widespread reporting in the media could, and did, have a radicalising effect. But generally speaking, the origins of radicalism were more complicated. The permissive ideology of youth culture contained no simple and direct lines into radical activity or political activism. It could just as easily lead into the self-centred sensualism of the drug culture or nomadic surfing along the east coast. The first issue of *Surf International* (1966) suggested the defence budget would be better spent on giving people access to the beach and the waves. The war in this magazine invoked fantasy rather than political action; 'Each time you hear or see the word Vietnam, cancel out the blackness with a picture of a beautiful man-shaped wave, a piece of love-nature. Make waves, not war." No broad sociological or demographic brush can explain why some took the political path and some pursued sensuality, whilst others vacillated, tried to find an amalgam, or kept out of it altogether. That level of explanation would call on biographical method and psychology. What we observe, at one remove from this, is how the Vietnam generation was rapidly and considerably politicised as the war went on. The war and conscription were coercive acts; they were inconsistent with the romanticism and idealism of many young people. The authorities who prosecuted the war and enforced conscription seemed alien in every way: embodiments of the materialism, the conventionality and the apparent hypocrisy of the system. In September 1969, Robert Wilton, the son of Australia's top soldier. General Sir John Wilton, burned his draft card on the steps of Parliament House.

Opposition to the war was generating a critical perspective on Australian society, a critique of the establishment, and a revolutionary outlook. When 69 anti-war demonstrators were arrested in Canberra after a sit-down protest outside the PM's lodge, they were brought before a magistrate. Mr Dobson SM, who wore an RSL badge. In a remarkable exercise of judicial neutrality. Mr Dobson told the demonstrators he was not going to convert any of them into martyrs, as the only heroes Australia recognised were fighting in Vietnam. The protesters replied later with an open letter to Mr Dobson. The letter referred to 'the out-modedness of the thought of people who make up the judicial system ... in bureaucracy-ridden Australia.' It claimed that the real heroes were the fighters of the NLF in Vietnam, and expressed solidarity 'with the forces of youthful revolutionary thought throughout the world, which are fighting the system of social and intellectual stratification that you and your ilk have imposed on us for far too long.'

Self-interest was equally important to the radicalisation of youth – every year a new cohort of young men was on the threshold of the conscription ballot when about 8000 of them would be called up. Their sisters and girlfriends were concerned – conscripts were coming home dead from May 1966 onwards, and by 1971 made up more than one-third of fatal casualties. The ballot also seemed grossly unfair – it was labelled the 'lottery of death'. The system's arbitrariness was evident in the courts, where the rules governing appeals for deferment of National Service were enforced with incredible inconsistency; and in the fitness medicals, where doctors, according to some critics, showed something of a sporting bias. Ron Saw in the *Sunday Telegraph* reported that bias as follows:

Show him [the Army doctor] an under-nourished, myopic, pigeon-toed asthmatic suffering from beri-beri, bilharzia, sprue, tickbite, boils, warts, furring of the tongue, grinding of the teeth, twitching of the nostrils, the heaves, the yelps and the snorts – and tell him that he's no more than a plasterer's apprentice – and he'll send him off to war marked A-1 Fit.

But show him a League footballer, a hairy throwback who regularly tackles Johnny Sattler without a second thought – presuming him to be capable of a first thought – and the doc will toss him out of Nasho for having a sore toe.

It was journalism such as this that helped conscription fall into disrepute. But the inconsistencies were very real and could seem terribly unfair; pig farmer Ronald Valentine Blundell applied for a one-year deferment on the grounds that his 230 pigs needed him. He had a mortgage to pay off; he would have to sell his pigs and pig prices were low at the time. The presiding magistrate rejected his application, saying it would cause 'hardship' but not 'exceptional hardship', therefore exemption under the Act was not possible. Ronald Valentine Blundell had to sell his pigs and go to war. But Rocky Gattelari, the boxer, got two years' exemption to pursue his 'career', and so did a dancer from Les Girls who had arrived for the medical in a dress. As late as 1971, polls showed that a large majority of Australian people (adults) continued to support universal conscription free of such prejudices, but that was not the way it worked.

There were other factors too: the Labor Party's continued electoral failure drove some young people into politics and further to the left: police violence at many demonstrations had a galvanising effect, and youth journalism became more and more vociferous in identifying the war as the key symbol for all that was evil in the system. *Go-Set* called it 'a dirty and dishonourable war' in July 1967; atrocities reported by the press and the judgement of an independent war crimes tribunal headed by Bertrand Russell seemed to confirm this. By 1970, sections of the mainstream press were swinging against the war, or at least following the Americans in accepting the imminence (and common sense) of troop withdrawal. Public opinion was swinging with it; draft resisters had embarked on a series of bold and defiant acts of non-compliance, burning draft cards in public and playing cat and mouse with the police. The press presented it as farce. It was good entertainment. The police looked clumsy, bad or brutal. The better known of the unshackled draft resisters, like Michael Matteson in Sydney and Harry Van Moorst in Melbourne, acquired something of folk hero status. Those in prison were martyrs. As momentum gathered, the style of the anti-war movement was increasingly assertive, dismissive, flippant and sarcastic. When Billy Snedden described intending Moratorium marchers as a bunch of 'Political bikies pack-raping Democracy', an elderly grey-haired woman replied by carrying a banner in the march which read, 'I am a pack-raping bikie.' By late 1971, defence lawyers were calling the failure to comply with the National Service Act a 'trivial offence', pointing out the authorities were not pursuing it and community standards did not hold it in scorn. The courts had become responsive to this mood. Six years after conscription had begun, twenty-year old men had almost doubled their chances of convincing the courts that they were genuine conscientious objectors, though the press continued to report the inconsistencies of court judgements. Youth had been politicised and it was instrumental in the wider mobilisation against the war, reaching a peak in the Moratoriums of 1970 and 1971.

The Slouch of Vietnam

Why should I wear the new slouch hat, the slouch of Vietnam,
Why should I share the napalm-guilt of blundering Uncle Sam,
Why should I hunt down peasant kids who fight for rights and rice,
Why should I spill this hard-earned blood in a sucker's sacrifice?
I think of my old uncles, and their mates who lie bone-white.
On the far-off fields of Flanders, now who promoted that fight?
They'll teach you that life is precious, then they'll brush it aside like dust.
But I won't give my life away 'cause a brass hat says I must.
A chilly dusk is falling here, the box-trees' shadows stretch.
And through the ring-barked clumps I see the vanished soldiers fetched.
The tall plume on the horseman, the slant brim down below.
As, through the mists of memory, the slaughtered slouches go.
There's young Mick, the cricketer, from frosty Eucumbene.
And 'Pally' Tom, the skinner, from the Southern Riverine.
And, troop by troop, the squadrons pass, the sun across their cheeks,
Clay-cold, and pale as cellar-grass, and not one soldier speaks.
The slouch of brave Gallipoli that blinded the digger's eyes,
The slouch of bloody Passchendaele where the shell-shock case still cries.
The martyrs hanged in Changi, the heroes killed at Lae,
But the slouch of jungle paddies is a slouch I cannot pay.
Why should I wear the new slouch hat, the slouch of Vietnam,
Why should I share the napalm-guilt of blundering Uncle Sam,
Why should I hunt down peasant kids who fight for rights and rice,
Why should I spill this hard-earned blood in a sucker's sacrifice?

Denis Kevans, *The Great Prawn War & Other Poems*, 1982

This poem was written in 1962 when 'advisers' were being sent to Vietnam by the Australian government.

SOLDIERING AND MANHOOD IN THE AGE OF AQUARIUS

In the midst of the Vietnam war period, recreational dress for officer trainees on leave from Scheyville was army black shoes, grey cuffed flannel trousers, white shirt, a Scheyville one-and-a-quarter inch-wide tie, and a dark blue blazer. As Gary McKay explains 'If you topped all that off with the incredibly short haircut we had, our chances of successful recreation on leave in the long-haired, flower-powered city of Sydney were minimal.' Soldiers found some ways around these restrictions, chiefly through non-compliance with regulation dress, but that only confirmed their alienation; it underlined the soldier's fall from grace in Australian culture.

In previous wars, the man in uniform was widely, almost universally, a figure of great appeal: a figure in step with his time. The political circumstances of the First World War made military tradition an important part of Australian culture. It imparted legendary qualities to the Australian soldier and it located him the Digger at the centre of our national mythology. Michael McKernan noted how, soon after Gallipoli, 'the propaganda became so intense that many soldiers actually resented the celebration and exaggeration of their exploits.' A mystique was built up around the returning soldier; its persistent elaboration put a soldierly masculinity at the centre of the national ethos. Going away to fight became the apotheosis of citizenship and manhood, a belief which corresponded to a deep vein in Western intellectual tradition. In twentieth-century Australia this vein was sustained by supportive social practices and successful contestation over many decades.

Until the sixties, the soldier was a model for men to follow and women to admire; the mystique of the male warrior was an important part of our culture that went deep into the Australian psyche. But in the sixties this kind of masculinity came under heavy fire for the first time. Alan Seymour's play. *The One Day of the Year* (meaning Anzac Day), anticipated the change to come with a savage attack on 'digger culture'. It was published in 1960. Later in the decade, draft resistance fused with the new currents of youth culture – drugs, surfing, hippiedom, campus life – to challenge the integrity of the soldier, to question the established connection between citizenship and military activity in Vietnam, to break up the strict standards of masculine conformity which had prevailed, it seemed, for eons. For many observers (and some soldiers), the Vietnam war would seriously discredit the style of aggressive masculinity that had been kept alive (and culturally dominant) by a succession of 'just wars' and the Cold War, for decades. It fused with other historical currents to precipitate a significant shift in the gender order. As Gary McKay put it. 'Men who fought in the Second World War didn't have to worry about being spat upon on Anzac Day because they were returned soldiers.' To parody conventional beliefs about military training. Moratorium marchers carried a poster which read. The Army made a Man of Him – A Dead Man'.

For those who were disturbed by street marchers, their banners and slogans, gender was never far off when it came time to count the cost of youth culture. This is partly why so much anxiety was evident on both sides of the barricades in this period. Not only politics was at stake, so also were core fundamentals relating to sexuality, family and lineage. 'No son of mine ... etc, etc' was a common enough formulation at the time. In the fifties and early sixties there was little of this in evidence. The dutiful breadwinning male seemed to have a mortgage on masculinity. Ideally he was strong, hard working, cautious tongued and abstemious – meaning somewhat resistant to the 'softening' effects of consumerism. What was not immediately apparent was the way that his efforts in the post-war context were financing a way of life that would radically separate his experience from that of his children, and probably require a second income (his wife's) if it was to be sustained. In both respects this would lead to a revaluation of his role in the home and society. His boys would grow up with a range of options – economic and cultural – too broad, too diverse, to permit the simple and uniform reproduction of traditional masculinity. And his wife might well take to permanent work which in turn could lead to a renegotiation of the marital pact. Traditional standards of masculinity were about to come under siege from all sides, and the consequences are still, today, working themselves through in society.

Consumerism had led the way with the marketing of hair dye and perms in unisex salons, coloured shirts and shorts. Gucci shoes, flared trousers and jewellery in men's boutiques. These things worked their way unevenly and randomly into many pockets of youth culture and the protest movement. Even the counter-culture was catered for, with Myers importing cheesecloth shirts in bulk from Asia, cotton trousers and sandals from India. Fashions suggested a rejection of the culturally dominant ideals of masculinity. Later, it would be backed by critiques coming out of feminism and gay liberation. In some respects, the Vietnam war was precipitate here, as it raised questions about soldiering and killing from the middle of the sixties, well before the counter-culture had built up steam and before feminism and gay liberation were organised and publicised. The war focussed attention on masculinity before other aspects of the male role were clearly on the political agenda. It was the dramatic centre of those sharp contrasts that emerged, in the latter half of the sixties, between army boots and bare feet, short-back-and-sides and hair long enough to stand on, hard steel and cheesecloth.

There were radicals in the anti-war movement who wanted to play the soldier at his own game. These wore army disposal gear, heavy boots, berets and sometimes ammunition belts. They talked seriously about revolutionary violence. But they were a tiny minority. The vast majority of the Vietnam generation saw military gear as fun, and identified instead with the parody of militaristic styles encouraged by the heroes of the youth culture. The Beatles in their Sergeant Pepper phase adorned old fashioned military uniforms in psychedelic surrounds; Jimi Hendrix did the same, wearing a bullet belt over his naked chest; The Animals appeared on an EP cover sitting on a railway track wearing Second World War military helmets; Crosby, Stills, Nash and Young posed with the weapons of the old West for their *Déjà Vu* album. Donovan translated this parody into critical lyrics directed at the soldier; 'He's the one who gives his body as a weapon of the war/And without him all this killing can't go on.'

The trauma of homecoming for some Australian soldiers was ample testimony to a new ambivalence in Australian society. Nowhere was this ambivalence sharper than at the airports when soldiers arrived from Vietnam to face demonstrations.

> I suppose I had this idea of coming home to a brass band and ticker-tape processions and women falling at your feet and guys coming up and shaking your hand and all that sort of stuff – the way it was for the Anzacs and the Second World War guys. I think we landed at Sydney airport about ten or eleven o'clock at night, went through customs, and got our pay. When the doors opened up there were these people waving placards and someone was holding up a page out of a newspaper about women and children being killed.

This testimony and others suggest the immense alienation experienced by returning soldiers who would not be fêted as their predecessors had been in earlier wars. But more important was the disinterest in

ABOVE LEFT: Private Ross McKay and his wife, Jo. Ross McKay went absent without leave in May 1970. A Vietnam veteran, he was prepared to face a court-martial in order to protest against Australia's commitment to the war.

ABOVE RIGHT: A young woman, riding on a young man's shoulders, displays placards outside the American consulate in Melbourne. Mass protest brought men and women together in collective action during the Vietnam years.

homecoming soldiers. There were a few protests, just as there were a few ticker-tape parades. But there was more indifference than either protests or parades. Not many really cared about soldiers when they came back. It was what they were doing abroad that really worried people. Soldiering was now a suspect game for many. The meaning and purpose of the war was hotly debated. Many saw it as immoral and its perpetrators as bullies and 'butchers'. The connection between soldiering and citizenship was no longer elevated as it had been. The integrity of soldiering was under fierce challenge. Sometimes the soldiers hit back with their own slogans – 'NLF kills Diggers' – or with their fists. Returning home from Vietnam their mates encouraged them to 'Wallop a Wharfie'. Gary McKay tells the story of how he went to a football match in Brisbane, accompanied by a nursing sister, after being invalided back to Australia. A student from the University of Queensland Rugby Club asked him how he came to be in a plaster cast. McKay told him, and the student allegedly replied, 'serves you bloody well right.' At the time McKay

Action and debate on the street during a Moratorium march in 1970.

could not believe that a fellow Australian would think like that. But some did, and many more were inclined in that direction.

In August 1969, on the release from prison of conscientious objector John Zarb, the *Sydney Morning Herald* ran an editorial in which it equated the courage of draft resisters with the action of a war hero in Vietnam. It was entitled 'two Kinds of Courage'. The editorial precipitated a furious and prolonged correspondence which resolved nothing, of course, but did indicate, as the editorial itself had indicated, that the digger was no longer a culturally secure symbol in Australian society. As Alan Stewart put it, in the Melbourne *Herald,* 'History proves it often takes guts to be a conscientious objector.'

Doubts about war and soldiering were evident in Vietnam as well as at home. The fighting in Vietnam was not cast in quite the clearcut way of previous wars when there was little question that it was a case of civilised man versus barbarian. There was still plenty of that, but there were also competing impressions, even within the military itself. A former Army officer comments that Australian advisers in Vietnam did not carry the same sense of rightness as did those of the two world wars, nor the same unqualified hatred and disdain for the enemy. After the battle of Hue, an officer wrote to his wife, saying. 'I have always had a grudging admiration for the VC in view of what they have accomplished in the face of what was against them.' He was able to add that this respect had now gone, following the atrocities of that battle, but the fact was 'the prevailing impression of soldiers experiencing war almost as a personal vendetta in the cause of God. King and Empire or in the defence of Australia against an inhuman enemy' did not carry through to Vietnam *in full force*. The horrors of the Hun and the Nip (bolstered by allied propaganda) and the might of their industrial backing made them fearsome opponents; equals in a way which helped sustain notions of manhood. Not so with the Vietnamese. Despite propaganda about Russian and Chinese support, the perception of the enemy could be very different. A soldier could find this war unnerving, disarming, shameful and emasculating. A veteran of successive tours reported on the enemy encountered in 1969:

> All the VC killed were very young. Clothes, khaki, weapons well kept. Some kids probably 14–16 (years), fought bravely. Very fair complexion and features more regular than our ARVN soldier... The hills in the DMZ are well fortified and bunkers and personnel are easily seen.

There was a questioning on the war front, as the David and Goliath dimensions of the fight sank into the military psyche. The reality of both 'child killing' and being killed by children (or grandmothers), took its effect. There is a story of how an American soldier tried to convey the toughness of the war. It was so tough he said, that his best buddy had to kill an eight-year-old boy, because the boy had a grenade and might have killed them. But what did that do to his manhood, asked one commentator? Prove it, or annihilate it? Australian soldiers were caught in the same war and a similar dilemma.

At the time, the RSL refused to acknowledge this. It recognised studies in America which showed that doubt about the war was a real psychological problem for returned soldiers, but insisted that Australian soldiers suffered no such torments. Evidence to the contrary has been accumulating ever since.

POSTSCRIPT: THE LEGACY OF THE SIXTIES

When Australian involvement in the Vietnam war began, our society was well advanced on its post-war transition into consumer culture. This transition was already threatening disorder by raising the challenge to established authority in many spheres of life – the family, the church, politics, the media and education. Any assessment of the social impact of the Vietnam war has to take these independent processes of challenge, disruption and reordering into account. Otherwise we will overestimate the impact of the war, which was not the cause of the transition, nor even the main engine.

On the other hand it is necessary to acknowledge the central place of anti-war activity in the public drama and tumult of the period; in the spirit of questioning and rebellion. The war radicalised people and brought them together, it linked fragments from factories, neighbourhoods, churches, schools and universities across the nation. New networks and alliances grew out of this, and a faith, wider spread than ever before, in the capacity to change things. The war became the focus and symbol of a broad range of discontents. The war sharpened and redirected critical inclinations that came out of the new permissive culture.

This cultural radicalism carried into the first half of the following decade, but it was beginning to fade

LET'S HAVE AN ADULT REVOLUTION

I am an 'Oldie'. I don't feel like one, but in the eyes of the student generation I am just that. I am also a 'square' – I don't like hippies, knockers and whingers.

I am tired of being blamed for all the ills of the world, and I refuse any longer to feel vaguely guilty and inadequate about what I and my generation have done. I am not in any way personally responsible for the Vietnam war, the sufferings of Biafra or the unhappy situation of our Aborigines.

For my own actions and mistakes I accept full responsibility – but there it is going to end.

We adults are allowing ourselves to be brainwashed into believing we are abject failures. As parents, are we not often too ready to accept the full blame for the actions of our children? Let a young unmarried girl become pregnant and the parents' immediate reaction is – 'Where did **we** go wrong?' 'Where did **we** fail?'

Why are they so ready to blame themselves when, in most cases, they have done everything in their power to prevent this thing happening? Why not blame the girl who was too smart to accept their good advice? Why not blame the man who seduced her?

Why not blame the teen-age vodka-drinking parties: the sex-orientated contents of the mass media: or the attitude of so many young people that all that is necessary for 'meaningful relationship' is a knowledge of the clinical, biological facts of sex without any thought about the social, moral or emotional aspects of the subject?

It is time that we took a good hard look at the situation. Thankfully, the greater percentage of the younger generation are fine studious young people – but a minority are not.

They are the ones who make all the noise and are constantly intruding their distasteful behaviour into the public view. It is time we called a halt to the antics of this minority who would have us believe we have achieved nothing except to get the world into a mess.

Achieved nothing? I have lived to see man walking on the moon and the killing diseases of diphtheria and polio wiped out. If we were to sit down and study the achievements of the past 20 years in the many fields of science, we would feel justly proud – not vaguely guilty.

Certainly we set values on our homes and possessions, but we work for them, we do not expect them by some divine right. If we had all sat around in grubby rags, smoking 'pot' and discussing philosophy, the present young generation would not have it so good.

Let's face it – by reason of their youth, they have contributed **nothing** to society so far. By what right then do they protest, demonstrate and blame: and degrade themselves and the halls of learning which they are privileged to inhabit? Why is their behaviour tolerated? What has happened to good old expulsion?

It's time we adults stopped playing chicken – time to hold up our heads with pride – time to be through with apology and denial of the good sense of maturity – time to back up the vast majority of fine, studious young people with firm authority – time to say to the whining minority: **'Wake up!' 'Grow up!' 'AND SHUT UP!'**

Mary Paterson
– from *reveille*, June 1971,
reprinted from *v.i.e.w. world*

This sit-down demonstration in 1970 shows the many faces of student protest during the Vietnam era.

virtually as Gough Whitlam took power in 1972. The end of conscription and the withdrawal of troops from Vietnam removed the symbolic centre of the protest movements. The protests were themselves an atypical upsurge. They grew out of a temporary alignment of forces which brought together youth culture and the over-reaction to it, the war and conscription, a full employment economy and educational expansion to match. It was a conjuncture that had to be short-lived. Those who had higher hopes – hopes of an enduring movement and a radical transformation – simply misunderstood the nature of the phenomenon. The solid core of activists were heavily politicised, but most of those who marched against conscription and the war were motivated by an intense humanism. They had no inclination to delve deep into political ideology; they knew next to nothing about Marx even when they had his poster on the wall: they knew being called a Trotskyite was an insult but were not sure why; they liked the sound of 'Property is Theft', but could not spell Proudhon. From this position it was not so hard to lose faith in politics and to fill the void with a retreat to individual satisfactions – to cults of expanded consciousness, health habits and personal growth programs. Some took this path and have remained on it.

    Events abroad encouraged their retreat. The war might have discredited American foreign policy but third-world resistance also lost its glow. In the seventies the hopes attached to liberation forces in Southeast Asia were one by one dashed as these forces came to power producing bloody aftermaths, totalitarian rule, and territorial feuds amongst themselves. Elsewhere, as in Chile, the right took a firm

The manager of a model agency protests against the war.

hold, reinforcing the demise of a once buoyant, progressive trend in the third world.

At home, there were cyclical changes as the Vietnam generation took jobs and settled down. Rising unemployment and, a little later economic rationalisation, began to assert a disciplining effect. There was renewed concern over work and careers. Some were exhausted, if not disillusioned, by years of around-the-clock activism. Some had paid a high price financially, vocationally, and in the courts. Some had moved on to home purchase and a family. For these people, political commitment, or the appearance of it, could be more easily sustained if it was reoriented to questions of private or personal morality and individual responsibility. Involvement in political organisation dropped off. The frantic, militant energies of 1968–71 vaporised quickly. And once the collective basis of sixties politics disappeared, conservatives were able to mobilise and reassert themselves in a very short time.

Some critics were in a hurry to conclude that protest had all been a fad. In doing so they imposed an unlikely uniformity on the diverse forces and motivations of the sixties upsurge. The fad theory claimed the participants had been in it for nothing more than amusement and self-gratification. Its proponents talk about 'youthful exuberance' and 'infantile behaviour' which in fact was easy enough to spot at the time but as a theory about what happened is totally misleading. Most people got involved as a matter of conscience, as the distinguished philosopher Hannah Arendt observed when commenting on the 'almost exclusively moral motives' of student movements around the world. A serious moral tone was an important part of the upsurge. 'Blue Poles', for example, was attacked by one group of the left, not because of its price, but because it was trivial and useless art' – because it diverted attention away from the real issues' of politics and war. Those who got involved deeply had to face hard work, vocational sacrifices and some very frightening harassment along with the so-called fun. The issues were solemn and important. Fad theory was (and is) generally employed by people who wanted (and still want) to efface the evils against which people rebelled and to trivialise that rebellion, 'to buttress the quiescence and resignation of the present,' to render the past dead and therefore safe.

Many who were politicking, demonstrating or experiencing new highs' in the sixties did drop out for good, some becoming totally absorbed in home renovations, restaurants and good wine, overseas travel, interior decoration and native plants. Of these, a small number got onto the Labor Party gravy train, took sinecures in Geneva or bought condominiums in Queensland. An insipid relativism could be heard around the traps: 'We don't like capitalism either but there's nothing better.' But a significant number – historians say 'significant number' when they do not really know how many – continued to be active in non-acquisitive ways, in reform activity and pressure groups at a community level. This has involved a certain quietening, a dilution of energies and a more philosophical approach to outcomes. The same energies are not evident on a mass scale. But a sense of political responsibility is widely evident. The middle order of the body politic is now heavily populated by the Vietnam generation. Some went into education and the arts, some into law, the administration of welfare and health. Whilst few Vietnam activists went in for parliament a lot of them did take new middle-class politics into the political bureaucracy. They have been incorporated and so their activity is harder to see. But they press on in an adverse climate. They continue to oppose the dismantling of welfare programs and of civil rights, the centralising tendencies in Canberra, the closing of schools and crèches, the withdrawal of funds for underprivileged groups, big spending in the defence sector and so on. Their lifestyles remain modest. On the definitive test of means and ends they are mostly consistent – *they represent what they believe in.*

Possibly the most enduring effect of the Vietnam generation is the way it has, along with the new middle class and the environmentally conscious trade unions, spread a wider belief in the individual's political rights and responsibilities. As a matter of course, the country now has a lot of grassroots political activity that it did not have in the fifties. People are active in community politics when a marina development is announced or a freeway threatens. Parks and forests are under a lot of watchful eyes. That does not guarantee their safety, but makes it a possibility. Lobbying is no longer the exclusive preserve of the rich. Australia is a less authoritarian and repressive place because popular opposition, albeit generally quieter and localised, has become part of the political fabric. The questioning of authority is more routine than ever before. This worries conservatives, who say we need strong rulers, obedient followers and traditional morality, otherwise society will fall apart. The achievement of the sixties, and of the Vietnam generation in particular, has been to insist that the terms for social cohesion be debated and if necessary contested. In most spheres of life the contest continues.

AUSTRALIA'S LEGACY

The Vietnam Veterans

Jane Ross

The Vietnam war was divisive. Being a veteran of that war is an ambivalent condition. A very small minority of the young men of Australia, half of them conscripted, served in a war which was ultimately unsuccessful, and discredited, at least in the eyes of many people in Australia and elsewhere.

The Vietnam war was an American idea, though the Australian government participated willingly in it. The Americans defined the nature of the problem at the time – communist aggression – and years later it seems to be on a largely American definition of the soldiers' post-war experiences that the Australian media draw. Even the term 'veteran' is an Americanism, supplanting the 'returned serviceman' of Australian usage, often shortened to the far more resonant 'returned man'.

The image of the Vietnam veteran was largely non-existent in the years immediately after the war, before the Vietnam Veterans Association (VVA) and the Agent Orange issues planted it firmly in the Australian mind. The idea of the veteran was filled out by images from American popular culture, just as the public knowledge of what the war had been like was probably taken almost exclusively from American movies.

The Australian war was often equated with the American war, though this is quite a distortion. Australian and American experiences were sometimes very different, though sometimes the same, just as the experiences of individual soldiers could vary widely. The different nature of each soldier's experiences during the war, and of his social milieu and acceptance on his return home, make it impossible to speak with assurance about the veteran of this war, as of any other.

This has not prevented the development of stereotypes about the returned soldier, the dominant one being that of the 'troubled veteran', as presented by the VVA. The actual typical veteran, in the sense of being the most commonly occurring case, may be somewhat more conventional. He may well be a reasonably adjusted, married forty-year-old with two children and a mortgage. He may belong to local organisations, march on Anzac Day and be proud to be part of a tradition going back to Gallipoli. Vietnam may be for him not a problematical issue, but merely one year, a long time ago.

There has been some indecision as to whether to treat the Vietnam veterans as just another group of returned servicemen. On the one hand, the veterans wish to be part of the Anzac tradition; on the other, their lobbying groups have pushed for special benefits on the grounds that they were subject to special stresses.

It would be hard to sustain the argument that experiences in Vietnam were unique, except for the fact of the overall lack of victory (a fact not usually emphasised by veterans themselves). Australian soldiers have experienced a very wide variety of horrors during the course of two world wars and other minor conflicts, to try to compare the indescribable is a futile exercise.

Australian Vietnam Veterans at a dawn service in 1988.

Currently, the dominant image of veterans may still be that fostered by the VVA, but this could well change in the future, as Vietnam veterans come to terms with their experiences through the passing of the years and a greater understanding of the meaning of the war for Australia.

COMING HOME

The popularly accepted stereotype of the returning Vietnam digger was that he was whisked from the jungle by helicopter and then flown home, to arrive at an airport at midnight, there to be met by family *and* demonstrators. Then he went back to normality where people either had not noticed that he had been away, or else attacked and jeered because he had been fighting in an unpopular war. His reaction, supposedly, was to deny his experiences, to himself and to others.

Stereotypes are hard to dispute because they invariably contain an element of truth, this is no exception. But this stereotype is also a gross distortion of the overall social reality of the soldiers' return home. The experiences of some soldiers *did* fit the stereotype: but the experiences of many, many more did not. The very complexity of the picture encourages its distortion. People want to get a fix on the veteran's experience – but no such one veteran exists.

The Australian Army in Vietnam prided itself on the performance of its units. There was good morale. There was virtually no drug problem because of good discipline and the widespread preference for alcohol. Even if half the troops were conscripted, there was no organised opposition to the war amongst those in Vietnam. There was pride in the group and a desire to do the best in a messy situation.

One of the organisational reasons why the Australian Army was not beset by the problems that American forces faced, was that the fighting units at least were rotated on a unit rather than an individual basis. Ideally, this meant that a whole battalion might train for twelve months, go to Vietnam for twelve months then return, still intact as a unit, to be welcomed in the streets of its own home city.

Yet, in practice, it did not work quite like this. The National Service scheme operated with four intakes per year and four corresponding discharge dates two years later. A soldier's discharge date was effective no matter where he was stationed, so the battalions, even in Vietnam, suffered from a constant trickle of expired conscripts leaving while new soldiers arrived to take their places. There was also a trickle of soldiers leaving for other reasons: through sickness or injury, being posted elsewhere or because they had been killed.

There are no figures readily available to show the extent of this trickle from units, except for the figures on 7 RAR contained in *The Mortality Report*. There, rather than a trickle, it appears to have been quite a flood. The battalion contained at any one time about 388 national servicemen; of these, 208 were posted in over the twelve months after the start of the battalion's tour in April 1967. So at least one-quarter of the battalion did not in fact stay with the unit for its full tour, and did not return home to march with it. Some of these soldiers returned in groups, there seem to have been strong bonds between recruits who trained together. Other soldiers, from combat and non-combat units, returned home as they had arrived in Vietnam: more or less alone. It is not possible to try to estimate the exact numbers in each of these categories.

Some soldiers returned quickly, by regular charter flights: others as casualties in 'medevac' Hercules. The lucky ones came by troopship, giving them a chance to begin to adjust to leaving the war zone. Some

Mr Gordon Grant of Wodonga shows the US Presidential citation presented to D Company, 6th Battalion, the Royal Australian Regiment, after the Battle of Long Tan. His son, Ernest, who was in D Company, was killed during the battle on 18 August 1966, while helping an injured comrade. The photograph of Ernest, shown here, was the last one taken by his parents before his departure for Vietnam.

soldiers did fly in to darkened airports, suddenly civilians again. All, however, had to return to the army after leave, for discharge procedures. Many, at least among the regulars, remained in the army, and are still serving today. No matter how they returned, readjustment was probably a difficult time. There were families and other civilians to befriend again: there was the Australian environment, so different from Vietnam, no matter whether the veteran was in the city or the country. Many veterans seem to have only very dim memories of this initial homecoming period, and they were perhaps too stunned to worry about much more than just coping. In some cases, veterans came home alone and were met by a singular lack of interest – or knowledge – about where they had been or what they had been doing. This, rather than hostility, was by far the more common reaction.

The Australian population at large was not opposed to the Vietnam war for most of the years of Australia's involvement, even less was it hostile to the soldiers who fought there. Returned servicemen in Australia have shared in the honour given to the original Anzacs, those returning from Vietnam were no exception. But the war did have a low profile in Australia, except for occasional outbursts in the media over either anti-war demonstrations or a jump in the Australian casualty rate. The newspapers at the time were very far from full of war reporting, the war was on American television sets, not in Australian living rooms. Only for opinion leaders, those with family involvement and for a small number with strong views on the commitment, was Vietnam of consuming importance.

For most of Australia, the Vietnam war years meant business-as-usual. Curiously, perhaps, the soldiers

A Moratorium march in Melbourne in May 1970, involving 70 000 people.

and the Moratorium marchers were united in wishing to see an end to this attitude. The Moratorium was to be a moratorium *on* business-as-usual.

Public opinion polls and two elections showed that the Australian electorate was not particularly opposed to the war. The reception given to those troops who *did* march on their return home, shows that there was abundant warmth and welcome in the community towards the soldiers. It is interesting that these earlier 'welcome home' marches seem to have been so comprehensively forgotten. All of the battalions marched when they returned home – sixteen marches in all – generally accompanied by other troops who had returned at or near that time. Most of these marches took place in Sydney and Brisbane, but there were some in Adelaide and Townsville. From the first march, in June 1966 in Sydney, to the last one, in December 1971 in Townsville, the troops were cheered and clapped by thousands of onlookers. There were occasional 'incidents', but of a very minor nature.

The first battalion to return home was 1 RAR. The soldiers had been warned by their Commanding Officer. Lieutenant-Colonel Preece, 'not to expect to be welcomed with open arms by all sections of the community ...

> When you go into a pub and during conversation mention that you have just returned from Vietnam, don't expect to be welcomed with open arms and be stood drinks for the rest of the day.
>
> People will try to argue with you on Australia's commitment to Vietnam. Most of them will start attacking those blokes Sukarno and Sihanouk. Pity their ignorance.
>
> There is a beatnik minority, who will challenge you on Australia's presence in Vietnam.

The soldiers must have been pleasantly surprised. The march in Sydney was televised live by the ABC. The

Twenty years on, a dawn march by Australian Vietnam Veterans.

crowd was estimated to be between 300 000 and 500 000, there was a band, streamers and confetti. True, a girl doused in red paint threw her arms round Preece. (The woman had no connection with any anti-war movement.) But this was the only recorded incident of its kind in all the years of the war, in spite of the apparently vivid memories of some later soldiers who believed it was re-enacted with their battalion.

This was not in fact the very first time that Sydney crowds had cheered Vietnam veterans. A few weeks before this, on Anzac Day:

> ... a handful of Vietnam veterans ... got a special cheer from the crowd. When the march ended ... old soldiers broke their ranks to shake hands with the young Vietnam veterans.

Similar scenes greeted 5 RAR nearly a year later. A front-page story and pictures showed *BIG CROWD CHEERS THE 'TIGERS'*.

> Hundreds of thousands of people packed the pavements along the three-mile route of the battalion's march from Garden Island through the city. This was one of Sydney's truly splendid occasions ...

That year's Anzac Day march had also shown public support for soldiers returned from Vietnam. The anti-war movement grew in strength as another year passed. Early 1968 saw the fragility of the Saigon regime and its allies exposed by the Tet Offensive. On 26 April 7 RAR returned and marched in Sydney.

> The crowd, estimated at about 6000 outside the Town Hall alone, treated the young Vietnam veterans to what was, in one way, an unusual Sydney welcome – they cheered.

Reportedly, shoppers in Sydney booed and jeered about 1000 anti-war marchers a day later. The anti-war marchers never had a good press, and they were abused by politicians as no soldiers ever were. In late 1969, a few weeks after 300 000 anti-war marchers besieged Washington, 9 RAR marched in Adelaide. About

200 protesters tried to join the march and were attacked by onlookers, the press describing it as a 'melee'.

In the next months, events moved quickly on the international scene. There were calls to revenge the killing of students at Kent State University and Nixon promised to be out of Cambodia by June. A Moratorium in May attracted an estimated 20 000 protesters to the Sydney Town Hall, and the Minister for National Service. Billy Snedden, made his notorious remarks about Moratorium organisers being 'political bikies pack-raping democracy'. There were other rallies: in Brisbane, crowds were shocked by marchers chanting an anti-war slogan containing an obscene seven-letter word.

Overall, the cities continued to welcome the soldiers home: 5 RAR in Sydney in March 1970, 8 RAR in Brisbane in November. The Brisbane march was a tumultuous affair, but there were no 'incidents'. One (police) officer said: 'the ratbags wouldn't have been game to try anything today.' Even near the end of the war – as far as Australia's combat troops were concerned – there was still a warm welcome. The Townsville *Daily Bulletin* describes the scene when some troops of 4 RAR and others marched shortly before Christmas 1971.

> Thousands of Townsville people turned on a rousing heroes' welcome. Cheering drowned the sound of marching feet for three city blocks as Townsville made the most of the last major parade by troops from Vietnam. The marchers were swamped with streamers and ticker-tape thrown from balconies and roadside vantage points. The crowd which packed the Flinders Street footpaths to capacity has been described as the largest ever to turn out and welcome troops returning from the war zone.

SPEAKING FOR THE VETERANS

After the final, low-key withdrawal of Australian troops from Vietnam, the whole episode was publicly forgotten. The men who had fought and returned, and the bereaved families of those who had not returned, were left to sort things out as best they could. At that time – in the early 1970s – there was no particular concept of 'the Vietnam veteran' in Australia, although the academic presses in America were already grinding out books on the traumas being experienced by their veterans. In a newspaper report on the 1970 Anzac Day March, the word 'veteran' was still presented in inverted commas.

At this stage, there seems to have been no feeling that the veterans of Vietnam presented a special problem. They were eligible to join the RSL, the 'natural' spokesman for all returned servicemen; the repatriation system was all in place; there was little unemployment; they were fit young men who had only done twelve months' service in what was a minor conflict anyway.

To trace the reasons why other groups besides the RSL, especially the VVA, came into being in the late 1970s, it is necessary to consider first, the nature of the RSL; and secondly the impact of the Agent Orange issue.

OPPOSITE PAGE: Crowds throng Sydney streets on 3 October 1987, during the Welcome Home march held to honour Australia's Vietnam veterans. Each of the flags carried – more than 500 in all – represented one of the Australians who lost their lives in the war.

LEFT: a front page of *The Bulletin* during the withdrawal of Australian troops from Vietnam.

ABOVE: Australian troops hold a service at the site of the Battle of Long Tan, three years after it was fought, on 18 August 1969.

A veteran speaks about Anzac Day and the RSL

I was asked to join (the RSL), I didn't run around volunteering to join it, but the bloke came up to me and asked me, and he said, 'You're a returned man now, you ought to come and join.' It sort of struck me then, yes, I was a returned man. At that stage you had to be a returned man to be in it. It gave me tremendous pride, especially on the first Anzac Day, to march with a bloke who'd served in Gallipoli, two or three other old fellows there and other blokes. You felt inferior to them, but it was good to feel eligible to line up. I'd never even been to an Anzac Day parade before, and it gave me a lot of pride. I've been proud to be associated with the RSL ever since.

THE VICTIMS

At the send off parties at home, the speeches at the local RSL we had a heritage to live up to and they knew we would do Australia proud. We the new breed of fighting Digger representing Australia in that rarely heard of country. South Vietnam.

So we left to the flag waving and pomp and ceremony, by plane and by ship, and arrived to the stink of the jungles, and drying fish in the shoreline villages.

We acclimatised to the country and then began the everlasting patrols, ambushes and village searches. Then the contacts began and our first casualties were brought in.

We didn't know that the defoliants that were being used to assist us, was also killing us, some quickly, others slowly, and the unlucky ones passing on unmentionable deformities to their children, or to how many more generations?

We weren't to know about the cancers some of us contracted after service in SVN, or the mental disorders caused by the booby-trapped bodies some of us came in contact with or by the general memories of our service.

But all these points are only a minor aspect, as there were only 423 killed in action of the 45 000 Australians who served with the Australian Forces in South Vietnam.

So therefore the higher suicide rate of our veterans must only be a coincidence with the rate compared to the general public.

Perhaps once again it is only a coincidence that the SVN veterans who attend as psychiatric patients compared to that of the general public is higher.

At times more publicity was given to the Save our Sons Movement, to the Jim Cairns Moratorium Marches, the postal strikes, and to the wharfie strikes, than to the members actually fighting there (whether those veterans agreed with the policies or not).

After all don't marriage break-ups occur in everyday life, so once again the suicides and divorces from the SVN veterans just because they are of a higher percentage, must also only be a coincidence.

Why is it like this, you ask yourself.

Is it just because the SVN veteran had such a large heritage to live up to or is it just that he has trouble explaining his feelings or that you just don't understand them.

Could it be the shame of the suicides, alcoholism, drug abuse, broken marriages, divorces, deformed children or psychiatric problems associated with the SVN veterans or the stigma attached to the Vietnam conflict that everyone wants to ignore and forget!

Or is it just the plain old reason that no one wants to remember and admit that Vietnam was the first losing war that Australian Diggers have been involved in?

Not only is the veteran a victim but also his wife and children, his parents and friends. They are all suffering.

– Russ Hollings

Ex 7 RAR SVN 1967–1968, 1970–1971
DEBRIEF, November 1983–January 1984

The organisers of a Vietnam Veterans International Reunion address veterans at a dawn service.

After the First World War, several groups organised to protect the interests of returned soldiers. Of these, the RSL emerged as the clear winner, with the government's seal of approval, and has become accepted by the public as the authority on ex-servicemen.

Like many large and established organisations, however, the League has gradually assumed more diverse functions and has taken upon itself to speak out on a wide range of political and social issues. A glance through the *Annual Reports* and the newspaper *Reveille* show just how far it spreads its interests from what could be construed strictly as 'welfare'. State and national leaders readily pronounce on issues of national importance such as multiculturalism, the flag, and defence.

All servicemen have undoubtedly benefited greatly from the RSL's hard-nosed lobbying on repatriation issues, even if the maximum League membership has only been around 50% of those eligible (in the 1920s): in recent years, it has been around 260–270 000 or some 30% of those eligible. The League claims Vietnam veterans are joining at the same rate as veterans of previous wars and in 1989 it had around 15 000 such members.

The VVA (originally the VVAA or Vietnam Veterans Action Association) had its beginnings in 1979–80 when groups of veterans around Australia began to meet because of their concern at what they saw as major health problems. Agent Orange, an issue imported from America, was undoubtedly the catalyst for the formation of the VVA branches (they federated in 1980), but from the outset they also provided self-help groups and crisis intervention counsellors. The theme of the VVA has remained constant: that Vietnam was a special war, and that its veterans require special help.

Vietnam veteran activists initially approached the Department of Veterans' Affairs (DVA) and the RSL, but their concerns over Agent Orange were not shared. This led to the VVA's bitter attacks on the more conservative organisation: the RSL had, in the VVA's thinking, 'betrayed' the veterans over the Agent Orange issue, by siding with those who saw no need for special action and argued that established channels could handle any problem. So the VVA decided to go it alone. It lobbied long and hard, and eventually gained some investigations into veterans' health (though the findings were not to their liking),

I Was Only Nineteen

Mum and Dad and Denny saw the passing out parade at Puckapunyal
(It was a long march from cadets).
The sixth battalion was the next to tour and it was me who drew the card.
We did Canungra and Shoalwater before we left.
    And Townsville lined the footpath as we marched down to the quay.
    This clipping from the paper shows us young and strong and clean.
    And there's me in my slouch hat with my SLR and greens.
    God help me, I was only nineteen.

From Vũng Tàu riding Chinooks to the dust at Núi Đắt,
I'd been in and out of choppers now for months.
But we made our tents a home, V.B., and pinups on the lockers.
And an Asian orange sunset through the scrub.
    And can you tell me, doctor, why I still can't get to sleep?
    And night-time's just a jungle dark and a barking M-16?
    And what's this rash that comes and goes, can you tell me what it means?
    God help me, I was only nineteen.

A four week operation, when each step can mean your last one
On two legs; it was a war within yourself.
But you wouldn't let your mates down 'til they had you dusted off
So you closed your eyes and thought about something else.
    Then someone yelled out 'Contact!', and the bloke behind me swore.
    We hooked in there for hours, then a God-almighty roar.
    Frankie kicked a mine the day that mankind kicked the moon.
    God help me, he was going home in June.

I can still see Frankie, drinking tinnies in the Grand Hotel
On a thirty-six hour rec, leave in Vũng Tàu.
And I can still hear Frankie, lying screaming in the jungle,
'til the morphine came and killed the bloody row.
    And the Anzac legends didn't mention mud and blood and tears.
    And the stories that my father told me never seemed quite real.
    I caught some pieces in my back that I didn't even feel.
    God help me, I was only nineteen.

    And can you tell me doctor, why I still can't get to sleep?
    And why the Channel Seven chopper chills me to my feet?
    And what's this rash that comes and goes, can you tell me what it means?
    God help me, I was only nineteen.

- John Schumann
This song was a hit in the early 1980s for Redgum, a group closely associated with the VVA.

Soldiers of the regular army take part in a march of Vietnam veterans.

and the establishment of the Royal Commission on the Use and Effects of Chemical Agents on Australian Personnel in Vietnam in 1983.

The RSL opposed the Royal Commission. The VVA called this a betrayal, while the RSL claimed three supposedly 'rational' reasons for its opposition. First, it pointed out that under the repatriation legislation of the time there was an onus of proof on the Commission to *disprove* any claims. A definite finding by the Royal Commission that Agent Orange had not damaged veterans' health would weaken a claimant's position. This is in fact what happened, although few claims had succeeded on Agent Orange grounds before the Royal Commission presented its findings. Secondly, the RSL feared that a close examination of the repatriation legislation might lead to calls to tighten it. Thirdly, the RSL maintained that the success rate of Vietnam veterans' claims to repatriation was 80%, a rate comparable to that of claimants from earlier wars. Unstated, but perhaps also on the agenda, was that a close examination of Agent Orange issues might have led to more criticism of Australia's involvement in the Vietnam war.

In addition to policy differences, there are more prosaic reasons for the hostility between the VVA and RSL. Initially, it seems, there were personality clashes. Added to this, the RSL is currently dominated by veterans of the Second World War (although in 1989 the national secretary and his predecessor were Vietnam veterans), and it has been hard for the younger and fewer Vietnam veterans to make their concerns felt. In future years, however, as the Second World War leadership ages, no doubt those from the Vietnam years will eagerly fill their places.

Some veterans undoubtedly have had bad experiences with the RSL (or perhaps more precisely, from members of RS clubs, which are not synonymous with the League itself). There has been a generation gap and also a war gap – 'You blokes never had it as hard as we did' – which also happened to the Second World War veterans when they came up against those from the First World War in the 1940s and 1950s. It seems that this unfriendliness is now breaking down, where it did exist, and the VVA's publicising of veterans' issues has no doubt helped.

The VVA is not representative of all Vietnam veterans, any more than is the RSL; not everyone agrees

THE COST OF OUR VIETNAM COMMITMENT – IN HUMAN TERMS

	Army			Army Only	Navy	Air	Total
	ARA	NS	CMF				
Killed in action	173	143	1	317	6	4	327
Killed accidentally	15	10	—	25	—	—	25
Died of wounds	40	31	—	71	—	—	71
Missing	1	1	—	2	—	2	4
Non-battle casualty deaths	49	15	—	64	2	8	74
Total Deaths	278	200	1	479	8	14	501
Wounded in action	1140	880	6	2026	13	30	2069
Injured/ill in action	171	150	1	322	9	—	331
NBC injured/ill	426	249	2	677	28	26	731
Total non-fatal casualties	1737	1279	9	3025	50	56	3131
Served in Vietnam				41 910	2858	4443	49 211

Source: Department of Defence

with its aims or its methods. Some veterans resent its portrayal of the 'troubled digger' and feel insulted by the image of a sick misfit with damaged children and a head full of bad dreams. Some dislike what they term the VVA's 'political' stance, which presumably means its abrasive and outspoken style and highly effective use of the media.

Hence the appearance of groups such as the Vietnam Legion of Veterans Association, who restrict themselves to welfare and social activities, acting almost as specialists on Vietnam in close harmony with the RSL. None of these organisations, including the VVA, are radical or political in their attitude to the Vietnam war, in the sense of being opposed to it. They all want recognition, reconciliation; they want the community to be grateful to ex-servicemen and respect them for having served in Vietnam.

The VVA does, however, maintain a bitterly cynical attitude towards both the politicians who sent them to Vietnam and then 'betrayed' them by losing the war; and towards the anti-war politicians who in general also 'betray' the veterans by criticising the rightness and usefulness of their war. Betrayal was a strong theme in the early American writing on the Vietnam veteran, and seems to have found fertile soil in the VVA.

The VVA has not been without its own internal problems. Like the RSL, it has a federal structure and there have always been differences of policy and personality between the various levels of the organisation. Like most voluntary organisations, too, it suffers a chronic shortage of funds and of experienced personnel, particularly for mounting and sustaining legal actions and publicity campaigns. (The VVA did receive some funding from the RSL and some legal aid, but this, too, seemed to be an occasion for acrimony between the two organisations.)

In assessing the effectiveness of the VVA as an organisation, the most striking thing is its success at defining 'the Veteran' image through the media. It also had considerable success in forcing the government to meet its demands for veteran health studies, for the VVCS (Vietnam Veterans Counselling Service) and for the Royal Commission. One could debate whether in fact the aim of making Agent Orange an important issue was desirable or not, but the VVA certainly achieved this. It has not, however, had the final vindication of seeing Agent Orange accepted as the cause of widespread health problems.

Since the findings of the Royal Commission were presented in 1985, the VVA has had less publicity, its membership has dropped, and it may be gradually becoming of less relevance to the veterans. There seems no likelihood that the VVA will attempt to emulate the RSL and adopt a stance on general political issues. Many veterans are members of both the RSL and other groups, and in future years, no doubt the relatively young Vietnam veterans will take over the RSL. There are increasing signs of cooperation, and some institutional pressures may force the organisations to work more closely. For example, the RSL and VVA are both represented on the Australian Vietnam War Veterans Trust Ltd, the body which will disburse the $3.3m received from the Agent Orange settlement in the American class action. It is easy to see the future VVA becoming like the VLVA, providing a low-profile, specialist input on Vietnam veterans and personalised counselling to them and their families. It is impossible, however, to look back on the story of the Vietnam veteran in Australia and not give a central place in its telling to the VVA.

AGENT ORANGE

Like Southeast Asia generally, Vietnam in the 1960s was a land of dense tropical forests. This lush growth posed problems for the attacking armies; it was used to advantage by the indigenous guerrilla forces, and the allies seemed to have a fear of jungle – a fear going back perhaps to the colonialists' association of jungle with the 'heart of darkness' – exacerbated by the Pacific war.

US forces began in the early 1960s to use the chemical defoliants and sterilants which had been developed since the latter years of the Second World War. The extent of this use can be gauged from figures presented in the *Macquarie Atlas:* before the 1960s. 65% of southern Vietnam (or some 16.8 million hectares) was covered by forests. Between 1965 and 1971 about 3.2 million hectares of this forest (nearly 20%) were destroyed by the extended use of defoliants. The chemicals were also used to destroy crops.

Are the chemicals a threat to human health? What degree of exposure constitutes a threat? These are the questions at the heart of the Agent Orange dispute. While they are more obviously pertinent to those who live in southern Vietnam, who breathe, eat, drink and reproduce under 'the deadly fog', they are of continuing importance to the visiting Australian soldiers who also, it seems certain, suffered *some* degree of exposure even if only indirectly during their time in Phước Tuy and adjacent provinces.

In this, though, they are not unique: one problem in assessing any effects which chemical exposure may have had is the background level of exposure to which all residents in a modem ecology may be subject.

The chemical at the heart of the eponymous dispute, Agent Orange, was the most widely used of several defoliants and sterilants. It consists of esters of the phenoxyacetic compounds 2,4,5-T and 2,4-D, both of which are still commonly used in Australian agriculture. A by-product of their manufacture,

Agent Orange

QUESTIONNAIRE
POSSIBLE ALLERGIC SYMPTOMS

1. **Skin:** Itching, burning, flushing, warmth, coldness, tingling, sweating behind neck, etc. Hives, blisters, blotches, red spots, 'pimples'.

2. **Ear, Nose and Throat:** Nasal congestion, sneezing, nasal itching, runny nose, post-nasal drip. Sore, dry or tickling throat, clearing of throat, itching palate, hoarseness, hacking cough. Fullness, ringing or popping of ears, earache, intermittent deafness, dizziness, imbalance.

3. **Eyes:** Blurring of vision, pain in eyes, watery eyes, crossing of eyes, glare hurting eyes, eyelids twitching, itching, drooping or swollen, redness and swelling of inner angle of lower lid.

4. **Respiratory:** Shortness of breath, wheeze, cough, mucus formation in bronchial tubes.

5. **Cardiovascular:** Pounding heart, increased pulse rate, skipped beats, flushing, pallor, warm, cold, tingling, redness or blueness of hands, faintness, precordial pain.

6. **Gastrointestinal:** Dryness of mouth, increased salivation, cancer sores, stinging tongue, toothache, burping, retasting, heartburn, indigestion, nausea, vomiting, difficulties in swallowing, rumbling in abdomen, abdominal pain, cramps, diarrhoea, itching or burning rectum.

7. **Gastro-Urinary:** Frequent, urgent or painful urination, inability to control bladder, vaginal itching or discharge.

8. **Muscular:** Fatigue, generalised muscular weakness, muscle and joint pain, stiffness, soreness, chest pain, backache, neck muscle spasm, generalised spasticity.

9. **Nervous System:** Headache, migraine, compulsively sleepy, drowsy, groggy, slow, sluggish, restlessness, jittery, convulsive, dull, depressed, serious, crying, tense, anxious, stimulated, overactive, head feels full or enlarged, silly, floating sensation, giggling, laughing, inebriated, unable to concentrate, feeling of separateness or apartness from others, amnesia for words or numbers or names, stammering or stuttering speech, temper rages.

– The veterans' magazine, *Debrief*, published this in 1982 to invite responses from possible victims of Agent Orange.

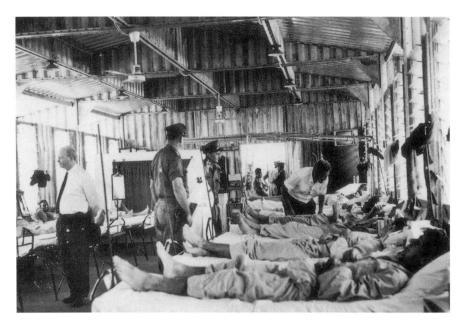

Prime Minister John Gorton visits 1st Field Hospital, Vũng Tàu, in 1968. A decade later, the soldiers' injuries and damaged health were once more an issue, this time because of the Agent Orange controversy.

contained in indeterminate quantities in the mixture, is the extremely poisonous substance TCDD or dioxin. Also used (though in smaller quantities) were other mixtures, code-named by the coloured bands on the drums: Agent Blue, an arsenical compound, cacodylic acid, mainly for destruction of rice crops; Agent White, a mix of 2.4-D and picloram, a persistent defoliator used particularly against forests. Bromacil and Monuron were soil sterilants.

American forces sprayed large quantities of these and other herbicides – more than eleven million gallons – officially with care and control, but in practice there could be little safety for those applying the chemicals, and even less safety for those on the ground. Much of the spraying was from relatively high-level, fixed-wing aircraft, with resultant drift and inaccuracies; there were ample opportunities for human error and carelessness.

Australian soldiers lived and worked in a province where the US spraying programs (mostly known as Ranch Hand) were active for several years. They also did their own defoliating, using their own chemicals which were similar to the American mixes, and probably also using the coloured agents themselves (Australians were constant users of most American material in Vietnam). There was also considerable use in Vietnam of various insecticides, both by individuals and on a larger scale.

It is hardly disputed that human factors vitiated the safety of the program. On policy grounds, too, there was probably minimal concern for the human and physical environments, since the herbicides were a weapon of war, being used against an enemy.

There was sufficient concern expressed by environmentalists and others to have the large-scale spraying programs in Vietnam abandoned in 1971. It was some years, however, before veterans in America began to make any claims against the chemical companies, or US agencies, on the basis that health problems had been caused by exposure to toxic chemicals.

The controversy in America entered a new phase with the TV program *Agent Orange – Vietnam's Deadly Fog,* made in Chicago in 1978. Veterans there began to make claims on the Veterans Administration,

> **Post Trauma Syndrome**
> AS DESCRIBED IN THE ROYAL COMMISSION REPORT XV-23
> Flashbacks to Terrifying Events • Nightmares • Irritability • Rage Reaction • Dizzy Spells • Anxiety • Insomnia • Depression • Guilt Feelings • Headaches • Low Back Pain • Ulcer • Migraine • Irritable Bowel Syndrome • Irritable Colon • Hypertension • Paranoia • Suspicion • Crowd Phobia • Alcoholism

and to demand scientific studies of their allegations; they also sought to use the court system by bringing a class action (including Australians and New Zealanders) for compensation from the chemical companies who manufactured and supplied Agent Orange. In the end they received an out-of-court settlement of $180 million, to be shared amongst the class of plaintiffs. As so often happens, both sides claimed they would have won and the lawyers seemed to be the chief beneficiaries from the court action.

In Australia, the veteran activists followed a different path but have also not succeeded in their aims of moral and financial vindication. In 1979, several factors came together to make Agent Orange an issue for Australian veterans. It then became the one issue for which veterans were known by the wider community, even though not all veterans supported the VVA in either their aims or methods. A controversy erupted in the Victorian town of Yarram over the alleged connection between the use of herbicides and a cluster of birth abnormalities. The TV documentary mentioned above, prompted investigations by Veterans Affairs and the US Air Force. Soon a group of veterans in Australia began to meet and to agitate: the VVA was born and Agent Orange has since been continually in the media.

Faced with claims from veterans that a variety of physical, neurological and psychiatric disturbances were the result of poisoning by Agent Orange, the Australian government at first unwisely denied that any Australian soldiers had ever been exposed. The claim was speedily retracted, but the government then insisted that established repatriation channels could handle the problem. The VVA continued to lobby, and instead of using the established channels – such as the RSL – it relied on media pressure and its own direct contacts with politicians and bureaucrats. (Relations with the RSL appear never to have been particularly cordial.) Its efforts were successful but not completely so. The VVA always wanted a judicial rather than scientific enquiry; the government referred the matter to the Senate Standing Committee on Science and the Environment (*Pesticides and the Health of Australian Vietnam Veterans*, 1982), and promised a comprehensive study into the health of veterans and their offspring. This study – the morbidity survey – unfortunately never eventuated. The other studies which were completed were the *Birth Defects Study* (1983) and the *Mortality Report* (1984). None of these studies has been accepted as valid by the VVA and it continued to push for a Royal Commission.

The Evatt Royal Commission (Royal Commission on the Use and Effects of Chemical Agents on Australian Personnel in Vietnam), established in 1983, heard evidence from many veterans and many experts; its report was released in July 1985 and did little, at least immediately, to defuse the issue. The

> ## CONCLUSIONS OF THE ROYAL COMMISSION
> So Agent Orange is Not Guilty and the chemical agents used to defoliate battle zones in Vietnam and to protect Australians from malaria are not to blame.
>
> No one lost.
>
> This is not a matter for regret but for rejoicing. Veterans and their wives are no more at risk of having abnormal offspring than anyone else.
>
> Veterans have not been poisoned. The number with general health problems is small, probably much smaller than amongst their peers in the community.
>
> The few that have psychological stress disorder can seek help freely and without shame and above all with hope of early relief and in the sure knowledge that no poisoning of their minds has occurred.
>
> This is good news and it is the Commission's fervent hope that it will be shouted from the roof-tops.

Royal Commission functioned, effectively, as a trial of Agent Orange. Counsel 'for' Agent Orange was briefed by various chemical companies; the case 'against' (and therefore 'for' the veterans) was argued by the VVA. The case against Agent Orange was found to be not proven – the chemicals were presumably innocent unless proven guilty! – and the verdict was announced by the Royal Commissioner in extravagant language.

The VVA claims that the onus of proof lay on the veterans – the plaintiffs – to show three things: first, that there were in fact health problems; second, that those suffering from these problems had been exposed in some way to herbicides; and third, that it was this exposure which had caused the individual's problems. The Commission found that the first had been demonstrated, but denied both sufficient exposure and connection between herbicides and ill-health. It did, however, validate the concept of post-traumatic stress disorder (PTSD) and also hinted at a possible carcinogenic effect of Dapsone, an antimalarial drug which was widely used.

The disquiet which greeted these findings was compounded by the discovery that large sections of the Report had been taken verbatim from the submissions of the Monsanto chemical company. This, and the treatment of some evidence and witnesses, reinforced the VVA in their view that the Commission was biased and that their case against Agent Orange would never be allowed to succeed, because of the alleged interlocking interests of companies, the military, and the government; and, the enormous implications for business and agriculture if Agent Orange were condemned.

Nevertheless, the case presented against Agent Orange was weak in several respects – which is not to say that the chemical should have been found not guilty, merely that the verdict should have been an open one. Yet, this also would have caused enormous political and human problems, providing no reassurance to veterans and their families in the years to come, perhaps, until the question is finally resolved.

The main problem with the veterans' case is the lack of watertight evidence of either an epidemiological or laboratory kind that there is in fact a medical problem related to chemical exposure. None of the government's studies has shown that veterans as a group have health problems out of the normal range, such as an increased risk of birth defective children. Moreover the scientific community is divided as to the toxicity of the chemicals at issue.

One of the problems which appears constantly in the literature is that of communication between the so-called experts and the lay community, including the veterans. Laboratory studies are highly technical, beyond the reach of most of us to query. The survey studies have similarly employed complex methodology, not commending themselves as easy reading. The VVA has, however, done its members a serious disservice by denying in principle the validity of all the studies whose findings do not accord with their own views. They appear to be wilfully bent on accepting the anecdotal evidence of sick veterans, while denying the results of any large surveys such as those of the national servicemen in the *Mortality Report*. The wider community, on the other hand, would probably agree with the Royal Commission in finding evidence such as that presented by the VVA in their Ten Best Shots (the ten veterans chosen as most likely to convince the Commission) singularly unconvincing. A well designed study of veterans' health would convince many people, but on past experience it is hard to see it being accepted by the VVA unless its findings pronounced Agent Orange guilty. We can question why some veterans seem to be intent on proving the guilt of Agent Orange almost to the point of obsession, when the Royal Commission findings mean that most claims will be allowed by the repatriation system on grounds other than toxicity of herbicides. The answer would seem to be that being able to blame a chemical, or some specific agent rather than 'just' the war, is important to a sufferer's self esteem, and the diagnosis of PTSD seems to have a definite stigma. Some veterans, too, may have hoped for some financial compensation if their claims against Agent Orange had succeeded.

While it would be tempting to see Agent Orange as simply a convenient issue on which to mobilise veterans, and the VVA as merely an opportunistic group which has exploited their anxieties, there is little doubt that those who believe in the guilt of Agent Orange do so passionately and sincerely.

Like many of the Australian veteran issues, the Agent Orange controversy was initiated in the United States – but then prosecuted with considerable vigour and effectiveness by Australians, those who formed the VVA. Ten years later, it would seem that we still have to await a definitive verdict on the safety or otherwise of the chemicals concerned; the answer, unfortunately, may lie with the future ill-health of veterans; but hopefully the future will validate the 'not guilty' finding of the Evatt Royal Commission.

THE HEALTH OF VETERANS

The Agent Orange campaign was based on the assumption that veterans of the Vietnam conflict, and their children, suffered ill-health as a result of exposure to chemicals during their service. But as the Royal Commission concluded, there is so far no evidence of large-scale health problems among Vietnam veterans. One can conclude from this, optimistically, as did the Royal Commission, that there *are* in fact no health problems; or one could leave it as an open question.

The VVA and other believers in Agent Orange have supplied anecdotal evidence of both physical and mental ill-health among veterans, and of birth abnormalities in their children conceived after service in Vietnam. None of these claims, however, has been substantiated in any large-scale studies. The VVA persuaded the government to undertake a study of veterans' health, and as a result the Australian Veterans Health Studies (AVHS) group was set up. The AVHS carried out the *Case Control Study of Congenital Anomalies and Vietnam Service* (Birth Defects Study), completed in 1983, which found that 'there is no evidence that Army service in Vietnam relates to the risk of fathering a child with an anomaly.' No subsequent research has invalidated this conclusion, and as the Royal Commission observed, the sad fact is that a normal incidence of birth defects among the children of Vietnam veterans would lead us to expect between 3% and 10% to suffer some malformation.

The second study carried out by the AVHS was a pilot morbidity study, designed to be the precursor to a major study of the health of veterans. The pilot study showed, basically, that there was no discernible pattern of ill-health among veterans. In spite of the Royal Commission's strong support, the government refused to give funding for the larger project, and it was finally abandoned.

The third study was, however, completed. Known as *The Mortality Report,* it compares the death-rates of veteran and non-veteran National Servicemen up to 1 January 1982. The Report is a mine of information on the career of the National Serviceman: on both the selection processes which carried him to Vietnam and the structure and function of units in Vietnam. The overall conclusions on mortality (as opposed to morbidity) are that veterans had slightly higher death rates than non-veterans, mainly because of increased alcohol-related sickness; but both groups of National Servicemen had lower mortality rates than non-servicemen of the same age group. Given the very good health of National Servicemen who were selected into the Army, and even more so, those who were sent to Vietnam, we would probably expect them to be healthier than the average citizen years later. The Report does suggest (though not conclusively) that Vietnam service had little adverse effect on mortality and by implication, therefore, on health. What effects it did have on health seem to be related to easy access to, and increased consumption of, those two widely used and harmful drugs alcohol and nicotine. Beer was cheap, available and by far the most common relaxant; cigarettes were supplied in both army ration packs and RSL and Red Cross 'comfort parcels'.

As with physical health, there has been almost no research in Australia on the mental health of veterans, though there have been studies of veterans undergoing psychiatric treatment. The Royal Commission seems to find it acceptable to use figures from the USA to estimate the probable levels of stress induced mental ill-health (summarised as Post Traumatic Stress Disorder, known earlier as Vietnam Veterans Syndrome). Yet, one could argue against this method on the grounds that both the war and the home front were different for Australian soldiers compared to US forces. According to evidence accepted by the Royal Commission, 23.5% of veterans would be expected to be complaining of symptoms (mostly of anxiety and depression); 12.2% would have sufficient symptoms to warrant a diagnosis; 5.9% would have chronic conditions; and 3.2% would be incapacitated. Most of these veterans would, however, be suffering from these symptoms even *without* having had Vietnam service, as the base male population percentages were respectively 20%, 99%, 4.9% and 2.4% (based apparently on a mental health survey carried out on a random sample of Botany Bay adults – who perhaps would not be completely representative of the general Australian population).

The Commissioner concluded:

> There is a Vietnam veterans' syndrome, broadly corresponding to PTSD. At this time about 25% of Vietnam veterans will have psychological symptoms requiring treatment, and this number may be expected to peak in 1988–89 and then gradually but steadily decline.

This is in line with the estimates of the VVCS that perhaps 20% of veterans are in need of some counselling.

The confusion over the possible levels of mental ill-health among veterans is understandable. First, measures of mental health in the general population are not noted for their reliability. There is little agreement on how to define mental health or how to measure it. Lay people, for instance, would probably be rather sceptical about the figures cited above showing 20% of the male population to be suffering from symptoms'; but we should remember that only a much smaller number find these symptoms in any way disabling, or seek treatment.

Secondly, most of the studies specifically on veterans' mental well-being are qualitative rather than quantitative. Certainly, they may show high levels of rage and violence, of guilt and distress because of combat experiences, but this is only among the population of those seeking counselling, or of those who are already psychiatric in-patients. These studies do not tell us anything about the other veterans, those who have not sought help. It is assumed, that they, like most people, are more or less adjusted; or more or less maladjusted, depending on one's view of the human condition.

THE REPATRIATION SYSTEM

For many returned soldiers, the central fact in being veterans is perhaps their contact with the repatriation system, the central focus for the activities of servicemen's lobby groups. The repatriation system was established in Australia during, and soon after, the First World War. A system of compensation for war service has continued since then, though with several changes to the names of the relevant Acts, commissions and departments.

Soldiers who went away to the First World War must have done so with little thought for the morrow. There was initially no system of disability pensions for servicemen, and no man could know how long he might be away. For a soldier going to Vietnam, there were fewer unknowns. As well as having a maximum of twelve months overseas, he knew that he would enter the repatriation system if wounded or otherwise disabled and he knew what other benefits would be available. War service home loans (now available to all service people) at low, fixed interest terms were an attraction, as were taxation benefits. There were some other resettlement benefits available to National Servicemen until 1972 when these were supposedly made redundant by schemes such as NEAT which were open to all.

The main categories of benefits for veterans are disability pensions, some with additional benefits, and service pensions (which will be of more relevance to Vietnam veterans in future years).

To qualify for a disability pension an applicant or his dependants need to show that an injury or disease (or death) has been, in general terms, 'war caused'. The precise definition of 'war caused' has changed somewhat in recent years. Until 1982, Vietnam veterans needed to have it accepted that death or incapacity resulted from an occurrence during the serviceman's eligible service; or that if the origin or cause of the disability existed prior to eligible service, it was aggravated by service. In 1982 the provision applying to Second World War veterans was extended to Vietnam veterans, whereby death or incapacity would be entitled to compensation if it 'had arisen out of, or was attributable to', service. This change was seen as significant by groups such as the VVA which had agitated for it.

Once entitlement to a disability pension has been accepted, the degree of incapacity is then assessed as being somewhere between nil and 100% in increments of 10% and a compensatory pension is paid accordingly. A large number of Vietnam veterans – more than 10 000 – receive disability pensions, but most of them only receive a small amount.

In addition to these disability pensions, there are benefits for veterans on 100% disability and whose working capacity is reduced to part-time or less because of the war-caused disability. These pensions are known as the Intermediate and Special Rates. Recipients of the latter are those formerly known as TPI (totally and permanently incapacitated), although a recent change means that those on only 70% disability can now apply to be considered for the Special Rate as well.

The numbers receiving these various pensions, and the current levels of benefit, are shown in the Table. As well as these income payments, there are also other benefits for the severely disabled and their dependants, including comprehensive medical care at the 'Repat' Hospitals, and by designated practitioners provided free regardless of the vagaries of the Medicare schemes.

Vietnam veterans and their dependants have also, since 1982, been entitled to free emergency hospital treatment even where the condition is not war-related. Separate from the Disability Pensions are the Service Pensions, similar to the age or invalid pension but payable at a younger age.

The steps which a veteran or his dependant goes through before receiving a repatriation pension can be quite complex. First, he approaches the Repatriation Commission with a claim. He may be immediately successful in having both his entitlement recognised and an acceptable level of pension paid. If he is not, he can begin the process of appeal, which goes through the following stages: Veterans Review Board, Administrative Appeals Tribunal, and on points of law, to the Federal Court, and finally the High Court. Largely because of this appeals system (and also of course because of changes to legislation and changes in medical fashions and knowledge), the complicated repatriation system is far from static. Changes to interpretation of law make their way through the whole system, and can have an impact on a large number of people. For example, the Federal Court's ruling on cigarette smoking in the *Law* case in 1981 came years too late for many veterans of the First and even the Second World Wars, but will presumably be to the benefit of many Vietnam veterans.

Some years ago there was something of a public opinion revolt against what were perceived as the over-generous provisions of the Repatriation Act. In 1969 John Whiting published *Be in it, mate!* describing some of the apparent rorts. Vietnam veterans perhaps felt that they entered the system at a bad time, that there would be tougher interpretations on their applications for benefit. The VVA has certainly promoted feelings of resentment towards the Department of Veterans Affairs DVA, the initial point of contact with government for those seeking a pension. The VVA has criticised both the Department's attitude towards Agent Orange claims and the alleged tightening up of repatriation legislation in 1985. It is perhaps inevitable that veterans lobby groups will attack the DVA, since it is in the position of giving or guarding the treasures of the public purse. It is difficult now at least, to see that overall there is any basis for the VVA's fears. To a civilian, the repatriation system seems quite generous in determining entitlements. If the rates of pension leave much to be desired, then that is in line with all other welfare assistance.

The 'repat' system has undergone several changes in the last few years, beginning with the ruling in the *Law* case. In this case the court found that the onus of proof lay on the commission to *disprove* a claimant's case. In the particular case, they would have had to prove that the claimant's lung cancer was not the result of his smoking habit, which he alleged he had taken up during his war service.

The ruling resulted in a very generous few years, 1981–85, when hardly any applications for pensions

RATES OF DISABILITY PENSIONS FOR VIETNAM VETERANS
June 1989

% of General Rate Pension being received	Number of Veterans	Cumulative % of Total	$ Benefit per week
10	2564	30	7.46
15–20	1762	51	14.92
25–30	1075	64	22.38
35–40	803	73	29.84
45–50	574	80	37.30
60	498	86	44.76
65–70	281	89	52.22
75–80	333	93	59.68
85–90	122	95	67.14
100	448	100	74.60
	8460		
Intermediate rate	36		136.25
Special rate (TPI)	678		197.90
	9174		

Source: Department of Veterans Affairs

were refused and it was during this period that some Agent Orange claims succeeded, notably that of *Simpson*. Then in 1985 the Act was reviewed, and the force of the new law was explained in the Federal Courts' case of *East*. A veteran is not required to *prove* his claim to a pension in the sense of there being an onus of proof on him. But he needs, as the Federal Court explained, to provide a 'reasonable hypothesis' linking his disability with some occurrence in his war service, 'to be reasonable,' the Court continued, 'a hypothesis must possess some degree of acceptability or credibility – it must not be obviously fanciful, impossible, incredible or not tenable or too remote or too tenuous ... At the same time, however, a hypothesis may be reasonable without having been proved ... to be correct as a matter of fact.'

What happens in practice in disputed claims, is that each side presents conflicting evidence from experts, and the determining board must reject some as not being reasonable and accept others, even though they may be in an area which is far from being scientifically or medically settled.

One might think that cases based on Agent Orange would be regarded as 'reasonable', given the above definition. This, however, is not the case; the repatriation system generally follows the Royal Commission's findings and disallows Agent Orange claims. The other side of this is that many claims can succeed which are based on stress, since the Royal Commission accepted that all soldiers in Vietnam did suffer stress, and stress in turn can be implicated, 'reasonably', in a wide variety of disorders. This is particularly so when

Crowds begin to line the streets of Sydney for the celebrated Welcome Home march of 1987.

smoking and alcohol consumption are also accepted as war-induced or aggravated behaviours in most cases, and are in turn accepted as causing or aggravating a wide range of health problems.

The repatriation system is impressive. Millions of dollars are disbursed each year, and a veteran certainly gets his day in court if he has the tenacity to pursue his claim through the Appeals system.

Nevertheless, urged by the VVA, the Liberal government in 1982 established the Vietnam Veterans Counselling Service (VVCS) as a semi-independent, twenty-four-hour, shopfront service for veterans and their families. The service seems to have fulfilled a much felt need, and has the support of all veterans' groups, although some would like the services to include all veterans.

The Service operates with an informal, client-centred style. It provides general counselling, crisis intervention, as well as individual and group therapy sessions. It follows very much the American model, and can also be seen as epitomising the anti-psychiatry, non-drug therapies of the 1970s and 1980s.

The VVCS has records on over 5000 clients, some of whom have minor problems with, for instance, home loans or repat claims; a large number have been diagnosed as having PTSD, after presenting with relationship problems, mood and sleep disturbances, and depression. Not all of these are 'cured' by the VVCS, but surveys of the clients show that a large majority rate the service overall as effective in helping them. The VVCS certainly has access to a large number of veterans, reporting over 23 000 contacts in each of recent years. The VVCS estimates that the 10% of all veterans – the number they have seen to date – represents perhaps half the total number in need of some counselling.

The future of the service now seems assured, with the Report *After the March* recommending its expansion and continuation for at least another ten years. This is confirmation of the limits of bureaucratised, establishment medical care as provided through the repatriation system.

A representative selection of British medals, awarded by the Australian government to Australians who served in Vietnam. Above, from left to right: The Victoria Cross (4 awarded); the Military Medal (84): the Distinguished Flying Cross (78). Below: the Campaign Service Medal, with Bar, South Vietnam, the Vietnam Medal 1964–73. The South Vietnam Campaign Medal, below right, was awarded by the Republic of South Vietnam.

A representative selection of US Medals, awarded to Australians who served in Vietnam. Above left, the United States Silver Star; above right, the United States Distinguished Flying Cross. Below, left to right: the United States Air Medal; the United States Bronze Star. Above, centred, is the National Order of the Republic of Vietnam, and below right is the Republic of Vietnam Gallantry Cross with Palm, both awarded by the Republic of South Vietnam.

WELCOME HOME

The government has provided reasonably well for its veterans of all wars. Soldiers have been compensated in large numbers for war-caused disabilities, though this compensation is not in any way comparable to the 'compo' of the civilian system. Perhaps there is some honourable instinct that shies away from attempting to recompense people, with cash, for the horrors of war. Nevertheless, returned soldiers are very much a 'motherhood' issue in Australian politics and no one will publicly decry the expenditures of repatriation or suggest that veterans have it too easy. In this, they are a privileged group.

Soldiers returning from the First and Second World Wars, like those returning from Vietnam, did so under many different circumstances. There were always small and large groups of men coming and going. Some returned wounded or unfit, some returned as heroes in their units; all had to make the difficult adjustment from overseas service life, maybe on the front line, to life as a civilian. To suggest that all veterans of the previous wars marched in victory parades is quite far from the truth. What *was* different about the First and Second World Wars had two major aspects. Firstly, the sheer size of the enterprise,

Australian and Vietnamese veterans of the war march together in Melbourne.

directly involving very significant proportions of the whole Australian population (in the First World War 13.4% of all men and in the Second World War 10.28% of the whole population enlisted, compared to around 0.4% of the population in the Vietnam era). Secondly, related to this, was the different outcome. The extent of relief and rejoicing which was felt on Armistice Day in 1918 and VP (Victory in the Pacific) Day in 1945 was immense; Australia was, after all, on the winning side, and both these wars had an unambiguous finish. By contrast. Australia's role in Vietnam ended – with a significantly named 'withdrawal' – before the war was over. The departure of the Task Force from Núi Đất was unheralded in the broadly pro-war Australian press; so, too, was the return to Australia of the last of the Task Force. The Australians did retain a small commitment of advisers after the Task Force withdrawal, but this group received almost no publicity. Their ultimate withdrawal came shortly after the election of the Whitlam Labor Government in December 1972.

Fighting continued in Vietnam between 'our side' and 'the enemy' until April 1975 when PAVN tanks rolled into Saigon. It became obvious, at last, that 'they' had won; Australian veterans of Vietnam seemed to be stunned and disbelieving. Many of them, even most, had seemed to genuinely believe that the Saigon regime would prevail. The patent and shamefaced collapse of the ARVN forces was to some veterans the final invalidation of their service for America's allies in Vietnam.

The events of 1975 seemed to mark the beginning of a quiet time for Vietnam veterans. Vietnam as an issue was now finally dead as far as the media were concerned, and the late 1970s were the time for new issues to assume public importance. It is this burying of Vietnam, the failure to confront the experience honestly and openly both on the social and individual levels, that is responsible for much of the simmering trauma and discontent which veterans felt and which was triggered into political action by the Agent Orange issue.

The gradual alteration in the treatment by the media of Anzac Day provides a neat illustration of the way political fashions changed in the later 1970s and early 1930s: foreign policy and defence have well and truly slipped off the front pages by the 1980s and their place has been taken by more domestic issues such as feminism, gay rights and lately multiculturalism.

Anzac Day is at the centre of 'old Australia' mythology. It is the time and place to parade old-fashioned virtues, to acknowledge the cultural supremacy of male doings and Anglo-Saxon policies. It is not the time and place for subtleties, for the celebration of differences, for pluralism. Vietnam, with all its ambiguities, fits uneasily into the sequence of Australia's wars. We were, after all, supposedly fighting *for* Asians, as well as against them; we did finally find ourselves part of the losing side (though many veterans still deny that we lost the war); and support for the war was at least equivocal both at home and abroad. But the soldiers themselves were perceived to fit in with the earlier Anzacs, at least by Anzac Day crowds and the media, from the very early years of Australia's involvement. Soldiers themselves were not radicals, though they found themselves at the heart of a divisive political issue. They stayed out of the issue by being 'professional', 'only doing a job'; although it seems that the vast majority were at heart active supporters of the war, and were only too eager to be returned diggers and so join the tradition of Anzac. As described earlier, the returning Vietnam soldiers were seen as giving new meaning to Anzac, as writing 'a new chapter in Anzac Tradition'. In 1967. '... in the continuing story of the Anzac tradition, soldiers returned from the conflict in Vietnam marched down Martin Place with veterans of Korea, Malaya and Borneo and members of the 3rd and 6th Battalions RAR.' According to a front-page *Sydney Morning Herald* report, the young people were the ones leading the cheers amongst the 100 000 onlookers.

> ... the strongest acknowledgment was for their own generation – the young Regulars and National Servicemen.
> Today, they are liable to be involved themselves. Today, their friends and relatives are being drawn into military commitment.
> In this non-militarist nation, on this day, military commitment had unified young and old.

In the following years of the Vietnam war, its veterans were always given special mention in the *Sydney Morning Herald* accounts of the Sydney Anzac March. In 1970, 'the biggest cheer or all was given the first of the Vietnam veterans' in the Korea, Malaya, Borneo and Vietnam troops ... A woman slipped under the barricades to throw confetti ...' then in 1972, after the withdrawal of most of the Australian troops from Vietnam, the youngest veterans were given the honour of leading the Sydney march. The number of veterans involved was not large – about 600 – but they were greeted enthusiastically by an estimated 150 000 spectators (a larger crowd than usual). Indeed, they instilled a new enthusiasm into the crowds, and received generous applause amidst cries of 'welcome back, boys!' and 'Good on you, fellers!' This year was the high point of Vietnam veteran participation in Anzac marches, at least as far as the media were concerned. In 1973 and 1974, they still rated a special mention in the *Sydney Morning Herald* reports. But in 1975 they did not; and from then onwards the press attention was drawn to the more dissident elements in Australia who began to attack, if not exactly Anzac Day, then at least the RSL's monopoly on defining how it was to be legitimately celebrated. The media's theme became 'peace and conflict' on Anzac Day, as women's groups such as Women against Rape in War, gay groups such as the Gay Ex-Servicemen's

Association, and various ethnic organisations began to demand the right to march or lay wreaths at the cenotaphs. An exception to the low-key treatment of Vietnam veterans was in 1980 when a group of about 100 marched in Sydney, wearing small pieces of orange paper on their jackets, in one of the earlier publicity moves in the Agent Orange saga. The organiser was eager to prove the group's Anzac *bona fides,* however:

> This is not a political protest. The crepe paper signifies our concern over the issue. We are the conservative element in Australia. We are members of RSL clubs. We served our country and we would like our country to serve us.

A brief glance through the newspaper files would emphasise that Vietnam veterans were not systematically ignored during the war years; they received as a group considerable public support during both battalion and Anzac marches, even though probably only a minority participated directly in these marches.

But from the time of its formation in 1980, the VVA was successful in defining the public image of the Vietnam veteran, and in depicting his experience of returning from the war as an overwhelmingly negative one. During the 1980s, almost the only discussions of Vietnam in the media have been in terms of 'the veteran and his problems', problems which have been seen as caused by either exposure to toxic chemicals and/or the unpopularity of the war. The images of the war which linger in the public mind – insofar as they do linger at all – are probably drawn more from North American than Australian experiences. The popular culture of the United States – its movies, pop music, and television – have been as important in depicting the nature of the war and the veteran experience as the US political leaders were in defining the nature of the Vietnam 'problem' years earlier. Independent analyses by Australians and for Australians might well have yielded more relevant results.

The Welcome Home March was, however, one American idea which did work well. Almost all American troops were individually rotated through their units in Vietnam, and their battalions did not have marches on their return home. It is no doubt true, too. That the war – and maybe the soldiers – were more unpopular in the USA than was the case in Australia, although there too the reaction may have been more one of ignorance and apathy than of open hostility.

US veterans organised a series of welcome home marches in 1986; the idea was taken up in Australia and a Welcome Home committee was formed. There was some backing from the NSW – not national – RSL, and, from some Sydney civilian groups. One of these groups, the Sydney City Council, was divided over the issue, and a veteran on the council accused the 'gay communist faction' of being opposed to the march. Another alderman who had been an anti-conscriptionist countered, 'there has never been an attempt at repatriation for those who chose the path which history has shown was the morally right path.'

The publicity in the months preceding the march employed the images supplied by the VVA – the troubled veteran, the unpopular war, the shame of having served …

Just before Anzac Day 1987, the *Sydney Morning Herald* reported on the visit by two of the organisers from the United States. Under the heading THE WAR IS HISTORY, WELCOME HOME, we learned that. 'For Australians who served in Vietnam the stench of a "dirty war" has been hard to shake. They have always trailed at the end of Army contingents in the Anzac Day parade – as if an afterthought.'

The Vietnam veterans led the 1987 parade, as they had the 1972 parade; and 1987 was a year of much discussion of the place of veterans generally. The editorial in the same newspaper a few days after Anzac Day (it wrongly stated, 'For the first time, Vietnam veterans led the Anzac Day march in Sydney') emphasised the potential of the Welcome Home march as a ritual to signify the reintegration of veterans into the community; but warned against believing that the parade was enough; the parade must be seen

> ... as a new beginning, a sign that we have all begun to gain a sense of historical perspective on the profound conflicts which the Vietnam War aroused.

Perhaps a decent interval does need to elapse before the mourning period is over. Anzac Day did not become a universal public celebration immediately after the end of the First World War; perhaps a public celebration will lay to rest more ghosts when some years of grieving and reflection have intervened.

Certainly the march was an unambiguous success for the veterans – about 22 000 or more of them – who participated. They came from all over Australia, and the march and reunions will no doubt provide them with warm memories for years to come. The city sparkled in the spring sunshine; the crowds cheered enthusiastically; there was a great feeling of goodwill. It was, as the *Sun-Herald* said, 'one of the greatest emotional outpouring Sydney has witnessed in decades.' For those who were unable to attend the march, the ABC transmitted a full coverage live to 288 TV stations.

The march was conceived as an occasion for honouring the soldiers, not the politicians and policies who sent them to fight in Vietnam. A member of the organising committee, Charles Wright, expressed in a letter to the *Weekend Australian* the spirit of reconciliation which motivated at least some of the marchers, accepting the oppositional activities of not only the Labor Party but even the 'wharfies' and postal unions; but not all commentators were so willing to let bygones be bygones.

Some organisers had feared that there might be 'incidents', that some old or new dissidents might seize the opportunity to protest the war yet again. But, on the contrary, the march seemed to provide more of a vehicle for the conservatives to express their conviction that Australia's commitment had been right all along. Thus Greg Sheridan in the *Australian* blamed 'Left-Liberal anti-South Vietnam, pro-Hanoi forces' who were traitors to their own troops. They are the ones who should apologise to our veterans and to the Vietnamese who marched with them last Saturday.' In the same paper on the day of the march. Kenneth Gee explained why, 'It was right for us to be there.'

Many veterans marching in the parade took delight in ignoring Prime Minister Hawke, who was taking the salute on the steps of the Sydney Town Hall. The march's chief organiser. Peter Poulton, interpreted the gesture as a final statement of 'resentment against the Labor Party, which had so strongly opposed the forces' presence in Vietnam.' Presumably these veterans would not have agreed with Senator Jo Vallentine, who remarked that, instead of a parade, these people deserve an apology for being sent to fight America's war.'

CONCLUSION

The cluster of red, white and blue flags in the Welcome Home March made a wonderful display. The symbolism of *pro patria mori* was moving if not overly subtle, the crosses on the flags falling gently to underline the supreme sacrifice made by the unlucky 500. But imagine if there were a march for First

World War veterans, with a flag being raised for each of the 60 000 dead, or for the Second World War and its 25 000. Vietnam was not a war to compare with our other wars: wars are measured by the body count, because they are about killing. Although individual families suffer just as much from the loss of their young man, a country as a whole is only affected by huge losses. The sheer inequality of sacrifice between those who die or are maimed, and those who are unharmed, is chilling.

Vietnam was not exactly what its veterans would have liked. It was unpopular – but not as unpopular as the Americanised version of its history would have them believe. It was unsuccessful – and even more so than many veterans seem to tell themselves.

The 50 000 veterans deal with their memories of the war in many different ways. For some, the full-time veterans, it becomes the defining element in their self-image. Some achieve peace by helping other veterans, a few by revisiting the battlefields in Phước Tuy. Some are damaged beyond cure, others live productive lives even though handicapped either physically or emotionally by their service. And for others, perhaps the largest number of veterans, their experience of the war in Vietnam is simply not an issue. For them, there is nothing to confront.

The Australians went to Vietnam with conservative political attitudes, and the war does not seem to have been a radicalising experience for them overall. There have been no 'veterans against the war' groups as there were in the United States, even though many individuals were no doubt disenchanted with Australian policy. The overall desire of Australian veterans seems to be for 'recognition'. Recognition would place them alongside the veterans of other wars. It involves defining the Australian commitment as being successful. For example, although Long Tan was a small engagement, it has been elevated to symbolise 'the legend of Anzac upheld', and other victories have been found too. The soldiers fought well and professionally, and they perhaps controlled Phước Tuy, even if only briefly.

The veterans want recognition (apart from the practical, welfare aspects) because they feel there has to be a meaning, that their service could not have been pointless. Recognition will validate and rationalise the Australian commitment retrospectively.

The marches and monuments giving tangible form to recognition in the future will, like all symbols and rituals, point to and reaffirm certain community values. Michael Clark has described the American memorials (both marches and monuments) as having 'the tendency to transform individual experience into an icon of communal redemption'. He describes the way the memories of the Vietnam war in the USA have been channelled, culturally, so that they fit the accepted historical pattern of American participation in other wars. The 'cultural apparatus' which has done this has:

> transformed guilt and doubt into duty and pride. And with a triumphant flourish it offered us the spectacle of its most successful creation, the veteran who will fight the next war.

If the same processes are successful in Australia, then the reintegration (or perhaps, more appropriately, the incorporation) of veterans will indeed have been successful.

AFTER THE WAR WAS OVER

Vietnamese in Australia

Nancy Viviani

LOOKING FORWARD, LOOKING BACKSS

There is a major discontinuity in how Australians saw the outcomes of the Vietnam war in 1975 and how those outcomes could be seen in 1989, nearly 15 years on.

Many of those Australians who had opposed the war saw April 1975 as the victory of the forces of liberation, the end of imperialist intervention in post-colonial regional disputes, the triumph of self-determination and a new future in the politics of Asia. The contending view maintained that the loss of Vietnam, which was ascribed to failures of political will in the United States and Australia, was but one episode in the historic struggle between capitalism and communism, between freedom and oppression. For those Australians, the struggle was by no means decided, even though they expected the new Vietnam to be both oppressive at home and expansionist abroad.

What these views shared was a common notion: that the world could be explained in terms of ideological struggle, not only for countries but for people's minds. In the succeeding decade and a half, the clarity of this world view, and thus its basis for deciding what was right and wrong in foreign policy, first dimmed and then began to evaporate.

In 1975 too, Australians did not envisage in any serious way that a refugee outflow of such magnitude would occur at the end of the war, or that it would continue in waves for another 15 years. Their earlier experience of refugees had come from the cataclysm of the division of Europe and its aftermaths of 1956 in Hungary and 1968 in Czechoslovakia. Thus, in Australian consciousness, refugees were principally a European phenomenon. Australians could not see then, in 1975, that they would be expected (because of, or perhaps despite their role in the Vietnam war) to take many Vietnamese refugees; they certainly could not see then how this would change the social and political landscape at home. The progressive abolition of the White Australia policy in the late 1960s and early 1970s had removed what was, for many, an uncomfortable stain on their consciences: but Australia had not envisaged having to put its principles into practice. People saw the Vietnam war as the central problem of their generation and thought that after it the world would return to a semblance of normality.

Looking back from 1989 reveals a different picture. The focus has shifted away from 'them', that is, the outside world, to 'us' and a preoccupation with Australian affairs. The end of the Vietnam war, the recognition of China, and temporary détente, all encouraged Australians to look inward: even a parliamentary committee decided that there were no foreseeable threats to the nation.

As the focus shifted to national affairs, after a time, the arrival and settlement of Vietnamese in Australia began to raise a question of community: 'we' as Australians, and 'they' as Asians, and thus what

An Australian seaman assists a Vietnamese refugee aboard the aircraft carrier HMAS *Melbourne* in 1981.

Vietnamese refugees arrive in Darwin in 1978 after a perilous voyage in a small vessel, under constant threat from pirates.

it means to be an Australian. This interminably difficult question of identity had been resolved in part for the Europeans who came as post-war migrants, by their being 'made' into Australians and by a half-hearted recognition of cultural pluralism. But Vietnamese migration raised the question of race, which somehow was a very different matter. While the issues of race and identity first arose with respect to Vietnamese migration, they were soon overtaken by a wider set of changes.

Other Asians, not refugees, were migrating to Australia in significant numbers in the 1980s. Some were rich business people, others were professionals, others specialised workers from a wide variety of national and ethnic sources. Confusion arose about the label 'Asian', about the middle-classness of these people, about the slipperiness of the idea of ethnicity. These confusions began to polarise attitudes in the community as attention focussed on the racial composition of the migration intake and on contending visions of a multiracial Australia. The Blainey debate of 1984 and the FitzGerald report on immigration of 1988 are the two hinges of the door opening, and then partly closing on these issues in the 1980s.

The angle of the backward-looking telescope needs to widen, however, Australia in the late 1970s and 1980s was a society experiencing the effects of major social change: in its demography, with low natural increase and an aging population; in family structure, with shifts in the status of women; with problems from previous waves of migration; and perceptions of disintegration in traditional social values. Rapid economic change was occur-ring as the economy was opened to international influences; the effects were clear in shifts in the manufacturing industry, the expansion of the services sector and the roller coaster of the balance of trade. The emblems of this open economy were the rise in Japanese tourism and investment,

ABOVE LEFT: Vietnamese refugees rescued in the South China Sea in July 1987 by the French patrol-boat, *La Moqueuse*.

ABOVE RIGHT: During Operation Boat People in 1987, organised by Bernard Kouchner, President of the French organisation Doctors of the World, the speed-boat from a French patrol-boat takes Vietnamese refugees in tow in the South China Sea.

the push to export to Asia and the stress on Asian studies to help gain a share of those expanding markets.

Suddenly it seemed that 'outside' had come inside; Asia was in Australia: its people, its business, its languages and its values. Of course, there is no 'Asia' except as a construct in people's minds: but in Australians' minds, it is a powerful, and contested image.

The uncertainties of rapid social change, the sense of vulnerability to 'them' (for example, Japanese investors or Asians more generally, appearing to do better than Australians), the attacks on multiculturalism and the stressing of community and identity are a powerful social and political brew in this country, one which helps to explain the rise of nationalism (the we-they response) and the way Australia celebrated its symbols in 1988.

In all of this the entry of Vietnamese to Australia in 1975 can be marked as one point of departure, one legacy of the Vietnam war. But what significance can be given to this in the wider story? One way is to look at the histories of the Vietnamese themselves in this country and to try to understand these in the wider context sketched above. There are difficulties in who is telling the story, in whose histories these are and in what can be known, given the lack of important pieces of information. Nevertheless, the story can begin with the Vietnamese leaving Vietnam and arriving in Australia, then go on to what happened to them here.

ABOVE: At a kindergarten run by the Metta Foundation, refugee children learn about Australia.

LEFT: Vietnamese tram conductors demonstrate how immigrants can adapt to typically Australian conditions.

ABOVE: Indochinese refugee children are shown new activities at a Canberra centre.

RIGHT: Vietnamese refugees arrive at Sydney airport to take up residence in Australia.

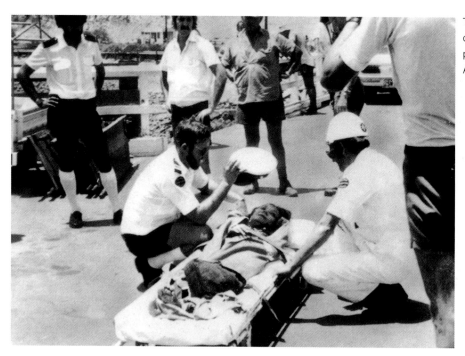

This refugee was one of the 'boat people' who arrived in Australia in 1979.

LEAVING VIETNAM, ARRIVING IN AUSTRALIA

It is noticeable now that new myths are being constructed about the Vietnam war: powerful images in films and TV series and the revision of history in books. For some Australians in middle age. Vietnam remains an icon of political struggle in the past; for others, it is a symbol of betrayal. For many young Australians, Vietnam seems as remote as the Peloponnesian wars. In the original myth making of the 1970s and the revised versions of the 1980s, the Vietnamese themselves remain bit players – voices off stage, as it were. Thus Vietnamese in Australia have a kind of myth-like origin in a past largely discarded by Australians.

The Vietnamese are bound tightly to that past. It is the reason they are here as refugees and, like the Australian veterans of Vietnam, it is the source of the legitimacy of their identity in this country. That legitimacy, because of the nature of the war, has been questioned or ignored by Australians. Those Vietnamese who arrived early were passionate initially in defence of their stances and their right to be heard. They are now mostly weary of this defence and have been forced to accept the marginalisation of their history.

In 1975, however, there was a period when the legitimacy of the refugees and the legitimacy of the Vietnam war were symbiotic issues. The Whitlam government had opposed Australian intervention in the war and had brought home the few remaining Australian troops. The question of whether Australia would take any refugees was very much bound up with attitudes to the war, and 1975 saw a divisive struggle over several issues. The refugee issue first arose before the fall of Saigon. Most Vietnamese and Cambodian students in Australia (there were over 300) sought to remain here permanently rather than return to a war-torn situation and the prospect of communist rule. The Whitlam government did not

Young Vietnamese refugees are welcomed into Australia.

accept these arguments at this time and only extended students' visas to the end of 1975 so as to reassess the situation later. Although the government's formal argument was that it was bound by intergovernmental agreement to return these students, the lack of empathy for their uncertain status was evident early. The issue of the 'baby flights' was a different matter. The Whitlam government was pushed into approving the entry of Vietnamese babies and young children by a well organised and extremely vocal adoption lobby: but this ceased when the Saigon government refused exit visas for these children and a plane carrying them crashed en route to the United States.

More telling was the government's stance on applications to enter Australia from Vietnamese linked in various ways to the previous Australian military and civil presence in Vietnam. The Australian embassy was besieged by such requests in the months before April 1975 but the government in Canberra would not approve these. In the event, at the fall of Saigon on 30 April, only about 30 Vietnamese nationals were permitted to enter Australia: Vietnamese wives of Australians and their children, some nuns (after pressure from the Catholic church hierarchy) and a few Vietnamese with close Australian links. Some others had had their entry approved, but too late for them to be evacuated.

The contrast with the stance of Australia's ally in Vietnam, the United States, was absolute. By various means, amid horrendous scenes of chaos, the Americans managed to evacuate some 130 000 Vietnamese to Guam and the mainland United States.

What can explain the Whitlam government's stance? First, although opinion in Australia had been sharply split over the war, a majority from both those opposed to, and in favour of, Australian intervention were prepared to have some Vietnamese enter as refugees. Jim Cairns, a leader of the anti-war movement and a minister in the Whitlam government, was representative of this view. Indeed, the press, groups such

An immigrant family arrives in Canberra, in 1980.

Shop fronts in Victoria Street, Abbotsford, in 1981.

as the RSL, student groups and many others urged the government to take refugees on humanitarian grounds. But Whitlam, and a group within the ALP, took a different view. They believed that there would be no bloodbath carried out by the new government, that Vietnam should be encouraged to enter relations with other regional countries, and that a new peaceful order should come about in Southeast Asia. To encourage refugee flows would work against these objectives. Whitlam's political foes saw this as plain pro-Hanoi partisanship. If this was the judgement in foreign policy terms, the domestic political calculation was perhaps more powerful. Despite the strength of expressions of opinion favouring the entry of Vietnamese, some in the ALP feared a racist reaction from Australians once Vietnamese arrived. Moreover, a group of rabidly anticommunist refugees conducting campaigns for the liberation of Vietnam was the last thing the Whitlam government wanted. It had suffered electorally from the DLP, supported by anticommunist East European refugees in the past, and would not itself add to that source of political opposition to the ALP. The racist epithet. 'Yellow Croats', summed up this opinion precisely – race and politics thus combined to help exclude Vietnamese.

Despite the public outrage expressed about this stance, the Whitlam government held firm. By the end of 1975, when the government was sacked, only about 1000 Vietnamese had been permitted to enter Australia, under pressure from the United Nations High Commission for Refugees (UNHCR), the Americans and the ASEAN countries (Association of South East Asian Nations). These people, who had left by boat at the fall of Saigon and found themselves in camps in Guam and various Asian countries, were able to enter on the basis of close family or other connections with Australians.

Though the claims of these Vietnamese to refugee status under international law were clear, their acceptance as legitimate refugees in Australia was uncertain, as they were seen by some as representative of a despised government in a hated war. These people, however, were not the Thiệus and the Kỳs who had fled to America. Some of those in Australia had army and government connections, mostly at middle levels: others were business people fearing government takeovers; some had got caught up in the exodus, while others took their chances for a better life in the West.

For the Fraser government in 1976 and for most of 1977, the issue of the entry of Vietnamese refugees retreated from the political agenda. Because there were so few of them in Australia, the problems of their settlement attracted little public attention.

The exodus of April and May 1975 did not end refugee flows from Vietnam. Poor economic conditions, political repression (especially in the form of re-education and imprisonment), and the new government's economic policies, which adversely affected private business, combined to give reason to leave. Increasing numbers of Vietnamese did leave, mostly by boat, fetching up in overcrowded refugee camps, principally in the ASEAN countries. This inflow built up inexorably as Western countries cut, rather than increased, their rates of settlement. Arrivals in camps were double the number of departures.

The ASEAN governments, fearful of a Palestine-type problem, began to press Western countries for increased resettlement rates – with little success – then began to prevent refugee boats from landing. They also encouraged those already on shore to voyage further. It was in this way that small boats carrying Vietnamese refugees began to arrive on the northern shores of Australia, on isolated occasions in 1976, more frequently in 1977 and on an almost daily basis in the months of October and November, before the December federal election.

The reaction to these arrivals was powerful and extreme. Australia's involvement in the war and the

Thai, Vietnamese and Australian employees work together on a Victa mower.

related responsibilities to refugees, which had been argued in 1975, were gone from public discussion. Only a few voices reminded Australians of their responsibility in international law not to turn refugees back. The clamour had ancient roots: the 'yellow peril', a peaceful but threatening armada, the end of splendid isolation. Australia's vulnerability to the other (Asia) were plain. The Vietnamese who arrived were said also not be 'real' refugees, they reportedly carried diseases and included the pimps and prostitutes of Saigon.

Those groups which had supported refugee entry in 1975 remained consistent, but were drowned out by the press, pusillanimous politicians and others.

This episode can be seen as a turning point in several respects. It was a demonstration that fears of Asians and the desire for a White Australia were not far below the surface, despite the generally pro-refugee opinion of the previous years. This revived Australians' concerns about their vulnerability and shifted opinion against refugee entry. It also acted to further deny the legitimacy of the refugees themselves.

The Fraser government sought to meet this danger to its electoral position in two ways. Ironically, but sensibly, it took more refugees from Southeast Asian camps and negotiated a deal in which Indonesia held boats bound for Australia in return for increased rates of resettlement from its camps. The deal held, and boat arrivals, which had permitted some 2000 Vietnamese to enter Australia, tapered off in 1978.

The problem, however, was not yet over. In March 1978, the government of Vietnam closed down private business and a new, much larger exodus from Vietnam began. Ethnic Chinese, who had controlled private business in the south of the country, took to the sea in tens of thousands. The developing conflict in 1978 in relations between Vietnam and China (principally over the problem of Cambodia) added to these refugee flows: a quarter of a million ethnic Chinese both fled, and were pushed, across the border to China. When Vietnam invaded Cambodia at the end of 1978, about 200 000 Cambodians crossed into Thailand. China responded to Vietnam's invasion by a three-week incursion into northern Vietnam, further increasing refugee flows. In 1979 alone, about a quarter of a million refugees from Vietnam, mostly ethnic Chinese, made landfall in the ASEAN countries. The numbers lost at sea were unknown, though some estimated that at least a tenth of those leaving died.

This was an exodus of huge proportions, with about half a million Indochinese people in all seeking refuge in ASEAN countries, none of whom could return home in the near future. This held a particular danger, for the exodus also included an organised trade in people, by means of large freighters, any of which could attempt to land in Australia as they did in the ASEAN countries.

The extremity of this situation forced an international solution in the form of the July 1979 Geneva Conference. The outcome was that Vietnam agreed to a 'moratorium' (another irony) on permitting Vietnamese to leave, in return for an orderly departure migration program (ODP). The Western countries agreed to settle a quarter of a million refugees as quickly as possible, while the ASEAN countries agreed to reinstate 'non refoulement' – that is, allowing refugees to land. Australia's 'fair share' of resettlement places was 15 000 a year for the next few years.

By this means, the crisis period was terminated. Vietnam succeeded in preventing most refugee departure, though agreed migration under the ODP did not generally work well. The majority of Vietnamese in ASEAN camps were resettled, though not the Cambodians camped on the Thai border. In this crisis period from 1979, Australia took a further 60 000 Indochinese refugees to 1982, of whom many were ethnic Chinese. For the entire 1975–86 period. Australia took about 120 000 Indochinese. In 1987 and 1988, the number of Indochinese refugees entering Australia fell to less than 4000 a year, although other Indochinese migrants entered under the family reunion and other programs.

In the period after the 1979 crisis, other issues arose: the problem of 'economic' refugees, the continuing low-level outflow of refugees from Vietnam, the renewed 'settlement fatigue' of Western countries and the unresolved problems of the Cambodians (some 300 000) in Thailand.

In 1988, and more acutely in 1989, the number of Vietnamese landing in Hong Kong and elsewhere in Asia has risen rapidly, posing another crisis for first asylum and resettling countries like Australia.

One legacy of the Vietnam war was yet more war; the Vietnamese occupation of Cambodia, a war with China, yet another massive exodus of refugees and polarisation in the politics of Asia.

The legacy of all this for Australia was a small group of Indochinese (about 130 000 in 1989) most of whom (some 105 000) were from Vietnam. Who these people were depended in part on when they left Vietnam: the early arrivals were principally ethnic Vietnamese, and mostly from the middle and lower classes, linked with the government and armed forces. Those arriving from 1980 to 1983 were mostly ethnic Chinese with their families, who had been in large or petty business in Vietnam; later arrivals saw the pattern established of young men sent out as 'anchors' for future family reunion. Among the Cambodians and Laotians were similar diversities of ethnicity, class and generation.

By 1988 then, this complex story of why people had left Vietnam, and why they were in Australia, had largely faded from public record. Australians, and Vietnamese, were more preoccupied by the tensions of settlement here.

SETTLING IN AUSTRALIA

Australians did not really focus on the settlement of Vietnamese in their community until about 1982. Before this. Vietnamese had been few in number and scattered across the states as a matter of policy. Their settlement problems of getting jobs and learning English had necessitated considerable efforts from the government and private groups. To the extent that they had a public image, it was as objects of compassion, requiring the help of Australians.

By 1982, their numbers had risen rapidly due to the flow-on from the 1979–80 exodus. Concentrations of Vietnamese communities began to appear and expand in Sydney (principally in Fairfield), Melbourne's Richmond and Darra in Brisbane. Vietnamese have been highly mobile across cities, and from rural to city areas, in search of employment, and for family reunion. These areas of Vietnamese settlement changed local environments rapidly, in urbanscape, retail trade and patterns of housing. The effects of the 1982 recession were dramatic for Australians and Vietnamese working in manufacturing industries located in, or near, these areas. Before 1982, many Vietnamese had been able to find jobs fairly easily, now it was much more difficult, with unemployment rife in these areas. The 1981 Census had shown high rates of unemployment among Vietnamese (around 25%), and low average household incomes. This situation was exacerbated by new groups of refugees entering an Australia in recession and with a poor long-term outlook for traditional refugee employment in manufacturing. By the mid 1980s, there were clear signs of social differentiation appearing among Vietnamese. Ethnic differences were clear: ethnic Chinese clustered together, formed their own associations, traded together and, with other Vietnamese and Australians, established a community with tenuous links to ethnic Chinese groups from other countries.

The ethnic Vietnamese also formed their own associations, weak and divided on class and status lines. Middle-class Vietnamese sought to regain a comparable position in Australian society. While some succeeded, the barriers of language and employment proved insuperable to many. Vietnamese were employed largely in blue-collar jobs in factories; women had also entered this segment of the work force in high proportions.

Vietnamese refugees had two major preoccupations: family reunion and economic security. Split families were very common, and reunion with family members could only be achieved by their escape from Vietnam with long waits in ASEAN camps or by the extreme uncertainties of the legal migration process. The preoccupation with family reunion touched almost every family and impeded the psychological process of settlement in Australia.

In their search for economic security, some Vietnamese did very well, especially in business, attracting the envy of both their compatriots and Australians. For the majority of families, however, the experience was either one of both parents working in low-paying jobs to make ends meet, or family welfare dependency. Young men, with little English and little education, fared badly in the employment market and became visible in the streets as 'Saigon cowboys'. Other family groups, dependent chiefly on welfare, also became visible as a distinct group in housing commission ghettoes.

Australian perceptions of this situation had already been shifting; in 1977 with the arrivals by boat in Darwin, in 1982 with the competition for jobs in recession conditions. By 1984, the government had slowed refugee migration, refusing also to take 'economic' refugees, further undermining the position of Vietnamese already here. Concern about 'Asian ghettoes' was already surfacing in the press and on

ABOVE: A Vietnamese proprietor stands by the counter of her fabric shop in Victoria Street, Richmond.

RIGHT: Doctor Dinh Quoc An in his surgery in Richmond, in 1988.

ABOVE: A Vietnamese family arrives at Canberra airport: in 1988, immigration from Southeast Asia was being hotly debated in Australia.

LEFT: A boy of Vietnamese parentage, Thanh Chi Nguyen, was awarded the first scholarship of the South Australian Cricket Association's Junior Cricket Foundation in 1987.

television. Then, in 1984, Professor Geoffrey Blainey encapsulated all these concerns in a speech which brought the issue of Asian migration back onto the top of the political agenda.

Blainey argued that the government had raised the proportion of Asians in the migration program at the expense of the British and that this did not have the support of the Australian people. He argued that Asian settlement was causing concern in the Australian community and would cause social divisions of the kind seen in other countries, for example, Fiji and Malaysia. He argued further that Asian migrants could lack a commitment to democratic values and that this would erode support for the Australian political and social system. Later, he argued that government policies of immigration and multiculturalism were transforming Australia into a 'nation of tribes', which would be vulnerable to influence, and even threat, from countries to our north.

These arguments polarised opinions in the community: the overtones of the reassertion of Anglo-Australian dominance, the question of what it is to be an Australian (with the implication that Asians can never be 'proper' Australians) and the lack of confidence in Australians' capacity to adapt to these kinds of social change, immediately caused a major political row. The quasi-consensus among the Australian elite that had underpinned political support for Asian migration since 1975 had been ruptured with devastating effect.

The Vietnamese communities were shocked and ill-prepared for this. Weak and divided, their response was little heard, though the migrant ethnic community associations rallied to their support. The problem was that, although Blainey was mistaken on several of his facts, public opinion polls did show a majority opposing further increases in all migration, including Asian migration. In addition, while about 30% of the total migration program was coming from Asian countries, only a small proportion of these were Vietnamese. Thus, in one sense. Vietnamese were being made a scapegoat for the new trends in other forms of Asian migration – business and skilled immigration especially.

There were two kinds of response to Blainey. Supporters such as Bruce Ruxton of the RSL and Ron Casey, a radio commentator, pursued the issue in racist terms, provoking a strong reaction from their opponents. Others sought to defuse and put the issue in a different perspective: after all, only 2% of Australians were of Asian origin; Asians were migrating precisely because of Australian democratic values and their desire to participate fully in social life here; Asian migrants (other than Vietnamese) were commonly Christian, middle-class, English-speaking and wanted to contribute to the development of Australia.

In this way, Vietnamese were again seen as separate and different, not only from Australians but also from other Asian migrants, who were part of the great middle class and were dispersing into Australian suburbia. Australians eventually made this class distinction about Vietnamese also: middle-class Vietnamese report Australians' surprise when they learn of their country of origin. Despite this, the image that all Vietnamese live in ghettoes, are on welfare and constitute a permanent underclass, is still fairly well entrenched.

This debate about race had another effect. It now became more respectable to practise racist behaviour, in word and deed, in schools, universities, the workplace, the street and on public transport. Though Australian and Vietnamese local community leaders worked to offset this, racist incidents apparently became more common.

The outcome of this debate, which continued, though less frenetically, in the years from 1985 to 1987, was a further questioning of the legitimacy of the Vietnamese community. The clear message was that they had better become Australian (whatever that might be) as soon as possible. The dice were loaded against this, however, because of the widespread expectation that such assimilation was not possible owing to differences in race, class and culture.

If Blainey had reopened the issue in 1984, the FitzGerald report of 1988 seemed to close it, at least for the time being. The commissioning of the FitzGerald inquiry into immigration rested on an attempt by the government to have Australians see migration as an instrument of economic policy rather than principally as a means of family reunion. The report itself tackled some contentious issues. It argued for a larger Australian population on economic grounds and an expanded migration program which it said would have ongoing economic benefits in terms of the size of the domestic market and upgrading of work-related skills. It argued for skills to be the dominant criterion for migrant entry, rejecting outright any notion of discrimination by race or country of origin. If the effect of a skill-dominated migration program was increased migration from Asia, then this was an acceptable outcome. The report also questioned the

A young Vietnamese woman works on the production line at the Nissan Motor Manufacturing Company in Victoria.

prominence of multicultural policies, reporting these as divisive in the community, and argued for an approach which stressed community cohesion.

Not surprisingly, these recommendations attracted criticism from a variety of sources, not least from ethnic groups concerned about family migration and the government's commitment to multicultural policies. Yet, Stephen FitzGerald had grasped the complexity of the race, culture and class concerns of Australians. By a commitment to social and cultural cohesion, he had undercut one concern voiced by Blainey and his followers. The uncompromising stance on race – that is, non-discriminatory entry – posed a challenge to opponents. The then Leader of the Opposition, John Howard, said in 1988 that when in government he would reassess the proportion of Asians in the total migration program, implying that he would reduce their numbers. This provoked such an antagonistic reaction from some in his party, and more broadly in the community, that the issue was allowed to subside. While the Labor Government held firm in 1989 to a non-discriminatory migration policy, it saw itself as holding the high moral ground. For the Opposition, by contrast, the electoral advantage from a discriminatory policy was uncertain. This was demonstrated in part in 1989 by Andrew Peacock when he unseated Howard as Leader of the Opposition: his first statement stressed adherence to a non-discriminatory policy on immigration, and a return to bipartisanship on this issue.

The FitzGerald report held no good news for Vietnamese, since it recommended a disengagement

Refugee children in a kindergarten painting group near Bondi Beach in Sydney.

from Indochinese refugee settlement. Although this does not seem to have become part of government policy, the general decline in the refugee part of the immigration program makes family reunion difficult.

These debates of 1984 and 1988 placed Vietnamese in Australia in an awkward position. They were signs of their non-acceptance by many Australians, an indication that other migrant groups, including other Asians, were to be preferred for their anticipated economic contribution to Australia and that somehow their presence and their settlement difficulties were the main 'Asian problem' in Australia. In this connection, business people from Hong Kong and professionals from Malaysia have been heard to argue for a cut in refugee entry, so as to better secure their middle-class future in Australia.

The debates of the 1980s ignored that aspect of Australian values which speaks of concern for the underdog, for those who suffer through no real fault of their own. Those who spoke out in the 1970s have been largely silent on this. Such opinions are, of course, currently unfashionable in an age of economic rationalism. But it is worth remembering that many Vietnamese are here involuntarily as an outcome of a war in which Australia was involved but which has been largely forgotten by Australians. The implication is that Australians have a responsibility for the Vietnamese, a responsibility that does not attach to other migrants who chose to settle in Australia. Refugeehood does, or should, make a difference. Given this, it is important to look more closely at the Vietnamese community in Australia, to see their problems and their possibilities in a wider context.

AUSTRALIAN VIETNAMESE TODAY

The Vietnamese in Australia are a small group, rather too small to hang such large myths on. The total Indochinese population in 1989 (that is, those born in Indochina) was 132 000 and Vietnamese made up some 105 000 of these – a group about the same size as the Dutch-born, Germans, Poles, and a little larger than the Lebanese-born. This Vietnamese group is young, relative both to Australians and to more settled migrant groups; the peak of its past migration was reached in the early 1980s and the family reunion phase is now also in a plateau stage. Barring another political or economic upheaval in Indochina, it will probably stay roughly the same relative size, because the Australian-born children of these Vietnamese (around 12 000) are of course, Australian and fertility patterns among Vietnamese in Australia appear to resemble those of the host population (that it, the two-child family is common). The majority of Vietnamese live in Sydney and Melbourne, though there are significant groups in Brisbane and Adelaide, with smaller groups in Perth and Darwin.

Within the four major cities there are areas of ethnic concentration of those born in Vietnam. Yet the data from the 1981 and 1986 censuses show that these patterns of spatial location are dynamic rather than static. First, the areas of major concentration have shifted: in some areas there has been a decline in the proportion of Vietnamese, while in others, there has been an increase. This may be largely an outcome of availability of housing and employment. Second, there is significant movement both in and out of these areas: newcomers head for the ethnic group, while some older residents find the means to move to better housing in other locations. What has appeared to be the solidification of a permanent ghetto is as much a transit point as a long term location. But this process, which we have seen before with other migrant groups, has its limits. English and jobs help social mobility but the unemployed, the non-English speakers, the widowed and divorced, the elderly and the young without families, cannot move. Unemployment rates for Vietnamese at around 35%, according to the 1986 census, had worsened since 1981. Lebanese had similar rates. It seems that not only does the continuing replenishment of the birthplace group keep these rates high but there is a core of people who cannot be employed. The effect of this is that average incomes for Vietnamese, like some other Asian groups, are somewhat lower than those for Australian-born, other established migrant groups and, of course, to some other Asian, predominantly middle-class, migrant groups.

It is really only in terms of birthplace that we can see Vietnamese as a group. In social terms, they are very diverse. Among the Vietnam-born, over 30% of whom are ethnic Chinese, the social division between them and the ethnic Vietnamese that was evident in Vietnam, persists in Australia. Class differences within both the ethnic Chinese and ethnic Vietnamese communities are now clearly evident in income, occupation, choice of housing, and the education of children. Class divisions in Australia based on income are not necessarily the basis for status within the Vietnamese communities. The division between the northerners and the southerners, which was so evident in the early arrivals, has lost much of its significance. The religious difference among Vietnamese, however, with the strong representation of Catholics among a majority of Buddhists, is still quite apparent. In some senses, being Catholic has helped in settlement, but being middle class may have conferred greater advantages.

Generation divisions among the Vietnamese are important both within the community and families. Within the Vietnamese community, the status that is owed to the elderly is not reinforced by the wider Australian community. The behaviour of many young men without families also cuts across Vietnamese norms. Within families, the usual cultural tensions between Australian and Vietnamese ways among the young are exacerbated because of the low status of Vietnamese in the wider Australian community.

Some Vietnamese look inward to their community, others look outward. Most Vietnamese take up citizenship as soon as they are able. In political attitudes, the anticommunist and conservative bent of the early arrivals has been tempered somewhat. Indications of voting patterns show Vietnamese voting rather like other Australians. They have not generally been as active in party organisations as the Eastern Europeans who migrated before them, but support several Vietnamese and Chinese language newspapers which express vigorous political viewpoints.

Patterns of education among Vietnamese show some interesting features. There is heavy emphasis, especially by middle-class parents, on their children's achievement so as to regain family status. This spills over into some preference for the Catholic education system, which even Buddhist Vietnamese see as maintaining desirable disciplinary standards. Most Vietnamese children are highly motivated and well socialised. But for those who came as unaccompanied minors, or with incomplete families, social mobility through education is very difficult.

Vietnamese families and communities stress reinforcement of cultural values. Part of this is reflected in children's attitudes to Vietnam: they are taught to revere the country and oppose the government. Generally, Vietnamese attitudes to Vietnam are ambivalent. Many Vietnamese in Australia support family members in Vietnam financially, and would like to return (at the least for a visit) were there not a communist government in power. Some have returned for a visit and to do business, but generally, the government there is hated and feared. After all, these Vietnamese either had to escape under extreme conditions, or felt forced to leave their homeland. While there are pragmatists among the Vietnamese, the exodus experience is still very close for most.

It is chiefly in this respect that Vietnamese are different from most other migrant groups. They have a history which is a central part of their identity in this country. Like the Eastern Europeans before them, they keep this history alive in their community, while Australians largely forget it.

What then is the significance of the Vietnamese in these wider histories? Though a small group in Australia, they took part in one of the largest movements of peoples in post-1945 history and represent the effects of the era of polarisation in Southeast Asia. That era may be fading but the world views that underpinned it are by no means gone.

In Australian history, the Vietnamese have a special place. They were the first to test whether the humanitarianism of Australians could extend across racial boundaries and whether the White Australia policy was really dead. As Charles Price has put it, while the great white walls are demolished, their foundations remain in good order in Australia.

The question of whether Australians had some special responsibility to Vietnamese refugees because of our involvement in the war has always been contentious. It is in this precise sense that the Vietnamese in Australia are the legacy of that war. Yet it is only right to recognise that while Australians had a choice about sending troops to Vietnam, the Vietnamese in Australia have had very little choice in being here. Thus it remains crucially important to resolve the problems of the settlement of Vietnamese in this country, not simply for their sakes, but as a sign of Australians' capacity to surmount their own history.

CONCLUSION

Australia's involvement in the Vietnam war was inspired by quite prosaic motives: essentially, to protect 'white' – that is, European – Australia by engaging American power to maintain Western dominance over Asia. Vietnam was a symbolic demonstration of America's willingness and ability to triumph over revolution worldwide and it was merely one part of a broader pattern of post-1945 American policies designed, in the words of President Truman, to 'run the world in the way the world ought to be run.' 'The only thing that made the Vietnam war unique for the United States,' says American historian Gabriel Kolko, 'was that it lost it completely.'

None of this is to suggest that American society was evil, or inherently worse than any other. Indeed, it was not. But in the post-1945 years it suffered, as did the world (especially Indochina), from its excess of power; just as Eastern Europe did from an excess of Soviet power. America was seeking to maintain its power over a sphere of interest, like all great powers before it, but over a far larger area – the whole world. The cost of asserting and maintaining its hegemony over much of the globe proved beyond even America's vast resources after 1945. The massive financial burden imposed by Vietnam (plus the Great Society program) was the last straw.

The decline in American global political and economic hegemony coincided with growing competition from an economically integrated Europe and a politically restive third world. Tensions in American society arising from the civil rights and anti-war movements (plus the imminent disintegration of the American army in Vietnam), encouraged but did not determine this process. In order to protect other international and domestic priorities, Washington decided to withdraw from Vietnam, cutting its losses and foregoing its objective of achieving a secure, separate southern Vietnam. 'Vietnamisation' was merely a cosmetic device to disguise this reality. Instead of seeking military victory, Washington embarked on a less costly alternative – diplomatic strategy. Notably, this meant acceptance of the fact of a communist China – indeed, a closer diplomatic relationship with it as a basis for a compromise settlement in Asia – and disarmament talks with the Soviet Union. The Cold War, in Asia at least, was over. Thereafter, once Vietnam lost its significance for America, the basis for close cooperation with Australia was gone.

For some time the Australian government failed to realise the winds of change. It had never made more than a token commitment to Vietnam, except in the rhetorical sense, so involvement imposed no great strain. Australia could have kept going forever, or at least as long as the Americans remained: the protest movement notwithstanding. Moreover, Southeast Asia remained Canberra's highest priority but not Washington's. Australia's leaders did not seem to sense the growing mood of futility in Washington. Ultimately, however, once America decided to withdraw, Australia had to follow suit, even though the professed objective of the original commitment (the security of the RVN) had not been achieved. The last Australian battalion departed Vietnam in December 1971. Australia withdrew from Vietnam, while still under a Liberal government, essentially because of profound changes in global politics, not because of the opposition at home. The withdrawal of the few Australians remaining in the Training Team, following the election of the Whitlam government in December 1972, was merely a symbolic gesture, ensuring only that Labor would share the credit and the blame for Australia's withdrawal.

Thus, it was the original architects of American and Australian involvement in Vietnam who orchestrated withdrawal and abandonment of their Saigon allies. Following successful negotiations with the DRV in October 1972, underlined by 40 000 tons of explosives dropped on DRV cities over eleven days, the Paris peace agreements were signed in January. The last American forces, except for 8500 civic action advisers, withdrew by March. With the Americans gone, General Thiệu reverted to form, abolishing village elections. Saigon had failed over 20 years, despite massive American backing, to build itself as a viable alternative to the revolutionary forces. The PLAF, however, was no longer strong enough to win by itself, being gravely weakened by combat losses from years of warfare, especially during the Tet Offensive, and the murderous 'Phoenix' program. Moreover, the ARVN was still better equipped and armed. So the *coup de grâce* was applied by the armour-led columns of the PAVN in early 1975. Denied by Congress the American air support which had saved it in 1972, the ARVN collapsed like a pack of cards. On 30 April, as Soviet-built tanks crashed through the gates of Independence Palace. General Minh announced the RVN's unconditional surrender. After nearly 30 years, Vietnam was reunited, although Hồ did not live to see the final realisation of his dream.

Defeat in Vietnam traumatised American society, including both 'doves' and 'hawks'. Revelations over Vietnam, notably the Pentagon Papers, were exacerbated by the exposure of 'Watergate', past and continuing activities of the CIA (including the overthrow of Chile's elected government in 1973), and other unsavoury aspects of the imperial 'presidency'. Accordingly, the Vietnam years helped unleash widespread criticism and questioning of established institutions, and of social practices and mores.

Australia was somewhat different. A token Australian involvement produced only a token reaction to defeat. Lacking the crusading idealism which underpinned American involvement, despite their extreme rhetoric at the time, supporters of Australia's Vietnam involvement not only were not traumatised by defeat, but either ignored it (as in 1975) or even denied it (as the RSL did more recently). During or since the war, no prominent Australian leader has ever expressed regret, moral or otherwise, over the commitment. The careers and reputations of the politicians, diplomats and senior officers who orchestrated Australia's involvement in Vietnam have not suffered like those of their American counterparts. One reason is that, in one sense, defeat in Vietnam did not prejudice the original objective of Australia's involvement. By the 1970s, the great threat, Indonesia, was under the control of its pro-Western military. With Asia 'stabilised' and relations with China burgeoning. American military involvement in Vietnam was no longer vital. A few still clung to old beliefs, however. Some of the right in Australia seized the occasion of Saigon's 'fall' to attack the Labor government, implying it had betrayed the West, and undoubtedly paranoia against it was heightened in financial, defence and security circles at home and abroad. The Whitlam government, although it contributed to its own defeat, was one of the last victims of the Cold War.

Although the final result in Vietnam inspired little reflection in 1975, it would be very wrong to deny the enormous impact that the Vietnam conflict, both home and abroad, had on Australian society. Its Shockwaves travelled far: questioning and criticism of other fundamental aspects of domestic society led to questioning and criticism of our military commitment, and vice versa. Criticism of official portrayals of Vietnam contributed greatly to the breakdown of the post-1945 anti-communist consensus, which in turn, broke down the wider consensus, that of the superiority of Western society, which lay behind it. Racism, sexism and consumerism are far from unique to Western imperialism: nevertheless they were an integral part of the authority structures and ideology in Australia. Challenges to them contributed to growing opposition to the war. Moreover, the war experience itself contributed to these wider processes of change. A belief in the ultimate virtue of the state lies at the core of anti-radical ideology; for many, the state had proven itself lacking in virtue over Vietnam.

Although these processes of change were often inspired and encouraged by parallel developments in other countries, notably (and perhaps ironically) the United States, they also had an independent life in Australia. Their continued existence, even after the commitment ended, constitutes one of the major legacies of the war for Australia. Many of these processes of change became solidified before, during and after the commitment to Vietnam. Many were implemented by Liberal governments, although it was the Whitlam government which really set free the forces of reform. For many voters it was domestic reform which mobilised their support – but Vietnam also held a central place as a symbolic national liberation struggle inspiring other struggles for liberation.

The struggle in Vietnam was part of the assertion of nationalist independence from European imperialism. This led, in turn, to the assertion of independence from the Cold War blocs created by American and Soviet power. In Australia, too, there was a growing mood of discontent with our subordination to British and American influence. The ties that bound Australia to Britain were steadily being loosened; the Labor government even asserted greater independence from Washington – violently attacking Nixon's bombing of Vietnam, raising doubts over the continuance of US bases in Australia and suggesting a break from US/British financial pre-eminence here – until it learnt the limits of freedom.

Although Australia remained firmly locked in the Western camp, America's defeat and withdrawal from Indochina, combined with Britain's decline, forced greater self-reliance on Australia in defence and foreign policy. 'Continental defence' replaced 'forward defence'. Australia had to chart a different course, developing its own policies towards its neighbours. It had to accept that its main effective relations were with Asian nations, notwithstanding the great symbolic importance of the American alliance. Notably, immigration laws were relaxed to allow entry of non-Europeans which, although it did not produce any great immediate racial changes in the migrant intake, was of great symbolic importance. A break was made with the white-supremacist South African and Rhodesian regimes. Since then, the flow of refugees from Indochina has forced Australians to re-examine the notion of preserving an essentially white Australia and has added new meaning to an old platitude – 'Australia, a part of Asia'.

'National' groups under colonial domination were not the only peoples seeking liberation at this time. Sub-national groups, the Indians in North America, the French in Canada and of course the Aboriginal people in Australia, all claimed rights of equality if not independence in this period. In the 1960s, the policy of assimilation faced mounting criticism both from liberal whites and increasingly politicised Aboriginal people. Indeed, the significant advances in the Aboriginal people's position in this period must be attributed not only to progressive governments but also to the growing activism of Aboriginal people themselves and the wish for self-determination.

Racism was not the only feature of traditional structures of authority and power in Australia under challenge. The traditional gender structure was another. The women's movement was revitalised through its experience in the anti-war movement, not just through criticism of the traditional patriarchal structures which had produced Vietnam, but also through criticism of the male domination of the anti-war movement itself. For many women, the war was the first time they were involved in political activity, certainly in a public way, often defying not only convention but also their peers, husbands and perhaps even their sons.

The emergence of youth as a new social category, produced a generation permeated with the liberal values of the marketplace but disillusioned with their parents and the values they expressed. Some young people adopted surfing, hippiedom and motorcycle gangs. Many others were politicised and radicalised by the Vietnam war and conscription. After that, some of this radical energy was channelled into other related political activities, for example, prison reform, welfare, women's or gay rights. Aboriginal issues or environmental concerns. Conservative elements in Australia would speak ruefully of having lost a generation over Vietnam.

The right was not alone in losing its sense of certainty after Vietnam. The broad coalition of liberal and left forces which united in opposition to Vietnam did not maintain its cohesion for long. The Soviet invasion of Czechoslovakia, and later Afghanistan, showed that imperialism was not confined to the West: the emergence of Idi Amin in Uganda and Colonel Gadaffi in Libya, as well as numerous African regimes, made people realise that domestic oppression was not confined either to colonial or Western-sponsored regimes. In Indochina, as Cambodia attacked Vietnam, prompting a Vietnamese counter-invasion, and China attacked Vietnam in 1979, it became difficult for many on the left to retain the certainty they had felt in previous years. The disillusionment experienced in these years, plus a deteriorating economic situation encouraging a more conservative political climate and criticism of the welfare state led to the emergence of the loose coalition known as the new right.

With the urging of the new right, there have been partial attempts in Australia, as elsewhere, to roll back some of the gains by Aboriginal people, women, gays, migrants, conservationists and others in Australian society. These have been only partially successful. The new right has a considerable constituency in terms of numbers and influence but has failed so far to win decisive support because the new middle class in particular (whatever its party allegiance), remains politically liberal. Even the conservative parties realise this and do not adopt the whole new right agenda, thereby accepting some of the gains made since Vietnam. The processes unleashed during the Vietnam years cannot be reversed. It is said that you cannot step into the same stream twice; try as some might. Australians cannot return to the Australia of the pre-Vietnam days.

This book stands as part of the record of an era which was divisive, disturbing and, for many Australians, deeply painful. It was a complex time, dominated by processes of change which only now, two decades later, are beginning to receive close evaluation.

Some of the research undertaken by authors in this volume has never been published before: new facts will continue to come to light in this way, adding to our understanding of what the Vietnam war really meant to Australians, at home and on the battlefields.

Reviewing the story of how Australia became involved, following the conflict from the first soldiers' arrival until the final withdrawal, tracing the patterns of confrontation at home, assessing the legacy of the war, for the returned servicemen and the refugees – these many views of one important period in the life of Australia add up to a larger picture, which deserves attention.

A nation's view of its past influences the policies of the present and future. Australia's Vietnam is no exception: the battles there are in the past, but the conflict continues today over our perception of the war. It is impossible not to mourn the sacrifices that were made during the war in Vietnam; it is equally important, looking back soberly, to perceive what the country may have gained from those divisive years.

NOTES

AUSTRALIA'S ROAD TO VIETNAM

East Wind prevails over West Wind Most of this chapter is my original work although I am indebted for inspiration for the ideas that lay behind my compilation of facts to the remarkable work by Kees van der Pijl, *The Making of an Atlantic Ruling Class*. London, 1984, in particular Chapters 6 and 7. The identification and translation of the quote from *Le Figaro*. I owe to Greg Lockhart. For the impact of these world changes on Australian policies. I drew upon Gregory Pemberton. *All the Way: Australia's Road to Vietnam*. Sydney, 1987. Chapters 2, 3 and 4. The quote, 'strategically, it was a defensive age even if the tactics were often aggressive', is from D. Calleo, *The Atlantic Fantasy: The U.S., NATO and Europe*. Baltimore/London, 1970, p. 45. The quote on 'golf' and the Eisenhower years comes from David Halberstam, *The Best and the Brightest*. New York, 1972. The quotes on Rostow are taken from van der Pijl, p. 196. Howard Beale's words on the Americans are from his book *This Inch of Time*. Melbourne, 1977, pp. 165–6.

For the early story of Australia's policy towards Vietnam see *All the Way*.

'Aggression from the North' The main official document setting out this central argument is the United States Department of State, Aggression from the North: *The Record of North Vietnam's Campaign to Conquer South Viet-Nam*, Washington, February 1965,

For the quote authentic Vietnamese nationalist government, see *Foreign Relations of the United States (FRUS)*, State Department. Washington D C., 1952–54, Vol. XVI, pp. 892–4: up to 'in case of bankruptcy... bankers have right to organize a receivership' see *FRUS*, 1952–54. Vol. XIII, pp. 1576–7: for nothing impresses him as much as gold' see *FRUS*, 1952–54. Vol. XIII, pp. 1616–18. For quote Hồ Chí Minh is the only Viet who enjoys any measure of national prestige' in the box on Diệm, see *FRUS*, 1951, vi, p. 385. For quote beginning favorably impressed' see *FRUS*, 1952–54, Vol. XIII, pp. 1608–9. For quote messiah without a message' and thereafter see *FRUS*, 1952–54, Vol. XIII, pp. 1616–18.

The reference to Diệm's regime as 'dictatorial, repressive and unpopular', is quoted from primary sources in *All the Way*, p. 164. The can of snakes' quote is from J.K. Galbraith, *Ambassador's Journal*. Boston, 1967, pp. 266–7.

For the arguments over the origins and nature of the second Indochina conflict', see Carlyle A. Thayer, The Origins of the National Front for the Liberation of South Viet-Nam, unpublished doctoral thesis. Australian National University. 1977 (to be published in 1989). See also Kolko, *Vietnam: Anatomy of a War 1940–1975*, especially Chapters 7 and 8. George McT, Kahin, *Intervention. How America Became Involved in Vietnam*. New York. 1986. Chapters III–VI, For a representative and contemporary work of the 'solely southern insurgency' school see George McT. Kahin and John Lewis, *The United States in Vietnam*, New York, 1967.

Changing Horses For the story of Australia's involvement see *All the Way*, especially Chapters 4–11. Also useful though less detailed are Glen St. John Barclay, *A Very Small Insurance Policy: The Politics of Australian Involvement in Vietnam. 1954–1967*. St Lucia. 1988 and *Friends in High Places*. Oxford, 1985; Michael Sexton. *War for the Asking*. Melbourne, 1981.

The leading detailed works on American (including allied) involvement in Vietnam are, in order of importance: Kahin, *Intervention;* George C. Herring, *America's Longest War: The United States and Vietnam 1950–1975*, 2nd ed., Philadelphia, 1986; Congressional Research Service, Library of Congress, *The U.S. Government and the Vietnam War: Executive and Legislative Roles and Relationships,* Parts 1 & 2, 1945–1964, are very good; dated but still useful is Leslie Gelb and Richard K. Betts, *The Irony of Vietnam, The* System *Worked,* Washington, 1979; Guenter Lewey, *America in Vietnam*, Oxford, 1978; a valuable short overview is William S. Turley, *The Second Indochina War: A Short Political and Military History 1954–1975,* Boulder, Colorado, 1986; Kolko, *Vietnam: Anatomy of a War 1940–1975* (especially Parts 2–6, provides a broad, conceptual understanding of all the detail); Stanley Karnow, *Vietnam, A History*, New York, 1986 (highly readable and wide-ranging but is only superficial in analysis); see also Michael Maclear, *Vietnam: The Ten Thousand Day War,* London, 1988; R.B. Smith. *An International History of the Vietnam War, Vols. 1 & 2, Revolution versus Containment, 1955–61*, New York, 1983 & 1986 (promises more than it delivers).

All the Way See the relevant parts of the works cited above. On the Tonkin Gulf Incident, Kahin. *Intervention*, pp. 219–26 is excellent. See also Congressional Research Service. Library of Congress. The U.S. Government and the Vietnam War: Executive and Legislative Roles *and Relationships*. Part 2. 1961–1964. Washington D.C., 1985, pp. 209–309. For the important American decisions of 1965 see Larry Berman. *Planning a Tragedy: The Americanization of the War in Vietnam*. New York, 1982.

INTO BATTLE

Dirt Boys' Stuff The main sources are as follows. Casey, R.G. Diaries, Manuscript Collection, National Library of Australia. MS 6150, Box 15, Vol. 12 for quotes relating to 'dirt boys' stuff'.

Lieutenant-General S.G. Savige, *Tactical and Administrative Doctrine for Jungle Warfare,* HQ 2 Aust Corps (AIF), 20 January 1945, which leaves no doubt about the Japanese influence on Australian tactical thinking. *The Australian Army Journal.* Sir William Slim, *Defeat Into Victory,* London: Cassell, 1956 on Japanese tactics and 'special Forces' in Burma. Charles Cruickshank, *SOE in the Far East,* Oxford University Press, 1983. For information on General Cawthorne see *Who's Who.* F. Spencer Chapman, *The Jungle is Neutral.* London: Chatto and Windus, 1949.

Numerous sources mention Serong's connection with the CIA and Ian McNeill, *The Team: Australian Army Advisers in Vietnam 1962–1972,* The Australian War Memorial, Canberra, 1984, on Serong in Burma. McNeill also on Warfe. R.J. Breen, *First to Fight – Australian Diggers, NZ Kiwis and US Paratroopers in Vietnam 1965–66,* Sydney: Allen and Unwin, 1988, for Essex-Clark, Barry Petersen with John Cribbin, *Tiger Men,* Melbourne: Macmillan, 1988, for ASIS sponsored Special Forces Training. D.M. Horner, *Australian Higher Command in the Vietnam War,* The Strategic and Defence Studies Centre, Australian National University, 1986, p. 1 for 'offshoot' of Malaya.

Frank Frost, *Australia's War in Vietnam,* Allen and Unwin, 1987 for counterinsurgency doctrine and analysis of *The Division in Battle, Pamphlet No. 11, Counter Revolutionary Warfare.*

You will tell the Soldiers Nothing The main sources are as follows, Horner, *Australian Higher Command,* p. 76, for Chiefs of Staff Directive. Breen, *First To Fight,* is the main source for all aspects of 1 RAR's experience, and p. 106 for the prostitute's assistance to 105 Field Battery. 5 RAR's difficulties with information and logistics are based on interviews with officers from the battalion. The other major source for 5 RAR's experience is Robert J. O'Neill, *Vietnam Task: The 5th Battalion The Royal Australian Regiment. 1966/67.* Melbourne: Cassell, 1968. The main source for 6 RAR's experience is Terry Burstall, *The Soldiers' Story,* University of Queensland Press, 1986.

On the location of the Task Force Base see Homer, *Australian Higher Command.* Peter G. Bourne's observation is quoted in Peter King ed., *Australia's Vietnam,* Sydney: Allen and Unwin, 1983, p. 83 in Jane Ross's essay. On principal tasks for the Australian Task Force see Homer, *Australian High Command,* pp. 28 and 79. On tasks, unclear aim, and unworkable command structure see Frost, *Australia's War in Vietnam.*

The basic sources on the Vietnamese side are Ban Chấp hành Đảng bộ Đảng Cong San Viet Nam Huyen Long Dat, *Lich Sự Dau Tranh Cach Mane của Huyen Long Dat So Thao* [Executive Committee of the Party Cell of the Communist Party of Vietnam in Long Dat District, *History of the Revolutionary Struggle on Long Dat District],* Dong Nai Publishing, House. 1986; Ban Chấp hành Đảng bộ Đảng Cong San Viet Nam Tinh Dong Nai, *Dong Nai 30 Nam Chien Tranh Giai Phong So Thao* (Executive Committee of the Party Cell of the Communist Party of Vietnam in Dong Nai Province, *A Draft History of Dong Nai's 30 Year War of Liberation],* Dong Nai Publishing House, 1986, p. 209 deals with the formation of D445. Pearson's quote comes from Frost, *Australia's War,* p. 65.

The information for 'the Big Picture' is based on William S. Thurley, *The Second Indochina War,* New York, 1980; Chapter 4.

Aimless Operations The main sources are as follows, Breen, *First to Fight,* for all 1 RAR actions; p. 46 for the Clive Williams quote; p. 57 for American casualties on 6 July. W.C. Westmoreland, *A Soldier Reports,* New York: Double Day, 1976, p. 258 for quote on Australian professionalism. Quote on people squatting in the fields comes from an interview with one of the 1 RAR officers. For American views of Australians, Breen, *First to Fight* is the best source.

Dong Nai, pp. 220–21 for operation At Zi Hoc (Hardihood); p. 220 for quotes on losses to American Army and presence of Australians and New Zealanders; p. 221 for quote on NZ artillery.

Dong Nai, p. 223 for quotes on Vietnamese intentions at the Battle for Long Tan; pp. 223–34 contains the 13-line reference. The main Australian sources on Long Tan are Burstall, *The Soldiers' Story;* Lex McAulay, *The Battle of Long Tan,* Melbourne: Hutchinson, 1986. *Dong Nai,* p. 224 for grossly exaggerated Vietnamese claims over Australian casualties.

Dong Nai, p. 227 for 'guerrilla conference' in October. Interviews with 5 RAR officers and O'Neill, *Vietnam Task,* for Cordon and Search operations. Burstall, *The Soldiers' Story,* p. 14 for Drinkwater quote. O'Neill, *Vietnam Task,* p. 182 for quote on Warr's questioning of the aim; pp. 224–25 for mine ambush of 21 February 1967.

For Australian views of the minefield see O'Neill, *Vietnam Task,* Chapter 16; Frost, *Australia's War,* Index; Homer, *Australian Higher Command,* pp. 29–30. For Vietnamese views of the minefield see *Dong Nai,* pp. 231–36; *Long Dat,* pp. 131–142. *Long Dat,* pp. 133–34 quote on initial effects of minefield; p. 136–38 on the lifting of the first mines, courses, and quote on relaying the mines to protect the Minh Dam base *Dong Nai*, p. 235 on the 'emulation movement' and quote on transforming the minefield into a Vietnamese base for hiding supplies. Homer, *Australian Higher Command*, p. 29 quotes the Task Force Commander on casualties 'from our own mines'.

Homer, *Australian Higher Command*, p. 20 for quote about Mackay's view of Saigon regime; p. 31 for Vincent's thoughts on Wilton's rejection of the American proposal on advisory functions.

CONSCRIPTION AND DISSENT

Early Anti-war Dissent Sources on early anti-war dissent in Australia are Malcolm Saunders and Ralph Summy. *The Australian Peace Movement: A Short History,* Peace Research Centre, Australian National University, Canberra 1986; Alan D. Gilbert and Ann-Mari Jordens, 'traditions of Dissent', in M. McKernan and M. Browne, *Australia Two Centuries of War and Peace,* Australian War Memorial in association with Allen and Unwin Australia, 1988; Ann Mari Jordens, 'Against the tide: the growth and decline of a liberal anti-war movement in Australia, 1905–1918'. *Historical Studies,* vol. 22 no. 88, April 1987; Ann Mari Jordens, 'Anti-war organizations in a society at war, 1914–18', *Journal of Australian Studies* (forthcoming); records of the Association for International Cooperation and Disarmament, boxes 4, 5 and 31, Mitchell Library manuscripts (ML MSS) 4342.

Conscription Proceedings of the January 1964 summer school of the Australian Institute of Political Science were published that year as *Australian Defence and Foreign Policy,* Angus and Robertson, Sydney. All information on public opinion in this chapter derives from Morgan Gallup Polls. For a detailed account of the relevance of the West New Guinea dispute to Australia's Vietnam involvement see Gregory Pemberton, *All the Way, Australia's Road to Vietnam,* Allen and Unwin, Sydney 1987, pp. 70–106.

Conscription for Overseas Service – Initial Acceptance The quotation by Paul Hasluck is from his article, 'Australia and Southeast Asia', *Foreign Affairs* (N.Y.) vol. 43, no. 1, October 1964, p. 57. For indications that overseas service meant action against Indonesia (text p. 8) see: *SMH,* 3, 8 (editorial), 12 (letter to editor), 13 (editorial) November 1964, F. Alexander, Problems in Australian Foreign policy, *Australian Journal of Politics and History,* vol. 7, April 1965, p. 1.

Statistics on army expenditure on recruitment activities are to be found in CPD vol. H of R 69, 19 August 1970, p. 215. Statistics of numbers and percentages of volunteers rejected by the Army 1959–69 were given in Parliament, CPD vol. H of R 69, 19 August 1970, p. 214.

For a detailed account of the debate over the conscription of Aborigines see Ann Mari Jordens, 'An administrative nightmare: Aboriginal conscription 1965–72', *Aboriginal History,* Volume 13, 1988. All statistics quoted in this chapter relating to the working of the National Service scheme are taken from Department of Labour and National Service press releases and from Commonwealth Parliamentary Debates 1965–72.

How Conscription worked A detailed account of the requirements of the conscription scheme to 1968 is given by Roy Forward in, 'Conscription, 1954–68', in Roy Forward and Bob Reece (eds), *Conscription in Australia,* University of Queensland Press 1968, pp. 79–142. For analyses of the US draft system see Stephen E. Fienberg, 'Randomization and Social Affairs: The 1970 Draft Lottery', *Science* vol. 171, 22 January 1971, pp. 225–61; John Whitely Chambers II, *To Raise an Army The Draft Comes to Modern America,* Macmillan, New York, 1987; J. Griffiths, *The Draft Law,* Graham R. Hodges, New York, 1969; Lawrence M. Baskir and William A. Strauss, *Chance and Circumstance. The Draft, the War and the Vietnam Generation,* Vintage Books, New York, 1978; Harry A. Marmion, *Selective Service: Conflict and Compromise,* John Wiley & Sons, New York, 1968; Arlo Tatum and Joseph S. Tuchinsky, *Guide to the Draft,* Beacon Press, Boston, 1970.

Allegations of cheating at medical examinations were made in *Australian Veteran's Health Studies. The Mortality Report,* part 1, Canberra 1984, p. 193. For casualty statistics of Australians in Vietnam see Ann-Mari Jordens, 'Conscription', in Graeme Aplin, S.G. Foster, Michael McKernan, *Australians: A Historical Dictionary,* Fairfax, Syme and Weldon, Broadway NSW, 1987. For inquiry into medical rejection rates in Queensland see: G. Chalk and S. Cullum, 'Morbidity among national service registrants'. *Medical Journal of Australia,* 6 April 1968, pp. 604–7.

Pro-war Organisations For an account of the provision of entertainers to Vietnam by the government and the RSL see Ann-Mari Jordens, 'Not *Apocalypse Now.* Government sponsored entertainers in Vietnam 1965–71', *Labour History* (forthcoming). For information on the attitudes and activities of the League in relation to the war see Peter Sekuless and Jacqueline Rees, *Lest We Forget. The History of the Returned Services League 1916–86,* Rigby, Sydney, 1986, pp. 140–43.

The Early Anti-war and Anti-conscription Movement For further information on Australian child care theories see the forthcoming thesis by Philippa Mein Smith, 'Infant survival in Australia 1900–1945', Australian National University.

The quotation by Robert Gould is from the *SMH*, 15 April 1966. The Anglican bishops' correspondence was published by the Prime Minister's Department on 20 April 1965 as *Vietnam: Exchange of letters between the Prime Minister, the Rt. Hon. Sir Robert Menzies, K.T., C.H., M.P., and the Rt. Rev. J.S. Moyes, C.M.G., and certain Archbishops and Bishops*. For an account of Catholic attitudes to the Vietnam war see Val Noone, 'Melbourne Catholics and the Vietnam War, 1965', MA prelim, History Department, La Trobe University, 1987.

The most detailed analysis of public opinion polls on conscription in the Vietnam period is to be found in M.E. Hamel-Green, 'the legitimacy of the 1964–72 Australian Conscription Scheme'. MA thesis, Political Science Department, University of Melbourne, 1975, pp. 34–142. The findings of the Victorian enquiry into police behaviour were published in the *Canberra Times*, 26 November 1966. Calwell's view of the war is quoted from CPD vol. H of R 46, 4 May 1965, pp. 1101–7 and Whitlam's views are from CPD vol. H of R 45, 25 March 1965, pp. 383–5 and vol. 47, pp. 288–96.

CONFLICT AND WITHDRAWAL

Note: The author wishes to thank Dr Greg Lockhart for the translation of the *Dong Nai* and *Long Dat* local histories used in this chapter (for complete bibliographic citations see the references to Dr Lockhart's chapter).

Tet-Ambiguous Offensive The main sources on the Tet Offensive are William S. Turley, *The Second Indochina War: A Short Political and Military History 1954–1975*, Boulder, Colorado, Westview Press, 1986; Gabriel Kolko, *Vietnam: Anatomy of a War*, London, Allen and Unwin, 1986; George C. Herring, *America's Longest War: The United States and Vietnam 1950–1975*, second edition, Philadelphia, Temple University Press, 1986. The analysis presented of the Tet Offensive draws heavily from Turley's excellent work. Kolko, *Vietnam*, p. 303 for quote on Tet as most important event of the war. Turley, *Second Indochina War*, pp. 81–84 on the background to Tet and pp. 98–100 on debates within the Party in late 1967. Kolko, *Vietnam*, p. 305, for the Americans' anticipation of an attack and Turley, *Second Indochina War*, pp. 103–106 on Khe Sanh and p. 105 for quote on 'the level of effort...'. Kolko, *Vietnam*, p. 306, for the quote from the Pentagon Papers editors and p. 333 for quote on the impact of the NLF's losses. Turley, *Second Indochina War*, pp. 113–114 for quote from Trần Văn Trà.

Homer, *Australian Higher Command*, p. 33, for Weyand quote and pp. 31–33 on pre-Tet activities by Task Force. John Rowe, *Vietnam: The Australian Experience*, Sydney, Time-Life Books in association with John Ferguson, Sydney, 1987, pp. 90–98 for accounts of Tet fighting in Baria and p. 93 for Shelton quote.

Dong Nai, p. 239 for quote on NLF preparations for Tet and p. 246 for quotes on the attack in Baria. *Dong Nai*, p. 250 for quote on the Australian counter-attack.

The main source on the operations at fire support base 'Coral' is Lex McAulay, *The Battle of Coral*, Hutchinson, Melbourne, 1988.

Pacification and Phước Tuy Neil Sheehan, 'Annals of War, An American Soldier in Vietnam : IV The Civilian General'. *The New Yorker*, 11 July 1988, p. 45, for quote by John Paul Vann. Turley, *Second Indochina War*, pp. 126–128 for communists' change in tactics. Kolko, *Vietnam*, pp. 386–400 on pacification. Serong's views on the post-Tet situation were presented in, 'the Strategic Necessities', *Vietnam Digest*, August 1969, pp. 5–8; quote is from p. 8, Herring, *America's Longest War*, p. 232, for quote by John Paul Vann. Kolko, *Vietnam*, pp. 396–397 for Komer quote.

A detailed account of the Đất Đỏ operations is provided in Frank Frost, *Australia's War in Vietnam*, Allen and Unwin, Sydney, 1987, pp 121–130. *Army press release*, 5838, Canberra, 21 June 1969, for quote on the Australian operational aim 'deny VC access...'. Pearson quote from an interview. *Long Dat*, p 163, for quote on the Australians' 'pill box' strategy and p. 162 for Australian attempts to find NLF cadres. *Long Dat*, p. 163, for the NLF's propaganda campaign in Đất Đỏ and p. 168 for the NLF's use of mines. Captain M.R. Battle, ed., *The Year of the Tigers: the Second Tour of 5th Battalion, the Royal Australian Regiment in South Vietnam, 1969–1970*. Printcraft Press, Sydney, 1970, p. 39 for quote on Operation Esso. Homer, *Australian Higher Command*, p. 41 for views of General Hay and p. 42 for quote from letter from General Hay to Brigadier Pearson. *Long Dat*, p. 174, on the NLF's use of mines to 'strike the enemy'.

For the account of the Long Hải hills operation, Homer, *Australian Higher Command*, p. 43, for quote from the Australian commander in Vietnam to the Chief of the General Staff on 1 March 1970 and for quote 'provided the opportunity...'. Major A. Clunies-Ross, ed., *The Grey Eight in Vietnam, The History of Eighth Battalion, Royal Australian Regiment, November 1969 – November 1970*, published by the battalion, Brisbane, 1970, p. 52, for quote on the 'elusive D445'. Quote by Brigadier Weir on B52 strike from interview. Clunies-Ross, *Grey Eight*, p. 54 for details of bunker clearing and mine casualties. Homer, *Australian Higher Command*, p. 42 for Chief of the General Staff's signal and p. 43 for Homer quote and for General Fraser's letter. Clunies-Ross, *Grey Eight,* pp. 109–114 for the Hoa Long ambush. August 1970. *Dong Nai,* p. 262, for quote on the severe situation in 1969.

Civic action is discussed in detail in Frost, *Australia's War in Vietnam,* pp. 164–177. General Gration's comments are from his speech at the launch of this book at the Australian War Memorial, Canberra, 7 July 1987.

Withdrawal For general accounts of 'Vietnamisation' see Turley, *Second Indochina War,* pp. 128–132 and Kolko, *Vietnam,* pp. 377–385. Homer, *Australian Higher Command,* p. 40 for Australian and New Zealand military attitudes to Vietnamisation. Statements by Prime Minister Gorton and Defence Minister Fraser from *Commonwealth Parliamentary Debates,* House of Representatives, Vol. 67, 22 April 1970, p. 1458 and Vol. 71, 24 February 1971, pp. 568–569. The Vietnamisation phase in Phước Tuy is covered in Frost, *Australia s War in Vietnam,* pp. 144–163. Ian McNeill, *The Team,* p. 449 and p. 452 for quotes on problems of the local forces and p. 407 for comment by General Daly. On the Phoenix Program in Phước Tuy, see Frost, *Australia's War in Vietnam,* pp. 152–158.

Gary McKay's account of the battle with the PAVN in 1971 is presented in *In Good Company* : *One Man's War in Vietnam,* Sydney, Allen and Unwin, 1987. Rowe, *Vietnam: The Australian Experience,* p. 162, for quote by Brigadier Geddes. *Long Dat,* p. 202 for Baria Party committee quote. See McNeill *The Team,* pp. 469–475 for the situation in Phước Tuy in 1972.

General Gration's comments were made in his speech at Australian War Memorial, 7 July 1987.

THE WAR THE MEDIA LOST

Lichty's summary of research findings on TV coverage of the war is found in Lawrence W. Lichty, 'Comments on the Influence of Television on Public Opinion', in Peter Braestrup (ed.), *Vietnam as History. Ten Years after the Paris Peace Accords,* University Press of America, January 1984.

The most extensive research project on US TV coverage of the war is David Hallin, *The 'Uncensored War' The Media and Vietnam,* New York, Oxford University Press, 1986.

Further material on Diệm's early positive press image can befound in Rodney Tiffen, 'News Coverage of Vietnam', in Peter King (ed.), *Australia's Vietnam,* Sydney, George Allen and Unwin, 1983.

Interesting accounts of this period by one of the participants can be found in David Halberstam, *The Making of a Quagmire,* London, Bodley Head, 1965, and his later *The Powers that Be,* New York, Alfred A. Knopf, 1979. The Halberstam 1962 quote and the impact of Ấp Bắc are from William M. Hammond, *The United States Army in Vietnam: Public Affairs: The Military and the Media 1962–1968,* Centre of Military History, United States Army, Washington DC, 1988, see p. 22 and p. 37.

A thorough study of Tet reporting is Peter Braestrup's *Big Story: How the American Press and Television Reported and Interpreted the Crisis of Tet 1968 in Vietnam and Washington,* 2 vols. New York, Anchor Books, 1979. Public opinion on Korea and Vietnam is summarised in John Mueller, *War, Presidents and Public Opinion,* New York, Wiley, 1973.

Limited Australian Media Capacities Quotations on Canberra TV coverage are from Clem Lloyd, *Parliament and the Press. The Federal Parliamentary Press Gallery 1901–88,* Melbourne University Press, 1988, pp. 211, 239.

See Cabinet Minute, Melbourne, 7 January 1955, Decision No. 262, Submission No. 241 'Australian Activities in the Cold War'.

On Intertel and Bidault, see K.S. Inglis, *This is the ABC. The Australian Broadcasting Commission 1912–1983,* Melbourne University Press, 1983. McEwen's speech is in *Commonwealth Parliamentary Debates,* vol. 38, 23 March 1963, p. 151.

The three examples of ABC managerial intervention in the text all come from Neville Petersen, 'the Vietnam War – Final Phase of ABC Paternalism?', Paper to the Australia and the Vietnam War conference, Macquarie University, 1987.

The Pathologies of Being a Junior Ally 'Hanoi was its puppet...' Gregory Clark, *In Fear of China,* Melbourne, 1967.

The 1963 Barwick quote is cited in David Marr, *Barwick,* Sydney, 1980.

Between Two Victories A more detailed comparison between the Australian and American governments' news management skills during Vietnamisation can be found in Rodney Tiffen, *op, cit,* More detailed material on coverage of the war's end is in Tiffen *ibid.,* and especially in Rodney Tiffen, *Symbolic Processes of Out-Group Politics, The Press, the Public and the Third World,* PhD thesis, Monash University, 1976. Box: Elegant, Westmoreland (1) quoted by Lichty in Braestrup (ed.), *op, cit.,* p. 158.

Nixon, Reston quoted by Hallin, *op, cit.,* p. 3.

Taylor (1) quoted from A. Lake (ed.), *The Vietnam Legacy,* New York. New York University Press, 1976.

Taylor, (2) quoted from M. Charlton and A. Moncrieff, *Many Reasons Why,* Harmondsworth, England, Penguin, 1977, pp. 150–51.

Westmoreland (2), Rusk (1) by Michael Maclear, *Vietnam: The Ten Thousand Day War,* London, Methuen, 1981, p. 295. Rusk (2) *ibid.,* p. 296.

Box: 'Winning' the War: Nearly all these quotations are taken from William G. Effros, *Quotations – Vietnam: 1945–1970,* New York, Random House, 1970.

Box: Tim Bowden, *One Crowded Hour. Neil Davis Combat Cameraman 1934–1985,* Sydney, William Collins Pty Ltd, 1987.

Box: Extracted from Pat Burgess, *Warco, Australian Reporters at War,* Richmond, Vic., William Heinemann Australia, 1986, pp. 124–25.

MOBILISING DISSENT

Many thanks to George Morgan, Emma Grahame, Joy Damousi, and John Docker for their assistance with this project. The literature on the anti-war movement in Australia includes unpublished theses such as those by Michael E. Hamel-Green. *The Legitimacy of the 1964–1972 Australian Conscription Scheme,* MA thesis, University of Melbourne, 1975; Malcolm Saunders, *The Vietnam Moratorium Movement in Australia; 1969–73,* PhD thesis, Flinders University, 1977; Julie Ockenden, *Anti-War Movement and the Student Revolt at Monash: an Examination of Contending Ideologies 1967–1970,* BA hons thesis, Monash 1985; Barry York, *Sources of Student Unrest in Australia, with Particular Reference to La Trobe University, 1967–73,* MA thesis, University of Sydney, 1983.

Journal articles and book chapters include: Michael E. Hamel-Green, 'the Resisters: a History of the Anti-conscription Movement, 1964–1972', in Peter King (ed.), *Australia's Vietnam,* Allen and Unwin, 1983; a series of articles by Malcolm Saunders including 'the ALP's Response to the Anti-Vietnam War Movement: 1965–73', in *Labour History,* no. 44, May 1983; 'Law and Order and the Anti-Vietnam War Movement: 1965–72': 'the Trade Unions in Australia and Opposition to Vietnam and Conscription: 1965–73', in *Labour History,* no. 43. November 1982; and 'Australia's Withdrawal from Vietnam: the Influence of the Peace Movement', in *Social Alternatives,* vol. 1, nos 6/7, 1980. See also Malcolm Saunders and Ralph Summy, 'One Hundred Years of an Australian Peace Movement, 1885–1984: Part II: From the Second World War to Vietnam and Beyond', in: Ralph Summy, 'Militancy and the Australian Peace Movement, 1960–1967', in *Politics,* November 1970, pp. 148–62; J.W. Berry, 'Who are the Marchers?', in *Politics,* vol. 3, no 2, November 1968; Barry York, 'sources of Student Dissent: La Trobe University, 1967–72', in *Vestes,* vol. 7, no. 1, 1984, pp. 21–31 and 'the Australian Anti-Vietnam Movement: 1965–1973'.

For Gregory Clark's statement see the *Australian,* November 1965 and also his 'Vietnam, China and the Foreign Affairs Debate in Australia: A Personal Account', in Peter King (ed.) *Australia's Vietnam.*

1966 Hyde Park demonstrators were reported in the *Sydney Morning Herald,* 17 March 1966.

ACTU policy against Australian involvement was hammered out in May 1965: see Saunders, 'the Trade Unions in Australia', pp. 65–7. For the demonstrations against Lyndon B. Johnson see *The Facts About the LBJ Demonstration,* published by Monash University SRC, 1966; *Sun Herald,* 23 October; *Sunday Mirror,* 23 October: *Australian,* 22 October, and *Sun,* 22 October 1966. Also Saunders, 'the ALP's Response', p. 79.

1967 For ALP's policy, see Saunders, 'the ALP's Response', pp. 81–83 and Summy, 'Militancy and the Australian Peace Movement', pp. 156–57. The article in *Lot's Wife* was 7 March 1967, on p. 2, For the move to the left, see Ockenden, *Anti-War Movement and the Student Revolt at Monash,* pp. 2–9, and Summy, 'Militancy and the Australian Peace Movement', p. 159. Julie Ockenden's statement occurs on page 4 of her thesis, and the Monash Labor Club's view is discussed on page 17.

For front-page student action see Warren Osmond, 'shock Therapy', in *Dissent,* no. 21, spring 1967. Also Ockenden, pp. 16–21. A pamphlet was issued by the Committee for Aid to the NLF on 28 August 1967, copy in *Vietnam Action,* vol. 1, no. 4, November 1967. Three members of the Labor Club were reprimanded and fined. See also Ockenden pp. 19 and 27.

Vietnam Day march, the *Australian,* 23 October 1967; quoted in Barry York, 'the Australian Anti-Vietnam Movement: 196573', p. 31.

For the Peace with Freedom movement, see Frank Knopfelmacher, 'Peace with Freedom' in *Quadrant,* July 1985, pp. 55–56, and reply by Alex Carey, *Of Professors and Pacification,* pamphlet, published by Carey, January 1968. The pamphlet reprinted a copy of an open letter from Professor Stove to academics.

1968 For Draft Resisters' movement see Hamel-Green, 'the Resisters', for a detailed account. For growing 'student power' see Rowan Cahill, 'Student Power', in *Outlook,* vol. 12, no. 4, August 1968, pp. 6–9, and *Dissent,* no. 23, spring 1968. For an analysis of the new left see John Docker,' "Those Halcyon Days": The Moment of the New Left', in Brian Head and James Walter (eds), *Intellectual Movements and Australian Society,* Oxford University Press 1988.

1969 For Don't Register appeal see Hamel-Green for a full account. See the *Australian,* 10 June 1969, re Nixon's announcement of withdrawal. See Saunders, 'Australia's Withdrawal from Vietnam', pp. 56–57.

For polls on bringing troops home, see Hamel-Green, 'the Resisters', p. 117: also Murray Goot and Rodney Tiffen, 'Public Opinion and the Politics of the Polls', in Peter King (ed), *Australian Vietnam,* p. 140, and Saunders, 'the ALP's Response', p. 84. For swing to Labor see G. Aplin et al, *Australians: Events and Places,* Fairfax, Syme and Weldon Associates, 1987, p. 192. For third stage of American withdrawal see the *Australian,* 17 December 1969, discussed in Saunders 'Australia's Withdrawal from Vietnam', p. 57, and for the fourth, Frank Frost, *Australia's War in Vietnam,* Allen and Unwin, 1987, p. 26.

1970 In protest at the news of the My Lai massacre, waterside workers, in defiance of ACTU and WWF policy refused to unload the *Jeparit* when it returned from Vietnam in December; Saunders, p. 69. See also the *Australian* 16, 17, 18 December 1969. See Saunders, 'the Trade Unions …', pp. 69–70. For Moratorium see Ockenden, p. 99 and Labor Club rhetoric, p. 97. For lists of signatories, see *SMH* 11 and 25 April 1970, and NSW Moratorium Sponsors' Newsletter, 13 April 1970. For suspension of students see Saunders, 'Australia's Withdrawal from Vietnam', pp. 59–60. For editorials on the Moratorium see *Outlook,* vol 14, no. 3, June 1970, p. 1.

Warren Osmond's comments appeared in *Old Mole,* no. 7, 26 October 1970. See also Warren Osmond, 'the State of Student Protest', *Current Affairs Bulletin,* vol. 46, no 8, 7 September 1970.

1971 For underground resistance to conscription, see Saunders, 'Australia's Withdrawal from Vietnam', pp. 56, 61. Also the debate between E.M. Schreiber and C.A. Rootes, in *Politics,* 1978/9, and Hamel-Green, 'the Resisters', p. 124. Michael Matteson's statement, *Nation Review,* 11–17 November 1972, pp. 120–1.

AT WAR AT HOME

Acknowledgement: For critical comments on an earlier draft of this essay thanks to Barry York, Ann Mari Jordens, Ken Inglis, Andrew Moore, John Herouvim, Fergus Robinson and Jane Ross.

The Sources of Discontent The most useful and readable text on the radical politics of the 1960s is Donald Horne, *Time of Hope Australia 1966–72,* Angus & Robertson, Sydney, 1980. Also important is Stephen Alomes, 'Cultural Radicalism in the Sixties', *Arena,* No. 62, 1983, pp. 28–54.

The term 'permissive consumerism' comes from Jill Matthews, *Good and Mad Women. The Historical Construction of Femininity in Twentieth Century Australia,* Allen & Unwin, Sydney, 1984, pp. 89–91. For Horne's comment on the new sexuality see *Time of Hope,* p. 13. See also John Berger, *Ways of Seeing,* Penguin, Harmondsworth, 1984. The selling of sex itself came in many forms: pornography for the mass market, new women's magazines such as *Cleo,* mainstream movies, sex therapy and birth control innovation, notably the Pill etc.

Herbert Marcuse was the author of *One Dimensional Man* (Boston, 1964), one of the most influential of new left texts. The quotation about 'beards, suede shoes and duffle coats…' is from Alomes, 'Cultural Radicalism in the Sixties', p 32. On the trade unions' part in anti-Vietnam protest see M. Saunders, 'the Trade Unions in Australia and Opposition to Vietnam and Conscription: 1965–73', *Labour History,* No. 43, November 1982, pp. 64–82. Possibly the most dramatic trade union intervention came in December 1969 when 300 union officials representing 32 unions and some 150 000 workers in Victoria passed a resolution calling on national servicemen in Vietnam 'to lay down their arms in mutiny against the heinous barbarism perpetrated in our name upon innocent aged men, women and children.' (See Saunders, p. 70.) But this was widely condemned by other sections of the union movement.

The use of the term 'generation' here is a deliberately narrow one. It signifies an age cohort distinguished by the dramatic conjuncture of youth culture and conscription. The narrow definition sustains the notion of a 'generation' gap signifying the space between youth and their parents. A.D. Hope's poem can be found in an anthology of anti-war writing. See S. Cass (et. al.), *We Took their Orders and are Dead. An Anti-War Anthology,* Sydney, 1971, p. 11. Hope's poem is cited in an important essay summarising the impact of the war on Australian writing, film and theatre. See Ann Mari Jordens, 'the Cultural Influence of the Vietnam War on Australia Since 1965', paper in *Journal of the Australian War Memorial,* No. 14, October 1989.

Figures for the rate of population growth have been calculated from the *Commonwealth Year Book,* No. 49, 1963, p. 318 and No. 54, 1968, p. 135. Figures for the growth of university numbers are from the *Commonwealth Year Book,* No. 37, 1946–7, p. 237 and No. 52, 1966, p. 607.

The discussion of youth culture here draws principally on two outstanding studies: Barry York, 'Sources of Student Unrest in Australia with Particular Reference to La Trobe University, 1967–73', MA thesis, University of Sydney, 1983; and, Megan Cronley, 'the Rise of the Surfing Subculture in Sydney, 1956–1966', BA Hons thesis, University of Sydney, 1983, esp. Chapter 3. The eye witness account of Malcolm Muggeridge's encounter with La Trobe University students is from York, 'Sources of Student Unrest ...', pp. 161–2. This thesis also contains an Appendix, Sample of Protest Songs to Enter the Top 40, 1966–72', p. 385.

'Almost Cut My Hair ...' For the quotation from *Go-Set*, see Vol. 1, No. 1, 2 February 1966, p. 3. The discussion of hair in this section centres on male youth and ties into later discussion of masculinity, soldiering and war. *Almost Cut My Hair* is a track from the Crosby, Stills, Nash and Young album *Deja Vu*. The cover script for the RCA album *Hair, The American Tribal Love-Rock Musical*, was written by Nat Schapiro. For Donald Home's comment on 'short-back-and-sides sober-suited puritanism', see *Time of Hope* ... pp. 34–5.

For *Go-Set's* advocacy of long hair see Vol. 6, No. 29, 17 July 1971, p. 3. The attitudes of police officers are discussed in Barry York, 'Baiting the Tiger. Police and Protest During the Vietnam War', in M. Finnane (ed.), *Policing in Australia. Historical Perspectives*, University of New South Wales Press, 1988, esp. p 172. The views of the RSL's National Secretary were expressed in July 1968. They were published in *Reveille* (Journal of the NSW Branch of the RSL), 1 November 1968, p. 24.

Gary Mackay's story about the new cadet officer at Scheyville is in his *In Good Company. One Man's War in Vietnam*, Allen & Unwin, Sydney, 1987, p. 28. William White's comment was quoted in the *Sydney Morning Herald*, 24 December 1966. The account of mistreatment of conscientious objectors in the Army and particularly in military prisons has been compiled from newspaper reports. For example see the various reports of the Phillipson case: *Sydney Morning Herald*, 18 July 1968, *Sun*, 5 June 1968, *Sunday Telegraph*, 10 January 1969. Note that conscientious objectors were only subject to military law for a short period. The National Service Act was amended in 1966 to make their actions a civil matter. For the quotation from *Surf International* see Vol. 1, No. 1, 1966, p. 9.

On Robert Wilton's draft card burning see *Sun Herald*, 14 September 1969, p. 3.

For the Canberra protest and Magistrate Dobson see *Canberra Times*, 20 May 1968, p. 1, and 21 May 1968, p. 3. The case is amplified by several undated newspaper clippings in the Jolliffe Papers, National Library of Australia. Ron Saw's report on the fitness medicals is in the *Sunday Telegraph*, 21 October 1971, p. 7.

The Gallup Poll on compulsory military training was carried out in September 1971. Details of the Poll were reported in the *Sun-Herald*, 3 October 1971, p. 3. The figures on investigations under the National Service Act were published in the *National Times*, 13 September 1971, p. 10. For the Blundell case see *Sydney Morning Herald*, 26 July 1968, p. 5.

The 'cat and mouse' game between draft resisters and the police was reported in the press under titles such as: 'Four Dodge Draft in Uni', *Sunday Telegraph*, 28 September 1971; 'Radio Jam for Jam Threat', *Australian*, 28 September 1971; 'Draft Resisters Defy Police', *Mirror*, 28 September 1971; 'students Guard Resisters', *Sydney Morning Herald*, 28 September 1971; 'search Police Accused of Harassing his Mother and Sisters', *Australian*, 8 October 1971; 'Resistance Runaround', *Australian*, 31 October, 1971; and 'Melbourne Raid: Waterloo for a Nonpolicy', *National Times*, 11 October 1971. The Moratorium banner 'I Am a Pack Raping Bikie' was reported in the Melbourne *Herald*, 8 May 1970, p. 3. The National Service Act described as a 'trivial offence' was reported in the *Sydney Morning Herald*, 29 October 1971 and the *Australian*, 30 October 1971. For continued reporting on the inconsistencies of court judgements see Alan Stewart, 'Any Objection?', *Herald*, 10 June 1971.

Soldiering and Manhood in the Age of Aquarius Gary McKay's thoughts on recreational dress for officer trainees are in *In Good Company*... p. 32.

Michael McKernan s comment on the aftermath of Gallipoli is in his *The Australian People and the Great War*, Nelson, Melbourne, 1980, p. 14. The connection between going away to fight, citizenship and manhood, is discussed by G. Lloyd in 'selfhood, War and Masculinity', in C. Pateman and E. Gross (eds), *Feminist Challenges. Social and Political Theory*, 1986, pp. 63–76.

The One Day of the Year was first performed in 1959.

Gary McKay's comment about being spat upon on Anzac Day is in *In Good Company* ... p. 187. The Moratorium slogan – 'the Army Made a Man of Him – A Dead Man'; was reported in the Melbourne *Herald*, 30 June 1971, p. 2.

The airport encounter with demonstrators is reported in S. Rintoul, *Ashes of Vietnam. Australian Voices*, Heinemann Australia, Richmond, 1988, p. 182. At other points Rintoul's book testifies further to the alienation suffered by many soldiers on returning home.

For Mackay's account of the football match in Brisbane see *In Good Company* ... p. 187. Soldiers who attacked Moratorium marchers in Adelaide were carrying the 'NLF kills Diggers' banner. See *Sunday Observer,* 10 May 1970, p. 2.

The editorial entitled 'two Kinds of Courage', appeared in the *Sydney Morning Herald* on 22 August 1969, p. 7. Stewart's precursor in the Melbourne *Herald* was on 2 May 1968.

The comparison with the experience of previous wars is based on Ian McNeill's, 'Australian Army Advisers. Perceptions of Enemies and Allies', in Kenneth Maddock and Barry Wright (eds), War, *Australia and Vietnam,* Harper and Row, Artarmon, NSW, 1987. Quotations in this paragraph come from pp. 39–43 of McNeill's article. Paul Fussell has tackled this comparison from another perspective: 'the Great War took place in what was, compared with ours, a static world where the values appeared stable and where the meanings of abstractions seemed permanent and reliable. Everyone knew what Glory was and what Honour meant.' (*The Great War and Modem Memory,* Oxford University Press, 1977, p. 21).

The story about the American soldier killing an eight-year-old boy is told in Barbara Ehrenreich, *The Hearts of Men. American Dreams and the Flight from Commitment,* Pluto Press, New York, 1983, p. 105.

For one instance of denial of post-war disorders among soldiers, see the comments of Colin Hines, NSW State President of the RSL, in *Reveille,* April 1972, p. 4. The matter is discussed in Jeffrey Streimer and Christopher Tennant, 'Psychiatric Aspects of the Vietnam War: The Effects on Combatants', in Kenneth Maddock and Barry Wright (eds), *War, Australia and Vietnam,* pp. 230–261.

Postscript: The Legacy of the Sixties Stephen Alomes, in Cultural Radicalism in the Sixties', has argued that sixties radicalism disintegrated, and that it disintegrated because its social constituency was too transient and diffuse to endure in the form of lasting political alliances. But there was never a political alliance. It was the *political demands* of sixties radicalism that were 'transient and diffuse', and never likely to endure. The new left, for example has been rightly described as 'a mood in search of a movement', and 'more a feeling than a programme'.

Fad theory is dispensed with in Part One of Barry York's thesis, 'sources of Student Unrest in Australia', mentioned above. For an important essay, hitting back at left intellectuals who have aligned themselves with fad theorists to disown their years in the anti-war movement see John Herouvim, 'Crossing the Bridge: Left to Right', *Arena,* No. 74, 1986, pp. 16–23. Marshall Berman has tackled the same problem at the level of intellectual fashion, observing for example, that Foucault's vision of the individual as the complete captive of the 'total institutions' of modem society has offered 'a generation of refugees from the 1960's a world-historical alibi for the sense of passivity and helplessness that gripped so many of us in the 1970 s.' Yet Foucault is by no means the only intellectual fashion to be utilised as a rationalisation for apathy. (See M. Berman, *All that is Solid Melts into Air. The Experience of Modernity,* Verso, London, 1983, pp. 34–35.)

AUSTRALIA'S LEGACY

Coming Home The mechanics of the posting system, etc. are described in detail in Volume III of *The Mortality Report,* Canberra 1984. On 1 RAR's return, *Courier Mail* 1 June 1966, *Sydney Morning Herald* and the *Australian* 9 June 1966. 5 RAR, *SMH* 13 May 1967. 9 RAR, the *Advertiser* (Adelaide) 10 December 1969. Mr Snedden is reported in *SMH* 8 May 1970 and the Moratorium a day later. 8 RAR, *Courier Mail,* 13 November 1970. Final march in Townsville, *Daily Bulletin* 18 December 1971.

Speaking for the Veterans The best sources on the servicemen's organisations are their own publications, such as *Reveille* and Annual Reports for the RSL; *Debrief* for the Vietnam Veteran's Association. Other material is in the Agent Orange Royal Commission report; Graham Walker 'the Vietnam Veteran's Association of Australia', in K. Maddock and B. Wright. *War: Australia and Vietnam,* Harper & Row, 1987; Ian Gollings (National Secretary of the RSL) 'the RSL of Australia and the Vietnam War', – During and Post War', paper presented to Conference on Australia and the Vietnam war, Sydney, 1987, 'the Victims' appears in full in *Debrief,* Nov. 1983-Jan. 1984. The Anzac Day quote is from a veteran interviewed by the author.

Agent Orange The published literature on Agent Orange is considerable. The most comprehensive treatment is in the nine volumes of the *Report of the Royal Commission on the Use and Effects of Chemical Agents on Australian Personnel in Vietnam,* AGPS 1985 (the Evatt Royal Commission). The VVA's case can be found in their journal *Debrief.* A critique of the Royal Commission is in Jock McCulloch's chapter 'Whistling in the Dark: the Royal Commission into Agent Orange', in K. Maddock and B. Wright (eds), *War: Australia and Vietnam,* Harper & Row, 1987. Two Australian publications give the story until the mid 1980s: John Dux and P.J. Young, *Agent Orange: The Bitter Harvest,* Hodder & Stoughton, 1980, and Jock McCulloch, *The Politics of Agent Orange,* Heinemann, 1984. Some of the ramifications of the case in the USA are discussed in James B. Jacobs and Dennis McNamara, 'Vietnam Veterans and the Agent Orange Controversy', *Armed Forces and Society*, 13(1), Fall 1986, pp. 57–80.

The Health of Veterans The AVHS studies are as cited in the text. There is a large literature on the physical and mental health of veterans in the USA; in Australia there is very little. The Report of the Royal Commission summarises material available up to 1985; later work on mental health is in Jeffrey Streimer and Christopher Tennant. 'Psychiatric Aspects of the Vietnam War: The Effect on Combatants', in K. Maddock and B. Wright (eds), *War: Australia and Vietnam*, Harper & Row, 1987. The quote on PTSD is from the Royal Commission Report, vol. V IX – 163. Information on the VVCS is in Report of the House of Representatives Standing Committee on Community Affairs, *After the March. Strengthening Support for the Veterans*, Canberra, 1988, and also Ric Marshall, 'Recovery from Vietnam: a Vietnam Veteran's Counselling Service Perspective'. AWM History Conference, July 1987. The best introductions to the vast American literature are perhaps: Charles R. Figley, *Stress Disorders Among Vietnam Veterans*, New York, 1978; and Josefina J. Card, *Lives After Vietnam*, Lexington, 1983.

The most recent study on birth defects is by Barbara Field and Charles Kerr, 'Reproductive behaviour and consistent patterns of abnormality in offspring of Vietnam veterans', *Journal of Medical Genetics*, 1988, 25, 819–26, which concludes that veterans do have unusual reproductive difficulties; the sample used, however, is not representative of the general veteran population.

The Repatriation System There is no published summary of the Repatriation system. I have relied heavily on the guidance of the staff at the Veterans' Review Board in Canberra, and on their publication *VeRBosity* which describes particular cases at appeals level. See also RSL Annual Reports, DVA pamphlets, and some historical material in Clem Lloyd and Jacqueline Rees, 'Repatriation and Australia'. AWM History Conference, 1987. On the VVCS see material cited in health section.

Welcome Home Anzac Day marches are reported in the relevant newspapers of 26 April each year. The report on the Sydney City Council's reaction to the Welcome Home March is in the *SMH*, 19 December 1986. The Welcome Home March is covered in newspaper reports of the weekend 3–4 October 1987, and the following day. The Welcome Home Committee has also published a book, *Welcome Home*. On the conservatism of the soldiers, see my 'Australian Soldiers in Vietnam: Product and Performance', in Peter King (ed.), *Australia's Vietnam*, Sydney, 1983, 'the legend of Anzac upheld' is on the cover of Lex McAulay's book, *The Battle of Long Tan*, Sydney, 1986. The quotes are from Michael Clark, 'Remembering Vietnam'. *Cultural Critique*, No. 3, spring 1986, pp. 49–69.

CONCLUSION

President Truman's 'run the world' quote is from W.A. Williams, *The Tragedy of American Diplomacy*, Cleveland, 1959, pp. 168–69. The quote from Gabriel Kolko comes from *Vietnam: Anatomy of a War 1940–1975*, London, 1986, pp. 72–73.

ABBREVIATIONS

The following abbreviations, referring to the military forces in Vietnam, appear in the text. **ARVN** Army of the Republic of Vietnam (army of the RVN). **COMAFV** Commander Australian Forces Vietnam. **DMZ** De militarised Zone. **DRV** Democratic Republic of Vietnam (Hanoi). **ICP** Indo-Chinese Communist Party. **MACV** Military Assistance Command Vietnam (United States' military command). **NLF** National Front for the Liberation of Southern Vietnam ('Viet Cong'). **PAVN** People's Army of Vietnam (army of the DRV). **PLAF** People's Liberation Armed Forces (Southern revolutionary forces). **RVN** Republic of Vietnam (Saigon). **VWP** Vietnam Workers' Party.

ROLL OF HONOUR

The following Australians died as a result of service in the Vietnam War.

Abbott D.E.
Abraham D.E.
Abraham R.J.
Adamczyk B.A.J.
Adams L.W.H.
Ahearn A.W.
Aldersea R.A.
Allen N.G.
Andrews J.H.
Annesly F.J.
Anton R.D.
Archer G.A.
Arnold K.J.
Arnold P.J.
Ashton W.J.
Attwood T.J.
Aylett D.R.
Ayres M.W.
Badcoe P.J. (VC)
Bade K.W.
Bailey E.J.
Baines G.T.
Bain J.
Baker D.A.
Bancks L.R.
Banfield D.J.
Barnett S.J.
Barrett J.J.
Bartholomew G.T.
Baudistel K.W.
Baxter L.J.
Beilken B.C.
Bell A.E.J.
Belleville G.R.
Bell R.J.
Betts R.W.
Binder B.G.F.
Bink M.
Binning R.P.
Birchell M.J.
Birnie T.
Birse R.G.
Black B.F.

Blackhurst T.D.
Black T.R.
Blanck W.A.
Bloxsom A.C.
Boardman K.J.
Bond J.A.
Borlace D.G.
Bourke M.A.
Bourne D.M.
Bowtell R.W.
Bracewell D.H.
Brady G.V.
Bramble P.J.
Brennan D.J.
Bressington J.
Brett W.J.
Brewer K.F.
Briggs D.J.
Brooks D.L.
Brophy E.F.
Brown A.R.
Brown I.R.
Brown L.N.
Buchan R.
Bullman J.H.
Bums R.
Butlin R.R.
Butterworth R.J.
Byrne B.E.
Byrne R.A.
Campbell J.A.
Carlyle H.
Carroll R.T.
Carroll W.T.
Carruthers J. (MID)
Carver R.C.
Casadio A.A.
Casey A.L.
Cashion G.O.
Cassano N.J.
Caston R.J.
Chant P.A.
Chapman R.S.

Checkley T.W.
Clark C.
Clark D.M.
Clark R.D.
Clark R.T.
Clements P.E.
Clifford L.I.
Cliff R.W.
Cock J.R.
Coles K.G.
Connors R.F.
Constable G.A.
Convery R.T.
Conway K.G.
Coombs G.J.
Cooper A.J.
Copeman R.J.
Coupe B.F.
Cox J.G.
Coxon R.E.
Cox R.J.
Craig P.
Crouch N.V.
Cullen B.T.
Cutcliffe T.J.
Danilenko A. (MID)
Davidson B.N.
Davies R.E.
Davies R.W.
Davison W.J.
Dawson I.K.
Dawson P.
Deed R.J.P.
Desnoy J.W.
De Vries van
Dewar K.I.
Dickson S.W.
Doherty J.A.
Donald B.C.
Donnelly D.J.
Donnelly W.W.
Doyle D.G.
Drabble G.A.

Driscoll R.W.
Drummond A.
Dubber D.J.
Duff J.
Duffy K.A.
Dufty M.R.
Duncuff A.L.
Duroux J.M.
Durrington J.T.
D'Antoine G.H.
Earle P.
Edwards B.P.
Engstrom R.J.
Evans P.
Evans T.A.
Fallon B.E.
Farren L.T.
Fewquandie F.J.
Field R.E.
Fisher D.J.E.
Fisher R.L.
Fitzgerald J.
Fitzpatrick B.F.
Fleming R.
Foster G.L.
Fotheringham A.H.
Fraser J.
Freeman J.W.
French V.A.
Gaffney R.J.
Galvin W.J.
Ganett J.E.
Gant K.H.
Garland B.A.
Garngan J.
George B.R.
Gibbs I.J.
Gibson A.J.
Gilbert G.G.
Gillard R.J.
Gillespie J.F.
Gill M.W.T. (MID)
Gillson P.R.

Godden G.R.
Gollagher P.J. (CMF)
Goody P.R.
Gould E.G.
Graham A.W.
Graham S.
Grant E.F.
Green G.B.
Green J.G.
Grice V.R.
Grills E.A.
Grist R.M.
Grose T.J.
Hacking W.F.
Halkyard E.
Hall J.
Hamersley F.G.
  (MID)
Hanley M.P.
Hannaford M.J.
Hansen A.R.
Hansen B.V.
Hansen P.R.
Harald N.S.
Hards E.W.G.
Harris R.A.
Harstad B.A.
Hartney G.J.
Hart P.R.
Hawker N.V.G.
Hayes J.F.
Hayes R.M.
Henderson M.A.
Hendle T.E.
Herbert M.P.J.
Hewitt R.D.
Hickey R.B.
Hill D.C.
Hillier R.H. (MID)
Hines P.A.
Hoare F.W.
Hoban W. (BEM)
Holland T.

Hollis A.E.
Holloway J.W.
Home N.W.
Hood R.D.
Houston J.M.
Houston K.R.
Hubble R.N.
Huelin A.J.
Hughes R.D.
Hughes R.E.
Hunt R.H.
Hurst H.W.
Hutchison M.J.
Hyland F.A.
Jackson P.J.
Jackson R.J.
James B.
Jellie A.D.
Jewry J.
Jones B.R.A.
Kalma J.H.
Kavanagh G.R.
Kelly B.W.
Kennedy J.J.
Kennedy R.J.
Kermode R.C.
Kerr J.K.
Key R.M.
Kingston-Powles K.
Kingston I.W.
Kirby J. (DCM)
Knight G.
Knight P.R.
Kowalski P.F.
La Grasta G.
Lance E.M.
Langlands T.E.
Large P.A.
Larsson S.G.
Le Bherz N.W.
Lee E.J.
Lees R.V.
Leeuwen T.J.

Lewis P.E.	Menz J.L.	Parker R.H.J.	Rich A.W.	Smith R.K.	Wales M.R.
Linton M.P.	Meredith T.F.	Parrello A. (MID)	Richardson N.T.	Smith R.S.	Walker B.G.
Lisle A.	Milford D.G.	Paterson D.	Richter P.M.	Sorrenson G.D.	Wallis A.J.
Lithgow C.T.	Milligan R.B.	Patten R.B.	Rijsewijk P.R.P.	Sprigg R.J.	Wallis D.A.
Lloyd A.	Mills N.R.	Pattison A.G.	Riley W.M.	Stahl D.M.	Walsh B. (MM)
Lloyd R.E.	Mitchell D.	Pearce J.G.	Rinkin K.P.	Stanczyk H.J.	Warburton G.F.A.
Locke G.R.	Mitchell W.D.	Pengilly B.M.	Rivett J.C.	Stanford G.I.	Waring A.E.L.
Logan B.A.	Mitchinson K.L.	Penn D.H.	Robertson A.J.	Steen D.J.	Waters B.D.
Loughman M.	Moore B.J.	Penneyston P.L.	Robertson M.R.	Stevens J.G.	Watson B.P.
Lowes N.	Moore R.J.	Perrin R.G.	Rogers J.	Stone J.M. (MID)	Watson R.C.A.
Lubcke R.J.	Moore S.T.	Pesonen T.E.A.	Rooney K.M. (MID)	Sukmanowsky M.	Webster D.R.
Luff N.F.	Morgan J.L.	Petersen B.O.	Roost C.W.	Sullivan P.C.	Webster J.C.
Lyddieth T.	Morrison D.W.	Petersen V.N.	Ross G.S.	Suter T.	West G.M.
Lyons P.	Moss A.B.	Petith T.G.	Ross T.	Suttor H.E.	Weston L.J.
Lyon T.E.	Moss G.J.	Pettit J.G.	Ruddy J.	Swanton R.J.	Weston R.B.
MacDonald J.	Mowbray B.G.	Pettit L.J.	Ruduss A.	Sweetnam J.R.	Wheatley K.A. (VC)
MacLennan L.J.	Muc M.	Pettitt N.C.	Salverson D.J.	Sykes A.	Wheeler J.W.
Malone P.A.	Muller H.L.	Phillips O'B.C.	Salzmann R.W.	Talbot A.	Whiston B.J.
Manicola J.G.	Munday B.J.	Phillips R.A.	Sandow R.W.	Taylor L.A.	Whiston C.J.
Manning P.	Murray P.E.	Phillips T.D.	Sawtell C.J.	Tebb P.	White H.W.
Marks-Chapman P.R.	Musicka H.R.	Pike G.A.	Scales G.J.	Teeling W.E.	White J.M.T.
Martin W.H.	Nagle G.	Plain D.B.	Schuit M.J.M.	Thomas D.J.	White M.P.
Mathers I.G.	Nalder W.L.	Plane B.J.	Scott I.J.	Thomas W.M.	Whitton J.H.
Mathews G.F.	Navarre P.J.	Polglase G.R.	Scott I.N.	Thompson B.J.	Wilkinson A.C.F.
Mathieson K.F.	Neal D.W.	Pomroy V.I.	Scott R.A.	Thompson D.L.	Williams A.S.
Maza R.N.	Needs J.D.	Poole M.D.	Scott T.R.	Thomson I.J.	Willoughby G.I.
McCarthy J.	Nelson D.E.	Pothof R.C.	Seiler R.	Tinkham J.R.	Wilsen R.P.
Mc Conachy M.	Niblett R.J.	Poulson D.	Seipel R.D.	Tobin V.J.	Wilson K.R.
McCormack A.	Nicholson K.R.	Power R.E.	Sharp G.C.	Tognolini M.P.	Wilson M.A.F.
McCormack D.	Nichols R.K.	Powter D.R.J.	Shaw K.C.	Tomas M.	Wilson R.B.
McDonnell L.C.	Nilsen E.H.	Pracy N.A.	Sheppard L.R.	Topp F.B.	Wojcik B.K.
McDuff P.E.	Nisbet C.R.	Prior K.J.	Sheriff P.J.	Towler M.	Womal N.J.
McGarry P.S.	Noack E.W.	Prowse L.	Shipp N.E.	Tregear B.	Woolford R.M.
McGoldrick W.	Noonan M.J.	Purcell A.T.	Siggers A.P.	Trimble B.M.	Woolley I.V.
McGuire R.A.	Norley G.L.	Quigley A.V.	Simpson T.	Troy K.J.	Worle J.T.
McInerney N.A.	Norris J.W.	Radomi S.E.	Slater H.L.	Trzecinski P.Z.	Wride D.S.
McLachlan C.W.	O'Brien J.A.	Raffen F.L.	Slattery J.M.	Tully D.J.	Young A.H.
McMillan J.C.	O'Connor J.M.	Ramsay J.S.	Smillie R.G.	Turner T.C.	Young B.T.
McMillan R.C.	O'Connor P.S.	Rands J.M.	Smith B.F.	Tweedie G.L.	Young R.G.
McNab R.L.	O'Dal S.J.	Rapp J.R.	Smith B.L.	Twomey J.W.Van	Yule R.J.
McNair D.G.	O'Hanlon R.M.	Reidy P.F.	Smith F.J.	Van Valen A.	
McPherson L.H.	O'Hara J.L.	Remeljej A.	Smith J.	Vickers P.J.	
McQualter M.B. (MID)	O'Neill A.L.	Rennie B.	Smith N.A.	Voyzey D.J.	
	O'Neill J.B.	Renshaw T.J.	Smith P.C.	Wagstaff V.N.	
McQuat J.L.	O'Shea G.	Rhodes M.L.	Smith P.L.	Waldock D.J.	

LEST WE FORGET

THOSE WHO SERVED

The following is a record of those on active service during the Vietnam War in the Royal Australian Navy, the Australian Army, and the Royal Australian Air Force. The names were kindly supplied by the Department of Veteran's Affairs and based on available records. These pages are intended to name all those who served in Vietnam, including members of the nursing corps. Please note that some service personnel have opted not to have their names included on the nominal roll for privacy reasons. Enquiries concerning the status of any names on or not on these pages should be forward to the Department of Veterans Affairs, Canberra, which administers this list.

Royal Australian Navy

JR Aaron, LB Abbey, AL Abbott, BD Abbott, RJ Abbott, TL Abbott, BJ Abel, DR Abel, PH Ablett, GJ Abnett, RG Abra, BE Abraham, BG Abraham, JL Abraham, NC Abraham, BK Abson, MK Ackland, RJ Ackroyd, JA Adam, M Adamcewicz, JAR Adames, BJ Adams, BL Adams, DC Adams, DI Adams, DJ Adams, DP Adams, GJ Adams, HJP Adams, IE Adams, KC Adams, LF Adams, MD Adams, MR Adams, PE Adams, PR Adams, R Adams, RG Adams, RJ Adams, RK Adams, SE Adams, WJ Adams, SJ Adamski, RG Adamson, AG Addison, S Addison, JA Adie, AD Adkins, RJ Adlard, WF Adler, BJ Affleck, TJ Agard, BG Agland, BJ Agnew, HA Ah Gee, AR Ahern, BL Aherne, DS Ahgee, SD Ahrens, RM Aiberti, GW Aikman, KJ Ainley, WC Ainsworth, TM Aird, BW Airey, RG Airey, LW Aisbett, AR Aitken, HT Aitken, JG Aitken, JM Aitken, MA Aitken, P Aitken, R Aitken, RW Aitken, WJ Aitken, J Aked, GK Akers, LR Albert, AA Albinson, RJ Alcock, MD Alcorn, JA Aldenhoven, BC Alderman, A Alderson, J Alderton, DA Aldridge, GE Aldridge, GR Aldridge, JA Aldridge, B Alexander, CV Alexander, GE Alexander, GG Alexander, KJ Alexander, PJ Alexander, PW Alexander, RS Alexander, SW Alexander, T Alexander, JR Alford, DS Allan, DW Allan, WA Allan, WK Allan, TJ Allard, VD Allard, RE Allchin, AL Allen, AS Allen, BG Allen, CJ Allen, DA Allen, DM Allen, DR Allen, EW Allen, G Allen, GJ Allen, GP Allen, GS Allen, J Allen, JD Allen, JE Allen, JS Allen, KJ Allen, KR Allen, LJ Allen, MG Allen, RB Allen, RDJ Allen, RG Allen, RJ Allen, RK Allen, RS Allen, WG Allen, WM Allen, SW Alleyn, FA Allica, NJ Allister, RB Allister, PR Allman, RJ Allom, JR Alloway, IG Allsop, M Allt-Graham, PK Alman, RG Althofer, RG Altorjay-Arnoul, M Altschul, JF Alvisio, JA Ambar, AE Ambler, S Ambler, DW Ambrey, DL Ames, OB Amjah, W Amjah, GC Amos, JR Amos, LL Amos, WJ Amos, JL Amourous, F Anchell, JA Anchor, TA Anchor, GE Andersen, WF Andersen, AJ Anderson, AK Anderson, AM Anderson, AT Anderson, BJ Anderson, BK Anderson, BT Anderson, CK Anderson, DA Anderson, DJ Anderson, EA Anderson, FC Anderson, G Anderson, GC Anderson, GD Anderson, GJ Anderson, GW Anderson, J Anderson, JFH Anderson, JG Anderson, JR Anderson, JWD Anderson, KG Anderson, LA Anderson, LC Anderson, M Anderson, MJ Anderson, NS Anderson, P Anderson, PA Anderson, PJ Anderson, RA Anderson, RC Anderson, RD Anderson, RG Anderson, TE Anderson, AH Anderson-Clemence, BJ Andrew, AJ Andrews, BJ Andrews, CA Andrews, ESF Andrews, HG Andrews, LJ Andrews, P Andrews, RL Andrews, RV Andrews, RW Andrews, TJ Andrews, AP Andrikonis, BW Andrzeiczak, GW Anesbury, RJ Anesbury, GJ Angel, RN Angel, JF Angelini, KD Angus, AW Anning, LE Ansell, PJM Ansen, PR Ansett, RD Anstee, DN Anthony, JG Anthony, JMG Anthony, TJ Anthony, AR Antoney, BR Appleby, GG Appleby, PS Appleby, TS Apted, AG Arabena, AM Archer, FO Archer, GC Archer, GP Archer, PM Archibald, PJ Arday, RW Ardern, DJ Ardrey, JF Arentz, MF Argent, RJ Argent, DB Argue, BM Arkinstall, RC Arklay, LR Armanasco, RF Armbruster, AE Armes, DJ Armes, RPL Armitage, FW Armour, KR Armour, BJ Armstrong, DP Armstrong, DW Armstrong, GJ Armstrong, GW Armstrong, LW Armstrong, PJ Armstrong, RC Armstrong, RE Armstrong, WL Armstrong, RR Arndt, EC Arnell, DJ Arnold, LG Arnold, PRS Arnold, RK Arnold, RP Arnold, SF Arnold, TJ Arnold, WGA Arnold, J Arnott, JA Arnott, M Arnott, TP Arnott, MD Arnoult, RJ Arriola, U Arro, PNF Arrowsmith, BJ Arthur, CJ Arthur, DG Arthur, E Arthur, GD Arthur, GM Arthur, PJ Arthur, RT Arthur, RAJ Arundel, PJ Ashburner, BR Ashby, PJ Ashby, SW Ashby, RAK Ashcroft, DJ Ashenden, FK Asher, WC Asher, DB Ashford, DJ Ashford, DJ Ashley, DN Ashley, E Ashman, GL Ashman, PJ Ashman, DK Ashmead, RE Ashmore, RW Ashmore, BE Ashpole, A Ashton, EJ Ashton, GD Ashton, GJ Ashton, HL Ashton, NA Ashton, PG Ashton, RD Ashton, RJ Ashton, RW Ashton, R Asimus, EM Asker, JE Asker, AD Aslat, RC Asmus, A Asplin, JJ Asplin, RL Asquith, LJ Assender, KR Assenheim, MJ Astbury, ID Astill, MF Astle, BJ Atkins, JC Atkins, JD Atkins, JF Atkins, KAR Atkins, KJ Atkins, NJ Atkins, PT Atkins, RL Atkins, TJ Atkins, TR Atkins, BR Atkinson, EB Atkinson, FC Atkinson, GB Atkinson, GD Atkinson, HS Atkinson, IE Atkinson, J Atkinson, JJ Atkinson, RJ Atkinson, RF Atlee, AG Attrill, AJ Attrill, M Attwood, KJ Atwell, HPF Auer, BJ Augostin, S Auguszczak, DE Austin, DR Austin, GT Austin, KJ Austin, NA Austin, RW Austin, RB Auston, FJ Auty, GJ Avard, MA Avard, WL A'vard, DR Avdall, NF Avent, BC Avery, GJ Avery, JR Avery, PE Avery, T Avery, MJ Aves, RS Avey, W Awyzio, PL Axten, CB Ayerst, MG Aylmer, MP Aylmer, WP Aylott, KJ Ayoub, EW Ayre, BJ Ayres, GA Ayres, JM Ayres, RJ Ayres, RN Ayres, WG Ayres, GM Azel, L Baba, RF Babarovich, KK Babington, BR Back, CE Back, R Bacon, RH Bacon, RW Bacon, WW Bacon, HH Baddams, RJO Badger, GW Badham, RRH Badman, M Bagdy, MG Baggott, J Bagnall, E Bahlij, A Bailey, BJ Bailey, BK Bailey, DW Bailey, EM Bailey, GR Bailey, GC Bailey, JD Bailey, HE Bailey, HL Bailey, JA Bailey, JW Bailey, KJ Bailey, KMG Bailey, MH Bailey, RC Bailey, RG Bailey, TJ Bailey, IW Baillie, LA Baillie, AJ Bain, DW Bain, KG Bain, MD Bain, RG Bain, RW Bainbridge-Fuller, JE Baines, PG Baines, GT Baird, HGM Baird, KA Baird, RA Baird, RM Baird, WJ Baird, NJI Baird-Orr, GR Bairnsfather, J Bajda, E Bak, AAJ Baker, AE Baker, AR Baker, BF Baker, C Baker, CH Baker, DA Baker, DJ Baker, DR Baker, DW Baker, FW Baker, HG Baker, JH Baker, JM Baker, JS Baker, KG Baker, M Baker, MB Baker, MG Baker, ND Baker, RD Baker, RJ Baker, RN Baker, RR Baker, SJ Baker, TA Baker, FE Balaam, BR Balchin, JW Balcomb, BJ Baldock, DW Baldwin, G Baldwin, MD Baldwin, WN Baldwin, KJ Bale, R Balemans, C Bales, JW Ball, PB Ball, RE Ball, SG Ball, BJH Ballantyne, PA Ballantyne, GW Ballard, KF Ballard, GW Ballhause, DC Balloch, LC Balven, AG Baly, DB Balzer, KB Bambrook, AL Bamford, RJ Bampton, MD Bancroft, RP Bancroft, GR Bandy, PH Banfield, JW Banister, JC Banks, RM Banks, SE Banks, EJ Bannister, PA Bannon, NG Banos, D Banu, GD Banyer, GR Baptie, C Baragwanath, MR Baranovsky, JC Barber, LJ Barber, R Barber, RH Barbour, JG Barclay, RA Barclay, SA Barden, JE Bardsley, PW Bardsley, JA Bargwanna, GC Barham, AE Barker, CR Barker, E Barker, EC Barker, GK Barker, GM Barker, J Barker, JC Barker, LW Barker, NC Barker, RE Barker, RP Barker, RW Barker, IJ Barkla, JF Barkley, SPA Barkley, JW Barling, RWC Barlow, WE Barlow, JL Barltrop, NR Barnard, PC Barnard, SG Barnard, BF Barnes, BG Barnes, BR Barnes, GA Barnes, GJ Barnes, HW Barnes, IK Barnes, JA Barnes, JR Barnes, K Barnes, KJ Barnes, LM Barnes, LT Barnes, NJ Barnes, PH Barnes, RA Barnes, RJ Barnes, RM Barnes, SK Barnes, WGT Barnes, KF Barnett, L Barnett, LC Barnett, RA Barnett, DJ Barnewall, TJ Barnfield, GB Barnier, AR Baron, AM Barr, CP Barr, RJ Barr, SM Barratt, TP Barratt, RS Barrell, AJ Barrett, BW Barrett, GC Barrett, GH Barrett, IG Barrett, LF Barrett, PW Barrett, SL Barrett, AA Barrie, CA Barrie, EH Barrie, BL Barrington, JN Barron, I Barrons, AA Barrow, GC Barrow, BL Barry, KJ Barry, KJP Barry, N Barry, PJ Barry, WR Barry, PA Barter, DK Bartholomai, JK Bartimote, BG Bartlett, CG Bartlett, KH Bartlett, LR Bartlett, MJ Bartlett, RMJ Bartlett, RN Bartlett, TJ Bartlett, BA Bartley, WW Bartley, KJ Barton, ME Barton, PJ Barton, EJ Bartrim, TJ Bartrim, BP Bartsch, RJ Barwick, JW Barwood, OS Barwood, DA Barzyk, GR Bascombe, DA Baskerville, RM Baskerville, LD Bass, GJ Bassett, WG Bassett, RA Bastian, WD Bastin, WJ Bastow, R Batchelor, WJ Batchelor, D Batchler, RJ Batchler, JA Bate, B Bateman, DE Bateman, RJ Bateman, WSG Bateman, CF Bates, D Bates, DAH Bates, GJ Bates, GL Bates, JA Bates, JE Bates, TJ Bates, L Bath, RC Bath, TW Bath, RC Bather, PJ Batman, J Batrachenko, G Batschowanow, AK Batt, RJ Batt, LR Batten, WK Battersby, VT Battese, CL Batty, JR Batty, CT Baty, KH Bauer, PR Bauers, VR Baugh, J Bauman, BR Baumgart, GJA Bawden, RC Bawden, GA Bawley, EW Baxter, IS Baxter, MC Baxter, R Baxter, L Bayley, NL Bayley, R Bayley, RJ Bayley, BJ Bayliss, GJA Bayliss, MJ Bayliss, SV Bayliss, CCE Bayly, IG Baynes, SWE Bazley, MJ Beach, DS Beadman, ID Beadman, HR Beagley, BR Beale, AS Beales, RB Beaman, FW Beament, DJ Beames, R Beamish, MH Bean, IJ Bear, JW Beard, BJ Beardman, HV Beardsell, BJ Beare, DW Beare, MJ Beasley, NL Beasley, KJ Beaton, AD Beattie, JR Beattie, KJ Beattie, NR Beattie, WH Beattie, AL Beaumont, GJ Beazley, SJ Beazley, VC Bechaz, JG Beck, PH Becker, DJ Beckett, RK Beckinsale, BP Beckwith, JR Bedford, MP Bedford, AJ Bedwell, GB Bedwell, RA Bedwell, GJ Bee, KW Bee, DL Beechey, AE Beeching, RB Beecroft, DL Beer, RG Beere, JF Beetham, DJ Beevers, TC Begley, RS Behrendt, G Beiger, AJ Belbin, LD Belbin, LW Belcher, WF Bele, GL Belgrove, JPM Belkner, BS Bell, CM Bell, CN Bell, CR Bell, CW Bell, D Bell, DJ Bell, DNW Bell, ES Bell, GT Bell, JD Bell, JN Bell, JR Bell, MW Bell, PR Bell, RT Bell, RTW Bell, RW Bell, SK Bell, WR Bell, W Bellamy, RR Bellay, SD Bellette, TB Bellette, DG Bellew, KJ Bellingham, JS Bellwood, JE Belton, GL Benbow, MJ Bence, RI Bence, IR Bendall, NG Bendall, WA Bender, B Benedetti, DM Benfield, LE Benfield, DT Benge, EV Beningfield, G Benington, DHJ Benjamin, LG Benn, WJ Benn, DT Bennet, AR Bennett, BE Bennett, CM Bennett, DP Bennett, FL Bennett, GD Bennett, GJ Bennett, JD Bennett, KT Bennett, LJ Bennett, LP Bennett, MJ Bennett, RA Bennett, RJ Bennett, WJ Bennett, DJ Bennetto, JL Bennetts, RK Bennetts, PB Benny, CA Benporath, J Benra, JJ Bensley, JD Benson, KP Benson, LA Benson, RA Benson, RJ Bentham, CJ Bentley,

IC Bentley, RE Bentley, TC Bentley, R Benton, RC Benton, M Benyk, RH Benzie, L Bereczkey, UW Berens, ID Beresford, NCE Beresford, LA Beresford-Maning, DW Berg, JE Berg, RA Berg, HJ Berger, HP Berger, M Berger, JB Berghuis, NRB Berlyn, DA Bermingham, GG Bermingham, JS Bernhard, LJ Bernhardt, RW Bernhardt, JH Berns, JM Berridge, JR Berridge, DC Berry, IR Berry, JR Berry, LF Berry, MJ Berry, MT Berry, PG Berry, RJ Berry, AB Berryman, GW Berryman, P Berserik, KF Bertoli, DL Bertram, RA Bertram, TA Bertram, TVJ Bertwistle, AP Berzins, JC Beslee, GS Besomo, GD Bessell-Browne, BA Best, LC Best, RG Best, DE Beswick, WJ Beswick, BJ Bettens, LG Bettess, JHL Betts, LF Betts, PB Betts, RJ Betts, KJ Beu, AE Beutel, DD Bevan, GR Bevan, KA Beven, KJ Beveridge, DN Bevins, JM Bevis, DG Bewert, RA Bezzant, DW Bible, AE Bichel, PN Bickley, BW Biddle, M Biddle, KR Bidgood, IK Biggs, JRS Biggs, TJ Biggs, JP Bignell, IP Bignold, CJ Billing, RA Billing, RM Billing, C Billingsley, RE Billingsley, GJ Billman, LL Billsborough, DG Bilton, AN Binder, JW Binder, KD Binding, MW Binding, AL Bindley, GC Bingham, EG Binney, LW Binnington, RL Binnington, AH Binns, DW Binns, PE Binns, RE Binns, GL Birch, GSE Birch, PJ Birch, RG Birch, RH Birch, WJ Birch, WJP Birch, AE Bird, BJ Bird, EJ Bird, ND Bird, PJ Bird, PW Bird, RH Bird, RS Bird, WK Bird, DS Birnie, MA Biro, IM Birrell, KJ Birss, FR Birt, AJ Birtchnell, FP Birtles, BD Birtwell, DB Birtwistle, GC Biscoe, RA Biscoe, AJ Bishop, GW Bishop, LE Bishop, RC Bishop, RD Bishop, RL Bishop, TW Bishop, JL Bizant, AD Black, DC Black, DS Black, G Black, GL Black, JT Black, JW Black, KJ Black, PS Black, PW Black, RM Black, RT Black, WJ Black, PR Blackband, B Blackburn, G Blackburn, GA Blackburn, RJ Blackburn, RD Blacker, AC Blackman, PV Blackman, TF Blackman, WJ Blackman, DG Blackmore, RJ Blackshaw, R Blackwell, BG Blackwood, HW Blad, DTV Blair, JA Blair, DK Blake, GJ Blake, LW Blake, PM Blake, RA Blake, AG Blakelock, KH Blakelock, AW Blanch, DG Blanch, JJ Blanch, PR Blanch, PA Blankesteijn, DJA Blankley, CT Blanning, JPJ Blansjaar, WD Blatch, LG Blaxter, A Blay, JW Blazer, DH Blazey, PJ Blenkinsopp, CC Blennerhassett, P Blennerhassett, HJ Blight, TD Blight, GK Blinkhorn, JM Blinkhorn, RC Bloffwitch, CT Blond, KP Blond, LE Blond, GR Blondel, JB Bloom, FJ Bloomfield, PK Bloomfield, TN Bloomfield, WS Bloomfield, WJ Blows, GJ Blucher, RS Blue, DG Bluhdorn, CL Blundell, BT Blunden, NB Blyth, GC Blyton, TB Blyton, GR Boag, MJD Board, RA Board, KJ Boardman, PE Boardman, JA Boase, PA Boase, FH Bobardt, MD Bobrige, PJ Bobroff, JJ Bobrowski, A Bock, BP Bock, DJ Bock, SF Bock, PS Boddington, WD Boden, WL Boden, PE Bodey, LJ Bodimeade, L Bodsworth, C Boekel, BJ Boettcher, P Boettcher, K Bogan, CF Bogg, JR Bogh, G Bogusz, HD Bohn, GJ Bohr, A Boiteau, RH Bojtschuk, DC Boland, LEA Bolden, EJ Boldery, DF Bolen, JR Bolger, MA Bolger, PR Boling, MD Bolitho, KE Boller, APF Bolton, BJ Bolton, CF Bolton, JR Bolton, WJ Bolton, DP Bond, GJ Bond, JJ Bond, MR Bond, VA Bond, RS Bonnar, LL Bonnett, KJ Bonning, AC Bonora, MF Bonser, MK Booby, IJH Booker, JH Booker, AN Boon, MJ Boon, RC Boon, TA Boon, H Boonstoppel, CJ Booth, CS Booth, EW Booth, IM Booth, RJ Boothey, LJ Boothman, F Boothroyd, JF Borbas, BL Border, VR Boreham, M Borg, H Borgardt, RS Borkowsky, E Boron, MJ Borthwick, RL Borthwick, AG Borwick, J Bos, R Bosboom, RJ Boserio, AR Bosson, MR Bosustow, GA Boswell, GL Botfield, BR Botham, FC Bothamley, JL Bothwell, L Botsman, DS Botwood, TJ Boucher, PC Boughton, JP Boulton, JW Boulton, RP Boulton, GL Bourke, ME Bourke, MJ Bourke, MT Bourke, TW Bourke, VC Bourke, AF Bourne, MR Bow, AM Bowden, AS Bowden, BJ Bowden, FW Bowden, GD Bowden, GR Bowden, ME Bowden, PJ Bowden, RJ Bowden, NK Bowe, CR Bowen, GD Bowen, GJ Bowen, GK Bowen, JA Bowen, PD Bowen, BJ Bowes, JHL Bowes, RB Bowes, JR Bowey, GD Bowkett, RJ Bowkett, PR Bowler, WG Bowles, RM Bowley, WC Bowley, WG Bowley, WR Bowley, JWA Bowling, BA Bowmaker, CN Bowman, DJ Bowman, DM Bowman, FM Bowman, PR Bowman, PV Bowman, GC Bown, MJ Bown, PC Bownas, AK Bowra, CC Bowyer, RN Boxall, RP Boxall, PV Boxhall, AO Boxsell, TL Boxsell, DG Boyce, G Boyce, RW Boyce, AJ Boyd, AW Boyd, GI Boyd, LD Boyd, LW Boyd, PA Boyd, PM Boyd, RA Boyd, RT Boyd, T Boyd, TS Boyd, WH Boyd, WJ Boyd, JJ Boyes, DG Boyington, EM Boyland, AR Boyle,

IJ Boyle, SK Boyle, TT Boyle, RM Boynton, AS Boyt-Cullis, SL Bracey, BR Bracken, GT Bracken, GR Bradbrook, MC Bradbrook, R Braddon, JT Bradford, MA Bradford, RJ Bradford, WF Bradford, BF Bradley, JG Bradley, KR Bradley, PH Bradley, JG Bradmore, JL Bradshaw, JM Bradshaw, PAW Brady, RG Bragge, AC Brailey, MS Brain, RJ Braithwaite, PR Bramley, JR Branch, AR Brandis, JL Brandl, SJ Brandt, HR Brankstone, RO Brasch, PJ Brassel, WJ Bratby, RJ Bratt, J Braun, CH Bray, GH Bray, MHW Bray, RD Bray, WF Brazell, K Brazier, BR Breach, ME Breakspear, MD Brebner, LD Bredhauer, GC Breen, JP Breen, MJ Breen, RJ Breen, PB Breeze, LMC Brelsford, DS Brennan, FJ Brennan, KJ Brennan, KP Brennan, LK Brennan, PE Brennan, RD Brennan, RMP Brennan, ED Brent, LJ Breslan, DC Brett, RJ Brett, MJ Brett-Young, DC Breugem, TJD Breukel, MTH Breukers, GF Brew, GR Brew, KN Brew, MG Brice, VC Brice, G Bridge, RG Bridge, GM Bridger, MT Bridges, LA Brien, A Briene, MT Brierley, MT Briers, DA Briggs, FJ Briggs, GK Briggs, LJ Briggs, PD Briggs, PR Briggs, RC Briggs, SM Briggs, G Brightman, KC Brinckman, DJ Brindley, ALJ Brine, DJ Brinkley, KB Briscoe, WA Briscoe, WL Bristow, CHE Britt, DH Britt, AR Brittain, BJ Brittain, P Brittain, D Brittan, DJ Britten, JW Britten, BJ Britton, P Britton, PD Britton, BJ Britz, OC Britz, DJ Broadbent, DV Broadbent, NJ Broadhurst, IG Broadsmith, MJ Broadsmith, H Broady, RJ Brockie, JTE Brodrick, MA Brodsky, CA Broekhof, AJ Brogan, TT Brogan, WJ Bromage, AM Bromilow, KP Bromilow, CG Bron, PG Brook, TJ Brooke, JR Brooker, SJ Brooker, TJ Brooker, WR Brookes, DC Brooklyn, BE Brooks, BP Brooks, DJ Brooks, DP Brooks, GW Brooks, JB Brooks, NP Brooks, PG Brooks, RA Brooks, RN Brooks, TE Brooks, W Brooks, WBR Brooks, IR Brooksby, CW Broome, AJ Broomhall, GN Broomhall, WN Brotton, D Brouff, RB Broun, W Brouwer, AG Brown, AJ Brown, AL Brown, B Brown, BA Brown, BE Brown, BJ Brown, CH Brown, CL Brown, CW Brown, DC Brown, DG Brown, DJ Brown, DM Brown, DN Brown, DW Brown, EJ Brown, ER Brown, FH Brown, FJ Brown, GC Brown, GD Brown, GK Brown, GL Brown, GP Brown, IA Brown, IC Brown, IR Brown, JA Brown, JC Brown, JR Brown, JV Brown, JW Brown, K Brown, KA Brown, KB Brown, KD Brown, KH Brown, KJ Brown, KT Brown, L Brown, LA Brown, LC Brown, LG Brown, LHR Brown, LW Brown, LWE Brown, MA Brown, MH Brown, MJ Brown, MR Brown, P Brown, PA Brown, PDC Brown, PF Brown, PJC Brown, R Brown, RA Brown, RAW Brown, RB Brown, RG Brown, RH Brown, RJ Brown, RJF Brown, RK Brown, RN Brown, SD Brown, SG Brown, SI Brown, SJ Brown, SK Brown, TG Brown, TJ Brown, TL Brown, TM Brown, W Brown, WF Brown, DJ Browne, GJ Browne, MR Browne, RJ Browne, AR Browning, IR Browning, TJ Browning, WJ Browning, MA Brownless, KJ Brownley, DL Broxholme, DW Bruce, GS Bruce, HD Bruce, JE Bruce, PG Bruce, WD Bruce, WL Bruckner, M Brueckner, CHS Bruggemann, BF Bruhn, SW Bruhn, GF Bruhwiller, MA Bruhwiller, AT Brumley, JR Brumley, DG Brunswick, D Brunton, GD Brushe, TC Bruyns, DB Bryan, GG Bryan, NA Bryan, AG Bryant, DE Bryant, DJ Bryant, JR Bryant, NJ Bryant, RW Bryce, GA Bryen, NW Bryson, R Brzeski, CJ Buchanan, DA Buchanan, DV Buchanan, JC Buchanan, JL Buchanan, KP Buchanan, LW Buchanan, RJ Buchanan, J Buchheim, K Bucholtz, RP Buck, MD Buckett, CE Buckingham, CS Buckingham, PR Buckingham, RK Buckingham, RH Buckland, JC Buckle, VJ Buckle, J Buckleigh, DG Buckley, EB Buckley, JR Buckley, PD Buckley, TJ Buckley, WR Buckley, WE Buckman, PIF Buckmaster, DR Budd, RJ Budd, WM Budden, DE Budworth, RJ Budworth, J Buesselmann, EEO Buethke, S Buglass, MCA Buhagiar, SV Buick, A Buks, GP Bulger, AJ Bull, GJ Bull, PG Bull, RA Bull, RL Bull, LW Bullen, I Bullivant, M Bullivant, GR Bullman, WJ Bulloch, AS Bullock, BJ Bullock, BK Bullock, EI Bullock, JR Bullock, K Bullock, KR Bullock, PS Bullock, DC Bulluss, KV Bulmer, CJ Bunch, RJ Bunker, VR Bunn, PF Bunt, TP Bunt, DG Burbidge, GG Burbidge, KC Burchall, TA Burchat, BJ Burchell, RJ Burden, KG Burdett, PD Burdett, RJ Burdett, DA Burdinat, DM Burdon, GT Burford, RJ Burge, RL Burge, AR Burgess, DW Burgess, HR Burgess, KJ Burgess, ND Burgess, NH Burgess, TE Burgess, TP Burgess, WB Burgess, LC Burggraaff, R Burggraaff, FM Burgin, RA Burk, CL Burke, GR Burke, RK Burke, WH Burke, NG Burkitt, KEA Burkwood, TE Burley, PJ Burn, BJ Burnet, MJ Burnet,

AE Burnett, BCT Burnett, P Burnett, PR Burnett, RW Burnett, WW Burnett, DT Burnheim, AJ Burns, B Burns, BE Burns, BFJ Burns, CM Burns, G Burns, GJ Burns, GR Burns, MGD Burns, RJ Burns, TE Burns, WJ Burns, WT Burns, IM Burnside, NB Burr, TK Burr, PG Burraston, GJ Burrell, SM Burrell, KE Burrett, AE Burridge, DR Burridge, GJ Burridge, LN Burridge, RS Burridge, W Burroughs, WJ Burrowes, A Burrows, AJ Burrows, GW Burrows, SR Burrows, WG Burrows, GR Burt, NL Burt, RA Burt, AT Burton, BS Burton, CW Burton, D Burton, GG Burton, JC Burton, JE Burton, JF Burton, JP Burton, MT Burton, MJ Burtonclay, RT Burtt, LW Bury, RJ Busbridge, EA Busby, M Busby, PA Busch, KR Buschmann, GL Bush, IJ Bush, JC Bush, JT Bush, TW Bush, JD Bushell, LE Bushell, PR Bushell, MJ Buss, R Bussenius, KH Bust, BJ Butcher, FR Butcher, LC Butcher, LG Butcher, PC Butcher, PM Butcher, RG Butcher, SW Butcher, DJ Butland, BJE Butler, DR Butler, GC Butler, GR Butler, GS Butler, HS Butler, IB Butler, J Butler, KC Butler, MV Butler, PH Butler, RJF Butler, RN Butler, RT Butler, SE Butler, WR Butler, PJ Butters, JEK Butterworth, RJ Butterworth, RS Butterworth, NR Buttfield, BJW Buttle, JA Buttle, DW Button, KJ Button, TJ Button, ER Buttress, WA Buttress, DH Buyrn, VE Buzza, HL Byass, JM Byatt, TJ Bycroft, PR Byden, CJH Bye, CJ Byles, E Bylett, A Byrne, DD Byrne, DF Byrne, FM Byrne, JD Byrne, JW Byrne, PG Byrne, SG Byrne, SH Byrne, TG Byrne, JB Byrnes, TW Byrnes, ND Byron, R Byron, ER Cabena, J Cacek, GF Cadd, KJ Caddaye, AL Cady-Ellis, PD Cahill, RM Cahir, TR Cain, J Caine, RJ Caines, MAA Cairney, BD Cairns, DS Cairns, GT Cairns, J Cairns, MA Cairns, PAA Cairns, CD Caisley, DG Calder, LJ Calder, RR Calder, GR Caldow, BA Caldwell, JLT Caldwell, PW Caldwell, DP Callaghan, IG Callaghan, JWH Callaghan, RC Callaghan, RE Callaghan, RF Callahan, WE Callan, EP Callanan, WJ Callanan, EJ Callander, LA Callander, IA Callaway, CK Callins, AE Callister, JS Calvert, B Calway, A Cameron, AI Cameron, AJ Cameron, DH Cameron, GL Cameron, ID Cameron, JC Cameron, JF Cameron, LFR Cameron, RJ Cameron, TG Cameron, VE Cameron, J Camilleri, KW Camm, P Campanaro, BH Campbell, C Campbell, CG Campbell, CT Campbell, DJ Campbell, DM Campbell, GAC Campbell, GE Campbell, GM Campbell, GP Campbell, HR Campbell, IA Campbell, IM Campbell, IP Campbell, ISB Campbell, J Campbell, JC Campbell, JCW Campbell, JF Campbell, KF Campbell, KW Campbell, M Campbell, PD Campbell, R Campbell, RC Campbell, RJ Campbell, RR Campbell, SG Campbell, DJ Camplin, JC Campman, RC Campton, AJ Canala, KK Candlin, DR Candy, TE Cangemi, RD Cann, RWJ Cannan, RL Canning, GR Cannon, JC Cannon, KJ Cannon, RJ Cannon, F Cannova, GA Canobie, WE Cant, GA Cantly, JJ Cantor, AR Cantwell, MM Cantwell, JJ Canty, GL Capeness, AR Capes, BR Caple, RA Caporn, WN Capple, BR Carden, RB Cardow, PL Cardwell, FBM Care, D Carew, DJ Carew, DH Carey, JG Carey, TJ Carey, DI Cargill, DR Cargill, RT Carkeet, BN Carleton, AJ Carley, CG Carlin, SJ Carlin, AC Carling, PL Carlow, AJ Carlson, RC Carlson, JD Carlton, R Carlton, T Carmady, DJ Carman, DR Carman, RA Carman, DS Carmichael, GJ Carmichael, IF Carmichael, PW Carmichael, JA Carnegie, KR Carnegie, BD Carney, JE Carolan, KS Carolan, JM Carpenter, N Carpenter, RJ Carpenter, TL Carpenter, CG Carr, DJ Carr, E Carr, WM Carr, MJ Carrel, BF Carrol, BJ Carroll, CM Carroll, CW Carroll, D Carroll, GJ Carroll, GW Carroll, J Carroll, JD Carroll, JM Carroll, JR Carroll, KE Carroll, NR Carroll, WL Carroll, GJ Carruthers, NM Carson, AD Carter, AW Carter, BW Carter, DC Carter, DJ Carter, EMJ Carter, GMF Carter, IG Carter, MD Carter, MP Carter, PJ Carter, RE Carter, TL Carter, WDW Carter, WR Carter, SW Carthew, AJ Cartwright, KH Cartwright, PJ Cartwright, RG Carty, AA Casadio, KS Casas, RA Case, AH Casement, AJ Casey, FJ Casey, MJ Casey, RD Casey, RH Casey, GH Cash, JWO Cash, NW Cash, DJ Cashman, R Cason, P Cass, WD Cass, H Cassa, MJ Cassidy, RJ Cassidy, IH Castens, KR Castle, RJ Castle, WP Castle, BS Castles, GS Cathcart, DJ Catling, RJ Cato, DA Caton, DPR Caton, LE Caton, W Caton, RH Cattermole, A Cattle, LK Catton, SL Caudery, RW Caudwell, RL Caulfield, WA Caulfield, BR Cavalier, GN Cavanagh, JE Cavanagh, MF Cavanagh, RL Cavanagh, RW Cavanagh, T Cavanough, JR Cavenett, R Cawthorn, JT Cecchi, MR Cechner, RJP Cecil, JD Celeban, RF Cerritelli, S Cesarec, E Ceslis, ZJ Cetera, RB Chadwick, T Chadwick, HD Chaffey, PD Chaffey, RK Chaffey,

JW Chalk, GG Chalklen, AJ Challis, DA Challis, AM Chalmers, DB Chalmers, RH Chalmers, IT Chaloner, CP Chamberlain, DG Chamberlain, GJ Chamberlain, GWE Chamberlain, RF Chamberlain, D Chambers, NW Chambers, WJ Chambers, JC Champion, PH Champness, CM Chance, GWT Chandler, IE Chandler, JD Chandler, KM Chandler, ND Chandler, RE Chandler, RTM Chandler, RC Channell, RH Channell, TM Channell, DM Channon, JMC Chant, R Chant, DE Chaplin, S Chaplin, TL Chaplin, L Chaplin-Ardagh, AD Chapman, B Chapman, DJ Chapman, GJH Chapman, JJ Chapman, JL Chapman, LH Chapman, PL Chapman, RJ Chapman, WJ Chapman, PA Chappell, A Chappelow, CG Chard, FB Charles, GT Charles, TN Charles, JEJ Charlesworth, MO Charlesworth, GW Charlston, DA Charlton, PJ Charlton, TM Charlton, AC Charlwood, RK Charters, ET Chatfield, MJ Chatfield, TL Chatterton, AG Chattington, WT Chatwin, KW Chay, JD Cheal, BG Cheers, PK Cheers, LB Cheetham, TJ Cheetham, WJ Cheetham, BJ Cheffins, PC Chegwidden, BJ Chelman, GJ Cheney, BR Chenoweth, RA Cherake, KP Cherwin, JA Chesson, AJ Chester, NW Chester, V Chetcuti, NL Chidgey, RJ Chilcott, BF Chilman, GR Chilman, KD Chilvers, NL Chipper, RK Chippindall, PK Chirgwin, JB Chisholm, B Chittock, TE Chitty, EK Chiverton, MT Chopping, RB Chorley, RR Choyce, AL Christensen, PM Christensen, WE Christensen, LV Christian, R Christian, PE Christianson, AM Christie, DJ Christie, GA Christie, RA Christie, RF Christie, RGS Christie, RJ Christie, TH Christie, WJS Christie, M Christofis, WFE Christopher, CD Church, LR Church, P Church, SJ Church, DJ Churches, LM Churches, NM Churches, GA Churchland, DR Churchward, J Cias, AJ Cichero, JB Cicolini, EW Ciemcioch, J Ciemcioch, GR Clampett, CR Clancy, NF Clancy, GR Clare, R Clare, SM Clare, RG Clarey, TE Clarey, AW Clark, B Clark, BF Clark, BV Clark, CR Clark, DWA Clark, EAF Clark, GM Clark, HR Clark, JF Clark, JS Clark, K Clark, LR Clark, P Clark, PA Clark, PJ Clark, PL Clark, RC Clark, RG Clark, RK Clark, RL Clark, RM Clark, RT Clark, RW Clark, ST Clark, TJ Clark, VR Clark, AJ Clarke, AK Clarke, AT Clarke, BDH Clarke, BJ Clarke, BT Clarke, DAH Clarke, DL Clarke, DR Clarke, DW Clarke, FR Clarke, KJ Clarke, LJ Clarke, MJ Clarke, NJ Clarke, PT Clarke, RA Clarke, RD Clarke, RF Clarke, RH Clarke, RJ Clarke, RN Clarke, TD Clarke, TJ Clarke, W Clarke, WC Clarke, RT Clarkson, MR Clasper, GJJ Claus, RJ Clauscen, WA Claxton, JB Claypole, JC Claypole, WL Clayton, DD Cleak, BJ Cleary, EV Cleary, GB Cleary, LJ Cleary, SD Cleary, JL Clegg, MW Clegg, S Clegg, PL Cleghorn, JW Clelland, RA Clelland, DH Clem, GH Clement, RL Clement, DN Clements, KV Clements, PP Clements, GL Clemson, WJ Clemson, T Clenton, CJ Cleveland, CG Cleverly, MB Clifford, RPH Clifford, TJ Clifford, JJ Clifton, RI Clifton, DE Clinch, WA Clogan, CPH Close, KA Close, MJ Close, WE Close, LA Clothier, BBS Clough, BR Clough, JT Clough, LW Clough, M Clough, PJ Clough, PR Clucas, GJ Clunes, BW Cluse, MJ Coad, BJ Coates, BR Coats, CI Coats, NJ Coats, GA Cobb, NHV Cobb, PW Cobb, RJ Cobb, LG Cobban, RJ Cobban, PJE Cobble, R Cochrane, SB Cocker, RJ Cocking, GE Cockram, PJ Cockroft, GA Cocks, RW Cocks, TW Code, MR Codling, RJ Cody, PJ Coe, JH Coff, EP Coffey, M Coffey, MJ Coffey, TP Coffey, NJ Coghlan, RW Coghlan, RJ Colbert, GM Colbran, RT Coldwell, AD Cole, AG Cole, BJ Cole, DP Cole, ER Cole, GAC Cole, GR Cole, JC Cole, JR Cole, JV Cole, PE Cole, RC Cole, RD Cole, RG Cole, B Coleman, BD Coleman, BT Coleman, CD Coleman, JAE Coleman, JC Coleman, M Coleman, NJ Coleman, NR Coleman, PA Coleman, RM Coleman, TN Coleman, TP Coleman, WT Coleman, CRJ Coles, EF Coles, LP Coles, RW Coles, JA Coley, SA Coll, JC Collas, LJ Colless, BP Collett, GJ Colley, TA Collicutt, WJ Collidge, RB Collie, EH Collier, TV Collier, AF Colligan, NL Colling, D Collingridge, AR Collings, PF Collings, AR Collins, B Collins, BJ Collins, DA Collins, DG Collins, EP Collins, F Collins, GG Collins, IM Collins, IS Collins, JO Collins, KJ Collins, NT Collins, P Collins, PA Collins, PJ Collins, PM Collins, PR Collins, RC Collins, RJ Collins, RM Collins, RS Collins, RW Collins, SC Collins, T Collins, WR Collins, MR Collinson, KC Collison, DN Collyer, PJ Collyer, RD Colman, SA Colman, WJ Colman, AE Colvin, BL Comerford, JT Comfort, IJ Conder, ED Condie, RE Condon, RF Condon, KJ Condren, N Conduit, KL Confoy, DB Conlin, WG Conlin, SJ Conlon, DM Conn, BA Connell, BC Connell, BR Connell, ID Connell, LJ Connell, LN Connell, JF Connellan, GA Connelly, JF Connelly, DB Connolly, DJ Connolly, J Connolly, KJ Connolly, SJ Connolly, VK Connolly, GV Connor, J Connor, SB Connor, AG Connors, DT Connors, GP Conole, IR Conole, BD Conroy, JE Conroy, G Consadine, PB Constable, AL Constance, ME Conway, RS Conway-Mortimer, A Cook, AJ Cook, BT Cook, CJ Cook, DJ Cook, DT Cook, EJ Cook, GW Cook, IR Cook, JL Cook, JP Cook, JR Cook, KJ Cook, LC Cook, LF Cook, MJ Cook, NJ Cook, RG Cook, SW Cook, TR Cook, WM Cook, B Cooke, GJ Cooke, GR Cooke, ML Cooke, RP Cooke, PJ Cooke-Russell, DG Coombe, GR Coombe, KL Coombe, WF Coombe, LJ Coomber, GW Coombes-Pearce, J Coombs, PW Coombs, RM Coon, AJ Cooney, A Cooper, BA Cooper, BM Cooper, CR Cooper, DA Cooper, DJ Cooper, EC Cooper, ER Cooper, FJ Cooper, GE Cooper, GF Cooper, GL Cooper, GM Cooper, IR Cooper, JC Cooper, JL Cooper, LJ Cooper, LR Cooper, MA Cooper, MJ Cooper, MR Cooper, OR Cooper, P Cooper, RB Cooper, RJ Cooper, SJ Cooper, TW Cooper, WH Cooper, WL Cooper, PR Coote, RJ Coote, KR Coots, MJ Copal, JH Cope, RDG Copeland, RR Copelin, SI Copp, FA Copping, MFK Coppins, PW Corbett, BE Corby, EJ Corby, JP Corby, RG Corby, CJ Corcoran, JB Corcoran, LG Cordner, MJ Cordwell, HG Cordy, RG Coremans, RW Coridas, RF Corish, RA Cork, GR Corker, LD Corkery, ME Corner, CC Corney, PR Corney, JR Cornish, MA Cornish, PL Cornish, RJ Cornish, D Corran, PL Corran, DJ Corrigan, PG Cory, BD Costa, IG Costa, GT Costello, ON Costello, RJ Costello, LN Coster, RF Coster, DB Cotsell, KJ Cottam, PJ Cottam, LL Cotterell, JJ Cotterill, ATB Cotton, G Cottrell, AJ Couch, SJ Couch, GE Coucill, BJ Coughlan, RJ Coughlan, BGC Coulson, GD Coulson, GJ Coulson, PK Coulson, RJ Coulson, TW Coulson, GF Coulthard, TR Coulthard, GM Counahan, DJF Couper, JH Courage, DJ Court, SB Courtier, ID Courtney, RJ Courtney, DJ Cousins, PN Cousins, RC Cousins, GD Coutts, RS Coutts, AR Cove, GA Coventry, RD Cowan, RJ Cowan, TM Cowan, MJH Coward, AD Cowell, GV Cowell, KJ Cowell, CW Cowie, RC Cowin, CW Cowland, BW Cowley, RH Cowley, AR Cowling, JG Cowlishaw, BD Cox, DA Cox, FD Cox, FW Cox, GM Cox, GN Cox, GT Cox, KR Cox, KT Cox, LA Cox, LC Cox, NC Cox, NE Cox, PF Cox, PM Cox, RJ Cox, RS Cox, TH Cox, WA Cox, WD Cox, WJ Cox, WR Cox, M Coyle, EM Coysh, ES Crabb, GJ Crabb, KH Crabbe, JH Cracknell, JW Cracknell, DJ Craggs, JL Craib, AH Craig, DM Craig, JST Craig, RA Craig, ST Craig, TN Craig, GR Craige, IK Craine, MN Craine, PS Craker, SJ Cramp, SE Cranage, AL Crandon, JC Crane, LF Cranston, CS Cranswick, NJ Craven, LR Crawfoot, AD Crawford, BC Crawford, FN Crawford, IM Crawford, KA Crawford, SK Crawford, A Crawley, EM Crawley, JA Crawley, MJ Crawley, TJ Crawley, BL Craymer, GL Craze, M Creagh, JE Creasey, RL Creber, WH Creedon, PM Creelman, D Crellin, TD Crellin, RE Cremer, AJ Cresp, JF Crew, BJ Crews, BM Cribbin, TW Crichton, GJ Criddle, RM Cripps, GA Crisp, ST Crisp, AD Critchley, IA Critchley, RL Critchley, RL Crocker, DW Crockett, GV Crockett, CJ Crockford, DC Crockford, R Croese, WG Croese, A Croft, DJ Croft, JW Croft, RF Croft, RJ Crofton, IG Crokam, WP Croke, IH Crombie, JM Crompton, CJ Cromwell, DA Cronin, DR Crook, GW Crook, D Crooks, AAM Croot, BD Cropley, AJ Croquett, AP Cross, B Cross, BT Cross, D Cross, DG Cross, DP Cross, ER Cross, MF Cross, MK Cross, PJ Cross, RF Cross, RJ Cross, SJ Cross, WH Cross, AFI Crossman, BH Crossman, PJ Crosswell, FJ Crouch, SC Crouch, IA Croucher, JC Croucher, JV Croucher, RK Crow, RW Crow, BG Crowe, GA Crowe, LV Crowe, RL Crowle, KF Crowley, DJ Crowther, M Crowther, RD Croxford, TW Cruise, MB Crummy, W Crutch, SE Cruttenden, JW Cruz, ND Ctercteko, B Cuculowsky, PA Cuddy, DN Cugley, RS Culbard, W Culbert, JM Cull, BA Cullan, BJ Cullen, BR Cullen, CH Cullen, DJ Cullen, J Cullen, JAO Cullen, JW Cullen, LJ Cullen, RK Cullen, OF Culley, PJ Cullinan, DG Culpan, TA Cumes, PG Cummin, D Cumming, DE Cumming, RR Cumming, GI Cummings, PT Cummings, RG Cummings, AR Cummins, BJ Cummins, DB Cundy, OO Cunliffe, BJ Cunningham, CJ Cunningham, DA Cunningham, JE Cunningham, LV Cunningham, NJ Cunningham, RW Cunningham, SW Cunningham, WJ Cunningham, BM Cunnington, G Cunnington, J Cunnington, LT Cupitt, DP Curbishley, FG Curbishley, JE Curbishley, AJR Curran, JD Curran, PD Currey, DM Currie, GA Currie, GD Currie, JF Currie, JW Currie, MJ Currie, P Currie, WR Currie, WJ Curry, AE Curtin, AG Curtis, BG Curtis, BP Curtis, EC Curtis, JL Curtis, MW Curtis, PG Curtis, RA Curtis, RC Curtis, RN Curtis, WPJ Curtius, AR Curyer, CJ Cusack, JE Cusack, RP Cussen, DM Cuthbert, AJ Cuthbertson, DM Cuthbertson, WJ Cutler, RA Cutting, I Cuttle, JR Da Costa, JM Da Silva, JMO Da Silva, ST Dacey, TW Dack, TL Dackiewicz, RT Dadd, GR Dade, TA Dadswell, MR Daetz, TW Daff, EF Dagan, J Dagwell, RG Dagworthy, PJ Dahlstrom, RH Daines, DW Daish, ER Dalby, RC Dalby, DJ Dale, MC Dale, PL Dale, RE Dale, PA Dales, CF Daley, KD Daley, MJ Daley, VW Daley, CR Dalgliesh, JW Dalgliesh, IR Dalglish, LM Dalle-Nogare, HHG Dalrymple, BJ Dalton, DJ Dalton, PJ Dalton, BJ Daly, CB Daly, GD Daly, GV Daly, MT Daly, VJ Daly, DW Dalziel, ENR D'Amato, RG Dance, CG Dangerfield, AWB Daniel, GA Daniel, GR Daniel, JC Daniel, NGR Daniel, AL Daniels, BC Daniels, G Daniels, PE Daniels, PT Daniels, MJ Danielson, CP Dann, JVM Dansey, DV D'Antoine, AM Danzi, M Darby, DJ Darcy, GJ Darcy, D Dargusch, GJ Dark, HP Darkiewicz, CL Darling, RT Darlington, GJ Darnell, JA Darnley-Stuart, JP Darrington, DG Dart, WE Dartnell, DC Darvell, RJ Darvell, R Dasczyk, JA Dau, KC Daunt, KJ Davenport, PJ Davenport, AG Davey, JA Davey, JK Davey, MJ Davey, PJ Davey, TR Davey, AD Davidson, CJ Davidson, DI Davidson, J Davidson, JM Davidson, RF Davidson, RJ Davidson, RM Davidson, S Davidson, WD Davidson, WM Davidson, DG Davie, A Davies, AE Davies, AM Davies, BA Davies, DR Davies, DT Davies, GL Davies, IG Davies, JB Davies, JE Davies, MR Davies, MW Davies, NE Davies, PJ Davies, PM Davies, RJ Davies, RK Davies, RT Davies, RW Davies, TA Davies, TG Davies, WMJ Davies, AG Davies-Graham, AA Davis, AE Davis, AG Davis, AJ Davis, AL Davis, AM Davis, B Davis, BF Davis, BJ Davis, BS Davis, BW Davis, CG Davis, CJL Davis, CS Davis, DB Davis, DRJ Davis, GJ Davis, GLJ Davis, GM Davis, J Davis, JDP Davis, KJ Davis, LG Davis, LJ Davis, LW Davis, ML Davis, MT Davis, PK Davis, RJ Davis, RL Davis, RLR Davis, RM Davis, RW Davis, TL Davis, GC Davison, J Davison, PJ Davison, RS Davison, RS Davson, KE Daw, J Dawe, KJ Dawes, SG Daws, AG Dawson, D Dawson, DG Dawson, DM Dawson, GD Dawson, GH Dawson, JG Dawson, KJ Dawson, M Dawson, PA Dawson, RT Dawson, BW Day, EW Day, HJ Day, IH Day, JG Day, JR Day, LD Day, RG Day, CJ Daylight, DJ Daylight, PJ De Abel, GAJ De Bakker, RC De Banks, LA De Bondi, JH De Gooijer, P De Graaff, JJ De Groot, PA De Jongh, HJ De Koning, PC De Kort, NG De Lacy, DK De Losa, AE De Luca, NP De Luca, WP De Munck, MG De Nooyer, DA De Rooy, RD De Ross, DF De Silva, MG De Smid, R De Smid, GR De Vaurno, RL De Vaurno, EA De Vere, TR De Voil, J De Vries, CWJ De Waard, AF Deacon, CE Deacon, CLA Deacon, GN Deacon, KF Deakin, P Deakin, CB Dean, DS Dean, GR Dean, LR Dean, RJ Dean, ST Dean, RA Deane, R Dearden, ID Deas, RA Deas, SA Debnam, GD Debney, DG Debus, PGV Dechaineux, TW Decini, BG Dedman, PH Dedourek, B Dedynskyj, JRC Dee, GR Deeble, GM Deegan, JL Deem, DA Dees, D Dejanovic, WN Dekker, JR Delahunty, MP Delahunty, DWJ Delaine, CW Delaney, JG Delaney, JR Delaney, K Delaney, RF Delaney, TJ Delaney, AW Dellamarta, JWA Dellar, SR Dellar, RA Delmenico, JE Delooze, R D'elton, GJ Demarco, VN Demczuk, IB D'emden, BFW Demeary, BA Demnar, GS Dempsey, AR Dempster, RD Denaro, SF Dendle, TJ Denham, A Denic, DA Denman, JLJ Denmead, HC Dennert, NL Dennett, IC Dennien, DG Denning, MD Denning, MJ Denning, LE Dennis, LJ Dennis, MJ Dennis, WF Dennis, DJ Dennison, HD Dennison, AG Denovan, CE Densley, FG Densten, PVD Denver, D Deppeler, DE Deppeler, TA Deppeler, RT Derbidge, PG Derby, D Dernedde, PL Derriman, PT Detering, JO Dettmann, DJ Dettmer, NH Devene, M Devenish, D Devenny, HJ Devereux, MJ Devine, NA Devitt, S Devjak, GJ Devlin, KR Devlin, PN Dewar, RJ Dewar, SS Dewar, DB Dewhurst, RK Dewis, SH Dexter, AG Di Betta, BJ Diamond, AP Diciunas, RA Diciunas, GA Dick, JA Dick, JS Dick, DG Dickens, CH Dicker, JG Dicker, CW Dicker-Lee, PWT Dickey, RL Dickfos, DNW Dickinson, RR Dickinson, JW Dickman, AG Dickson, GJ Dickson, JC Dickson, JS Dickson, KG Dickson,

RJ Dickson, RW Dickson, JH Diefenbach, TJ Diehm, HJM Diekema, J Dietmann, JR Diffen, AJ Diggelman, JG Diggerson, AB Diggle, ML Diggle, RJ Dight, KC Digney, LJ Digney, GJ Dikkenberg, C Dillon, CR Dillon, EJ Dillon, JC Dillon, LJ Dillon, MJ Dillon, PG Dilworth, PC Dine, RJ Dine, KC Ding, NHA Dingle, RC Dingle, JA Dini, LA Dinsdale, ML Dinsdale, DL Dinte, K Dios-Brun, MC Disney, WC Diston, DK Ditchburn, MA Divertie, GW Dix, RC Dix, AL Dixon, DJ Dixon, GE Dixon, HK Dixon, JA Dixon, LC Dixon, PG Dixon, R Dixon, WEJ Dixon, PAG Dlask, J Dobbie, KE Dobbie, PL Dobbie, AF Dobbs, T Dobos, HE Dobosz, W Dobosz, O Dobrowolski, BC Dobson, JB Dobson, KJ Dobson, LG Dobson, LL Dobson, WE Dobson, AF Docherty, EA Docherty, W Docherty, AM Dodd, DJ Dodd, JA Dodd, JL Dodd, KJ Dodd, AT Dodds, CJ Dodds, GW Dodds, RD Dodds, M Dodsworth, LW Dodt, TD Doessel, A Doherty, BT Doherty, J Doherty, JF Doherty, RF Doherty, JCM Dohmen, BW Dole, GJ Dollar, JFC Dollar, SN Dollard, ET Domanski, A Donald, BJ Donald, GA Donald, IK Donald, JG Donald, JR Donald, BM Donaldson, CG Donaldson, G Donaldson, IR Donaldson, MG Donaldson, NJ Donaldson, RT Donaldson, WJ Donaldson, JM Donato, BL Donchi, KE Doncon, AR Donnan, RA Donne, RJ Donne, AF Donnelly, F Donnelly, GJ Donnelly, JB Donnelly, KM Donnelly, NJ Donnelly, PB Donnelly, RJ Donnelly, RP Donnelly, WG Donnelly, EK Donoghue, RW Donoghue, BJ Donohue, HJ Donohue, KM Donohue, R Donohue, AS Donovan, BJ Donovan, FJ Donovan, JC Donovan, JW Donsworth, P Donzow, JR Doohan, KA Doolan, TJ Doolin, TW Dorain, MC Doran, PJ Dorante, RJ Dore, RW Dore, AN Dorey, RJ Dorham, AJ Dorhauer, JD Dorsett, DR Dorward, BJ Double, JA Doudle, JR Doudle, IR Dougall, JA Doughty, BN Douglas, IC Douglas, JAT Douglas, JC Douglas, JR Douglas, KA Douglas, PG Douglas, CK Douglass, A Doust, G Doust, BR Douthwaite, GK Dove, JJ Dover, AD Dow, AR Dow, RF Dow, MFP Dowd, LA Dowdell, TN Dowdell, KD Dower, PS Dower, W Dower, BR Dowling, DR Dowling, JHF Dowling, PJ Dowling, LG Down, RJ Down, GJ Downes, T Downie, RCJ Downing, PA Downs, RG Downton, WC Downton, AC Downward, SA Downward, AD Dowsett, BM Dowsing, JR Dowson, GC Doyle, GP Doyle, HS Doyle, JE Doyle, JR Doyle, MC Doyle, PH Doyle, PR Doyle, RLG Doyle, SA Doyle, SJ Doyle, WC Doyle, HL Drabble, DJ Drane, B Dransfield, BG Draper, G Draper, AS Dray, KR Drechsler, BP Drew, DJ Drew, JA Drew, KE Drew, KW Drew, PM Drew, WL Drew, LJ Dreyer, RJ Drinan, JA Drinkwater, KJ Drinkwater, LN Drinkwater, FJ Driscoll, GB Driscoll, VL Driscoll, F Driver, WH Driver, EA Drohan, AC Drover, GA Drudge, HC Drummond, AR Drury, GJ Dryden, DJ Drysdale, PT Du Guesclin, DA Dubbeld, EL Ducat, GA Ducker, N Duckworth, PB Dudley, KR Dudman, R Duesing, PA Duff, GA Duffey, JR Duffey, IR Duffner, EK Duffy, KJ Duffy, KVC Duffy, LJ Duffy, BE Duggan, ND Duguid, AJ Duke, FJ Duke, RE Duke, JH Dukes, HJL Duley, BA Dun, LG Dunbar, WG Dunbar, BM Duncan, CW Duncan, ER Duncan, JC Duncan, JH Duncan, JW Duncan, LA Duncan, LJ Duncan, MM Duncan, RV Duncan, JD Dundas, CR Dunham, A Dunlop, CJ Dunlop, DA Dunlop, DJ Dunlop, JC Dunlop, R Dunlop, BGJ Dunn, BJ Dunn, C Dunn, CR Dunn, CS Dunn, DB Dunn, DL Dunn, GF Dunn, IL Dunn, JP Dunn, KC Dunn, LW Dunn, MD Dunn, OS Dunn, PJ Dunn, G Dunnachie, JO Dunne, JP Dunne, MT Dunne, RO Dunne, ST Dunne, MJ Dunner, EAG Dunstan, JF Dunstan, WG Dunster, J Dunthorne, M Dunton, AH Durant, GC Durdin, JM Durick, PJ Durran, JH Durrant, A Durston, LD Durston, KW Dusting, PW Dusting, B Duszynski, BA Dutch, RM Dutton, SJ Dutton, DP Dwiar, AR Dwojacki, DG Dwyer, GM Dwyer, RA Dwyer, SM Dwyer, RF Dybala, GT Dybing, LM Dybing, JD Dyer, JG Dyer, JT Dyer, W Dyksma, AF Dykstra, CG Dykstra, AA Dyson, J Dyson, JG Dyson, KM Dyson, PR Dyson, V Dzodz, S Eades, T Eades, KP Eagan, JR Eagland, BL Eagles, JH Eagles, WCS Eaglesham, AW Eakins, KC Eales, AJ Eames, RD Eames, MEH Earlam, LJ Earle, GJ Earley, PJ Earnshaw, DG Easom, PJ East, TM Eastcott, JE Easter, DH Eastgate, FJ Eastwell, BT Eastwood, CP Eastwood, TC Eather, WB Eaton, GD Eaves, H Ebdon, AW Eberhardt, RE Eberhardt, AL Eccleston, AG Eckel, EJ Eckermann, WT Eckhardt, BE Eddes, DB Eddington, AJ Eddy, KJ Eddy, A Edgar, AJ Edgar, G Edge, J Edge, PJ Edge, GS Edgecombe, GW Edgell, LW Edgerton, MD Edgeworth, DM Edhouse, DHS Edson, DH Edwardes, AE Edwards, AJ Edwards, AT Edwards, B Edwards, CJ Edwards, D Edwards, DC Edwards, DR Edwards, GA Edwards, GJ Edwards, IG Edwards, J Edwards, JA Edwards, JG Edwards, KF Edwards, KJ Edwards, KRA Edwards, LJ Edwards, LW Edwards, MI Edwards, MJ Edwards, N Edwards, NWR Edwards, PCD Edwards, PGF Edwards, PJ Edwards, RD Edwards, RH Edwards, RJ Edwards, RP Edwards, SP Edwards, WJ Edwards, PJ Eerden, BF Egan, BP Egan, CH Egan, JF Egan, JJ Egan, PF Egan, RJ Egan, RV Egan, H Egberts, LW Eggins, MR Egginton, G Eglitis, P Eimer, SL Eisenhuth, BP Ekin, J Ekman, FV Elarde, GA Elcoate, DG Elder, JB Eldershaw, RJ Eldridge, WJ Eldridge, PAL Eley, RJ Eley, PJ Elffmoff, WE Elgey, G Elias, FO Eliason, PL Elion, GPM Elix, RA Elkington, ED Elks, AC Ellard, BD Ellaway, HJ Ellem, PA Ellem, RE Ellen, WH Ellery, RJ Elley, SJ Ellingford, F Ellingworth, JR Elliot, R Elliot, AR Elliott, CF Elliott, DJ Elliott, DR Elliott, FE Elliott, JC Elliott, P Elliott, PJ Elliott, PL Elliott, BN Ellis, CJ Ellis, DP Ellis, GT Ellis, JW Ellis, LF Ellis, NW Ellis, P Ellis, PD Ellis, PS Ellis, SH Ellis, BC Elliss, DR Elliss, AJ Elms, BB Elphick, I Elsley, PJ Elsley, CJ Elsmore, GC Elstob, PR Elton, TRA Elverd, JC Elvish, TJ Elwell, VR Elwell, RS Ely, W Emans, EA Emery, RM Emery, TH Emery, LM Emmerson, AL Emmerton, SF Emmett, FW Emms, M Emslie, ML Endersby, PF Endicott, KW Engelking, KB Engelsman, BR Engert, RC England, RJ England, LJ English, RD English, RF English, AG Ennis, PT Ennis, SP Ennor, BL Enright, TJ Epis, LF Erbacher, MJ Erceg, GB Erickson, KKW Ericson, JV Eriksson, RC Errington, AC Erskine, DJ Erskine, ID Erskine, GR Erwin, WR Espin, NS Esson, AP Etherington, AJ Euling, KN Eustance, AF Evans, AH Evans, BW Evans, DJ Evans, DP Evans, DR Evans, DS Evans, EA Evans, EB Evans, G Evans, GC Evans, GD Evans, GW Evans, JH Evans, JR Evans, JWR Evans, KE Evans, KL Evans, L Evans, MJ Evans, NA Evans, NC Evans, NH Evans, NJ Evans, NT Evans, PC Evans, PH Evans, PL Evans, PW Evans, RA Evans, RC Evans, RD Evans, RE Evans, RJ Evans, RL Evans, RW Evans, SB Evans, TJS Evans, WL Evans, PJ Eveille, DR Evelyn-Liardet, KG Everett, RT Everett, PJ Everist, JC Everitt, CG Everson, MA Every, AJ Evett, RA Evison, SW Ewen, JD Exley, AL Ey, CJ Ey, DE Ey, MH Ey, PR Ey, FA Eyck, LFA Eyck, I Ezergailis, J Ezergailis, V Ezergailis, N Ezzy, JB Faber, JR Face, AG Facey, WG Facey, RJ Fadden, MR Fagg, WJ Fail, RG Fairbairn, RW Fairbairn, DP Fairfax, DJ Fairhurst, DH Falconer, DW Falconer, JE Falk, EG Falla, JR Falloon, PA Falzun, CF Fanker, KJ Fanker, W Farenik, EG Farmer, KJ Farmer, PL Farmer, PR Farmer, SD Farmer, MJC Farnan, AS Farnell, HG Farquhar, JW Farquhar, SH Farquhar, VJ Farquhar, ID Farquharson-Scott, DB Farr, HD Farrant, RG Farraway, B Farrell, JC Farrell, JF Farrell, MJ Farrell, PT Farrell, RJ Farrell, WW Farrell, LF Farrelly, GW Farrow, A Farrugia, P Farrugia, DD Farthing, K Farthing, BJ Fathers, TA Fauchon, SG Faulder, CJ Faulkner, DA Faulkner, FT Faulkner, AP Faulks, RJ Faunce, B Faust, JV Favaloro, GF Fawdry, AR Faye, RW Fayers, RC Fazackerley, VB Fazio, LW Fearn, GM Fearne, R Featherstone, JW Fegan, RV Feil, MK Felgate, KR Fellenberg, NJ Felsch, NH Fenn, J Fennell, JK Fenner, HA Fenske, BR Fenton, PH Fenton, TJ Fenton, KP Fenwick, TJ Fenwick, B Ferguson, CS Ferguson, DJ Ferguson, DW Ferguson, IC Ferguson, IK Ferguson, J Ferguson, JM Ferguson, JS Ferguson, JT Ferguson, KR Ferguson, LH Ferguson, PIM Ferguson, RA Ferguson, SA Ferguson, WH Ferguson, KJ Fergusson, JA Fern, GP Fernihough, R Fernley, PMW Fernyhough, JGM Ferrari, PJ Ferres, JE Ferrier, AG Ferris, G Ferris, LK Ferris, ML Feutrill, GH Fewkes, RF Fidler, BD Fidock, AG Field, AI Field, DA Field, JW Field, KR Field, M Field, RH Field, JD Fielder, EL Fielding, IF Fielding, JF Fielding, KI Fielding, JP Fields, LR Figg, DK Filgate, JA Filipek, E Filippetti, R Filmer, GB Finch, JH Finch, JR Finch, JW Finch, GW Findlater, H Findlay, JB Findlay, JW Findlay, JB Finlay, JM Finlay, KD Finlay, D Finn, JF Finn, AGK Finnemore, JP Finucane, SF Firman, GJ Firth, JD Firth, JW Firth, RJ Firth, BF Fischer, CA Fischer, J Fischer, P Fischer, WB Fischer, MR Fish, MC Fishbourne, AL Fisher, BJJ Fisher, BP Fisher, CR Fisher, DG Fisher, G Fisher, GL Fisher, GW Fisher, HT Fisher, JGA Fisher, KE Fisher, LV Fisher, MA Fisher, MK Fisher, RD Fisher, TR Fisher, AC Fishwick, GJ Fitch, WG Fitness, RE Fittler, BJ Fittock, B Fitton, BJ Fitzgerald, CW Fitzgerald, FB Fitzgerald, JF Fitzgerald, KJ Fitzgerald, MJ Fitzgerald, J Fitzgibbon, DB Fitzpatrick, FC Fitzpatrick, JF Fitzpatrick, RJ Fitzpatrick, RL Fitzpatrick, TF Fitzpatrick, TJ Fitzpatrick, IR Fitzsimmons, AL Flaherty, CI Flaherty, SJM Flak, BW Flanagan, GT Flanagan, MD Flanagan, MJ Flanagan, TG Flanagan, MJ Flassman, PA Flatley, WG Flatt, DJ Fleet, AR Flegg, BK Fleming, DA Fleming, JQ Fleming, JR Fleming, MJ Fleming, T Fleming, AE Fletcher, AR Fletcher, D Fletcher, DTW Fletcher, GTM Fletcher, HB Fletcher, JA Fletcher, LG Fletcher, NC Fletcher, PR Fletcher, RF Fletcher, T Fletcher, MJ Flett, RL Flett, K Flindell, DV Flint, GC Flint, WGC Flint, RM Flisher, PJ Flockhart, BP Flood, JG Flood, JW Flowers, AR Fluris, CB Flux, BC Flynn, P Flynn, RJ Flynn, KJ Foale, HJ Foeken, KJ Fogarty, PL Fogarty, TW Fogg, VC Fogliani, GR Fogo, SH Fogo, CJ Foley, LJ Foley, MW Foley, TF Foley, BJ Folkes, ACE Foord, RC Foord, TJ Foord, HJ Foot, PK Foote, GA Forbes, RA Forbes, RM Forbes, JA Ford, JC Ford, JH Ford, RT Ford, SJ Ford, TC Ford, TL Ford, VG Ford, W Ford, EH Forder, W Forder, MG Fordham, VH Forman, GD Forno, CM Forrest, LWF Forrest, MB Forrest, RC Forrest, WP Forrest, DJ Forster, RA Forsyth, RB Forwood, DAF Foster, DJ Foster, GW Foster, HCM Foster, IT Foster, JD Foster, RA Foster, RB Foster, RG Foster, SJ Foster, TJ Foster, WR Foster, J Fotek, T Fotek, CW Fothergill, CR Foulis, RL Fountain, DN Fourmile, PF Fowler, RD Fowler, WJ Fowler, WJ Fowles, AA Fox, FT Fox, HE Fox, ID Fox, KR Fox, LG Fox, LN Fox, MJ Fox, NH Fox, PG Fox, RCT Fox, RJ Fox, RO Fox, SE Fox, WT Fox, LA Foxon, JF Fraher, EG Frain, BJ Frame, IG Frame, EJ France, CF Francis, CH Francis, DA Francis, FN Francis, HJ Francis, JW Francis, LG Francis, P Francis, RJ Francis, RW Francis, WJ Francis, K Frank, DC Frankcombe, TC Frankland, GA Franklin, GSA Franklin, JO Franklin, KJE Franklin, PJ Franklin, PN Franklin, RJ Franklin, WP Franklin, TM Franks, CR Frape, A Fraser, B Fraser, DE Fraser, DK Fraser, KS Fraser, NW Fraser, P Fraser, RH Fraser, RJ Fraser, RW Fraser, MA Frauenfelder, BM Frawley, AJ Frazer, BC Frazer, G Frazer, DK Frazier, KJ Frazier, RJM Frederiks, MJ Free, AP Freebody, GE Freebody, TJ Freebody, LG Freeleagus, MR Freeman, RB Freeman, TH Freeman, KR Freemantle, DJ Freer, RJ Freer, RW Freer, JE Freestone, BJ Fregon, DT Freiboth, BR Freier, BR French, GA French, GF French, GJ French, KJ French, MG French, PA French, WR French, HE Frey, NH Friebe, GL Friedman, GO Friedrich, DW Friend, FW Frimston, HJ Frings, JS Frith, KE Fritsch, BP Frizell, GF Frost, GR Frost, HD Frost, PD Frost, PL Frost, RA Frost, AD Froude, CN Fry, J Fry, K Fry, MD Fry, MJ Fry, PF Fry, RC Fryer, AF Fuchs, MR Fudge, JM Fuhrmann, JC Fullard, JH Fullard, BA Fuller, DF Fuller, DP Fuller, EJ Fuller, GM Fuller, HE Fuller, JE Fuller, MH Fuller, RI Fuller, SC Fuller, GR Fullerton, LM Fullerton, RJ Fullgrabe, PG Fulton, TR Fulton, GV Funnell, RL Funston, WC Furey, PC Furk, GW Furlong, MPC Furlong, PRJ Furnell, BJ Furner, AJ Furness, AJ Furze, CD Fuss, WJ Futcher, AE Fuz, AJS Fyfe, WH Fyffe, BM Gabb, D Gacesa, GH Gadd, SM Gadd, WD Gadd, M Gaffney, TP Gaffney, MK Gahan, P Gaias, JS Gaides, GS Gain, SW Gainey, AFB Gale, DK Gale, MF Gale, RD Gale, RR Gale, RW Gale, JG Galea, PA Galea, R Gall, RC Gall, JJ Gallacher, CD Gallagher, GW Gallagher, JA Gallagher, JE Gallagher, MP Gallagher, PF Gallagher, PJ Gallagher, TF Gallagher, KA Gallasch, KM Gallegos, KR Galligan, PM Gallon, AA Galloway, EC Galloway, IM Galloway, RR Galloway, GM Galpin, KM Galpin, SJ Galpin, RW Galt, WA Galvin, PJ Gange, LS Garbutt, R Garbutt, DJ Gardiner, DR Gardiner, JS Gardiner, K Gardiner, NJ Gardiner, RA Gardiner, TIN Gardiner, AJ Gardner, F Gardner, GA Gardner, GWS Gardner, JC Gardner, PH Gardner, WD Gardner, AJ Garing, CB Garner, FAM Garner, PK Garner, WF Garner, MJF Garrad, RG Garrard, TS Garrard, EJ Garrett, JL Garrett, RG Garrick, RGF Garrick, IG Garry, GHP Garstin, PR Garth, RH Gartlan, MS Garvan, KC Gascoigne, KJ Gascoine, PJ Gassman, JL Gaston, RGO Gatacre, JW Gates, JW Gauci, DJ Gaul, JH Gault, TJ Gavan, KPF Gay, RT Gaydon, RV Gayford, PL Gaylard, TJT Gealy, KN Gear, ACP Geason, D Geddes, DF Gedling, MG Gee, KE Geer, EW Geesing, DFR Geeson, MR Geeves, KE Geipel, IJ Gell, EC Genn, DV Genrich, K Genrich, GA Gent, PJ Geoghegan, RA Geoghegan, SW Geoghegan, TJ Geoghegan, CJ George, D George, DE George, DJ George, DM George, EP George, GR George, NR George, TA George, TH George, WG George, WF Geradts, GJC Geraghty, JP Geraghty,

TA Gerding, RAF Gerdtz, HF Gerekink, PO Gerholt, JCA Gerlach, B Germain, GD Gerrard, TE Gerrard, R Geuenich, JD Geverding, HJ Gewohn, NP Geyer, IB Ghea, RJ Gherardin, L Giannini, DI Gibb, RG Gibb, DB Gibbons, DH Gibbons, KA Gibbons, NJH Gibbons, BG Gibbs, NR Gibbs, TJ Gibbs, AJ Gibson, BW Gibson, DA Gibson, DB Gibson, GC Gibson, HJ Gibson, ID Gibson, JA Gibson, JR Gibson, MJ Gibson, RE Gibson, TR Gibson, WJ Gibson, KR Gibsone, RJ Gibsone, RG Giddings, TP Giddings, GC Giddy, GJ Giddy, RT Giffen, AR Gifford, WJ Gigney, LE Gilbee, AP Gilbert, DC Gilbert, DG Gilbert, WJ Gilbert, KE Gilby, IA Gilchrist, J Gilchrist, JJ Gilchrist, RC Gildare, GE Giles, LG Giles, WF Giles, JR Gilfellon, M Gilfoyle, D Gilkinson, BC Gill, BJ Gill, FW Gill, GV Gill, NR Gill, R Gill, RE Gill, BJ Gillard, MJ Gillen, KJ Gillespie, PG Gillespie, RA Gillespie, LB Gillett, DC Gillies, DW Gillies, G Gillies, MG Gillies, RM Gillies, RMS Gillies, FD Gilligan, RE Gilling, KR Gillis, SD Gillis, ID Gillon, DJ Gilmore, V Gilmore, MJ Gilmour, RJ Gilmour, PAJ Gilmour-Walsh, GL Gilpin, JM Gilshenen, MC Gilson, JA Giltrap, LG Giltrap, HF Gilvarry, RH Ginbey, DH Ginger, HR Ginn, MJ Ginnane, GG Ginniff, JM Ginniff, DE Girvan, PJ Girven, DJ Giste, E Giuliani, F Giusti, RL Giusti, RR Giveen, SF Given, BG Gladin, DJ Gladman, GJ Glancy, DJ Glasby, RK Glasby, FM Glaskin, CJ Glass, JS Glass, RJ Glass, DJ Glasson, PJ Glazier, GR Gleadhill, BW Gledhill, JW Gledhill, LJ Gledhill, DA Gleeson, TJ Gleeson, RIA Glen, RD Glendening, PJ Glendenning, CJ Glenn, KB Glennon, DR Glew, DW Glew, RV Glew, J Glossop, CJ Glover, GT Glover, IW Glover, PG Glover, SM Glover, TJ Glover, WR Glover, MW Glynn, NW Goad, BE Goble, JD Goble, JE Godbold, FJH Goddard, PF Goddard, CR Godden, HJ Gode, WA Godenzie, AJ Godfrey, AK Godfrey, DJ Godfrey, PC Godfrey, RJ Godfrey, GT Goding, HL Godwin, JA Godwin, JR Godwin, RA Godwin, RV Goeldner, BK Goener, BPN Goener, PJ Gogol, RP Golden, JF Golder, DA Golding, JA Goldsmith, PAS Goldsmith, SBJ Golinski, AE Golledge, A Golles, JD Golotta, SP Gomes, PR Gomm, AL Gooch, EG Gooch, P Gooch, AS Good, C Good, KR Good, MF Good, NC Good, JA Goodacre, HA Goodall, JA Goodall, RL Goodall, PL Goodchild, FW Goode, RJ Goode, RJ Goodfellow, TA Goodley, RL Goodluck, D Goodman, DV Goodrich, JM Goodridge, BM Goodwin, CG Goodwin, CJ Goodwin, GE Goodwin, GK Goodwin, JL Goodwin, KP Goodwin, MG Goodwin, RW Goodwin, WA Goodwin, BG Goopy, GJ Gordes, BG Gordon, BW Gordon, DH Gordon, JG Gordon, LJ Gordon, NJ Gordon, PJ Gordon, RG Gordon, RW Gordon, TW Gordon, SE Gore, RA Gorman, WJ Gorman, BK Gorringe, JJ Gorski, C Gorst, GL Gosden, LK Gosling, ME Goss, PR Gostlow, JP Gough, NJ Gough, RJ Gough, TR Gough, RS Gould, AR Goulding, BH Goulding, B Gourlay, PD Gourlay, RG Gourley, PA Gover, RL Gover, PA Gow, PH Gower, PR Gowers, R Gowers, BF Grace, JE Grace, KR Grace, NM Graetsch, DR Graffin, AJ Graham, DR Graham, EL Graham, G Graham, GR Graham, JC Graham, JT Graham, KC Graham, KJ Graham, KJW Graham, KM Graham, LB Graham, LC Graham, MA Graham, MR Graham, MS Graham, PN Graham, RG Graham, CR Graham-Measor, BL Grainger, K Grainger, SJ Grainger, TP Granland, DE Grant, DF Grant, G Grant, ND Grant, PJ Grant, R Grant, SM Grant, J Grantins, DL Gration, PJ Gratte, NA Grau, JR Graves, AP Gray, BW Gray, CJ Gray, DK Gray, DR Gray, EJJ Gray, EW Gray, FJ Gray, GA Gray, GJ Gray, IP Gray, JCO Gray, JE Gray, JT Gray, JW Gray, KD Gray, MC Gray, P Gray, PJ Gray, RJJ Gray, RN Gray, RW Gray, TE Gray, TJ Gray, TS Gray, WR Gray, AJ Grayson, JP Grayson, JA Greacen, KD Grealy, DB Greatrix, AJ Greaves, GN Greaves, GR Greaves, GT Greaves, KW Greber, AW Greedy, A Green, AT Green, B Green, BR Green, DG Green, DJ Green, DR Green, DT Green, EJ Green, GM Green, HC Green, HW Green, J Green, JE Green, JW Green, JWE Green, KI Green, KR Green, LE Green, PT Green, R Green, RA Green, RD Green, RF Green, RJ Green, RMC Green, RP Green, RW Green, SA Green, SE Green, TR Green, KG Greenaway, NW Greenaway, R Greeneklee, PR Greenfield, VJ Greenfield, AJ Greenhalgh, PJ Greenhalgh, AJ Greenham, ES Greenhill, AE Greenwood, GA Greenwood, K Greenwood, DR Greer, GCL Greer, AJ Gregg, AD Gregory, B Gregory, FP Gregory, GC Gregory, KJ Gregory, PJ Gregory, RR Gregory, RJK Gregson, RK Gregson, KBM Greig, KJ Greig, RJ Greig, MJT Grelis, JG Grenfell, JH Gresty, AC Grevell, LC Gribben, AJ Grice, DAP Grice, AJC Griegg, A Griepsma, B Grierson, L Grierson, BA Griffin, DJ Griffin, FE Griffin, GJ Griffin, J Griffin, KJ Griffin, KW Griffin, PM Griffin, RE Griffin, TP Griffin, AW Griffith, GR Griffith, S Griffith, WJ Griffith, DC Griffiths, GR Griffiths, GWC Griffiths, MJ Griffiths, RD Griffiths, RJ Griffiths, WB Griffiths, WC Griffiths, BA Grigg, JM Grigg, KF Griggs, NC Grimditch, IR Grimes, JF Grimmond, LR Grimmond, WJ Grimsey, MK Grimshaw, SR Grindrod, JG Griskauskas, SJ Grochowski, PJ Groen-int-woud, PA Groessler, RJ Groombridge, RW Groome, AJ Groves, DAJ Groves, DT Groves, JM Groves, JW Grubb, WT Grundy, EA Grusauskas, SP Guerin, IL Guest, RG Guest, PJR Guilford, AB Guilk, L Guise, NC Gullick, MS Gulliford, IR Gulliver, KA Gulliver, FW Gulson, JT Gumley, JJ Gunn, RT Gunn, VW Gunnee, AR Gunning, RS Gunter, MJ Gunther, NW Gunthorpe, TL Gunton, DW Guppy, RW Guppy, KC Gurnett, W Gurnett, DS Gurr, J Gurr, BC Guthrie, BG Guthrie, WA Guthrie, CP Gutteridge, GA Gutteridge, FG Guy, H Guy, PM Guy, VB Guy, JV Guyenette, GJ Gwynne, SD Gwynne, AFW Gysen, RH Gyton, MF Haala, AN Haas, F Habenschuss, EG Hack, WG Hack, RJ Hackett, TJ Hackett, W Hackworth, WL Hadden, JF Haddin, IG Haddon, DL Hadfield, JP Hadler, PJ Hadler, MD Hadley, NFK Hadley, NG Hage, S Hagedorn, EJ Haggart, RM Hagley, MC Haglund, G Hagstrom, SN Haidle, WC Haidon, PJR Hain, DB Haines, DJ Haines, GJ Haines, GL Haines, GW Haines, JJ Haines, JW Haines, MS Haines, NE Haines, DG Haining, MJ Haining, SL Hair, PR Haisman, GP Hajek, JA Hakkennes, AD Haldane, FR Hale, JT Hales, RJ Hales, DJ Hall, ES Hall, GAC Hall, GAF Hall, GC Hall, GJ Hall, HAL Hall, IW Hall, JM Hall, PD Hall, PJ Hall, PR Hall, R Hall, RC Hall, RG Hall, RJ Hall, RL Hall, RN Hall, RS Hall, RVR Hall, SJ Hall, TA Hall, W Hall, WJ Hall, DT Hallam, MWJ Hallen, J Halley, BC Halliday, DW Halliday, ME Halliday, RJ Halliday, CA Halliwell, B Halloran, DJ Halloran, RC Halloran, RL Halls, AC Halpin, JP Halpin, BE Halsey, FE Halsey, AR Halton, DG Halton, ND Halton, WM Halvorsen, PR Hambleton, WJ Hambling, BJ Hambour, DH Hamburger, BN Hamden, G Hamel, MF Hamer, J Hamill, AC Hamilton, AL Hamilton, BR Hamilton, CJ Hamilton, DA Hamilton, DG Hamilton, IJ Hamilton, NJ Hamilton, PN Hamilton, RV Hamilton, JD Hamilton Smith, TH Hamilton, GK Hamlyn, WB Hamlyn, RC Hammal, CAA Hammer, GDR Hammer, KD Hammerich, GG Hammett, AJ Hammond, EA Hammond, KJ Hammond, KW Hammond, MI Hammond, NDH Hammond, RC Hammond, PO Hamon, MA Hampson, G Hampstead, S Hampstead, DT Hampton, JC Hampton, RI Hampton, WF Hampton, PE Hamrol, NF Hams, AC Hancock, JA Hancock, JF Hancock, PG Hancock, R Hancock, PH Hancox, WC Handfield, LH Handicott, TE Handke, PSJ Handley, GA Hanisch, CM Hankin, TF Hankin, KR Hankinson, KW Hanley, A Hanlon, DE Hanlon, MF Hanlon, RJ Hanlon, RW Hanlon, TJ Hanlon, BD Hanmer, DW Hanmer, PG Hanmer, AVE Hann, BJ Hann, DM Hannaford, PB Hannaford, SC Hannant, GA Hanneford, D Hannigan, JS Hannigan, MK Hannigan, PJ Hannon, JA Hanratty, MJ Hansch, BF Hansell, DI Hansen, DJ Hansen, GC Hansen, GJ Hansen, HC Hansen, IM Hansen, KMA Hansen, NR Hansen, PG Hansen, VGF Hansen, AL Hansford, GEG Hanson, JHT Hanson, LJ Hanson, OG Hanson, RJ Hanson, MA Happy, LH Harber, GA Harbert, C Hardie, PJ Hardiman, D Harding, JL Harding, KG Harding, PG Harding, IK Harding-Colliss, AT Hardinge, ID Hardinge, GJ Hardman, JG Hardman, JW Hardman, RA Hardstaff, G Hardwick, RJ Hardwick, WJ Hardwick, WM Hardwick, CW Hardwicke, MR Hardwicke, RA Hardwicke, AK Hardy, D Hardy, DJ Hardy, PA Hardy, PR Hardy, PW Hardy, RE Hardy, SEG Hare, MJ Haren, JA Harford, AC Hargood, JC Hargraves, GR Hargreaves, LA Hargreaves, PM Hargreaves, MJ Harker, HR Harkness, DJ Harland, BC Harley, PE Harley, RJ Harley, JG Harlock, AF Harman, HP Harman, JH Harman, JD Harmer, AG Harms, JA Harms, GJ Harmsworth, AJ Harnett, DJ Harnett, PJ Harney, BG Haron, NV Harp, CR Harper, DV Harper, PB Harper, RW Harper, NH Harraway, AW Harrell, MR Harrhy, DA Harries, JM Harries, CSH Harrington, PF Harrington, RJ Harrington, NG Harrip, AB Harris, AW Harris, BE Harris, CH Harris, DJ Harris, DW Harris, EJ Harris, GJ Harris, GW Harris, HP Harris, JB Harris, JC Harris, JE Harris, JF Harris, JM Harris, KM Harris, L Harris, M Harris, NL Harris, PA Harris, PG Harris, RB Harris, RG Harris, RH Harris, RJ Harris, RW Harris, WE Harris, WL Harris, AG Harrison, AJ Harrison, AL Harrison, AV Harrison, BG Harrison, D Harrison, FJ Harrison, J Harrison, JE Harrison, JF Harrison, JJ Harrison, JL Harrison, ME Harrison, MJ Harrison, NF Harrison, NK Harrison, NP Harrison, PA Harrison, RC Harrison, W Harrison, WJ Harrison, WT Harrison, KM Harriss, TJ Harriss, GW Harrod, RL Harrod, S Harrod, BR Harrold, AP Harste, BE Hart, BM Hart, GJ Hart, GK Hart, HC Hart, ID Hart, JMW Hart, JVW Hart, LR Hart, MF Hart, NJ Hart, PHK Hart, T Hart, TR Hart, CW Hartcher, BSS Hartfield, KJ Hartigan, CJ Hartland, AD Hartley, EL Hartnett, GR Hartnett, CR Hartwell, G Hartwell, KJ Hartwell, PJ Hartwell, N Hartwig, BLG Harvey, BWA Harvey, CN Harvey, IE Harvey, J Harvey, JG Harvey, LW Harvey, MG Harvey, NW Harvey, PJ Harvey, RA Harvey, RW Harvey, WT Harvie, EW Harwood, FW Harwood, RA Harwood, E Hasch, DRF Hase, NF Haseldine, GJ Haselwood, RF Haskett, D Haskings, GW Hasler, MH Hasler, MG Hassall, PC Hassall, JW Hassam, KJ Hasson, MJ Hasson, A Hastie, AJ Hastie, GR Hastwell, CTV Hatch, EW Hatch, RW Hatch, AR Hatcher, EJ Hatchman, NR Hatchman, CR Hateley, PR Hateley, R Hateley, EO Hately, BWF Hathaway, PA Hattenfels, RA Hattenfels, JA Hatter, LM Hatwell, GP Haughey, J Haughey, SFH Haughton, SJ Hausfeld, C Hausmann, TB Havelberg, JG Haverkate, FP Havey, MR Hawes, RNJ Hawke, DD Hawker, RJ Hawker, MJ Hawkes, WE Hawkes, AW Hawkins, CT Hawkins, JT Hawkins, LD Hawkins, RB Hawkins, TJ Hawkins, CJ Hawley, JS Hawley, EJ Haworth, EJ Hay, RH Hay, SD Hay, VT Hay, WB Hay, CH Hayden, WE Hayden, BF Haydon, CB Hayes, DL Hayes, DW Hayes, EJ Hayes, GC Hayes, GF Hayes, LM Hayes, MJ Hayes, RA Hayes, RS Hayes, TG Hayes, WJ Hayes, JW Hayler, AL Hayles, CJ Hayman, LA Hayman, DJ Haynes, GM Haynes, KC Haynes, KL Hays, AR Haysom, WS Haysom, AW Hayton, KG Hayton, AW Hayward, BJ Hayward, DJ Hayward, KB Hayward, KWG Hayward, P Hayward, RA Hayward, SR Hayward, WCJ Hayward, RL Haywood, G Hazelden, AJ Hazell, JP Hazell, RR Hazell, AG Head, EB Head, RJ Head, KV Headlam, BT Headridge, JD Heald, AE Healey, PJ Healey, WJ Healey, PA Healy, PF Healy, RA Heanes, A Heaney, MJ Heaney, RE Heaney, NH Heard, J Hearn, JE Hearn, P Hearps, RD Hearps, KB Heath, R Heath, RE Heath, DH Heathcote, CWB Heaven, PM Heavey, RC Heazlewood, KP Heberle, PW Hedger, EK Hedges, B Hedley, PM Heeb, KR Heffernan, DR Hegarty, KJ Hegarty, PC Heilman, H Heim, RF Heindorff, W Heinrich, JW Heinze, IC Heiser, TP Helion, G Hellmrich, EA Helm, RG Helm, NF Helyer, EM Hemingway, MJ Hemmy, KM Hemsley, RP Hemsley, A Henderson, AD Henderson, AG Henderson, BS Henderson, D Henderson, EW Henderson, HF Henderson, JJ Henderson, N Henderson, GJ Henderson-Smith, GN Henderson-Smith, GK Hendle, AP Hendricks, DM Hendry, JM Hendry, LAM Hendy, CV Henkel, KH Henkel, FAJ Henley, RF Henley, TJ Henley, P Hennings, LE Henny, MR Henricks, AB Henricus, DB Henry, JR Henry, JW Henry, KB Henry, GS Hensby, LR Hensby, AJ Henson, RM Henson, AJ Henstock, GA Henstock, RJ Henwood, RM Hepburn, SJ Hepburn, LP Hepworth, RW Herbener, AEL Herbert, DJ Herbert, RL Herbert, TW Herbert, BM Herd, KA Herd, PJ Heritage, GH Hermsen, JM Heron, CAC Herrald, BJ Herrenberg, BM Herrett, GT Herring, IL Herrington, JI Herriot, MJ Herrmann, ER Herrod, BJ Herron, RA Hersel, RW Heslop, RJ Hespe, J Hetherington, ME Hetzel, JW Hewett, GL Hewitt, G Hews, C Hey, WT Hey, NC Heyhorn, G Heyink, KL Heylbut, DJ Heymer, KJ Heynatz, G Heys, K Heys, I Heywood, HRF Heyworth, RE Hibberd, JF Hibbert, KH Hibbert, PS Hibbert, RJ Hibbert, AP Hibbitt, CB Hibbitt, DA Hick, JPT Hickey, KJ Hickey, KW Hickey, N Hickey, MT Hickie, GW Hickling, KC Hickling, HJ Hickman, WG Hickman, AR Hicks, BJ Hicks, FJ Hicks, GJ Hicks, H Hicks, JV Hicks, MCL Hicks, MR Hicks, RF Hicks, RK Hicks, BJ Hiddins, D Hide, RJ Higginbottom, AR Higgins, DA Higgins, DJ Higgins, DR Higgins, EA Higgins, GC Higgins, MG Higgins, R Higgins, RJ Higgins, SJ Higgins, MG Higgison, LW Higgon, MJ Higgs, DC Highnam, BJ Hildebrand, PR Hilder, AA Hill, AH Hill, AJM Hill, AO Hill, ARC Hill, BG Hill, BJ Hill, CR Hill, DL Hill,

EA Hill, GD Hill, GP Hill, GW Hill, HN Hill, JR Hill, JS Hill, KG Hill, KN Hill, MR Hill, NJ Hill, PA Hill, PD Hill, PJ Hill, RC Hill, RG Hill, RJ Hill, SF Hill, TJ Hill, WA Hill, WB Hill, WT Hill, B Hillan, BW Hillard, LA Hillhouse, T Hilliar, DG Hilliard, RI Hilliard, AJ Hillier, FW Hillier, KJ Hillier, RA Hillier, RR Hillier, W Hillis, AL Hillman, NJ Hill-Norton, A Hills, AGF Hills, BE Hills, KB Hills, PJ Hills, SA Hills, K Hillyard, PJ Hilton, WG Hilzinger, R Himbury, RE Hinch, WA Hind, NR Hindle, RJ Hindle, PL Hindley, VL Hinds, WR Hinds, DG Hine, JL Hine, RJ Hine, MG Hines, PG Hines, SL Hinkley, R Hinnrichsen, JG Hinrichsen, JW Hinson, DH Hinton, DJ Hinton, AA Hintz, AG Hipkiss, W Hipkiss, GR Hipper, GC Hipwell, DE Hiron, MP Hirsh, L Hirst, IA Hislop, KJ Hislop, JP Histon, BP Hite, RE Hoad, BS Hoare, DK Hoare, EG Hoare, GJ Hoare, RG Hobba, JC Hobbelen, BJ Hobbs, KJ Hobbs, M Hobbs, NR Hobbs, PJ Hobbs, RJ Hobbs, WR Hobby, GD Hobden, BD Hobsbawn, BL Hobson, RL Hobson, WD Hobson, LRA Hock Hing, DB Hockham, DJ Hockham, BJ Hockley, DE Hodder, LG Hodder, AC Hodge, GM Hodges, JM Hodges, RC Hodges, STG Hodges, TA Hodgetts, P Hodgkinson, JR Hodgkison, CA Hodgson, JM Hodgson, MA Hodgson, ML Hodgson, E Hodikin, RE Hodson, NI Hoey, TW Hoey, LA Hoffmann, MJ Hogan, TM Hogan, D Hogben, JE Hogben, AW Hogg, JS Hogg, LG Hogg, EW Holbrook, RT Holdcroft, AJ Holden, GH Holden, PN Holden, RG Holden, ME Holder, PA Holding, W Holding, LP Holdsworth, CMG Hole, RS Holiga, AG Holland, BH Holland, CR Holland, DJ Holland, DW Holland, ER Holland, GR Holland, JF Holland, NC Holland, PC Holland, PL Holland, PR Holland, SD Holland, TJ Holland, GJ Hollas, WJ Hollas, DC Holliday, ED Holliday, JA Holliday, PA Holliday, AJ Hollier, MT Hollis, PW Hollitt, JR Hollow, GR Holloway, HW Holloway, JA Holloway, LC Holm, RW Holman, R Holme, B Holmes, CWA Holmes, DA Holmes, DRG Holmes, FA Holmes, GG Holmes, IF Holmes, J Holmes, JR Holmes, LE Holmes, RD Holmes, RJ Holmes, WJ Holmes, WK Holmes, PR Holmesby, DWV Holmstrom, ID Holmwood, S Holswilder, G Holt, LJ Holt, PB Holt, R Holt, DG Holthouse, I Holthouse, NC Holton, LJ Holzhauser, MR Holzl, RH Homer, CDM Hone, DA Honess, PAF Honeysett, LE Hood, IT Hoof, GW Hoogenboom, PH Hoogland, PR Hoogland, WM Hook, SH Hooke, DL Hooper, GD Hooper, L Hooper, RE Hooper, SB Hooper, DWR Hooton, AH Hope, E Hope, GDM Hope, JA Hope, PW Hope, VM Hope, BF Hopkins, GG Hopkins, JD Hopkins, ML Hopkins, MR Hopkins, IA Hopkinson, LV Hoppe, FJ Hopper, RW Hopton, LL Hopwood, GB Horan, JPW Horan, LJ Horbal, LW Horby, BR Hore, T Horgossy, DB Horn, SA Hornbuckle, AL Horne, AVR Horne, DN Horne, DRS Horne, EA Horne, GR Horne, KC Horne, KL Horne, MR Horne, PM Horniblow, M Hornibrook, HR Hornig, JC Hornsby, JR Hornsby, N Hornsby, W Hornstra, EW Horridge, LR Horrobin, LR Horrocks, RH Horsburgh, LA Horsfield, VP Horsfield, GG Hortle, AR Horton, DJ Horton, JT Horton, LW Horton, PB Horton, RL Horton, RT Horton, L Horvath, SW Hoskin, SW Hosking, WA Hosking, NC Hoskins, AW Hoswell, SF Hotop, GJ Houldsworth, JH Houldsworth, SR Houldsworth, TG Houldsworth, CR Houlgrave, LE Houlgrave, RA Hoult, DC Hounsome, JR Hourigan, LM Hourigan, RJ Hourigan, MJ Hourihan, DC House, WH Houssenloge, CNL Houston, HM Houston, MWR Houston, RGD Houston, GC Hoving, AJ Howard, AW Howard, BA Howard, DG Howard, DJB Howard, DN Howard, GO Howard, HM Howard, J Howard, LD Howard, RG Howard, SJ Howard, SC Howarth, RL Howden, SJ Howden, A Howe, DJ Howe, WE Howe, JH Howell, JW Howell, RE Howell, CGD Howes, FCL Howes, GT Howgate, ES Howie, JF Howie, RJ Howie, P Howis, RB Howitt, RA Howland, SV Howland, DM Howlett, JA Howlett, RS Howlett, AR Hoy, FJ Hoy, K Hoy, PW Hoy, RM Hoy, WJ Hoye, SG Hoyle, R Hrycyk, JR Hubner, KJ Hubner, AL Huby, KJL Huckstepp, CJ Hudson, JB Hudson, KJ Hudson, ML Hudson, MW Hudson, AJ Huelin, TJ Huf, B Huggett, DW Huggins, RS Huggins, WJ Huggins, AD Hughes, AJ Hughes, AM Hughes, AN Hughes, AR Hughes, BK Hughes, CE Hughes, CL Hughes, DM Hughes, HF Hughes, IL Hughes, JE Hughes, JR Hughes, JW Hughes, KN Hughes, M Hughes, MR Hughes, NT Hughes, OG Hughes,

OJ Hughes, RC Hughes, S Hughes, WK Hughes, BK Hughes-Gage, PJ Hugonnet, DRJ Hulance, BJ Hull, DL Hull, JR Hull, MG Hull, GJ Hulls, LJ Hulme, AR Humble, JM Hume, TD Hume, WJ Hume, TJ Hummerston, CA Humphrey, CR Humphrey, DI Humphrey, PJF Humphrey, AK Humphreys, M Humphreys, MG Humphries, MJ Humphries, NF Humphries, JH Humphris, LT Humphris, KJ Humphrys, ND Hunnam, AL Hunt, BD Hunt, DJ Hunt, DT Hunt, EW Hunt, GB Hunt, GE Hunt, HJ Hunt, JL Hunt, KW Hunt, LV Hunt, RH Hunt, TC Hunt, WE Hunt, BK Hunter, DJ Hunter, GJ Hunter, IB Hunter, MJ Hunter, PJ Hunter, RW Hunter, TJ Hunter, TR Hunter, WJ Hunter, RT Huntriss, WD Huntriss, RL Huppatz, RJ Hurdle, JP Hurst, NW Hurst, PE Hurst, PS Hurt, HN Husk, KJ Husking, AE Hussey-Smith, CC Hussey-Smith, GF Hussey-Smith, GR Hustwaite, RA Hustwaite, J Huszcza, J Huszczo, PJ Hutch, A Hutchcraft, AG Hutchings, LD Hutchings, NG Hutchings, RP Hutchings, KW Hutchins, AF Hutchinson, I Hutchinson, PJ Hutchison, RL Hutchison, RN Hutchison, GE Hutton, JP Huxham, CB Huxtable, RC Hyde, BJ Hyland, JE Hynes, EP Hytten, WL Ibbotson, BL Iceton, AS Ide, LA Ide, PE Ievers, RT Ifould, P Ignatiew, KN Ikin, DH Iles, JJ Iles, PJ Iles, CJ Iliffe, AC Imlach, GC Imms, PJ Imms, BA Inall, KE Inall, MJ Inall, AL Ingham, RJ Ingledew, GJ Inglis, RJ Inglis, EJ Ingram, JE Ingram, JG Ingram, PG Ingram, KA Ings, AP Inman, D Innes, DA Innes, PW Inns, JF Inskip, AJ Ireland, BH Ireland, LW Ireland, SC Irish, KG Ironmonger, BJ Irons, LA Irons, ME Irvin, FVS Irvine, GJ Irvine, J Irvine, T Irvine, RG Irvine-MacDonald, AG Irving, IW Irving, MD Irving, GR Irwin, WR Irwin, AJ Isaac, CA Isard, BK Iselin, RW Ison, R Isselmann, CF Isted, G Ivanoff, T Ivanoff, RS Iverson, GE Ives, RD Ivory, R Izard, ICE Izat, KR Jackel, DA Jacklin, CC Jackman, PA Jacks, AF Jackson, AL Jackson, AV Jackson, BA Jackson, BDC Jackson, BP Jackson, BS Jackson, C Jackson, DA Jackson, DG Jackson, DJ Jackson, DK Jackson, DM Jackson, EN Jackson, GA Jackson, GN Jackson, GR Jackson, IC Jackson, IM Jackson, KI Jackson, L Jackson, LHE Jackson, MD Jackson, MR Jackson, MT Jackson, PF Jackson, PR Jackson, RA Jackson, RG Jackson, RK Jackson, RL Jackson, RS Jackson, RV Jackson, WJ Jackson, WN Jackson, JA Jacobi, AJ Jacobs, BJ Jacobs, JH Jacobs, KE Jacobs, RJ Jacobs, RP Jacobs, EW Jacobson, RE Jacobson, TA Jacobson, WL Jacobson, KC Jaekel, SJ Jaenke, KG Jaffers, RG Jaffray, RA Jaggers, KM Jago, BJ Jahnsen, CA James, CW James, DW James, EM James, ET James, GF James, HT James, IB James, IG James, JE James, JJ James, KA James, LM James, MR James, NA James, PG James, R James, RA James, RN James, RW James, T James, TJ James, TR James, WC James, WK James, WP James, GPC Jameson, AD Jamieson, CFL Jamieson, CR Jamieson, DH Jamieson, FC Jamieson, HTU Jamieson, PJ Jamieson, RG Jamieson, SR Jamieson, BJ Janczewski, BR Janes, KL Janiszewski, WJ Jankiwskyj, J Jankowski, ER Jans, RC Jansen, KF Janson, CIH Jansz, MR Jarrett, PW Jarrett, E Jarvie, KG Jarvis, PE Jarvis, RN Jarvis, J Jasper, E Jastrzebski, FC Jeanes, PW Jeckeln, T Jeckeln, JM Jeff, GT Jefferies, JC Jefferson, NM Jefferson, DG Jeffery, DM Jeffery, DW Jeffery, MR Jeffery, RL Jeffery, VM Jeffery, FA Jeffree, RJ Jeffree, BR Jeffrey, DA Jeffrey, DR Jeffrey, MG Jeffrey, EC Jeffreys, RJ Jeffreys, RM Jeffreys, RJ Jeffries, GA Jehn, TF Jehn, R Jellett, RJ Jelly, RM Jemesen, DO Jenetsky, A Jenkins, AN Jenkins, BT Jenkins, DW Jenkins, GP Jenkins, HC Jenkins, JE Jenkins, KE Jenkins, RC Jenkins, TJ Jenkins, ML Jenkinson, WK Jenkinson, JW Jenks, BT Jenner, DH Jenner, EJ Jenner, DR Jennings, HJ Jennings, RC Jennings, TA Jennings, WJ Jennings, GA Jenno, AC Jensen, DS Jensen, EC Jensen, GM Jensen, IB Jensen, PC Jensen, RA Jensen, MJ Jeppesen, H Jerke, RN Jermyn, JF Jersovs, A Jerzyna, GR Jesser, AP Jessop, MS Jessop, TE Jessop, J Jewczenko, TM Jimmieson, RJF Jobson, RN Jocumsen, DR Joel, DH John, DR John, RN John, BG Johns, DW Johns, GA Johns, GR Johns, KS Johns, RJ Johns, AR Johnson, AT Johnson, BF Johnson, BJ Johnson, BS Johnson, C Johnson, CD Johnson, CS Johnson, DC Johnson, DH Johnson, DL Johnson, DS Johnson, GB Johnson, GD Johnson, GW Johnson, IG Johnson, JA Johnson, JP Johnson, JW Johnson, KE Johnson, KG Johnson, KJ Johnson, KR Johnson, KW Johnson, LA Johnson, LF Johnson, LM Johnson, NB Johnson, PF Johnson, PG Johnson, PJD Johnson, PL Johnson, PRE Johnson, R Johnson, RA Johnson, RE Johnson,

RJ Johnson, RW Johnson, TM Johnson, TW Johnson, WG Johnson, WR Johnson, AH Johnston, AS Johnston, BCW Johnston, BD Johnston, CW Johnston, EE Johnston, GR Johnston, JD Johnston, KLE Johnston, KR Johnston, LS Johnston, MA Johnston, MI Johnston, MJ Johnston, NB Johnston, PL Johnston, RB Johnston, RE Johnston, RJ Johnston, RS Johnston, TA Johnston, TE Johnston, WJP Johnston, GA Johnstone, GF Johnstone, JC Johnstone, DS Joicey, LJ Joliffe, NA Jollie, R Jolliffe, RC Jolly, SR Jolly, A Jones, AG Jones, AN Jones, AS Jones, BC Jones, BJ Jones, BS Jones, C Jones, CE Jones, CG Jones, CP Jones, CR Jones, DA Jones, DB Jones, DJ Jones, DK Jones, DT Jones, DW Jones, E Jones, GA Jones, GD Jones, GK Jones, HE Jones, HW Jones, IB Jones, IM Jones, IR Jones, JL Jones, JM Jones, JP Jones, JW Jones, KA Jones, KC Jones, KE Jones, L Jones, LA Jones, LC Jones, LJ Jones, LR Jones, LW Jones, M Jones, MB Jones, N Jones, NP Jones, PB Jones, PD Jones, PE Jones, PEL Jones, PG Jones, PGC Jones, PR Jones, PT Jones, PW Jones, RA Jones, RC Jones, RD Jones, RH Jones, RL Jones, RM Jones, RW Jones, SL Jones, SR Jones, TJ Jones, TN Jones, VT Jones, VW Jones, WD Jones, WE Jones, WT Jones, CFA Jongebloed, OP Jongewaard, GKG Jonnek, D Jonusaitis, RB Joplin, AR Jordan, BD Jordan, CJ Jordan, DC Jordan, GC Jordan, LE Jordan, SR Jordan, AJ Jorgensen, RJ Jorgensen, WJ Jose, RD Joseph, WR Joseph, HA Josephs, RE Josey, RK Josey, WG Josey, RJ Joslin, GJ Joss, IK Josselyn, RT Joughin, CW Joy, PL Joy, BA Joyce, WW Joyce, JA Joynes, GK Judd, RP Judd, GM Jude, CT Judge, WF Julius, OK Jurd, RW Jurey, SR Justice, VR Justice, GP Kable, EB Kaczmarsky, JF Kaehler, PK Kairl, DW Kakoschke, V Kalceff, PGM Kalkman, RP Kalman, DL Kalwig, J Kaminski, BW Kane, DA Kane, PW Kane, W Kane, JR Kapel, BZ Kapral, RM Karandrews, SM Karow, FR Kassulke, RF Kattenberg, DE Kavanagh, EM Kavanagh, JM Kavanagh, AT Kay, MR Kay, PT Kay, RJ Kay, TG Kay, AI Kazuberns, JA Kean, MJ Kean, ET Keane, BR Kear, BJ Kearins, KV Kearney, MD Kearney, RT Kearney, KG Kearsley, BE Keating, JK Keats, FF Keavy, MJS Keay, JC Kedge, JM Kee, J Keefe, PA Keefe, WJ Keegan, JL Keeley, PL Keeley, TJ Keeley, RH Keeling, J Keen, WA Keen, DH Keeton, AJ Keevers, CS Keevers, KC Keft, GJ Keighley, AHE Keily, WC Keleher, GJ Kelleher, MA Kelleher, DW Kellett, BAR Kelly, BJ Kelly, D Kelly, EJ Kelly, GA Kelly, GR Kelly, JA Kelly, JD Kelly, JF Kelly, JG Kelly, JM Kelly, JP Kelly, KL Kelly, M Kelly, MC Kelly, MD Kelly, MJ Kelly, MW Kelly, OA Kelly, PB Kelly, PJ Kelly, PL Kelly, PM Kelly, RAC Kelly, RD Kelly, RE Kelly, RH Kelly, SH Kelly, SW Kelly, TF Kelly, VH Kelly, CM Kelson, DK Keltie, PC Kember, CRG Kemp, CW Kemp, FBR Kemp, J Kemp, JD Kemp, NL Kemp, WA Kemp, KF Kempnich, LG Kempster, CR Kendall, RR Kendall, EH Kendall-Torry, JE Kendon, MJ Kenna, JR Kennaway, AG Kennedy, AGL Kennedy, AL Kennedy, DH Kennedy, DK Kennedy, DN Kennedy, EF Kennedy, GD Kennedy, GW Kennedy, JP Kennedy, JS Kennedy, JW Kennedy, MB Kennedy, PGN Kennedy, PJ Kennedy, RJ Kennedy, RR Kennedy, WG Kennedy, IJ Kennett, BC Kennewell, GJ Kenney, DG Kenny, G Kenny, MJ Kenny, PN Kenny, RW Kensey, DJ Kent, JL Kent, PE Kent, KJ Kenyon, MH Keogh, GP Keough, RC Ker, WN Kermode, BE Kern, MW Kernaghan, BK Kerr, G Kerr, GJ Kerr, GM Kerr, GR Kerr, GV Kerr, JL Kerr, K Kerr, PJ Kerr, RJ Kerr, RK Kerr, WC Kerr, KH Kerrigan, SD Kershaw, JW Kershler, RJ Kessenich, KP Kesters, RP Kesting, BW Ketchell, MJ Ketchell, EJ Kettle, M Kettle, BS Kew, WF Keys, RJ Keyte, AR Khan, CWL Khan, H Kibbler, LA Kidd, PJ Kidman, JA Kielbicki, M Kielty, PR Kiely, BJ Kiem, T Kiiver, MC Killeen, JT Killen, DD Kilmister, FM Kilmister, D Kilpatrick, WJ Kilpatrick, RJ Kilsby, JOT Kimball, MJ Kimball, WM Kimpton, AA Kindelan, MT Kinder, DA Kindon, AT King, BD King, BTM King, DR King, F King, GN King, GS King, JK King, JN King, JS King, KD King, KW King, LJ King, MJ King, NI King, NS King, PE King, PJ King, PR King, RC King, RG King, RH King, RJ King, TA King, WE King, WM King, LGJ Kingma, M Kingsley, AU Kingston, G Kingston, LE Kingston-Kerr, RA Kinkade, KA Kinloch, GJ Kinnane, DF Kinnear, JM Kinnear, VJ Kinnear, LJ Kinnest, RJ Kinross, WAE Kinross, NC Kinsey, GR Kipling, AD Kirby, CW Kirby, LT Kirby, WP Kirby, HJ Kirk, HJ Kirkland, MW Kirkland, AP Kirkman, BJ Kirkman, HJ Kirkman, LJ Kirkman, RC Kirkman, D Kirkpatrick, S Kirkpatrick, NR Kirkwood, R Kirkwood, RHS Kirkwood, EE Kirstenfeldt, A Kish, DWK Kissick, D Kitchen, GJ Kitchener, KS Kite, TW Klan,

RC Klease, AG Kleidon, RE Kleidon, M Klein, LR Klem, J Klich, BHG Klimpel, RJ Klose, TK Klose, G Kluyt, WL Kmon, DS Knape, SL Knapp, WF Knapp, PH Knauth, M Kneale, D Kneeves, YRP Knezy, PA Knife, AC Knight, AG Knight, AJ Knight, BSJ Knight, DJ Knight, GR Knight, GV Knight, JM Knight, K Knight, MA Knight, PA Knight, RJ Knight, D Knights, RS Knights, K Knott, PH Knott, KB Knowler, SJ Knowler, DA Knox, IW Knox, AE Knudsen, AE Knutsen, DJ Knutsen, BM Kobylas, BM Koch, IV Kocins, GR Koehler, A Koenders, CNF Koeneman, FAJ Koeneman, V Koest, J Koina, MJ Kokles, AJ Kolder, WJ Kolpak, JL Komarek, CD Konemann, NA Konemann, WD Konemann, GB Kong, B Konicanin, PE Konrath, H Koopman, D Kooyman, BK Kopp, GH Kopp, KA Koschel, V Koskovic, KR Kotz, GJ Kousbroek, S Kowal, RW Kraal, TM Kraal, F Krainoff, A Kramer, BG Kramer, SA Kramer, JB Kramme, GR Krause, GS Krause, WL Krause, L Krawczyk, G Kreicbergs, DR Kreitling, A Krenn, W Krist, B Kristensen, J Kroeger, M Kroeger, RJ Krog, PA Krollig, M Krompic, BA Kroning, P Kroon, NF Kropp, N Kruck, HPB Kruger, RW Kruger, KH Krummel, BHS Kruse, RJ Krygsman, Z Krzywowzyja, L Kuhn, M Kuhnast, TJ Kuiters, E Kukla, NG Kunde, NW Kuskey, IJ Kwiatkowski, AL Kyd, RJ Kyle, PJ Kyte, PT La Roche, A Labady, DW Lacey, JF Lacey, JV Lacey, DJ Lackey, AF Lade, LA Ladner, KJ Lahz, JA Laidlaw, KJ Laidlaw, IT Laidler, P Laidler, A Laing, AR Laing, DIF Laing, DJ Laing, RR Laing, G Laing-Schofield, D Laird, KR Laity, CG Lakatos, AO Lake, GS Lake, LP Lake, RC Lake, RK Lake, TA Lally, PJ Lalor, RAA Lalor, R Lamacraft, AF Lamb, E Lamb, GW Lamb, PR Lamb, RD Lamb, WP Lamb, CJ Lambert, ED Lambert, IW Lambert, JG Lambert, KJ Lambert, R Lambie, AC Lamble, DG Lambourn, TM Lambourne, JL Lamey, MS Lamey, CF Lammers, RA Lamond, IM Lamont, R Lamont, BW Lamp, SJ Lampe, GR Lamperd, ML Lampo, ARW Lamshed, MJ Lancaster, P Lancaster, SA Lancaster, DA Lancelott, RE Lander, DC Landrigan, DC Landy, AA Lane, CJ Lane, DJ Lane, DW Lane, EM Lane, JE Lane, JR Lane, KV Lane, MJ Lane, PS Lane, RB Lane, RRW Lane, SW Lane, TP Lane, AJ Lang, GR Lang, RI Lang, RW Lang, GB Langan, GK Lange, JK Langfield, KE Langford, WG Langford, JL Langham, B Langley, RC Langley, JF Langridge, JR Langsford, RP Langsford, AC Langstone, JM Langton, IR Langtree, JMW Langtry, JF Lankford, HE Lansdown, SJ Lapere, DE Lapham, LR Larder, A Large, JH Large, R Large, RL Lark, JH Larkham, A Larkin, RD Larnach, A Larsen, RP Larson, FC Larter, P Lashko, S Lasoryzak, GD Lassau, RW Lastelle, MI Latimer, P Latimer, PG Latimer, JN Lattin, LJ Laub, PJ Launder, EJ Laundess, GM Laurance, AG Laurenson, BM Laurie, DH Laurie, KJ Lavelle, MG Lavender, R Laverty, BR Law, KG Law, MJ Law, GR Lawford, PF Lawford, RJ Lawford, SJ Lawford, BL Lawler, PJ Lawler, CJ Lawless, JJ Lawley, BJ Lawlor, GV Lawrance, EJ Lawrence, FJ Lawrence, O Lawrence, PA Lawrence, PG Lawrence, RN Lawrence, BH Lawrie, JN Lawrie, AJ Laws, GL Laws, B Lawson, BJ Lawson, BL Lawson, DJ Lawson, KL Lawson, PG Lawson, RK Lawson, WA Lawson, DC Lawton, F Lawton, T Lawton, TWD Lawton, RG Laxton, PP Laycock, RC Layfield, RM Layton, RW Layton, RT Le Cren, LJ Le Dan, JR Le Hunt, NJ Le Lievre, JC Le Page, WR Le Page, GA Le Pavoux, IFD Le Raye, AR Le Rutte, RE Lea, DW Leach, MF Leach, TA Leach, GA Leader, MF Leahy, JM Leak, S Leake, NR Leaney, PR Lear, RG Lear, B Learoyd, WL Leary, DW Leat, JF Leate, HT Leathan, ME Leathan, BC Leavy, JE Leck, JM Leckie, AL Ledden, B Ledgerwood, BF Ledlie, AN Lee, BE Lee, BL Lee, DC Lee, EJ Lee, GB Lee, GC Lee, GH Lee, GJ Lee, JKH Lee, JP Lee, JW Lee, KG Lee, M Lee, MA Lee, ND Lee, NW Lee, PG Lee, RE Lee, RJ Lee, SJ Lee, I Lee-Conway, TK Lee-Conway, GF Leek, IR Leeming, KEW Leendertz, AJ Lees, AR Lees, JD Lees, TJ Lees, WDH Lees, RJ Lee-Tet, EJ Legg, JH Legg, RW Legg, PL Leggat, AR Leggate, RM Leggatt, GF Legge, GL Legge, JW Legge, MO Legge, SC Legge, LM Leggett, LT Leggett, RC Leggett, TJ Leggo, AJ Lehman, PB Lehman, BE Lehmann, DP Lehmann, GC Lehmann, MJ Lehmann, MA Leibick, W Leijen, AD Leis, GM Leis, JD Leisk, GR Leitch, MF Leitch, SM Leitl, J Lenard, AO Lenartas, GW Lenihan, JK Lennon, GA Lennox, TR Lennox, RW Lenson, KJ Lentell, JW Lenton, GW Leo, RK Leon, DE Leonard, FA Leonard, JA Leonard, L Leonard, NJ Leonard, RJ Leonard, RK Leonard, GM Leonhardt, KA Lepley, CR Lerstang, PG Leslie, RW Leslie, WA Leslie, BJ Lester, GA Lester,

MG Lester, MN Lester, FN Letchford, GR Lethbridge, BF Letherbarrow, RJ Letts, TJ Leuenberger, J Levay, JA Lever, LW Lever, WL Leverett, BW Levett, AW Levy, JW Levy, ND Levy, LM Lewandowski, RJ Lewer, RG Lewin, RJ Lewin, N Lewington, AR Lewis, BA Lewis, DJ Lewis, FF Lewis, GJ Lewis, GP Lewis, JB Lewis, JE Lewis, JF Lewis, KG Lewis, KRG Lewis, LJ Lewis, MA Lewis, MG Lewis, NS Lewis, PG Lewis, RE Lewis, RJT Lewis, RP Lewis, SM Lewis, TE Lewis, NG Leworthy, PG Lewry, P Lewsley, J Lia, LD Libbesson, IJ Liccioni, VJ Liddell, CW Liddicoat, W Liddle, KH Lide, AJ Lidgard, HB Lidgard, RJ Lidsey, J Lightowlers, K Lightowlers, JG Lilley, AA Lillicrap, BC Lillyman, GAJ Limburg, JN Lincoln, TWE Lincoln, VC Lind, RK Lindberg, PJ Lindenberg, AR Lindley, DC Lindquist, JAC Lindridge, CP Lindsay, FS Lindsay, JC Lindsay, RD Lindsay, RH Lindsay, TE Lindsay, HM Linfoot, GJ Linford, DW Ling, R Lingard, DW Linguey, MJ Linke, HH Linkins, RV Linnane, M Linnell, GW Linnett, IE Linning, EW Linton, GA Linton, NM Lipman, DA Lipscombe, RAC Lipscombe, WA Lipscombe, N Lis, RJ Lister, JJ Litchfield, BR Litherland, LN Lithgow, D Little, HR Little, DJ Littlechild, VJ Littlefield, JW Littler, CJ Littleton, PA Littlewood, VR Littlewood, EH Lively, DW Livingstone, J Livingstone, NIJ Livingstone, AJ Livmanis, GP Llewellen, WR Llewellyn, D Lloyd, G Lloyd, GG Lloyd, HD Lloyd, JH Lloyd, LC Lloyd, SJ Lloyd, WJ Lloyd, WT Lloyd, JM Loader, GE Loan, RJ Loane, IF Lobley, P Loch, IJ Lock, GP Locke, RM Locke, PJ Lockey, CN Lockton, MJ Lockwood, RJ Lockwood, SJ Lockwood, NK Lockyer, DR Lodding, WM Loechel, W Loeckenhoff, RL Lofthouse, PA Lofts, WB Loftus, WW Loftus, GA Logan, JG Logan, KR Logan, R Logan, SM Logan, TJ Logan, PE Loimaranta, PTW Loker, JT Lomas, SP Lomas, JC Lomax, B Lomulder, TJ London, CW Loney, AR Long, LW Long, RH Long, AG Longbotham, BV Longbotham, JG Longden, PG Longden, PA Longdon, CR Longley, W Longmuir, JD Looby, WS Look, RJ Looke, EJT Loomes, TE Loose, RG Loosli, MV Loram, CG Lord, FF Lord, JC Lord, JR Lord, KW Lord, LJ Lord, PW Lord, RI Lord, WA Lord, MH Lorenz, DL Lorimer, IG Lorimer, HH Lorson, A Losew, EA Lougher, SD Loughran, CJL Lourey, RJ Louth, F Lovasz, RD Love, WJV Love, GP Lovekin, C Lovell, RB Lovett, RC Lovitt, BM Low, JA Low, PR Low, RD Low, RJ Low, AW Lowe, BE Lowe, D Lowe, DF Lowe, GG Lowe, GM Lowe, JKW Lowe, JS Lowe, MG Lowe, WS Lowe, AT Lowes, T Lowes, KJ Lowien, G Lowin, RE Lowth, W Lozberis, W Lozowy, RW Lucanus, GPC Lucas, LH Lucas, MJ Lucas, PN Lucas, RH Lucas, BJ Luck, BM Luck, D Luck, RB Luck, P Lucken, GR Luckey, NJC Lucock, TE Ludwick, JB Luff, PT Lugsden, L Luhrmann, V Lui, RG Lukasiewicz, DA Luke, JWM Luke, KJ Luke, LL Luke, MAP Luke, BF Lukey, JE Lumb, MA Lumsden, SJ Lumsden, CJ Lunardi, P Lunardi, T Lund, J Lungo, FW Lunn, GR Lunn, KF Lunn, LJ Lunn, WJF Lunney, DO Lunniss, PD Lunt, JA Luobikis, MJ Lusham, GD Lusk, C Luther, JE Luthy, AL Lutton, LP Lutton, PD Lutton, WL Luttrell, JH Lutze, RD Luxford, PC Luxton, RJ Luxton, GR Lyell, HH Lyford, GM Lyle, EF Lymbery, RE Lyme, C Lymn, GT Lymn, PJ Lymn, BJ Lynch, EJ Lynch, FJ Lynch, GAT Lynch, GF Lynch, GIL Lynch, JA Lynch, LK Lynch, MA Lynch, NR Lynch, PJJ Lynch, RE Lynch, RF Lynch, SJE Lynch, AC Lyne, NM Lyne, PR Lyneham, PJ Lyngcoln, AJ Lynn, KTA Lynn, GN Lyon, F Lyons, JB Lyons, JF Lyons, PJ Lyons, TJ Lyons, WR Lyons, P Lysaght, JF Lysle, WR MacAfee, GD MacAndrews, IL MacAndrews, DJJ MacAngus, JR Macartney, JW Macaskill, MJ MacBean, F Maccione, BA MacCormack, AF MacDonald, AJ MacDonald, BE MacDonald, EL MacDonald, GF MacDonald, JC MacDonald, JM MacDonald, JR MacDonald, K MacDonald, MR MacDonald, N MacDonald, NR MacDonald, RA MacDonald, RAC MacDonald, MP MacDouall, KW Mace, WB MacFarlane, J MacGregor, RJ MacGregor, RL MacGregor, RFB Machan, PJ Machin, JF Macinally, GJ Mackay, KM Mackay, MGK Mackay, PA Mackay, RM Mackay, WC Mackay, MA Mackay-Blair, C Mackenzie, GE Mackenzie, GJ Mackenzie, WA Mackenzie, D Mackenzie-Forbes, MJ Mackey, CG Mackie, RJ Mackie, G MacKinnell, AB MacKinnon, AD MacKinnon, JH MacKinnon, RG MacKinnon, RG Mackintosh, DR Macklin, RW Macklin, SJ Mackness, AW Maclachlan, GF Maclean, RM Maclean, BL Maclennan, AL Macleod, IR Macleod, MO Maclure, NA Macmillan, RG MacNevin, RFS Maconachie, RJE Macpherson, RP Macpherson,

NBD Macrae, JL Macsporran, JE Madden, PV Madden, RE Madden, SJ Maddison, FA Maddox, AP Madej, P Madejewski, ED Madigan, SC Magdalinski, LK Maginnity, PA Magnuson, MR Magor, DC Maguire, RJ Maguire, TJ Maguire, WJ Maguire, BW Maher, G Maher, JS Maher, P Maher, MN Mahnkoph, DR Mahoney, JM Mahoney, HJ Maidens, GA Maier, RS Mailo, RR Main, AG Maine, RH Mair, GJ Maisey, GRE Majaura, LJ Major, ADR Makin, TJ Makings, T Maksimovic, TN Malby, PRC Malcolm, NE Maley, TG Mallaghan, BR Mallett, PW Mallie, DL Mallyon, NM Mallyon, AMT Maloney, KJ Maloney, PI Maloney, WEG Malouf, DE Malpas, JV Malysz, PJ Mander, TN Mander, WE Mander, TM Manders, VR Mandic, PJ Mangan, JI Maniana, JP Manley, PJ Manley, CD Mann, CE Mann, DP Mann, PI Mann, WR Mann, BCB Manning, DC Manning, KD Manning, KEJ Manning, MA Manning, PR Manning, RW Manning, WR Manning, BT Mannion, PR Manoel, GB Manoi, DJ Manolas, CRL Mansbridge, DC Mansell, G Mansell, GW Mansell, JG Mansell, R Mansell, BC Mansfield, FD Mansfield, LT Mansfield, RC Mansfield, J Mansom, AJ Manson, CA Manson, MR Manson, AJ Manteit, GR Mant-Old, AJ Mapson, AR March, DJ March, JC March, RL March, G Marchant, JS Marchant, RJ Marchant, WL Marcroft, JA Marcus, JR Marcus, E Marecki, J Marecki, J Marek, V Marek, K Marengo, D Mariner, G Mariotto, GR Mark, MP Mark, JK Markham, RS Markiewicz, BJ Marks, DC Marks, EK Marks, LB Marks, LR Marks, PL Marks, TJ Marks, RG Markwell, PD Marlborough, RG Marlow, RF Marnham, HK Marques, DDJ Marrable, KJ Marren, PW Marriner, JA Marrison, JC Marrs, DD Marsen, DW Marsen, DL Marsh, DM Marsh, FJ Marsh, G Marsh, GJ Marsh, JD Marsh, MP Marsh, RJ Marsh, CT Marshall, FA Marshall, GP Marshall, GW Marshall, IF Marshall, LR Marshall, MB Marshall, NS Marshall, RJ Marshall, SJR Marshall, W Marshall, M Marsham, PH Marsman, L Martain, JA Martens, AR Martin, BM Martin, C Martin, CJ Martin, D Martin, DA Martin, DC Martin, DE Martin, DJ Martin, DR Martin, ED Martin, G Martin, GJ Martin, GP Martin, GT Martin, J Martin, JB Martin, JF Martin, JJ Martin, JL Martin, JR Martin, KL Martin, LG Martin, LR Martin, ME Martin, MF Martin, MH Martin, MW Martin, PE Martin, PH Martin, PR Martin, PW Martin, RF Martin, RJ Martin, RP Martin, TL Martin, VJ Martin, WJ Martin, N Martino, C Martschenko, E Martschenko, GC Martyn, RK Marum, MJ Marwick, DJ Mascord, RD Maskall, RJ Maskell, GA Maskey, CW Maslen, DE Maslen, DR Maslin, AC Mason, AJ Mason, AR Mason, BK Mason, BR Mason, BW Mason, D Mason, DR Mason, DW Mason, GB Mason, GF Mason, JW Mason, LW Mason, MF Mason, MGK Mason, RD Mason, RE Mason, RT Mason, WR Mason, GAR Massie, BR Masson, H Mast, AF Masters, DW Masters, EJ Masters, MH Masters, RN Masters, SJ Masters, RK Masterton, SL Masterton, N Matchett, W Matczak, RC Mather, BR Mathers, AA Matheson, GJ Matheson, L Matheson, RJ Mathew, BJ Mathews, DJ Mathews, JH Mathews, KC Mathews, RA Mathews, AG Mathewson, GD Mathie, S Mathieson, JS Mathwin, RG Matsen, RJ Matson, LD Matterson, GJ Matthes, R Mattheus, MT Matthew, S Matthew, AB Matthews, AW Matthews, B Matthews, BF Matthews, BJ Matthews, C Matthews, CR Matthews, E Matthews, GR Matthews, GWC Matthews, IR Matthews, JE Matthews, MJ Matthews, PF Matthews, RJ Matthews, SW Matthews, TE Matthews, WJ Matthews, WR Matthews, RJ Mattson, BL Maughan, RT Maughan, RW Maughan, BL Maultby, IJ Maunder, TE Maunder, RG Mawer, IP Mawson, DJ Maxton, DR Maxwell, GR Maxwell, GS Maxwell, JR Maxwell, MC Maxwell, PA Maxwell, PJ Maxwell, RP Maxwell, TW Maxwell, WI Maxwell, AG May, DL May, JR May, PJ May, RJ May, RR Maybury, WJ Maybury, MG Maycock, AW Mayes, RJ Mayes, RE Maynard, GC Mayne, GF Mayne, C Mayo, DS Mays, GJ Mays, HJ Maziarz, JE Mazlin, DJ McAdam, GK McAdam, J McAdam, CS McAlister, KB McAlister, SC McAlister, DS McAllister, WE McAllister, LJ McAnally, GAV McArthur, GJ McArthur, ID McArthur, NA McArthur, MT McAuley, KD McAuliffe, RD McBay, GJ McBroom, PJ McBurney, JL McCabe, JT McCabe, MF McCabe, KA McCallum, LR McCallum, PJ McCallum, DJ McCann, JJ McCann, JB McCarthy, JE McCarthy, KC McCarthy, PM McCarthy, TG McCarthy, MJ McCaskill, NA McCaskill, FW McCaul, MA McCaul, RL McCay, KR McClarty, AJ McClelland, DR McClelland, KF McClelland, RG McClelland,

MJ McClory, PH McCloskey, JW McClure, JB McClymont, PJ McColl, SU McColl, J McColm, I McCombe, CR McConnachie, IP McConnochie, KD McConnon, CW McConville, IG McCormack, J McCormack, PV McCormack, DJ McCormick, I McCormick, JC McCormick, JE McCorriston, JL McCorriston, LF McCourt, DM McCowat, JR McCoy, KG McCoy, CG McCracken, JP McCracken, LT McCracken, FC McCreanor, I McCrindle, JR McCrohon, PB McCullen, D McCulloch, JL McCulloch, KR McCulloch, RL McCullough, MI McCune, LG McCurley, D McCutcheon, GT McCutcheon, IW McCutcheon, JH McDade, VM McDade, WJ McDeed, GC McDermid, WJ McDermid, GR McDermott, JG McDermott, PA McDermott, RJ McDermott, RK McDermott, LJ McDiarmid, R McDiarmid, A McDonald, AD McDonald, AK McDonald, BJ McDonald, DJ McDonald, DR McDonald, GE McDonald, GR McDonald, GW McDonald, HMR McDonald, IR McDonald, JA McDonald, JD McDonald, JNR McDonald, KC McDonald, LJ McDonald, LN McDonald, NE McDonald, PM McDonald, PW McDonald, RG McDonald, TJ McDonald, WJ McDonald, TE McDonell, BF McDonnell, AG McDonough, JH McDonough, IR McDougall, LGR McDougall, M McDougall, SJ McDougall, WA McDougall, PM McDowall, WL McDowall, GJ McDowell, RK McDowell, KN McEacharn, EF McEvoy, RF McEvoy, ML McFadden, AG McFarland, I McFarlane, KJ McFarlane, SH McFarlane, KAJ McFarlane-Peacock, IRS McFawn, J McFeeters, RH McFerran, WJ McFerran, MJ McFie, GA McGahan, JD McGarry, WJ McGarry, RD McGaw, JR McGee, LJ McGee, RC McGhee, RM McGillvery, GD McGilvery, IR McGilvray, WJ McGinlay, RJ McGinley, PD McGinniss, LG McGlenchy, DR McGlinn, GA McGlinn, AD McGowan, AP McGowan, TM McGowan, AS McGown, LI McGown, BJ McGrade, GJ McGrath, JL McGrath, MGJ McGrath, PM McGrath, RA McGrath, RL McGrath, TG McGrath, TJ McGrath, CK McGregor, GJ McGregor, I McGregor, JA McGregor, JD McGregor, KW McGregor, PM McGregor, RR McGregor, J McGrigor, AJ McGrory, IJ McGuckin, PJ McGuckin, BJ McGufficke, RJ McGuffie, KJ McGuiness, M McGuinness, CB McGuire, IL McGuire, LT McGuire, PF McGuire, T McGuire, TF McGuire, BP McGurgan, PC McGurk, RS McHue, AR McInnes, B McInnes, BWC McInnes, DS McInnes, ER McInnes, IS McInnes, NA McInnes, DM McIntosh, DT McIntosh, GS McIntosh, M McIntosh, PJ McIntosh, RT McIntosh, SJ McIntosh, IM McIntyre, IS McIntyre, J McIntyre, RS McIntyre, W McIntyre, AJ McKandie, TR McKaskill, AV McKay, B McKay, DR McKay, IR McKay, JEL McKay, LI McKay, N McKay, PD McKay, RJ McKay, RC McKeag, AB McKean, DE McKee, PJ McKee, DA McKeen, LC McKeen, TP McKeever, AM McKelvie, PR McKendrick, KM McKenna, PJA McKenna, AD McKenzie, AJ McKenzie, CJ McKenzie, CR McKenzie, DJE McKenzie, EP McKenzie, FH McKenzie, IC McKenzie, J McKenzie, JA McKenzie, JK McKenzie, KHJ McKenzie, MA McKenzie, MD McKenzie, RA McKenzie, RG McKenzie, WB McKenzie, WH McKenzie, WK McKenzie, WT McKenzie, BS McKeough, GR McKeown, PJ McKeown, VJ McKerchar, TD McKerlie, GW McKewen, RJ McKewin, RJ McKibbin, IF McKie, IWL McKie, RF McKinna, R McKinney, DJ McKinnon, M McKinnon, JJ McLachlan, SJ McLachlan, JCO McLaine, KH McLaine, DC McLaren, LS McLaren, RM McLaren, RT McLaren, BM McLauchlan, DC McLaughlin, GR McLaughlin, IR McLaughlin, RJ McLaughlin, RM McLaurin, DJ McLean, DP McLean, DR McLean, G McLean, GM McLean, GT McLean, IR McLean, JA McLean, JAF McLean, KL McLean, MC McLean, NA McLean, NF McLean, NRJ McLean, R McLean, RA McLean, RG McLean, RJ McLean, TE McLean, WL McLean, RL McLear, PJ McLeish, T McLellan, BA McLennan, GF McLennan, RJ McLennan, AB McLeod, CD McLeod, DA McLeod, GB McLeod, GM McLeod, JS McLeod, KD McLeod, NF McLeod, PJ McLeod, PK McLeod, RJ McLeod, SJ McLeod, T McLeod, FI McLeod-Dryden, BH McLernon, GW McLure, RE McMah, BD McMahon, DJ McMahon, RF McMahon, RJ McMahon, RP McMahon, TJ McMahon, AC McManus, BR McManus, I McManus, EL McMaster, RSH McMaster, KJ McMiles, AB McMillan, DJ McMillan, DM McMillan, JW McMillan, PJ McMillan, R McMillan, RJ McMillan, WK McMillan, AF McMullen, LJ McMurdo, BW McMurtrie, A McNab, P McNair, PD McNair, TD McNair, WD McNair, ELJ McNally, GR McNally, JP McNally, P McNally, BJ McNamara, DJ McNamara, DN McNamara, DR McNamara, JK McNamara, PA McNamara, RG McNamara, JW McNamee, WJ McNamee, DG McNaught, H McNaught, PF McNay, AMB McNeill, BR McNeill, DRC McNeill, NW McNeill, R McNeill, WJ McNeill, DE McNeilly, J McNicol, AWR McNicoll, J McPhail, G McPhee, BE McPherson, DJ McPherson, LM McPherson, RCJ McPherson, TM McQuade, AA McQueen, IA McQueen, P McQueen, IG McQuiston, KJ McRae, RC McRae, G McRobb, E McShane, PR McShane, MB McSweeney, TC McSweeney, ID McTaggart, CJ McVea, NM McVee, PJ McVee, AR McVicar, KR McWade, RK McWaters, JW McWha, NE McWilliams, GSW Meacham, DJ Mead, JB Mead, PE Mead, PJ Mead, PJ Meade, MR Meades, IA Meadowcroft, I Meadows, TW Meagher, RM Meaker, TJ Meany, CD Meares, RB Meares, J Medaris, RF Medcalf, OG Medcraft, CJ Medway, A Meehan, JS Meehan, TJ Meehan, A Meek, RW Mees, JW Megow, IG Meighen, DT Meiklejohn, PA Meiklejohn, RD Melaney, JM Meldrum, DJ Melia, EG Mellish, FA Mellish, P Mellish, DW Mellowship, BE Melrose, BJ Melville, RL Melville, RBC Melville-Main, DG Memory, GA Mende, RL Meneely, W Mengele, WJ Menhennett, GJ Menteith, E Mentz, WJ Menz, LK Menzies, PF Menzies, BA Meotti, JN Mercer, RW Mercer, BJ Merchant, DG Merchel, M Mercurio, DT Meredith, JA Meredith, JW Meredith, RT Meredith, MJ Merefield, JA Merlin, NS Merrifield, S Merrilees, JS Merrillees, DJ Merritt, VGJ Merryweather, JLW Merson, KGJ Mesecke, GJ Messell, GI Meszaros, DC Metcalf, GW Metcalf, PC Metcalf, E Metcalfe, RT Metcalfe, GE Mewett, ID Mewett, AG Meyer, SH Meyer, BR Meyers, GK Meyers, VE Miatke, LG Michael, AC Michel, JM Michelson, SH Michod, LW Mickan, RJ Micke, L Middis, AR Middleton, KJ Middleton, MJ Middleton, W Middleton, WA Middleton, RG Midford, EC Midgley, RC Midgley, LH Midson, RJ Miers, W Mieszkuc, M Mihaljcek, TV Mihaly, S Mika, SG Milazzo, JE Mildner, TD Mildren, YH Milenz, DA Miles, KS Miles, SF Miles, BA Milford, DW Milford, JD Milgate, PJ Milgate, A Miliaresi, PC Millane, AJ Millar, BJ Millar, GM Millar, HK Millar, HW Millard, IW Millard, PT Millen, AA Miller, ATH Miller, AW Miller, BEJ Miller, DD Miller, DK Miller, E Miller, G Miller, GE Miller, GH Miller, GJ Miller, GL Miller, GO Miller, GP Miller, IH Miller, JA Miller, JW Miller, KF Miller, KL Miller, LJ Miller, MA Miller, MB Miller, RD Miller, RG Miller, RJ Miller, RW Miller, TJ Miller, WR Miller, RC Millers, DW Millett, RJ Millhouse, D Millington, AJ Mills, AM Mills, CAR Mills, CD Mills, CM Mills, DL Mills, DW Mills, FJ Mills, GA Mills, GW Mills, J Mills, LM Mills, MW Mills, P Mills, PE Mills, RA Mills, RB Mills, RC Mills, RL Mills, TA Mills, MA Millsom, MK Milne, RJ Milner, AL Milroy, DG Milroy, JW Milton, LB Minchin, PR Minchin, BW Minck, R Minette, TM Miniken, B Minogue, TN Minogue, DG Minto, BJ Mirtschin, JL Miscamble, R Mischlewski, RE Misell, IC Misfeld, AD Mitchell, AG Mitchell, AJ Mitchell, AW Mitchell, BA Mitchell, BMG Mitchell, C Mitchell, CB Mitchell, CD Mitchell, D Mitchell, DC Mitchell, DH Mitchell, DR Mitchell, E Mitchell, GF Mitchell, GJ Mitchell, HW Mitchell, JA Mitchell, JE Mitchell, JW Mitchell, KR Mitchell, LJ Mitchell, LL Mitchell, MD Mitchell, PC Mitchell, PS Mitchell, RAB Mitchell, RJ Mitchell, RT Mitchell, TP Mitchell, RJ Mitten, RL Mitting, JM Mitton, SJ Moar, IR Moate, RS Mobbs, ME Mobley, RL Mock, HA Modin, FL Moffatt, MS Moffatt, CD Moffitt, NG Moffitt, RG Moffitt, RH Moffitt, AC Mohamad, RM Moir, EW Mol, DW Mole, GJ Mole, PL Mole, FM Molean, I Molineaux, A Moller, JM Moller, KJ Molloy, GC Mollross, JL Moloney, JR Moloney, MG Moloney, IJG Molony, RE Monaghan, WJ Monaghan, RJ Monck, RM Mondey, RW Monery, WH Money, KA Monk, KL Monk, MJ Monson, C Montaldo, TR Monteith, DF Montgomery, DN Montgomery, JHH Montgomery, LS Montgomery, RH Montgomery, RP Montiglio, AJ Monty, IL Moodie, RD Moodie, CWH Moody, P Mooi, AM Moon, JRF Moon, JW Moon, MC Moon, RD Mooney, TA Moonie, JW Moorcroft, AK Moore, BJ Moore, BL Moore, DBL Moore, DE Moore, DR Moore, DY Moore, EGL Moore, GJ Moore, GLG Moore, HJ Moore, IJ Moore, J Moore, JA Moore, JH Moore, JL Moore, LJ Moore, MAC Moore, MJ Moore, P Moore, PH Moore, R Moore, RB Moore, RD Moore, RH Moore, RK Moore, LJ Moorfoot, RF Moran, CFP Morbey, PA Morcom, JS More, T Morehead, DW Moreland, HCW Morey, DC Morgan, DL Morgan, EJ Morgan, EL Morgan, GA Morgan, GE Morgan, GJ Morgan, HE Morgan, HR Morgan, J Morgan, JG Morgan, JP Morgan, KD Morgan, L Morgan, MJ Morgan, PR Morgan, RD Morgan, RL Morgan, TA Morgan, WR Morgan, GJ Moriarty, LF Moriarty, DE Morison, AN Morley, RD Morley, DJ Moroney, JH Moroney, LJ Morony, M Moros, RN Morphett, FA Morrah, RJ Morrall, JO Morrice, AG Morris, BG Morris, CJR Morris, CR Morris, DF Morris, DJ Morris, DR Morris, FT Morris, GD Morris, JD Morris, JL Morris, JO Morris, JP Morris, JR Morris, KF Morris, KJ Morris, NH Morris, RJ Morris, TJ Morris, TL Morris, TTP Morris, WG Morris, WK Morris, WR Morris, GM Morrison, NR Morrison, RW Morrison, SG Morrison, TK Morrison, AJ Morriss, KL Morrissey, RV Morritt, DG Morrow, DL Morse, RC Morse, DG Mortimer, P Mortimer, TE Mortimer, WD Mortimer, RF Mortison, GE Mortlock, BJ Morton, GA Morton, KH Morton, R Morton, SJ Morton, BA Moseley, TR Moseley, AJ Moser, IW Mosey, M Moskal, DJ Mosman, BJ Moss, DJ Moss, RP Moss, LE Mossman, SHT Mossman, PR Moulden, RM Moule, DJ Mounsey, N Mount, A Mowatt, JD Moy, PJ Moy, TR Moyes, RT Moyle, RL Moynihan, SJ Moyns, GM Mozol, AD Muddle, LG Mudge, EP Mudry, EJ Mueller, RT Mueller, BJ Muggleton, GE Mugridge, PE Muhlhan, TG Muhlhan, RC Muir, PM Mulcare, L Mulder, GJ Muldoon, JW Muldoon, JJ Mulhall, PM Mulheren, WIT Mulholland, DR Muller, JL Muller, LJ Muller, NP Muller, PJ Mulley, MJ Mullice, MW Mulligan, PO Mulligan, TD Mullineux, MR Mullinger, MM Mullins, SJ Mullins, SN Mullins, CK Mulquiney, PJ Mulquiney, A Mulroy, DC Mulvihill, LW Mumme, CP Munday, IA Munday, CJ Mundt, AC Mundy, PJ Mundy, RD Mundy, LH Mungovan, T Munneke, PK Munnery, KW Munnings, HG Munnink, DD Munro, GR Munro, JD Munro, JG Munro, LI Munro, ME Munro, PC Munro, RKF Munro, SN Munro, WE Munro, WJ Munro, BT Munt, R Munton, W Muras, RD Murchie, KF Murcutt, PV Murdoch, RH Murdock, AJ Murgatroyd, AJ Murphy, AP Murphy, AT Murphy, BJ Murphy, BM Murphy, CG Murphy, CL Murphy, DF Murphy, DJ Murphy, JB Murphy, JC Murphy, JG Murphy, JJ Murphy, JM Murphy, JT Murphy, KR Murphy, PD Murphy, PW Murphy, RG Murphy, RJ Murphy, TP Murphy, WF Murphy, AR Murray, BS Murray, CD Murray, DJ Murray, GF Murray, GR Murray, IF Murray, IM Murray, IR Murray, ME Murray, RG Murray, SP Murray, TW Murray, JR Murrell, KM Murrell, PJ Murrell, GF Murtagh, GG Murton, BOC Musch, RJ Muscio, WK Musson, GA Mustow, RW Muus, W Mycio, AM Myers, B Myers, BA Myers, GL Myers, JW Myers, LN Myers, NC Myers, SAW Myers, WK Myers, JB Mylan, G Myors, J Nable, S Nagy, S Naisby, JJ Nankervis, GR Nanscawen, GLH Nantes, JD Napier, JG Napier, PC Narramore, GR Nash, JB Nash, JJB Nash, GW Nason, RJ Nattey, AD Naughton, J Naughton, DP Nay, MJ Nay, AE Naylor, JR Naylor, TH Naylor, R Neagle, BJ Neal, KG Neal, MJF Neal, RW Neal, TW Neal, AR Neale, WJ Neale, PP Neary, KE Neath, DL Neck, A Needham, HM Needham, KV Needham, P Needham, WA Needham, DF Neenan, HGW Neervoort, DR Neich, JC Neil, KA Neil, TG Neil, DLG Neild, WF Neill, FL Neilsen, GP Neilsen, ARP Neilson, BC Neilson, JK Neilson, NM Neilson, PT Neilson, G Nekrasov, JC Nelms, AJ Nelson, GA Nelson, GJ Nelson, KWJ Nelson, GE Nepean, PA Nesbitt, DA Nettle, MWN Neumann, RG Nevell, BE Neville, GJ Neville, IW Neville, AH Newberry, BG Newbold, JG Newby, PT Newby, JRA Newcomb, PA Newcomb, AE Newcombe, AR Newell, H Newell, JR Newell, RRJ Newell, GA Newey, RP Newey, DB Newham, PL Newland, AD Newlands, DN Newman, EJ Newman, JGJ Newman, MJ Newman, N Newman, PR Newman, TJ Newman, WR Newman, RJ Newnham, NJ Newsham, BJ Newton, CR Newton, DJ Newton, MJ Newton, MTO Newton, PE Newton, RA Newton, RC Newton, RF Newton, SC Newton, TC Newton, RI Niblett, BR Nichol, RM Nichol, BF Nicholas, G Nicholas, JD Nicholas, P Nicholas, BW Nicholls, DG Nicholls, DGH Nicholls, GW Nicholls, LKW Nicholls, WJ Nicholls, BR Nichols, BWJ Nichols, DA Nichols, JE Nichols, RH Nichols, SJ Nichols, WJ Nichols, AE Nicholson, DR Nicholson, IH Nicholson, JA Nicholson,

JP Nicholson, LK Nicholson, P Nicholson, DJ Nicol, IF Nicol, RJ Nicolai, JWJ Nicoll, MW Nicoll, DAI Nicolson, GR Niehus, AC Nielsen, G Nielsen, LH Nielsen, PLP Nielsen, WJ Nielsen, PGJ Nienhuys, ST Nihill, GM Nikolic, KG Nilsen, KN Nilsen, CE Nilsson, TK Nilsson, IJ Nimmo, BW Nipperess, CJ Nisbet, W Nissel, A Nistico, A Nits, T Niven, AJ Nixon, DR Nixon, PJ Nixon, NA Noack, R Noakes, CV Nobbs, B Nobes, CS Noble, DJ Noble, LD Noble, PD Noble, R Noble, RD Noble, RS Noble, BJ Nolan, CT Nolan, D Nolan, JE Nolan, LD Nolan, PG Nolan, PJ Nolan, VM Nolan, VW Nold, WH Noll, KP Noonan, RV Noonan, DL Norbury, GL Nordberg, RK Nordberg, RF Nordsvan, G Norley, A Norman, DA Norman, R Norman, RCT Norman, RJ Norman, TA Norman, BF Normington, DJ Norquay, CB Norris, EC Norris, KL Norris, LP Norris, PE Norrish, RC Norrish, WJJ North, JB Northcote, SJ Northey, B Northover, GE Northrop, BR Northrope, BF Norton, BM Norton, DV Norton, GF Norton, JN Norton, KD Norton, PJ Norton, RA Norton, RB Norton-Baker, AG Nosse, JF Nothdurft, RJ Nothdurft, DJ Nothrop, RT Nott, M Novak, SS Nowicki, DW Nowland, GD Noyes, HJ Nugent, MR Nugent, NC Nugent, TB Nugent, LW Nurse, PP Nurse, GW Nuss, PAF Nuss, GJ Nuthall, JG Nuttman, BGJ Nye, CR Oakes, JW Oakes, LJ Oakey, GW Oakley, IH Oakley, SJ Oates, WT Oates, M O'Beirne, RJ Oberman, W Obernier, JE Oborne, AV O'Brien, B O'Brien, D O'Brien, DW O'Brien, J O'Brien, JL O'Brien, JP O'Brien, KF O'Brien, KJ O'Brien, MH O'Brien, MJ O'Brien, PB O'Brien, PJ O'Brien, PJC O'Brien, PK O'Brien, PL O'Brien, RJ O'Brien, RP O'Brien, FJ O'Bryan, GL Obst, C O'Callaghan, GL O'Callaghan, JBA O'Callaghan, HF Ochremienko, GW Ockwell, DK O'Connell, HD O'Connell, KF O'Connell, MJ O'Connell, TH O'Connell, BP O'Connor, EJ O'Connor, JB O'Connor, JM O'Connor, JW O'Connor, KS O'Connor, LK O'Connor, N O'Connor, RPH O'Connor, RC O'Day, WA O'Day, JL O'Dea, K Odell, EJ O'Doherty, PA O'Donahoo, CH O'Donnell, DW O'Donnell, KM O'Donnell, LJ O'Donnell, NP O'Donnell, RM O'Donnell, TPC O'Donnell, WJ Odonnell, JM O'Donoghue, PD O'Dowd, LP O'Driscoll, BP O'Dwyer, JW O'Dwyer, NW O'Dwyer, CC O'Farrell, JA O'Farrell, GE Offord, B O'Flaherty, NA O'Flaherty, CF O'Flynn, GR Ogg, CL Ogle, MP O'Gorman, PJ O'Grady, RP O'Grady, KP O'Hagan, BS O'Halloran, MJ O'Halloran, EJW O'Hara, JS O'Hara, RS O'Hara, KJ O'Hare, CR O'Hora, FJ O'Kane, CJ O'Keefe, GFL O'Keefe, KR O'Keefe, VL O'Keefe, DP O'Keeffe, PJ O'Keeffe, ER Okely, LW Olah, JM Olchowik, RH Old, DT Olden, MG Olden, R Oldham, WR Oldmeadow, JD O'leary, N O'leary, PM Oleson, PJ Oliffe, F Olinga, A Oliver, AJ Oliver, D Oliver, DA Oliver, DL Oliver, GF Oliver, J Oliver, KW Oliver, PR Oliver, RV Oliver, SJ Oliver, TL Oliver, RC Ollenburg, BL Olney, EC Olney, PA O'loghlin, PJ O'loughlin, PA Olrich, BA Olsen, BL Olsen, GJ Olsen, KR Olsen, RM Olsen, WAE Olsen, WG Olsen, KJ Olson, BG O'Mahony, WN O'Malley, AE O'Meagher, GK O'Neal, BC O'Neill, BP O'Neill, CW O'Neill, JA O'Neill, JG O'Neill, JL O'Neill, LR O'Neill, MJ O'Neill, PB O'Neill, PR O'Neill, DE Oner, AG Ongley, PJ Onley, A Oosting, RJ Opalinski, M Opassi, WW Oppenhuis, PL O'Rance, GF Orchard, KR Orchard, A Ordelman, RD O'Regan, VD O'Regan, DF O'Reilly, DM O'Reilly, JJ Orford, LW Orford, PJ O'Riordan, P Ormerod, JA Ormes, JJ Ormes, P Ormsby, TJ O'Rourke, HJ Orozco, ML Orpin, B Orr, BJ Orr, DJ Orr, ET Orr, RA Orr, RJ Orr, SC Orr, M Oryszczyn, BD Osborn, L Osborn, RA Osborn, DA Osborne, JR Osborne, JT Osborne, PA Osborne, RS Osborne, DM O'Shannessy, EE O'Shannessy, JT O'Shannessy, MJ O'Shannessy, WA O'Shannessy, J O'Shaughnessy, B O'Shea, JJ O'Shea, MF O'Shea, PB O'Shea, PJ O'Shea, WL O'Sing, V Osis, FJ Osland, SA Osment, C Osmon, JW Ostenfeld, IL Oster, CA Ostrowski, FMS Ostrowski, DP O'Sullivan, EA O'Sullivan, PJ O'Sullivan, RP O'Sullivan, T O'Sullivan, CJ O'Toole, MD Otter, L Oudenryn, KJ Ousley, RJ Ovans, RG Overhall, S Oversby, WR Overson, JT Overton, WE Overton, WR Overton, DW Owen, JA Owen, PW Owen, RTA Owen, SJ Owen, DH Owens, DT Owens, GR Owens, GW Owens, RJ Owens, LJ Owler, RM Oxborrow, CJ Oxenbould, WJ Oxey, DD Oxford, R Oxley, CG Oyston, BS Oytaben, E Ozols, JP Pacey, GR Packanen, R Packham, JO Paddon, JA Padersen, P Paech, PMS Paffard, A Page, BH Page, CA Page, HG Page, JS Page, MJ Page, NG Page, PJ Page, RF Page, SK Page, WJ Page, LK Pagett, PC Pagett, BL Paine, BN Pallier, WE Pallot, A Palmer, AAA Palmer, AL Palmer, CR Palmer, DB Palmer, GF Palmer, GH Palmer, GR Palmer, GS Palmer, GW Palmer, JRV Palmer, LG Palmer, R Palmer, RJ Palmer, RT Palmer, TM Palmer, WA Palmer, DN Paloff, BB Pankhurst, TE Pankhurst, GA Pannell, DJ Pannowitz, RJ Pantlin, SJ Panton, PG Paprotny, GE Pardy, BB Pareezer, RL Pares, RW Parici, GM Parish, RT Parish, KS Park, SR Park, BR Parke, SJ Parke, B Parker, BJ Parker, DR Parker, G Parker, GD Parker, GJ Parker, JF Parker, JN Parker, JR Parker, KLE Parker, LR Parker, NV Parker, PJ Parker, R Parker, VA Parker, WB Parker, WG Parker, WJ Parker, BJ Parkes, GF Parkes, RJ Parkes, J Parkhill, GL Parkin, JV Parkins, PJ Parkins, DL Parkinson, JM Parkinson, KE Parkinson, LJ Parkinson, RJ Parkinson, D Parks, LG Parks, D Parnell, KL Parr, P Parr, AV Parrett, JH Parrott, BL Parrotte, BA Parry, CG Parry, GA Parry, SH Parslow, JT Parsonage, B Parsons, G Parsons, GJ Parsons, GL Parsons, JE Parsons, JEA Parsons, JM Parsons, LE Parsons, RF Parsons, RR Parsons, PM Parsonson, RE Partington, RN Partington, MP Pascoe, PR Pascoe, SW Pascoe-Lambert, RV Pasfield, SJ Pasfield, FJ Pashen, RJ Paskevicius, JH Passehl, FG Passmore, PF Passmore, JG Pasztor, LN Pataky, DL Patch, RA Patch, AR Paterson, GR Paterson, I Paterson, IR Paterson, JW Paterson, KJ Paterson, JWC Patison, GW Patman, RA Patmore, MR Patnaude, AD Paton, BLJ Paton, GJ Paton, GM Paton, N Patriarca, CJ Patrick, IN Patrick, AR Patten, CRL Patten, DR Patten, IW Patten, CJ Patterson, JL Patterson, JP Patterson, LG Patterson, M Patterson, PA Patterson, RJ Patterson, A Pattison, JR Pattison, NW Pattison, GD Pattle, MA Patton, BF Paul, BH Paul, WJ Paul, IW Paulet, DW Paull, BP Paulsen, RF Paulus, GL Pavett, AD Payne, AE Payne, BA Payne, CH Payne, EJ Payne, EM Payne, G Payne, GA Payne, GN Payne, JC Payne, JG Payne, NA Payne, NH Payne, RJ Payne, TL Payne, TW Payne, AG Payton, KR Payton, RD Peach, KD Peacock, DN Peak, GF Peake, RTM Peake, JH Pearce, JR Pearce, MJ Pearce, RH Pearce, RM Pearce, PW Peard, CS Pearn, BAL Pearson, DJ Pearson, G Pearson, JD Pearson, JF Pearson, JH Pearson, NE Pearson, RA Pearson, RS Pearson, JGJ Peart, DW Pease, ID Pechey, L Pechotsch, AP Peck, GH Peck, PE Peck, RJ Peckitt, TW Peckover, AB Pedder, GE Pedder, AB Pedersen, CM Pedersen, HM Pedersen, JPW Pedgeon, NJ Pedler, RJ Pedler, RI Peek, TJ Peek, EJ Peel, DJ Peers, GJ Peers, VS Peet, KHJ Peever, R Pegg, LJ Pegler, WK Pegus, TM Peisley, LW Pelham, RG Pelham, DW Pemberton, RA Pendal, GT Pendreigh, LW Pendrick, PV Penfold, CM Penglase, RI Penglase, SM Penman, B Penn, RJ Pennell, AG Penney, DW Penney, G Pennicuik, TS Pennington, RJR Pennock, AC Penny, P Penny, TH Penridge, RP Penrose, DL Pepper, M Peppernell, LE Pepyat, LN Percival, RH Percy, PS Pergunas, BP Perkins, CW Perkins, MS Perkins, OE Perkins, RG Perkins, RJ Perkins, RM Perkins, RP Perkins, RC Perks, JK Perrett, DF Perrin, GN Perrin, TJ Perrin, F Perrott, MA Perrott, AC Perry, DR Perry, JA Perry, KJ Perry, MA Perry, MD Perry, NM Perry, DS Pert, MWW Pes, HC Pesch, LJ Peschek, MJ Petch, JJ Peter, LJ Peterie, GF Peters, GJ Peters, GW Peters, MR Peters, RG Peters, RP Peters, SA Peters, CL Petersen, KA Petersen, MJ Petersen, RD Petersen, BR Peterson, CC Peterson, DN Peterson, FW Peterson, G Peterson, JG Peterson, KH Peterson, LA Peterson, WG Peterson, DC Petherick, JW Pethers, JA Petkevicius, N Petraccaro, BM Petrie, DJ Petrie, JS Petrie, LC Petrie, RW Petrie, RC Pettersen, K Petterson, BRE Pettifer, CM Pettigrove, GJ Pettit, TJ Pettit, BB Pettitt, AE Petty, HE Petty, RJ Petty, GB Peut, WJ Phalp, BJ Phefley, AA Philip, LM Philip, R Philip, S Philip, PJ Philippe, CA Philippson, KWW Philipson, HL Philistin, ANH Phillips, CR Phillips, DAS Phillips, DR Phillips, EJ Phillips, EL Phillips, JH Phillips, JM Phillips, KD Phillips, KT Phillips, LG Phillips, ME Phillips, MJ Phillips, MT Phillips, N Phillips, NW Phillips, OCI Phillips, PAK Phillips, PH Phillips, PL Phillips, RA Phillips, RB Phillips, RC Phillips, RJ Phillips, RN Phillips, RV Phillips, RW Phillips, TJ Phillips, WK Phillips, EJ Philp, JH Philp, WR Philp, WJ Philpott, DJ Phipps, D Phizacklea, JR Piccles, N Pickard, CJ Pickering, D Pickering, NH Pickering, AH Pickett, KR Pickett, DA Pickford, RJ Pickles, GJ Picone, KM Pidgeon, CC Pidler, WJF Pierce, RN Pierson, HW Pietras, EL Pietsch, PJ Pietzsch, A Piggott, GA Piggott, KJ Piggott, DGM Pigot, AG Pike, TC Pike, L Pilaczynski, DJ Pilkington, SG Pilling, TJ Pillinger, OG Pincott, DK Pink, RR Pinkstone, DG Piper, LAC Piper, TJ Piper, VN Piper, AL Pirie, JJ Pitcher, GJ Pitman, RH Pitt, TJ Pitt, NW Pittaway, PJ Pittaway, RE Pittaway, SW Pittaway, A Pittman, W Pittman, MJ Pitts, TG Place, KR Plain, CJ Plaisted, EJ Plant, GE Plant, GLH Plant, JD Platten, JR Platten, KS Playford, PI Playford, BJ Pleash, JW Pleiter, IR Plews, JP Ploszczyniec, CW Plummer, KS Plumridge, PE Plumridge, DO Plunkett, NJ Plunkett, PJ Plunkett, J Plunkett-Cole, PJ Plunkett-Cole, T Plymin, RH Poat, CB Pobje, JC Pocklington, MJ Pocock, AW Podmore, GT Polding, R Polglaze, TS Polkinghorne, AI Pollard, GW Pollard, JG Pollard, LG Pollard, NP Pollard, RF Pollard, JT Polley, JC Pollitt, DJ Pollock, GA Pollock, RJ Polo, DM Ponsonby, OH Pontin, D Pool, DM Pool, CJ Poole, LF Poole, RA Poole, RJ Poole, LA Poore, R Poore, TJ Poore, AJ Pope, CR Pope, M Pope, RK Pope, VG Pope, DJ Popp, L Porcu, RJ Portakiewicz, RH Porteous, BG Porter, GL Porter, HG Porter, KE Porter, WGH Porter, GJ Porzuczek, PCA Potaczala, G Pothoven, DP Potter, IKL Potter, IT Potter, JF Potter, NE Potter, SJ Potter, JP Potterat, BF Potts, BG Potts, R Potts, RW Potts, BJ Powell, CA Powell, DM Powell, DW Powell, EE Powell, KP Powell, KT Powell, LE Powell, RA Powell, RN Powell, RT Powell, TJM Powell, B Power, BD Power, BP Power, DW Power, EA Power, MJ Power, RA Power, DE Pownall, RF Poynting, G Poyzer, TR Prasolik, GD Prass, GF Prass, BE Pratt, JD Pratt, JR Predl, DJ Preece, GEC Preece, JK Prendergast, G Presland, JS Presland, LM Presland, EW Pressley, BJ Preston, RR Prestwidge, E Pretty, JC Pretty, GJ Price, LJ Price, MBJ Price, MR Price, PC Price, WR Price, RA Price-Beck, W Priddis, CR Pride, HJ Pride, JM Pridgeon, BD Priest, FG Priest, LJ Priest, RJ Priest, RP Priest, JT Priestly, RH Priestly, EB Princ, G Prince, P Prince, RJ Prindiville, DHJ Pringle, IG Pringle, LB Pringle, NL Prior, RT Prior, TE Prior, G Pritchard, JA Pritchard, KF Pritchard, RJC Pritchard, RL Pritchard, RS Pritchard, PM Procopis, GH Procter, PJ Procter, KF Prophet, PA Prosser, TS Proud, NB Prout, VW Provost, MP Prowse, WJ Prudham, GD Pryke, K Pryor, TC Pryor, H Przetocki, V Przetocki, GR Puckeridge, ME Pudney, AA Pugh, GD Pugh, JA Pugh, RW Pugh, RG Puller, RL Pulling, KJ Puls, RJ Pummell, KH Pumpa, AL Punch, BW Pung, CJ Purcell, GL Purcell, PT Purcell, LJ Purdie, GE Purkiss, PJ Purnell-Webb, LF Pursell, VB Purvey, KR Pusser, PN Puxty, AJ Pye, LR Pye, MA Pye, S Pye, GG Pyke, KC Pyke, WR Pylypiak, CE Pyne, DH Quaile, RJ Qualtrough, LW Quarrell, JW Quaylee, RA Que, IF Quelch, GJ Quick, JL Quick, RG Quick, RA Quigley, RA Quill, JJ Quilty, PJ Quin, MJ Quinlan, AP Quinn, DFS Quinn, DP Quinn, GPS Quinn, IK Quinn, JF Quinn, JL Quinn, MJ Quinn, PA Quinn, RL Quinn, SA Quinn, WR Quinn, PF Quinton, KJ Raabe, C Raams, CL Raatz, JL Rackstraw, TJ Radel, RJC Rademakers, EG Radford, LS Radford, K Radke, BC Radnidge, AH Radojkovic, JB Rae, JC Rae, RM Rae, SP Raepa, CC Raff, WAE Raff, GJ Rafferty, J Rafferty, TJ Raffo, TS Raftery, LJ Rago, MR Rain, PF Rainbird, GB Rainbow, A Raines, JC Raines, A Rainford, HE Rakow, JL Raleigh, ER Ralph, GE Ralph, L Ralph, N Ralph, RHG Ralph, WE Rampal, BR Ramsay, DJ Ramsay, DM Ramsay, GL Ramsay, PM Ramsay, RA Ramsay, RI Ramsay, RWJ Ramsay, JW Ramsey, AJ Ramseyer, EH Randel, AJ Rankin, GD Rankin, NG Rankin, MJ Rankine, VN Rann, EJ Ranson, GD Ranson, PJ Rapinett, MT Rapp, AV Rashleigh, DG Rasmussen, JL Raspe, KD Ratcliff, RH Ratcliffe, SR Rathbone, PCL Rattray, RM Raue, PG Rawlings, PJ Rawlings, MJ Rawlinson, SP Rawlinson, JH Rawson, AJ Ray, DR Ray, PJ Ray, RG Ray, GJ Rayfield, MB Rayment, VJ Raymer, DJT Raymond, TJ Raymond, EW Rayner, GJ Rayner, RL Rayner, WM Rayner, BJ Read, CM Read, GC Read, GP Read, MC Read, RP Read, RS Read, TM Read, EC Reading, JM Reading, DG Rear, DG Reardon, DR Reardon, J Reardon, P Reay, IS Rector, RN Reddacliff, VH Reddacliff, DW Reddick, BF Redenius, JC Redfern, JD Redman, DR Redshaw, WVL Redshaw, JD Reece, MEA Reece, WB Reece, GJ Reed, JA Reed, PE Reed, LR Reedman, DJ Rees, DW Rees, JF Rees, PT Reeve, R Reeve, BWA Reeves, CR Reeves, J Reeves, JA Reeves, JCW Reeves, JD Reeves, JH Reeves, JL Reeves, RM Reeves, RN Reeves, AW Regan, ME Regan, AI Reid, CA Reid, CWM Reid, DA Reid, DJ Reid, GDJ Reid, GJ Reid, GS Reid, JA Reid, JE Reid, JL Reid, KR Reid, MP Reid, PRC Reid, R Reid, RA Reid, RG Reid, RI Reid, TW Reid, DR Reidy, GN Reidy, FS Reilly, K Reilly, KO Reilly, LM Reilly, MJ Reilly, PA Reilly, WJ Reilly, HAU Reinecker,

LW Reinhard, HW Reinhardt, OB Reinhold, TB Reinhold, U Reinhold, GP Reinke, RJ Reinke, ES Reksmiss, J Rem, SR Renagi, RP Renaud, AG Rendell, JT Renfrey, LW Renfrey, NL Renfrey, IR Rennie, JW Rennie, LJ Rennie, MJ Rennie, RJ Rennie, CW Renshaw, GN Renshaw, PBM Repschlager, PLF Retallick, E Retford, VB Reutens, KH Reuter, CR Rex, DC Reynolds, GL Reynolds, JA Reynolds, JFW Reynolds, MF Reynolds, MJ Reynolds, PL Reynolds, PM Reynolds, T Reynolds, VL Reynolds, DN Rhook, BVM Rice, GT Rice, GW Rice, LV Rice, ML Rice, RB Rich, RE Rich, DP Richards, EC Richards, FW Richards, GT Richards, HL Richards, IR Richards, MRA Richards, NA Richards, PA Richards, R Richards, RB Richards, RL Richards, RN Richards, TW Richards, A Richardson, BJ Richardson, CL Richardson, DL Richardson, GE Richardson, GJ Richardson, IG Richardson, JF Richardson, LJ Richardson, MG Richardson, PJ Richardson, RJ Richardson, WJ Richardson, KG Richer, WC Richer, GH Riches, RJ Richey, LR Richmond, GR Richter, MJ Rick, DR Rickard, GG Rickard, P Rickard, DJ Rickards, WK Rickards, LA Rickert, RW Ricketts, DJ Rickman, JL Rickman, GR Rickwood, JW Ridd, RJ Riddell, KM Ridding, JE Riddle, D Riddock, JN Riddock, GG Rider, WA Ridgers, MR Ridgewell, JF Ridgway, GM Ridgwell, DR Ridings, SI Ridland, JD Ridler, GJ Ridley, RWC Ridley, GE Ridout, KW Ridout, TK Rieck, WT Rieken, RW Rielly, GP Riethmuller, CA Rigg, ET Rigg, RS Rigg, RS Rigney, WB Rignold, A Riley, AJ Riley, BT Riley, DG Riley, IG Riley, JS Riley, N Riley, SJ Riley, JP Rimmer, JW Rinaldi, LJ Rinehart, DJ Ring, WJ Ringholt, PJ Ringold, PJ Rinkin, RJ Ripper, MAW Riseley, PR Riseley, RP Riseley, JW Ritchey, CA Ritchie, CJ Ritchie, JB Ritchie, MJ Ritchie, TW Ritchie, WG Ritchie, PE Riters, RH Ritter, SA Ritter, WC Rivett, J Rix, DJ Rixon, JF Rixon, RJN Rixon, RL Rixon, B Roach, DR Roach, RE Roach, RW Roach, MJ Roadley, JE Robb, TN Robb, AR Robbins, CJ Robbins, MJ Robbins, TJ Robbins, AF Roberts, AP Roberts, B Roberts, BCA Roberts, BJ Roberts, CI Roberts, DAG Roberts, DF Roberts, DJ Roberts, DN Roberts, DR Roberts, EC Roberts, GB Roberts, GJ Roberts, GP Roberts, GR Roberts, JH Roberts, JM Roberts, KJ Roberts, KR Roberts, MA Roberts, MF Roberts, NDM Roberts, PD Roberts, RA Roberts, RJ Roberts, TW Roberts, WJ Roberts, WOC Roberts, DRE Robertshaw, AE Robertson, AJ Robertson, BD Robertson, BM Robertson, DN Robertson, GG Robertson, GJ Robertson, GS Robertson, HB Robertson, IB Robertson, IM Robertson, JA Robertson, JAD Robertson, NB Robertson, NJ Robertson, PD Robertson, PJ Robertson, RJ Robertson, SFH Robertson, SM Robertson, TW Robertson, WJR Robertson, WM Robertson, AL Robeson, C Robins, AB Robinson, AD Robinson, AJ Robinson, AK Robinson, BD Robinson, BT Robinson, BW Robinson, DL Robinson, GLS Robinson, GM Robinson, GN Robinson, IH Robinson, IJ Robinson, JD Robinson, JE Robinson, MJ Robinson, MP Robinson, N Robinson, NJ Robinson, P Robinson, PD Robinson, PR Robinson, RA Robinson, RB Robinson, RJ Robinson, SW Robinson, WA Robinson, WJ Robinson, WL Robinson, B Robson, DJ Robson, DST Robson, EN Robson, JL Robson, M Robson, RC Robson, SC Robson, DR Roche, MD Roche, PC Roche, HL Rochester, B Rochford, TJ Rochford, DE Rochow, GE Rodda, RR Rodda, RG Roddie, GT Rodger, WJ Rodger, AP Rodgers, BJ Rodgers, CA Rodgers, DN Rodgers, DW Rodgers, LJ Rodgers, PAC Rodgers, SD Rodgers, RP Rodriguez, MT Rodsted, RH Rodwell, GR Roe, KG Roe, S Roe, RR Roebig, RG Roebuck, HG Roelofs, WMM Roestenburg, KE Roffey, AG Rogers, BJ Rogers, BR Rogers, GG Rogers, GH Rogers, GW Rogers, JH Rogers, KR Rogers, MJ Rogers, O Rogers, PJ Rogers, PR Rogers, RA Rogers, RJ Rogers, RN Rogers, TC Rogers, WW Rogers, BH Rogge, BA Rogotzki, GR Rohrsheim, MB Roland, JW Roles, EJ Rolfe, H Rollinger, HF Rollinson, RO Rollinson, JG Rollnik, DJ Rolt, BS Romaine, I Roney, LJ Ronning, AW Rooke, MW Rooks, KA Rooney, RC Roots, GJ Roper, KF Roper, M Rosch, BE Rose, CB Rose, CM Rose, DC Rose, EW Rose, GA Rose, JB Rose, KW Rose, LAW Rose, LJ Rose, ML Rose, PL Rose, KG Rosen, DJ Rosenberg, MJ Rosenberg, GA Rosengreen, CM Rosenthal, RF Rosenthal, RW Roser, T Roser, KG Rosevear, BA Rosewarne, AW Rosier, WJ Rosier, SJ Rosmalen, WJ Rosolen, A Ross, AE Ross, AG Ross, B Ross, FE Ross, IM Ross, JT Ross, KJ Ross, KJC Ross, NA Ross, PA Ross, PR Ross, PW Ross, R Ross, RM Ross, TR Ross, WH Ross, WJ Ross, WL Ross, MJ Rosser, DJ Rossi, GP Rossi, MJ Rossiter, RC Rossiter, SB Rosta, CJ Rothwell, WE Rothwell, BE Rottinger, G Roudenko, AC Rough, FR Round, JR Rounsevell, WJ Rourke, RW Rouse, BW Router, AG Row, KJ Row, A Rowan, MJ Rowan, P Rowan, RB Rowcroft, BL Rowe, BM Rowe, BNJ Rowe, CD Rowe, CJ Rowe, CP Rowe, GJ Rowe, HG Rowe, HR Rowe, IRA Rowe, JA Rowe, KG Rowe, KJ Rowe, LJ Rowe, RJ Rowe, RR Rowe, RT Rowe, SJ Rowe, TG Rowe, TJ Rowell, AM Rowland, C Rowland, GJ Rowland, KJ Rowland, B Rowlands, GD Rowles, AFC Rowley, LS Rowley, NF Rowley, TG Rowley, BL Rowling, TD Rowling, DJ Rowston, PR Royall, GB Royle, FI Rubly, H Ruckert, AB Rudd, C Rudd, RW Rudd, JJ Ruddy, MJ Rudling, SJ Ruff, DH Ruffin, WR Rufus, P Ruhl, BP Rule, PI Rule, WL Rumbel, AN Rumble, NA Rumble, DJ Rumel, WG Rundell, RJC Rundle, SR Rundle, W Rupenovic, TR Rusden, RQ Rush, SJ Rush, ED Rushton, IA Rushton, RE Rushton, WR Rushton, KM Rushworth, RL Russ, BK Russell, BL Russell, GA Russell, GK Russell, K Russell, LC Russell, LF Russell, MD Russell, ME Russell, N Russell, NW Russell, PD Russell, PG Russell, PR Russell, RK Russell, RL Russell, SI Russell, VC Russell, WA Russell, WP Russell, F Russo, AD Rust, ID Rutherford, T Rutherford, AL Rutledge, HR Rutt, AJM Rutten, HJ Rutter, GA Rutterman, NG Rutzou, SJ Ruwoldt, RK Ryall, A Ryan, AJC Ryan, AS Ryan, B Ryan, BR Ryan, CG Ryan, CJ Ryan, DG Ryan, DJ Ryan, DL Ryan, DQ Ryan, DW Ryan, EW Ryan, GV Ryan, JB Ryan, JF Ryan, JP Ryan, JR Ryan, JW Ryan, KD Ryan, KF Ryan, KN Ryan, KW Ryan, MP Ryan, PJ Ryan, PW Ryan, RJ Ryan, RW Ryan, H Rybalka, JD Ryder, TM Ryder, KN Rylands, JL Ryley, WJ Ryley, R Ryman, AD Rynan, LK Rynne, H Ryschka, G Rywak, J Rzeznik, DM Saffell, JP Sage, S Sakker, WR Sale, DB Salisbury, GW Salkeld, PA Salkeld, GR Salmeri, CG Salmon, DV Salmon, KS Salmon, MD Salmon, RFC Salmon, RT Salmon, GW Salter, KD Salter, RA Salter, RT Salter, JRN Salthouse, K Saltor, JR Salvesen, P Samelowski, NT Sampson, RK Sampson, RL Sampson, RS Sampson, AJ Sams, DT Sams, JL Samuel, PJ Samuel, SK Samuel, HB Sandall, GA Sandeman, GD Sander, LN Sander, F Sanders, FS Sanders, IR Sanders, JJ Sanders, KJR Sanders, PM Sanders, R Sanders, RE Sanders, WB Sanders, AR Sanderson, DJ Sanderson, KA Sanderson, NB Sanderson, DL Sandery, RT Sandford, RN Sandiford, BR Sandlant, DN Sando, DR Sando, PR Sandona, DR Sandquest, JR Sands, RJ Sands, CJ Sandy, IJ Sangwell, R Sankey, FP Sanney, MJ Sansom, J Sanzone, C Sappelli, AW Sara, TC Sard, GJ Sargant, RE Sargant, JR Sargeant, CJ Sargent, BHL Sargeson, AB Sariago, B Saric, WB Sartori, WH Sass, AW Saunders, DL Saunders, FW Saunders, G Saunders, GD Saunders, GJ Saunders, GW Saunders, JA Saunders, JE Saunders, JF Saunders, KJ Saunders, NF Saunders, PW Saunders, RE Saunders, RF Saunders, RG Saunders, RH Saunders, RS Saunders, RW Saunders, SWR Savage, WJ Savill, KWJ Saville, IS Saw, BC Sawyers, CJ Saxby, JM Sayers, JR Scanlan, DA Scanlon, DJ Scarborough, JA Scarborough, AL Scarce, KJ Scarce, JA Scarlett, DE Scarr, AMK Schaefer, RW Schahinger, GG Schapel, RW Scharper, JH Schattiger, RG Schefe, FR Scheibel, BW Scherf, GL Scherf, PJV Scherini, KH Schierenbeck, PI Schilling, PD Schindler, PA Schipanski, IR Schleicher, LJ Schloithe, COL Schluenz, K Schmack, EHC Schmidt, GL Schmidt, JT Schmidt, RM Schmidt, HG Schneider, WE Schodel, MC Schoer, HS Schofield, PA Schofield, RJ Schofield, TB Schofield, RJ Scholberg, JL Scholz, J Schoneveld, PM Schonhardt, E Schoo, F Schoo, J Schreiber, GR Schuback, JJ Schubel, H Schubert, RA Schubert, VR Schubert, GC Schuberth, RL Schuh, AM Schultz, DI Schultz, JW Schultz, KL Schultz, RJ Schultz, RP Schultz, WJ Schultz, G Schumacher, MR Schumacher, V Schut, L Schwaiger, AB Schwarze, AA Scott, AJ Scott, AW Scott, BW Scott, DP Scott, DT Scott, DTG Scott, FG Scott, FK Scott, GD Scott, JC Scott, JE Scott, JH Scott, KJ Scott, KR Scott, LA Scott, ME Scott, MM Scott, PC Scott, PE Scott, PM Scott, RA Scott, RG Scott, RH Scott, RHG Scott, TG Scott, TJ Scott, WK Scott, AE Scovell, RP Scovell, GW Scown, PO Screen, RJ Scrivenor, HC Scroop, GH Sculley, TK Sculley, J Scullion, ET Scully, PG Scully, LW Scutts, WH Seabrook, JM Seach, MS Seadon, MAW Sealby, A Seaman, GJ Seaniger, JM Searl, DJ Searle, PD Searle, JH Sears, DJM Seaton, GJ Seaton, GR Secombe, GK Sedunary, SJ Seed, RJ Seers, J Selby, JS Selby, PG Selby, RJ Selfe, L Selke, GJ Selkirk, ES Sell, AG Sellars, GD Sells, MC Sells, AJ Sellwood, GW Selway, LH Selwood, ML Semfel, DR Semmens, EH Semmens, RJ Semmens, TW Semmens, GJ Semple, TR Semple, M Senczak, JP Sendy, CA Senior, WE Senn, MP Sennett, PW Sercombe, WM Serisier, RH Sernig, JJL Serre, MC Sessions, GF Setch, F Settele, DA Seward, KS Seward, RJ Sewell, SA Sewell, TJ Sewell, PA Sexton, RJ Sexton, RJ Seyde, FJ Seymour, DJ Shackleton, NJ Shackleton, KT Shadforth, DJH Shakeshaft, RE Shalders, KW Shands, GJ Shankley, DJ Shanks, WT Shanks, GF Shannon, R Shannon, RL Shannon, TP Shannon, WE Shannon, AJ Shanny, TV Sharkey, JJ Sharman, PA Sharman, DR Sharp, F Sharp, FWC Sharp, GV Sharp, HW Sharp, KR Sharp, RW Sharp, BW Sharpe, KR Sharpe, N Sharpe, REJ Sharpe, TM Sharples, G Sharrock, FJ Sharwood, AJ Shaw, DJ Shaw, EJ Shaw, ER Shaw, FH Shaw, G Shaw, GD Shaw, GR Shaw, JE Shaw, JV Shaw, KG Shaw, L Shaw, RI Shaw, RL Shaw, RM Shaw, SC Shaw, TJ Shaw, TV Shaw, WE Shaw, WJM Shaw, WM Shaw, DF Shea, BE Sheard, WB Sheard, JJ Shearer, RH Sheargold, AW Shearman, HG Shearman, CO Shears, GD Shearsmith, GN Sheath, BJ Sheather, WK Sheather, EC Sheavils, REJ Shee, CP Sheehan, GM Sheehan, JT Sheehan, PA Sheehan, MK Sheely, MJ Sheil, DJ Shelley, ED Shelley, RB Shenton, CD Shephard, LG Shephard, PH Shephard, A Shepherd, BL Shepherd, DF Shepherd, JA Shepherd, JR Shepherd, KG Shepherd, LA Shepherd, N Shepherd, PWH Shepherd, SJ Shepherd, RF Shepley, TJ Shepley, AM Sheppard, CM Sheppard, RJ Sheppard, RR Sheppard, RJ Shepperd, GL Sheridan, JB Sheridan, AJ Sherlock, FH Sherlock, L Sherlock, G Sherringham, BA Sherry, KM Sherwin, HH Sherwood, JF Sherwood, RW Sherwood, RH Shewan, BW Shields, CW Shields, GR Shields, J Shields, PJ Shields, PS Shiels, RJ Shilcock, G Shimmen, DH Shine, NE Shipp, C Shires, LW Shirley, DJ Shirvill, KJ Shoobridge, JC Shooter, AJ Shoppee, DE Short, DW Short, IJH Short, JL Short, MTE Shotter, J Shrapnel, BR Shrimpton, H Shukosky, WJ Shurey, PS Shute, PW Shuttleworth, O Siedlarczyk, RE Siemsen, TE Siemsen, N Sierak, B Sierek, VJ Sikarew, JK Silver, JR Sim, GH Simes, GH Simm, TS Simm, AGG Simmonds, BJ Simmonds, FJ Simmonds, JK Simmonds, KJR Simmonds, RJ Simmonds, GD Simmons, JR Simmons, WP Simmons, WR Simmons, RI Simms, RJ Simms, AT Simons, G Simons, GB Simons, MW Simons, PAH Simons, JD Simounds, AW Simpson, BE Simpson, BG Simpson, BW Simpson, DF Simpson, DW Simpson, JA Simpson, JW Simpson, L Simpson, LE Simpson, MC Simpson, PC Simpson, PC Simpson, RJ Simpson, SR Simpson, VL Simpson, WA Simpson, WJ Simpson, WT Simpson, AC Sims, BG Sims, LJ Sims, IA Sinclair, ID Sinclair, JF Sinclair, MF Sinclair, PR Sinclair, CT Sincock, JE Sincock, TP Sincock, PC Sincocks, JN Sinfield, PR Sinfield, RF Singleton, SJ Singleton, GR Singline, CL Siniuk, RB Sinnamon, WJ Sissing, J Sitkei, T Sitkei, A Sivell, KS Skaar, J Skeen, AJ Skelton, AJ Skene, DK Skene, DR Skene, J Skene, NV Skene, RB Skennerton, J Sketchley, DP Skewes, GW Skey, MG Skidmore, KR Skimmings, AC Skinner, AJ Skinner, CJ Skinner, DL Skinner, JN Skinner, LG Skinner, MJ Skinner, RT Skinner, BR Skipworth, MS Skopal, M Skuba, A Skudutis, AF Slade, BC Slade, KD Slade, ND Slade, RG Slapp, AG Slater, CJ Slater, EJ Slater, GA Slater, RJ Slatter, TJ Slattery, IS Sleeman, PC Sleeman, AC Slingsby, JW Sloan, RK Sloan, AR Sloper, BR Sloper, GV Sloper, JM Sloper, JK Slotboom, HA Sluiter, BA Sly, J Sly, RF Sly, RL Slyney, RA Slywa, JR Smail, GM Smales, AC Small, GA Small, HT Small, J Small, BJ Smallacombe, D Smart, EB Smart, SB Smart, T Smart, TR Smart, WJ Smart, WT Smart, JM Smeets, RL Smerdon, SE Smidt, RJ Smit, A Smith, AA Smith, AE Smith, AHM Smith, AJ Smith, AL Smith, AM Smith, AR Smith, AS Smith, B Smith, BA Smith, BE Smith, BG Smith, BR Smith, CG Smith, CH Smith, CJ Smith, CP Smith, DA Smith, DB Smith, DC Smith, DCS Smith, DE Smith, DG Smith, DJ Smith, DPL Smith, DR Smith, DW Smith, EF Smith, EJ Smith, EP Smith, FR Smith, GA Smith, GC Smith, GD Smith, GF Smith, GH Smith, GHB Smith, GHH Smith, GJ Smith, GK Smith, GM Smith, GR Smith, GW Smith, HA Smith, HL Smith, ID Smith, IF Smith, IL Smith, IM Smith, J Smith, JH Smith, JJ Smith, JL Smith, JM Smith, JW Smith, KG Smith, KR Smith, KW Smith, LCG Smith, LCP Smith, LG Smith, LJ Smith, LP Smith, MC Smith, MK Smith, NG Smith, NJ Smith, NP Smith, NSC Smith, OV Smith, PC Smith, PD Smith, PH Smith, PJ Smith, PJ Smith,

PL Smith, PM Smith, PR Smith, PS Smith, RA Smith, RAC Smith, RD Smith, REJ Smith, RF Smith, RH Smith, RJ Smith, RK Smith, RL Smith, RM Smith, RN Smith, RS Smith, RT Smith, SG Smith, SJ Smith, TA Smith, TN Smith, TP Smith, TR Smith, TV Smith, VA Smith, WA Smith, WG Smith, WH Smith, WL Smith, WS Smith, WW Smith, GR Smithard, G Smitheman, IP Smithers, MJ Smithies, JD Smoothy, RH Smyrk, AW Smyth, JD Smyth, CWR Snadden, NF Snashall, MD Sneath, PC Sneath, PK Sneddon, GE Snell, BJ Snoad, BB Snodgrass, NJ Snook, A Snow, AN Snow, KI Snowden, MI Snowden, DM Snowdon, J Soban, CP Soden, WN Sojan, AT Solaga, NM Soley, CR Solomons, EJ Solway, IF Somers, JM Somers, BR Somerville, LWT Somerville, RD Somerville, G Sommer, WA Sonsee, DR Soper, CJ Sorensen, NA Sorensen, RF Sorensen, NG Sorrenson, Z Sosnowski, V Soszynski, RJ Soutar, CSH Souter-Robertson, JL South, KS South, BA Southam, JC Southey, JLC Sowden, KJ Sowden, AJ Spackman, NE Spackman, RJ Spaeth, TJ Spain, JR Spalding, RK Spalding, RA Spargo, AW Sparks, EW Sparks, JT Sparks, GK Sparrow, D Sparshott, IG Spaulding, AG Spearpoint, GP Spears, PN Spears, JH Spee, RC Speed, IM Speedy, RA Speight, KH Speirs, KW Spence, AC Spencer, DA Spencer, DP Spencer, GT Spencer, KJ Spencer, PJ Spencer, RRP Spencer, BE Spender, PA Spender, JL Sperring, RD Spethman, PN Spiby, FJ Spicer, RH Spicer, RA Spillard, RA Spilstead, RG Spindler, JW Spinks, MA Splatt, FA Spong, RH Spotswood, AA Spowart, RD Spratt, WL Spreadborough, GB Spresser, GD Spring, RG Spring, M Springham, WD Sprlyan, RM Sproge, DM Sproule, GW Sproule, RJ Sproule, BG Spry, JL Spulis, NPJ Spurling, RJM Spurr, RW Spurway, CC St Clair, PD St John, ID Stabb, JA Stables, CL Stace, JB Stacey, JG Stacey, MJ Stacey, IB Stacker, AM Stackpool, J Stadler, AJ Stadoliukas, K Staff, DN Stafford, LJ Stafford, SD Stafford, TJ Stafford, TO Stafford, KA Stagg, LA Stahlhut, KB Staib, L Stakenburg, TA Staker, FL Stall, HA Stallard, JA Stallard, TG Stanbridge, JC Stanbury, BN Standen, M Standen, JB Standfield, E Standing, KJ Standring, BA Stanford, MG Stangret, MJ Staniland, FA Stanitzki, Z Stankowski, AJ Stanley, EJ Stanley, GJ Stanmore, LA Stanton, MD Stanton, JA Stanyer, BC Staples, BW Staples, GJ Stapleton, J Stapleton, JR Stapleton, KA Stapleton, BD Stapley, JM Stapley, NA Star, GE Starcevich, AM Stark, BW Stark, DJM Stark, JW Stark, LF Stark, T Stark, YA Stark, GH Starling, AJ Starr, BP Starr, PE Starr, PW Starr, R Starr, RA Starr, KJ Starrit, PKG Staunton, E Stavleu, BJ Stead, RE Stead, RF Steedman, A Steegstra, CT Steele, I Steele, M Steele, NJ Steele, RL Steele, PJ Steen, AD Steer, RL Steer, G Stefanov, OW Steggles, PH Stehn, AW Stehr, JL Stein, LJ Stein, B Stelfox, SP Stenton, BL Stephens, D Stephens, JA Stephens, JP Stephens, RJ Stephens, WC Stephens, BT Stephensen, GW Stephenson, HG Stephenson, JR Stephenson, PD Stephenson, PJ Stephenson, RT Stephenson, J Sterger, S Sternbeck, A Stevens, AJ Stevens, AL Stevens, BN Stevens, C Stevens, CRG Stevens, DJ Stevens, EJ Stevens, GF Stevens, GS Stevens, JB Stevens, JD Stevens, JM Stevens, LC Stevens, R Stevens, RD Stevens, RF Stevens, RW Stevens, WR Stevens, A Stevenson, DJI Stevenson, GJ Stevenson, HD Stevenson, JM Stevenson, KJ Stevenson, P Stevenson, RB Stevenson, RK Stevenson, TJ Stevenson, RH Steward, AJ Stewart, CH Stewart, CJ Stewart, DG Stewart, DJ Stewart, EJC Stewart, FJ Stewart, G Stewart, GH Stewart, GJ Stewart, JB Stewart, JE Stewart, JR Stewart, MJ Stewart, MK Stewart, NI Stewart, PG Stewart, PJ Stewart, RA Stewart, RC Stewart, RH Stewart, RJ Stewart, RT Stewart, RW Stewart, WW Stewart, WJ Stewien, JP Steyn, NHP Steyn, H Stiklus, GR Stiles, LA Stiles, TJ Stiles, DI Still, J Still, MR Still, PP Stilwell, JG Stirling, JW Stock, MJ Stock, PD Stock, BJ Stockdale, JR Stockings, GW Stocks, CWT Stockwell, JA Stockwin, S Stojanovic, NJ Stoker, AJ Stokes, AJJ Stokes, EJ Stokes, GE Stokes, JF Stokes, WH Stokes, MB Stokoe, CWL Stolk, P Stolp, CD Stone, D Stone, DC Stone, DL Stone, DR Stone, DV Stone, DW Stone, GR Stone, HN Stone, KD Stone, PM Stone, GJ Stoneham, DA Stonehouse, K Stopford, RNW Storer, MC Storey, RE Storey, LOG Storm, JM Storrie, MJ Storrs, GF Story, AR Stott, JFD Stott, RL Stout, LF Stovold, W Stowell, A Strachan, LJ Strachan, WS Strachan, JK Stracke, WJ Strahan, CB Strang, RJ Strang, AK Strange, T Strasser, IEG Strathie, R Strating, RL Stratton, SA Stratton, GA Strawhan, KJ Strawn, KA Strazdins, DG Street, KA Street, MJ Street, PR Street, NJ Streeter, TR Strettles, SC Strevens, J Strickland, RN Stride, AR Stringer, BJ Stringer, BR Stringer, GM Stringer, PJ Stringer, TM Stringer, BW Stringfellow, A Strong, RV Strong, PU Strunz, RF Stuart, MD Stubbington, DC Stubbs, LD Stubbs, PW Stubbs-Mills, EG Stubington, WM Studley, JZ Stulik, JP Stupple, R Stupple, JS Sturgess, RL Sturmer, IN Sturtevant, AJ Styles, BJ Suckling, CA Sugden, KW Sugden, AR Sullivan, CJ Sullivan, DJ Sullivan, HJ Sullivan, J Sullivan, JA Sullivan, JJ Sullivan, JL Sullivan, MD Sullivan, MJ Sullivan, RV Sullivan, T Sullivan, WR Sullivan, LM Sulman, RA Sulman, GB Summerhayes, PJ Summerill, AMF Summers, GF Summers, JD Summers, PFJ Summers, PK Summers, RJ Summers, SJ Summers, EL Summerton, DP Sumner, WE Sumner, I Sunaklis, B Sunderland, RJ Sunderland, JA Sundholm, JG Sundman, MJ Supple, TF Supple, JD Sur, RN Surridge, G Sutak, DV Sutcliffe, JR Sutcliffe, DA Sutherland, JH Sutherland, JJ Sutherland, KM Sutherland, LF Sutherland, SK Sutherland, DC Sutton, ER Sutton, FJ Sutton, GJ Sutton, HJA Sutton, IE Sutton, JW Sutton, PJ Sutton, RE Sutton, DA Svatos, GA Swadling, BA Swain, BT Swain, GC Swain, KA Swain, GN Swaine, JR Swaine, DS Swales, E Swalue, PD Swalwell, B Swan, BL Swan, GR Swan, RC Swan, W Swan, JF Swanbury, HG Swanson, KP Swanson, NE Swanson, RS Swanson, TA Swanton, W Swanwick, MJ Sward, AJ Sweeney, AV Sweeney, GS Sweeney, DW Sweet, R Sweet, GP Sweetapple, JC Swinbourne, BJ Swinburne, DJ Swindells, FM Swinfield, JD Swingler, NW Swinnerton, RE Swinnerton, JJ Sykes, L Sykes, RJ Sykes, T Sykes, RV Sylvester, DJ Symes, FJ Symes, ID Symington, B Symmons, MR Symon, CW Symonds, NE Symonds, J Symons, P Symons, WE Symons, AM Synnot, PD Sypek, HC Szaja, P Szarko, WB Szarszewski, Z Szczesniak, MJ Szemiot, BJ Szirt, CT Sztorch, GE Taarnby, FW Tabb, C Tabbernor, RJ Tabe, TW Tabuai, H Tacey, TB Tadman, CB Taeuber, TE Taggart, A Tahija, A Taiono, AD Tait, AM Tait, AP Tait, CW Talbot, MJ Talbot, RD Talbot, HNF Tallack, IW Tallis, H Tanava, BC Tancock, GW Tancock, GC Tancred, RP Tandy, TE Tangen, J Tangwei, MM Tanner, PT Tanner, SL Tanner, JL Tant, NK Tape, RG Tapp, SC Tapp, JC Tapping, V Taran, MJ Targett, RE Tarry, BA Tarticchio, PL Tascas, AK Tassell, NS Tatarinoff, RC Tate, JM Taubman, PJ Taudevin, HHJ Taulien, MS Tavener, RS Tayler, AJ Taylor, AK Taylor, AM Taylor, AP Taylor, AR Taylor, B Taylor, BA Taylor, BE Taylor, BH Taylor, BJ Taylor, BL Taylor, BW Taylor, DA Taylor, DGF Taylor, DR Taylor, EI Taylor, EJ Taylor, FL Taylor, GA Taylor, GD Taylor, GJ Taylor, GR Taylor, GT Taylor, GTH Taylor, GW Taylor, H Taylor, J Taylor, JE Taylor, JH Taylor, JS Taylor, KA Taylor, KB Taylor, KMA Taylor, KT Taylor, KV Taylor, LFW Taylor, MB Taylor, MJ Taylor, NC Taylor, PA Taylor, PG Taylor, R Taylor, RF Taylor, RG Taylor, RJ Taylor, RL Taylor, RLM Taylor, RM Taylor, RN Taylor, SN Taylor, SP Taylor, T Taylor, TA Taylor, VJ Taylor, W Taylor, TA Teague, RJ Teale, EF Tearle, GF Tearle, G Tedford, PA Teichmann, JMO Teivonen, GT Telfer, GB Telford, GL Tempest, M Templeman, DC Tennent, A Tentori, HG Ter Rahe, MH Terare, GV Terrell, AP Terry, LG Terry, RW Terry, J Teske, JA Tester, KJ Tester, CK Tetis, PL Teuma, TA Teys, JW Thackray, KD Thamm, BJ Thatcher, DJ Thatcher, M Thatcher, PA Thatcher, WM Thatcher, R Theeuf, CR Thelan, HHG Theunens, GT Thick, WJ Thiedeman, EE Thirkell, MJ Thistlewaite, MA Thode, BE Thomas, CJ Thomas, CJB Thomas, CT Thomas, GF Thomas, GG Thomas, GN Thomas, GW Thomas, KCF Thomas, KJ Thomas, LD Thomas, NW Thomas, PN Thomas, PR Thomas, R Thomas, RC Thomas, RF Thomas, RG Thomas, RJ Thomas, RK Thomas, RW Thomas, TJ Thomas, TR Thomas, VB Thomas, WG Thomas, WJ Thomas, JCR Thomasson, AL Thompson, AS Thompson, BD Thompson, BR Thompson, CMG Thompson, CR Thompson, DG Thompson, EN Thompson, EV Thompson, FV Thompson, G Thompson, IJ Thompson, IR Thompson, JC Thompson, JL Thompson, JW Thompson, K Thompson, KG Thompson, LD Thompson, LG Thompson, MJ Thompson, NJ Thompson, PA Thompson, RJ Thompson, RL Thompson, S Thompson, SJ Thompson, TS Thompson, WC Thompson, WH Thompson, WM Thompson, WR Thompson, PC Thomsen, HW Thomsett, DH Thomson, DM Thomson, GH Thomson, IJ Thomson, IR Thomson, JH Thomson, JL Thomson, JO Thomson, LJ Thomson, P Thomson, PC Thomson, RE Thomson, RH Thomson, RN Thomson, SG Thomson, GR Thorburn, RW Thorburn, BW Thorley, DJ Thorley, ER Thorley, JE Thorley, MT Thorne, CT Thornton, DJ Thornton, DM Thornton, FC Thornton, RW Thornton, JH Thorp, M Thorpe, P Thorpe, PKR Thorpe, WJ Thorpe, PG Thorsen, PJ Thorsen, DL Thorssell, GW Threlfall, PL Threlfall, SJ Threlfall, B Thrippleton, L Thurgood, P Thurgood, R Thurgood, RJ Thurgood, WJ Thurgood, DS Thurkle, P Thurley, LG Thurlow, DJ Thuroczy, GGS Thurstans, KS Thurstans, BR Thurston, DW Thurston, JM Tibballs, JR Tickner, MRH Tickner, RM Tidy, PJ Tie, AT Tierney, RK Tierney, MA Tiffen, RI Tighe, J Tilden, DJ Tiley, JT Tilley, RP Tilley, AC Tillgren, GD Tillman, GJ Tilly, GR Tilney, EWJ Tilt, CC Timmins, RW Timms, IJ Timson, DR Tindale, MW Tindale, DF Tindall, KW Tinson, LL Tippet, RE Tipping, DB Tippo, GG Tirrell, MB Tischler, RM Titcombe, RJ Titman, BA Tobin, RL Tobin, BAN Todd, BW Todd, DT Todd, GAD Todd, RJ Todd, PR Toet, GD Toft, AJ Tolhurst, JA Tolley, MH Tolley, GG Tolliday, DR Tolson, O Tomaschewsky, RE Tomblin, DJ Tomich, ED Tomkins, PJ Tomkins, SC Tomkins, DJ Tomkinson, DC Tomlinson, DH Tomlinson, K Tomlinson, PW Tomlinson, LH Toms, BH Tonkin, BS Tonks, PF Tonks, CJ Toohey, JL Toohey, LJ Toohey, MJ Toohey, TE Toohey, AF Tooke, D Toolan, A Toolen, JS Tooley, RL Tootell, HEF Tooth, ER Toovey, RJ Toovey, NL Toplis, DJ Topp, R Topperwien, KJ Torney, IF Torrance, KK Torrens, MS Torry, JW Toshach, ER Totman, R Totterdell, AR Toulmin, RS Towell, BES Towler, CT Town, SG Town, BJ Townley, GW Townley, PW Townley-Jones, R Townley-Jones, DR Townsend, DW Townsend, ER Townsend, FX Townsend, RJ Townsend, SR Townsend, SV Townsend, E Toyer, WL Tozeland, BW Tozer, MR Tracey, DJ Tracy, LJ Traeger, JC Trafford, I Trail, K Traill, FT Trainor, J Trajdos, AD Trapp, NE Trapp, BF Trappett, GE Trappett, IC Trappett, RC Trautmann, MR Traves-Taylor, MP Travis, KM Traviss, WM Treadgold, RG Treasure, JT Tredrea, PE Tregarthen, RB Tregear, DP Tregellis, LA Treleaven, GH Treller, MF Treloar, W Treloar, GH Tremenheere, GD Tresidder, GR Trethewey, EJ Trevaskis, JH Trevena, WJ Trevethan, RW Trevitt, GN Trevor, DM Trew, BG Trewhella, JW Trewhella, CR Trickett, AJ Triffett, NBW Triffitt, DJ Trigg, ME Trigge, O Trimble, RP Triming, KE Trinder, WJ Tripcony, SW Tripney, JN Tripp, GB Trippett, FH Tritton, DC Trompp, JS Trood, JC Troost, S Trott, WJH Trott, RN Trotter, BA Trouchet, KG Trousselot, DR Trout, RM Trower, EC Trudgett, RM Trunkfield, GI Tryde, PT Tschirpig, N Tubecki, BJ Tucker, GR Tucker, QW Tucker, KS Tuckey, TG Tuckfield, RC Tuckwell, J Tucs, BA Tulip, RJ Tulip, RM Tulip, AV Tulk, RS Tulk, GA Tullemans, MA Tullier, DV Tully, CR Tumath, VT Tumath, PD Tumbers, AB Tumminello, PR Tunbridge, RJ Tunbridge, FV Tunney, MW Tuohy, TE Turcsanyi, EF Turk, SP Turkenburg, PJ Turley, D Turnbull, DH Turnbull, IA Turnbull, IS Turnbull, RJ Turnbull, AC Turner, AF Turner, AJ Turner, BJ Turner, DT Turner, DW Turner, I Turner, JA Turner, JC Turner, JR Turner, KJ Turner, KW Turner, MC Turner, ME Turner, MG Turner, MR Turner, MS Turner, N Turner, NG Turner, NH Turner, NPK Turner, PJ Turner, RC Turner, RJ Turner, TF Turner, TL Turner, TM Turner, GN Turnley, EH Turnwald, IJ Turton, SJ Turton, VT Turton, KG Turvey, SHR Tuttiett, BF Tweddle, JM Tweedie, RJ Tweedie, RJ Twell, EW Twells, PD Twigg, Q Twigg, DW Twiss, JT Twist, GJ Twohill, JL Twyford, DJ Tye, GL Tye, BA Tylee, CR Tyler, PB Tyndall, MP Tyrrell, PW Tyrrell, LE Tysoe, RE Tyson, RP Udo, PJ Uglow, V Uksi, DP Ulstrup, RJ Underdown, RV Underhill, BE Underwood, BN Underwood, IC Underwood, DJ Uney, IJ Unwin, TJ Uppington, EJ Urmston, AW Urqhart, AM Urquhart, RC Usback, AG Usher, DA Utber, AJ Uthenwoldt, LJ Utterson, KJ Uttley, VR Uyeda, WA Uyeda, ER Uzzell, PJ Vacchiano, G Vafiopulous, WE Vafiopulous, CS Vagg, GJ Vagg, DA Vail, PP Valcke, BR Vale, MH Valent, JW Valentine, AD Vallins, MJ Vallis, GH Van Baast, W Van Beekum, PJ Van Bladel, RF Van Bodegraven, P Van Boheemen, WM Van Boheemen, JG Van de Kolk, JH Van de Velden, GA Van Den Bogaart, R Van Den Brand, FJW Van der Hoek, HSH Van der Hoek, RA Van der Lelie, MJM Van der Pas, JA Van der Putten, PL Van der Togt, TA Van der Velde, P Van der Wal, WG Van der Wel, JZ Van der Zyden, ER Van Doorn, H Van Dreven, JL Van Dyk, L Van Dyken, GJH Van Eyck, JG Van Eyck, JNW Van Eyck, WA Van Gennip, RC Van Lawick, LF Van Loggerenberg, MJ Van Loggerenberg, AF Van Maanenberg, F Van Mastrigt, LA Van

Poeteren, L Van Thiel, JW Van Trigt, G Van Velthuizen, JM Van Vliet, CFR Van Wezel, MH Van Wyck, GP Van Zandbergen, JC Van Zetten, KJ Vandenberg, BF Vandepeer, PN Vanderkyl, K Vandermolen, G Vandersluys, RG Vandervelden, HL Vandervord, WJ Vanderwolf, J Van't Hoff, PC Van't Hoff, G Varga, DN Varley, JW Varley, KW Varley, P Varley, RJ Varley, FJ Varris, JG Varro, JA Vasalauskas, MJ Vasek, JA Vasey, RJ Vass, WG Vass, AR Vaughan, TE Vaughan, DW Vayro, DL Veach, AJ Veacock, LH Vear, PA Veen, J Veigel, JS Veitch, WA Veitch, D Vella, TE Vellacott, J Veltmeyer, LJ Veltmeyer, VD Venaglia, AH Veneman, BJ Venn, RW Venn, RE Venning, EJ Venus, GC Venus, JL Venus, AAT Verbeeten, RJ Vercoe, T Verdon, C Vergeer, W Vergeer, G Verheyden, N Verity, DE Vernals, FW Vernon, AN Versace, CPJ Vervaart, BL Verwayen, WN Vesty, FJ Vett, JO Vianello, JG Vickers, PJ Vickers, TW Vickers, GES Vidal, AE Vidler, FG Vidler, FP Vidler, WH Vierveyzer, JD Villiers, AJ Vincent, AN Vincent, GH Vincent, JT Vincent, PW Vincent, VW Vincent, C Vines, CG Virgo, DAP Visser, RB Vitenbergs, RG Vivian, RI Vizard, DF Vizzard, AD Vodic, GH Voelker, TJ Vogler, JC Vogt, GH Voigtlander, AG Volk, RC Volker, P Volkov, GM Vollmer, J Von der Putter, JE Von Stein, RJ Vonarx, K Vonthethoff, G Vorisek, KJ Vote, P Vouvoulis, RJ Voyzey, DA Vujadinov, LJ Vyner, RE Waack, GR Waddell, RA Waddell-Wood, AM Wade, BR Wade, JJ Wade, JM Wade, KJ Wade, RA Wade, FA Wagner, J Wagner, LAG Wagner, WG Wailes, JM Wain, AK Wait, GL Waite, MJ Waite, PD Waite, JAH Wake, JG Wake, BJ Wakefield, GJ Wakefield, WE Wakefield, SD Wakeling, R Walczak, BG Walden, JW Walden, KT Walden, CJ Walder, WB Waldock, GD Waldron, RK Waldron, BD Waldron-Lamotte, HT Wale, TL Walford, A Walker, AJ Walker, AOF Walker, BH Walker, CJ Walker, CT Walker, CW Walker, DJ Walker, EF Walker, FW Walker, G Walker, GC Walker, GG Walker, GJ Walker, JA Walker, JD Walker, JJ Walker, JW Walker, KE Walker, KJ Walker, LA Walker, MC Walker, PJ Walker, R Walker, RN Walker, RS Walker, RW Walker, WJ Walker, TN Walkerden, DG Walkington, W Walkley, JR Walkom, BJ Wall, GJ Wall, GS Wall, NW Wall, RG Wall, RJ Wall, TJ Wall, AC Wallace, AJ Wallace, BJ Wallace, DA Wallace, MJ Wallace, TF Wallace, GD Wallbank, RJ Wallent, PM Walliker, AJ Wallis, F Wallis-Tayler, RAK Walls, TA Walmsley, D Walpole, GR Walpole, AG Walsh, CR Walsh, GF Walsh, GJ Walsh, JF Walsh, JT Walsh, KG Walsh, PJ Walsh, RG Walsh, RJ Walsh, PR Walshaw, RA Walshe, CP Walsingham, DE Walter, GL Walter, JR Walter, KJ Walter, PV Walter, BR Walters, GJ Walters, PC Walters, R Walters, SE Walters, AE Walton, ALA Walton, G Walton, GC Walton, JD Walton, L Walton, MB Walton, PJ Walton, RH Walton, RR Walton, GWT Wanders, PJ Want, PA Waplington, M Warburton, RB Warburton, WG Warburton, BA Ward, BD Ward, CR Ward, DK Ward, J Ward, JD Ward, JF Ward, JM Ward, LA Ward, LJ Ward, M Ward, MA Ward, MB Ward, MD Ward, MJ Ward, PC Ward, PL Ward, RJ Ward, RL Ward, SR Ward, TW Ward, WT Ward, GB Warden, AJR Wardle, FJ Wardle, KR Wardle, LT Wardle, SN Wardle, PJ Ware, RV Ware, CJ Wareham, SJ Wareham, R Waring, GK Warmoll, CN Warn, WJR Warncke, GJ Warne, IB Warne, PJ Warne, AJ Warner, D Warner, J Warner, RA Warner, RJ Warner, TJ Warner, BT Warnest, HO Warnick, MC Warr, AJ Warren, BN Warren, CLF Warren, DG Warren, DJ Warren, FJ Warren, JH Warren, JR Warren, KS Warren, RA Warren, RD Warren, RJ Warren, RW Warren, TB Warren, TL Warrener, RE Warrick, J Warrington, FJ Warry, GM Washbourne, BM Washbrook, I Waskiw, D Wasley, RA Wass, DJ Wassell, FJ Wasson, DL Waterhouse, BG Waterman, IJ Waters, RW Waters, PR Waterworth, AJ Watkins, BM Watkins, JR Watkins, P Watkins, R Watkins, S Watkins, SW Watkins, HE Watling, AV Watson, BA Watson, BF Watson, CL Watson, CR Watson, CW Watson, DA Watson, DB Watson, DF Watson, DJP Watson, DN Watson, DR Watson, EA Watson, EP Watson, ET Watson, GK Watson, HK Watson, IC Watson, IW Watson, JR Watson, LD Watson, MC Watson, PC Watson, PJ Watson, PL Watson, RC Watson, RE Watson, SE Watson, SJ Watson, WR Watson, AJ Watt, ES Watt, GD Watt, PA Watt, RC Watt, RJ Watt, DE Watters, DJ Watters, MR Watters, MP Watterson, IC Wattle, DG Watts, IM Watts, JE Watts, JR Watts, LRJ Watts, PE Watts, RA Watts, TJ Watts, WS Watts, NFJ Watty, AJ Waugh, GH Waugh, FG Wawszkowicz, JN Way, RS Way, LT Waye, OL Waywood, LR Weate, RJ Weathered, GH Weaver, TE Weaver, A Webb, AR Webb, CR Webb, DC Webb, DF Webb, DG Webb, EW Webb, GA Webb, GJ Webb, GW Webb, IJ Webb, JP Webb, NDR Webb, P Webb, PL Webb, PM Webb, PT Webb, RC Webb, RJ Webb, RT Webb, SA Webb, TA Webb, AT Webber, ME Webber, PJ Webber, RA Webber, WJ Webber, ML Webcke, BJ Weber, JE Weber, TJ Weber, DC Webster, GP Webster, GS Webster, HJ Webster, LA Webster, LG Webster, LT Webster, MC Webster, PB Webster, RD Webster, CB Wedlock, DW Weeden, GJ Weedon, RJ Weekes, BL Weeks, JG Weeks, RJ Ween, IL Wegener, CW Wegner, TAM Wegwermer, NH Wehrmann, JR Weiberle, PR Weidenhofer, DP Weil, RE Weinhofen, F Weir, GA Weir, GH Weir, MS Weir, AS Welbourne, PB Welburn, RJ Welch, J Weldon, D Weller, R Weller, WT Weller, GA Wellham, AW Wells, CJ Wells, DC Wells, DJ Wells, HW Wells, IG Wells, JB Wells, JI Wells, JW Wells, KJ Wells, LT Wells, RJ Wells, RM Wells, W Wells, WJ Welman, BJ Welsh, DB Welsh, PW Welsh, R Welsh, RJA Welten, NL Wenban, RA Wendt, AL Went, KH Went, SC Went, JO Were, DJ Werner, JL Werner, OPJ Werner, P Werner, KS Wernert, WE Wernert, DJ Wescombe, WR Wessman, A West, CR West, DA West, DG West, DW West, JC West, KD West, LJ West, PH West, RT West, RW West, ST West, AH Westbury, J Westerhof, KO Westerland, SA Western, WP Western, MJ Westerside, RP Westneat, NJ Westnedge, AT Weston, JG Weston, PJ Weston, GA Westthorp, RD Westthorp, JF Westwood, JW Westwood, CH Weyling, P Weyling, AT Whalan, BR Whalley, KS Wharton, CC Whatley, SW Whatley, MJ Wheat, SA Wheatley, WT Wheeldon, DA Wheeler, GJ Wheeler, KR Wheeler, M Wheeler, MG Wheeler, PN Wheeler, RH Wheeler, RW Wheeler, WR Wheeler, DC Whelan, GL Whelan, GN Whelan, JP Whelan, RW Whelan, MJ Wheldon, JM Whenan, RJ Whillock, L Whinnen, BC Whitaker, RA Whitaker, NL Whitburn, A White, AE White, AJ White, AM White, AR White, BA White, BJ White, BM White, BW White, CA White, CD White, CI White, DB White, DG White, DLC White, ED White, FG White, FR White, GD White, GG White, GJ White, HG White, HW White, I White, ID White, J White, JA White, JG White, JH White, JO White, JP White, JR White, JW White, KJ White, LJ White, LT White, MJ White, MW White, NJ White, PHC White, PR White, PW White, R White, RA White, RE White, RG White, RH White, RJ White, RS White, RW White, SF White, SK White, TB White, W White, WA White, GC Whitechurch, D Whitehead, RJ Whitehead, NK Whitehill, M Whitehorn, CA Whitehouse, EA Whitehouse, IA Whitehouse, PF Whitehouse, JD Whitelaw, CJ Whiteman, KJ Whiteway, HPJ Whitfield, WT Whitfield, GJ Whitford, B Whitham, MR Whitham, AG Whiting, JL Whiting, PA Whitmore, WM Whitmore, AF Whitney, GFJ Whitney, J Whitney, FW Whittaker, JB Whittaker, PJ Whittaker, WT Whittaker, AC Whitten, KVK Whitten, RJ Whitten, RB Whittet, KMG Whitting, CC Whittington, IJ Whittington, IM Whittle, RG Whittle, TJ Whittle, GJ Whitton, IK Whitty, IS Whitty, CVM Whitworth, BS Whyatt, AJ Whyte, D Whyte, MR Whyte, BA Wickham, JC Wickham, K Wickham, PR Wickham, RN Wickham, JP Wicks, MW Wicks, PA Wicks, H Wieringa, J Wigfield, KR Wightwick, JL Wignell, MT Wignell, PA Wignell, TJ Wigney, C Wilcock, R Wilcock, GW Wilcox, TM Wild, MR Wilde, J Wilden, EK Wile, G Wiley, U Wilken, JWL Wilkie, KP Wilkie, GR Wilkin, MG Wilkin, CRH Wilkins, N Wilkins, AJ Wilkinson, BR Wilkinson, CR Wilkinson, GT Wilkinson, IR Wilkinson, JD Wilkinson, JE Wilkinson, JL Wilkinson, TH Wilkinson, TM Wilkinson, JM Wilks, PM Willard, EN Willcox, SP Willcox, JE Willding, TNN Willett, AS Willey, BJ Willey, A Williams, AC Williams, AGC Williams, B Williams, BC Williams, BJ Williams, BM Williams, BR Williams, BV Williams, CD Williams, CR Williams, CT Williams, DA Williams, DE Williams, DG Williams, DJ Williams, DL Williams, DM Williams, DP Williams, DR Williams, EGC Williams, GA Williams, GE Williams, GJ Williams, GM Williams, HE Williams, HR Williams, IL Williams, JA Williams, JB Williams, JC Williams, JCE Williams, JE Williams, JEC Williams, JH Williams, JL Williams, JM Williams, JR Williams, LJ Williams, MG Williams, MJ Williams, MR Williams, NS Williams, NT Williams, P Williams, PE Williams, PJ Williams, R Williams, RC Williams, RF Williams, RG Williams, RI Williams, RJ Williams, RW Williams, SF Williams, TJ Williams, TM Williams, TV Williams, WC Williams, WH Williams, WT Williams, DB Williamson, DJ Williamson, DT Williamson, LG Williamson, PD Williamson, PL Williamson, PLR Williamson, RE Williamson, RJ Williamson, TJ Williamson, W Williamson, WC Williamson, KW Willick, AL Willingham, AA Willis, BG Willis, GJ Willis, LD Willis, RA Willis, RG Willis, RJ Willis, AE Williscroft, R Willmot, DJ Willmott, AS Willoughby, EH Wills, LA Wills, RB Wills, RF Wills, MC Willshire, JF Willson, SFJ Wilmore, GN Wilsdon, AF Wilson, AJ Wilson, B Wilson, BH Wilson, BI Wilson, BJ Wilson, BM Wilson, BR Wilson, BW Wilson, D Wilson, DA Wilson, DC Wilson, DG Wilson, DJF Wilson, DL Wilson, DW Wilson, E Wilson, EJ Wilson, FM Wilson, G Wilson, GA Wilson, GJ Wilson, IA Wilson, IK Wilson, IR Wilson, JAK Wilson, JE Wilson, JLJ Wilson, JM Wilson, JP Wilson, JR Wilson, KDT Wilson, KN Wilson, LAJ Wilson, LG Wilson, MA Wilson, MH Wilson, PB Wilson, PJ Wilson, PK Wilson, PM Wilson, R Wilson, RA Wilson, RE Wilson, RG Wilson, RH Wilson, RJ Wilson, RS Wilson, RT Wilson, RWC Wilson, SJ Wilson, SS Wilson, TW Wilson, VFC Wilson, WC Wilson, WDK Wilson, WFA Wilson, WM Wilson, ZR Wilson, JA Wilton, CF Wiltshire, JW Winch, PA Winch, RA Winch, AM Winchcombe, DW Winchester, IG Winchester, DW Winckle, GR Windebank, BJ Windle, AJ Windsor, DJ Wingrove, HJ Winkeler, OF Winkleman, GH Winn, NJ Winn, TJ Winner, BG Winnett, GE Winning, W Winning, AA Winstanley, RW Winston, G Winter, RE Winter, TA Winterbottom, TJ Winterbottom, GD Winterson, KA Wintle, GR Winton, VJ Winton, RGA Wintour, FG Wintzloff, DS Winzar, IG Winzar, DR Wirges, TLR Wirth, P Wischeropp, GJ Wise, GN Wise, KR Wise, TB Wise, JJ Wisely, RL Wiseman, RM Wiseman, WF Wiseman, J Wishart, TC Wisman, MH Witcher, BL Wither, DA Withers, JA Withers, PK Withers, RJ Withers, RW Withers, RE Withnell, WN Withnell, PE Witt, KF Wittek, R Wittholz, HW Woelke, JW Woithe, BK Wojcik, H Wolarczuk, MB Woldseth, JP Wolford, RE Wollerman, HS Wolski, SR Wolski, LJ Wolter, CJ Wolzak, AJ Wood, BC Wood, BF Wood, BJ Wood, CV Wood, ED Wood, ES Wood, FC Wood, FJ Wood, GC Wood, GR Wood, GW Wood, KR Wood, MJ Wood, MR Wood, NR Wood, PA Wood, PR Wood, RB Wood, RG Wood, RS Wood, SJH Wood, TF Wood, WF Wood, LL Woodard, HR Woodbridge, B Woodbury, DW Woodcraft, GJ Wooders, JER Woodforde, MD Woodham, AIR Woodhouse, BG Woodhouse, DM Woodruff, AC Woods, BR Woods, FR Woods, GJ Woods, JC Woods, K Woods, KJ Woods, LC Woods, MS Woods, N Woods, PJ Woods, RF Woods, RK Woods, RL Woods, T Woods, BJ Woodsell, GR Woodward, PR Woodward, AD Woodyard, JP Woodyard, CJ Wooler, GA Woollard, IH Woollard, WE Woollcott, RF Woolnough, RL Woolnough, GJH Woolrych, SR Woolrych, DR Worboys, CE Worcester, GR Worden, LC Worden, MJ Worrad, D Worrall, NR Worrall, J Worseling, JA Worstencroft, AT Worth, BJ Worth, CT Worth, GI Worth, MJ Worth, MH Wortham, LA Wotzko, RC Woulfe, BN Wray, IJ Wray, K Wren, BJ Wriggles, AD Wright, BJ Wright, BL Wright, BT Wright, CE Wright, CW Wright, DE Wright, DJ Wright, FW Wright, G Wright, GB Wright, GR Wright, ID Wright, IM Wright, JA Wright, JG Wright, KA Wright, KC Wright, KJ Wright, KWC Wright, LC Wright, LHL Wright, MC Wright, MT Wright, NA Wright, PJ Wright, PL Wright, RE Wright, RJ Wright, RN Wright, SG Wright, TC Wright, TJ Wright, TRR Wright, VJ Wright, WJ Wright, MS Wrigley, RF Wrobel, DJ Wuillemin, KJ Wuillemin, SW Wulff, KC Wunsch, AFS Wyatt, TW Wyatt, CJ Wykes, GAO Wylie, WA Wylie, FJ Wyllie, RL Wymond, TB Wynberg, CJ Wynn, HS Wynne, DV Wynne-Allen, JB Wynne-Markham, H Wyver, JM Xavier, TW Yabsley, LB Yagmich, JH Yaldren, AF Yalg, MP Yantsch, AE Yates, JM Yates, NJ Yates, WJ Yates, WNM Yates, AM Yearby, LJ Yellema, CC Yench, BA Yeo, RC York, RJ York, RD Youens, MJ Youl, SJ Youll, AJ Young, BC Young, C Young, CD Young, CM Young, DR Young, GR Young, J Young, JD Young, JE Young, JK Young, JR Young, KA Young, LJ Young, M Young, NG Young, PJ Young, PR Young, RA Young, RF Young, RH Young, RL Young, RS Young, SR Young, TL Young, TS Young, WJ Young, AP Younglove, TJ Youngnickel, WEF Youngs, SG Yovan, PW Yuen, LE Yuke, JJ Yukich, NC Zahn, VM Zak,

MP Zammit, TL Zanich, K Zarubin, G Zarzycki, PJ Zegenhagen, JA Zeiher, BG Zemek, PRH Zeptner, LJ Zielinski, MH Zillman, WA Zimmer, EL Zinga, B Zintschenko, GA Zio, WM Zollner, E Zubreckyj, F Zuccala, JM Zwiers.

Royal Australian Army

PJ Aarons, TL Abberfield, MB Abbey, BV Abbott, DR Abbott, EF Abbott, FG Abbott, GB Abbott, GF Abbott, IG Abbott, KB Abbott, MN Abbott, ND Abbott, NE Abbott, RL Abbott, WA Abbott, WK Abbott, WA Abboud, GC Abdoo, DP Abe, CF Abel, CJ Abel, LT Abel, RJG Abel, AAG Abeleven, AD Aberdeen, DS Abernethy, L Abernethy, WJ Abernethy, PJ Abigail, WH Abigail, EH Ablett, RE Abnett, EV Abolins, DE Abraham, RJ Abraham, SE Abrahamffy, AL Abrahams, BL Abrahamson, KR Abrahamson, AR Absalom, GK Absalom, JD Absalom, BH Absolon, IS Absolon, TD Ace, AA Achammer, JW Achilles, AA Achmat, ME Acker, J Ackerley, AA Ackerman, RE Ackermann, AR Ackland, GJ Ackland, JE Ackland, MC Ackland, LR Acord, RG Acreman, IH Adair, PN Adair, R Adair, LD Adam, RW Adam, T Adamcewicz, BAJ Adamczyk, PA Adamowicz, A Adams, AC Adams, AH Adams, AJ Adams, AM Adams, BH Adams, BJ Adams, BS Adams, C Adams, CJ Adams, CR Adams, CS Adams, DG Adams, E Adams, GJ Adams, GL Adams, GR Adams, GT Adams, GW Adams, HJ Adams, IC Adams, IR Adams, J Adams, JC Adams, JCS Adams, JH Adams, JW Adams, KJ Adams, LA Adams, LJ Adams, LP Adams, LWH Adams, MH Adams, PH Adams, PJ Adams, PN Adams, RA Adams, RE Adams, RF Adams, RH Adams, RJ Adams, RL Adams, RN Adams, RP Adams, RS Adams, RT Adams, SD Adams, TC Adams, TJ Adams, VJ Adams, W Adams, WEJ Adams, WJ Adams, WN Adams, W Adamski, B Adamson, CJ Adamson, CS Adamson, GA Adamson, JW Adamson, M Adamson, PW Adamson, DF Adcock, DJ Adcock, RP Adcock, R Addenbrooke, JTW Addicott, BC Addington, B Addis, GW Addison, RE Addison, GF Addley, WR Ade, DB Adlam, WG Adlam, GJ Adler, CM Adriaansen, AW Adsett, BA Adshead, PJ Aebersold, DW Aesche, FA Affleck, JRR Affleck, MJ Afflick, LJ Agar, CL Agent, FR Agius, N Agius, PB Agland, BB Agnew, DAW Agnew, GA Agnew, JA Agnew, JJ Agnew, KL Agnew, SS Agnew, SR Agnola, KR Agombar, RP Agombar, AW Ahearn, IF Ahearn, PJ Ahearn, BE Ahern, FJA Ahern, MF Ahern, NJ Ahern, AA Ahrens, HR Ahrens, MA Ahrens, NW Ahrens, SA Aiken, AA Aikman, RJ Ainscough, B Ainsley, CT Ainslie, DC Ainsworth, JE Ainsworth, JF Ainsworth, RW Ainsworth, D Aird, LG Aird, RJ Aird, FJ Airey, KR Airs, WG Airton, A Aisthorpe, BC Aitchison, DJ Aitchison, KT Aitchison, BR Aitken, CF Aitken, DB Aitken, DE Aitken, DJ Aitken, G Aitken, GA Aitken, GD Aitken, JF Aitken, JH Aitken, JM Aitken, LR Aitken, LS Aitken, MA Aitken, MJ Aitken, PW Aitken, RJ Aitken, RW Aitken, TR Aitken, W Aitken, WM Aitken, WB Aitkenhead, C Aked, WA Akell, CJ Akeroyd, GP Akins, PMA Aksila, GJ Alberd, DJ Albert, RA Albert, RK Albert, DE Albrecht, E Albrecht, EG Albrecht, IC Albrecht, RE Albrecht, SR Albrecht, TA Albrecht, CT Albrighton, FR Albury, BT Alchin, RD Alchin, EE Alcock, HV Alcock, JE Alcock, KG Alcock, KM Alcock, PR Alcock, RF Alcock, RM Alcock, IC Alcorn, JA Alcorn, KJ Alcorn, R Alcorn, FX Alcorta, ED Alcott, B Aldcroft, GW Alden, A Aldenhoven, LP Aldenhoven, BK Alderman, FD Alderman, RA Aldersea, GP Alderson, PT Alderson, DC Alderton, GL Alderton, KJ Alderton, DJ Aldis, DC Aldous, E Aldred, NE Aldred, JR Aldridge, LJ Aldridge, RJ Aldridge, DJ Aldworth, J Aleksic, ME Aleman, BJ Alexander, CE Alexander, D Alexander, DT Alexander, FW Alexander, GB Alexander, GC Alexander, GF Alexander, GJ Alexander, HJ Alexander, I Alexander, J Alexander, JG Alexander, JK Alexander, JR Alexander, JW Alexander, KJ Alexander, KR Alexander, KT Alexander, ME Alexander, MJ Alexander, MR Alexander, NJ Alexander, PJ Alexander, R Alexander, RC Alexander, RG Alexander, RI Alexander, RJ Alexander, RM Alexander, RW Alexander, TG Alexander, W Alexander, PS Alford, RA Algar, RW Algie, Z Ali, HN Alidenes, RW Alison, FJ Alizzi, DI Allan, DM Allan, FJ Allan, G Allan, GD Allan, GJ Allan, GM Allan, GT Allan, J Allan, JS Allan, KA Allan, LJ Allan, MD Allan, MK Allan, MR Allan, RA Allan, RD Allan, RF Allan, RJ Allan, WL Allan, EF Allanson, JB Allard, RI Allardice, KI Allchurch, JA Allday, NR Alldis, DG Alldridge, RJ Alldridge, AD Allen, BF Allen, BM Allen, BP Allen, BW Allen, CD Allen, CN Allen, D Allen, DC Allen, DG Allen, DJN Allen, DL Allen, DP Allen, DV Allen, E Allen, EA Allen, FC Allen, FT Allen, GD Allen, GJ Allen, GL Allen, GR Allen, HW Allen, JAR Allen, JD Allen, JE Allen, JG Allen, JJ Allen, JP Allen, K Allen, KR Allen, KS Allen, LA Allen, LE Allen, LK Allen, LR Allen, LT Allen, LW Allen, MD Allen, MF Allen, MI Allen, NG Allen, NL Allen, PC Allen, PD Allen, PH Allen, PL Allen, PM Allen, PR Allen, PRD Allen, R Allen, RA Allen, RB Allen, RC Allen, RD Allen, RE Allen, RG Allen, RJ Allen, RP Allen, RT Allen, RW Allen, SJ Allen, SR Allen, T Allen, TJ Allen, VC Allen, VE Allen, WF Allen, WH Allen, WL Allen, FBJ Allender, KL Allender, DP Allgood, DS Allie, RN Allie, GB Allingame, DJ Allingham, GR Allinson, MW Allis, BH Allison, EC Allison, IG Allison, RA Allison, JR Allman, CJ Allmark, WR Alloway, RJ Allport, BJ Allsop, GR Allsop, JC Allsopp, MHW Allsopp, WD Allsopp, EM Allum, BJ Allwell, GB Allwood, JR Allwood, DB Allwright, MA Allwright, NR Allwright, B Almond, KG Almond, LM Almond, NN Almond, RM Almond, TR Almond, T Alonzo, CR Alpen, VJJ Alsbury, PC Alsford, K Alsop, WJ Alston, BR Altham, RG Althaus, J Altorjay, BJ Altus, LC Alver, JD Alvey, PL Alvin, RJ Alway, RT Aly, F Amato, FP Amato, GA Amber, DJ Ambler, DI Ambrose, FJT Ambrose, JS Ambrose, RG Ambrose, DL Amies, MJ Amiss, J Amitrano, GJ Amm, RO Ammer, HJ Amor, JJ Amor, A Amorim, AJ Amos, BJ Amos, D Amos, DM Amos, GT Amos, IR Amos, J Amos, JA Amos, JR Amos, MT Amos, P Amos, PJ Amos, RC Amos, RJ Amos, HHG Amtsberg, VP Amtsberg, AG Amundsen, A Andaloro, J Anders, DA Andersen, JS Andersen, KJ Andersen, MC Andersen, PC Andersen, RA Andersen, RC Andersen, TR Andersen, AC Anderson, AD Anderson, AE Anderson, AF Anderson, AG Anderson, AGM Anderson, AJ Anderson, AK Anderson, AM Anderson, AN Anderson, AW Anderson, BL Anderson, CJ Anderson, D Anderson, DC Anderson, DG Anderson, DJ Anderson, DM Anderson, DR Anderson, DS Anderson, DW Anderson, ES Anderson, FE Anderson, FJ Anderson, GD Anderson, GJ Anderson, GL Anderson, GN Anderson, GP Anderson, GS Anderson, GV Anderson, H Anderson, I Anderson, IC Anderson, IG Anderson, IK Anderson, IL Anderson, J Anderson, JE Anderson, JG Anderson, JL Anderson, JP Anderson, JR Anderson, JS Anderson, JT Anderson, JV Anderson, KA Anderson, KB Anderson, KC Anderson, KD Anderson, KG Anderson, KJ Anderson, KK Anderson, KW Anderson, LC Anderson, LE Anderson, LG Anderson, LH Anderson, LJ Anderson, LN Anderson, LR Anderson, MD Anderson, MJ Anderson, MR Anderson, NB Anderson, NC Anderson, NE Anderson, NG Anderson, NL Anderson, OD Anderson, OE Anderson, P Anderson, PA Anderson, PB Anderson, PC Anderson, PI Anderson, PJ Anderson, PO Anderson, PT Anderson, R Anderson, RA Anderson, RB Anderson, RC Anderson, RD Anderson, RG Anderson, RJ Anderson, RL Anderson, RT Anderson, RV Anderson, RW Anderson, SG Anderson, TG Anderson, TJ Anderson, TPP Anderson, VF Anderson, W Anderson, WE Anderson, WF Anderson, WJ Anderson, WM Anderson, WS Anderson, C Andersonpeters, CHM Andersson, KH Anderton, RB Anderton, RJ Anderton, GW Andrea, GW Andrew, JD Andrew, PD Andrew, PG Andrew, RN Andrew, R Andrewartha, RJ Andrewartha, AD Andrews, AJ Andrews, AP Andrews, BA Andrews, CG Andrews, DH Andrews, DW Andrews, EJ Andrews, G Andrews, GC Andrews, GE Andrews, GJ Andrews, GP Andrews, GS Andrews, HA Andrews, IM Andrews, J Andrews, JC Andrews, JH Andrews, JR Andrews, KV Andrews, LCJ Andrews, NJ Andrews, PS Andrews, RG Andrews, RJ Andrews, RK Andrews, AP Andriejunas, A Andriessen, TWA Andriessen, N Andropof, V Andryc, BK Anesbury, DK Anfield, DC Angel, CM Angeles, DP Angell, LE Angell, MJ Angell, PA Angell, EJ Angelo, P Angelo, S Angelopoulos, J Angely, G Angi, BM Angove, JE Angove, IR Angow, DJ Angus, DR Angus, GN Angus, HS Angus, JG Angus, MG Angus, MS Angus, P Angus, RA Angus, RJ Angus, FA Angyal, J Anictomatis, SJ Aniol, PR Anketell, TP Anlezark, DR Annells, BH Annels, FJ Annesley, LS Annesley, P Annetta, DG Annette, D Anning, PA Anning, N Annison, P Annison, WJ Anns, RJ Anock, CR Ansell, GH Ansell, GR Ansell, MA Ansell, SV Ansell, MJ Ansen, AC Anset, PN Ansett, DJ Anspach, KE Anstee, MG Anstee, NJ Anstee, WG Anstee, DB Anstey, JK Anstey, TK Anstey, KB Answer, BR Anthes, GW Anthes, PA Anthes, WG Anthes, RL Anthoney, EJ Anthony, G Anthony, JJ Anthony, KJ Anthony, RW Anthony, RF Antley, DS Antney, LP Antoine, G Anton, RD Anton, VT Antoniades, RW Antonio, R Antonis, GM Antonovich, AR Antony, IG Apathy, M Apfelbaum, A Aplin, B Aplin, FH Aplin, PJH Aplin, LE Appelbee, BF Appelkamp, AD Appleby, CI Appleby, GR Appleby, MC Appleby, RH Appleby, RR Appleby, BR Appleford, DN Appleford, NR Appleton, RE Appleton, RL Appleton, JE Appleyard, PA Appleyard, RC Appo, AL Apps, RK Apps, J Aprile, RH Apted, JW Arahill, LJ Arblaster, SA Arblaster, AA Arbon, BGH Arbon, GJ Arbuckle, WF Arbuckle, CJ Arbuthnot, A Arcella, ML Arch, EJ Archbald, JS Archbold, AP Archer, DA Archer, DJ Archer, FJ Archer, GA Archer, GD Archer, GM Archer, IR Archer, J Archer, JC Archer, KL Archer, PR Archer, PT Archer, SC Archer, SW Archer, WL Archer, EL Archinal, AR Arday, A Arden, MC Ardrey, A Arena, A Argent, RJ Argent, RL Argent, A Argyropoulos, BJ Arkell, JP Arkell, NG Arkinstall, G Arlotta, SH Armbrust, JF Armer, RL Armfield, AJ Armistead, SR Armistead, TJ Armistead, EG Armitage, RG Armitage, WJ Armitage, IF Armitt, KR Armitt, PF Armitt, BJ Armour, CW Armshaw, D Armstead, AE Armstrong, AR Armstrong, BJ Armstrong, D Armstrong, DB Armstrong, DG Armstrong, DJ Armstrong, DR Armstrong, DT Armstrong, ER Armstrong, GD Armstrong, GE Armstrong, GK Armstrong, GL Armstrong, JB Armstrong, JE Armstrong, JN Armstrong, LB Armstrong, LNT Armstrong, LR Armstrong, LW Armstrong, MJ Armstrong, NAH Armstrong, P Armstrong, R Armstrong, RAP Armstrong, RB Armstrong, RJ Armstrong, RT Armstrong, WB Armstrong, GC Armytage, RD Armytage, VC Arnall, FS Arndt, RA Arnel, DG Arneman, K Arnett, LH Arnfield, PM Arnison, EA Arnol, AJ Arnold, B Arnold, BG Arnold, BJ Arnold, BM Arnold, CJ Arnold, DB Arnold, DL Arnold, DS Arnold, GR Arnold, JK Arnold, JL Arnold, JM Arnold, JR Arnold, KJ Arnold, KR Arnold, MW Arnold, ND Arnold, OR Arnold, PJ Arnold, RA Arnold, RD Arnold, RL Arnold, RS Arnold, RT Arnold, SR Arnold, WFL Arnold, AE Arnott, DR Arnott, JB Arnott, JW Arnott, KD Arnott, NR Arnott, RJ Arnott, TW Arnott, L Arnould, DM Arratta, BE Arrow, EW Arrow, GA Arrowsmith, R Arrowsmith, RE Arrowsmith, TH Arrowsmith, BC Arthur, BJ Arthur, DC Arthur, GL Arthur, GP Arthur, H Arthur, JM Arthur, KP Arthur, PC Arthur, PD Arthur, R Arthur, RJ Arthur, RN Arthur, VJ Arthur, WP Arthur, S Arthurson, AH Arthy, AJ Arthy, GL Artis, BR Artup, KW Asbury, PD Asbury, WH Asbury, MJA Asche, DJ Ash, DM Ash, JW Ash, PJ Ash, RA Ash, E Ashby, GJ Ashby, OJ Ashby, TR Ashby, WP Ashby, DB Ashcroft, GV Ashcroft, JC Ashcroft, PM Ashcroft, RT Ashdown, BH Ashe, BG Ashen, CG Ashenden, JA Asher, RJ Ashfield, AW Ashford, CA Ashley, MJ Ashlin, KC Ashman, PWJ Ashman, RB Ashman, NJ Ashmead, AL Ashmore, DJ Ashmore, AL Ashton, DJ Ashton, GE Ashton, HD Ashton, J Ashton, JD Ashton, JN Ashton, KJ Ashton, KM Ashton, PJ Ashton, PK Ashton, WJ Ashton, B Ashworth, RG Ashworth, RJ Ashworth, RR Ashworth, JT Askew, RW Askew, MW Askey, PJ Askey-Doran, DG Askin, RJ Askin, RF Aslan, O Asmanis, GW Asmus, RJ Asmus, DG Aspden, PR Aspery, KR Aspin, AC Aspinall, DI Aspinall, DJ Aspinall, HJ Aspinall, KD Aspinall, KHL Aspinall, KL Aspinall, PC Aspinall, ES Asplin, BA Asplund, B Asquith, M Asquith, RA Asquith, RJ Assan, WV Assange, J Asselman, DG Assheton, PJ Astell, GP Astill, NA Astill, GS Astin, GA Astle, KG Aston, MR Aston, GA Astridge, MJ Atchison, KR Atfield, A Athanatos, DA Atherden, BA Atherton, JWN Atherton, NP Atherton, HA Athorn, BH Atkin, CJ Atkin, JN Atkin, KR Atkin, RJ Atkin, AJ Atkins, AP Atkins, C Atkins, DJ Atkins, GA Atkins, HR Atkins, IC Atkins, JA Atkins, JM Atkins, MJ Atkins, MW Atkins, PR Atkins, RJ Atkins, TD Atkins, TF Atkins, BG Atkinson, BM Atkinson, DK Atkinson, EA Atkinson, GC Atkinson, GE Atkinson, GJ Atkinson, GR Atkinson, HW Atkinson, IG Atkinson, J Atkinson, JA Atkinson, JE Atkinson, JF Atkinson, JN Atkinson, JP Atkinson, JR Atkinson, K Atkinson, KF Atkinson, KG Atkinson, L Atkinson, LJ Atkinson, MA Atkinson, NE Atkinson, NP Atkinson, NR Atkinson, P Atkinson, PE Atkinson, PN Atkinson, RA Atkinson, RF Atkinson, RJM Atkinson, RL Atkinson, RN Atkinson, RW Atkinson,

TW Atkinson, WR Atkinson, WS Atkinson, PA Atley, J Atrens, G Attenborough, KB Attewell, EA Attridge, AD Attrill, PF Attwill, DJ Attwood, TJ Attwood, JW Atwell, WD Atwell, WL Atwell, ET Aubrey, RJ Aubrey, RL Auburn, TA Aucher, JP Auditore, PA Auer, RG Auer, RJ Auer, M Augello, AM Augustes, ML Augustus, E Augustyn, GP Auhl, P Aukstinaitis, BD Auld, DG Auld, IR Auld, JL Ault, WJ Aulton, BM Aumann, KR Aumann, TH Aunger, DG Aurisch, DL Aurisch, RA Aurisch, PJ Ausling, PR Austen, RJ Austen, A Austin, AD Austin, AK Austin, DI Austin, EG Austin, EJ Austin, GJ Austin, JG Austin, JR Austin, KW Austin, M Austin, MF Austin, ML Austin, NB Austin, PG Austin, R Austin, RSS Austin, WB Austin, WG Austin, KS Austwick, HG Auton, FS Autunno, JW A'vard, GH Avern, BD Avery, BJ Avery, C Avery, DJ Avery, EJ Avery, JE Avery, L Avery, RG Avery, TC Avery, BI Avis, JC Avis, DP Avon, I Avotins, WJ Awcock, JR Awege, HK Axelsen, EJ Axford, WH Axford, KJ Axisa, M Axleby, AW Ayerbe, MW Ayers, TG Ayers, F Aylen, GJ Aylen, DB Ayles, JE Ayles, PN Ayles, DR Aylett, PC Aylett, RD Aylett, KR Ayliffe, W Ayliffe, FJ Ayling, PB Aylward, DC Ayoub, G Ayre, MW Ayres, RL Ayres, KF Ayris, GJ Ayson, JA Azzaro, BA Azzopardi, JL Azzopardi, PF Azzopardi, SP Azzopardi, H Baart, H Baayens, RJ Babb, DW Babbage, JR Babbage, WT Babbs, CH Babington, G Bacales, DW Bachelor, GW Bachman, IR Bachmann, HE Back, K Back, WC Back, RK Backen, HJ Backers, KE Backhouse, KJ Backhouse, SE Backhouse, ND Backman, DP Backwell, AL Bacon, CJ Bacon, MJ Bacon, RA Bacon, RC Bacon, AL Bacskai, BD Badcock, CS Badcock, PG Badcock, PJ Badcoe, KW Bade, RW Bade, IR Badenoch, WJ Badger, WE Badior, GN Badke, KN Badke, NC Badman, PR Badman, AA Bagdonas, EG Baget, HC Baggaley, KJ Baggott, PE Baggott, AW Baggs, CR Baggs, AW Baglin, GH Bagnall, HM Bagnall, JD Bagnall, TW Bagnall, GL Bagnell, GM Bagot, VL Bagust, CP Bahnerth, TJ Bahnsen, CV Bahr, AR Baich, TC Baigent, RI Baihn, RB Baikie, P Bail, RG Bail, AH Bailey, BJ Bailey, BK Bailey, BP Bailey, BR Bailey, CAM Bailey, CL Bailey, DA Bailey, DG Bailey, DJ Bailey, DM Bailey, DR Bailey, DW Bailey, EJ Bailey, FJ Bailey, GK Bailey, GL Bailey, HW Bailey, JC Bailey, JF Bailey, JH Bailey, JR Bailey, JW Bailey, KD Bailey, LA Bailey, LD Bailey, LF Bailey, LR Bailey, MJH Bailey, ND Bailey, PG Bailey, PR Bailey, RAH Bailey, RF Bailey, RH Bailey, RI Bailey, RJ Bailey, RL Bailey, RP Bailey, RW Bailey, RWH Bailey, TS Bailey, WE Bailey, RJ Baillie, SA Baillie, SM Baillie, TP Baillie, CM Bain, D Bain, GG Bain, J Bain, NJ Bain, RH Bain, TR Bain, GC Bainbridge, NK Bainbridge, NW Bainbridge, GB Baines, GR Baines, GT Baines, PL Baines, AC Baird, BD Baird, BP Baird, CW Baird, DJ Baird, GW Baird, HA Baird, J Baird, JC Baird, JD Baird, JK Baird, RA Baird, RH Baird, RJ Baird, TO Baird, H Bajars, DL Bajenoff, AC Baker, AG Baker, AJ Baker, AR Baker, BC Baker, BJ Baker, BK Baker, BP Baker, BW Baker, CJ Baker, DA Baker, DC Baker, DE Baker, DJ Baker, DK Baker, DP Baker, EJ Baker, ET Baker, FG Baker, FR Baker, GC Baker, GJ Baker, GL Baker, GR Baker, GV Baker, HJ Baker, IR Baker, JA Baker, JG Baker, JS Baker, KA Baker, KJ Baker, KL Baker, KW Baker, LAD Baker, LK Baker, LP Baker, LR Baker, MR Baker, N Baker, NB Baker, NE Baker, NW Baker, OK Baker, PA Baker, PD Baker, PF Baker, PH Baker, PW Baker, RAL Baker, RB Baker, RG Baker, RJ Baker, RR Baker, RW Baker, SD Baker, SL Baker, VD Baker, VE Baker, WA Baker, WB Baker, WD Baker, WH Baker, WP Baker, WWG Baker, L Bakker, LA Bakker, TJ Bakker, JA Baklarz, FL Balcombe, GD Balcombe, S Balcombe, GR Bald, V Baldacchino, L Baldizzone, JR Baldock, RW Baldock, DP Baldry, PJ Baldry, AJ Baldwin, AT Baldwin, CA Baldwin, GE Baldwin, GR Baldwin, IJ Baldwin, JW Baldwin, KT Baldwin, MJ Baldwin, N Baldwin, RB Baldwin, RF Baldwin, RH Baldwin, WC Baldwin, WE Baldwin, GD Bale, J Bale, P Bale, TE Bale, WJ Bale, WM Balfe, D Balfour-Ogilvy, JP Baliga, A Baljas, JM Balk, WR Balks, AC Ball, AJ Ball, CE Ball, ET Ball, FP Ball, GA Ball, GE Ball, GF Ball, GG Ball, GJ Ball, GW Ball, JA Ball, KA Ball, KC Ball, KF Ball, KR Ball, MJ Ball, MP Ball, PC Ball, PF Ball, R Ball, TA Ball, ML Ballans, AW Ballantine, TJ Ballantine, DJ Ballantyne, HJ Ballantyne, IJ Ballantyne, JM Ballantyne, LE Ballantyne, MA Ballantyne, R Ballantyne, RA Ballantyne, BA Ballard, DJ Ballard, IR Ballard, RJ Ballard, KJ Ballenden, GKW Ballentine, GJ Ballinger, LT Ballinger, DR Ballment, JR Ballment, IS Balmer, PL Balmer, RG Balmer, RM Balmer, TJ Balmer, AJ Balsillie, DW Balsley, TR Balston, J Balzan, PJ Balzary, NJ Balzer, BJ Bamblett, CDV Bamblett, RR Bamblett, BJ Bambrick, CJ Bambrick, GJ Bambridge, BR Bament, RC Bament, RJ Bament, A Bamford, KG Bamford, RH Bamford, RT Bamford, VG Bampton, DJ Bancks, LR Bancks, D Bancroft, GW Bandy, RA Bandy, RCS Bandy, I Banfalvi, CT Banfield, DJ Banfield, TP Banfield, LP Bang, DA Banham, DC Banham, DP Banister, AJ Banks, CJ Banks, DG Banks, DL Banks, DP Banks, EC Banks, JL Banks, JR Banks, KW Banks, MC Banks, PL Banks, RC Banks, RH Banks, RJ Banks, SR Banks-Smith, J Bankuti, ML Bann, RF Bannan, CH Banner, B Bannerman, HC Bannerman, WH Bannerman, W Bannigan, LW Banning, DG Bannister, KL Bannister, ML Bannister, PL Bannister, TC Bannister, W Bannon, T Banytis, J Baranowski, PJ Barbary, IT Barbato, DC Barber, DJ Barber, ED Barber, ID Barber, JR Barber, LC Barber, MR Barber, RA Barber, RC Barber, RH Barber, RP Barber, RS Barber, RW Barber, TC Barber, VG Barber, BAH Barbour, DP Barbour, PT Barbour, AM Barclay, DJ Barclay, DT Barclay, IR Barclay, KJ Barclay, MJ Barclay, RG Barclay, FB Barcovich, DL Barden, JA Barden, EJ Bardsley, SW Bardsley, DR Bardwell, IC Bardwell, RG Barfield, JL Barfoot, MW Barfoot, RJ Barfoot, PJ Barham, AA Barich, PL Barke, AW Barker, BD Barker, BJ Barker, BL Barker, CW Barker, DB Barker, DH Barker, EJ Barker, EV Barker, GF Barker, HF Barker, HL Barker, I Barker, IT Barker, IW Barker, JB Barker, JE Barker, JH Barker, JWC Barker, KE Barker, KK Barker, KW Barker, LJ Barker, MH Barker, MM Barker, NM Barker, PW Barker, RE Barker, RS Barker, TE Barker, TF Barker, TL Barker, WC Barker, WJ Barker, J Barkle, CJ Barling, JA Barling, WT Barling, AA Barlow, FC Barlow, FS Barlow, GL Barlow, GP Barlow, JAC Barlow, JC Barlow, JS Barlow, KW Barlow, LR Barlow, MC Barlow, MG Barlow, RJ Barlow, RS Barlow, SJ Barlow, TN Barlow, WA Barlow, GJ Barn, DA Barnard, G Barnard, WC Barnard, EH Barnard-Brown, M Barnbaum, DR Barnby, A Barnes, AR Barnes, BC Barnes, BW Barnes, CE Barnes, CF Barnes, DC Barnes, DG Barnes, DJ Barnes, FE Barnes, GC Barnes, GJ Barnes, GL Barnes, GM Barnes, H Barnes, JA Barnes, JF Barnes, JG Barnes, JJ Barnes, JL Barnes, JT Barnes, JV Barnes, K Barnes, MJ Barnes, PG Barnes, PH Barnes, PJ Barnes, RA Barnes, RE Barnes, RJ Barnes, TA Barnes, TJ Barnes, TM Barnes, VG Barnes, AM Barnett, CE Barnett, CT Barnett, ED Barnett, EJ Barnett, ER Barnett, HB Barnett, IA Barnett, IR Barnett, JG Barnett, LJ Barnett, LR Barnett, MR Barnett, PH Barnett, SJ Barnett, WR Barnett, LA Barnfield, NK Barnier, RE Barnier, GT Barnsley, PR Barnsley, MJ Barnwell, AM Barr, BC Barr, GJ Barr, IF Barr, WG Barr, WH Barr, GR Barrance, TR Barratt, BC Barrett, BL Barrett, C Barrett, CT Barrett, DL Barrett, DW Barrett, GS Barrett, GX Barrett, JF Barrett, JJ Barrett, JKJ Barrett, JP Barrett, JR Barrett, MW Barrett, NC Barrett, NG Barrett, NJ Barrett, NV Barrett, PJ Barrett, R Barrett, RB Barrett, RC Barrett, RF Barrett, RL Barrett, SJ Barrett, SP Barrett, TL Barrett, TP Barrett, TW Barrett, VP Barrett, WR Barrett, R Barrett-Lennard, AF Barrie, PW Barrie, RS Barrie, WJ Barrie, SC Barringhaus, BU Barron, CJ Barron, HD Barron, RL Barron, TD Barron, K Barrott, MJ Barrott, DJ Barrow, EF Barrow, JK Barrow, P Barrow, PJ Barrow, ID Barrowclough, DG Barry, EL Barry, GE Barry, JA Barry, JE Barry, JF Barry, KJ Barry, P Barry, PM Barry, R Barry, RJ Barry, TE Barry, TV Barry, VB Barry, AJ Barselaar, TR Barsenbach, W Barsley, L Bartal, LP Bartel, BG Bartels, NO Bartels, DR Barter, MJ Barter, JC Bartholomai, FJ Bartholomew, GT Bartholomew, K Barthram, W Bartkiw, C Bartkus, R Bartkus, AG Bartlett, CJ Bartlett, GD Bartlett, GJ Bartlett, IR Bartlett, JA Bartlett, JH Bartlett, JW Bartlett, KC Bartlett, LDJ Bartlett, LJ Bartlett, RA Bartlett, RK Bartlett, RT Bartlett, WJ Bartlett, BD Bartley, EJ Bartley, GJ Bartley, RD Bartley, RJ Bartley, VE Bartley, BG Barton, EG Barton, FC Barton, FP Barton, GN Barton, JC Barton, KL Barton, RE Barton, F Bartos, I Bartos, JC Bartos, AD Bartram, GW Bartram, W Bartram, J Bartrim, JB Bartrim, BK Bartsch, BT Bartsh, LC Bartz, RG Barwald, GR Barwell, BW Barwick, KW Barwick, MG Barwick, PG Barwick, RG Barwick, TP Barwick, S Baryla, J Barylka, BA Bascombe, NE Basedow, LC Basell, G Basford, BE Basham, PJ Bashford, RJ Basman, JG Bass, RAJ Bass, TR Bass, WF Bassam, RN Bassan, BA Basset, DR Bassett, GJ Bassett, LJ Bassett, MW Bassett, PR Bassett, TE Bassett, TR Bassett, JR Bassford, AP Bassham, ADF Bastiaanse, AJ Bastian, DM Bastian, FL Bastin, NR Bastin, FJ Bastock, RJ Bastock, AR Batchelor, DV Batchelor, GF Batchelor, GR Batchelor, RJ Batdorf, KJ Bate, RD Bate, B Bateman, BW Bateman, GR Bateman, JL Bateman, P Bateman, PJ Bateman, RB Bateman, RJ Bateman, SJ Bateman, TJ Bateman, WP Bateman, AG Bates, AI Bates, BR Bates, CE Bates, DG Bates, DK Bates, FB Bates, GB Bates, HJ Bates, I Bates, IB Bates, JA Bates, JF Bates, JH Bates, JH Bates, JP Bates, LA Bates, LJ Bates, PG Bates, PW Bates, RF Bates, RG Bates, RL Bates, RP Bates, RW Bates, TJ Bates, TP Bates, TR Bates, RH Bateup, AW Bath, GL Bath, IC Bath, DF Bathersby, G Bathgate, FG Bathis, G Batiste, GW Batiste, M Batson, TW Batson, AJ Batt, AK Batt, AM Batt, LW Batt, RW Batt, KR Battaglia, RA Battaglin, MJ Battams, BN Batten, MW Batten, PJ Batten, RAF Batten, EL Batterbury, JE Batterbury, KM Batters, KR Battersby, RR Battersby, RJ Battese, GW Battis, DP Battisson, MR Battle, PC Battle, LF Battley, LH Battley, TE Battley, K Battmer, BL Batty, DE Batty, GJ Batty, JA Batty, P Batty, GK Battye, L Battye, PW Battye, CP Baty, JR Baty, L Batze, W Batze, GF Batzloff, KW Baudistel, M Baudzus, BR Bauer, DN Bauer, HWH Bauer, EF Baulch, PJ Baulch, RC Baulch, BS Bauld, FJ Baum, JD Baum, AD Bauman, AJ Bauman, JN Baumann, F Baumeister, AE Baunach, B Bavcevich, J Bavell, KO Bavin, RS Bavington, NW Bavister, CS Bavistock, CR Bawden, MJ Bawden, TL Bawden, SJ Bawn, ACD Baxter, AJ Baxter, BA Baxter, BE Baxter, BJ Baxter, D Baxter, DH Baxter, EH Baxter, GJ Baxter, IA Baxter, JS Baxter, LJ Baxter, LL Baxter, MC Baxter, MD Baxter, PR Baxter, PT Baxter, RG Baxter, RS Baxter, TG Baxter, WM Baxter, WT Baxter, GD Bayes, JA Bayford, ID Bayles, GM Bayley, KJ Bayley, MW Bayley, RJ Bayley, W Bayley, TI Bayliff, ER Baylis, RE Baylis, CB Bayliss, CR Bayliss, DG Bayliss, GD Bayliss, GV Bayliss, JT Bayliss, PG Bayliss, PJ Bayliss, RW Bayliss, KW Bayly, ER Bayne, HG Bayne, LJ Baynham, TC Bayo, RJ Bayre, R Baysinger, PE Bazarow, RA Bazley, R Bazzo, RL Beacall, GK Beach, JJ Beach, RO Beacham, EC Beacroft, PC Beacroft, CT Beadle, FR Beadle, PC Beadle, WJ Beagley, DF Beahan, KG Beahan, IR Beal, L Beal, PJ Beal, DG Beale, PB Beale, PW Beale, KJ Beaman, KT Beaman, JF Beames, J Beamish, MEJ Beamont, BL Bean, CR Bean, GA Bean, LK Bean, MJ Bean, TJ Bean, DW Bear, RK Bear, TL Bear, AV Beard, DD Beard, EG Beard, JM Beard, LF Beard, PB Beard, RC Beard, RH Beard, RJ Beard, RK Beard, WG Beard, AT Beare, KR Beare, ND Beare, TH Beare, TG Bearne, DL Beasley, EJ Beasley, IK Beasley, MG Beasley, RJ Beasley, RR Beasley, RW Beasley, TJ Beasy, J Beath, GM Beaton, FJ Beattie, JD Beattie, JG Beattie, JN Beattie, JW Beattie, K Beattie, R Beattie, RC Beattie, RP Beattie, WE Beattie, WH Beattie, KJ Beatty, KL Beatty, RD Beatty, W Beatty, GR Beauchamp, PW Beauchamp, RW Beauglehole, KT Beauman, GD Beaumont, IJ Beaumont, PJ Beaumont, R Beaumont, RW Beaumont, TJ Beaumont, PG Beaven, AR Beaver, DM Beavis, EN Beazley, RP Beazley, LJ Bebb, TR Bechaz, AW Beck, CD Beck, DG Beck, DW Beck, HJC Beck, J Beck, LJM Beck, MJ Beck, RJ Beck, HO Becke, CE Becker, CH Becker, IR Becker, JR Becker, TD Becker, LF Beckerath, GD Beckett, I Beckett, JD Beckett, KJ Beckett, L Beckett, FK Beckhaus, AJ Beckingham, WJ Beckwith, JW Becus, SJ Beddoe, DJ Bedford, JR Bedford, ME Bedford, RG Bedford, TA Bedford, C Bednarczyk, S Bednarczyk, JS Bednarski, RG Bednarski, AP Bednarz, CJ Bedwell, EP Bedwell, KT Bedwell, WW Bedwell, R Bee, AE Beebar, BE Beech, CJ Beech, AF Beecham, JS Beecham, M Beeching, AJP Beecroft, B Beecroft, D Beecroft, JF Beekmeyer, AJ Beer, FA Beer, JK Beer, PG Beer, RL Beer, RO Beer, RW Beer, SE Beer, TE Beer, JE Beere, PF Beere, RP Beesley, RL Beeson, AJ Beeston, HM Beeston, PG Beetham, WF Beetham, AJ Beeton, CG Beeton, DI Beeton, ES Beeton, WD Beeton, DJ Beetson, JJ Beevis, HH Beezley, J Beezley, AE Begbie, DR Begg, GL Beggs, GR Beggs, JE Beggs, WV Beggs, TJ Begley, GW Beh, PJ Beh, AG Behan, CE Behan, LE Behan, RV Behan, LC Behm, DJ Behncke, CJ Behr, JD Behrend, KD Behrend, D Behrends, RJ Behrendt, G Beilby, WD Beilby, BC Beilken, W Beinhauer, RA Beischer, DA Beitsch, BJ Beitzel, G Bekendam, M Belajich, CE Belcher, DC Belcher, DJ Belcher, JW Belcher, WA Belcher, JL Belfield, JW Belford, SR Belford, RS Belgrove, AA Bell, AD Bell, AEJ Bell, AR Bell, AS Bell, AT Bell, C Bell, CD Bell, CE Bell, CJ Bell, CL Bell, CR Bell, DA Bell, DB Bell, DC Bell, DJ Bell, DS Bell, FE Bell, FJ Bell, FK Bell, GA Bell, GE Bell, GM Bell, GR Bell, HL Bell, IL Bell, JC Bell, JH Bell, JM Bell, JW Bell, K Bell, KC Bell, KE Bell, KW Bell, LF Bell, MJ Bell, MS Bell, NA Bell, NJ Bell, NM Bell, NR Bell, OW Bell, PR Bell, PW Bell, R Bell, RF Bell, RH Bell, RJ Bell, RK Bell, RL Bell,

RRN Bell, RS Bell, RV Bell, SE Bell, SJ Bell, TSB Bell,
VF Bell, CW Bellaart, DW Bellairs, EJ Bellamy, MD Bellamy,
RG Bellamy, RT Bellamy, WA Bellamy, DR Bellchambers,
JJ Bellchambers, JWH Bellert, GW Bellette, JS Bellette,
GR Belleville, GW Belleville, GW Belling, R Bellinger,
AR Bellingham, MF Bellingham, CJ Bellis, J Bellis, RV Bellis,
R Bellman, RS Bellott, KR Below, JW Belsey, PL Belt,
GJ Beltrame, RJ Bemmer, TJ Benardout, Z Ben-Avi,
GN Benbow, AL Bence, JC Bendall, JA Bendeich, D Bender,
WB Bender, J Bending, NWP Benedict, A Benes, MD Benfer,
FH Benfield, SJ Benfield, DJ Benford, AG Benham,
GJ Benham, KA Benier, KR Benier, PD Benier,
JA Beningfield, W Benington, GV Benjamin, FT Benko,
DL Benn, DW Bennallack, TG Benne, RC Bennedick,
AW Bennell, JC Bennell, MD Benness, AD Bennett,
AE Bennett, AJ Bennett, AS Bennett, AW Bennett,
BC Bennett, BJ Bennett, CA Bennett, CTE Bennett,
DF Bennett, DL Bennett, DV Bennett, DW Bennett,
EE Bennett, EJ Bennett, GJ Bennett, GL Bennett,
GW Bennett, JK Bennett, JM Bennett, KJ Bennett,
KO Bennett, KS Bennett, LF Bennett, LG Bennett,
LN Bennett, LW Bennett, ML Bennett, N Bennett,
NF Bennett, NJ Bennett, NR Bennett, PA Bennett,
PE Bennett, PG Bennett, PH Bennett, PJ Bennett,
PR Bennett, PS Bennett, R Bennett, RI Bennett, RL Bennett,
RM Bennett, S Bennett, TF Bennett, TJ Bennett,
VH Bennett, WL Bennett, WR Bennett, J Bennettburleigh,
LD Bennetto, JJ Bennetts, PR Bennetts, RA Bennetts,
RG Bennetts, BW Bennier, AR Bennion, RW Bennion,
MW Benporath, E Bensi, AB Bensley, BV Bensley,
EO Bensley, PA Bensley, BJ Benson, BV Benson, DL Benson,
HAF Benson, I Benson, J Benson, JJ Benson, KJ Benson,
KR Benson, MJ Benson, NC Benson, DG Bent, DA Bentham,
CA Bentley, GA Bentley, JS Bentley, JW Bentley, MJ Bentley,
NE Bentley, RA Bentley, RN Bentley, W Bentley, JL Benton,
JW Benton, NH Benton, RB Benton, KG Benzie, RE Benzie,
PG Beohm, WJ Beohm, GJ Beplate, PF Beraldo, AJ Berbers,
PG Bercene, DW Beresford, RL Beresford, AE Berg, BL Berg,
CR Berg, HJ Berg, JO Berg, RA Berg, HA Berger, PE Berger,
RF Berger, W Berghammer, GM Berghofer, MP Bergin,
NR Bergin, DB Bergman, DJ Bergman, GD Bergman,
BC Bergmann, PH Bergmann, JA Bergmans, PG Berk,
WD Berkrey, G Berman, BJ Bermingham, CR Bermingham,
LG Bermingham, W Bernadine, MP Bernasconi,
AG Bernauer, PR Bernays, G Berne, KB Berney, FE Bernhardt,
JC Bernhardt, KG Bernhardt, AS Bernotas, WJ Berntsson,
TG Berrick, MJ Berridge, MJ Berrigan, SJ Berrigan, PJ Berrill,
MA Berriman, TR Berriman, AB Berry, AK Berry, AL Berry,
AR Berry, DG Berry, DJ Berry, DM Berry, GA Berry,
GFG Berry, GK Berry, HA Berry, HW Berry, J Berry,
JH Berry, KH Berry, LJ Berry, MD Berry, PS Berry,
TW Berry, LE Berryman, GF Berson, JS Bert, DL Bertholli,
JL Bertini, BM Bertram, JF Bertram, KS Bertram,
RG Bertram, IR Bertrand, AB Bertucci, PH Bertuch,
WJ Bertuch, NP Berzinski, GE Besford, R Besier, M Beslagic,
KR Besley, IA Bessant, DL Bessell, GM Bessell, PW Bessell,
KA Bessen, EB Bessey, AR Best, BE Best, CI Best, D Best,
DDF Best, FL Best, GA Best, GD Best, GE Best, GH Best,
GR Best, J Best, JF Best, JR Best, KA Best, KJ Best, LJ Best,
PJ Best, RA Best, BL Bester, GW Bester, DG Bestwick,
RR Beswick, MK Bethune, JH Bett, RJ Bettany, JJ Bettens,
IC Betteridge, M Betteridge, JW Betterman, JR Bettridge,
AW Betts, BE Betts, BT Betts, DM Betts, FG Betts, FJ Betts,
JE Betts, JS Betts, LJ Betts, MC Betts, MF Betts, P Betts,
PN Betts, RG Betts, JF Betzel, GA Beulah, R Beumer,
JH Beus, G Beuzeville, PJ Beuzeville, BA Bevan, BN Bevan,
HF Bevan, JR Bevan, PR Bevan, RJ Bevan, ET Bevans,
KR Bevans, CA Beveridge, DG Beveridge, DW Beveridge,
GC Beveridge, IR Beveridge, ML Beveridge, RV Beveridge,
P Bevilacqua, AA Bevis, MG Bevis, KJ Bevitt, CT Bew,
AW Bewley, JS Bewley, PJ Bewley, AT Bewry, NW Bextream,
NR Bextrum, MG Bey, RT Beyer, DL Beynon, KH Beynon,
MC Beynon, RD Beynon, RW Beynon, TH Beynon,
EA Bialek, T Bialkowski, HH Bianchi, MJ Biancotti,
K Biberian, DS Bice, R Bicheno, BD Bickel, BA Bicket,
JL Bickford, BE Bickham, DL Bickle, AJ Bickley, CC Bicknell,
CM Bicknell, GJ Bicknell, NA Biddle, RL Biddle,
GS Biddlecombe, IH Biddolph, C Bidewell, MD Bidey,
AC Bidgood, CM Bidgood, RL Biele, BA Bierton, NR Biffen,
RJ Bigby, WD Biggar, IR Biggins, NA Biggins, GH Biggs,
PJ Biggs, RL Biggs, WB Biglands, IL Bignall, MF Bignall,
BD Bignell, KC Bignell, MR Bignell, RM Bignell,
RA Bigwood, M Bikoff, S Bilbrough, WD Bilby, JW Biles,
RW Biles, RS Billett, RA Billiards, BJ Billing, J Billing,
JW Billing, PG Billing, RE Billing, TG Billing,
FW Billinghurst, BC Billings, D Billings, JW Billingsley,
EW Billingsly, BE Billington, EC Billington, RP Billington,
WAP Billington, RL Billman, AR Bills, RL Bilsborough,
EH Bilsborrow, RG Bilsby, JE Bilston, LG Bilton,
RW Bimrose, BGF Binder, G Binder, HHB Binder,
TR Binder, BJ Bindley, GH Bindley, MJ Bindley, KJ Bineham,
EN Bing, BW Binge, AJ Bingham, FW Bingham,
LC Bingham, TC Bingham, WD Bingham, PM Binion,
M Bink, GA Binks, DJ Binney, TR Binney, WW Binney,
ADH Binnie, AJ Binnie, MR Binning, RP Binning,
WH Binning, AN Binnoore, DC Binns, G Binns, PJ Binns,
WM Binns, T Binyon, KM Birbeck, CS Birch, DJ Birch,
EAP Birch, GD Birch, IG Birch, JA Birch, KC Birch,
PR Birch, RL Birch, MJ Birchell, MH Birchenall, D Bird,
DA Bird, DH Bird, DR Bird, HG Bird, JHA Bird, JR Bird,
JW Bird, KF Bird, LW Bird, ND Bird, PA Bird, PJ Bird,
RAJ Bird, RE Bird, RF Bird, RJ Bird, RO Bird, RR Bird,
RW Bird, TL Bird, TW Bird, VA Bird, WJ Bird, AJ Birkbeck,
J Birkett, WJ Birkett, WR Birkett, CJ Birmingham,
JM Birmingham, JS Birnie, NJ Birnie, SA Birnie, T Birnie,
GD Birrell, HW Birrell, RC Birse, RG Birse, KA Birt,
NL Birt, RJ Birt, GD Birthisel, RC Birtles, GP Birtles-Crute,
LL Bisa, J Bisaro, MJ Bisby, A Bishop, AG Bishop, AJ Bishop,
B Bishop, BM Bishop, DA Bishop, DJ Bishop, DM Bishop,
EJ Bishop, GR Bishop, JF Bishop, JG Bishop, JR Bishop,
JW Bishop, LE Bishop, LK Bishop, LW Bishop, PA Bishop,
PD Bishop, RB Bishop, RC Bishop, RJ Bishop, RL Bishop,
TJ Bishop, WH Bishop, WL Bishop, WR Bishop, MT Bisits,
WM Biskup, JG Bitcon, P Bitmead, OA Biziak, CJ Bizzaca,
AJ Black, AR Black, AS Black, BC Black, BF Black, BJ Black,
BR Black, CL Black, CW Black, DJ Black, GA Black,
GE Black, GJ Black, GR Black, IM Black, IS Black, JR Black,
KJ Black, KR Black, KT Black, LC Black, LW Black,
MA Black, MJ Black, MT Black, PJ Black, RA Black,
SA Black, SJ Black, TI Black, TR Black, VG Black, WJ Black,
WN Black, SJ Blackbourn, AJ Blackburn, G Blackburn,
PJ Blackburn, R Blackburn, TR Blackburn, AM Blacker,
BF Blacker, EC Blacker, EN Blacker, TT Blacker, CR Blacket,
BJ Blackett, CD Blackford, DW Blackford, JT Blackford,
RB Blackford, TA Blackhurst, TD Blackhurst, SC Blackie,
C Blackley, CM Blackley, GI Blackman, ID Blackman,
JAT Blackman, KB Blackman, P Blackman, PJ Blackman,
GD Blackmore, JC Blackmore, LD Blackmore,
MC Blackmore, MJ Blackmore, RG Blackmore,
WA Blackmore, DJ Blackney, P Blackstock, TS Blackstock,
AD Blackwell, AS Blackwell, CR Blackwell, DJ Blackwell,
GG Blackwell, JW Blackwell, PH Blackwell, PF Blackwood,
KA Blade, KJ Bladen, AJ Blades, JI Blades, AJ Blaik, DR Blaik,
NJ Blaik, TE Blaikie, WK Blaikie, MR Blain, DI Blair,
DP Blair, EA Blair, GD Blair, GE Blair, GJ Blair, GM Blair,
GS Blair, GW Blair, IR Blair, JF Blair, KR Blair, R Blair,
RL Blair, SJ Blair, TH Blair, A Blake, BD Blake, BH Blake,
C Blake, FB Blake, GW Blake, JA Blake, JT Blake, KG Blake,
MP Blake, PC Blake, RF Blake, SS Blake, VN Blake,
KW Blakeley, IJ Blakeney, NE Blakeney, RT Blakeway,
DA Blakey, J Blakey, JL Blakley, DA Blanch, DC Blanch,
EJ Blanch, GA Blanch, GC Blanch, KRH Blanch, PJ Blanch,
PW Blanch, P Blanchard, PJ Blanchard, SE Blanchard,
AS Blanche, BR Blanchette, DA Blanchonette, WA Blanck,
AC Blanco, EK Bland, GE Bland, NL Bland, RDJ Bland,
RF Bland, JW Blandford, HD Blandthorn, A Blaney,
RA Blank, DC Blanksby, JJ Blanshard, PJ Blaskett,
MJ Blaszkow, DB Blatch, TR Blay, EA Blayney,
JB Blayneymurphy, S Blazek, CE Blazely, DJ Blazely,
KB Blazely, NR Blazely, VL Blazely, AA Blazevicius,
PRG Blazley, GE Bleakley, RW Bleakley, JE Blechynden,
K Bleechmore, RC Bleechmore, RL Blencowe, DR Blenkiron,
PD Blenkiron, PR Blennerhassett, CF Blewden, AD Blewer,
AW Blewitt, RE Blewitt, AD Bligh, DA Bligh, RH Bligh,
C Blight, GP Blight, R Blight, RG Blight, BA Blinco,
GD Blinco, BE Blink, PM Blissett, PJ Blizzard, EF Blocksidge,
NE Bloffwitch, GA Blok, GL Blok, M Blokland, AN Blom,
KJ Blom, GT Blomeley, J Blomley, P Blood, RS Blood,
AW Bloom, BD Bloom, DW Bloom, GJ Bloom, GW Bloom,
LN Bloom, SL Bloomer, DL Bloomfield, PG Bloomfield,
RJ Bloomfield, SG Bloomfield, DG Bloor, JG Blount,
AG Blow, SN Blowers, KG Blowes, RJ Bloxsome, J Blucher,
KR Bluck, L Bluff, WM Blumenfeld, DA Blumer,
A Blumfelds, GN Blumson, GD Blundell, JP Blundell,
JW Blundell, SW Blundell, WF Blundell, BR Blunden,
FJ Blunden, FK Blunden, HA Blunden, PJ Blunden,
WJ Blunt, J Bluzer, AJ Blyth, AT Blyth, DG Blyth, PW Blyth,
ES Blythe, RO Blythe, GJ Blythman, JD Blythman,
NH Blyton, DM Boaden, TJ Boaden, JW Boag, KJ Boag,
LC Boag, LG Boag, WJS Boag, KL Boaler, RF Boaler,
IK Board, PM Board, DW Boardman, KJ Boardman,
TD Boardman, TW Boardman, BW Boast, RJ Boast,
AW Boaz, L Bobako, A Bobets, JW Bobongie, PA Boccabella,
P Boccamazzo, LF Bocchino, GR Bock, L Bockisch,
J Boddam-Whetham, RB Boddenberg, KE Bode, JL Bodey,
WRT Bodger, JW Bodinnar, KJ Bodkin, AL Bodley,
BM Bodley, A Bodnar, DA Bodsworth, RB Bodsworth,
RL Bodsworth, DN Body, VJ Body, W Boeder, WA Boelen,
R Boerman, GR Boettcher, N Boettcher, PH Boeyen, FJ Boff,
BJ Bofinger, T Bogacki, VA Bogar, G Bogdan, NM Bogdan,
RN Bogg, GM Boggie, RT Bogle, AJ Bognar, G Bogodoohoff,
T Bogunovich, PG Bohan, A Bohdan, MO Bohl, JF Bohle,
HW Bohlmann, MW Bohn, F Bohoslavsky, P Bohrnsen,
GFD Boileau, J Bojarski, AP Boland, DL Boland, G Boland,
GE Boland, GT Boland, JF Boland, MD Boland, MJ Boland,
WP Boland, JM Bolas, SW Boldiston, PJ Bolger, RW Bolger,
GE Bolitho, MC Bolitho, MR Bolitho, PW Bolitho,
RJ Bolitho, RJ Bolland, JW Bollard, ML Bollenhagen,
JL Bolst, BW Bolt, JS Bolt, PR Bolt, TC Bolte, EA Bolton,
JC Bolton, LJ Bolton, MC Bolton, MG Bolton, W Bolton,
WR Bolton, THM Boltong, BJ Bom, S Bombell, JR Bomford,
A Bomm, G Bona, GD Bonar, A Bonavita, BG Bond,
BR Bond, CE Bond, DW Bond, FW Bond, JA Bond,
KG Bond, NG Bond, P Bond, PB Bond, PW Bond, RA Bond,
RG Bond, A Bondar, W Bondarczuk, LM Bondin, A Bone,
AW Bone, CJ Bone, KL Bone, LW Bone, RJ Bone, WS Bone,
JC Boneham, LA Boneham, NW Bonell, RC Boness,
VJ Bonett, TL Bongers, FA Bongiorno, FR Bonham,
JA Boniface, KB Bonnefin, NW Bonnell, RC Bonner,
RJ Bonner, DW Bonnes, JT Bonnett, MJ Bonney, NE Bonney,
PB Bonney, CE Bonnici, JJ Bonnici, SP Bonnici, RN Bonny,
BD Bonser, DH Bonser, LJ Bonser, A Bonvino, RR Bony,
CS Bonython, CP Bonzas, DJ Booby, BJ Boocker, KW Boog,
AJ Booker, AM Booker, JT Booker, JC Bookless, PL Bool,
A Boone, DR Boorman, PJ Boorman, JH Boot, BE Bootes,
LN Bootes, PH Bootes, BT Booth, BW Booth, DN Booth,
GA Booth, GD Booth, JE Booth, JL Booth, JS Booth,
KJ Booth, LG Booth, LT Booth, MJ Booth, MW Booth,
PJ Booth, RE Booth, RF Booth, RR Booth, S Booth,
VJG Booth, RP Boothroyd, JH Booton, J Booty, RK Border,
GJ Boreham, RW Boreland, A Borg, JJ Borg, L Borg, N Borg,
OA Borg, TS Borg, KJ Borger, LF Borger, KH Borgges,
WS Borham, TJ Borich, RJ Borinelli, BJ Borkiewicz,
A Borkovic, E Borkowski, DG Borlace, CW Borland,
KD Borland, CW Borlase, GR Borlase, JM Borlase,
RG Borradale, DR Borrett, VG Borrett, BL Borrie,
WW Borserini, KJE Borserio, J Borshoff, R Bos,
SH Bosanquet, GM Boscacci, BJ Bosci, GW Boscoe,
GB Boseley, RF Boserio, DF Bosher, BJ Bosley, PJC Bosley,
JM Boss, LJ Boss, KJ Bosse, GH Bostock, NLJ Bostock,
WJ Bostock, WR Bostock, LC Boston, AR Bosustow,
BM Bosustow, BF Boswell, LV Boswell, HJ Botcher,
IT Botfield, MW Botfield, AG Both, IC Botham,
NH Botheras, JF Bothwell, DN Bott, KR Bott, RR Bott,
WE Bott, JS Botterell, KA Botterill, RL Bottin, PJ Bottrell,
VG Bottrell, PF Bottroff, G Botwright, GJ Boucaut,
A Boucher, DC Bouchier, BT Boughton, C Boughton,
HK Boulding, CH Boully, JG Boulter, B Boulton, I Boulton,
MR Boulton, PE Boulton, RK Boulton, RT Boulton,
TW Boulton, CJ Boundey, DP Boundey, LN Bounds,
RP Bounds, JL Boundy, DE Bourchier, RG Bourchier,
BA Bourke, BE Bourke, BF Bourke, DCT Bourke, DF Bourke,
DM Bourke, HJ Bourke, J Bourke, JE Bourke, JR Bourke,
KJ Bourke, KL Bourke, MA Bourke, MH Bourke, P Bourke,
PJ Bourke, PL Bourke, PW Bourke, RJ Bourke, RM Bourke,
RV Bourke, RW Bourke, SR Bourke, TM Bourke, TS Bourke,
TW Bourke, WJ Bourke, CW Bourn, DH Bourne,
DM Bourne, DW Bourne, ID Bourne, LV Bourne,
RA Bourne, JA Bouse, S Boutlis, GL Bouttell, MC Bouttell,
GJ Bouveng, JL Bouveng, HA Bouwhuis, TK Bouwman,
LR Bovey, KA Bovill, L Bowater, JW Bowbrick,
GW Bowcock, RE Bowd, RM Bowd, A Bowden,
AH Bowden, AM Bowden, AP Bowden, BJ Bowden,
BS Bowden, CP Bowden, D Bowden, DJ Bowden,
DR Bowden, FW Bowden, RA Bowden, TA Bowden,
TM Bowden, VC Bowden, WM Bowden, FA Bowder,
BP Bowe, DW Bowe, PG Bowe, RE Bowe, DM Bowen,
F Bowen, GJ Bowen, IH Bowen, JK Bowen, JP Bowen,
KF Bowen, KP Bowen, L Bowen, N Bowen, NG Bowen,

PR Bowen, RJ Bowen, RW Bowen, B Bower, FE Bower, GA Bower, RJ Bower, S Bower, SA Bower, KN Bowerman, R Bowerman, SB Bowerman, NA Bower-Miles, AT Bowers, CL Bowes, DG Bowes, DW Bowes, RT Bowes, BJ Bowie, JD Bowie, EJ Bowkett, GH Bowler, IR Bowler, KP Bowler, PL Bowler, DC Bowles, JC Bowles, JH Bowles, SN Bowles, JH Bowley, RR Bowley, JG Bowling, M Bowmaker, BA Bowman, CJ Bowman, DJ Bowman, EJ Bowman, FE Bowman, GJ Bowman, JH Bowman, L Bowman, PD Bowman, RL Bowman, SH Bowman, TJ Bowman, PS Bowring, GC Bowser, WF Bowser, FE Bowtell, RL Bowtell, RW Bowtell, AR Bowtellharris, JS Bowthorpe, A Bowyer, JC Bowyer, LW Bowyer, GD Box, JE Box, JW Box, PF Box, PG Box, RE Box, RE Boxall, TJ Boxall, DS Boxer, IC Boxhall, BF Boxsell, RH Boxsell, AL Boxshall, K Boxshall, PW Boxshall, DG Boyce, GJ Boyce, KW Boyce, R Boyce, RJ Boyce, TJ Boyce, A Boyd, AA Boyd, AN Boyd, B Boyd, BG Boyd, DD Boyd, DW Boyd, E Boyd, EL Boyd, EW Boyd, FW Boyd, GH Boyd, GM Boyd, HA Boyd, IM Boyd, IR Boyd, JR Boyd, KL Boyd, KR Boyd, LP Boyd, P Boyd, PI Boyd, RD Boyd, SA Boyd, SM Boyd, WA Boyd, WGS Boyd, JC Boyer, D Boyes, R Boyes, SR Boyes, T Boylan, AH Boyle, AJ Boyle, AP Boyle, BA Boyle, BK Boyle, DJ Boyle, JA Boyle, JC Boyle, KJ Boyle, MF Boyle, MG Boyle, RJ Boyle, RT Boyle, TM Boyle, WD Boyle, WM Boyle, JR Boyles, WF Boyling, RK Boyne, PT Boyns, BG Boys, RM Boys, GM Boyt, GV Bozinis, WM Brabant, RR Brabants, CA Brabham, AG Braby, GC Bracegirdle, GJ Bracegirdle, DH Bracewell, JR Bracher, AG Brack, CBR Bracken, CM Bracken, IW Bracken, BA Brackenreg, BW Brackin, RH Bradbery, RW Bradbery, NG Bradbrook, AJ Bradbury, KJ Bradbury, M Bradbury, RN Bradbury, TJ Bradbury, TM Bradbury, GE Bradd, WH Bradd, GK Braddock, EC Braddon, RH Bradfield, DL Bradford, EJ Bradford, JC Bradford, JW Bradford, P Bradford, PL Bradford, RB Bradford, RC Bradford, SM Bradford, B Bradley, CA Bradley, DE Bradley, DN Bradley, EJ Bradley, JM Bradley, M Bradley, MS Bradley, NT Bradley, PE Bradley, PJ Bradley, RA Bradley, RC Bradley, RL Bradley, RW Bradley, S Bradley, T Bradley, RL Bradmore, B Bradshaw, MS Bradshaw, N Bradshaw, P Bradshaw, T Bradshaw, TG Bradshaw, TR Bradshaw, TW Bradshaw, HA Bradstreet, AW Brady, BP Brady, DR Brady, ER Brady, FW Brady, GJ Brady, GV Brady, IJ Brady, J Brady, JM Brady, JW Brady, KJ Brady, MTJ Brady, NM Brady, R Brady, RA Brady, RE Brady, RT Brady, TL Brady, WF Brady, GF Braendler, RA Braendler, AR Bragg, RJ Bragg, TW Bragg, TJ Braham, GH Braid, RJ Braid, KD Braidwood, AE Brailsford, JR Braimbridge, DJ Brain, JA Brain, MJ Brain, RS Brain, P Braiotta, M Braithwait, EH Braithwaite, RJ Braithwaite, JJ Brak, CJ Brakell, KR Brakewell, SB Bramah, PJ Bramble, BL Brame, JH Brameld, CM Bramley, DG Bramley, GB Bramley, KF Bramley, RW Bramley, GJ Brammer, PJ Brammer, JL Bramston, GR Branch, KD Branch, LG Branch, RC Branch, RJ Branch, DM Brand, G Brand, GC Brand, GJ Brand, MG Brand, MO Brand, TA Brand, BJ Brandenburg, JJ Brander, CD Brandham, DJ Brandie, IJ Brandis, LJ Brandis, JN Brandon, PJ Brandon, RN Brandon, ECM Brandon-Cramer, L Brandsma, AB Brandt, RJ Brandt, HD Brandy, JE Braniff, JE Brankstone, AE Brann, KJ Brann, WE Brannan, ES Brannigan, DL Branson, FLR Branson, V Brase, R Brassen, GJ Brassil, PJ Brassington, PR Brassington, WJ Bratby, GR Brathwaite, RG Bratley, IW Bratt, GC Bratz, JC Brauer, LH Brauer, RM Braumann, JJ Braumberger, JW Braun, M Braun, PL Braun, L Braut, RE Bravo, RJ Bravo, MJ Brawn, WW Brawn, AB Bray, AR Bray, DJ Bray, EJ Bray, JA Bray, JH Bray, LA Bray, LC Bray, PJ Bray, RJ Bray, WE Bray, RJ Brayshaw, JJ Brazel, CL Brazier, PT Brazier, PV Brazionis, J Breacher, GR Breaden, BJ Breadmore, JM Breadsell, TH Breakwell, JD Brearley, MG Brearley, RJ Brearley, AJ Brebner, RE Brebner, BR Breddin, NJ Bredhauer, RH Bredl, W Bree, PC Breed, AJ Breen, CW Breen, F Breen, KM Breen, RJ Breen, SJ Breen, GM Breeze, JAE Breeze, SL Breeze, AG Breglec, J Bregonje, MW Breheny, K Breitkopf, JM Bremner, PC Bremner, GA Brendish, AB Brennan, AF Brennan, CE Brennan, DJ Brennan, DP Brennan, HF Brennan, IJ Brennan, JA Brennan, JE Brennan, JF Brennan, JH Brennan, LE Brennan, NJ Brennan, PL Brennan, PM Brennan, R Brennan, RF Brennan, S Brennan, TH Brennan, TJ Brennan, WG Brennan, WR Brennan, TF Brennand, DH Brenneke, KJ Brens, BJ Brent, SH Brent, GF Brenton, CR Brereton, MK Brereton, WG Brereton, BJ Breslin,

DJ Bresnan, A Bresser, AR Bressington, J Bressington, AJ Bretherton, MH Bretherton, GA Brett, JD Brett, JR Brett, RA Brett, RC Brett, RG Brett, RH Brett, SJ Brett, WJ Brett, LR Brettle, JL Bretz, GE Bretzke, NA Bretzke, JG Breust, RJ Brevitt, P Breward, A Brewer, BA Brewer, CB Brewer, CJ Brewer, CS Brewer, GW Brewer, JA Brewer, JEP Brewer, JR Brewer, KF Brewer, NFT Brewer, RG Brewer, WR Brewer, RE Briais, DC Brian, MR Brian, SN Briansky, KT Briant, B Brice, EP Brice, PG Brice, RF Brice, GT Brick, RJ Brickle, WJ Bricknall, RL Bricknell, AG Bride, RD Brideson, AJ Bridge, AR Bridge, CW Bridge, DR Bridge, LF Bridge, LW Bridge, NB Bridge, PJ Bridge, AR Bridgehouse, JA Bridger, AE Bridges, AW Bridges, FJ Bridges, KJ Bridges, LW Bridges, TR Bridges, WS Bridgewater, CV Bridgford, GS Bridgland, BR Bridgman, JW Bridgman, AE Bridle, B Bridle, RB Bridle, PL Bridley, JR Brien, RG Brien, PW Brier, HL Brierley, JL Briers, NW Briers, RT Briese, A Briffa, GGC Briffa, GC Brigden, DA Briggs, DJ Briggs, EJ Briggs, GS Briggs, IA Briggs, IJ Briggs, JD Briggs, JJ Briggs, JW Briggs, KC Briggs, KW Briggs, LA Briggs, R Briggs, RC Briggs, RJ Briggs, SJ Briggs, TL Briggs, BJL Bright, DP Bright, GA Bright, JA Bright, KW Bright, LB Bright, PJ Bright, RE Bright, TA Bright, NC Brightman, CD Brighton, RJ Brightwell, IL Brignell, JAA Brill, DJ Brindley, RA Brine, CC Brines, JW Brinkworth, SP Brinkworth, RA Brinton, BR Brisbane, DM Briscoe, JK Briskey, LG Bristol, RJ Bristow, RK Bristow, DW Bristowe, GJ Bristowe, OE Britnell, AD Britt, LR Britt, R Britt, RA Britt, AJ Brittain, CR Brittain, RJ Brittain, DR Brittan, DC Britten, RD Britten, TJ Britten, BF Britton, DJ Britton, JA Britton, JR Britton, RE Britton, RW Britton, BW Broad, DW Broad, PJ Broad, RC Broad, TW Broad, WFC Broad, DM Broadbent, I Broadbent, RG Broadbent, CJ Broadhead, RT Broadhurst, BE Broadribb, AJ Broatch, CJ Brock, DC Brock, JK Brock, MW Brock, PA Brock, RJ Brock, TR Brock, O Brockenhuus-Schack, RJ Brockett, PA Brockhoff, J Brockman, RNJ Brockman, GS Brockway, BM Brockwell, ER Brockwell, B Broderick, G Broderick, J Broderick, WP Broderick, AJ Brodie, CR Brodie, RE Brodie, IC Brodribb, MA Brodziak, WH Broekhof, WH Broekstra, JA Brogan, MF Brogan, RD Brogan, T Brogan, G Brokate, GM Bromage, JW Broman, DT Bromell, M Bromet, ER Bromfield, KW Bromham, MP Bromhead, WA Bromiley, GL Bromley, HW Bromley, I Bromley, RL Bromley, TH Bromley, DM Brook, DN Brook, FN Brook, GT Brook, I Brook, PJ Brook, PR Brook, WR Brook, A Brooke, PR Brooke, RL Brooke, AW Brooker, BD Brooker, CL Brooker, JW Brooker, PG Brooker, RC Brooker, RJ Brooker, WS Brooker, BJ Brookes, BW Brookes, D Brookes, IN Brookes, JE Brookes, PR Brookes, J Brookfield, MJ Brooking, C Brooks, CL Brooks, D Brooks, DB Brooks, DE Brooks, DI Brooks, DJ Brooks, DL Brooks, DW Brooks, GR Brooks, GW Brooks, HA Brooks, HJF Brooks, HW Brooks, IS Brooks, JC Brooks, KA Brooks, KW Brooks, MR Brooks, RJ Brooks, RL Brooks, RT Brooks, RW Brooks, S Brooks, SG Brooks, TF Brooks, WJ Brooks, SR Brooksby, WS Broom, A Broome, DJ Broome, DS Broome, JW Broome, BR Broomfield, BW Broomfield, GD Broomfield, B Broomhall, WJ Broomhall, KJ Broomham, EF Brophy, GW Brophy, MP Brophy, CJ Brosnan, KJ Brosnan, MG Brotherton, DK Brough, BC Broughton, J Broughton, JT Broughton, RA Broughton, WR Broughton, AA Brown, AD Brown, AE Brown, AH Brown, AJ Brown, AM Brown, AQ Brown, AR Brown, AW Brown, AY Brown, BA Brown, BC Brown, BE Brown, BJ Brown, BL Brown, C Brown, CA Brown, CE Brown, CK Brown, CR Brown, CVH Brown, CW Brown, DC Brown, DE Brown, DF Brown, DG Brown, DJ Brown, DK Brown, DM Brown, DN Brown, DR Brown, DV Brown, DW Brown, EG Brown, EH Brown, EW Brown, F Brown, FR Brown, G Brown, G Brown, GB Brown, GC Brown, GD Brown, GF Brown, GG Brown, GH Brown, GJ Brown, GM Brown, GP Brown, GR Brown, GT Brown, GV Brown, GW Brown, HA Brown, ID Brown, IN Brown, IR Brown, IT Brown, IW Brown, J Brown, JA Brown, JC Brown, JD Brown, JH Brown, JI Brown, JJ Brown, JK Brown, JL Brown, JM Brown, JR Brown, KE Brown, KG Brown, KJ Brown, KP Brown, KR Brown, KS Brown, KW Brown, LC Brown, LG Brown, LJ Brown, LJT Brown, LN Brown, LR Brown, MA Brown, MD Brown, ME Brown, MG Brown, MJ Brown, ML Brown, N Brown, NB Brown, NE Brown, NH Brown, NI Brown, NJ Brown, NL Brown, NM Brown, NW Brown, OC Brown, OW Brown, P Brown, PC Brown, PH Brown, PJ Brown, PL Brown, PR Brown,

PT Brown, R Brown, RA Brown, RB Brown, RD Brown, RE Brown, RG Brown, RH Brown, RI Brown, RJ Brown, RJ Brown, RK Brown, RL Brown, RM Brown, RN Brown, RO Brown, RP Brown, RR Brown, RS Brown, RSJ Brown, RW Brown, SH Brown, SK Brown, SL Brown, SP Brown, SR Brown, TC Brown, TD Brown, TG Brown, TJ Brown, TN Brown, VJ Brown, W Brown, WA Brown, WC Brown, WD Brown, WJ Brown, WL Brown, WM Brown, WR Brown, WS Brown, AV Brownbill, CA Browne, CJ Browne, DJ Browne, DN Browne, GL Browne, IJ Browne, JA Browne, JL Browne, MB Browne, MCL Browne, MG Browne, MJ Browne, R Browne, TC Browne, TE Browne, TH Browne, WV Browne, CFM Brownhill, CM Browning, EA Browning, HG Browning, J Browning, KD Browning, NA Browning, R Browning, WD Browning, ML Brownlee, RE Brownley, AS Brownlie, RJ Brownlie, ER Brownlow, PB Brownrigg, BG Bruce, CG Bruce, CH Bruce, CR Bruce, ID Bruce, JE Bruce, JL Bruce, KF Bruce, PJJ Bruce, PR Bruce, R Bruce, RA Bruce, RK Bruce, RW Bruce, TJ Bruce, TW Bruce, WJ Bruce, IL Bruckshaw, PT Brudell, RMD Brudenell, RG Bruellke, NJ Bruggeman, MJ Bruggemann, D Bruhn, MJ Bruhwiller, GJ Bruin, J Bruin, IRW Brumfield, KR Brumfield, RA Brumm, W Brunalli, MB Brunckhorst, NA Brundle, G Brunelli, KS Brunette, R Brunner, BN Brunning, MD Brunning, J Bruno, JO Bruns, AJ Brunt, AD Brunton, PN Brunton, DJ Brushe, GE Bruton, LA Bruty, AP Bruzga, AF Bryan, BR Bryan, DA Bryan, DJ Bryan, DW Bryan, GA Bryan, JS Bryan, LR Bryan, MR Bryan, PF Bryan, WJ Bryan, AG Bryant, AS Bryant, CKR Bryant, DB Bryant, DW Bryant, EF Bryant, FP Bryant, GD Bryant, GH Bryant, GJ Bryant, GW Bryant, IJ Bryant, JA Bryant, JC Bryant, JE Bryant, JK Bryant, K Bryant, KK Bryant, MJ Bryant, MJT Bryant, MTJ Bryant, NR Bryant, RCG Bryant, RD Bryant, RF Bryant, RJ Bryant, RK Bryant, TM Bryant, VM Bryant, RJ Bryar, BG Bryce, J Bryce, KA Bryce, PA Bryce, TJ Bryceson, CA Bryde, JF Bryden, R Bryden, WA Brydie, C Brydon, DW Brydon, NA Brydon, WJ Brydon, ES Bryon, IEL Bryson, K Bryson, RC Bryson, WJ Bryson, MA Bubacz, AK Bubb, IL Bubb, MD Bubear, BW Bubner, JG Buchan, R Buchan, RS Buchan, BE Buchanan, BJ Buchanan, CEC Buchanan, GA Buchanan, GC Buchanan, JA Buchanan, JL Buchanan, KB Buchanan, MD Buchanan, RJ Buchanan, RN Buchanan, TJ Buchanan, WB Buchanan, K Buchmaier, R Bucik, DL Buck, IE Buck, LG Buck, R Buck, DG Buckby, BA Buckell, AG Buckingham, PG Buckingham, R Buckingham, C Buckland, FD Buckland, GB Buckland, PL Buckland, WR Buckland, BF Buckle, FR Buckle, JF Buckle, TC Buckler, ACS Buckley, AK Buckley, AP Buckley, BR Buckley, CM Buckley, DJ Buckley, GLT Buckley, GW Buckley, H Buckley, HJ Buckley, JM Buckley, JW Buckley, LG Buckley, MJ Buckley, MR Buckley, PG Buckley, PJ Buckley, RG Buckley, RW Buckley, TJ Buckley, W Buckley, CA Buckman, RW Buckman, JF Bucknall, MW Bucknall, RW Bucknall, TR Bucknall, RJ Bucknar, PJ Buckney, K Buckolz, PD Buckthorpe, DM Buckwalter, DN Budd, EA Budd, J Budd, RL Budd, RP Budd, BF Budden, RA Budden, R Budge, TN Budge, P Budworth, RC Buerckner, GJ Buffa, DJ Buffett, MF Buffham, FJ Bugby, WH Bugert, PL Bugg, JA Bugge, MG Bugge, MJ Buggy, EK Bugis, PM Bugler, TL Bugslag, JS Buhagiar, JH Buhmann, RS Buick, TM Buick, TR Buick, DJ Buik, PC Buik, AT Builder, J Bujnowski, ES Bulbeck, A Bulcock, W Buldo, GGO Bulger, JL Bulkeley, AJ Bull, DJ Bull, FR Bull, JR Bull, LD Bull, MN Bull, PJ Bull, RA Bull, RJ Bull, SC Bull, WA Bullard, JE Bullen, MA Bullen, NR Bullen, RJ Bullen, WR Bullen, ID Buller, KG Buller, AF Bullis, PW Bullis, RI Bullis, MG Bullivant, JH Bullman, ID Bulloch, RJ Bulloch, AG Bullock, AR Bullock, BW Bullock, CF Bullock, GJ Bullock, GR Bullock, IA Bullock, DW Bullow, RJ Bullpitt, IR Bulmer, RR Bulmer, KA Bulow, G Bulsing, BF Bultitude, KG Bultitude, JR Bumpstead, WR Bungate, BC Bunker, DK Bunker, I Bunn, P Bunn, DE Bunney, MD Bunney, JT Bunning, DB Bunny, MR Bunt, RE Bunt, INH Bunter, SJ Bunter, DW Buntine, RL Buntine, PJ Bunting, RA Bunting, RB Bunting, RM Bunting, WA Bunting, DJ Bunton, RS Bunton, L Bunworth, PEJ Bunyan, WA Bunyan, JR Buratowski, G Burbidge, GC Burbury, MB Burcham, TH Burchell, RN Burcher, IG Burchill, KJ Burchill, JA Burdell, G Burdett, H Burdett, KJ Burdett, RC Burdett, JC Burdeu, GR Burdon, PJ Burdon, BR Burford, MA Burford, PS Burford, RA Burford, RJ Burford, WA Burford, DC Burg, BJ Burge,

BR Burge, D Burge, KW Burge, ME Burge, RD Burge, SL Burge, WJ Burge, GR Burger, NW Burgerhof, BJ Burgess, BR Burgess, BW Burgess, CE Burgess, CR Burgess, DC Burgess, DF Burgess, DW Burgess, FKT Burgess, GA Burgess, GC Burgess, GD Burgess, GF Burgess, GK Burgess, JE Burgess, KJ Burgess, KL Burgess, MC Burgess, MI Burgess, MJ Burgess, P Burgess, PML Burgess, RE Burgess, RJ Burgess, RN Burgess, RP Burgess, SR Burgess, WJ Burgess, WL Burgess, WT Burgess, HA Burghardt, DJ Burgher, WD Burgher, JL Burgin, PR Burgis, PJ Burgmann, NW Burgoyne, DLH Buring, AG Burk, AJ Burke, AR Burke, BJ Burke, BP Burke, BV Burke, BW Burke, CP Burke, D Burke, DJ Burke, DL Burke, DP Burke, GJ Burke, JMD Burke, JP Burke, JV Burke, PA Burke, PE Burke, PF Burke, PJ Burke, RC Burke, RD Burke, RJ Burke, TB Burke, TW Burke, WE Burke, HR Burkenhagen, AR Burkhill, AW Burland, DN Burley, KA Burley, KD Burley, PG Burley, PJ Burley, RF Burley, BD Burling, IR Burling, JA Burling, RD Burling, PE Burls, AT Burman, IC Burman, LD Burman, EJ Burn, TW Burn, RL Burnard, WF Burnard, H Burnell, JW Burnell, S Burnell-Jones, IMF Burner, JH Burness, RK Burness, WR Burness, D Burnet, RAG Burnet, SM Burnet, BG Burnett, DP Burnett, DR Burnett, GC Burnett, GJ Burnett, GL Burnett, J Burnett, K Burnett, KJ Burnett, NM Burnett, RA Burnett, RG Burnett, TW Burnett, WJ Burnett, CM Burney, RC Burney, AM Burnicle, PJ Burnie, RA Burnie, AC Burns, AJ Burns, BG Burns, BL Burns, CE Burns, CI Burns, CR Burns, DH Burns, EC Burns, JC Burns, JK Burns, JL Burns, JW Burns, KJ Burns, KO Burns, KR Burns, LW Burns, NA Burns, PA Burns, PD Burns, PJ Burns, PR Burns, R Burns, RG Burns, RJ Burns, RM Burns, SR Burns, TC Burns, VH Burns, WJ Burns, MK Burnside, RC Burnside, DJ Burow, PA Burquest, AM Burr, MF Burr, RW Burr, WC Burr, DL Burrage, AW Burrell, IJ Burrell, J Burrell, LR Burrell, ID Burrett, LB Burrett, BR Burridge, JDC Burridge, KG Burrill, RR Burriss, JF Burrough, BB Burrow, GC Burrow, AV Burrowes, CF Burrowes, JL Burrowes, AO Burrows, DA Burrows, GJ Burrows, GW Burrows, JD Burrows, JJ Burrows, JS Burrows, KC Burrows, LJ Burrows, LM Burrows, WO Burrows, NA Burstall, PF Burstall, RT Burstall, MJ Burston, R Burston, BC Burstow, AA Burt, BR Burt, DJ Burt, DW Burt, FD Burt, G Burt, KR Burt, LF Burt, LW Burt, MG Burt, RJ Burt, BF Burton, BJ Burton, BL Burton, BS Burton, BW Burton, DC Burton, DF Burton, FC Burton, FW Burton, G Burton, GA Burton, HA Burton, JR Burton, JW Burton, KB Burton, KT Burton, LA Burton, MJ Burton, MP Burton, MR Burton, P Burton, PT Burton, RG Burton, RJ Burton, RW Burton, SJ Burton, TL Burton, TV Burton, VC Burton, WA Burton, WT Burton, RH Burton-Bradley, PC Burton-Gibbs, HK Burtt, DJ Burvill, DR Bury, R Bury, DL Burzacott, RS Busbridge, AE Busby, FM Busby, PN Busby, RW Busch, JW Buscumb, BL Bush, CB Bush, KJ Bush, PJS Bush, R Bush, RJ Bush, RR Bush, WT Bush, PW Bushby, RW Bushby, JF Bushell, D Bushman, AL Busk, JL Buss, P Buss, PJ Buss, BC Bussenschutt, B Bussingham, JC Butchart, JT Butchart, CJ Butcher, D Butcher, GD Butcher, GJ Butcher, GW Butcher, JR Butcher, KJ Butcher, LA Butcher, PA Butcher, RV Butcher, W Butcher, G Butera, L Butera, JB Butland, AG Butler, AL Butler, AR Butler, AW Butler, BJ Butler, BR Butler, CJ Butler, DC Butler, DD Butler, DF Butler, DG Butler, DM Butler, DR Butler, DW Butler, FJ Butler, GH Butler, GI Butler, GJ Butler, JA Butler, JL Butler, JT Butler, KD Butler, KJ Butler, KR Butler, KS Butler, M Butler, MH Butler, MJ Butler, MK Butler, MW Butler, NM Butler, OD Butler, PC Butler, PE Butler, PG Butler, PJ Butler, PL Butler, PR Butler, RD Butler, RE Butler, RF Butler, RH Butler, RJW Butler, RM Butler, RW Butler, TB Butler, TJ Butler, WE Butler, WH Butler, WJ Butler, IF Butlin, RR Butlin, PR Butorac, VB Butsch, BG Butt, GD Butt, PT Butt, RJ Buttel, WE Butterfield, KJ Butterley, IA Butterly, AD Butters, CW Butterworth, H Butterworth, M Butterworth, NJ Butterworth, WA Butterworth, GL Buttery, JSH Buttifant, PPA Buttigieg, NR Buttimer, GJ Buttner, DJ Button, F Button, PG Button, TP Button, WJ Button, PD Buttrose, MR Butts, AJ Butun, DM Buxallen, EF Buxton, JG Buxton, PA Buxton, RC Buxton, RJ Buxton, PA Buykx, RB Buzacott, JP Buzelin, N Buzza, P Buzza, B Buzzard, GP Byard, JR Byars, RL Bycroft, NR Bye, PF Bye, RJ Bye, DR Byers, PM Byers, RG Byers, WC Byers, W Byfield, JM Bygrave, RG Byles, GD Byng, JL Byng, M Byng, TW Byng, VE Byquar, BE Byrne, BJ Byrne, CF Byrne, DK Byrne, DL Byrne, DW Byrne, FJ Byrne, GE Byrne, JF Byrne, JM Byrne, JW Byrne, KB Byrne, KL Byrne, KM Byrne, KP Byrne, MB Byrne, MJ Byrne, MP Byrne, PA Byrne, PD Byrne, PJ Byrne, PR Byrne, PV Byrne, RA Byrne, SD Byrne, SJ Byrne, TF Byrne, TJ Byrne, TKK Byrne-King, AD Byrnes, C Byrnes, DP Byrnes, JD Byrnes, JK Byrnes, K Byrnes, MR Byrnes, PJ Byrnes, RA Byrnes, RF Byrnes, RJ Byrnes, RM Byrnes, JD Byrom, K Byrom, KW Byron, ME Byron, RV Byron, PA Bysouth, GM Byth, JV Bywater, WV Bywater, PM Bywaters, T Bywaters, AJ Caban, AL Cabban, JB Cable, M Cace, PM Cachia, WJ Cadd, LJ Caddell, ML Cadden, ID Caddies, RJ Caddies, BJ Caddle, PF Caddy, RG Caddy, JA Cadge, PS Cadge, A Cadger, GF Cadman, WP Cadogan, BV Cadusch, LJ Cadzow, RL Cafe, BD Caffery, PW Caffery, FW Cage, DM Cahalan, BE Cahill, CD Cahill, DJ Cahill, FB Cahill, GG Cahill, GJ Cahill, IJ Cahill, JG Cahill, LJ Cahill, NE Cahill, JT Cahir, AP Cain, CF Cain, J Cain, JA Cain, JG Cain, MJ Cain, PJ Cain, RF Cain, RM Cain, IF Caines, RA Caines, RC Cains, GN Cairncross, BW Cairnes, P Cairnes, V Cairney, RH Cairnie, AJ Cairns, BJ Cairns, EJ Cairns, FAC Cairns, KR Cairns, NJ Cairns, ON Cairns, PH Cairns, PS Cairns, RJ Cairns, RW Cairns, PJ Caisley, D Cakoliris, CE Calcraft, JS Calcutt, B Calder, DH Calder, JH Calder, MJ Calder, WW Calder, DJ Calderwood, DA Caldwell, GI Caldwell, PC Caldwell, RA Caldwell, RJ Caldwell, DC Calear, BJ Caligari, AA Caljouw, AJ Callaghan, DA Callaghan, DN Callaghan, EJ Callaghan, H Callaghan, J Callaghan, JL Callaghan, JP Callaghan, JS Callaghan, KP Callaghan, LL Callaghan, LP Callaghan, MAJ Callaghan, ME Callaghan, MR Callaghan, PF Callaghan, RA Callaghan, MJ Callanan, ML Callanan, RE Callanan, FAG Callander, IM Callander, IR Callaway, JH Callcott, MM Calleja, D Callen, KJ Callinan, RE Callinan, DJ Callison, NJ Calliss, AE Callister, J Callister, J Callow, P Callow, DR Callum, A Callus, PJ Callus, JM Calnin, PJ Calvert, RW Calvert, MR Calvett, FG Calway, AJ Cambey, JD Cambridge, JR Cambridge, AJ Cameron, AK Cameron, AT Cameron, B Cameron, BI Cameron, BJ Cameron, D Cameron, DD Cameron, DG Cameron, DJ Cameron, DM Cameron, DR Cameron, E Cameron, EG Cameron, G Cameron, G Cameron, GC Cameron, GM Cameron, HJ Cameron, IG Cameron, IL Cameron, JD Cameron, JL Cameron, KS Cameron, LG Cameron, MA Cameron, NL Cameron, PD Cameron, PJ Cameron, PJG Cameron, PL Cameron, PR Cameron, RA Cameron, RB Cameron, RC Cameron, RD Cameron, RE Cameron, RJ Cameron, SP Cameron, TJ Cameron, TS Cameron, VM Cameron, WA Cameron, WDB Cameron, WR Camilleri, NT Camin, NC Camm, RW Camm, TC Camm, TH Campain, SG Campani, A Campbell, AG Campbell, AJ Campbell, AL Campbell, AN Campbell, AW Campbell, B Campbell, BA Campbell, BC Campbell, BD Campbell, BJ Campbell, C Campbell, CJ Campbell, CM Campbell, CR Campbell, DA Campbell, DC Campbell, DE Campbell, DG Campbell, DH Campbell, DI Campbell, DM Campbell, DR Campbell, EF Campbell, EH Campbell, EN Campbell, GB Campbell, GC Campbell, GD Campbell, GG Campbell, GR Campbell, GS Campbell, I Campbell, IG Campbell, IJ Campbell, IL Campbell, ILG Campbell, IM Campbell, IR Campbell, J Campbell, JA Campbell, JD Campbell, JE Campbell, JK Campbell, JW Campbell, KG Campbell, KJ Campbell, LM Campbell, MB Campbell, MG Campbell, MI Campbell, MJ Campbell, MR Campbell, ND Campbell, NJ Campbell, NW Campbell, PJ Campbell, R Campbell, RA Campbell, RB Campbell, RD Campbell, RE Campbell, RJ Campbell, RK Campbell, RL Campbell, RW Campbell, SR Campbell, SW Campbell, TC Campbell, TR Campbell, W Campbell, WG Campbell, WJ Campbell, WM Campbell, CS Campbellfraser, CDT Campey, RO Campey, V Campisi, TE Camplin, SC Campling, PJ Campman, DG Camps, BL Campton, P Canakis, M Canavan, PJ Canavan, RL Canavan, DN Candow, GW Candy, WH Candy, BD Cane, RA Cane, WJ Cane, LA Canham, FW Cann, RA Cann, CS Cannan, EJ Cannan, PR Cannane, DJ Cannard, PL Canney, CF Cannin, DA Canning, MC Canning, PJ Canning, JS Cannon, MJ Cannon, RJ Cannon, BJ Cannons, DO Canny, RJ Canobie, GJ Cant, RL Cantamessa, BG Canton, GR Cantrill, FW Cantwell, DJ Canute, JG Canuto, EDM Cape, TF Cape, RF Capel, E Capobianco, A Capogreco, D Capogreco, IC Caporn, JH Caporn, PC Capp, GL Capper, JE Cappler, LJ Capra, JS Capuano, M Caravias, MP Carberry, RL Carberry, JG Carbery, KB Carbery, SR Carbines, RG Carbins, AD Carbis, BJ Carbone, RT Carbury, TD Card, P Cardona, PS Cardone, DK Cardow, JD Cardwell, P Cardwell, C Care, AR Carew, WH Carewreid, GJ Carey, GK Carey, GW Carey, KJ Carey, KPR Carey, LB Carey, MH Carey, P Carey, PJ Carey, RJ Carey, RM Carey, RW Carey, LG Cargeeg, RG Cargill, TW Cargill, FR Carl, KC Carl, RI Carl, R Carlin, CJ Carling, PD Carlisle, RJG Carlisle, AC Carlon, JK Carlow, CS Carlsen, BF Carlson, DG Carlson, FJ Carlson, GH Carlson, JR Carlson, RJ Carlson, RG Carlsson, JD Carlton, RG Carlton, WG Carlton, BR Carlyle, H Carlyle, DW Carlyon, LN Carlyon, MJ Carlyon, RG Carlyon, T Carlyon, RT Carman, RP Carmichael, DM Carmody, EK Carmody, GM Carmody, ME Carmody, MJ Carmody, TJ Carmody, TR Carmody, BLJ Carn, JW Carn, DL Carne, GJ Carne, RC Carne, DP Carnegie, DJ Carnes, JE Carnes, JT Carnes, JW Carnes, D Carney, JR Carney, JW Carney, TF Carney, W Carney, WD Carney, AD Carns, BM Carolan, BJ Carpenter, CG Carpenter, CR Carpenter, DJ Carpenter, EJ Carpenter, GJ Carpenter, HC Carpenter, JR Carpenter, PEC Carpenter, PM Carpenter, RJ Carpenter, RL Carpenter, SR Carpenter, WG Carpenter, AD Carr, AG Carr, B Carr, BJ Carr, EW Carr, F Carr, GE Carr, GH Carr, JD Carr, JJ Carr, JN Carr, JR Carr, JS Carr, MI Carr, RV Carr, RW Carr, SN Carr, WA Carr, DW Carra, S Carrabba, J Carreras, GR Carrick, MW Carrigan, NP Carrington, R Carrod, PJ Carrodus, AJ Carroll, BD Carroll, BF Carroll, CD Carroll, CP Carroll, DJ Carroll, DN Carroll, DP Carroll, EL Carroll, FA Carroll, GJ Carroll, GL Carroll, JF Carroll, JG Carroll, JJ Carroll, KJ Carroll, LR Carroll, MC Carroll, MCM Carroll, MJ Carroll, MO Carroll, MP Carroll, MR Carroll, MV Carroll, OM Carroll, PD Carroll, PW Carroll, RA Carroll, RH Carroll, RJ Carroll, RT Carroll, TH Carroll, TR Carroll, W Carroll, WT Carroll, RG Carrott, JD Carruth, CC Carruthers, CS Carruthers, IJ Carruthers, J Carruthers, JR Carruthers, JS Carruthers, LJ Carruthers, SJ Carruthers, BF Carson, DL Carson, DR Carson, DS Carson, GJ Carson, JL Carson, JV Carson, LW Carson, MD Carson, PG Carson, RA Carson, RJ Carson, AJR Carstairs, C Carstairs, GA Carstairs, DB Carswell, WD Carswell, AA Carter, AB Carter, AR Carter, BF Carter, BJ Carter, BL Carter, BM Carter, BR Carter, CJ Carter, CL Carter, DJ Carter, E Carter, EG Carter, GC Carter, GD Carter, GH Carter, GR Carter, IG Carter, JA Carter, JAR Carter, JD Carter, JH Carter, JW Carter, KA Carter, KD Carter, KJ Carter, MG Carter, MJ Carter, MS Carter, NG Carter, NW Carter, PA Carter, PK Carter, RA Carter, RC Carter, RD Carter, RF Carter, RG Carter, RH Carter, RJ Carter, RL Carter, SL Carter, TE Carter, WK Carter, WW Carter, PW Carters, GS Carthew, JG Carthew, PR Carthew, RG Carthew, AW Carthy, P Carthy, CR Cartledge, PM Cartledge, RG Cartledge, TJ Cartlidge, KS Cartmell, S Cartner, A Cartoon, BJ Cartwright, BM Cartwright, GR Cartwright, JM Cartwright, K Carty, PR Carty, JP Caruana, NL Carvell, GE Carver, BT Carvey, AH Carvill, K Carville, LC Casboult, BJ Case, LJ Case, NJ Case, TE Case, GL Casemore, AL Casey, BW Casey, DA Casey, DB Casey, DJ Casey, GB Casey, GR Casey, JD Casey, JTE Casey, KJ Casey, KL Casey, KR Casey, LA Casey, MP Casey, PJ Casey, RA Casey, RJ Casey, RL Casey, TJ Casey, TM Casey, CB Cash, JC Cash, MJ Cash, PF Cashin, GO Cashion, KJ Cashion, RJ Cashmere, FC Cashmore, DCQ Caskey, GS Cass, JW Cass, ML Cass, NP Cass, RW Cass, PW Cassady, NJ Cassano, C Cassar, AP Cassidy, CJ Cassidy, D Cassidy, GJ Cassidy, J Cassidy, JA Cassidy, LA Cassidy, MK Cassidy, RJ Cassidy, KG Casson, DP Castelanelli, KR Casteldine, CJ Castle, DE Castle, DH Castle, ED Castle, JJ Castle, MJ Castle, RA Castle, RF Castle, RM Castle, EH Castledine, LR Castlehow, BM Castles, DK Castles, JC Castles, JF Castles, JG Castles, RI Castles, RJ Castles, PF Castley, RJ Caston, CC Caswell, RJ Caswell, SW Caswell, WJ Caswell, C Cataldo, CB Catchpole, AR Cater, DR Cathcart, JJ Cathcart, LM Cathcart, RB Cathcart, RW Cathcart, RJ Cather, NW Catheray, MR Catlett, BP Catley, NE Cato, GT Catsacos, GL Catt, WP Cattach, RJ Cattana, CJ Cattanach, JG Cattanach, KA Cattell, D Catterall, DF Catterall, JW Catterall, PJ Catterall, ERA Cattermole, JJ Cattermole, JS Catton, JW Catton, JC Cauchi-Gera, DJ Caudle, KD Caughey, NR Caulfield, BW Caulley, DM Causby, MB Causer, PA Caust, RA Causton, BD Cavanagh, BJ Cavanagh, BR Cavanagh, CJ Cavanagh, CW Cavanagh, EJ Cavanagh, KJ Cavanagh, KL Cavanagh,

LG Cavanagh, RA Cavanagh, RJ Cavanagh, TP Cavanagh, WR Cavanagh, IJ Cavanough, RA Cavanough, GG Cave, GW Cave, PJ Cave, SM Cave, R Cavell, BJ Caven, ID Caverswall, RN Cavill, MJ Cawley, RA Cawood, JC Cawston, WB Cawthorne, VW Cazaly, JN Cazey, KD Cazzy, MJ Cebalo, WJ Cebula, AG Ceccato, RB Cecchini, DJ Cecil, BA Celedin, DP Celler, PM Cerdapavia, A Cerone, DGP Ceruti, P Cervinski, AJ Chaberka, GJ Chad, MR Chad, P Chadbourne, RW Chadburn, CP Chadwick, WD Chadwick, WF Chadwick, LW Chaffey, RJ Chaffey, JH Chainey, RD Chaisty, M Chajka, AJ Chalk, DJ Chalk, MR Chalk, CC Chalker, DM Chalker, GA Chalker, JA Chalker, PJ Challands, G Challen, JF Challenger, TJ Challenger, AG Challenor, DWA Challons, DB Chalmers, EM Chalmers, G Chalmers, KJ Chalmers, LW Chalmers, ND Chalmers, RE Chalmers, RJ Chalmers, SG Chamarette, BW Chamberlain, CF Chamberlain, DA Chamberlain, EP Chamberlain, EW Chamberlain, GC Chamberlain, GR Chamberlain, HB Chamberlain, JG Chamberlain, JN Chamberlain, MJ Chamberlain, RW Chamberlain, BAJ Chambers, BJ Chambers, BW Chambers, CA Chambers, CC Chambers, DE Chambers, DM Chambers, DR Chambers, FG Chambers, GA Chambers, GP Chambers, IB Chambers, ID Chambers, JF Chambers, JR Chambers, LC Chambers, LE Chambers, LJ Chambers, MD Chambers, ME Chambers, MG Chambers, MR Chambers, RH Chambers, RT Chambers, SA Chambers, TR Chambers, AJ Champ, BP Champion, GJ Champion, S Chamulko, LI Chan, RJ Chan, CW Chanalgie, RJ Chance, AE Chandler, BW Chandler, CH Chandler, DE Chandler, DW Chandler, GG Chandler, J Chandler, RC Chandler, RG Chandler, RM Chandler, RW Chandler, DR Channell, GC Channells, RMJ Channells, CA Channon, GB Channon, AW Chant, BE Chant, PA Chant, RJ Chant, GT Chaplin, JS Chaplin, NM Chaplin, RA Chaplin, RM Chaplin, AA Chapman, AD Chapman, BA Chapman, BC Chapman, BE Chapman, BK Chapman, C Chapman, CA Chapman, CF Chapman, DD Chapman, DJ Chapman, DW Chapman, EA Chapman, FA Chapman, G Chapman, GC Chapman, GJ Chapman, GK Chapman, GN Chapman, JC Chapman, JN Chapman, JS Chapman, JW Chapman, L Chapman, LJ Chapman, ME Chapman, MG Chapman, MK Chapman, MW Chapman, NR Chapman, PG Chapman, PJ Chapman, PR Chapman, PV Chapman, PW Chapman, RA Chapman, RF Chapman, RJ Chapman, RP Chapman, RS Chapman, SW Chapman, TC Chapman, TD Chapman, TJ Chapman, TR Chapman, VE Chapman, MB Chappel, AJ Chappell, BA Chappell, DR Chappell, GD Chappell, RG Chappell, CE Chapple, SJ Chapple, JE Chard, RT Chard, M Charenko, PA Charge, BA Charles, CK Charles, HJ Charles, MP Charles, PR Charles, RG Charles, RJ Charles, RRC Charles, SR Charles, TJ Charles, RJ Charleston, NR Charlesworth, RJ Charlesworth, BJ Charlton, BR Charlton, CR Charlton, EJ Charlton, JH Charlton, JM Charlton, JW Charlton, KD Charlton, RE Charlton, WL Charlton, JT Charter, NW Charter, RJ Charters, C Chase, CL Chase, EG Chase, KC Chase, GAC Chasling, WA Chater, DR Chatfield, GF Chatfield, KR Chatfield, BW Chatman, H Chattillon, BJ Chattin, JF Chattin, TS Chatwin, BJ Chatwood, AD Chaunavel, R Cheal, JR Checkley, TW Checkley, KG Cheers, BW Cheeseman, PG Cheeseman, PT Cheeseman, SH Cheeseman, TW Cheeseman, AJ Cheesman, AM Cheetham, BJ Cheetham, G Cheetham, NJ Cheetham, TJ Chell, AJ Chelo, RC Chenery, RR Chenery, WE Chenery, CW Cheney, ET Cheney, GA Cheney, JM Cheney, JR Cheney, WJ Cheney, GF Chenhall, JH Chenoweth, PN Chenoweth, D Chequer, F Cherepandoff, J Cherne, DR Cherry, LJT Cherry, RN Cherry, RP Cherry, PE Cheshire, CA Chesser, MA Chesson, JC Chessor, GR Chessum, BR Chester, FA Chester, GR Chester, JN Chester, KC Chester, KG Chester, RE Chesterman, AN Chesters, AP Chesters, C Chesterton, JT Chestnut, RB Chestnut, RM Chettle, WJ Chettle, GG Chevalley, WM Chevis, RE Chew, CL Cheyne, JR Cheyne, MG Cheyne, NM Cheyne, RJ Cheyne, DB Chick, JM Chick, LP Chick, MO Chidgey, AA Chiementon, N Chiew, GW Chiffey, SN Chignell, MG Chigwidden, GD Chilcott, PG Chilcott, RW Chilcott, DB Child, JT Child, KK Child, MJ Child, RE Child, SJ Child, WJ Child, DL Childs, RI Childs, PJ Chiles, GD Chillingsworth, CJ Chilton, JL Chilton, BA Chinn, DA Chinn, GE Chinn, JJ Chinner, KL Chinnery, LM Chinnick, PI Chinquan, KG Chipchase, BE Chipman, GE Chipman, JA Chipman, TM Chipman, GA Chippendale, GW Chippindall, AL Chisholm, F Chisholm, GJ Chisholm, GK Chisholm, GS Chisholm, HJ Chisholm, JF Chisholm, JJ Chisholm, NR Chisholm, RE Chisholm, JA Chislett, JF Chisnall, EA Chitham, DR Chitty, GR Chitty, R Chivers, RP Chivers, G Chohan, BW Chong, R Chonka, JW Chopping, MC Chopping, LJ Choppy, DF Choyce, HD Choyce, NJ Choyce, D Chrisp, NL Chrisp, R Christen, DA Christensen, DJ Christensen, DL Christensen, DW Christensen, J Christensen, K Christensen, KJ Christensen, M Christensen, PC Christensen, HG Christgoergl, B Christian, EW Christian, GR Christian, MJ Christian, PE Christian, T Christian, R Christiansen, A Christie, CR Christie, CV Christie, D Christie, DC Christie, DE Christie, DJ Christie, GJ Christie, GP Christie, HS Christie, JDN Christie, L Christie, PB Christie, PG Christie, SL Christie, WD Christie, WJ Christie, RG Christmass, GR Christoffel, LL Christopher, GJ Christopherson, LC Christopherson, P Christopoulos, LM Chromiak, HA Chrust, M Chudiak, B Chudiakow, V Chumak, DF Church, DK Church, EG Church, JM Church, MK Church, RM Church, RW Church, AD Churchett, DH Churchett, DJ Churchill, DW Churchill, PN Churchill, WJ Churchin, WF Churchland, BH Churchley, D Churchley, S Churchyard, AV Ciancio, G Ciantar, VA Ciccolella, MN Cielens, TG Ciesniewski, HJ Ciezak, K Cimdins, JC Cini, JT Cini, R Cinque, JP Cioccarelli, AH Ciotucha, EB Ciracovitch, HF Cislowski, M Cisternino, JW Cizzio, HC Claassen, RJ Clack, RJ Cladingboel, KJ Claffey, PJ Clague, LW Clampett, BF Clancy, BP Clancy, BPJ Clancy, DP Clancy, DR Clancy, JR Clancy, NJ Clancy, PM Clancy, RJ Clancy, BT Clapham, RA Clapham, GW Clapp, WF Clappers, DC Clapperton, PI Clapson, MW Clapton, DP Clare, GA Clare, GJ Clare, JA Clare, NG Clare, NH Clare, CA Clarey, BA Claridge, EV Claridge, A Clark, AD Clark, AH Clark, AJ Clark, AM Clark, BC Clark, BD Clark, BJ Clark, BL Clark, BV Clark, C Clark, CF Clark, CR Clark, DA Clark, DF Clark, DM Clark, DR Clark, FB Clark, FR Clark, G Clark, GA Clark, GC Clark, GD Clark, GH Clark, GJ Clark, GR Clark, GW Clark, GWR Clark, HB Clark, IB Clark, IG Clark, IJ Clark, IM Clark, J Clark, JA Clark, JD Clark, JE Clark, JF Clark, JG Clark, JH Clark, JP Clark, JR Clark, JT Clark, JW Clark, KB Clark, KC Clark, LA Clark, LC Clark, LG Clark, MC Clark, ML Clark, MP Clark, MR Clark, NJ Clark, P Clark, PA Clark, PJ Clark, R Clark, RA Clark, RB Clark, RD Clark, RF Clark, RJ Clark, RN Clark, RP Clark, RS Clark, RSJ Clark, RT Clark, RW Clark, SA Clark, SC Clark, SN Clark, T Clark, TB Clark, TJ Clark, TW Clark, WA Clark, WK Clark, WV Clark, A Clarke, AG Clarke, AJ Clarke, AJB Clarke, AN Clarke, AT Clarke, BH Clarke, BJ Clarke, BJG Clarke, BV Clarke, C Clarke, CA Clarke, CD Clarke, CJ Clarke, CR Clarke, DE Clarke, DJ Clarke, DL Clarke, DT Clarke, EAN Clarke, EG Clarke, EV Clarke, EW Clarke, FH Clarke, FJ Clarke, GA Clarke, GD Clarke, GE Clarke, GG Clarke, GJ Clarke, GK Clarke, GL Clarke, GP Clarke, GR Clarke, GT Clarke, GW Clarke, IR Clarke, J Clarke, JA Clarke, JC Clarke, JE Clarke, JF Clarke, JM Clarke, JP Clarke, JR Clarke, KF Clarke, KJ Clarke, KL Clarke, KR Clarke, KW Clarke, L Clarke, LA Clarke, LHJ Clarke, MG Clarke, MI Clarke, MW Clarke, N Clarke, P Clarke, PA Clarke, PB Clarke, PC Clarke, PJ Clarke, PM Clarke, PS Clarke, PT Clarke, PW Clarke, RA Clarke, RC Clarke, RD Clarke, RG Clarke, RH Clarke, RJ Clarke, RJH Clarke, RN Clarke, RR Clarke, SJ Clarke, SW Clarke, TE Clarke, TJ Clarke, W Clarke, WA Clarke, WD Clarke, WL Clarke, WM Clarke, AI Clarkson, JP Clarkson, MJ Clarkson, NC Clarkson, PJ Clarkson, RA Clarkson, W Clarkson, HW Clarry, HJ Clarsen, WM Clary, FA Clasie, JR Classon, GJ Claughton, RG Clauscen, RE Clausen, SH Clavan, RA Claxton, RJ Claxton, VL Claxton, PG Clay, CWT Claydon, KP Claydon, MJ Claydon, RF Claydon, WB Claydon, AG Clayton, AJ Clayton, BJ Clayton, FS Clayton, GJ Clayton, GK Clayton, IJ Clayton, JM Clayton, LJ Clayton, MK Clayton, PH Clayton, PJ Clayton, PM Clayton, RA Clayton, RN Clayton, WH Clayton, G Cleak, JA Clear, K Clearihan, BM Cleary, DJ Cleary, GS Cleary, JW Cleary, KJ Cleary, PJ Cleary, RD Cleary, VP Cleary, AR Cleasby, AE Cleasby-Jones, MK Cleave, AM Cleaver, AR Cleaver, BJ Cleaver, MW Cleaver, PM Cleaver, RJ Cleaver, CF Clee, MJ Clee, J Cleere, CW Clegg, NJ Clegg, RE Clegg, VS Clegg, RJ Cleggett, MD Cleland, PJ Cleland, LG Clem, DM Clemens, KA Clemens, AW Clement, JA Clement, BA Clements, BL Clements, IG Clements, JA Clements, JT Clements, KN Clements, PE Clements, PW Clements, RD Clements, SA Clements, PM Clemson, AW Clendinen, JJ Clendinen, PJ Clerk, RW Clewer, T Clewes, BP Clewley, CS Clewley, LJ Clewley, PG Cliff, RW Cliff, LJ Cliffe, JP Cliffe-Hickling, DJ Clifford, LI Clifford, RG Clifford, SR Clifford, TV Clifford, WA Clifford, IW Clift, RJ Clift, C Clifton, CW Clifton, DW Clifton, GA Clifton, J Clifton, K Clifton, KL Clifton, MJ Clifton, PC Clifton, RC Clifton, GJ Clinch, FJ Cline, RN Clinghan, RJ Clink, BJ Clinton, JJ Clinton, GA Clipston, IR Clisdell, PR Clisdell, BF Clissold, HD Clively, NJ Clively, JC Clodd, PJ Clohesy, RJ Cloke, WJ Cloney, BG Close, JG Close, MW Close, PD Close, JA Closter, WE Closter, MF Clothier, MR Clothier, RC Cloudsley, GE Clough, GH Clough, IR Clough, M Clough, RC Clough, RJ Clough, BW Cloughley, BV Clover, PJ Clover, P Clowes, PJ Clowry, CJ Clowser, CL Clues, BR Clugston, B Clulow, RW Clunes, WD Cluney, A Clunies-Ross, JE Cluning, KR Cluning, MC Cluss, AB Clutterbuck, EC Clutterbuck, GA Clyde, IM Clyde, AJ Clyne, AP Clyne, BR Clyne, IN Clyne, PD Clyne, EE Coady, CJ Coakes, CJ Coapesmith, MJ Coastergarton, GL Coat, BC Coates, CJ Coates, DJ Coates, DN Coates, GL Coates, HJ Coates, RA Coates, SG Coates, W Coates, DJ Coats, PH Coats, PJ Coats, AM Cobb, BJ Cobb, CA Cobb, GE Cobb, RC Cobb, LD Cobban, TJ Cobby, BF Coble, JW Coble, ME Coble, B Cochran, DJ Cochran, JD Cochran, PL Cochran, WK Cochran, AS Cochrane, DA Cochrane, DM Cochrane, DR Cochrane, DS Cochrane, GS Cochrane, ID Cochrane, J Cochrane, LA Cochrane, PC Cochrane, PJ Cochrane, RC Cochrane, RM Cochrane, AD Cock, IJ Cock, JR Cock, A Cockburn, T Cockburn, D Cocker, DR Cocker, RM Cocker, SJ Cocker, D Cockerell, G Cockerell, RP Cockerell, RB Cockerill, CD Cocking, D Cocking, R Cocking, CW Cockram, DM Cockram, PJ Cockram, AF Cockroft, RJ Cockroft, HW Cocks, KG Cocks, AT Cocodis, BJ Cody, SJ Cody, BK Coe, DL Coe, GT Coe, IG Coe, JJ Coe, KT Coe, RC Coe, RP Coe, WA Coe, CJ Coelli, PL Coen, MJ Coetzee, LJ Coff, AM Coffey, CS Coffey, DB Coffey, DP Coffey, JP Coffey, M Coffey, MJ Coffey, PA Coffey, RC Coffey, TA Coffey, PPA Cogan, RJ Cogan, AR Coggan, JL Coggan, RH Coggan, LG Coggins, RJ Coggins, RE Coghill, BR Coghlan, DW Coghlan, JA Coghlan, PJ Coghlan, R Coghlan, SG Coghlan, SJ Coghlan, CJR Cogswell, KR Cogzell, AJ Cohen, DB Cohen, GF Cohen, PD Cohen, PN Cohen, RC Cohen, WAR Cohen, EW Coit, RJ Coker, SJ Coker, N Colasante, BJ Colbert, GJ Colbert, GP Colbert, KE Colbert, PK Colbert, TJ Colbert, J Colborne-Veel, DJ Colbran, RN Colburn, SM Colburn, RK Colclough, PJ Coldwell, BL Cole, DA Cole, DB Cole, DJ Cole, FK Cole, FR Cole, G Cole, GF Cole, GM Cole, GT Cole, GW Cole, IR Cole, JF Cole, JW Cole, KJ Cole, KR Cole, LJ Cole, ME Cole, PD Cole, PF Cole, PG Cole, RE Cole, RJ Cole, RR Cole, SH Cole, SJ Cole, SL Cole, TJ Cole, W Cole, WH Cole, RG Colebatch, BE Coleclark, BT Colegate, ML Colegrave, CJV Colelough, PF Colelough, AD Coleman, AJ Coleman, AS Coleman, BC Coleman, CF Coleman, DA Coleman, DF Coleman, DW Coleman, EA Coleman, FG Coleman, GJ Coleman, JH Coleman, JS Coleman, KC Coleman, KRG Coleman, LH Coleman, MW Coleman, N Coleman, NRB Coleman, PM Coleman, R Coleman, RA Coleman, RC Coleman, RJ Coleman, RL Coleman, RR Coleman, WG Coleman, WJ Coleman, M Coleridge, AS Coles, JL Coles, KG Coles, LR Coles, RC Coles, WL Coles, RC Colgrave, NW Collard, RL Collard, RN Collard, WJ Collard, PJ Collas, GB Coller, MA Colles, DS Colless, LA Colless, BJ Collett, GE Collett, GJ Collett, HE Collett, JA Collett, RA Collett, SH Collett, R Collette, SC Colley, WJ Colliar, DR Collie, ME Collie, TM Collie, DA Collier, DJ Collier, JE Collier, N Collier, RD Collier, WJ Collier, DJ Collin, JA Collin, EJ Collings, JR Collings, AB Collins, AD Collins, AE Collins, AJ Collins, AM Collins, AR Collins, AT Collins, B Collins, BA Collins, BG Collins, BH Collins, BJ Collins, BL Collins, BR Collins, CW Collins, DA Collins, DB Collins, DG Collins, DH Collins, DJ Collins, DL Collins, DN Collins, DW Collins, EJ Collins, FJ Collins, G Collins, GA Collins, GG Collins, GJ Collins, GW Collins, IJ Collins, IW Collins, J Collins, JE Collins, JM Collins, JP Collins, K Collins, KB Collins, KC Collins, KD Collins, L Collins, LG Collins, LR Collins, M Collins, MA Collins, MF Collins, MJ Collins, MN Collins,

PFX Collins, PG Collins, PJ Collins, PM Collins, PT Collins, PV Collins, RA Collins, RC Collins, RE Collins, RG Collins, RH Collins, RJ Collins, RM Collins, RS Collins, RT Collins, RW Collins, S Collins, SJ Collins, T Collins, TJ Collins, TK Collins, TP Collins, TW Collins, WJ Collins, WM Collins, C Collinson, RH Collinson, RJ Collinson, PF Collise, B Collison, DJ Collison, IR Collison, MG Collison, CRM Collum, WS Collum, DC Collyer, JJ Collyer, RJ Collyer, CJ Colman, PW Colman, RA Colman, EW Colmer, LR Colmer, PB Coloretti, AB Colquhoun, AC Colquhoun, JF Colquhoun, N Colquhoun, RT Colson, RA Colston, GF Colton, EJ Columbus, JE Colvin, TG Colwill, AJ Colyer, PA Coman, RG Coman, D Combe, DR Combe, EJ Combe, AT Comben, RE Comben, KV Comber, GB Combes, MA Combes, NJ Comenos, GE Comer, RG Comerford, RE Comin, TJ Comini, AD Comley, DJ Commerford, PW Commerford, GA Commisso, KR Commonsfidge, RV Comollatti, J Compe, RJ Compston, KR Compt, KS Comrie, RK Comrie, PR Conabeer, AC Conacher, IF Conaghan, LJ Conaghan, MA Conaghan, MT Conaghan, HT Conant, PJ Conboy, MP Conchie, RL Conde, GJ Condely, GA Conder, DF Condon, DG Condon, GL Condon, ID Condon, JH Condon, MJ Condon, RJ Condon, PM Condrick, WA Conduit, BR Coneybeare, DG Congram, GM Conley, JA Conley, PW Conley, AJ Conlon, NK Conlon, SR Conlon, WS Conlon, BD Connell, BP Connell, DA Connell, DB Connell, EF Connell, EJ Connell, GJ Connell, J Connell, JT Connell, KG Connell, LP Connell, LT Connell, MR Connell, MV Connell, NA Connell, PJ Connell, RE Connell, AH Connellan, JM Connellan, MA Connellan, B Connelly, BW Connelly, CJB Connelly, DK Connelly, JA Connelly, JF Connelly, MP Connelly, PT Connelly, RJ Connelly, WJ Connelly, DR Conner, JR Connery, LJ Connolley, AJ Connolly, DV Connolly, GJ Connolly, GR Connolly, JA Connolly, JM Connolly, MD Connolly, RJ Connolly, SM Connolly, WJ Connolly, A Connor, AS Connor, CFP Connor, CSS Connor, GI Connor, JB Connor, KJ Connor, KR Connor, LP Connor, NR Connor, P Connor, PA Connor, RJ Connor, SR Connor, TA Connor, VP Connor, BJ Connors, CW Connors, GB Connors, KE Connors, M Connors, MP Connors, PA Connors, RF Connors, KC Conole, BH Conradi, PR Conradi, DL Conroy, DP Conroy, IW Conroy, J Conroy, MF Conroy, NP Conroy, PJ Consalvo, L Conserdyne, JB Considine, RE Considine, BC Constable, CL Constable, GA Constable, GW Constable, MJ Constable, RG Constable, RP Constable, WD Constable, GR Constant, DS Constantine, EP Constantine, LH Constantine, C Constantinides, AM Conte, S Contessa, JAP Conti, TC Contor, BJ Convery, PJ Convery, RT Convery, TM Convery, EJ Conway, GD Conway, GJ Conway, JG Conway, KG Conway, LA Conway, LH Conway, PJ Conway, PL Conway, PR Conway, RD Conway, RG Conway, WJ Conway, GC Conyers, RK Coogan, AGH Cook, AJ Cook, AP Cook, AW Cook, BJ Cook, BM Cook, BR Cook, BW Cook, CB Cook, CC Cook, CD Cook, CJ Cook, CW Cook, D Cook, DA Cook, DC Cook, DE Cook, DJ Cook, DN Cook, DR Cook, DW Cook, GA Cook, GJ Cook, GLJ Cook, GR Cook, H Cook, HH Cook, IH Cook, IW Cook, J Cook, JA Cook, JB Cook, JE Cook, JF Cook, JJ Cook, JT Cook, KG Cook, LF Cook, LR Cook, MJ Cook, ML Cook, OJ Cook, PH Cook, RA Cook, RC Cook, RE Cook, RG Cook, RJ Cook, RL Cook, RM Cook, RO Cook, RS Cook, RT Cook, RW Cook, T Cook, TJ Cook, WA Cook, WG Cook, AC Cooke, AG Cooke, AL Cooke, AT Cooke, B Cooke, BL Cooke, DF Cooke, KG Cooke, KJ Cooke, NC Cooke, PJ Cooke, PR Cooke, RA Cooke, RB Cooke, RC Cooke, TH Cooke, RG Cooksley, SBJ Coolahan, CW Coolburra, TL Cooley, HR Cooling, PR Coombe, WB Coombe, JR Coomber, AK Coombes, IC Coombes, RJ Coombes, RS Coombes, TW Coombes, TH Coombley, BD Coombs, CH Coombs, FG Coombs, GA Coombs, GJ Coombs, JD Coombs, JH Coombs, R Coombs, RJ Coon, BC Cooney, MJ Cooney, WJ Cooney, AF Cooper, AJ Cooper, AN Cooper, AR Cooper, BA Cooper, BC Cooper, BF Cooper, BH Cooper, BJ Cooper, BL Cooper, BN Cooper, CA Cooper, CD Cooper, CW Cooper, D Cooper, DC Cooper, DJ Cooper, DN Cooper, DW Cooper, EB Cooper, GA Cooper, GM Cooper, GN Cooper, GP Cooper, GT Cooper, GW Cooper, I Cooper, ID Cooper, JA Cooper, JC Cooper, JE Cooper, JF Cooper, JM Cooper, JR Cooper, JW Cooper, KC Cooper, KD Cooper, KE Cooper, KFW Cooper, KJ Cooper, KW Cooper, LA Cooper, LE Cooper, LF Cooper, LJ Cooper, M Cooper, MN Cooper, MR Cooper, MS Cooper, NE Cooper, NH Cooper, NM Cooper, NW Cooper, PB Cooper, PC Cooper, PD Cooper, PJ Cooper, R Cooper, RC Cooper, RG Cooper, RJC Cooper, RL Cooper, RR Cooper, SG Cooper, SJ Cooper, SR Cooper, T Cooper, TP Cooper, WA Cooper, WAE Cooper, WD Cooper, WH Cooper, WJ Cooper, WW Cooper, GE Coops, JJ Coorey, JP Coort, KA Coote, RC Coote, SW Coote, TM Coote, TR Cootes, GF Copas, RA Cope, WR Cope, AS Copeland, HB Copeland, MJ Copeland, NJH Copeland, RB Copeland, JVE Copeman, RJ Copeman, G Copley, KJ Copley, L Copley, RJ Copley, DR Copp, WT Coppin, JC Coppleman, PG Coppleman, PA Coppock, MJ Coppola, RM Corban, D Corbett, EJ Corbett, GC Corbett, IL Corbett, JA Corbett, JD Corbett, KG Corbett, KJ Corbett, WJ Corbett, RJ Corbey, GA Corbin, AJ Corboy, DW Corboy, KM Corby, LG Corby, PS Corby, RJ Corby, WC Corby, AT Corcoran, BM Corcoran, JF Corcoran, TL Corcoran, WJ Corcoran, RD Cordell, GJ Corderoy, CL Cordery, D Cordier, JF Cordrey, RB Cordwell, VP Cordwell, AG Cordy, GE Cordy, GT Core, KE Core, PJ Core, GC Coret, KB Coridas, BJ Cork, WG Corker, BJ Corkeron, MJ Corkeron, MA Corkery, M Corkhill, JC Corkran, JG Corless, S Corlett, GP Corlis, NJ Cormack, PM Cormack, AR Cornelius, TC Cornelius, KT Corneliusen, CA Cornell, DG Cornell, EG Cornell, IM Cornell, JS Cornell, OM Cornell, WA Cornell, GS Cornes, EJ Cornford, WF Cornford, BL Cornish, CB Cornish, G Cornish, PD Cornish, PJ Cornish, PR Cornish, RJ Cornish, RS Cornish, WG Cornish, DW Cornock, MJ Cornock, GD Cornwall, GL Cornwill, AJ Corones, GA Corr, RC Corran, BW Corric, LL Corrie, ES Corrigan, F Corrigan, MW Corrin, OFM Corry, RJ Corry, RN Corry, B Corse, CS Corser, EL Corser, BF Cory, DM Cosgriff, AJ Cosgrove, B Cosgrove, C Cosgrove, DA Cosgrove, DG Cosgrove, GM Cosgrove, OJ Cosgrove, PJ Cosgrove, TM Cosgrove, VJ Cosgrove, PR Cosh, RY Coshott, R Cosier, G Cosis, BW Cossar, APF Cossardeaux, GD Cossey, JH Cosstick, GD Costa, LP Costa, PJ Costa, TJ Costa, BJ Costello, GJ Costello, JF Costello, JJ Costello, P Costello, PW Costello, RJ Costello, KJ Costelloe, SR Costelow, NC Coster, DJ Costigan, GS Costin, R Costmeyer, RK Costolloe, PJ Cotchett, HB Cother, GA Cottam, KE Cottam, WA Cottam, RM Cottee, W Cottee, GA Cotter, JR Cotter, JS Cotter, JW Cotter, KE Cotter, MD Cotter, MH Cotter, MJ Cotter, PJ Cotter, PL Cotter, AJ Cotterell, FF Cotterell, JJ Cotterell, AJ Cotterill, GC Cotterill, AD Cottier, DG Cottingham, TC Cottingham, GG Cottle, JS Cottom, BG Cotton, IS Cotton, JE Cotton, JW Cotton, RW Cotton, GJ Cottrell, JW Cottrell, EJ Cottrill, RW Couacaud, NF Couch, PE Couchman, WK Couchman, RW Coughlan, WM Coughlan, AJ Coughlin, JE Coughlin, MJ Coughlin, NTE Coughlin, WJ Coughlin, RA Coughran, TE Coulcher, GD Couley, DC Coulson, DJ Coulson, JC Coulson, KJ Coulson, MW Coulson, BJ Coulter, ER Coulter, GD Coulter, JH Coulter, NB Coulter, NJ Coulter, TJ Coulter, BC Coulton, MR Counsell, MA Count, BF Coupe, AB Couper, HJ Couper, JG Couper, JK Couper, MS Couper, RA Couper, RF Couper, RK Couper, GL Coupland, WG Coupland, AJ Court, GJ Court, RJ Court, RW Court, CE Courtney, CJ Courtney, PJ Courtney, WL Courtney, D Cousins, GL Cousins, JR Cousins, KL Cousins, PC Cousins, RA Cousins, RJ Cousins, DF Coustley, DK Couston, BA Coutman, RDP Couttie, AP Coutts, AW Coutts, GIG Coutts, JR Coutts, MA Coutts, TJ Coutts, TP Coutts, DG Couzens, WR Cove, LW Covell, DL Coventry, MD Coventry, RD Coventry, RE Coventry, AD Covey, LW Covill, BW Cowan, CG Cowan, CJ Cowan, CL Cowan, G Cowan, J Cowan, JM Cowan, LRJ Cowan, LT Cowan, PG Cowan, PM Cowan, RC Cowan, VG Cowan, WR Cowan, BC Coward, BM Coward, JH Coward, TC Cowburn, DT Cowdrey, MJ Cowdroy, BA Cowell, BE Cowell, EC Cowell, JH Cowell, LL Cowell, MG Cowell, NH Cowell, RJ Cowell, CW Cowen, DG Cowen, FN Cowen, GJ Cowen, JC Cowen, JJ Cowen, WS Cowen, WW Cowie, AB Cowin, JD Cowin, RD Cowles, IS Cowley, PJ Cowley, RE Cowley, TW Cowley, BS Cowling, DC Cowling, DE Cowling, LE Cowling, PM Cowling, LG Cownie, DP Cowper, JG Cowper, AJ Cox, AR Cox, AS Cox, BA Cox, BD Cox, BH Cox, BJ Cox, BW Cox, CJ Cox, CR Cox, DF Cox, DG Cox, DJ Cox, DL Cox, EA Cox, EV Cox, GAK Cox, GD Cox, GE Cox, GJ Cox, GM Cox, GN Cox, GR Cox, I Cox, IC Cox, IW Cox, JA Cox, JC Cox, JG Cox, KJ Cox, KP Cox, LC Cox, LJ Cox, LM Cox, LP Cox, LW Cox, M Cox, MG Cox, MH Cox, MM Cox, MW Cox, NJ Cox, PD Cox, PJ Cox, PM Cox, PR Cox, R Cox, RA Cox, RC Cox, RD Cox, RJ Cox, SV Cox, TJ Cox, WA Cox, WE Cox, WF Cox, WJ Cox, WP Cox, DF Coxhead, LH Coxhill, RE Coxon, RF Coxon, ED Coy, JP Coy, VP Coy, AJ Coyle, AW Coyle, BA Coyle, MA Coyle, TT Coyle, B Coyne, JT Coyne, KA Coyne, KP Coyte, AA Crabb, JSL Crabb, NE Crabb, RAM Crabb, SNR Crabb, GK Crabbe, JRS Crabbe, TB Crabtree, G Crack, J Cracknell, PD Craddock, CH Craddon, LE Cradock, IR Craft, GD Cragan, MG Craib, PW Craib, AD Craig, AG Craig, AGH Craig, AM Craig, AR Craig, CF Craig, EG Craig, GR Craig, GW Craig, IW Craig, JD Craig, KJ Craig, LD Craig, LW Craig, MD Craig, MJ Craig, P Craig, PJ Craig, RC Craig, SJ Craig, TC Craig, TH Craig, WP Craig, TJ Craike, RW Crain, WT Cram, TR Crammond, HB Cramp, J Cramp, PN Cramp, P Crampton, BF Crane, GM Crane, JF Crane, JJ Crane, KL Crane, MJ Crane, N Crane, OJ Crane, PM Crane, RA Crane, RB Crane, RJJ Crane, RK Crane, SR Crane, JT Cranfield, IP Crangle, DG Crank, DT Cranmer, RG Cranna, RJ Cranney, AN Cranston, EH Cranston, JA Cranston, MB Cranston, WD Cranston, BTP Cranwell, IJ Cranwell, GJ Crapp, WR Crapp, CW Crapper, KG Crase, JA Craufurd, B Craven, GA Craven, KR Craven, RJ Craven, NN Craven-Griffiths, CJ Cravino, PI Craw, AP Crawford, AR Crawford, BM Crawford, C Crawford, DK Crawford, DL Crawford, FW Crawford, GH Crawford, IC Crawford, JA Crawford, KJ Crawford, MA Crawford, MC Crawford, MJ Crawford, NL Crawford, PA Crawford, PG Crawford, RA Crawford, RB Crawford, RG Crawford, RI Crawford, RJ Crawford, RR Crawford, TC Crawford, MJ Crawley, RB Crawshay, ME Craze, RJ Creagh, V Creagh, MA Creamer, JL Creasey, JR Creber, AM Credlin, DJ Cree, L Creece, JH Creed, PD Creedon, P Creedy, EA Creegan, DC Creek, GM Creek, RJ Creek, RN Creek, IJ Creelman, RJ Creelman, PR Crees, P Creevey, RJ Creevey, DB Creighton, IJ Creighton, MM Creighton, RW Crelley, NJ Crellin, RJ Crellin, N Cremen, AE Cremer, HJ Cremin, MW Cremin, DJ Crennan, KN Crerar, T Cresdee, J Cressey, RJ Cresswell, W Cressy, L Crestani, CO Creswell, JA Creswell, A Creswick-Jackson, JE Creusot, BW Crew, PA Crew, RG Crew, RJ Crewe, WJ Crews, BJ Cribb, DG Cribb, MS Cribb, WJ Cribbes, BW Cribbs, JL Crichton, LE Crichton, GC Crick, GG Crick, GR Cridge, GA Crighton, WW Crighton, DJ Crilley, PV Crilley, DM Crimmins, DA Cripps, RR Cripps, AP Crisp, BW Crisp, DM Crisp, HM Crisp, IS Crisp, KL Crisp, PM Crisp, RJ Criss, DG Critchley, DL Critchley, B Critchlow, R Critchlow, MC Crittenden, M Crnkovic, RG Croall, CW Crocker, DW Crocker, EJ Crocker, GV Crocker, J Crocker, JA Crocker, JF Crocker, JJ Crocker, JK Crocker, DN Crockett, MJ Crockett, PW Crockett, VB Crockett, CT Croese, BW Crofft, CR Croft, DA Croft, DR Croft, JF Croft, RF Croft, RW Croft, AT Crofts, PV Crofts, PJ Croke, PT Croke, MH Croker, NA Croker, PA Croker, PJ Croker, TJ Croker, H Cromar, LA Cromarty, NB Cromarty, RC Cromarty, DJ Cromb, JA Cromb, WH Crombie, T Cromie, DH Crompton, DJR Crompton, DN Crompton, IV Crompton, LR Crompton, FT Cron, FC Cronin, JE Cronin, NT Cronin, RE Cronin, AJ Crook, BG Crook, CD Crook, CT Crook, DW Crook, G Crook, IW Crook, J Crook, JR Crook, KT Crook, PC Crook, PL Crook, BG Crooks, D Crooks, EG Crooks, W Crooks, HJ Crosbie, MJ Crosbie, WA Crosbie, AD Crosby, RA Crosby, REJ Crosby, WJ Crosby, FD Crosdale, JL Crosling, AC Cross, AJ Cross, BJ Cross, CD Cross, DA Cross, FJ Cross, GL Cross, GR Cross, GT Cross, JA Cross, JD Cross, JE Cross, JL Cross, KE Cross, MG Cross, PF Cross, PS Cross, RA Cross, RG Cross, RP Cross, TE Cross, TH Cross, WD Cross, WH Cross, WL Cross, WR Cross, WV Cross, JD Crossan, NT Crossett, DA Crossfield, FR Crossingham, PA Crossingham, A Crossley, JK Crossley, LW Crossley, PS Crossley, RH Crossley, WM Crossley, BD Crossman, DK Crossman, JF Crossman, TJ Crossman, DA Crosthwaite, IP Crosthwaite, RC Crosthwaite, RD Crosthwaite, WR Croston, IH Crothers, RA Crothers, RW Crothers, TA Croton, IR Crotty, KG Crotty, LR Crotty,

PB Crotty, SL Crotty, DL Crouch, GR Crouch, KA Crouch, KJ Crouch, NV Crouch, PD Crouch, RC Crouch, RD Crouch, RJ Crouch, WE Crouch, DA Croucher, PJ Croucher, PJ Crough, RJ Crough, JE Crow, JM Crow, WP Crow, AT Crowe, BJ Crowe, BR Crowe, DB Crowe, DJ Crowe, EJ Crowe, FX Crowe, GL Crowe, GW Crowe, LS Crowe, PP Crowe, RG Crowe, WA Crowe, RF Crowell, GF Crowhurst, TS Crowhurst, BJ Crowley, BS Crowley, GA Crowley, JP Crowley, KJ Crowley, LP Crowley, P Crowley, WC Crowley, WD Crowley, GK Crowther, GV Crowther, JA Crowther, JB Crowther, JF Crowther, RD Crowther, T Crowther, WD Crowther, JF Croxford, GJ Croyden, GJ Croydon, JA Croymans, GA Crozier, LG Cruckshank, DM Cruden, F Cruden, EJ Cruickshank, JA Cruickshank, JJ Cruickshank, JL Cruickshank, BJ Cruickshanks, RK Cruickshanks, BJ Cruikshank, RN Crum, AR Crummer, T Crummey, AK Crump, PL Crump, RS Crump, AJ Crumpton, JD Crundall, DW Cruse, GP Cruse, RJ Cruse, TA Cruse, JT Crust, LJ Crutchfield, DA Crute, FH Cruwys, WR Cruwys, J Cruz, BR Cryer, AF Crynes, W Crystal, L Csibi, A Csivincsik, JA Csorba, PT Cubbin, SA Cubillo, RM Cubis, MJ Cubit, NW Cubit, RJ Cubitt, WD Cubitt, RJ Cuddihy, DH Cudmore, GA Cudmore, WJ Culbertson, LN Culbong, PB Culey, A Culham, PD Culhane, AJ Culkin, BR Cullam, AG Cullen, B Cullen, BT Cullen, DJ Cullen, GH Cullen, GJ Cullen, GT Cullen, GW Cullen, IRE Cullen, JA Cullen, JF Cullen, KJ Cullen, KM Cullen, LP Cullen, MB Cullen, NJ Cullen, RJ Cullen, RT Cullen, TB Cullen, TK Cullen, WF Cullen, J Cullens, MJ Culley, TW Culley, RSW Culliford, MJ Cullinan, BL Culling, A Cullino, F Cullum, JF Cully, PF Culnane, A Culph, EJ Culpitt, RD Culton, JG Cumbrae-Stewart, BA Cumine, BS Cumming, K Cumming, KW Cumming, NG Cumming, BK Cummings, CM Cummings, CR Cummings, HJ Cummings, PG Cummings, RP Cummings, WE Cummings, AJ Cummins, BF Cummins, GP Cummins, JW Cummins, LM Cummins, RJ Cummins, DB Cumner, RF Cumper, GR Cuneo, KW Cuneo, TJ Cunich, PF Cunliffe, WA Cunliffe, MP Cunnane, JM Cunneen, LP Cunneen, WJ Cunneen, AB Cunningham, AG Cunningham, AJ Cunningham, AM Cunningham, BE Cunningham, BG Cunningham, BP Cunningham, BR Cunningham, DP Cunningham, DWT Cunningham, FW Cunningham, GD Cunningham, GE Cunningham, GJ Cunningham, GL Cunningham, GRD Cunningham, H Cunningham, JP Cunningham, PC Cunningham, PH Cunningham, R Cunningham, RJ Cunningham, W Cunningham, WN Cunningham, DA Cunnington, JE Cunnington, PJ Cunnington, EW Cupitt, KH Cupitt, MT Cupitt, RI Cupitt, KK Cupples, NL Curby, G Curcuruto, LG Curd, ML Curley, PR Curley, SN Curley, TC Curley, TL Curley, TM Curley, DK Curnoe, DJ Curnow, FS Curnow, MD Curnow, MJ Curnow, EH Curphey, F Curphey, RJ Curphey, PN Curr, RW Currall, CB Curran, CJP Curran, DJ Curran, DR Curran, MH Curran, NS Curran, PB Curran, PJ Curran, RB Curran, RJ Curran, TS Curran, VB Curran, SJ Currell, DA Currey, IC Currey, TJ Currey, DR Currie, GJ Currie, JA Currie, JG Currie, MD Currie, NB Currie, RC Currie, TA Currie, TG Currin, AR Curry, MJ Curry, RJ Curry, WJ Curry, AJ Curtain, AT Curtain, PD Curtain, BL Curtin, JB Curtin, JP Curtin, RW Curtin, TJ Curtin, AA Curtis, AJ Curtis, AK Curtis, CH Curtis, DC Curtis, DG Curtis, DL Curtis, FJ Curtis, GB Curtis, GE Curtis, HC Curtis, JA Curtis, JN Curtis, JW Curtis, KJ Curtis, KV Curtis, MJ Curtis, MK Curtis, RF Curtis, RG Curtis, RJ Curtis, RS Curtis, RW Curtis, TJ Curtis, TR Curtis, WJC Curtis, GH Cusack, GK Cusack, IN Cusack, OJ Cusack, PJ Cusack, RJ Cusack, DA Cush, NP Cush, BA Cushing, BM Cushing, GJ Cuskelly, KJ Cuskelly, CJ Cust, JS Custance, MS Custance, JL Cutbush, TJ Cutcliffe, CJ Cuthbert, DC Cuthbert, NP Cuthbert, KJ Cuthbertson, PF Cuthbertson, LK Cutler, RA Cutler, RC Cutler, RR Cutler, WL Cutler, WR Cutler, A Cutmore, AJ Cutmore, AE Cutten, GB Cutter, AW Cutting, GI Cutting, BR Cutts, JR Cuzens, RG Cuzzubbo, CJ Cybulski, GL Cybulski, W Cyc, EC Cymbalak, ZJ Czapracki, V Czerepaszenko, ES Czerwinski, BT Czislowski, GS Czislowski, JM Da Costa, GV Da Silveira, S Daanen, RB Dabinett, P Dabnor, CR Dacey, PA Dacey, RJ Dacey, MG Dachs, D Dacre, IN Dadd, MJ Dadd, NA Daddow, GC Dadds, R Dadds, GA Dadson, P Daff, JC Daffy, WJ Daffy, V Dagata, MF Dagge, PJ Dahl, RJ Dahl, MC Dahler, TJ Dahler, C Dahl-Helm, MH Dahl-Helm, HJ Dainton, RH Dakers, DK Dakin, RE Dakin, AM Dakos, BW Dalby, BH Dale, BW Dale, KTV Dale, M Dale, PR Dale, RA Dale, RG Dale, T Dale, VC Dale, I Dales, BJ Daley, DJ Daley, EG Daley, EN Daley, ET Daley, GB Daley, JE Daley, JP Daley, K Daley, KJ Daley, M Daley, NF Daley, PF Daley, R Daley, WPN Daley, AR Dalgairns, DR Dalgairns, BA Dalgleish, WD Dalgleish, PT Dalgrin, C Dalino, T Dalitz, WP Dallas, F Dallasanta, RJ Dallaway, HR Dalley, J Dalley, RG Dalley, JH Dallimore, RJ Dally-Watkins, RJ Dally, SG Dally, PJ Dalmau, ML Dalterio, AK Dalton, DC Dalton, DJ Dalton, HT D'Alton, JM Dalton, LF D'Alton, LW Dalton, MB Dalton, MG Dalton, NP Dalton, PJ Dalton, RA Dalton, BD Daly, BJ Daly, BM Daly, BP Daly, DM Daly, EH Daly, EI Daly, G Daly, GA Daly, GC Daly, GJ Daly, GP Daly, JJ Daly, JK Daly, JP Daly, KF Daly, KJ Daly, LJ Daly, ME Daly, MJ Daly, NG Daly, RE Daly, RM Daly, SN Daly, TF Daly, TJ Daly, K Dalzell, GL Dalziel, GJ Damm, KP Damm, W Damsma, DO Danaher, PM Danaher, WJ Danaher, F Danby, J Danby, TJ Dancer, VC Dand, B Dando, MK Dando, RM Dando, RD Dangaard, S Dangelo, TC Danger, CD Dangerfield, WV Dangerfield, BL Daniel, BRC Daniel, DJ Daniel, IC Daniel, RA Daniel, WC Daniel, J Daniell, AJ Daniels, BR Daniels, GS Daniels, GW Daniels, LW Daniels, NJ Daniels, NT Daniels, PJ Daniels, RA Daniels, RR Daniels, RT Daniels, T Daniels, WB Daniels, A Danilenko, V Danko, MG Danks, DW Dann, HR Dann, IR Dann, J Dann, KG Dann, NJB Danne, CW Dans, DG Dans, FL Dans, JE Danskin, GH D'Antoine, J Danyluk, BJ Daphne, GJ Dapiran, J Darby, NR Darby, PF Darby, RR Darby, GP Darcy, HT Darcy, LA Darcy, LC Darcy, LG D'Arcy, MB D'Arcy, PD D'Arcy, RE D'Arcy, RJ Darcy, WF D'Arcy, DL Dare, EW Dare, KH Dare, PM Dare, RA Dare, RR Dare, RL Dargavel, RJ Darge, WJ Dark, MJ Darkin, GJ Darley, KJ Darling, LR Darling, DJ Darlington, GJ Darlington, GR Darlington, IG Darlington, JR Darlington, LW Darlington, RJ Darlington, WM Darmanin, MJ Darmody, JW Darney, SJ Daros, BD Darr, WW Darr, MD Darragh, RC Darragh, GLG Darrall, J Darren, JD Darrington, RK Darrington, GK Dart, JN Dart, JR Dart, MF Dart, PB Dart, RM Dart, TL Dart, GJ Dartnell, CB Darts, RJ Dash, PS Dass, PV Dass, GJW Date, RD Date, WC Date, KW Datson, A Daubaras, WFR Dauk, GF Daunt, GJ Daunt, GA Daven, JBS Davenport, LA Davenport, P Davenport, R Davenport, RG Davenport, TJ Davern, AR Davey, BP Davey, BR Davey, DJ Davey, DW Davey, GJ Davey, J Davey, JS Davey, MJ Davey, PR Davey, PV Davey, RA Davey, RF Davey, RJ Davey, WS Davey, PH David, AR Davidson, BN Davidson, BR Davidson, BW Davidson, CR Davidson, DF Davidson, DJ Davidson, DM Davidson, EV Davidson, G Davidson, GE Davidson, GJ Davidson, HJH Davidson, J Davidson, JF Davidson, JG Davidson, JM Davidson, JS Davidson, JW Davidson, KF Davidson, L Davidson, MA Davidson, MC Davidson, MD Davidson, NT Davidson, PW Davidson, RB Davidson, RW Davidson, SR Davidson, T Davidson, TJ Davidson, DR Davie, JF Davie, RG Davie, A Davies, B Davies, CJ Davies, DW Davies, EH Davies, EK Davies, EW Davies, GA Davies, GC Davies, GR Davies, GRH Davies, HT Davies, IR Davies, IT Davies, J Davies, JC Davies, JE Davies, JH Davies, JM Davies, JN Davies, JR Davies, JS Davies, JW Davies, KG Davies, KGT Davies, KJ Davies, M Davies, MF Davies, P Davies, PS Davies, RA Davies, RD Davies, RE Davies, RG Davies, RH Davies, RJ Davies, RN Davies, RW Davies, TD Davies, TF Davies, W Davies, WA Davies, WG Davies, WJ Davies, WL Davies, WS Davies, DC Daviescolgate, AB Davis, AJ Davis, AR Davis, AS Davis, BA Davis, BE Davis, BF Davis, BJ Davis, BL Davis, C Davis, CB Davis, CC Davis, DC Davis, DG Davis, DJ Davis, DWP Davis, EB Davis, EW Davis, FG Davis, GC Davis, GE Davis, GJ Davis, GK Davis, GL Davis, GR Davis, GS Davis, GW Davis, HJ Davis, HK Davis, IF Davis, J Davis, JE Davis, JH Davis, JJ Davis, JK Davis, JL Davis, JM Davis, JR Davis, K Davis, KC Davis, KF Davis, KG Davis, KK Davis, KR Davis, LC Davis, LJ Davis, LK Davis, LM Davis, LR Davis, LW Davis, M Davis, MA Davis, MJ Davis, MS Davis, MT Davis, N Davis, NC Davis, NH Davis, NPA Davis, NR Davis, OL Davis, PA Davis, PC Davis, PH Davis, PJ Davis, PR Davis, PT Davis, RB Davis, RF Davis, RG Davis, RJ Davis, RK Davis, RL Davis, RN Davis, RP Davis, RW Davis, SG Davis, SJ Davis, TG Davis, TJ Davis, VW Davis, W Davis, WB Davis, WR Davis, A Davison, GH Davison, GI Davison, JP Davison, KJ Davison, M Davison, PA Davison, PO Davison, PR Davison, RA Davison, TW Davison, WA Davison, WJ Davison, DP Davoren, PJ Davoren, PJ Davy, W Davy, G Daw, MG Daw, NL Daw, LS Dawber, NR Dawe, PV Dawe, AJ Dawes, AM Dawes, DD Dawes, GN Dawes, PWS Dawes, RE Dawes, RN Dawes, JM Dawidowicz, AJJ Dawkins, JA Dawkins, M Dawkins, AG Dawson, BH Dawson, BL Dawson, CE Dawson, CJ Dawson, CR Dawson, DA Dawson, DB Dawson, DS Dawson, FR Dawson, GH Dawson, GK Dawson, GL Dawson, GV Dawson, GW Dawson, IK Dawson, JA Dawson, JF Dawson, KA Dawson, LB Dawson, MB Dawson, MC Dawson, MG Dawson, MJ Dawson, MR Dawson, P Dawson, PD Dawson, PE Dawson, PR Dawson, RC Dawson, RI Dawson, RJ Dawson, TA Dawson, TE Dawson, TM Dawson, A Day, BR Day, CJ Day, DC Day, DR Day, GC Day, GG Day, GJ Day, HT Day, JM Day, JR Day, KR Day, KW Day, LA Day, LG Day, LT Day, MJ Day, P Day, PJ Day, PL Day, PR Day, RB Day, RC Day, RE Day, RG Day, RJ Day, RL Day, RM Day, AE Dayas, RG Dayhew, JD Dayman, PR Daymond, KJ Dayton, M Dazkiw, FD Dcosta, WG De Mamiel, C De Ridder, LM De Bari, R De Boer, JPA De Bont, A De Catania, RA De Gabriele, SA De Gabrielle, RW De Gray, AW De Greef, JJ De Guara, RA De Haas, DV De Heer, LWA De Jong, PJ De Jong, WJ De Jong, CG De Jussing, J De Kaste, NF De La Hunty, NR De La Motte, NW De La Rue, PB De Launay, U De Longis, PG De Masson, AW De Niet, RG De Pasquale, PRG De Pierres, PD De Renzy, MA De Ridder, DG De Somer, ML De Souza, TJ De Vries Van Leeuwen, AA De Weger, GS Deacon, KJ Deacon, KM Deacon, R Deacon, RM Deacon, RS Deacon, SJ Deacon, PJ Deagan, MGJ Deak, AC Deakin, TJ Deally, PL Dealy, A Dean, AA Dean, AL Dean, AM Dean, BJ Dean, CJ Dean, DA Dean, DJ Dean, DW Dean, EM Dean, FW Dean, GJ Dean, J Dean, JC Dean, JD Dean, JE Dean, JJ Dean, KL Dean, L Dean, LJ Dean, MH Dean, P Dean, PG Dean, RB Dean, RG Dean, RJ Dean, RK Dean, RM Dean, TM Dean, EL Deane, F Deane, FW Deane, LJ Deane, TH Deane, WR Deane, JH Deane-Butcher, C Deans, WLG Deanshaw, AF Deany, MP Dear, CD Dearling, RE Deas, AG Death, FT Death, DJ Deathe, KW Deavin, DR Debeen, JH Debelle, BV Debomford, AJ Debont, JA Debreceny, D Decarli, JC Decharmoy, TG Dechaufepie, KR Declerck, GN Declosey, PF Decure, J Dedman, BJ Dee, BR Dee, GC Dee, D Deebank, LJ Deeble, BW Deed, R Deed, RJP Deed, IM Deegan, RW Deegan, JW Deelen, GP Deem, RP Deem, JV Deen, PF Deeran, GI Defaveri, BMP Defreitas, PT Degaris, GF Degering, JJ Degering, P Degiorgio, GJ Degrassi, PC Degroot, RJ Degroot, NS Degrussa, GE Deguet, RJ Dehle, DCJ Deighton, HJ Deighton, JPA Deighton, PJ Deimos, PB Dejersey, HP Dejong, A Dekaste, GC Dekker, JN Dekker, RM Dekok, JJ Delacey, RR Delaforce, WH Delaforce, JL Delahunty, MP Delahunty, RL Delaland, AT Delaney, BJ Delaney, J Delaney, JP Delaney, MJ Delaney, RJ Delaney, RL Delaney, KR Delany, RJ Delarue, CF Delbridge, GC Delcourt, A Deleeuw, PC Delforce, I Delfos, BJ Delgado, V Delgado, P Delhaas, AR Dell, DH Dell, EJ Dell, L Dell, RH Dell, DJ Della Mora, JV Dellaca, BL Dellar, AA Dellasantina, AR Deller, BD Deller, LR Dellit, R Dellit, JK Dellow, BC Delmas, KW Delofski, GP Deloryn, PB Deloryn, PH Delph, BR Delsar, AP Deluca, GK Delves, P Delyster, DM Delzoppo, D Demarchi, S Dembowski, J Demczuk, PM Demerlo, E Demestichas, JG Demetrovics, JR Demmery, EE Demmler, NW Demorton, GW Dempsey, JP Dempsey, MJ Dempsey, PC Dempsey, RG Dempsey, B Dempster, QE Dempster, WH Dempster, J Den Besten, L Den Hoedt, AA Denbigh, MA Dench, PR Dencher, NJ Dendle, DJ Denehey, WH Denford, PJ Dengate, CR Denham, NR Denham, RL Denham, RC Denholm, RS Dening, JA Denison, M Denison, F Denley, MV Denley, AH Denman, KL Denman, RJ Denman, GRA Denmeade, KJ Denmeade, WG Denne, RA Dennehy, LM Denneman, RL Denner, F Dennert, LJ Dennert, RC Dennett, AJ Denney, DG Denning, GL Denning, J Denning, A Dennis, AJ Dennis, AM Dennis, BE Dennis, BW Dennis, CB Dennis, DC Dennis, DJ Dennis, FN Dennis, GR Dennis, GW Dennis, HE Dennis, JD Dennis, JJ Dennis, LT Dennis, REJ Dennis, RJ Dennis, RL Dennis, RS Dennis, WW Dennis, CF Dennison, LR Denniss, WT Denny, JA Densley, LG Densten, GH Dent, RJ Dent, RR Dent, KO Dentith, BM Denton, CM Denton, PS Denton, RW Denton, ADG Denvil, OG Denys, P Denysiuk, TW Denzel,

GT Depiazzi, J Derbyshire, WP Derdowski, R Dere, PE Deres, V Derewianka, JP Derksen, CD Dermody, JG Dermody, WH Dermody, CJ Derrick, EBD Derrick, PT Derrick, TF Derrick, GF Derry, NW Derry, GJ Desantis, EL Desfontaines, JE Deshon, JE Deshong, GW Desmet, PJ Desmond, JN Desnica, JW Desnoy, AP Dessaix, PJ Dessent, RH Detering, DA Detloff, GW Detmar, PH Dettmann, R Dettmer, JF Deturt, RA Devaise, DS Devantier, SR Devenish, GA Devenny, GE Devenport, RR Devenport, AJ Dever, KL Dever, R Devere, NJ Devereux, RJ Devereux, RM Devers, RN Devers, ME Devery, IE Deveson, JF Deveson, ME Deveson, AL Devine, DJ Devine, HJ Devine, JE Devine, JP Devine, KH Devine, PB Devine, PF Devine, PJ Devine, PK Devine, RG Devine, RJ Devine, RT Devine, TP Devine, WP Devine, RA Devink, JH Devitt, RJ Devitt, BK Devlin, FC Devlin, KJ Devlin, SL Devlin, BJ Devos, GA Devries, RG Devries, RTC Devries, PJ Dew, AR Dewar, B Dewar, JD Dewar, JM Dewar, JS Dewar, KI Dewar, TE Dewar, TM Dewar, RF Dewhurst, GS Dewick, JC Dewing, RA Dewing, L Dewitte, PH Deworboies, RG Dewsbery, LB Dewsnap, K Dexter, JCE Dey, JG Dey, JD Deykin, S Dezso, AS D'hage, RA Dhu, RM Dhu, DT Dial, JD Dial, JT Dial, RA Dial, BJ Diamond, EJ Diamond, GW Diamond, PC Diamond, PL Diamond, JE Dibb, TE Dibben, CR Dibden, TE Dibdin, GA Dibley, NH Dibley, AC Dick, BJ Dick, BT Dick, CM Dick, D Dick, DWR Dick, GA Dick, GC Dick, GD Dick, PC Dick, PF Dick, PW Dick, WA Dick, LI Dicken, AC Dickens, RB Dickens, DT Dicker, GJ Dicker, RA Dicker, WA Dickerson, MJ Dickeson, RL Dickeson, WS Dickey, MK Dickfos, AJ Dickinson, EJ Dickinson, JW Dickinson, KJ Dickinson, RG Dickinson, W Dickinson, W Dickinson, JSP Dickman, LT Dickman, RJ Dickman, DR Dicks, AJ Dickson, CG Dickson, DW Dickson, GJ Dickson, GRC Dickson, JS Dickson, KL Dickson, MJ Dickson, ML Dickson, ND Dickson, NJ Dickson, NR Dickson, PG Dickson, PL Dickson, SG Dickson, SW Dickson, TAS Dickson, RA Dickson-Battye, MK Dicton, PF Diddams, JV Didsman, LO Didsman, MH Didsman, RL Diebert, BEL Diehl, RA Diener, LJ Dienhoff, M Diepenbroek, R Diflorio, RD Digance, JW Digby, RJ Diggens, J Diggins, IJ Diggle, HM Dighton, T Digiovanni, GC Dignam, JF Digweed, RJ Dihm, R Dikes, HJ Dikkenberg, D Diklich, BW Dillon, DL Dillon, DR Dillon, HF Dillon, KE Dillon, KL Dillon, PR Dillon, RM Dillon, T Dillon, TJ Dillon, RE Dillow, G Dimasi, A Dimitrijevic, RW Dimmack, IL Dimmock, ID Dimond, RWL Dimond, WR Dineen, LT Dingle, NT Dingle, SG Dingle, RD Dingley, DB Dingwall, J Dingwall, NJ Dingwall, PM Dinham, TE Dinneen, C Dinoto, GR Dinte, W Dinys, A Dionysius, AL Dipede, L Dippel, N Dippel, VG Dipper, BE Diprose, KW Diprose, P Diprose, GJ Direen, RG Direen, RJ Direen, K Disbery, NW Dishon, R Disibio, PJ Disney, IS Diss, RP Ditcham, DJ Ditchburn, EA Ditchfield, RC Dittman, RB Dittmar, RL Ditton, RA Dive, KE Divola, BJ Diwell, NJ Dix, TG Dix, PE Dixey, ACW Dixon, BC Dixon, BJ Dixon, CTW Dixon, EV Dixon, G Dixon, GB Dixon, GL Dixon, HH Dixon, I Dixon, JE Dixon, JW Dixon, KC Dixon, LC Dixon, MA Dixon, MR Dixon, NT Dixon, PE Dixon, PR Dixon, RB Dixon, RC Dixon, RE Dixon, RF Dixon, RJ Dixon, RM Dixon, VR Dixon, WB Dixon, WR Dixon, RT Dixson, L Djatschenko, MHJ Djukic, PH Dlugosz, AJ Doak, JC Doalman, DF Dobbin, JS Dobbin, G Dobbs, MG Dobbs, PE Dobbs, RJ Dobe, JE Dobeli, LJ Dobell, WJ Dobell, AT Dobie, CG Dobie, RJ Dobie, HV Dobinson, KW Doble, KW Dobransky, S Dobrowolski, AJ Dobson, B Dobson, DA Dobson, DT Dobson, GE Dobson, GR Dobson, KD Dobson, KG Dobson, KL Dobson, P Dobson, PN Dobson, RG Dobson, SP Dobson, WJ Dobson, WL Dobush, AS Docen, RA Docen, S Docen, EF Docherty, JT Docherty, N Docherty, RF Docherty, BR Docksey, GW Docksey, RG Docksey, B Doctor, AJ Dodd, BC Dodd, DR Dodd, HG Dodd, JC Dodd, ML Dodd, PJ Dodd, PS Dodd, RA Dodd, RWP Dodd, AD Dodds, AJN Dodds, CF Dodds, GRA Dodds, KL Dodds, PG Dodds, PR Dodds, RJ Dodds, TR Dodds, WA Dodds, WJ Dodge, EM Dodgshun, FJ Dodson, K Dodsworth, RW Dodwell, BB Doeblien, KH Doehrmann, W Doeland, FE Doerr, BJ Doherty, J Doherty, JA Doherty, JR Doherty, KF Doherty, P Doherty, PJ Doherty, RJ Doherty, MF Dohnt, AN Doidge, JD Doidge, JR Doidge, IR Dolan, NE Dolan, TF Dolan, TJ Dolbel, MP Dolensky, BJ Dolgan, CG Doll, LR Dollery, G Dollin, AJ Dollman, CT Dolphin, HJ Dolsen, JT Dolton, M Domarecki, LB Domaschenz, EJ Dombrose, PJ Domingo, JH Dominish, RL Domjahn, LL Donaghey, AF Donaghy, DJ Donahay, MF Donahoo, AO Donald, BC Donald, DR Donald, GD Donald, GJ Donald, GR Donald, KF Donald, LG Donald, RG Donald, TJ Donald, GM Donaldson, IJ Donaldson, KT Donaldson, PJ Donaldson, RB Donaldson, RG Donaldson, ME Donchi, PC Donchi, RJ Done, AR Donegan, JP Donegan, MJ Donegan, MG Dong, ET Donges, DWB Donkin, RJ Donkin, JM Donlen, GN Donley, JT Donley, CJ Donne, BM Donnellan, MA Donnellan, BR Donnelly, DJ Donnelly, EB Donnelly, FP Donnelly, JA Donnelly, JC Donnelly, JF Donnelly, JG Donnelly, K Donnelly, KJ Donnelly, KP Donnelly, LJ Donnelly, M Donnelly, MM Donnelly, P Donnelly, PB Donnelly, PJ Donnelly, PW Donnelly, RB Donnelly, RF Donnelly, RK Donnelly, RT Donnelly, SD Donnelly, SJ Donnelly, TB Donnelly, TJ Donnelly, TM Donnelly, WW Donnelly, RE Donnes, AR Donnison, DP Donoghue, GR Donoghue, JJ Donoghue, RH Donoghue, TE Donoghue, BB Donohoe, FM Donohoe, JJ Donohoe, MJ Donohoe, PA Donohoe, PJ Donohoe, D Donohue, JJ Donohue, MT Donohue, WJ Donohue, BJ Donovan, CD Donovan, D Donovan, DP Donovan, EWP Donovan, FA Donovan, JT Donovan, KE Donovan, KJ Donovan, PJ Donovan, PR Donovan, ST Donovan, TFF Donovan, TK Donovan, GR Doodson, PJ Doody, JB Doohan, LT Doohan, F Doolan, GJ Doolan, JW Doolan, KP Doolan, MS Doolan, RF Doolan, BJ Dooley, MJT Dooley, NJ Dooley, GF Doolin, RK Doonan, PE Doorey, JA Doorley, AA Doran, D Doran, DJ Doran, JG Doran, KF Doran, M Doran, MA Doran, RJ Doran, AR Dorber, EW Dore, LW Dore, PA Dore, PT Dore, RA Dorey, PD Dorfield, MJ Dorian, DH Doring, RJ Dorizzi, DJ Dorling, BR Dorman, KC Dorman, LM Dorman, PJ Dorman, PR Dorman, J Dorn, RR Doroszuk, KW Dorotich, EJ Dorrington, GT Dorrington, JG Dorrington, H Dorrough, BRT Dorsett, GJ Dorsett, PC Dorter, BB Dorward, KR Dorward, JE Dossetor, SP Dossetor, AA Dotter, RE Dotter, GD Douce, MM Doudle, RC Doudle, JG Doudney, M Dougall, MS Dougall, AD Dougherty, BJ Dougherty, DJ Dougherty, GK Doughty, WC Doughty, B Douglas, BJ Douglas, CL Douglas, DI Douglas, E Douglas, FA Douglas, G Douglas, GE Douglas, GI Douglas, GJ Douglas, GR Douglas, IJ Douglas, IR Douglas, J Douglas, JA Douglas, JM Douglas, JR Douglas, KS Douglas, KW Douglas, LG Douglas, LJ Douglas, LR Douglas, LS Douglas, PM Douglas, PN Douglas, PT Douglas, RE Douglas, RG Douglas, TB Douglas, TR Douglas, WJ Douglas, WN Douglas, WO Douglas, WT Douglas, IH Douglass, JF Douglass, JW Douglass, RL Douglass, WT Douglass, J Doulis, GJ Doulton, JM Douma, MW Doupain, TJC Dousi, CR Doust, EG Doust, MC Doust, RE Doust, JWV Doutch, A Dove, RC Dove, CH Dover, D Dover, WT Dover, DCN Dow, RB Dow, BC Dowd, GS Dowd, MB Dowd, PJ Dowd, GP Dowdell, TJ Dowdle, LJ Dowell, WW Dowell, K Dower, PJ Dowie, JR Dowler, AR Dowley, DJ Dowling, DJP Dowling, KJ Dowling, PF Dowling, PR Dowling, TJ Dowling, GR Down, AE Downes, BJ Downes, JH Downes, JW Downes, KM Downes, LJ Downes, MR Downes, AR Downey, AW Downey, GR Downey, HR Downey, JA Downey, JR Downey, L Downey, MJ Downey, MS Downey, PJ Downey, GF Downie, IS Downie, LD Downie, N Downie, PA Downie, SA Downie, TB Downie, WA Downie, WL Downie, DJ Downing, JR Downing, MA Downing, MP Downing, RE Downing, RPV Downing, GJ Downs, PS Downs, KR Downward, RL Dowse, B Dowsett, D Dowsett, LJ Dowsett, SG Dowsett, AJ Dowson, JW Dowson, MC Dowson, AR Doyle, BP Doyle, BS Doyle, D Doyle, DG Doyle, DH Doyle, DW Doyle, FW Doyle, GE Doyle, GL Doyle, GLP Doyle, GT Doyle, JA Doyle, JJ Doyle, JM Doyle, JO Doyle, KL Doyle, LG Doyle, LJ Doyle, ML Doyle, ND Doyle, P Doyle, PA Doyle, PB Doyle, PJ Doyle, RA Doyle, RD Doyle, RS Doyle, SM Doyle, TM Doyle, TR Doyle, WF Doyle, DG Drabble, GA Drabble, HL Drabble, DA Drabsch, GP Dragon, BR Dragunaitis, MJ Drain, DMJ Drake, DW Drake, LA Drake, AJ Drakefield, JW Dransfield, CW Draper, D Draper, GM Draper, HJ Draper, IT Draper, RJ Draper, RL Draper, TJ Draper, DM Dray, NJ Dray, KL Drayton, HP Drazek, EE Dreger, WT Dreier, CA Dreis, CL Dreis, DW Drennan, KD Drennan, WT Drennan, JH Drennert, AP Drew, C Drew, IM Drew, JM Drew, JP Drew, KJ Drew, P Drew, RJ Drew, TL Drew, VR Drew, WE Drew, PF Drewe, WR Drewe, CJ Drewett, GL Drewett, WD Drewett, GF Drews, R Drews, CE Dries, MC Driffield, PC Driffield, N Drimatis, FR Dring, AM Drinkwater, JF Drinkwater, L Drinkwater, MB Drinkwater, WV Drinkwater, RA Drinnan, JH Dripps, JD Driscoll, RW Driscoll, ED Driver, IWF Driver, RD Driver, CM Drochmann, G Drochmann, JM Drolz, PR Droop, I Dropulic, PC Druce, JM Druhan, LJ Drumgold, A Drummond, IG Drummond, NC Drummond, PG Drummond, PJ Drummond, RG Drummond, RJ Drummond, RK Drummond, SW Drummond, TH Drummond, TJ Drummond, IC Drury, RA Drury, TE Drury, G Drusetta, R Druszcz, MF Dryden, RC Dryden, EM Dryer, JJ Drysdale, RL Drysdale, S Dryza, J Duance, R Duane, M Dubajic, HJ Dubbeld, PJ Dubourg, RC Dubsky, HRJ Ducasse, AJ Ducat, TA Ducat, MD Duce, RA Ducie, DG Duck, JA Duck, RA Duck, CH Ducker, RJ Duckford, NJ Duckwitz, AJ Duckworth, DA Duckworth, JL Duckworth, I Duda, C Dudden, NB Dudgeon, AG Dudley, CE Dudley, DN Dudley, MB Dudley, SJ Dudley, L Duell, PR Duell, WHJ Duell, WM Duell, AK Duerdoth, IW Duers, DA Dufall, DP Duff, GR Duff, IJ Duff, J Duff, JE Duff, JR Duff, PJ Duff, RW Duff, SM Duff, TJ Duff, WH Duff, DA Duffey, JP Duffey, MP Dufficey, JAF Duffield, JE Duffield, RG Duffield, RC Duffin, TM Duffin, DJ Duffus, AJ Duffy, BO Duffy, JJ Duffy, KA Duffy, PM Duffy, PR Duffy, TJ Duffy, MJ Dufty, MR Dufty, PSW Dufty, GM Dugan, GA Dugdale, AEA Duggan, AF Duggan, CD Duggan, MJ Duggan, MP Duggan, PS Duggan, RK Duggan, RW Duggan, TF Duggan, TL Duggan, AJ Duggin, PE Duggin, NE Dugley, DH Duguid, WM Duguid, HI Duhigg, TF Duhring, JH Duiker, AJ Duke, DH Duke, RF Duke, WA Duke, AJ Dulczewski, RA Duldig, JP Dullard, W Duma, JT Dumble, R Dumesny, A Dumetz, NE Dummett, RE Dummett, TR Dummett, GP Dumpleton, FA Dunbar, GT Dunbar, WR Dunbar, J Dunbarreid, AB Duncan, AC Duncan, AF Duncan, AJ Duncan, AS Duncan, BG Duncan, BJ Duncan, BM Duncan, CA Duncan, CG Duncan, DM Duncan, FR Duncan, GE Duncan, GH Duncan, GR Duncan, IJ Duncan, J Duncan, JA Duncan, JM Duncan, JN Duncan, JR Duncan, KL Duncan, RB Duncan, RF Duncan, WB Duncan, LG Duncanson, RW Duncombe, AL Duncuff, PJ Dundas, RW Dunford, MP Dungan, LA Dungate, AC Dungey, GL Dungey, BT Dunham, JP Dunhill-Martin, TH Duniam, RL Dunk, COR Dunker, SE Dunker, CC Dunkley, G Dunkley, HT Dunkley, HV Dunkley, MF Dunkley, PLE Dunlevie, AJ Dunlop, BA Dunlop, BW Dunlop, CC Dunlop, GJ Dunlop, IJ Dunlop, RI Dunlop, AC Dunn, AD Dunn, AR Dunn, BC Dunn, BL Dunn, D Dunn, GJ Dunn, GR Dunn, IM Dunn, JA Dunn, JB Dunn, JH Dunn, JJ Dunn, JT Dunn, K Dunn, LW Dunn, ME Dunn, MR Dunn, MV Dunn, NI Dunn, PJ Dunn, PL Dunn, PM Dunn, R Dunn, RB Dunn, RJ Dunn, RK Dunn, RL Dunn, RM Dunn, RN Dunn, RT Dunn, RW Dunn, VJ Dunn, W Dunn, BR Dunne, DT Dunne, ER Dunne, G Dunne, GN Dunne, JM Dunne, JRW Dunne, KR Dunne, LW Dunne, NB Dunne, PJ Dunne, PT Dunne, RJ Dunne, SG Dunne, TJ Dunne, AP Dunnett, KJ Dunnicliffe, GC Dunning, IR Dunning, MJ Dunning, GN Dunsford, JHS Dunshea, PJ Dunsire, AL Dunsmuir, K Dunstall, PK Dunstall, CN Dunstan, DB Dunstan, JA Dunstan, JL Dunstan, JM Dunstan, LJ Dunstan, RE Dunstan, RJ Dunstan, WL Dunstan, PB Dunstone, NJ Dunton, VT Dunwoodie, DK Dupille, AL Dupree, RE Dupuy, DC Duquemin, R Durance, DN Durant, JR Durant, SA Durant, AC Durbidge, T Durbidge, CJ Durbridge, CT Durdin, JMP Durdin, RA Durdin, HN Duren, IL Durham, DF Durie, MAJ Durie, GJ Durkin, RJ Durkin, GW Durnford, PJ Durnford, JM Duroux, LG Duroux, DP Durrant, JH Durrant, RJ Durrant, JT Durrington, RJ Durrington, PS Dury, DJ Duscher, TJ Dusci, AL Dusting, JG Dusting, JM Duthie, KD Duthie, MJ Duthie, RKD Duthie, DS Dutka, BJ Dutko, GR Dutton, KG Dutton, MJ Dutton, RG Dutton, RJ Dutton, RM Duurland, GM Duus, AR Duval, A Duwakin, MD Dux, RVM Dux, RW Dux, J Dvoracsek, ET Dwan, JT Dwan, JW Dwenger, RG Dwenger, GC Dwiar, GE Dwight, MJ Dwight, AD Dwyer, AF Dwyer, AH Dwyer, BE Dwyer, BM Dwyer, C Dwyer, CD Dwyer, CJ Dwyer, DJ Dwyer, EW Dwyer, GP Dwyer, ID Dwyer, JJ Dwyer, JP Dwyer, JR Dwyer, KM Dwyer, KR Dwyer, MB Dwyer, MN Dwyer, PA Dwyer,

PB Dwyer, PR Dwyer, RG Dwyer, RJ Dwyer, RP Dwyer, RPT Dwyer, RV Dwyer, TB Dwyer, WJ Dwyer, KJ Dyas, WRH Dyball, J Dyce, B Dye, DJ Dye, TG Dye, GC Dyer, JM Dyer, KF Dyer, KJ Dyer, LN Dyer, MG Dyer, PG Dyer, RL Dyer, WJ Dyer, DI Dyke, JT Dyke, R Dyke, ID Dykes, JG Dykyj, A Dylewski, IG Dymock, HJ Dynarzewski, RJ Dyne, ZV Dyrynda, BK Dyson, BM Dyson, D Dyson, IF Dyson, JB Dyson, JK Dyson, JT Dyson, KJ Dyson, PG Dyson, RW Dyson, J Dziedzic, J Dziki, LJ Dziukas, MA Dziurek, JP Dzwonkowski, AC Eacott, CJ Eacott, GF Eacott, RW Eacott, AJ Eade, DJ Eade, R Eade, WA Eade, DC Eades, EA Eadie, FK Eadie, MC Eadie, GC Eady, AR Eagle, GR Eagles, RC Eagles, WFJ Eaglesham, J Eagleton, D Eakins, MC Eales, MK Eales, PH Eales, BJ Eames, KG Eames, PF Eardley, JR Earea, PE Earea, RE Earea, RC Earixson, DA Earl, DF Earl, JL Earl, LB Earl, RJ Earl, BG Earle, DK Earle, GJ Earle, IR Earle, P Earle, RM Earle, SE Earle, TL Earle, DH Earley, JM Earley, GS Earney, KL Earney, GW Earnshaw, MD Earnshaw, RJ Earnshaw, RL Earnshaw, CB Earp, BG Earwicker, JM Easlea, AP Eason, KL Eason, RB Eason, DJ Eassie, MI Eassie, A East, CHA East, RW East, TJ East, WH East, GR Eastall, B Easter, JN Easter, AJ Easterbrook, GS Easterbrook, TW Easterby, DA Eastham, GL Eastham, PJ Eastham, A Easthope, PJ Eastlake, BK Eastley, DE Eastley, GJ Eastley, RJ Eastman, RJ Eastment, RK Eastment, LG Eastoe, AD Easton, GH Easton, GN Easton, JF Easton, EC Eastwell, LL Eastwell, WJ Eastwell, AJ Eastwood, RC Eastwood, RJ Eastwood, TJ Eastwood, AL Eather, AR Eather, DW Eather, MJ Eather, OM Eather, PJ Eather, R Eather, RFJ Eather, R Eatock, AS Eaton, CJ Eaton, DL Eaton, GR Eaton, J Eaton, KJ Eaton, MP Eaton, RW Eaton, SC Eaton, SQ Eaton, TA Eaton, WR Eaton, KV Eatt, RT Eaves, JW Eayrs, H Ebbelaar, JJ Ebbs, JG Ebden, RW Ebdon, RA Eberhard, FK Eberle, KR Eberle, DW Ebert, RP Ebert, CE Ebner, DJ Eborall, CR Ebsworth, IC Ebzery, R Ebzery, BT Eccles, CR Eccles, KT Ecclestone, FA Echlin, RG Eckermann, RW Eckert, LC Eckett, B Econonidis, MT Edbrooke, P Edden, RW Eddington, WL Eddington, JD Eddleston, BR Eddy, GF Eddy, JF Eddy, LG Eddy, MR Eddy, PR Eddy, WJ Eddy, R Edelman, E Eden, AB Edgar, AJ Edgar, B Edgar, RJ Edgar, CG Edge, CJ Edge, TR Edge, W Edge, RD Edgell, AK Edgelow, SLC Edgelow, GL Edgerton, MJ Edghill, AC Edgley, DJ Edgley, DW Edgley, LR Edie, PL Edie, GJM Edis, MJ Edmiston, D Edmond, DW Edmond, AW Edmonds, D Edmonds, DN Edmonds, EG Edmonds, EJ Edmonds, GH Edmonds, PC Edmonds, PL Edmonds, PT Edmonds, RG Edmonds, RJ Edmonds, RM Edmonds, RS Edmonds, JL Edmondson, AR Edmondstone, BW Edmondstone, BL Edmunds, KH Edmunds, LM Edmunds, BM Edney, HM Ednie, JW Ednie, J Edson, PJ Edson, PH Edstein, GW Edward, WG Edward, WV Edward, A Edwards, AJ Edwards, AV Edwards, AW Edwards, B Edwards, BJ Edwards, BM Edwards, BP Edwards, BS Edwards, CD Edwards, CJ Edwards, CW Edwards, DA Edwards, DB Edwards, DG Edwards, DJ Edwards, DR Edwards, EF Edwards, EH Edwards, EJ Edwards, F Edwards, FE Edwards, FG Edwards, FJ Edwards, FN Edwards, GA Edwards, GB Edwards, GD Edwards, GJ Edwards, GL Edwards, GT Edwards, HR Edwards, IL Edwards, JC Edwards, JH Edwards, JJ Edwards, JP Edwards, JR Edwards, JT Edwards, KA Edwards, KW Edwards, LC Edwards, LG Edwards, MH Edwards, MJ Edwards, MP Edwards, ND Edwards, P Edwards, PA Edwards, PC Edwards, PE Edwards, PG Edwards, PJ Edwards, PJ Edwards, PN Edwards, PT Edwards, PW Edwards, R Edwards, RA Edwards, RC Edwards, RF Edwards, RG Edwards, RJ Edwards, RK Edwards, RS Edwards, SE Edwards, TE Edwards, TM Edwards, TR Edwards, WA Edwards, WE Edwards, WH Edwards, WJ Edwards, WR Edwards, WT Edwards, IH Edwardson, JO Edwick, LA Edyvane, NSG Eekhoff, MJ Eele, PB Eeles, RN Eeles, AG Efimov, NF Efremoff, J Efstathiou, A Egan, AL Egan, BE Egan, BJ Egan, EK Egan, GP Egan, HC Egan, JF Egan, JK Egan, JP Egan, KJ Egan, KT Egan, KWC Egan, PF Egan, PJ Egan, PR Egan, PT Egan, RH Egan, TJ Egan, WJ Egan, G Eggington, KE Eggins, AE Eggleston, MJ Eggleston, RK Eggleston, RR Eggleston, SS Eggleston, RJ Eggleton, EJ Eggmolesse, AJ Eglinton, BA Eglinton, RM Eglinton, M Ehlefeldt, EG Ehlers, J Ehlers, HE Ehnhuus, LB Ehrlich, AP Ehrnholm, PJ Ehsman, NR Eiby, TJ Eichler, KW Eichner, DR Eickenloff, KM Eickenloff, AF Eilola, HN Eilola, RA Eime, EC Einam, WW Einthal, PJ Eisele, JT Eisentrager, RL Eiszele, AA Eitmann, R Eitmann, RE Ekberg, JF Eke, BN Ekelund, BC Eklom, MFG Ekman, BE Elari, DB Elbourne, R Elbourne, MMP Elcoate, BA Elder, DD Elder, DE Elder, IC Elder, RG Elder, TJ Elder, C Eldridge, DC Eldridge, GM Eldridge, NJ Eldridge, PR Eldridge, RJ Eldridge, RW Eldridge, J Elek, TT Elemes, AJ Eley, LA Eley, RA Eley, HR Elfenbein, DW Elford, JM Elford, CR Elfverson, SA Elfverson, LA Elgar, JJ Elias, H Elings, RM Elkington, JE Elkins, NP Ellaby, L Ellcombe, MC Elledge, BH Ellem, ER Ellem, LF Ellem, MJ Ellem, RJ Ellen, JP Eller, HF Ellerbock, F Ellero, CW Ellery, DJ Ellery, RF Ellery, RJ Ellery, RJ Ellett, RC Ellevsen, GR Ellice-Flint, FJ Ellingham, CJ Elliot, D Elliot, L Elliot, RA Elliot, RC Elliot, A Elliott, AR Elliott, AW Elliott, BW Elliott, CD Elliott, D Elliott, DA Elliott, DW Elliott, EG Elliott, F Elliott, GR Elliott, HJ Elliott, JF Elliott, JM Elliott, JN Elliott, KR Elliott, MB Elliott, MD Elliott, NL Elliott, R Elliott, RA Elliott, RD Elliott, RF Elliott, RH Elliott, RS Elliott, SJ Elliott, TD Elliott, TJ Elliott, WJ Elliott, WO Elliott, WR Elliott, AC Ellis, AH Ellis, AJ Ellis, AL Ellis, AP Ellis, AW Ellis, BF Ellis, BJ Ellis, BM Ellis, BW Ellis, CF Ellis, CH Ellis, CJ Ellis, D Ellis, DE Ellis, DJ Ellis, EJ Ellis, FK Ellis, G Ellis, GC Ellis, GD Ellis, GG Ellis, GN Ellis, GP Ellis, GR Ellis, GS Ellis, HV Ellis, IM Ellis, J Ellis, JB Ellis, JC Ellis, JF Ellis, JM Ellis, JR Ellis, KJ Ellis, KR Ellis, KW Ellis, MJ Ellis, PE Ellis, RAG Ellis, RC Ellis, RG Ellis, RH Ellis, RJ Ellis, RK Ellis, RS Ellis, S Ellis, SL Ellis, TC Ellis, TJ Ellis, TR Ellis, DW Ellison, PA Ellnor, C Ellul, E Ellul, L Ellul, VW Ellul, RL Ellwood, W Ellwood, IB Ellyard, EC Elmes, MR Elmslie, AD Elphick, B Elphick, DJ Elphick, RJ Elphick, CR Elphinston, GC Elphinstone, F Elrington, RJ Elrington, GG Elsbury, JA Elsbury, JG Elsden, PJ Elsegood, JC Elsmann, DE Elson, JA Elson, KT Elson, TF Elstob, G Elston, JA Elston, DJ Elsum, GM Elt, CJ Elton, CT Elton, SE Elvey, C Elwell, EH Elwell, LJ Elwell, RW Elworthy, RC Ely, PM Elzas, GP Elzinga, S Elzinga, RJ Embelton, BC Emberson, KJ Emberson, DE Emblem, JA Embleton, RW Embrey, JA Emerson, PJ Emerson, RW Emerson, SM Emerson, WL Emerson, AJ Emery, CF Emery, G Emery, GA Emery, HJ Emery, KJ Emery, PS Emery, TK Emery, CA Emes, PP Emmanuel, DR Emmerton, AG Emmett, JG Emmett, BL Emonson, JW Emslie, DJ Enderby, RW Enderby, KR Enders, DK Endersbee, PF Endicott, RJ Endicott, RJ Endicotte, GK Enever, LC Enfield, DFW Engel, MG Engel, GF Engelman, RM Engelman, FL Engelsma, CM England, JB England, JR England, P England, GJ Engleby, IJ Engleby, AG English, BJ English, BP English, BR English, DV English, DW English, GL English, GS English, JA English, JW English, LJ English, MC English, MP English, NR English, RM English, RP English, SRC English, BE Englund, RJ Engstrom, BR Enkelman, KL Ennis, WD Ennis, KA Enno, D Enright, JG Enright, RJ Enright, T Entwistle, PJ Eppel, CJ Epskamp, MA Epton, HE Erbacher, NR Erbacher, PA Erbs, TH Erbs, SM Erceg, M Erdmanis, CF Erhardt, GJ Erhardt, GB Ericksen, DW Erickson, PG Erickson, JE Ericsson, HC Erkelens, JD Erkelens, E Ermanis, C Ermert, DJ Ernst, GA Ernst, RD Ernst, DA Errington, PJ Errington, WA Errington, WR Errington, JR Erwin, UD Eschholz, DK Escott, GJ Escott, GR Escott, GR Escreet, RB Esdale, GR Esler, HT Esler, EP Esmonde, GJ Esmonde, L Espie, NJ Espie, DW Essenhigh, J Essex-Clark, MD Estella, JG Estreich, JA Etchell, D Etchells, JH Etchells, RA Etherington, RJ Etherington, WR Ettles, DT Ettridge, H Euscher, HWB Eustace, BG Eva, A Evans, AD Evans, AF Evans, AG Evans, AR Evans, AW Evans, BD Evans, BG Evans, BJ Evans, CA Evans, CG Evans, CJ Evans, D Evans, DC Evans, DD Evans, DF Evans, DG Evans, DJ Evans, DN Evans, DR Evans, DT Evans, DV Evans, DW Evans, E Evans, ED Evans, EJ Evans, F Evans, FR Evans, GB Evans, GD Evans, GJ Evans, GR Evans, GT Evans, HC Evans, HD Evans, IR Evans, JA Evans, JB Evans, JD Evans, JM Evans, JR Evans, K Evans, KA Evans, KD Evans, KJ Evans, LA Evans, LT Evans, LW Evans, MA Evans, MC Evans, MD Evans, MD Evans, MF Evans, MG Evans, MH Evans, MJ Evans, NF Evans, NL Evans, NR Evans, OB Evans, P Evans, PG Evans, R Evans, RB Evans, RC Evans, RD Evans, RF Evans, RG Evans, RJ Evans, RS Evans, RV Evans, RW Evans, SA Evans, T Evans, TA Evans, TB Evans, TE Evans, TH Evans, TJ Evans, TW Evans, WA Evans, WC Evans, WD Evans, WG Evans, JS Eveleigh, PA Evenden, RHC Evennett, FJ Evens, BG Everard, RE Everes, AM Everett, GM Everett, GT Everett, IW Everett, JE Everett, KV Everett, PJ Everett, SR Everett, WR Everett, R Everhardus, MS Everill, JD Everingham, RJ Everington, DF Everitt, DJ Everitt, GR Everitt, JM Everitt, S Everitt, JH Evers, KH Everson, RJ Everts, PG Every, NA Eves, KJ Evorall, KD Ewart, M Ewart, KL Ewell, RL Ewell, FB Ewing, JC Ewing, MJ Ewing, PJ Ewington, JR Excell, RW Excell, C Exindaris, AA Exley, SW Exon, GR Eyers, AT Eyles, FG Eyles, JW Eyles, LA Eyles, OF Eyles, RE Eyles, SJ Eyles, WS Eyles, KJ Eylward, PD Eylward, EW Eyre, JR Eyre, LM Eyre, TJ Eyre, AA Eyssens, DJ Ezzy, MJ Ezzy, N Ezzy, R Ezzy, RC Ezzy, DP Fabian, MB Fabian, PJ Fabian, HS Fabisiak, M Fabricato, FG Facey, RL Facey, CR Fackender, RM Fadden, PL Faddy, BJ Fagan, MB Fagan, RJ Fagan, PR Fagerlund, WD Fagerlund, FW Fagg, BJ Fahey, RA Fahey, WJ Fahey, BJ Fahy, CJ Fahy, E Fahy, EJ Fahy, JJ Fahy, KJ Fahy, JS Fainges, AD Faint, AG Faint, DJ Faint, JA Faint, G Fairall, AR Fairbanks, TA Fairbanks, AH Fairbrother, B Fairbrother, RJ Fairbrother, RL Fairchild, B Fairclough, MA Fairey, MJ Fairfax, TH Fairfax, TV Fairfax, AJ Fairhall, MJ Fairhall, BL Fairhead, MF Fairhead, MWL Fairless, GW Fairley, J Fairley, JG Fairley, JH Fairley, NA Fairley, EE Fairman, PJ Fairon, J Fairway, DJ Fairweather, JF Fairweather, MA Fairweather, RS Fairweather, SG Fairweather, PE Faithfull, RG Faithfull, PW Falconbridge, GJ Falconer, JD Falconer, AB Falk, GS Falk, L Falkai, P Falkland, CE Falla, LJ Falla, TA Fallance, V Fallins, GR Fallis, G Fallo, BE Fallon, GE Fallon, GR Fallon, JG Fallon, JW Fallon, PJP Fallon, RS Fallon, BJ Falvey, KJ Falvey, PE Falzon, RJ Famlonga, AS Famularo, L Fan, WN Fancourt, SB Fanetti, DA Fanker, CM Fankhauser, FC Fanna, LE Fanning, LW Fanning, A Fantis, JW Faram, GW Farbridge, RA Fardell, TJ Fardell, GJ Fardy, JE Farenden, S Farkas, CF Farley, GA Farley, GC Farley, JW Farley, L Farley, NGW Farley, RG Farley, RJ Farley, JT Farmelo, AE Farmer, AF Farmer, BA Farmer, CW Farmer, DW Farmer, G Farmer, JG Farmer, LF Farmer, MD Farmer, MW Farmer, NE Farmer, RG Farmer, RF Farnes, JS Farnham, GR Farnsworth, HC Farnsworth, AJ Farquhar, NP Farquhar, RA Farquhar, AB Farquharson, WJ Farquharson, FM Farr, JL Farr, LJ Farr, MK Farr, PR Farr, IR Farrall, RL Farrand, EH Farrands, ID Farrant, R Farrant, MN Farrar, MT Farrar, RT Farrar, WF Farrar, CM Farrell, IE Farrell, JP Farrell, KJ Farrell, M Farrell, PJ Farrell, PR Farrell, PT Farrell, RA Farrell, RC Farrell, RH Farrell, RS Farrell, RW Farrell, SP Farrell, TF Farrell, TJ Farrell, P Farrelly, LT Farren, CL Farrer, RF Farrier, GA Farrington, JS Farrow, ME Farrow, MG Farrow, SR Farrow, BS Farrugia, JD Farr-Wharton, DR Farry, JJ Farry, GL Farthing, FJ Fatches, LJ Fatone, GH Faul, R Faulds, GC Faulkhead, BA Faulkner, DF Faulkner, DJ Faulkner, DM Faulkner, LV Faulkner, NH Faulkner, NJ Faulkner, R Faulkner, RA Faulkner, RJ Faulkner, RE Faulks, JC Faull, TR Faull, RP Fauntleroy, D Faust, KL Faust, R Faustmann, RJ Favell, LA Faver, N Fawcett-Smith, C Fawcett, DJ Fawcett, DE Fawkner, MP Fawkner, RA Fawns, JA Fay, JF Fay, RA Fay, RG Fay, KT Fayle, DR Fazackerley, F Fazekas, EE Fea, RJ Feain, WD Feakes, CEJ Fealy, RA Fear, NN Fearn, DJ Fearne, DG Fearnhead, WH Fearnhead, WD Fearnley, WW Fearon, WE Featherby, KF Featherston, BM Featherstone, G Featherstone, JJ Featherstone, J Fedorowytsch, VW Fedoryschyn, CG Fedrick, MA Fee, EJ Feebrey, JD Feeney, PJ Feeney, HJ Feening, WJ Feenstra, BR Fegan, PJ Fegan, LJ Fehon, JF Feint, BE Feldman, RW Feldman, SR Feldman, A Feleppa, WJ Felke, TW Felkin, A Fell, KA Fell, RC Fell, RF Fellenberg, RM Fellows, TJ Fellows, JL Felsman, WJ Felstead, AJ Feltham, LG Feltham, NA Feltham, RG Feltham, IN Felton, JM Felton, JP Felton, JS Fenby, A Fenech, FL Fenech, J Fenech, W Fenech, AJ Fenerty, FW Fenn, BR Fennell, GM Fennell, MR Fennell, RA Fennell, ID Fenner, PJ Fennessy, NC Fennis, AL Fensom, SA Fensom, JD Fentiman, AJ Fenton, BR Fenton, EH Fenton, JC Fenton, JE Fenton, JW Fenton, LOJ Fenton, RJ Fenton, BA Fenwick, DC Fenwick, MV Fenwick, RA Fenwick, GR Ferdinand, FA Ferdinands, AM Ferguson, BD Ferguson, BJ Ferguson, BW Ferguson, D Ferguson, DB Ferguson, DM Ferguson, DP Ferguson, DR Ferguson, FL Ferguson, FT Ferguson, G Ferguson, GG Ferguson, GM Ferguson, GR Ferguson, HR Ferguson, IG Ferguson, IP Ferguson, J Ferguson, JJ Ferguson, JM Ferguson, JV Ferguson, KG Ferguson, LJ Ferguson, MJ Ferguson, ML Ferguson, NR Ferguson, NS Ferguson, PA Ferguson, PJ Ferguson, PK Ferguson, RA Ferguson, RJ Ferguson, RL Ferguson, RS Ferguson, RM Ferguson-McLellan, DW Fergusson, JRA Fergusson, MN Fergusson, PA Fergusson, RN Fergusson,

RM Ferluga, VD Fermaner, JA Fernandes, GH Fernando, MR Fernando, KJ Fernie, AJ Fernihough, DA Ferrari, RK Ferrari, A Ferraro, PJ Ferre, JL Ferres, ML Ferres, PR Ferriday, RJ Ferrier, KG Ferris, MW Ferris, PR Ferris, RC Ferris, RG Ferris, TG Ferry, MC Festing, GB Fettell, ND Fettes, RM Feverbach, AJ Fewings, HW Fewings, FJ Fewquandie, JD Fewson, GT Fewster, RF Fewster, UEA Fey, PG Fidden, DM Fiddes, A Fiddian, PS Fiddler, TR Fidge, MT Fidler, DMH Fiechtner, CB Fiedler, WA Fiedler, M Fieg, B Field, BH Field, CH Field, DK Field, DS Field, DW Field, EA Field, GD Field, JF Field, KG Field, MP Field, PR Field, PW Field, RE Field, RJ Field, WG Field, WR Field, PJ Fielden, DA Fielder, BN Fieldhouse, DJ Fieldhouse, JA Fieldhouse, G Fielding, LE Fielding, RH Fielding, DJ Fields, PG Fields, WV Fields, PE Fienberg, WH Fietz, VR Fifield, R Figliomeni, RB Fihelly, G Fikerle, A Filardi, MJ Filby, BWD Filce, GP Files, WE Files, BG Filewood, SJ Filewood, GB Fill, BJ Filmer, RE Filmer, BA Filsell, BJ Finch, BW Finch, F Finch, GD Finch, IF Finch, IW Finch, LR Finch, LW Finch, NJ Finch, P Finch, M Fincham, ER Findlay, IM Findlay, JD Findlay, JG Findlay, JK Findlay, JL Findlay, MA Findlay, R Findlay, RR Findlay, G Findlayson, LR Findley, R Finedon, GC Finegan, LL Finger, R Finkelde, BF Finlay, BM Finlay, CJ Finlay, DH Finlay, DK Finlay, IA Finlay, IT Finlay, JD Finlay, KR Finlay, R Finlay, WJ Finlay, GP Finlayson, WJ Finlayson, AG Finley, EO Finn, GW Finn, JL Finn, PV Finn, R Finn, RA Finn, JC Finnegan, TJ Finnegan, SM Finnelley, WJ Finnemore, MJ Finnerty, N Finney, RJ Finney, SW Finney, LM Finnie, RJ Finnie, FT Finnigan, JJ Finnigan, DJ Finning, BL Finniss, KJ Finucane, A Fior, JR Fiorio, RR Firehock, JM Firman, LE Firman, TJ Firmin, BJ Firns, BW Firns, CP Firriolo, BD Firth, GN Firth, HC Firth, LB Firth, NR Firth, VW Firth, GI Fischer, LJ Fischer, ND Fischer, P Fischer, PJ Fischer, TA Fischer, TE Fischer, AE Fish, JJ Fish, RG Fish, GG Fishburn, WJ Fishburn, A Fisher, AD Fisher, AJ Fisher, BR Fisher, BSE Fisher, CA Fisher, D Fisher, DB Fisher, DG Fisher, DJ Fisher, DL Fisher, DM Fisher, FJ Fisher, GA Fisher, GJ Fisher, ID Fisher, IS Fisher, J Fisher, JA Fisher, JE Fisher, JF Fisher, JH Fisher, JJ Fisher, JN Fisher, KJ Fisher, LD Fisher, LGA Fisher, MJW Fisher, NHG Fisher, PF Fisher, PR Fisher, RA Fisher, RC Fisher, RH Fisher, RJ Fisher, RL Fisher, RR Fisher, RW Fisher, SN Fisher, TJ Fisher, TW Fisher, VW Fisher, WG Fisher, WJ Fisher, WR Fisher, WS Fisher, WW Fisher, MC Fishlock, F Fisicaro, CA Fisk, JE Fisk, PA Fiske, FT Fitch, JS Fitch, RJ Fittler, AJ Fittock, B Fitton, RG Fitts, R Fitz, MJ Fitzallen, A Fitzgerald, CR Fitzgerald, DJ Fitzgerald, G Fitzgerald, GJ Fitzgerald, GW Fitzgerald, HL Fitzgerald, J Fitzgerald, JG Fitzgerald, JJ Fitzgerald, JT Fitzgerald, JW Fitzgerald, LP Fitzgerald, LR Fitzgerald, ME Fitzgerald, MK Fitzgerald, MP Fitzgerald, MW Fitzgerald, PJ Fitzgerald, RH Fitzgerald, RM Fitzgerald, SM Fitzgerald, ST Fitzgerald, TG Fitzgerald, TPM Fitzgerald, WJ Fitzgerald, MA Fitzgibbon, NG Fitzgibbon, DG Fitzhenry, AF Fitzpatrick, BS Fitzpatrick, BT Fitzpatrick, BW Fitzpatrick, CM Fitzpatrick, D Fitzpatrick, DJ Fitzpatrick, GJ Fitzpatrick, IRW Fitzpatrick, JG Fitzpatrick, JJ Fitzpatrick, LT Fitzpatrick, MD Fitzpatrick, MJ Fitzpatrick, MJP Fitzpatrick, NE Fitzpatrick, NJ Fitzpatrick, NP Fitzpatrick, PJ Fitzpatrick, RD Fitzpatrick, RJ Fitzpatrick, TJ Fitzpatrick, BJ Fitzsimmons, BWV Fitzsimmons, JA Fitzsimmons, LJ Fitzsimmons, PJ Fitzsimmons, PW Fitzsimmons, RWM Fitzsimmons, SB Fitzsimmons, JA Fitzsimon, AR Fixter, C Fizzell, GE Fizzell, AG Flack, AJD Flack, EDH Flack, LR Flack, MB Flack, P Flack, RJ Flack, AJ Flaherty, KB Flaherty, PJ Flaherty, AJ Flanagan, AM Flanagan, AP Flanagan, EJ Flanagan, G Flanagan, PA Flanagan, PJ Flanagan, TJ Flanagan, GG Flanders, MT Flanders, GA Flannery, HJ Flannery, J Flannery, BD Flatman, RJ Flaton, CJ Flatters, BJ Flavel, GD Flavel, RA Flavell, EM Fleay, PN Flecker, JC Fleer, FJ Flegg, RJ Fleiner, B Flematti, A Fleming, AG Fleming, AK Fleming, BS Fleming, CL Fleming, DC Fleming, DJ Fleming, DK Fleming, GJ Fleming, JG Fleming, JR Fleming, KJA Fleming, ME Fleming, NA Fleming, PT Fleming, PV Fleming, PW Fleming, R Fleming, RG Fleming, RJ Fleming, RL Fleming, RR Fleming, SR Fleming, WG Fleming, GW Flemming, GW Flemming, DT Flentjar, AT Fletcher, B Fletcher, BA Fletcher, BE Fletcher, CA Fletcher, CC Fletcher, CM Fletcher, DJ Fletcher, DW Fletcher, GC Fletcher, GK Fletcher, GL Fletcher, IF Fletcher, IJ Fletcher, IP Fletcher, J Fletcher, JE Fletcher, JG Fletcher, JL Fletcher, JR Fletcher, JRS Fletcher, KG Fletcher, KJ Fletcher, LJ Fletcher, ME Fletcher, MJ Fletcher, NF Fletcher, NJ Fletcher, PG Fletcher, PJ Fletcher, PL Fletcher, PR Fletcher, PS Fletcher, PW Fletcher, RC Fletcher, RE Fletcher, RJ Fletcher, SC Fletcher, SW Fletcher, WJ Fletcher, KJ Fletchett, RA Fletchett, EE Flett, RG Flett, DG Flew, RJ Flew, BE Flewell-Smith, JJ Flewers, MJ Flight, CF Flint, GM Flint, GR Flint, RS Flint, WJ Flippence, DJ Flissinger, BW Flockhart, FM Flockhart, K Flockton, AJ Flohr, AA Flood, BT Flood, JR Flood, AK Floor, R Flor, PR Florance, RJG Florance, BG Florence, JJS Florent, DG Florian, MV Flower, PJ Flower, RG Flowers, AR Floyd, CE Floyd, DT Floyd, GJ Floyd, JGT Floyd, JH Floyd, LJ Floyd, TW Floyd, WR Flugge, AJ Flux, AJ Flynn, BM Flynn, BP Flynn, JA Flynn, P Flynn, PE Flynn, PJ Flynn, TW Flynn, VM Flynn, DJ Foale, LT Foale, NT Foale, TM Foale, GD Foat, D Fock, CH Fogarty, EJ Fogarty, JW Fogarty, T Fogarty, TB Fogarty, WL Fogarty, RA Fogg, WR Foggin, GK Fogwell, AR Folbigg, WJ Folder, KJ Foletta, AL Foley, CI Foley, DL Foley, G Foley, GJ Foley, JM Foley, KP Foley, LJ Foley, MH Foley, PL Foley, PR Foley, ML Folkard, BP Folkes, WK Folland, DK Follett, BG Follington, AE Followes, MC Folster, Z Foltyn, WT Fong, J Fongkee, PG Fontanini, CJF Fooks, LF Fooks, MG Foot, RS Foot, BJ Foote, LH Foote, ML Foote, RA Foote, WJ Foote, GL Footer, PR Footner, IW Foran, JA Foran, AS Forbes, AV Forbes, BA Forbes, BJ Forbes, DA Forbes, JJ Forbes, KCG Forbes, KJ Forbes, KR Forbes, NF Forbes, PJ Forbes, RA Forbes, RJ Forbes, RW Forbes, TN Forbes, TR Forbes, WN Forbes, WW Forbes, F Forcucci, BC Ford, BL Ford, C Ford, CW Ford, DC Ford, DF Ford, DW Ford, FH Ford, GJ Ford, GM Ford, GR Ford, HJ Ford, JA Ford, JD Ford, JE Ford, JFL Ford, JM Ford, JS Ford, JW Ford, KN Ford, KP Ford, KR Ford, LG Ford, MJ Ford, MN Ford, NE Ford, P Ford, PD Ford, RB Ford, RD Ford, RT Ford, RJ Ford, SP Ford, TR Ford, CH Forde, TJ Forde, TJ Forde, KW Forden, JR Fordham, RJ Fordham, P Fordzun, AC Foreman, IL Foreman, JS Foreman, KI Foreman, KL Foreman, JE Forestal, AJ Foresto, BC Forlonge, DL Forman, JC Forman, DA Formby, HE Forno, BJ Forrest, CD Forrest, DC Forrest, EW Forrest, GE Forrest, GP Forrest, IJ Forrest, J Forrest, JR Forrest, KG Forrest, LW Forrest, PA Forrest, TJ Forrest, WJ Forrest, AD Forrester, AR Forrester, KL Forrester, LT Forrester, RI Forrester, WA Forrester, NF Forsberg, AJ Forsdike, RL Forshey, AJD Forster, AR Forster, BR Forster, DB Forster, DJ Forster, GG Forster, GT Forster, IG Forster, JL Forster, JM Forster, KC Forster, MJ Forster, MR Forster, RC Forster, RD Forster, RJ Forster, TA Forster, WES Forster, AR Forsyth, BD Forsyth, CP Forsyth, DR Forsyth, LR Forsyth, PD Forsyth, RL Forsyth, SG Forsyth, T Forsyth, NL Forth, RW Forth, BC Forward, CV Forward, EH Forward, GJ Forward, R Forwood, L Fossati, PJ Fossey, WL Fossey, AH Foster, B Foster, BA Foster, BN Foster, CA Foster, CT Foster, DC Foster, DC Foster, DJ Foster, GF Foster, GI Foster, GL Foster, GT Foster, GW Foster, JC Foster, JK Foster, JR Foster, KH Foster, KS Foster, ME Foster, MJ Foster, PK Foster, RB Foster, RG Foster, RJ Foster, RW Foster, SM Foster, SS Foster, TJ Foster, W Foster, WC Foster, WJ Foster, NJT Fothergill, AH Fotheringham, BJ Fotheringham, JA Fotheringham, P Fottrill, N Foukas, EC Foulds, TC Foulkes, BE Fountain, GWJ Fountain, KD Fountain, NS Fountain, PD Fountain, R Fountain, WJ Fountain, ARG Fowler, BA Fowler, CR Fowler, DF Fowler, GD Fowler, GJ Fowler, GP Fowler, KL Fowler, LK Fowler, MA Fowler, MB Fowler, MI Fowler, PE Fowler, RD Fowler, RJ Fowler, RK Fowler, RT Fowler, S Fowler, GR Fowles, KF Fowles, WL Fowles, AH Fox, AJ Fox, BE Fox, BL Fox, BW Fox, DR Fox, FJ Fox, FW Fox, GD Fox, GJ Fox, JA Fox, JE Fox, JL Fox, JM Fox, JR Fox, KR Fox, LC Fox, NB Fox, NW Fox, PH Fox, PJ Fox, PJT Fox, R Fox, RF Fox, RJ Fox, SG Fox, TD Fox, WC Fox, WF Fox, WP Fox, B Foxall, WJ Foxall, A Foxley, DH Foxwell, JM Foxwell, GT Foy, GR Foyle, RJ Fozzard, P Fradgley, D Fragnito, C Fragomeni, RJ Frahm, ET Frampton, KE Frampton, AD France, AJ France, PA France, SC France, WP France, CL Frances, DL Frances, DP Francesconi, M Francetich, AM Francis, BJ Francis, DH Francis, DK Francis, DMM Francis, DW Francis, G Francis, GA Francis, GJ Francis, J Francis, JR Francis, JS Francis, JW Francis, KJ Francis, KW Francis, LC Francis, LN Francis, LW Francis, NJ Francis, PJ Francis, RE Francis, RH Francis, RI Francis, RJ Francis, RN Francis, RV Francis, TS Francis, RS Franck, V Franco, DC Frangos, JD Frangos, H Franke, JWR Frankel, RS Frankel, R Frankiewicz, A Frankland, BA Frankland, BE Franklin, D Franklin, EJ Franklin, GA Franklin, GJ Franklin, GW Franklin, HC Franklin, IF Franklin, KA Franklin, LK Franklin, MJ Franklin, MW Franklin, RG Franklin, RS Franklin, TG Franklin, WG Franklin, AB Franks, AH Franks, GP Franks, ML Franks, EA Frantz, SR Franzi, F Frasca, AK Fraser, AR Fraser, BD Fraser, BM Fraser, CA Fraser, CAE Fraser, DJ Fraser, DM Fraser, DP Fraser, EB Fraser, ED Fraser, EJ Fraser, FB Fraser, GB Fraser, GF Fraser, GN Fraser, GW Fraser, IG Fraser, J Fraser, JA Fraser, JC Fraser, JM Fraser, JW Fraser, KL Fraser, KR Fraser, L Fraser, LE Fraser, LW Fraser, MR Fraser, NA Fraser, NW Fraser, P Fraser, PH Fraser, PR Fraser, RB Fraser, RC Fraser, RJ Fraser, RL Fraser, RN Fraser, RS Fraser, T Fraser, JP Fraser-Byass, DJ Fratus, VP Fratus, RW Frauenfelder, KJ Frawley, RJ Frawley, DG Frazer, JA Frazer, KA Frazer, KN Frazer, MP Frazer, NH Frazer, PJ Frazer, RJ Frazer, IE Frazierroxburgh, K Freakley, TJ Frearson, RA Freckleton, JG Frederiksen, PE Frederiksen, JR Fredrick, WJ Free, RS Freebairn, HL Freeburn, JA Freeburn, RE Freeburn, LG Freeland, RD Freeland, CG Freeman, EM Freeman, GJ Freeman, GL Freeman, GW Freeman, JE Freeman, JM Freeman, JV Freeman, JW Freeman, KH Freeman, KJ Freeman, KP Freeman, KR Freeman, KW Freeman, NV Freeman, PG Freeman, RJ Freeman, RR Freeman, SR Freeman, TR Freeman, TV Freeman, WK Freeman, AW Freemantle, B Freer, KF Freer, SD Freese, BT Freestone, G Freestone, JB Freestone, RJ Freestone, G Freethymansfield, EJ Freid, DL Freier, RS Freight, AW Fren, AD French, AR French, AV French, BA French, BJ French, CF French, CS French, DJ French, DV French, GR French, M French, MB French, MG French, RB French, RJ French, RL French, S French, TF French, VA French, WJ French, RC Frencham, GG Frencken, DT Frensham, RJ Freriechs, RM Freshfield, KN Freshwater, DD Frew, GJ Frew, SB Frew, SM Frew, JJ Frewen, MX Frichot, JA Fricke, NJ Frickmann, GR Friday, HA Friday, MJ Fridolf, JW Friebel, DG Friend, GR Friend, H Friend, LA Friend, NM Friend, RJ Friend, GC Friese, FP Frigerio, PT Frisby, RA Frisby, RH Frisch, P Frisina, GC Friske, IB Friske, ER Frisken, RG Fritchley, MA Frith, AJ Fritsch, PG Fritsch, EC Fritz, TJ Fritz, BJ Froben, RA Frohlich, DH Frohmuller, FT Frok, GM Fromm, MA Frood, GA Froome, BJ Frost, DJ Frost, FR Frost, GT Frost, JG Frost, JW Frost, K Frost, LD Frost, LJ Frost, MA Frost, MJ Frost, PG Frost, PN Frost, PR Frost, RB Frost, RT Frost, W Frost, WD Frost, WR Frost, PL Froud, IK Fruend, HL Frugtniet, AD Fry, DJ Fry, LC Fry, PJ Fry, WG Fry, C Fryc, G Frydrych, AB Fryer, D Fryer, GA Fryer, IW Fryer, RA Fryer, RG Fryer, PJ Fryers, JZ Fudali, GL Fudge, JR Fuge, AW Fuhlbohm, IE Fuhrmann, PR Fuhrmann, RG Fulcher, RI Fulford, JP Fulham, BR Fullagar, WR Fullagar, BE Fullard, DN Fullbrook, BJ Fuller, BW Fuller, DA Fuller, GE Fuller, JD Fuller, JE Fuller, JR Fuller, LE Fuller, LG Fuller, LW Fuller, QR Fuller, R Fuller, RJ Fuller, RL Fuller, RR Fuller, SR Fuller, TB Fuller, TR Fuller, WG Fuller, WM Fuller, GN Fullerton, RK Fullford, LJ Fullgrabe, DRJ Fullick, JR Fullwood, A Fulton, BJ Fulton, GG Fulton, JL Fulton, JS Fulton, KG Fulton, PW Fulton, R Fulton, RH Fulton, RJ Fulton, FA Funnell, DJ Furletti, CW Furlong, GA Furmston, JO Furner, AR Furness, BJ Furness, GJ Furness, JN Furness, NR Furness, PW Furness, RC Furness, DC Furneyvall, R Furno, RR Furtner, AS Furze, P Fuschtei, AC Futcher, LW Futcher, PF Futcher, AG Fyfe, BJ Fyfe, DH Fyfe, JD Fyfe, PJ Fyfe, NG Fyffe, AJ Fysh, GR Fysh, TG Fysh, GC Gaal, RG Gabel, JW Gabelish, DJ Gablonski, KJ Gablonski, RF Gablonski, KA Gabriel, WB Gabriel, EF Gadd, VJ Gadd, TM Gadean, PA Gaden, PM Gadsden, RA Gaehl, PE Gaff, HB Gaffney, RJ Gaffney, RE Gagan, SM Gage, V Gagliardi, WW Gahagan, GA Gailer, GJ Gailey, DR Gainer, MFF Gainer, LW Gainey, PJ Gainsford, BW Gair, RN Gair, RW Gair, CE Gaitskell, FS Gal, T Gal, C Galakos, JJ Galati, JE Galbraith, NS Galbraith, TE Galbraith, DW Gale, GA Gale, GW Gale, JH Gale, NA Gale, RN Gale, RW Gale, WL Gale, WM Gale, A Galea, AD Galea, PJ Galea, S Galea, VP Galea, RO Galilee, D Gall, JC Gall, W Gall, JNM Gallacher, WC Gallacher, AJ Gallagher, GF Gallagher, GK Gallagher, J Gallagher, KG Gallagher, KJ Gallagher, MJ Gallagher, MK Gallagher, MW Gallagher, PA Gallagher, PJ Gallagher, PL Gallagher, PN Gallagher, PR Gallagher, RL Gallagher, WA Gallagher, WJ Gallagher, WR Gallagher, AL Galland, PJB Galland, KE Gallard, NK Gallard,

BM Gallasch, KE Gallasch, AJ Gallegos, AM Gallio, ER Galloway, LE Galloway, MR Galloway, W Galloway, JK Galpin, MW Galt, DJ Galvin, F Galvin, PJ Galvin, RJ Galvin, WJ Galvin, BC Gamble, GR Gamble, ME Gamble, RC Gamble, RE Gamble, TJ Gamble, BW Gambold, CK Gameau, AJ Gamlin, AW Gammelgaard, DG Gammie, RL Gammie, DJ Gammon, DN Gammon, PG Gammon, RC Gander, JG Ganderton, FG Gane, KW Gane, PJ Gane, PR Gane, BJ Ganley, MRN Ganly, KD Gann, RW Gann, PG Gannan, KJ Gannaway, BD Gannon, CJ Gannon, FR Ganser, DH Gant, KH Gant, LC Gant, LC Ganter, LE Gapes, G Garard, SA Garard, S Garay, AG Garbett, KE Garbutt, L Garbutt, KJ Garcia, PE Garcia, RJ Garcia, KR Gard, IR Gardam, NL Gardam, NE Gardem, PJ Gardener, WDJ Gardener, AG Gardiner, AR Gardiner, BJ Gardiner, BK Gardiner, BS Gardiner, C Gardiner, DR Gardiner, GJ Gardiner, GL Gardiner, GW Gardiner, HR Gardiner, JC Gardiner, JD Gardiner, JW Gardiner, KF Gardiner, PL Gardiner, R Gardiner, R Gardiner, RJ Gardiner, TG Gardiner, TJ Gardiner, WF Gardiner, WR Gardiner, WS Gardiner, AG Gardner, BG Gardner, BL Gardner, CH Gardner, GH Gardner, JR Gardner, KI Gardner, MJ Gardner, RB Gardner, RH Gardner, RJ Gardner, TK Gardner, V Gardner, S Gargano, AB Garland, AM Garland, BA Garland, EJ Garland, N Garland, PK Garland, PR Garland, RD Garland, RM Garland, RS Garland, SA Garland, DJ Garlin, GF Garner, JA Garner, JK Garner, JT Garner, KW Garner, MS Garner, PJ Garner, AW Garnham, RW Garnish, DM Garrard, WE Garrard, BA Garratt, BT Garratt, EJ Garratt, RJ Garratt, DW Garraway, RM Garraway, AW Garrett, JE Garrett, MA Garrett, MH Garrett, NP Garrett, TC Garrett, WJ Garrett, TA Garrick, J Garrigan, DJ Garrow, AJ Garside, WJ Garside, T Garson, GS Garth, LA Garth, RE Garth, RG Gartner, A Garton, PL Garton, BJ Gartside, GR Gartside, DK Garvey, AG Garvin, W Garwoli, JS Garwood, HW Gascoigne, KJ Gascoigne, RT Gaske, RW Gaskell, PE Gaskin, RC Gaskin, RI Gaskin, PH Gasmier, EW Gason, JE Gason, A Gasparovic, J Gasperowicz, JG Gass, JG Gasson, IC Gatehouse, PJ Gately, AR Gates, D Gates, JJ Gates, JW Gates, LA Gates, LE Gates, PK Gates, RJ Gatherer, JA Gatt, LP Gatt, GJ Gauci, FR Gaudet, J Gaudion, JL Gaudion, RB Gauld, B Gault, JS Gault, PS Gault, KJ Gaulton, GM Gaunson, G Gaunt, ISM Gaunt, JH Gaunt, KJ Gaunt, PS Gaunt, RK Gaunt, KA Gaut, HL Gauvin, KB Gavan, BE Gavin, J Gavin, AS Gavine, M Gavrilovic, H Gawel, RA Gawley, AK Gay, BA Gay, CDR Gay, EW Gay, IM Gay, MR Gay, NA Gay, NW Gay, RE Gay, RR Gay, RW Gay, T Gay, TJ Gay, LJ Gaylard, RM Gaylard, GJ Gayler, VJ Gaynes, MM Gaynor, RJ Gaze, RF Gazzara, AR Gazzard, DE Gazzard, LW Gazzard, RB Geaghan, WM Geaghan, DR Geale, JK Geale, RN Geale, KBG Gealy, CR Geappen, KM Gear, RG Gear, VL Gear, MW Gearring, DR Geary, GP Geary, NJ Geary, AR Geatches, FC Gebbett, NF Gebbett, J Gebhardt, JA Gebhardt, IA Geddes, IM Geddes, KR Geddes, KW Geddes, A Gee, AE Gee, AW Gee, BA Gee, BR Gee, C Gee, CB Gee, GM Gee, NW Gee, RD Gee, TA Gee, J Geedrick, PJ Geelen, RF Geeman, TB Geer, AG Geernaert, RH Geeves, JP Gehle, PA Gehle, AL Geia, PJ Geil, P Geisel, WH Geisel, BJ Geisler, JP Geisler, PW Gejas, M Geldart, AP Geldens, WG Gelhaar, CC Geljon, RA Gell, AL Gellie, KE Gelling, PL Geltch, DW Gemmell, JC Gemmell, WE Genninges, JF Genovese, KE Gent, KL Gentle, RJ Gentle, JC Gentles, AE Gentry, CD Gentrypike, K Geoffrey, JJ Geoghegan, KD Geoghegan, KP Geoghegan, RM Geoghegan, WE Geoghegan, AE George, AJ George, AR George, BA George, BC George, BM George, BR George, D George, DJ George, DL George, EJ George, FE George, GA George, GS George, JF George, MG George, MJ George, RD George, RG George, RI George, RJ George, RP George, RS Georgekennedy, FA Gepp, RW Geppert, BF Geraghty, DJ Geraghty, MK Geraghty, P Geraghty, TR Geraghty, SR Gerahty, DE Gerard, JB Gerber, J Gerbes, BE Gerecke, BE Gerhard, DJ Gerhardt, RE Gerhardt, WR Gerhardt, RM Gerhardy, M Geri, EJ Gerke, G Gerlach, VH Germaine, MW Gernhoefer, JG Gerrans, DM Gerrard, JA Gerrard, JH Gerrard, TJ Gerrish, W Gerritsen, DW Gersbach, RW Gertzel, MA Gervase, AAM Gerzina, JW Gestier, RG Geutner, EJ Gewin, LJ Geyer, JA Geytenbeek, PR Geytenbeek, GW Ghent, WP Ghersi, JF Ghilotti, S Giacomantonio, A Giacomel, RP Gialanze, TJ Giamalis, JL Gianatsis, AS Gibb, IL Gibb, TN Gibb, WH Gibbens, CL Gibbings, RJ Gibbings, DW Gibbins, K Gibbins, RH Gibbins, RJ Gibbins, DG Gibbons, GD Gibbons, IC Gibbons, JE Gibbons, JL Gibbons, JM Gibbons, MJ Gibbons, MR Gibbons, PA Gibbons, PD Gibbons, RJ Gibbons, BA Gibbs, IJ Gibbs, J Gibbs, KA Gibbs, KP Gibbs, SR Gibbs, EM Giblett, AH Gibson, AJ Gibson, BJ Gibson, BP Gibson, BS Gibson, BW Gibson, CM Gibson, CW Gibson, DB Gibson, DE Gibson, DF Gibson, DN Gibson, EG Gibson, FM Gibson, G Gibson, GA Gibson, HJ Gibson, IW Gibson, J Gibson, JAJ Gibson, JM Gibson, JS Gibson, KA Gibson, LJ Gibson, M Gibson, MC Gibson, ML Gibson, MO Gibson, MR Gibson, NL Gibson, NR Gibson, PJ Gibson, PM Gibson, PN Gibson, RC Gibson, RG Gibson, RJ Gibson, RK Gibson, RM Gibson, RW Gibson, SR Gibson, TD Gibson, TJ Gibson, TR Gibson, WD Gibson, WF Gibson, WR Gibson, GH Giddens, GA Giddins, RP Gidman, JE Giersch, L Giesen, WG Giesler, CJ Giezen, E Giffin, NJ Giffin, RJ Giffin, D Gifford, JE Gifford, PA Gifford, PJ Gifford, RC Gigg, RC Giggins, RS Giglio, HC Gilbank, BL Gilbert, CB Gilbert, CR Gilbert, EN Gilbert, GG Gilbert, GJ Gilbert, GV Gilbert, GW Gilbert, JE Gilbert, JR Gilbert, KF Gilbert, LW Gilbert, RM Gilbert, RN Gilbert, RW Gilbert, WS Gilbert, DJ Gilbey, JA Gilchrist, JJ Gilchrist, RJ Gilchrist, TL Gilchrist, TS Gilchrist, DA Gilday, JV Gildea, RE Gilder, WH Gilders, KD Gildersleeve, R Gildersleeve, ME Gildersleeves, BA Giles, BG Giles, DG Giles, DP Giles, ER Giles, GJ Giles, I Giles, J Giles, JR Giles, KW Giles, LJ Giles, LW Giles, PH Giles, PR Giles, PS Giles, RP Giles, SC Giles, WJ Giles, J Gilewicz, DR Gilfedder, RT Gilfillan, P Gilfoyle, AR Gilham, L Gilkinson, AG Gill, BE Gill, BJ Gill, BS Gill, CL Gill, GG Gill, GJ Gill, GL Gill, GW Gill, ID Gill, KJ Gill, MJ Gill, MWT Gill, NF Gill, R Gill, RH Gill, RJ Gill, RL Gill, RM Gill, RR Gill, TW Gill, WCJ Gill, WR Gill, GD Gillam, RL Gillam, RM Gillam, JW Gillan, LJ Gillan, J Gillanders, KJ Gillard, RC Gillard, RJ Gillard, RL Gillard, BP Gillespie, BR Gillespie, GB Gillespie, JF Gillespie, JM Gillespie, LJ Gillespie, MJ Gillespie, RJ Gillespie, RM Gillespie, AA Gillett, DH Gillett, JG Gillett, KJ Gillett, MA Gillett, CJ Gillham, GL Gillham, WS Gillham, RI Gillian, MJ Gillick, GG Gillie, DJ Gillies, DR Gillies, EJ Gillies, K Gillies, RM Gillies, WA Gillies, KT Gilligan, RJ Gilligan, TJ Gilligan, JD Gilliland, RA Gilliland, WJ Gilliland, DM Gillings, CG Gillis, FJ Gillis, RP Gillis, RWJ Gillis, TE Gilliver, BWF Gillman, KJ Gillman, FA Gillow, PR Gillson, R Gillson, DJ Gilmer, AM Gilmore, GC Gilmore, IGC Gilmore, JK Gilmore, JR Gilmore, JA Gilmour, K Gilmour, RC Gilmour, AB Gilmour-Walsh, FE Gilpatrick, MJ Gilpin, DJ Gilroy, DI Gilshenan, FT Gilshenan, DP Gilshenen, PF Gilson, JD Giltrow, SR Ginbey, BF Ginn, RL Ginn, GF Ginnivan, JL Ginnivan, EV Giosserano, WG Girdwood, EG Giri, JD Giroud, RM Girvan, DJ Gisborne, GJ Gissane, TP Gissane, BJ Gissell, AG Gissing, NS Gist, JS Gittings, LG Gittins, PH Gittus, G Giuliani, ARW Gizycki, CJ Gladman, NL Gladman, RA Gladman, MA Gladwell, BA Glance, FM Glancy, RJ Glanfield, GR Glanville, RW Glanville, BJ Glare, KE Glascock, AF Glascott, B Glass, DH Glass, EJ Glass, LD Glass, RJ Glass, BJ Glassenbury, G Glassford, JL Glasson, KJ Glatz, RS Glaubitz, JE Glazebrook, TA Gledhill, D Gleeson, DB Gleeson, DG Gleeson, DJ Gleeson, I Gleeson, IM Gleeson, JF Gleeson, LWJ Gleeson, MA Gleeson, MB Gleeson, MFK Gleeson, PR Gleeson, TJ Gleeson, WP Gleeson, JH Gleich, ADM Glendenning, WP Glendenning, RP Glenn, JE Glennon, WE Glenny, CJ Glenwright, PJ Glenwright, RE Glew, P Gligorevic, HA Gloede, RR Gloede, RW Gloss, BW Glossop, LJ Glossop, BA Glover, BE Glover, CG Glover, DJ Glover, GE Glover, JL Glover, JT Glover, KP Glover, NJ Glover, RC Glover, RJ Glover, RJ Glover, RM Glover, SR Glover, TR Glover, WF Glover, GM Gluche, P Gluhin, BD Glyde, DW Glyde, JT Glyde, KP Glynn, KA Glynne, P Gniatkiewicz, ZJ Gniot, GR Goater, PD Gobetti, BC Goble, JM Goc, JA Godbaz, NJ Godbold, HP Godbolt, B Goddard, DO Goddard, M Goddard, ME Goddard, P Goddard, RJ Goddard, TA Goddard, TJ Goddard, WS Goddard, RM Godde, TR Godde, WJ Godde, BJ Godden, DI Godden, GR Godden, JR Godden, TW Gode, WS Gode, JR Godfredson, BA Godfrey, BC Godfrey, CJ Godfrey, DC Godfrey, G Godfrey, J Godfrey, JD Godfrey, NJ Godfrey, PC Godfrey, PJ Godfrey, RJ Godfrey, RR Godfrey, LJ Goding, C Godlee, DR Godley, EA Godsall, MB Godsell, PG Godwill, ML Godwin, H Godycki, F Goedhart, DM Goetze, AK Goff, BJ Goff, DA Goff, GV Goff, KB Goff, RA Gogan, GM Goggins, PR Goggins, TP Gogoll, MJ Goiser, NH Goiser, GF Gojanovich, A Gold, CW Gold, PR Gold, CD Golden, HE Golden, PJF Golden, RA Golden, JS Goldfinch, KR Goldfinch, B Golding, BB Golding, CB Golding, JJ Golding, LF Golding, RT Golding, W Golding, DM Goldman, DR Goldman, PJ Goldman, BL Goldring, B Goldsbury, AV Goldsmith, JR Goldsmith, LJ Goldsmith, MN Goldsmith, NR Goldsmith, PW Goldsmith, WC Goldsmith, NH Goldspink, RD Goldspink, WP Goldstone, AH Goldsworthy, AJ Goldsworthy, DJ Goldsworthy, R Golebiowski, WJ Golla, PJ Gollagher, MI Golland, SW Golland, BJ Golledge, NM Goller, IJ Gollings, K Gollschewski, SP Golosky, CD Golsby, S Golubenko, HJO Gomer, NF Gomm, HJ Gommermann, RA Gonano, V Goncharow, G Gontar, EJ Gooch, H Gooch, K Gooch, RG Gooch, WR Gooch, AJ Good, CJ Good, J Good, ME Good, SJ Good, SR Good, VM Good, L Gooda, RS Goodacre, TJ Goodacre, BM Goodall, DA Goodall, DB Goodall, LA Goodall, RB Goodall, FG Goodchap, B Goodchild, JB Goodchild, MD Goodchild, PG Goodchild, LW Goode, TDM Goode, CJ Goodear, SJ Gooden, BJ Goodes, RJ Goodes, WJ Goodes, AJ Goodey, WA Goodey, GJ Goodfellow, R Goodger, GL Goodhew, NJ Goodhew, RG Goodhew, DW Gooding, GJ Gooding, NH Gooding, DF Goodings, DC Goodliffe, DJ Goodman, DS Goodman, GJ Goodman, IC Goodman, MH Goodman, PC Goodman, RR Goodmanson, BC Goodrich, TJ Goodrich, BR Goodrick, S Goodridge, AT Goodsell, BE Goodsell, DN Goodson, BD Goodwin, BI Goodwin, BR Goodwin, CN Goodwin, DA Goodwin, DR Goodwin, GM Goodwin, GW Goodwin, JA Goodwin, JB Goodwin, JN Goodwin, MJJ Goodwin, NJ Goodwin, PJ Goodwin, RW Goodworth, PR Goody, BJ Goodyear, JJ Goold, RJ Goold, PJ Gooley, ZJ Gorbunovs, JMP Gorczynski, BD Gordon, BE Gordon, BJ Gordon, BT Gordon, CB Gordon, CH Gordon, CJ Gordon, DJ Gordon, FW Gordon, GF Gordon, GM Gordon, IA Gordon, J Gordon, JCH Gordon, JW Gordon, KG Gordon, KS Gordon, LS Gordon, PD Gordon, RB Gordon, REK Gordon, RJ Gordon, RR Gordon, RSN Gordon, RW Gordon, TG Gordon, TJ Gordon, WC Gordon, WJ Gordon, WJS Gordon, WG Gordon-Brown, AB Gore, GJ Gore, IW Gore, KJ Gorham, JJ Goritchan, A Gorman, BG Gorman, FJ Gorman, G Gorman, LN Gorman, RK Gorman, TJ Gorman, WE Gorman, BJ Gornik, JS Goroncy, DG Gorrick, RL Gorrie, AL Gorringe, TB Gorringe, JA Gorsch, H Gorski, AG Gosby, RG Goschiniak, JR Goslett, JF Gosling, MT Gosling, BA Gosman, WD Gosney, GD Gosper, TH Gosper, DS Goss, IG Goss, JA Goss, JB Goss, KV Goss, PR Goss, RG Goss, SJ Goss, JJ Gossage, KG Gosschalk, AK Gostelow, RJ Gostling, J Gostynski, BH Gotch, PW Gothard, GJ Gott, GT Gott, T Gott, LJ Gotting, A Gottschling, MJ Gottwaltz, NA Gottwaltz, RM Goubareff, RL Goudey, KJ Goudie, A Gough, AJ Gough, DA Gough, GI Gough, GR Gough, IJ Gough, JM Gough, KR Gough, L Gough, RL Gough, AJ Gould, AN Gould, CD Gould, CM Gould, DR Gould, EC Gould, EG Gould, EJ Gould, FJ Gould, J Gould, JR Gould, JW Gould, KJ Gould, MB Gould, MJ Gould, MW Gould, NL Gould, PA Gould, PJ Gould, PJJ Gould, M Goulden, R Goulden, RJ Goulden, JE Goulder, KE Goulder, CW Gouldson, AJ Goulevitch, DD Gourlay, GJ Gourlay, JC Gourlay, DJ Gourley, DR Gourley, RG Gourlie, AG Govan, T Govorcin, AR Gow, DG Gow, DJ Gow, GM Gow, N Gow, PA Gow, PW Gow, RD Gow, PTF Gowans, RE Goward, BE Gower, PR Gower, RO Gower, SN Gower, PR Gowie, CL Gowing, ID Gowing, R Gowland, ID Gowlett, RG Gowley, RH Gowling, P Gowran, DJ Goy, CA Goyne, P Grabb, WS Grabda, RN Grabham, H Grabowski, BF Grace, EC Grace, F Grace, GM Grace, JB Grace, JO Grace, JR Grace, LJ Grace, LL Grace, WJ Grace, TG Gracie, K Gradon, FJ Grady, RM Grady, TW Grady, GH Graefling, RJ Graetz, AB Graf, F Graf, RD Graf, AM Grafton, JM Grafton, MJ Grafton, A Graham, AB Graham, AK Graham, AM Graham, AR Graham, AW Graham, BJ Graham, BT Graham, BV Graham, C Graham, D Graham, DA Graham, DD Graham, DF Graham, DG Graham, DJ Graham, DK Graham, DL Graham, DR Graham, EH Graham, EL Graham, ER Graham, FA Graham, G Graham, GB Graham, GDJ Graham, GE Graham, GH Graham, GP Graham, GR Graham, I Graham, ID Graham, IM Graham, JA Graham, JG Graham, JS Graham, JW Graham, KD Graham, KR Graham, KT Graham, KW Graham, LA Graham,

LG Graham, LJ Graham, LW Graham, ME Graham, NC Graham, ND Graham, NF Graham, PB Graham, PJ Graham, RG Graham, RJ Graham, RM Graham, RP Graham, RW Graham, RWR Graham, S Graham, SC Graham, SL Graham, TA Graham, TJ Graham, TW Graham, BE Grahame, G Grail, PF Grainger, PG Grainger, RR Grainger, SJ Grainger, PJ Grainger-Smith, T Grall, PN Grambower, ID Grandison, DJ Graney, DG Granfelt, D Granger, EC Granger, BF Granland, IH Granland, SS Granne, AK Grant, B Grant, C Grant, C Grant, CR Grant, DB Grant, DM Grant, EF Grant, FC Grant, GA Grant, GAG Grant, GD Grant, GH Grant, GK Grant, HS Grant, JB Grant, JR Grant, JS Grant, KJ Grant, LR Grant, NC Grant, PA Grant, PF Grant, PJF Grant, PS Grant, RH Grant, RI Grant, RJ Grant, RL Grant, RV Grant, TJ Grant, WE Grant, WL Grant, NE Granter, KJ Grantham, AG Grant-Smith, JC Grasby, WJ Grassick, PC Gration, RF Gratton, RH Gratton, AB Gratwick, DP Gratwick, RJ Graupner, V Gravelis, WN Gravener, A Graveson, A Gray, AC Gray, AE Gray, AK Gray, AM Gray, BC Gray, D Gray, D Gray, DB Gray, DM Gray, DN Gray, DS Gray, EF Gray, EJ Gray, ERG Gray, G Gray, GA Gray, GL Gray, ID Gray, IM Gray, JS Gray, KD Gray, LG Gray, LJ Gray, LK Gray, MC Gray, MJ Gray, MW Gray, NR Gray, P Gray, PA Gray, PD Gray, PJ Gray, R Gray, RA Gray, RC Gray, RD Gray, RDE Gray, RE Gray, RF Gray, RJ Gray, RS Gray, RW Gray, SP Gray, SR Gray, TJ Gray, WM Gray, WR Gray, JR Graydon, WG Graydon, DA Grayson, GR Grayson, KG Grayson, TC Grayson, RM Greagen, AG Grealey, MV Grealy, RJ Grealy, AJ Greaney, BM Grear, A Greaves, AH Greaves, AR Greaves, BL Greaves, DR Greaves, HG Greaves, IJ Greaves, J Greaves, LD Greaves, RJ Greaves, WJ Greaves, ER Greay, JJ Grech, M Grech, S Grech, AC Grecian, DJ Grecian, A Green, AR Green, AS Green, AT Green, AW Green, BA Green, BJ Green, BP Green, CJ Green, DA Green, DJ Green, DL Green, EA Green, EG Green, FP Green, GB Green, GC Green, GG Green, GM Green, GN Green, GR Green, GS Green, GW Green, H Green, H Green, HD Green, HM Green, IW Green, JA Green, JC Green, JF Green, JG Green, JP Green, JR Green, JW Green, K Green, KB Green, KD Green, KR Green, KSF Green, KW Green, LB Green, LD Green, LM Green, LR Green, MJ Green, MJA Green, ML Green, MW Green, NL Green, OB Green, ON Green, PD Green, PE Green, PJ Green, PM Green, PP Green, PR Green, PS Green, RA Green, RC Green, RJ Green, RL Green, RN Green, RR Green, RS Green, RV Green, RW Green, SCA Green, TJ Green, TP Green, TS Green, WC Green, WR Green, WW Green, JD Greenaway, ID Greenbank, BN Greenberger, PJ Greenbury, BM Greene, IP Greene, JG Greene, RJ Greene, RW Greene, CW Greenhalgh, DW Greenhalgh, JR Greenhalgh, KA Greenhalgh, MR Greenhalgh, PJ Greenhalgh, PN Greenhalgh, AW Greenham, RS Greenhill, AJ Greening, GW Greenland, J Greenough, JA Greenshields, JC Greensill, DS Greentree, IG Greentree, LS Greentree, PD Greentree, AM Greenway, FDL Greenway, JN Greenway, MJ Greenway, DJ Greenwell, AD Greenwood, AJ Greenwood, BJ Greenwood, EW Greenwood, GN Greenwood, K Greenwood, KJ Greenwood, M Greenwood, RJ Greenwood, RK Greenwood, RT Greenwood, SC Greenwood, WC Greenwood, WJ Greenwood, DL Greer, KM Greer, RG Greer, B Greetham, PE Greethead, ID Gregg, JR Gregg, KH Gregg, KJ Gregg, PJ Gregg, RC Gregg, RF Gregg, SP Gregg, WJC Gregg, GD Gregor, GS Gregor, PG Gregor, AJ Gregory, AW Gregory, DA Gregory, GB Gregory, GJ Gregory, GR Gregory, GW Gregory, HD Gregory, HM Gregory, IJ Gregory, JD Gregory, JK Gregory, KA Gregory, PL Gregory, PR Gregory, RL Gregory, SC Gregory, WR Gregory, WS Gregory, AW Gregson, GF Gregson, KG Gregson, PC Grehan, RA Greig, RG Greig, RJ Greig, WF Greig, HK Greinke, DJ Greiveson, JV Grelck, PR Grelck, PE Grenenger, PB Grenfell, RC Grenfell, WL Grenfell, AB Greshner, CJ Greville, LR Greville, PJ Greville, EC Grew, DA Grey, EN Grey, GR Grey, JC Grey, KJ Grey, MJ Grey, RA Grey, RC Grey, WG Grey, TE Gribbin, MH Gribble, SR Gribble, J Gribbon, A Grice, AS Grice, EJ Grice, KL Grice, TA Grice, VR Grice, WJ Grice, GA Gridley, KR Gridley, MG Gridley, U Grieco, LE Grierson, AC Grieve, BE Grieve, CR Grieve, LH Grieve, NG Grieve, RE Grieve, DJ Grieves, EM Griff, MS Griffen, TJ Griffen, ID Griffey, BA Griffin, BT Griffin, FI Griffin, JT Griffin, MD Griffin, MJ Griffin, NJ Griffin, PD Griffin, PR Griffin, TD Griffin, WC Griffin, BB Griffith, BJ Griffith, BM Griffith, JH Griffith, AA Griffiths, AD Griffiths, B Griffiths, BK Griffiths, CA Griffiths, CL Griffiths, D Griffiths, DJ Griffiths, DL Griffiths, GD Griffiths, GJ Griffiths, GL Griffiths, GR Griffiths, GT Griffiths, JH Griffiths, JL Griffiths, JMM Griffiths, JW Griffiths, KB Griffiths, KF Griffiths, LC Griffiths, LW Griffiths, NE Griffiths, PR Griffiths, PV Griffiths, PWC Griffiths, RB Griffiths, RE Griffiths, RJ Griffiths, S Griffiths, SR Griffiths, TA Griffiths, TM Griffiths, VJ Griffiths, IR Grigg, PA Grigg, RH Grigg, TJ Grigg, GR Griggs, HA Griggs, JH Griggs, RK Griggs, WN Griggs, FA Grigonis, WJ Grigor, AK Grikis, EA Grills, KS Grills, P Grills, TE Grills, JP Grimblot, KF Grime, DJ Grimes, HD Grimes, NJ Grimes, WH Grimes, GL Grimish, DG Grimley, MA Grimmer, RG Grimmer, GV Grimmond, EA Grimshaw, RJ Grimshaw, TR Grimsley, LR Grimstone, GJ Grimwood, RR Grindal, JK Grindley, DT Grindrod, R Grindrod, VG Grinham, AM Grinter, WJ Grinter, RJ Grinyer, BL Grisdale, RM Grist, RD Grivell, BD Groat, PF Grob, AJ Groessler, AJ Grogan, JF Grogan, RM Grogan, WJ Grogan, AD Gronow, AJ Gronow, RT Groombridge, AF Groome, KT Grose, LR Grose, MH Grose, PW Grose, TJ Grose, PN Grosfeld, BB Gross, FG Gross, RJ Gross, SP Gross, TF Gross, C Grosse, MA Grosse, RJ Grosseibl, MJ Grosser, DJ Grosvenor, FL Grosvenor, WA Grosvenor, GJ Groth, MO Groth, DL Groundwater, MG Groundwater, NB Groundwater, RD Groundwater, DJ Grove, JC Grove, RA Grove, MJ Grovenor, RE Grover, AC Groves, AJ Groves, BW Groves, JR Groves, N Groves, ND Groves, PK Groves, PW Groves, RG Groves, SEF Groves, SR Groves, G Growden, KM Growden, D Grubb, JC Grubb, JR Grubb, PA Grubb, WT Grubb, EP Grube, JG Grudzinskas, HJ Grueninger, N Gruetzner, KK Grula, AW Grulke, NH Grummett, M Grund, HNW Grundell, PM Grundman, R Grundy, P Grygiel, LG Grygierczyk, H Grzegozewski, LW Gubbin, DH Gudde, KR Gudgeon, JL Guerin, LR Guerin, PJ Guerin, RJ Guerin, AG Guest, GC Guest, GD Guest, GT Guest, JW Guest, LF Guest, NR Guest, PK Guest, RL Guest, TP Guest, WJ Guest, PJ Guider, AM Guiffre, IM Guild, JA Guild, MF Guillot, BE Guise, TW Guivarra, AM Gul, P Gulbransen, RL Guldbransen, LG Guley, PR Gulley, RJ Gulley, IR Gully, F Gulyas, BC Gum, GG Gumley, PR Gumprich, J Gumulak, WM Gunder, GR Gundry, CJ Gunn, DW Gunn, GC Gunn, GM Gunn, KR Gunn, RJ Gunn, R Gunnell, FW Gunning, KH Gunning, RR Gunning, TH Gunning, LC Gunns, VG Gunnulson, AA Gunson, WP Gunsser, D Gunst, JE Gunst, BA Gunston, GR Gunthorpe, GJ Gunton, JW Gunton, NW Guppy, PL Gurd, CM Gurner, KS Gurner, AR Gurnett, DR Gurney, JP Gurney, K Gurney, P Gurney, PL Gurney, RK Gurney, RP Gurney, PT Gurr, R Guse, AS Guster, BJ Guthrie, CWW Guthrie, DH Guthrie, L Guthrie, PC Guthrie, RB Guthrie, HD Gutjahr, W Gutjahr, J Gutschmidt, BH Gutteridge, G Gutteridge, AF Guy, CA Guy, FE Guy, IJ Guy, JD Guy, JW Guy, KR Guy, LR Guy, PJ Guy, PL Guy, TLJ Guy, PD Guyatt, DJ Guye, AE Guyer, RC Guymer, BJ Guzder, J Gwynn, TJ Gygar, DV Gynther, J Gyory, TC Gysbers, AP Haabjoern, GF Haack, SK Haas, MW Habben, AV Habel, NF Haberfield, AA Haberley, BC Haberley, DW Habgood, DP Habler, CA Habraken, GR Hack, RC Hack, B Hackett, GK Hackett, KC Hackett, PJ Hackett, R Hackett, WT Hackett, AM Hacking, WF Hacking, R Hackman, PE Hacon, GR Hadaway, JE Hadaway, PF Haddad, JD Hadden, TR Haddleton, BW Haddock, GC Haddock, A Haddon, JAD Haddon, JL Haddon, RG Haddow, DG Haddrell, EF Haddrick, JG Haddrick, DI Hadley, GR Hadley, MJ Hadley, RV Hadley, WR Hadley, DE Haebich, JD Hafemeister, EJ Hagan, JR Hagan, RL Hagan, TF Hagan, TP Hagan, DJ Hage, JP Hagean, N Hagel, CP Hagenbach, RE Hagerty, R Haggart, WJ Hagger, RG Haggerty, J Hagston, BH Hague, RI Hague, DR Hahn, DS Hahn, J Hahn, EF Haidley, EMM Haig, LE Haig, PW Haig, PJ Haigh, PL Hailes, JR Haim, KMD Haimes, DP Haines, JE Haines, RC Haines, WG Haines, DJ Haining, CP Hains, KM Hains, K Hainsworth, MT Hainsworth, CJ Hair, SJ Hair, G Hajdu, ME Halbreiner, TJ Halcroft, MJ Haldane, RL Haldane, DJ Haldon-Hodge, A Hale, AE Hale, BF Hale, CA Hale, CR Hale, D Hale, JF Hale, LS Hale, PJ Hale, RC Hale, RJ Hale, TH Hale, TM Hale, AJ Hales, BG Hales, DW Hales, JK Hales, AHJ Haley, RJ Haley, TR Halfacree, LT Halford, WA Halfpenny, E Halkyard, RC Halkyard, A Hall, AB Hall, AL Hall, AR Hall, AT Hall, BD Hall, BG Hall, BP Hall, C Hall, CJ Hall, DLJ Hall, DW Hall, EA Hall, ED Hall, EJ Hall, EV Hall, GD Hall, GJ Hall, GNG Hall, GR Hall, HR Hall, HW Hall, IG Hall, IM Hall, IW Hall, J Hall, JC Hall, JF Hall, JH Hall, JR Hall, JR Hall, KA Hall, KJ Hall, KL Hall, KN Hall, KP Hall, KR Hall, KW Hall, LA Hall, LJ Hall, LN Hall, LR Hall, MC Hall, MG Hall, MJ Hall, N Hall, NT Hall, OH Hall, PB Hall, PJ Hall, PL Hall, PR Hall, R Hall, RA Hall, RE Hall, RG Hall, RJ Hall, RJG Hall, RK Hall, RL Hall, RN Hall, RW Hall, SD Hall, SI Hall, SK Hall, SM Hall, SR Hall, TE Hall, WE Hall, WG Hall, WL Hall, WM Hall, CE Hallam, GE Hallam, GRS Hallam, JA Hallam, JE Hallam, PJ Hallam, JB Hallas, JA Hallett, RK Hallett, RW Hallett, TJ Hallewell, PJ Halley, RW Hallgath, BJ Halliday, D Halliday, F Halliday, J Halliday, KJ Halliday, PA Halliday, PV Halliday, RJ Halliday, RJP Halliday, D Hallifax, KW Halligan, RM Hallin, JC Hallinan, VE Hallinan, FS Hallissy, DJ Halliwell, F Halliwell, KF Halloran, RL Halloran, B Halls, J Halls, LC Halls, MK Halls, RC Halls, RJ Halls, SAC Hallstrom, CT Halmarick, DJ Halmarick, AR Halpin, ID Halpin, WA Halpin, SG Halse, GL Halsey, T Halstead, BW Halsted, MJ Halton, PR Halton, RJ Halverson, PA Halvorsen, CN Ham, PJ Ham, RJ Ham, RC Hamann, RL Hamann, BR Hambleton, NL Hamblion, JP Hambly, SH Hambly, RJ Hamblyn, GA Hamburger, IG Hamdorf, IJ Hamdorf, DJ Hameister, RV Hameister, RD Hamence, CR Hamer, KN Hamer, FG Hamersley, RE Hamerton, RG Hames, WJ Hames, DG Hamill, G Hamill, PH Hamill, AD Hamilton, AR Hamilton, B Hamilton, BA Hamilton, BJ Hamilton, DB Hamilton, DI Hamilton, DJ Hamilton, EJR Hamilton, GE Hamilton, GF Hamilton, GJ Hamilton, GL Hamilton, IJ Hamilton, JD Hamilton, JG Hamilton, JH Hamilton, KJ Hamilton, KR Hamilton, MB Hamilton, PA Hamilton, RA Hamilton, RI Hamilton, RJ Hamilton, RP Hamilton, WE Hamilton, WJ Hamilton, WR Hamilton, CV Hamlet, DP Hamlin, EA Hamlin, AG Hamlyn, JS Hamlyn, RD Hamlyn, DE Hammat, JL Hammer, EG Hammerton, AW Hammett, RJ Hammett, RV Hammett, RC Hammill, AM Hammond, C Hammond, CJ Hammond, DA Hammond, DJ Hammond, GJ Hammond, HW Hammond, JE Hammond, PG Hammond, RG Hammond, RJ Hammond, RS Hammond, TF Hammond, WG Hammond, PS Hamon, JN Hamood, DH Hampshire, BC Hampson, EB Hampson, JF Hampson, KB Hampson, NA Hampson, PK Hampson, TJ Hampson, VLW Hampson, B Hampstead, BV Hampstead, JG Hampstead, TC Hampstead, DL Hampton, GE Hampton, JE Hampton, NW Hampton, JE Hams, KP Hams, NR Hamson, LS Hana, AJ Hanbridge, B Hanbury, DG Hanchard, A Hancill, AI Hancock, DG Hancock, DJ Hancock, FL Hancock, JF Hancock, JJ Hancock, JR Hancock, KA Hancock, KC Hancock, LA Hancock, MW Hancock, RC Hancock, RE Hancock, RG Hancock, TS Hancock, RS Hancy, DJ Hand, RJ Hand, DJ Handbury, JAM Handby, AFJ Handley, AR Handley, DJ Handley, DW Handley, GB Handley, GE Handley, KB Handley, M Handley, WC Handley, WT Handley, DH Hands, IG Hands, PL Handy, J Hanek, JL Hanely, AH Haneveld, RG Hanham, RJ Hanisch, P Hankel, CL Hankin, L Hankin, AJ Hankinson, IF Hankinson, NS Hankinson, AK Hanks, DR Hanks, JW Hanks, DT Hanlen, DT Hanley, JJ Hanley, LR Hanley, MP Hanley, P Hanley, PE Hanley, RC Hanley, TJ Hanley, DW Hanlin, GW Hanlin, PS Hanlin, AC Hanlon, DW Hanlon, JJ Hanlon, KJ Hanlon, RH Hanlon, RJ Hanlon, FJ Hanly, GH Hann, RJ Hann, TI Hann, ID Hanna, BJ Hannaford, DJ Hannaford, GE Hannaford, MJ Hannaford, TP Hannaford, GK Hannah, JJ Hannah, MP Hannah, PW Hannah, RJ Hannah, RS Hannah, TI Hannah, RJ Hannam, AT Hannan, I Hannay, BT Hannebery, DM Hannell, RG Hannett, NJ Hanney, P Hanney, RR Hannigan, JP Hannon, JL Hanns, CP Hanrahan, JD Hanrahan, JM Hanrahan, P Hanratty, LD Hansch, CE Hansell, AR Hansen, BJ Hansen, BR Hansen, BV Hansen, C Hansen, CJ Hansen, DA Hansen, DJ Hansen, GC Hansen, GJ Hansen, GR Hansen, JA Hansen, JC Hansen, JP Hansen, KR Hansen, NR Hansen, PD Hansen, PR Hansen, RJ Hansen, RK Hansen, RM Hansen, RS Hansen, TJ Hansen, WP Hansen, HR Hansford, RF Hansford, KP Hanslow, BJ Hanson, BN Hanson, DD Hanson, G Hanson, GJ Hanson, GW Hanson, NB Hanson, RA Hanson, RJ Hanson, SJ Hanson, TG Hanson, TL Hanson, WD Hanson, WJ Hanson, BT Hansson, PH Hanstock, S Hanuszewicz,

SE Hanvey, AP Hanway, PD Happ, NS Harald, P Haran, RJ Harbach, BC Harbeck, PN Harbeck, RA Harbeck, W Harbers, HG Harberts, CG Harbinson, LP Harbinson, B Harbour, EH Harbour, RG Harbourd, RC Harbourne, L Harbridge, GW Harcla, KW Harcoan, ALN Harcombe, AJ Harcourt, GD Harcus, JL Harcus, K Harcus, LF Hardacre, RC Hardaker, CJ Harden, NH Harden, ES Hardgrave, AR Hardgrove, FR Hardidge, DB Hardie, J Hardie, REJ Hardie, VJ Hardie, AP Hardiman, EB Hardiman, RK Hardimon, LG Hardin, AM Harding, AR Harding, DG Harding, DH Harding, DJ Harding, DW Harding, G Harding, GW Harding, IL Harding, JA Harding, JC Harding, JW Harding, KW Harding, LA Harding, LJ Harding, LT Harding, MG Harding, MJ Harding, MR Harding, PB Harding, PG Harding, PH Harding, R Harding, RA Harding, RK Harding, RR Harding, TE Harding, WP Harding, MW Hardless, BE Hardman, C Hardman, DJ Hardman, JC Hardman, RB Hardman, EW Hards, JT Hards, W Hards, AJ Hardstaff, CW Hardwick, PT Hardwick, TC Hardwick, TH Hardwick, BC Hardy, CT Hardy, DJ Hardy, IA Hardy, JD Hardy, JK Hardy, JW Hardy, KJ Hardy, M Hardy, NE Hardy, NW Hardy, PD Hardy, PM Hardy, WFJ Hardy, AJ Hare, DC Hare, JE Hare, KJ Hare, KW Hare, RA Hare, BJ Harford, DV Harford, DJ Hargans, B Hargense, GJ Hargrave, GL Hargrave, RA Hargrave, AR Hargraves, MW Hargraves, GM Hargreaves, HD Hargreaves, RW Hargreaves, TA Hargreaves, M Harken, GM Harker, KB Harker, LJ Harker, D Harkin, DA Harkin, E Harkin, DB Harkins, KM Harkins, A Harkness, GG Harkness, HL Harland, JT Harland, RB Harland, RR Harland, TM Harland, L Harler, BM Harley, EA Harley, EJ Harley, HD Harley, NE Harley, PA Harley, PG Harley, WDA Harley, BA Harlock, BC Harlond, RP Harlor, HD Harlow, JH Harlow, RT Harlow, IH Harm, ER Harman, KT Harman, LC Harman, T Harmansmith, DF Harmer, DJ Harmer, GK Harmer, HJ Harmer, JB Harmer, MF Harmer, WJ Harmer, RW Harmes, GJ Harmon, AR Harms, J Harms, JS Harms, RP Harms, LT Harmsworth, AF Harney, GF Harney, PJ Harnwell, BC Harper, BJ Harper, CR Harper, DG Harper, DM Harper, DR Harper, JR Harper, JS Harper, JT Harper, JW Harper, LA Harper, P Harper, RJ Harper, RT Harper, RW Harper, SM Harper, TJ Harper, WJ Harper, JJ Harpley, WB Harpley, AH Harpwood, JH Harrap, RE Harriden, DW Harries, WF Harrigan, RE Harring, CJ Harrington, CM Harrington, EJ Harrington, GW Harrington, JH Harrington, JP Harrington, MH Harrington, P Harrington, WA Harrington, MJ Harriott, A Harris, AF Harris, AJ Harris, AL Harris, AT Harris, BA Harris, BC Harris, BK Harris, BW Harris, CJ Harris, CL Harris, DA Harris, DE Harris, DJ Harris, DL Harris, DR Harris, DW Harris, DWV Harris, EFW Harris, FJ Harris, G Harris, GD Harris, GI Harris, GJ Harris, GPL Harris, GR Harris, GW Harris, HB Harris, HL Harris, HM Harris, IH Harris, IM Harris, IS Harris, J Harris, JC Harris, JH Harris, JS Harris, JW Harris, K Harris, KG Harris, KJ Harris, L Harris, LE Harris, LG Harris, LJ Harris, MJ Harris, MR Harris, MW Harris, N Harris, NB Harris, NE Harris, NJ Harris, NR Harris, P Harris, PG Harris, PJ Harris, PK Harris, PM Harris, PR Harris, PW Harris, QP Harris, RA Harris, RC Harris, RD Harris, RG Harris, RH Harris, RIK Harris, RJ Harris, RM Harris, RS Harris, RW Harris, RWR Harris, SD Harris, SG Harris, SP Harris, ST Harris, TJ Harris, TM Harris, VB Harris, VL Harris, WE Harris, WR Harris, AR Harrison, BW Harrison, C Harrison, D Harrison, DA Harrison, DC Harrison, DR Harrison, DV Harrison, DW Harrison, EJ Harrison, EM Harrison, EWD Harrison, FA Harrison, G Harrison, GT Harrison, IG Harrison, IJ Harrison, ITT Harrison, JI Harrison, JM Harrison, JR Harrison, JVL Harrison, JW Harrison, KC Harrison, KD Harrison, KJ Harrison, KR Harrison, MN Harrison, MT Harrison, P Harrison, PJ Harrison, PM Harrison, R Harrison, RB Harrison, RD Harrison, RE Harrison, RG Harrison, RH Harrison, RI Harrison, RN Harrison, RP Harrison, SL Harrison, TD Harrison, TG Harrison, TH Harrison, TJ Harrison, WE Harrison, WM Harrison, WN Harrison, WR Harrison, NK Harriss, PR Harriss, RW Harriss, DA Harrod, DH Harrod, BE Harrold, KW Harrold, LF Harrold, TN Harrold, CH Harrop, MJ Harrop, N Harrop, JN Harrower, PW Harrower, GJ Harry, WJ Harsh, BA Harstad, AM Hart, BP Hart, CW Hart, DF Hart, DJ Hart, G Hart, GJ Hart, GL Hart, IR Hart, JJ Hart, LG Hart, LJ Hart, NJ Hart, PC Hart,

PR Hart, PT Hart, RJ Hart, SD Hart, SE Hart, SW Hart, TA Hart, TJ Hart, BJ Hartas, EG Hartas, MG Hartas, JF Harte, RJ Harte, GJ Hartigan, ND Hartigan, PM Hartigan, RB Hartigan, J Hartingdon, ML Hartl, EA Hartley, FJ Hartley, GR Hartley, I Hartley, JC Hartley, JF Hartley, JS Hartley, JW Hartley, LD Hartley, PE Hartley, RG Hartley, RJ Hartley, RN Hartley, RW Hartley, WJ Hartley, HJ Hartman, RD Hartman, RA Hartmann, VJ Hartmann, JF Hartnack, FD Hartnell, GWJ Hartnett, LJ Hartnett, CN Hartney, GJ Hartney, JGE Hartney, MM Hartney, RP Hartney, PM Hartrick, FJ Hartridge, DF Hartshorn, DM Hartshorn, IP Hartshorn, P Hartung, JA Hartwell, AF Hartwig, KR Hartwig, IC Harty, JD Harverson, B Harvey, BR Harvey, BT Harvey, D Harvey, DF Harvey, ET Harvey, G Harvey, GA Harvey, GE Harvey, GG Harvey, GM Harvey, J Harvey, JE Harvey, JF Harvey, JG Harvey, JH Harvey, JS Harvey, K Harvey, KB Harvey, KJ Harvey, KM Harvey, LA Harvey, LF Harvey, MJ Harvey, O Harvey, PJ Harvey, PK Harvey, R Harvey, RC Harvey, RJ Harvey, RJH Harvey, RM Harvey, RP Harvey, SP Harvey, TJ Harvey, WC Harvey, WJ Harvey, WR Harvey, WR Harvey-Hall, HA Harvey-Sutton, FG Harvie, FG Harvison, AA Harwood, AC Harwood, BC Harwood, D Harwood, GC Harwood, KW Harwood, TR Harwood, BE Haseldine, GW Haselgrove, AT Haseloff, RJ Haskard, DM Haskett, LV Haskett, NWA Haskett, NM Haskins, IR Haslam, P Haslau, JA Hasler, JJ Hasler, BK Haslett, JR Haslett, RJ Haslett, BAJ Hassall, GF Hassall, JPL Hassard, FG Hassett, JP Hassett, ML Hassett, RW Hassett, PK Hassgall, GN Hasted, NM Hasted, GD Hastie, KJ Hastie, RF Hastie, SJ Hastie, BL Hastings, DJ Hastings, GG Hastings, IJ Hastings, IR Hastings, LD Hastings, NS Hastings, TP Hastings, PR Hastwell, G Haswell, J Hatch, MR Hatch, NH Hatch, RJ Hatch, OF Hatchard, GJ Hatcher, MW Hatcher, WJ Hatcher, BM Hateley, P Hateley, DL Hathaway, KA Hatherley, BW Hatherly, RF Hattander, RJ Hattley, LJ Hatton, JE Hatwell, FS Hatzel, M Hau, JC Hauck, WG Hauck, BW Haug, ML Haug, RL Haughey, GJ Haupt, GM Haupt, WR Hauser, BG Havers, CW Havers, MJ Havey, PR Haw, MJ Haward, AA Hawes, JL Hawes, RJ Hawes, WH Hawes, IG Hawke, KC Hawke, AN Hawken, ER Hawken, LB Hawken, FA Hawker, GJ Hawker, NV Hawker, PW Hawker, S Hawker, EC Hawkes, FCA Hawkes, JM Hawkes, RW Hawkes, LR Hawkett, BJ Hawkey, DG Hawkey, DR Hawking, AE Hawkins, AR Hawkins, BA Hawkins, BM Hawkins, BR Hawkins, BW Hawkins, DJ Hawkins, EJ Hawkins, GE Hawkins, GW Hawkins, JW Hawkins, KE Hawkins, NH Hawkins, NR Hawkins, PE Hawkins, PJ Hawkins, RA Hawkins, RC Hawkins, RJ Hawkins, RK Hawkins, S Hawkins, TC Hawkins, WP Hawkins, WT Hawkins, AL Hawksford, DI Hawksworth, EA Hawksworth, EM Hawley, MF Hawley, KD Haworth, BR Hawthorne, KE Hawthorne, DR Hawtin, JE Hawton, BG Hay, BF Hay, DG Hay, GW Hay, J Hay, JCJ Hay, MA Hay, MJ Hay, PD Hay, RA Hay, RJ Hay, RR Hay, TJ Hay, TW Hay, WE Hay, IM Hayat, IJ Haycock, BC Hayden, CJ Hayden, E Hayden, JA Hayden, PJ Hayden, RE Hayden, RJ Hayden, C Haydock, AJ Hayes, BE Hayes, CE Hayes, CJ Hayes, DG Hayes, DL Hayes, DW Hayes, EG Hayes, FS Hayes, FV Hayes, GW Hayes, HJ Hayes, HR Hayes, JF Hayes, JR Hayes, KL Hayes, KP Hayes, KS Hayes, LC Hayes, LV Hayes, P Hayes, PJ Hayes, RC Hayes, RG Hayes, RJ Hayes, RW Hayes, SJ Hayes, TD Hayes, TF Hayes, TJ Hayes, TJM Hayes, WGC Hayes, LJ Hayesstclair, IR Hayles, GE Haylock, IW Haylock, PF Haylock, PJ Haylock, AL Hayman, DG Hayman, GM Hayman, IH Hayman, JA Hayman, MW Hayman, RS Haymen, J Hayne, NP Hayne, CD Haynes, DJ Haynes, FJ Haynes, GL Haynes, JD Haynes, JK Haynes, JS Haynes, KG Haynes, PH Haynes, PJ Haynes, W Haynes, EC Hays, RG Hays, HJ Hayter, DF Hayward, DJ Hayward, E Hayward, FC Hayward, GR Hayward, JB Hayward, JD Hayward, JG Hayward, JL Hayward, JR Hayward, KD Hayward, LR Hayward, MA Hayward, RA Hayward, RF Hayward, SC Hayward, GE Haywood, ID Haywood, MR Haywood, PA Haywood, RJ Haywood, AJ Hazel, EG Hazel, GA Hazel, JR Hazel, FG Hazelager, DM Hazell, NJ Hazell, PT Hazell, RA Hazell, SE Hazell, WR Hazell, FC Hazelwood, KR Hazzard, CJ Head, J Head, JH Head, JL Head, RJ Head, SJ Head, TM Head, VH Head, WA Head, GJ Heading, AW Headley, BK Headley, BAF Heal, DJ Heald, AL Heales, DG Healey, GF Healey, HF Healey, J Healey, KA Healey, LF Healey, MD Healey, PJ Healey, RGC Healey, RP Healey,

TC Healey, DL Healy, DM Healy, JB Healy, JD Healy, LP Healy, MG Healy, PJ Healy, PL Healy, RM Healy, RW Healy, TA Healy, TJ Healy, KN Heanes, CR Heaney, JJ Heaney, PJ Heaney, BE Heap, WJ Heapy, AB Heard, BC Heard, IG Heard, KW Heard, MD Heard, NJ Heard, RF Heard, RG Heard, SR Hearder, BR Hearn, IJC Hearn, JR Hearn, RJ Hearn, RL Hearn, TJ Hearn, A Hearne, GD Hearne, RJ Hearne, VEJ Hearne, AM Heaslip, BJ Heath, BK Heath, BR Heath, DJ Heath, DW Heath, GD Heath, JT Heath, KS Heath, WS Heath, BE Heathcote, C Heathcote, GJ Heathcote, RA Heathcote, RE Heathcote, JW Heather, NC Heather, DJ Heatley, PJ Heatly, EM Heaton, AW Heaver, NL Heavisides, DJ Heazlewood, JS Hebbard, TC Hebbard, KJ Hebblewhite, DN Hebden, IJ Heberle, LJ Hebert, RW Hebert, PR Hecker, JR Hector, TD Hedderman, DP Hede, LR Hedge, NV Hedge, RG Hedge, PA Hedgecock, GF Hedger, RG Hedger, DF Hedges, KA Hedges, PJ Hedges, RW Hedges, MC Hedley, PJ Hedrick, RJ Heeb, BJ Heenan, DF Heenan, KL Heenan, MN Heenan, PD Heenan, PW Heenan, TV Heenan, PJ Heeney, WA Heeps, TI Heesom, BJ Heffernan, EBA Heffernan, GM Heffernan, GP Heffernan, MJ Heffernan, R Heffernan, JA Hefford, WA Heffy, C Hegarty, H Hegarty, JJ Hegarty, MJ Hegarty, PJ Hegarty, FC Hegerty, BR Heggie, RT Heggie, BA Hehir, GA Hehir, RJ Hehr, LJ Heid, L Heidenreich, JA Heidt, EK Heieck, DR Height, RW Heiler, B Heine, K Heiniger, CA Heinrich, DR Heinrich, WF Heinson, JJ Heinze, RE Heinze, ED Heise, LT Heiskanen, RL Heit, EE Held, CR Heldon, KJ Heldon, FP Hele, P Helenis, CG Heley, DF Heley, Z Helinski, D Hellen, ME Hellessey, FC Hellier, PE Hellmrich, GR Hellwig, DW Hellyer, GLA Hellyer, JA Hellyer, MA Hellyer, PR Hellyer, NJ Helm, DG Helmrich, VR Helps, RJ Helyar, MJ Helyard, CG Hemberg, KD Hemburrow, JN Hemerik, DS Heming, JC Hemmens, MR Hemmens, LG Hemming, SG Hemming, FA Hempel, DM Hempenstall, JP Hempenstall, GA Hemphill, JH Hemphill, R Hemphill, DA Hemsley, KJ Hemsley, PW Hemsworth, DW Henchie, DJ Hend, AB Henderson, AH Henderson, AJ Henderson, AS Henderson, B Henderson, BJ Henderson, CL Henderson, D Henderson, DG Henderson, DJ Henderson, DR Henderson, FC Henderson, FG Henderson, FJ Henderson, GB Henderson, GD Henderson, GS Henderson, HE Henderson, HG Henderson, IM Henderson, J Henderson, JP Henderson, JS Henderson, JV Henderson, KJ Henderson, LA Henderson, LD Henderson, LW Henderson, MA Henderson, ML Henderson, NA Henderson, NF Henderson, NW Henderson, PF Henderson, PI Henderson, RE Henderson, RG Henderson, RH Henderson, RJ Henderson, RW Henderson, SJ Henderson, TG Henderson, TM Henderson, W Henderson, WG Henderson, WJ Henderson, WR Henderson, TE Hendle, KG Hendley, JJ Hendrick, AB Hendrickson, GF Hendrickson, RT Hendrie, CJM Hendriks, DW Hendry, RGJ Hendry, A Hendy, PA Hendy, RAL Hendy, LRJ Heness, LW Heness, BG Henkel, BJ Henley, GR Henley, HJ Henley, JAT Henley, JB Henley, JN Hennebery, RJ Hennegan, PJ Hennessey, AJ Hennessy, BJ Hennessy, GE Hennessy, HK Hennessy, JJ Hennessy, LW Hennessy, R Hennessy, RFJ Hennessy, RP Hennessy, WR Hennessy, WC Henney, NJ Hennigan, RW Henning, SE Henning, GG Henricksen, PS Henriksen, RR Henriksen, AJ Henry, BR Henry, ET Henry, GS Henry, J Henry, JB Henry, MJF Henry, MP Henry, PE Henry, PM Henry, PR Henry, RG Henry, RJ Henry, SA Henry, DJ Henrys, ME Henrys, VP Henrys, PB Hensell, AJ Henshall, BM Henshall, IJ Henshall, G Henshaw, GM Henshaw, JW Henshaw, W Henshaw, DJ Henson, ES Henson, RJ Henson, T Henson, PL Henssler, BL Henstridge, ME Hentschke, GD Henzell, GG Hepburn, JB Hepburn, RJ Hepburn, CR Hepenstall, A Hepple, GR Hepple, SE Hepple, W Herasymowicz, AA Herbert, BL Herbert, CH Herbert, DA Herbert, EA Herbert, EJ Herbert, GP Herbert, JA Herbert, LMC Herbert, LR Herbert, MJ Herbert, NL Herbert, OJ Herbert, PP Herbert, RR Herbert, RW Herbert, TJ Herbert, WR Herbert, KF Herbig, RD Herd, TC Herd, KJ Herdman, KW Hergenhan, RG Heriot, NE Heritage, EF Herlihy, JD Herlihy, RJ Herlihy, B Herman, CJ Herman, M Herman, BR Hermann, JF Hermann, AJ Hermanson, HW Hernaman, BD Heron, D Heron, DP Heron, JE Heron, JW Heron, WA Heron, JR Herrick, CN Herring, LJ Herring, RA Herring, RF Herring, RH Herring, DE Herrington, B Herrmann, NR Herrmann, RH Herrod, IJ Herron,

LA Herron, LM Herron, WL Herron, GL Herschell, TL Herse, AD Hersey, J Herzen, KJ Herzig, PM Herzig, KJ Herzog, HJ Hese, C Heseltine, M Heseltine, MS Hesketh, GR Heskett, DE Heslewood, JE Heslewood, AW Heslin, EMH Heslin, PJ Heslin, NK Heslington, HS Heslop, IL Hespe, TF Hesse, SJ Hessey, JG Hession, PB Hession, BV Hester, G Hester, PD Hester, LDP Hesterman, JW Hetherington, MB Hetherington, R Hetherington, W Hetherington, WR Heugh, GW Heuston, LJ Hevey, WJ Hewat, BR Hewer, RA Hewer, DH Hewett, GL Hewett, JR Hewett, NA Hewett, R Hewett, RW Hewett, RA Hewitson, DJ Hewitt, PM Hewitt, PR Hewitt, RG Hewitt, RJ Hewitt, RK Hewitt, RL Hewitt, RMW Hewitt, TJ Hewitt, B Hewson, EB Hewson, JW Hewson, RJ Hewson, DA Hewton, NB Hexter, RJ Hexter, RS Heyde, JJ Heydon, TR Heydon, HC Heyer, JV Heyes, BC Heyhoe, JK Heyhoe, DW Heys, F Heys, AB Heywood, GPJ Heywood, RT Heywood, TA Heywood, FV Hiatt, BJ Hibbard, PC Hibbard, RC Hibben, LL Hibberson, MJ Hibbins, BJC Hickey, BW Hickey, D Hickey, DJ Hickey, FN Hickey, GM Hickey, JF Hickey, JP Hickey, KD Hickey, KL Hickey, ME Hickey, RB Hickey, RJ Hickey, SA Hickey, AR Hickinbotham, TJ Hickinbotham, HG Hicklin, FJ Hickling, DG Hickman, RG Hickman, AR Hicks, BJ Hicks, BS Hicks, CJ Hicks, DR Hicks, GF Hicks, GL Hicks, JJ Hicks, MJ Hicks, PD Hicks, RA Hicks, RB Hicks, RJ Hicks, RL Hicks, TH Hicks, W Hicks, WF Hicks, WIN Hicks-Hall, HW Hickson, PA Hickson, PR Hickson, RC Hickton, LJ Hiddins, R Hiddlestone, RH Hider, RJ Hidgcock, P Hiebler, PR Hielscher, NA Higginbotham, TG Higginbotham, AB Higgins, AG Higgins, AJ Higgins, BJ Higgins, C Higgins, DWT Higgins, GB Higgins, GJR Higgins, JF Higgins, JP Higgins, JR Higgins, JT Higgins, KW Higgins, LA Higgins, LF Higgins, LJ Higgins, MA Higgins, PJ Higgins, RG Higgins, RW Higgins, WD Higgins, DC Higginson, LF Higgisson, RL Higgs, FE High, A Higham, WD Highland, JW Hignett, JB Hiho, D Hilber, U Hilbert, TW Hildebrand, DL Hildebrandt, RJ Hildebrandt, RJ Hilder, RR Hilditch, DW Hile, R Hiles, P Hiley, G Hill-Smith, AJ Hill, AL Hill, AM Hill, AR Hill, AS Hill, B Hill, BC Hill, BJ Hill, BL Hill, BR Hill, CB Hill, CC Hill, CD Hill, CJ Hill, CJH Hill, CL Hill, D Hill, DC Hill, DE Hill, DG Hill, DJ Hill, DL Hill, DM Hill, DR Hill, DT Hill, DV Hill, DW Hill, EG Hill, GDW Hill, GF Hill, GG Hill, GH Hill, GK Hill, GL Hill, GR Hill, GTM Hill, GV Hill, GW Hill, I Hill, IJ Hill, JE Hill, JJ Hill, JL Hill, JR Hill, KE Hill, KJ Hill, KM Hill, LJ Hill, MA Hill, MJ Hill, NA Hill, NI Hill, PA Hill, PO Hill, RA Hill, RAE Hill, RD Hill, RE Hill, RG Hill, RI Hill, RJ Hill, RK Hill, RN Hill, RS Hill, RW Hill, SH Hill, TA Hill, WJ Hill, WR Hill, RB Hillard, JR Hillary, LR Hillberg, PH Hillbrick, DC Hille, KI Hiller, BP Hillery, CT Hilliard, AD Hillier, DE Hillier, GA Hillier, JR Hillier, ND Hillier, NR Hillier, R Hillier, RF Hillier, RH Hillier, TM Hillier, JR Hillman, REG Hillman, WA Hillman, G Hillowens, C Hills, CA Hills, KC Hills, KR Hills, MA Hills, PA Hills, RC Hills, RR Hills, SA Hills, TJ Hills, WM Hills, C Hillyer, GA Hilt, BE Hilton, BJ Hilton, CG Hilton, GT Hilton, GW Hilton, RA Hilton, SER Hilyander, K Himing, NB Hince, TJ Hinch, TJ Hinchcliffe, AJ Hinchey, A Hinchliffe, DR Hinchliffe, KG Hinchliffe, WL Hinchsliff, PL Hincks, A Hind, AJ Hind, CP Hind, GW Hind, WM Hind, DJ Hinde, PD Hinde, RC Hinde, MJ Hindle, PJ Hindle, RS Hindle, SL Hindle, A Hindley, DG Hindmarch, CM Hindmarsh, JS Hindmarsh, R Hindmarsh, WL Hindmarsh, AJ Hinds, ASF Hinds, DG Hinds, DM Hinds, HF Hinds, R Hinds, GC Hindson, MD Hindson, PC Hindson, WF Hindson, JT Hine, PA Hines, RA Hines, RB Hines, RE Hines, AG Hingst, JF Hingst, DJ Hinkley, EB Hinkley, GA Hinkley, KM Hinkley, D Hinnrichsen, AG Hinson, AJ Hinton, AR Hinton, C Hinton, KC Hinton, RJ Hinton, SR Hinton, TE Hinton, DJ Hinze, WJ Hipkin, CR Hipper, TW Hippisley, KT Hipwell, TE Hird, JP Hirrison, ED Hirst, JR Hirst, MC Hiscocks, KG Hiscoxprice, GL Hislop, JG Hislop, RA Hislop, M Hitch, MJ Hitch, GE Hitchcock, NJ Hitchcock, SB Hitchcock, E Hitchings, RG Hite, WA Hixon, B Hnatyszyn, L Hoad, CC Hoade, GB Hoadley, PJ Hoadley, CR Hoar, AE Hoare, DJ Hoare, DP Hoare, EB Hoare, FW Hoare, GB Hoare, JC Hoare, MJ Hoare, PJ Hoare, RE Hoare, AP Hoban, JV Hoban, WJ Hoban, RF Hobart, JR Hobbin, MR Hobbin, FJ Hobbins, BR Hobbs, DG Hobbs, DJ Hobbs, DR Hobbs, GJ Hobbs, JH Hobbs, JL Hobbs, RG Hobbs, RJ Hobbs, RS Hobbs, RW Hobbs, SV Hobbs, TJ Hobbs, WA Hobbs, JP Hobday, KL Hobday, GA Hobley, GR Hobley, EE Hobson, IA Hobson, LT Hobson, RD Hobson, SH Hobson, GJ Hockam, KM Hockey, KW Hockey, LC Hockey, MT Hockey, WJ Hockey, JH Hockham, DJ Hocking, DL Hocking, FJ Hocking, JW Hocking, KM Hocking, PA Hocking, PJ Hocking, RI Hocking, RR Hocking, WJ Hocking, CR Hockings, RJ Hockings, GA Hockley, BH Hockney, DM Hodda, DC Hodder, S Hodder, HH Hoddy, WD Hodgart, BV Hodge, GJ Hodge, IS Hodge, KJ Hodge, LG Hodge, MJ Hodge, PA Hodge, RC Hodge, RD Hodge, RW Hodge, WD Hodge, AB Hodges, AH Hodges, CG Hodges, DF Hodges, JE Hodges, JF Hodges, JR Hodges, JW Hodges, KB Hodges, KJ Hodges, PE Hodges, PJ Hodges, RJ Hodges, RW Hodges, TK Hodges, DA Hodgetts, GD Hodgins, IRJ Hodgkinson, RE Hodgkinson, BJ Hodgson, CW Hodgson, GH Hodgson, GI Hodgson, GR Hodgson, GV Hodgson, JAA Hodgson, JE Hodgson, JF Hodgson, JW Hodgson, KB Hodgson, KJ Hodgson, MC Hodgson, PF Hodgson, RF Hodgson, RJ Hodgson, S Hodgson, BA Hodson, GR Hodson, HPM Hoebee, HP Hoefnagels, MM Hoenselaars, RG Hoey, GW Hofert, LC Hoff, AC Hoffman, DC Hoffman, FJ Hoffman, GD Hoffman, GM Hoffman, NW Hoffman, P Hoffman, RH Hoffman, WG Hoffman, WH Hoffman, JN Hoffmann, KD Hoffmann, MC Hoffmann, TW Hoffmann, WJ Hoffmann, WS Hoffrichter, JR Hofman, AJ Hogan, AP Hogan, AW Hogan, CB Hogan, GK Hogan, GL Hogan, GP Hogan, IR Hogan, JA Hogan, JF Hogan, JP Hogan, MS Hogan, MW Hogan, NR Hogan, PD Hogan, PW Hogan, RC Hogan, RED Hogan, RJ Hogan, SJ Hogan, ST Hogan, TJ Hogan, BME Hogarth, CJ Hogarth, DA Hogarth, F Hogarth, GS Hogarth, RR Hogarth, R Hogben, RT Hogben, JC Hogbin, RM Hogden, PJ Hogeboom, HW Hoger, RP Hoger, AL Hogg, DF Hogg, EW Hogg, GR Hogg, JA Hogg, JW Hogg, TD Hogg, JA Hoggart, LJ Hogno, WO Hogue, GJ Hohnen, DA Hohnholt, TJ Hoile, BR Holahan, PH Holberton, BP Holborow, DT Holbrook, N Holbrook, P Holcroft, S Holcroft, AM Holden, BE Holden, D Holden, G Holden, HJ Holden, JG Holden, JL Holden, KJ Holden, KR Holden, LAC Holden, M Holden, PD Holden, PG Holden, RJ Holden, RW Holden, TJ Holden, LR Holder, PR Holder, J Holding, RL Holdman, DC Holdom, GB Holdom, ER Holdsworth, JR Holdsworth, N Holdsworth, RJ Holdsworth, EF Hole, JJ Holeszko, DE Holford, TC Holford, TR Holford, J Holgate, TJ Holl, AL Holland, BI Holland, BJ Holland, BP Holland, GJ Holland, JE Holland, JJ Holland, JP Holland, JTA Holland, JW Holland, KC Holland, M Holland, MG Holland, PR Holland, R Holland, RA Holland, T Holland, TH Holland, BL Hollands, WG Hollands, M Hollaway, HH Holle, J Hollett, LR Holley, NJ Holley, RG Holley, SR Hollick, DA Holliday, DJ Holliday, PE Holliday, RA Holliday, RJ Holliday, NA Hollindale, ND Hollindale, RW Hollingbery, NH Hollingdrake, RJ Hollingdrake, JA Hollings, RJ Hollings, WR Hollings, IM Hollingsworth, JT Hollingsworth, PG Hollington, AE Hollis, GA Hollis, JL Hollis, PL Hollis, PT Hollis, RJ Hollis, RW Hollis, PG Hollister, BG Hollitt, DJ Hollonds, MJ Hollow, AK Holloway, BG Holloway, BJ Holloway, DN Holloway, GR Holloway, HG Holloway, JW Holloway, KM Holloway, ML Holloway, PB Hollows, RJ Hollway, BC Holly, LM Holm, RR Holm, DJ Holman, GA Holman, JL Holman, LB Holman, WR Holman, WW Holman, AJ Holmberg, DW Holme, A Holmes, CJ Holmes, DA Holmes, DG Holmes, DJ Holmes, DWG Holmes, ED Holmes, GJ Holmes, GN Holmes, HJ Holmes, HP Holmes, IW Holmes, JR Holmes, KE Holmes, LA Holmes, LJ Holmes, LR Holmes, MG Holmes, ML Holmes, PE Holmes, PL Holmes, RA Holmes, RAJ Holmes, RF Holmes, RJ Holmes, RT Holmes, RW Holmes, TJ Holmes, TL Holmes, WJ Holmes, BW Holmshaw, B Holscher, EW Holst, JA Holst, KH Holst, MH Holstein, A Holster, AL Holt, BA Holt, DR Holt, ES Holt, GJ Holt, JV Holt, KE Holt, KG Holt, MD Holt, RA Holt, RB Holt, RJ Holt, T Holt, TM Holt, VJ Holt, GS Holtby, RJ Holten, RJ Holtham, JW Holthouse, JF Holtman, TJ Holtom, DJ Holton, GM Holton, MG Holton, CV Holtsbaum, GH Holusa, RA Holyoak, RR Holyoak, PJ Holywell, PJ Holz, GAG Holzberger, RJ Holze, HFC Holzer, AM Holzhauser, CR Holzheimer, EP Holzheimer, K Holzigal, KJ Holzworth, WJ Holzworth, KD Homan, DL Homann, AR Homer, EJ Homer, FW Homer, JC Homer, FR Homewood, KG Homewood, RG Homewood, RJ Homewood, BE Hondow, RW Hone, KA Honess, JG Honey, JP Honey, KJ Honeybrook, DJ Honeychurch, ENA Honeyman, JD Honeysett, RF Hong, RJ Hong, SL Hong, MA Honinger, BR Honner, GJ Honour, D Hood, DM Hood, JF Hood, OA Hood, RD Hood, RW Hood, WJ Hood, AJ Hoogenboom, H Hoogkamer, CR Hook, DV Hook, JJ Hook, MK Hook, RJ Hook, WE Hook, AG Hooke, DM Hooker, JJ Hooker, PW Hoolahan, GJ Hooley, JT Hoolihan, AA Hooper, BE Hooper, BM Hooper, DJ Hooper, GA Hooper, GD Hooper, GJ Hooper, GT Hooper, JA Hooper, JD Hooper, LR Hooper, RAW Hooper, RG Hooper, RI Hooper, RJ Hooper, TL Hooper, WJ Hooper, G Hoopert, JG Hooton, DS Hope, GG Hope, HR Hope, JL Hope, JR Hope, PB Hope, PJ Hope, RC Hope, TR Hope, AI Hopkins, AR Hopkins, BF Hopkins, BT Hopkins, DJ Hopkins, GA Hopkins, GR Hopkins, JG Hopkins, KD Hopkins, KJ Hopkins, RH Hopkins, RJ Hopkins, VE Hopkins, WK Hopkins, WV Hopkins, IR Hopley, JH Hopman, KR Hoppe, CG Hopper, GE Hopper, PD Hopper, PS Hopper, RA Hopper, TF Hopper, CR Hoppner, LH Hoppner, GJ Hoppo, RJ Hoppo, LC Hopson, RK Hopson, LI Hopton, JL Hopwood, JE Horan, JG Horan, KA Horan, AJ Horder, AT Horder, JW Horder, LJ Horder, NW Horder, RB Horder, RJ Horder, BR Hore, DT Hore, GR Hore, MJ Hore, RD Hore, RH Hore, RA Horgan, DA Horkan, JW Horlock, RL Horlock, TS Horlock, DE Horn, MJ Horn, NL Horn, P Horn, RA Horn, TF Hornbuckle, DM Horne, EJ Horne, GJ Horne, GS Horne, JC Horne, JO Horne, JW Horne, MLS Horne, NW Horne, PC Horne, RB Horne, RJ Horne, TW Horne, AJ Horner, AR Horner, DC Horner, DM Horner, JL Horner, LG Horner, SR Horner, RW Hornery, WF Hornett, CR Hornsby, RE Hornsby, BG Hornung, DW Horrigan, P Horrocks, SJ Horsburgh, RC Horsell, RK Horsell, CG Horsey, JL Horsfall, RG Horsfall, RS Horsfall, RW Horsfall, DD Horsley, DKL Horsley, MG Horsten, RD Horsten, CW Horton, DH Horton, L Horton, LM Horton, RA Horton, RH Horton, RP Horton, RK Horwell, JC Horwood, JL Horwood, GA Hose, GW Hose, RG Hose, AJ Hoseasonsmith, MJ Hoseasonsmith, SD Hoseason-Smith, IR Hosie, JG Hosie, BK Hoskin, BR Hoskin, JD Hoskin, JW Hoskin, M Hoskin, PC Hoskin, TA Hoskin, GT Hosking, HA Hosking, MJ Hosking, JC Hoskins, PE Hoskins, WG Hoskins, PR Hoskinson, JK Host, WJ Host, VC Hotchkiss, IF Hotschilt, PA Hotton, AJ Hough, JL Hough, MJ Hough, DW Houghton, FC Houghton, J Houghton, KS Houghton, RJ Houghton, NR Houlahan, PJ Houlahan, A Houldridge, KF Houley, EJ Houlihan, KJ Houlihan, JB Houliston, JF Hounslow, JT Hounslow, M Hourigan, DR House, GT House, GW House, AK Houseman, HM Houstein, AR Houston, FRT Houston, JM Houston, JP Houston, KC Houston, KR Houston, LD Houston, MC Houston, RJ Houston, BR Houting, RJB Houting, H Houtsma, JN How, KE How, MR How, AJ Howard-Osborne, AJ Howard, BW Howard, CB Howard, CJ Howard, EJ Howard, G Howard, GK Howard, JA Howard, JF Howard, JP Howard, JR Howard, JT Howard, KC Howard, KJ Howard, MJ Howard, MW Howard, NL Howard, PE Howard, PJ Howard, PV Howard, RA Howard, RJ Howard, RT Howard, RW Howard, SJ Howard, TL Howard, TW Howard, WJ Howard, ZA Howard, AJ Howarth, DM Howarth, KJ Howarth, NS Howarth, PA Howarth, WJ Howarth, WL Howarth, BF Howden, GJ Howden, JM Howden, A Howe, BR Howe, CB Howe, DF Howe, DL Howe, GJ Howe, JN Howe, KK Howe, MA Howe, P Howe, RJ Howe, RL Howe, DA Howell, DC Howell, DK Howell, FJ Howell, GA Howell, GW Howell, KR Howell, LD Howell, PR Howell, RC Howell, RD Howell, RI Howell, RJ Howell, RS Howell, RW Howell, WA Howell, BD Howells, DG Howells, DL Howells, PR Hower, AR Howes, BJ Howes, EJ Howes, JG Howes, FH Howett, MF Howie, RB Howie, B Howieson, JW Howieson, C Howis, MS Howitt, PG Howitt, PR Howkins, AJ Howland, RC Howle, DJ Howlett, DN Howlett, GN Howlett, HN Howlett, MG Howlett, RJ Howlett, TJ Howlett, WC Howlett, WR Howlett, WE Howman, GW Howson, NW Howson, RV Howson, CJ Hoy, IR Hoy, JF Hoy, PF Hoy, RA Hoy, JL Hoyes, JB Hoyle, K Hoyle, PJ Hoyne, JJ Hryc, J Hryhorec,

B Hubbard, DJ Hubbard, JW Hubbard, KB Hubbard, B Hubble, RN Hubble, HP Hubner, RG Huckauf, RA Hucker, S Huckin, JH Huddleston, CT Huddy, WJ Hudnott, AG Hudson, AJ Hudson, BG Hudson, BL Hudson, BR Hudson, CJ Hudson, DR Hudson, DW Hudson, HF Hudson, JM Hudson, JP Hudson, KJ Hudson, LC Hudson, LRP Hudson, LT Hudson, NF Hudson, PR Hudson, RE Hudson, RK Hudson, TF Hudson, TJ Hudson, TD Hudspith, DG Huebsch, RG Huender, MN Hueppauff, JT Huet, LR Hufer, RW Huggan, PW Huggett, AN Huggins, IJ Huggins, JE Huggins, JL Huggins, NL Huggins, PC Huggins, AD Hughes, AF Hughes, AJ Hughes, AR Hughes, AW Hughes, BB Hughes, BFP Hughes, BJ Hughes, BM Hughes, CA Hughes, CC Hughes, CE Hughes, CJ Hughes, CM Hughes, CN Hughes, DG Hughes, DJ Hughes, DR Hughes, EJ Hughes, GE Hughes, GL Hughes, GM Hughes, GR Hughes, HE Hughes, J Hughes, JC Hughes, JF Hughes, JG Hughes, JH Hughes, JM Hughes, JN Hughes, JW Hughes, KE Hughes, KJ Hughes, KR Hughes, KW Hughes, LJ Hughes, MF Hughes, MJ Hughes, MM Hughes, MR Hughes, NK Hughes, PJ Hughes, PM Hughes, PR Hughes, R Hughes, R Hughes, RA Hughes, RC Hughes, RD Hughes, RE Hughes, RF Hughes, RJ Hughes, RL Hughes, RM Hughes, SH Hughes, TD Hughes, TJ Hughes, TW Hughes, W Hughes, WE Hughes, WG Hughes, BM Hughson, BJ Huhse, JP Huigens, GN Huish, PE Hulbert, TG Hulcup, MD Hulett, PM Hulett, JR Hulin, AJ Hull, BG Hull, DS Hull, G Hull, KD Hull, PN Hull, J Hulls, RC Hulm, GJ Hulme, JM Hulme, K Hulme, GL Hulse, HJ Hulse, MJ Hulse, F Hulshof, P Hulsing, HA Hulskamp, JA Humberstone, RJ Humble, TR Humble, WJ Humble, RJ Humbles, IG Humby, JA Humby, RJ Humby, JB Hume, JJ Hume, WM Hume, JB Humffray, J Hummel, BJ Humphrey, GH Humphrey, JH Humphrey, LC Humphrey, MJ Humphrey, BJ Humphreys, BR Humphreys, BW Humphreys, GR Humphreys, JA Humphreys, JB Humphreys, JD Humphreys, LG Humphreys, NB Humphreys, NR Humphreys, RJ Humphreys, WJ Humphreys, EJ Humphries, IG Humphries, JC Humphries, JF Humphries, PT Humphries, RD Humphries, RL Humphries, TR Humphries, WJ Humphries, RJ Humphris, L Humphry, RE Humphrys, MAP Hundt, TG Hung, FL Hungerford, HJ Hungerford, IS Hungerford, JWB Hungerford, PJ Hungerford, RM Hungerford, DJ Hunnam, RJ Hunnisett, AH Hunt, AT Hunt, BC Hunt, BJ Hunt, DJ Hunt, EW Hunt, FJ Hunt, GC Hunt, GD Hunt, GE Hunt, GR Hunt, JA Hunt, JW Hunt, KG Hunt, KJ Hunt, ML Hunt, MT Hunt, NG Hunt, P Hunt, PE Hunt, PJ Hunt, PR Hunt, PW Hunt, RA Hunt, RD Hunt, RF Hunt, RV Hunt, TE Hunt, TJ Hunt, TT Hunt, VG Hunt, WA Hunt, WG Hunt, WJ Hunt, WL Hunt, A Hunter, AJ Hunter, AK Hunter, AL Hunter, AW Hunter, BS Hunter, BW Hunter, CH Hunter, CJ Hunter, DC Hunter, DF Hunter, DJ Hunter, DM Hunter, G Hunter, GF Hunter, GG Hunter, GJ Hunter, GL Hunter, IJ Hunter, IR Hunter, IW Hunter, JC Hunter, JE Hunter, JM Hunter, JP Hunter, KJ Hunter, KK Hunter, KR Hunter, MA Hunter, MC Hunter, MR Hunter, MW Hunter, NC Hunter, NJ Hunter, NL Hunter, PF Hunter, PJ Hunter, PN Hunter, R Hunter, RE Hunter, RF Hunter, RJ Hunter, RM Hunter, RW Hunter, SR Hunter, TJ Hunter, TN Hunter, WJ Hunter, WR Hunter, BL Hunting, LJ Hunting, RR Hunting, NJ Huntley, WE Huntley, AJ Huntsman, TR Hupalo, TB Huppatz, GJ Hura, D Hure, AJ Hurford, GW Hurford, RB Hurford, TH Hurford, HJ Hurij, BT Hurkens, MA Hurl, A Hurley, AR Hurley, BF Hurley, CF Hurley, JA Hurley, PM Hurley, RN Hurley, KA Hurling, FV Hurman, KG Hurn, GR Hurnall, VA Hurrelbrink, AA Hurrell, FG Hurren, PC Hurren, TR Hurrey, RE Hursey, CG Hurst, G Hurst, GA Hurst, HW Hurst, JM Hurst, JR Hurst, KJ Hurst, PR Hurst, SN Hurst, CS Hurstfield, J Husband, AW Hush, JR Hush, KB Hussell, BH Hussey, DM Hussey, IM Hussey, PD Hussey, PG Hussey, T Hussey, AB Huston, AG Hutchens, FG Hutcheon, AJ Hutcheson, JM Hutcheson, RS Hutchesson, JJ Hutchieson, PC Hutchings, RA Hutchings, AJE Hutchins, CT Hutchins, GR Hutchins, JB Hutchins, AG Hutchinson, BL Hutchinson, BV Hutchinson, EN Hutchinson, GC Hutchinson, GJ Hutchinson, GS Hutchinson, IJ Hutchinson, IT Hutchinson, JC Hutchinson, KD Hutchinson, LD Hutchinson, PW Hutchinson, R Hutchinson, RI Hutchinson, RJ Hutchinson, RK Hutchinson, RW Hutchinson,

WT Hutchinson, IE Hutchison, IG Hutchison, KR Hutchison, MJ Hutchison, RA Hutchison, RC Hutchison, RH Hutchison, RP Hutchison, WA Hutchison, JG Hutley, JF Hutson, LG Hutson, RW Hutson, DG Hutton, GR Hutton, H Hutton, JD Hutton, JW Hutton, LG Hutton, PH Hutton, PV Hutton, RA Hutton, RC Hutton, RG Hutton, RH Hutton, BJ Huxley, DE Huxley, PJ Huxley, WK Huxley, WL Huxley, GM Huxtable, KA Hyam, LF Hyatt, LK Hyatt, A Hyde, AR Hyde, DJ Hyde, E Hyde, GJ Hyde, GW Hyde, IC Hyde, KG Hyde, L Hyde, RJ Hyde, TD Hyde, TF Hyde, WF Hyde, BJ Hyland, DC Hyland, FA Hyland, FD Hyland, JH Hyland, JR Hyland, JS Hyland, RC Hyland, RJ Hyland, WJ Hyland, RM Hylard, GD Hyles, J Hynd, RJ Hynd, EF Hynds, DJ Hynes, EH Hynes, JA Hynes, RF Hynson, WG Hynson, J Hys, HW Hyslop, MF Hyson, J Iacono, CV Iannuzzi, JP Ianson, JR Ibbetson, PJ Ibbotson, SW Ibbotson, WD Ibbs, AG Ible, LT Icke, H Iddon, LJ Idiens, DM Iffla, HJ Iglinski, RW Ihlein, RJ Ikin, P Ilacqua, PG Iland, EW Ilett, R Ilett, G Iliopoulos, A Illin, B Illingworth, BM Illingworth, JT Illingworth, AM Illman, CM Illman, DG Illman, NJ Ilnyckyi, C Ilsley, GJR Ilsley, DM Iltscheff, AA Ilyin, ZJ Imaks, CH Imberger, BW Imlach, DE Imlach, MJ Imlach, RJ Imlach, NA Imlay, PS Impey, AD Inall, AL Inall, IJ Inall, VR Inch, HW Ind, DE Ineson, P Infalletta, AW Ing, TB Inge, MF Ingham, PJ Ingham, FN Ingle, TP Ingle, RW Ingleby, DW Ingles, ML Ingles, RJ Ingleton, AR Inglis, DJ Inglis, F Inglis, GB Inglis, GGJ Inglis, NR Inglis, RW Inglis, TJ Inglis, AA Ingram, AC Ingram, AE Ingram, BGW Ingram, BJ Ingram, EL Ingram, GG Ingram, MJ Ingram, PM Ingram, PV Ingram, RB Ingram, SG Ingram, TJ Ingram, WG Ingram, PD Ingrey, OD Inman, PE Inman, RG Inman, B Innes, DA Innes, JC Innes, JH Innes, KL Innes, KN Innes, NK Innes, RD Innes, SC Innes, SW Innes, WA Innes, JP Insull, MS Inwood, SN Ionn, CN Iozzi, FJ Ipsa, MP Iredale, BN Ireland, DA Ireland, E Ireland, GA Ireland, JR Ireland, MS Ireland, PE Ireland, RD Ireland, JR Irish, KW Irons, RJ Irons, PA Ironside, GWK Irvin, BD Irvine, D Irvine, GDW Irvine, GK Irvine, J Irvine, JE Irvine, JF Irvine, JR Irvine, L Irvine, LG Irvine, LJ Irvine, LS Irvine, MD Irvine, MR Irvine, PJ Irvine, SJ Irvine, WR Irvine, BC Irving, DJ Irving, JS Irving, SI Irving, DB Irwin, GJ Irwin, HW Irwin, IK Irwin, JD Irwin, JH Irwin, RF Irwin, RJ Irwin, SA Irwin, TJ Irwin, VJ Irwin, WE Irwin, FS Iry, AR Isaac, EW Isaac, JL Isaac, IJ Isaacs, JV Isaacs, KG Isaacs, PJ Isaacs, RJ Isaacs, JC Isager, OH Isaksson, BC Iselin, KJ Iselin, TS Isherwood, KL Ising, P Isle, CJ Ison, DJ Ison, JR Ison, KL Ison, P Ison, GM Israel, PJ Israel, TA Issanchon, DM Isted, IJ Iszlaub, KW Iszlaub, NW Iszlaub, GM Ithier, GM Itzstein, PJ Itzstein, RJ Ivanecky, YM Ivanovic, RW Iverach, MG Ivers, BT Ives, JD Ives, KJ Ives, DJ Ivey, DP Ivey, RJ Ivey, RR Ivey, P Ivory, WR Ivory, J Iwankiw, JJ Iwanko, DJ Izatt, IS Izatt, DJ Izod, L Jaago, JJ Jablonski, SA Jablonski, GC Jabs, DG Jack, DR Jack, RA Jack, A Jacka, DL Jacka, GI Jacka, SRE Jacka, KG Jackat, GR Jackett, Z Jackiewicz, DW Jackman, GR Jackman, MA Jackman, R Jackman, A Jackson, AE Jackson, AF Jackson, AP Jackson, AR Jackson, AT Jackson, AW Jackson, B Jackson, BD Jackson, BJ Jackson, BM Jackson, C Jackson, CC Jackson, CJ Jackson, DL Jackson, DR Jackson, DV Jackson, DVV Jackson, FR Jackson, G Jackson, GA Jackson, GE Jackson, GJ Jackson, GK Jackson, GL Jackson, GR Jackson, GW Jackson, HA Jackson, HB Jackson, HE Jackson, IJ Jackson, J Jackson, JA Jackson, JB Jackson, JC Jackson, JL Jackson, JR Jackson, KG Jackson, KH Jackson, KJ Jackson, KL Jackson, L Jackson, MJ Jackson, NR Jackson, NV Jackson, OD Jackson, P Jackson, PA Jackson, PG Jackson, PI Jackson, PJ Jackson, RA Jackson, RB Jackson, RE Jackson, RG Jackson, RH Jackson, RJ Jackson, SE Jackson, TJ Jackson, TJH Jackson, TM Jackson, TR Jackson, VJ Jackson, WA Jackson, WH Jackson, WJ Jackson, WN Jackson, WP Jackson, A Jackway, NJ Jackway, KW Jackwitz, MC Jacob, ED Jacobs, JA Jacobs, LT Jacobs, PJ Jacobs, RS Jacobs, TJ Jacobs, DM Jacobsen, GJ Jacobsen, JF Jacobsen, RJ Jacobsen, BJ Jacobson, HT Jacobson, IT Jacobson, NC Jacobson, RC Jacobson, R Jacombs, A Jacques, K Jacques, NR Jacques, RF Jacques, PC Jaekel, KG Jaenke, WJ Jaenke, LS Jaffe, HD Jager, MJ Jagers, LG Jaggar, NC Jaggar, JW Jaggard, LR Jagger, AJ Jago, DJ Jago, GD Jago, K Jago, LP Jago, NO Jago, WJ Jago, AR Jagoe, PK Jahnes, PG Jahnke, RJ Jakeman, WD Jakeman, A Jakiel, ZS Jakiel, V Jakowenko, AM James, AR James, AW James, B James, BK James, CA James, D James, DA James, DM James, DP James, DS James, E James, ES James, GB James,

GG James, GK James, GR James, HG James, HR James, IR James, IS James, JE James, JH James, JL James, JR James, JV James, JWH James, KA James, KW James, LR James, LRG James, LTL James, MJ James, MR James, NF James, NR James, PC James, PJ James, PM James, PSN James, RB James, RC James, RD James, RF James, RG James, RJ James, RM James, RS James, S James, SD James, T James, TA James, TD James, TH James, TJ James, TM James, TR James, WB James, WHR James, WJ James, DG Jameson, IS Jameson, PW Jameson, AH Jamieson, CH Jamieson, GY Jamieson, IJ Jamieson, J Jamieson, JR Jamieson, NJ Jamieson, PJ Jamieson, PM Jamieson, RF Jamieson, RJ Jamieson, RL Jamieson, TJ Jamieson, VJ Jamieson, WD Jamieson, DK Jamison, LS Jamvold, JP Janas, KH Janczyk, AE Jane, BW Jane, IP Jane, B Janic, B Janisch, VA Jankovic, KG Jankowski, P Janout, NA Jans, BJ Jansen, BT Jansen, CM Jansen, HJ Jansen, JAR Jansen, K Jansen, MR Jansen, P Jansen, PJ Jansen, AB Janssen, HJM Janssen, UK Janssen, M Jansson, PJ Jansz, AR Jantzen, RP Janvrin, GJ Janz, AV Jaques, J Jaques, KS Jaques, MK Jaques, RD Jaques, RG Jaques, EJ Jarden, D Jardine, NM Jardine, AR Jarman, KA Jarman, MR Jarman, GB Jarmyn, RJ Jaroszczuk, AE Jarrad, FW Jarrad, LG Jarratt, PC Jarratt, KC Jarred, JT Jarrett, KG Jarrett, KW Jarrett, MJ Jarrett, RA Jarrett, W Jarrett, WD Jarrett, KE Jarrold, LC Jarrold, RP Jarrott, S Jaruga, AN Jarvis, CW Jarvis, KJ Jarvis, MA Jarvis, NS Jarvis, PF Jarvis, RK Jarvis, RL Jarvis, RW Jarvis, TJ Jarvis, GK Jasch, E Jasen, JP Jasinski, M Jasinski, THV Jason, PN Jasper, WL Jasper, AP Jasse, B Jaudzemis, JAJ Jauncey, MG Jauncey, B Jay, PW Jay, RE Jay, NM Jeanes, J Jeans, PW Jeans, GA Jebb, JW Jebb, RL Jecks, K Jede, S Jedrzejczyk, TW Jefferies, C Jeffers, JR Jeffers, RD Jeffers, WJ Jeffers, TW Jefferson, WW Jefferson, AJ Jeffery, BW Jeffery, DG Jeffery, GJJ Jeffery, GL Jeffery, HS Jeffery, K Jeffery, PM Jeffery, RJ Jeffery, SR Jeffery, W Jeffery, WC Jeffery, JA Jefferys, RF Jefferys, BS Jeffress, GR Jeffress, BN Jeffrey, BR Jeffrey, DA Jeffrey, E Jeffrey, ML Jeffrey, PR Jeffrey, RC Jeffrey, RD Jeffrey, RJ Jeffrey, RP Jeffrey, ZR Jeffrey, SR Jeffreys, RJ Jeffries, SA Jeffries, KL Jeffs, LS Jeffs, R Jeffs, TP Jeisman, FJ Jelen, AS Jelleff, GJ Jellett, KR Jelley, AD Jellie, PJ Jellis, TM Jelly, G Jelsma, RG Jemerson, GP Jeney, DK Jenkin, DW Jenkin, G Jenkin, GC Jenkin, HR Jenkin, RS Jenkin, VC Jenkin, BD Jenkins, CR Jenkins, DA Jenkins, DJ Jenkins, DW Jenkins, G Jenkins, GW Jenkins, JE Jenkins, JR Jenkins, JW Jenkins, K Jenkins, KW Jenkins, PD Jenkins, PJ Jenkins, PR Jenkins, PW Jenkins, R Jenkins, RJ Jenkins, RL Jenkins, SA Jenkins, SJ Jenkins, W Jenkins, DC Jenkinson, DW Jenkinson, KL Jenkinson, PC Jenkinson, SR Jenkinson, MT Jenner, TJ Jenner, CW Jennings, DG Jennings, DR Jennings, FG Jennings, G Jennings, TJ Jennings, WJS Jennings, GD Jennion, CA Jennison, AH Jensen, AP Jensen, CA Jensen, DH Jensen, DJ Jensen, GD Jensen, GW Jensen, IP Jensen, JC Jensen, KS Jensen, MT Jensen, NA Jensen, NO Jensen, PA Jensen, RA Jensen, RP Jensen, RW Jensen, TJ Jensen, FR Jenson, RF Jenson, J Jenusch, JE Jenvey, JR Jepson, N Jeremenko, DL Jericho, WE Jerome, F Jeromel, BJ Jerrard, AL Jervis, RV Jervis, PE Jesperson, AD Jessen, DS Jessen, RP Jessen, FW Jessep, BW Jesser, DL Jesser, GH Jesser, ID Jesser, JR Jesser, JS Jesser, JS Jesson, AJ Jessop, MC Jessop, R Jessop, GS Jessup, RC Jessup, DA Jewell, GJ Jewell, IJ Jewell, JA Jewell, JL Jewell, RH Jewell, RW Jewell, J Jewry, EL Jeynes, RG Jeziorny, CC Joannides, LV Job, CD Jobling, LJ Jobling, TE Jobling, CJ Jobson, GT Jobson, TK Jobson, TW Jobson, EJ Jocelyn, TR Jochinke, BF Jocumsen, RJ Jocumsen, FC Joel, RC Joel, SS Joel, J Jogar, GJ Johannesen, ES Johansen, JR Johansen, TL Johanson, EJ Johansson, RG Johansson, MR John, PA John, AF Johns, BM Johns, CH Johns, CM Johns, DH Johns, DW Johns, GA Johns, GC Johns, IC Johns, JR Johns, KL Johns, KR Johns, MN Johns, MR Johns, NR Johns, NR Johns, PD Johns, RA Johns, RJ Johns, RL Johns, SR Johns, TR Johns, WM Johns, KW Johnsen, AB Johnson, AD Johnson, AF Johnson, AJ Johnson, AL Johnson, B Johnson, BA Johnson, BC Johnson, BE Johnson, BJ Johnson, BP Johnson, BW Johnson, C Johnson, CA Johnson, CB Johnson, CEL Johnson, CR Johnson, CT Johnson, CW Johnson, D Johnson, DC Johnson, DG Johnson, DGH Johnson, DJH Johnson, DL Johnson, DTA Johnson, DW Johnson, EJ Johnson, EL Johnson, F Johnson, F Johnson, FA Johnson, GA Johnson, GC Johnson, GD Johnson, GE Johnson, GK Johnson, GR Johnson, GV Johnson, GW Johnson, IE Johnson, IK Johnson, IM Johnson, IP Johnson, IR Johnson,

IW Johnson, JC Johnson, JF Johnson, JJ Johnson, JV Johnson, K Johnson, KC Johnson, KD Johnson, KP Johnson, KR Johnson, KW Johnson, LA Johnson, LC Johnson, LD Johnson, LF Johnson, LW Johnson, MA Johnson, MJ Johnson, MK Johnson, ML Johnson, MM Johnson, MR Johnson, MS Johnson, NE Johnson, NF Johnson, NJ Johnson, NJA Johnson, PH Johnson, PL Johnson, PM Johnson, PR Johnson, R Johnson, RA Johnson, RB Johnson, RC Johnson, RE Johnson, RF Johnson, RH Johnson, RJ Johnson, RL Johnson, RM Johnson, RN Johnson, RP Johnson, RR Johnson, RS Johnson, RW Johnson, SJ Johnson, T Johnson, TA Johnson, TB Johnson, TC Johnson, TF Johnson, TG Johnson, TW Johnson, W Johnson, WA Johnson, WC Johnson, WE Johnson, WF Johnson, WH Johnson, WJ Johnson, WM Johnson, ZJ Johnson, GVT Johnsson, WM Johnsson, AF Johnston, AG Johnston, AJ Johnston, AP Johnston, AR Johnston, AS Johnston, AWB Johnston, B Johnston, BA Johnston, BE Johnston, BM Johnston, BR Johnston, CE Johnston, CH Johnston, DA Johnston, DB Johnston, DC Johnston, DF Johnston, DI Johnston, DR Johnston, DS Johnston, DT Johnston, DW Johnston, EG Johnston, ER Johnston, EW Johnston, FC Johnston, FJ Johnston, FSK Johnston, GG Johnston, GL Johnston, GR Johnston, GS Johnston, HB Johnston, HL Johnston, IJ Johnston, IL Johnston, IW Johnston, JG Johnston, JM Johnston, JW Johnston, KN Johnston, KR Johnston, KW Johnston, LA Johnston, LF Johnston, LN Johnston, MP Johnston, N Johnston, PH Johnston, PJ Johnston, PL Johnston, PT Johnston, PW Johnston, R Johnston, RA Johnston, RB Johnston, RC Johnston, RJ Johnston, RK Johnston, RN Johnston, TE Johnston, TL Johnston, WJ Johnston, WR Johnston, BG Johnstone, BR Johnstone, C Johnstone, GH Johnstone, JD Johnstone, LD Johnstone, LR Johnstone, M Johnstone, MW Johnstone, PA Johnstone, PJ Johnstone, RK Johnstone, TK Johnstone, W Johnstone, WS Johnstone, D Joiner, H Joksimovic, BE Jolley, KC Jolley, RJ Jolley, RM Jolley, RT Jolley, GJ Jolliffe, KJ Jolliffe, N Jolliffe, AM Jolly, CJ Jolly, DL Jolly, JM Jolly, PJ Jolly, RJ Jolly, TH Jolly, GR Jonas, ML Jonas, MW Jonas, BF Jonathan, FJ Jonczyk, AA Jones, AD Jones, AE Jones, AF Jones, AJ Jones, AK Jones, AP Jones, AR Jones, AT Jones, AV Jones, AW Jones, B Jones, BA Jones, BB Jones, BC Jones, BG Jones, BJ Jones, BK Jones, BN Jones, BR Jones, BRA Jones, BS Jones, CA Jones, CD Jones, CE Jones, CF Jones, CJ Jones, CL Jones, CM Jones, CW Jones, DA Jones, DB Jones, DE Jones, DF Jones, DI Jones, DJ Jones, DL Jones, DN Jones, DW Jones, EA Jones, EF Jones, EJ Jones, EP Jones, FA Jones, FB Jones, FD Jones, FE Jones, G Jones, GA Jones, GC Jones, GD Jones, GD Jones, GF Jones, GGA Jones, GJ Jones, GN Jones, GP Jones, GR Jones, GV Jones, GW Jones, HD Jones, HF Jones, I Jones, IA Jones, IJ Jones, IM Jones, J Jones, JA Jones, JC Jones, JD Jones, JE Jones, JG Jones, JL Jones, JO Jones, JP Jones, JR Jones, JT Jones, JW Jones, K Jones, KA Jones, KB Jones, KH Jones, KJ Jones, KL Jones, KM Jones, KP Jones, KR Jones, KS Jones, KW Jones, L Jones, LG Jones, LH Jones, LL Jones, LR Jones, LW Jones, ME Jones, MG Jones, MI Jones, MJ Jones, N Jones, NB Jones, NH Jones, NJ Jones, NK Jones, NT Jones, PC Jones, PD Jones, PF Jones, PG Jones, PJ Jones, PL Jones, PM Jones, PR Jones, PW Jones, R Jones, R Jones, RA Jones, RB Jones, RC Jones, RE Jones, RG Jones, RI Jones, RJ Jones, RK Jones, RL Jones, RM Jones, RR Jones, RS Jones, RW Jones, SL Jones, SW Jones, T Jones, TA Jones, TD Jones, TG Jones, TH Jones, TM Jones, TO Jones, TR Jones, VG Jones, VW Jones, W Jones, WH Jones, WJ Jones, WM Jones, WT Jones, J Jongedijk, A Jonita, V Jonkaitis, SW Jonsson, RP Jopling, A Jordan, DE Jordan, DJ Jordan, DP Jordan, EE Jordan, GW Jordan, JCT Jordan, JP Jordan, JS Jordan, JT Jordan, K Jordan, LW Jordan, M Jordan, MJ Jordan, PE Jordan, PW Jordan, R Jordan, RJ Jordan, T Jordan, WV Jordan, DJ Jordon, RF Jordon, AJ Jorgensen, JH Jorgensen, KA Jorgensen, KJ Jorgensen, LR Jorgensen, PE Jorm, TB Jorna, PW Joscelyne, DA Jose, PJ Jose, RL Jose, RM Jose, KR Joselin, AJ Joseph, EB Joseph, GN Joseph, MW Joseph, PC Joseph, T Joseph, VJH Joseph, G Josephs, WE Josephs, WC Josephsen, R Joshua, PW Josling, BA Joss, BJ Joss, JF Joss, KJ Joss, JW Joughin, RF Jourdain, KD Jovanovic, MG Jovicic, KG Joy, TS Joy, A Joyce, AJ Joyce, BB Joyce, BE Joyce, BF Joyce, BJ Joyce, DL Joyce, DM Joyce, GK Joyce, IA Joyce, JP Joyce, K Joyce, KR Joyce, P Joyce, R Joyce, RJ Joyce, GJ Joycey, S Jozwiak, A Jubb, AW Jubber, WA Jucha, DH Juckel, GC Juckert, CB Judd, DJ Judd, EH Judd, MS Judd, RW Judd, VD Judd, KE Judge, DA Juers, WH Juhas, DJ Juillerat, LA Jukes, AH Junge, PM Juniper, DE Jupp, PJ Jupp, B Jurcun, BJ Jurd, CJ Jurd, LR Jurd, ZR Jurkiewicz, IM Jury, J Jury, ME Just, MR Justice, AE Jux, JG Kaarsberg, PM Kable, KJ Kachel, W Kaczmarek, D Kaddatz, DJ Kadel, RO Kadletz, PJ Kadow, FE Kaesler, CF Kahl, GA Kahler, MK Kahler, SJ Kaighin, LC Kail, K Kain, WE Kaine, PAF Kaineder, CS Kaiser, RA Kaiser, RG Kaiser, RB Kajar, E Kakafikas, AK Kalb, GJ Kalemba, S Kaliczinsky, DC Kalis, BG Kalisperis, TM Kallas, H Kallergis, JH Kalma, AR Kalman, PA Kalms, A Kalnins, J Kalnins, S Kalpidis, J Kamenek, RS Kamid, LS Kaminski, NJ Kaminski, AJ Kamphius, AJ Kamphuis, MK Kanake, AT Kane, BT Kane, GE Kane, JE Kane, NL Kane, PJ Kane, RL Kane, WR Kannar, JW Kanowski, MJ Kanowski, J Kantor, Z Kaplon, LA Kapp, BL Kappler, A Karas, E Karasoulos, M Kargas, TC Karl, D Karleusa, I Karlich, GJ Karner, M Karolak, RL Karpin, NA Karpowicz, JP Karpuska, SS Karsai, HW Karwowski, HK Kaselow, JZ Kasiniak, HJS Kasteel, H Katala, FP Katers, L Katona, GE Kaufmann, WR Kaukianen, KJ Kauschke, BW Kavanagh, GD Kavanagh, GR Kavanagh, BJ Kay, BW Kay, JJ Kay, KR Kay, LN Kay, MJ Kay, NJ Kay, NL Kay, PA Kay, RC Kay, RJ Kay, RM Kay, SR Kay, SW Kay, DA Kaye, SN Kaye, SP Kaye, CD Kayler-Thomson, JA Kazimierowicz, DG Keall, JG Keall, C Kealy, GR Kealy, LJ Kealy, JM Kean, RA Kean, DC Keane, JFN Keane, M Keane, MJ Keane, MJ Keane, MS Keane, OW Keane, PA Keane, TM Keane, W Keane, G Kearnes, DL Kearney, EJ Kearney, FJ Kearney, PF Kearney, PJ Kearney, RS Kearney, TW Kearney, JF Kearns, LC Kearns, PC Kearns, RP Kearns, PG Kearsley, DJ Kearton, WE Kearvell, TT Keary, CL Keast, PW Keat, RJ Keates, B Keating, CR Keating, DA Keating, KJ Keating, LJ Keating, MJ Keating, BJ Keatley, GF Keaton, GC Keats, AN Keddie, BR Keddie, SM Kee, AB Keech, DD Keech, IF Keech, PN Keech, DP Keefe, JH Keefe, GM Keeffe, MA Keegan, MG Keegan, NS Keegan, RA Keegan, CJ Keel, AJ Keele, MKE Keeler, SR Keeler, G Keely, EJ Keen, HF Keen, JW Keen, KH Keen, PN Keen, RK Keen, RM Keen, DR Keena, E Keenahan, BH Keenan, IC Keenan, MF Keenan, WE Keenan, R Keens, PJ Keep, RM Keep, WJ Keepkie, W Keers, RW Kees, AJ Keevers, AO Keevers, BR Keevers, BV Keevers, EW Keevers, NE Keevers, DW Keft, RJ Keft, FT Kehoe, LJ Kehoe, MJ Keighran, RW Keightley, AJ Keiley, PR Keillor, HJP Keimeier, CF Keioskie, GG Keir, JR Keirnan, DJ Keirs, JJC Keisler, D Keith, DJ Keith, AE Kelaher, JD Keldie, G Keleris, K Keliher, IR Kelk, BM Kelleher, DM Kelleher, DW Kelleher, J Kelleher, DJ Keller, GH Keller, KB Keller, AP Kellett, D Kellett, DS Kellett, T Kellett, G Kellner, JC Kellner, GJ Kells, AJ Kelly, AM Kelly, BD Kelly, BE Kelly, BJ Kelly, BL Kelly, BM Kelly, BP Kelly, BR Kelly, BW Kelly, CB Kelly, CC Kelly, CP Kelly, DE Kelly, DH Kelly, DJ Kelly, DR Kelly, DWA Kelly, E Kelly, EJ Kelly, ER Kelly, FJ Kelly, GA Kelly, GH Kelly, GP Kelly, GR Kelly, GW Kelly, HJ Kelly, IF Kelly, J Kelly, JA Kelly, JC Kelly, JD Kelly, JE Kelly, JF Kelly, JJ Kelly, JL Kelly, JP Kelly, JW Kelly, KJ Kelly, LA Kelly, LB Kelly, LN Kelly, M Kelly, MJ Kelly, MM Kelly, MP Kelly, MR Kelly, MS Kelly, ND Kelly, NJ Kelly, NM Kelly, P Kelly, PA Kelly, PJ Kelly, PO Kelly, PR Kelly, PS Kelly, R Kelly, RB Kelly, RC Kelly, RD Kelly, RE Kelly, RG Kelly, RH Kelly, RJ Kelly, RK Kelly, RP Kelly, SJ Kelly, TC Kelly, TJ Kelly, TR Kelly, TV Kelly, W Kelly, WA Kelly, WJ Kelly, MG Kelman, JA Kelsey, LG Kelsey, DP Kelso, KJ Kelso, BR Kelson, JE Kelton, GF Kelty, MJ Kelty, GM Kember, RA Kember, GM Kemble, J Kembrey, BM Kemp, CB Kemp, CJ Kemp, EJ Kemp, GE Kemp, GHV Kemp, GL Kemp, GP Kemp, JB Kemp, JD Kemp, JF Kemp, JH Kemp, JP Kemp, JW Kemp, KC Kemp, MV Kemp, RB Kemp, RC Kemp, RH Kemp, RI Kemp, RW Kemp, KJ Kempin, MC Kemsley, SJ Kenafack, GR Kenafacke, JW Kenafacke, RT Kenane, MJ Kendal, AR Kendall, DL Kendall, GJ Kendall, GM Kendall, J Kendall, JE Kendall, LO Kendall, M Kendall, RJ Kendall, WJ Kendall, WT Kendall, JS Kendell, RJ Kendell, AM Kendrick, GA Kendrick, GJ Kendrick, RN Kendrick, GH Kendrigan, DJ Kenealy, LS Kenfield, WJ Kenihan, BF Kenna, BJ Kenna, NS Kenna, GD Kennan, JW Kennard, RS Kennard, JA Kenneally, W Kenneally, A Kennedy, AB Kennedy, AK Kennedy, B Kennedy, BJ Kennedy, BM Kennedy, BP Kennedy, BS Kennedy, BW Kennedy, CF Kennedy, CI Kennedy, CR Kennedy, DC Kennedy, DE Kennedy, DJ Kennedy, DL Kennedy, DM Kennedy, DW Kennedy, EJ Kennedy, EM Kennedy, GE Kennedy, GT Kennedy, ID Kennedy, IM Kennedy, J Kennedy, JA Kennedy, JDB Kennedy, JJ Kennedy, JR Kennedy, KA Kennedy, KW Kennedy, LJ Kennedy, LN Kennedy, MA Kennedy, MH Kennedy, MJ Kennedy, NP Kennedy, NT Kennedy, PC Kennedy, PG Kennedy, PJ Kennedy, PM Kennedy, PN Kennedy, PR Kennedy, RA Kennedy, RE Kennedy, RG Kennedy, RJ Kennedy, RR Kennedy, VJ Kennedy, W Kennedy, WD Kennedy, WE Kennedy, WF Kennedy, WJ Kennedy, WL Kennedy, WS Kennedy, WW Kennedy, HS Kennell, AJ Kennett, GN Kennett, PL Kennett, RJ Kennett, AE Kennewell, DT Kennewell, NH Kennewell, MD Kenney, WF Kenney, DA Kenniff, GW Kenning, J Kennison, AJ Kenny, BL Kenny, DE Kenny, DP Kenny, IF Kenny, KD Kenny, KJ Kenny, LJ Kenny, R Kenny, RE Kenny, RS Kenny, RW Kenny, TJ Kenny, CW Kensey, AH Kent, BS Kent, CR Kent, DA Kent, DJ Kent, DK Kent, FJ Kent, GJ Kent, GN Kent, JE Kent, NR Kent, PJ Kent, PN Kent, RG Kent, RH Kent, ST Kent, R Kentler, PW Kentwell, GB Kenworthy, JM Kenworthy, D Kenyon, GE Kenyon, JR Kenyon, SWN Kenyon, BJ Keogh, GM Keogh, J Keogh, PJ Keogh, JC Keoller, DR Kepper, C Keratzis, TS Kerby, GA Kercher, PJ Kercher, A Kerekes, GJ Kerford, BM Kerin, MJ Kerin, M Kerkez, R Kerkez, JJS Kerkman, PJ Kerley, NB Kerlin, TJ Kerlin, KR Kermode, RC Kermode, AJ Kernaghan, LA Kerney, WJ Kernoczy, PC Kerntke, ND Kernutt, AG Kerr, BL Kerr, DA Kerr, DE Kerr, DK Kerr, DN Kerr, DV Kerr, ICR Kerr, J Kerr, JK Kerr, JL Kerr, JM Kerr, JW Kerr, LD Kerr, LG Kerr, NE Kerr, RJ Kerr, RT Kerr, WL Kerr, WW Kerr, PW Kerridge, R Kerrigan, LF Kerrison, N Kerrison, D Kershaw, KR Kershaw, RA Kershaw, DJ Kerslake, DW Kerslake, RW Kerslake, AAH Kersten, JJ Kerwick, MG Kerwin, RJ Kerwin, PJ Kesby, RB Kessell, JA Kester, BG Kesterton, L Ketelaar, WM Kett, JD Ketteringham, AE Kettle, VE Keusemann, LMJ Kevalaitis, DS Kew, GH Kewin, RA Key, RM Key, EA Keygan, LC Keynes, RT Keynes, AD Keys, AL Keys, JG Keys, PV Keys, RS Keys, SW Keys, TC Keys, W Keyser, RJ Keyte, RS Keyte, CN Khan, DW Kibbey, SD Kibble, IC Kibblewhite, JA Kibby, RR Kickett, DG Kidd, DM Kidd, DR Kidd, GH Kidd, GRM Kidd, JF Kidd, JK Kidd, LJ Kidd, PD Kidd, RC Kidd, TA Kidd, J Kidner, BE Kidney, RI Kidston, W Kidston, HJ Kiehn, GC Kiehne, WT Kiehne, JH Kiel, EJ Kiellerup, P Kielly, CJ Kielman, EE Kiely, PE Kiely, PR Kiely, SA Kiely, J Kiene, LE Kiernan, PJ Kiernan, J Kijko, CN Kikeros, JW Kilbourne, MA Kilburn, AJ Kilby, BR Kilby, PB Kilby, MJ Kilcoyne, J Kilday, WP Kilday, CF Kilduff, JV Kiley, BB Killalea, JF Killalea, IT Killeen, BJ Killen, P Killen, JR Killian, FW Killick, WG Killick, DG Killion, RW Killoran, BE Killworth, DW Kilner, LE Kilner, RV Kilner, AR Kilpatrick, BG Kilpatrick, DR Kilpatrick, FR Kilpatrick, J Kilpatrick, ND Kilpatrick, PD Kilpatrick, PI Kilpatrick, PR Kilpatrick, RG Kilsby, JA Kilworth, DG Kimball, AD Kimber, GC Kimberley, JF Kimberley, JL Kimberley, CR Kimble, EL Kime, MG Kimlin, JM Kimmorley, PR Kimmorley, AR Kimpton, M Kinang, BR Kincade, AF Kinch, WJ Kinchin, JD Kinder, RC Kindness, RE Kindred, AAF King, AE King, AF King, AJ King, AR King, BG King, BJ King, BL King, BM King, C King, CE King, DJ King, DK King, DM King, DRM King, DW King, DWF King, EB King, ECJ King, EE King, EM King, GE King, GF King, GG King, GH King, GJ King, GN King, GP King, HA King, HR King, ID King, IN King, IS King, IT King, J King, JA King, JB King, JC King, JF King, JK King, JL King, JM King, JR King, JV King, KD King, KJ King, KO King, LA King, LE King, LF King, M King, MD King, ME King, MG King, MR King, MS King, ND King, NJ King, PJ King, PL King, PT King, RA King, RB King, RD King, RE King, RJ King, RM King, RN King, RP King, RR King, RV King, RW King, SA King, T King, TC King, TD King, TJ King, TR King, TW King, VG King, WH King, AJ Kingdom, GF Kingdon, GF Kinggee, RM Kinggee, RC Kingsbury, IW Kingston, JW Kingston, LL Kingston, TA Kingston, WL Kingston, KM Kingston-Powles, RN Kinley, GC Kinmonth, MG Kinna, DA Kinnaird, MJ Kinnaird, BJ Kinnane, NJ Kinnane, WA Kinnane, RJ Kinnear, PJ Kinney, D Kinniburgh, JF Kinsela, MJ Kinsela, BE Kinsella, MVS Kinsella, PA Kinsella, T Kinsella, RK Kipp, PW Kippax, DH Kippen, RD Kippen, JD Kipper, NE Kipps, BA Kirby, BJ Kirby, GG Kirby, JW Kirby, MJ Kirby, PT Kirby, RJ Kirby, RW Kirby, WE Kirby, GH Kirk, GJ Kirk, MG Kirk, R Kirkbright, DH Kirkby, GP Kirkby, KJ Kirkby, QV Kirkby, RA Kirkby, N Kirke, KH Kirkham, RF Kirkham, S Kirkitscha, AG Kirkland, BE Kirkland, KH Kirkland, RM Kirkland,

TJ Kirkland, DJ Kirkman, DW Kirkman, HR Kirkman, JJ Kirkman, DA Kirkpatrick, DL Kirkpatrick, T Kirkpatrick, WJ Kirkpatrick, JL Kirkup, KJ Kirkup, JL Kirley, V Kirsch, RJ Kirshaw, D Kirtley, AJ Kirwan, RF Kirwin, A Kish, ER Kisir, V Kisler, DT Kissick, VL Kissin, R Kitchen, RI Kitchener, JF Kitchin, LM Kitchin, JM Kite, D Kitley, PM Kitschke, IJ Kitson, JT Kitson, DR Kitt, KM Kittle, NJ Kitto, WS Kitto, DR Kittyea, S Kiyose, EJ Kjellgren, RW Kjellgren, MJ Klaassens, RR Klan, JR Klar, MJ Klas, E Klass, WC Klass, DR Klatt, HA Klaws, RJ Kleidon, B Klein, CG Klein, J Klein, JE Klein, JM Klein, KJ Klein, MD Klein, RJ Klein, OE Kleinig, SJ Kleinig, JK Kleinschmidt, RR Klem, BF Klemm, PE Klemm, W Kleszcz, TB Kliese, WEA Klimisch, PC Kline, DH Klingbiel, HG Klinkert, T Klisc, NP Klitscher, HJ Klopcic, RG Klopp, RW Klopp, JFT Klopper, JD Klose, R Kluczniak, KE Kludas, RW Klupp, SW Klysz, W Kmetyk, RCG Knaggs, DW Knapp, GR Knapp, MD Knapp, RJ Knapp, KD Kneebone, BA Kneeves, GR Knell, J Knell, AT Kneller, DA Kneller, AC Knight, AD Knight, AG Knight, AT Knight, B Knight, BA Knight, BD Knight, BF Knight, DC Knight, DG Knight, DH Knight, DJ Knight, DL Knight, DR Knight, EE Knight, EJ Knight, G Knight, GD Knight, GM Knight, GR Knight, HR Knight, JC Knight, JR Knight, JS Knight, JW Knight, LB Knight, LJ Knight, LW Knight, MC Knight, MJ Knight, NG Knight, PD Knight, PJ Knight, QJ Knight, RB Knight, RC Knight, RD Knight, SG Knight, T Knight, TF Knight, WR Knightbridge, GL Knighton, JR Knights, J Knightsmith, KJ Knipe, MG Knispel, GJ Knobben, KD Knop, DW Knopke, KG Knopp, AS Knott, CJ Knowles, J Knowles, JA Knowles, JH Knowles, KC Knowles, KW Knowles, RA Knowles, RE Knowles, CL Knox, DM Knox, GM Knox, JD Knox, RP Knox, WC Knox, CS Knuckey, GK Knuckey, RD Knuckey, H Koblitz, HA Koch, JF Koch, LJ Koch, PF Koch, WF Koch, RJ Kochowiec, DEJ Kock, JR Kocka, B Koczyrkewycz, JF Koek, PA Koekoek, GJ Koenig, WL Koetter, RM Koffel, RM Kofoed, A Kohary, AN Kohler, DG Kohler, RW Kohlhagen, R Kohn, JR Kohnke, B Kohut, I Kohut, V Kojevnikoff, DH Kokegei, E Kokins, J Kokoschko, B Kolasa, A Kolbuch, CR Kolderie, H Kolek, J Kolenberg, S Koliba, GI Kollar, BC Kollias, NH Kollias, GG Kolln, J Kolodziejski, VJ Komarowski, CTP Kondratowicz, S Konefal, K Konemann, P Kongras, W Konias, S Koning, R Konopacki, W Konowec, WM Kontor, B Konz, AH Koo, CJ Kook, G Kool, JC Kool, C Koolen, JK Koop, R Koops, JF Koosache, W Koot, L Kop, AJ Kopacz, JJ Kopec, SJ Koper, P Kopievsky, W Kopp, AM Koppen, MP Koppman, J Korczak, J Kordupel, W Kordupel, RH Korff, JR Korn, V Korney, M Kornitschuk, ZJH Korol, I Korpos, IW Kortlang, WA Koscielecki, P Kosenko, AJ Koster, PA Koster, JA Kostera, JL Kostin, M Kostiuk, W Kostiw, G Kotlarski, AZ Kotlarz, I Kotsopoulos, T Kotynia, PA Kotz, C Koulouris, RT Koutchavlis, JPA Kouwenhoven, F Kovaleff, I Kowalczyk, J Kowalczyk, JS Kowalczyk, BG Kowald, J Kowalenko, PF Kowalski, J Kowcun, RI Kraehe, BM Kraft, EJ Krahnert, DR Krake, BR Kramer, HH Kramer, MG Kramer, PW Kramer, RJ Kramer, A Krantis, ME Kranz, S Krasnoff, JR Krason, M Krasowski, N Krassos, MR Krassovsky, KR Kratz, BL Kratzmann, LE Kratzmann, RW Kratzmann, DH Krause, GRR Krause, JW Krause, MA Krause, NL Krause, PC Krause, EC Kraut, HWP Krautheim, O Krawec, AM Krawtshuk, GL Krebs, HJ Kreemers, AJ Kregor, OG Krenke, RP Kriedemann, RJ Krieg, LG Krieger, BW Kriesel, WB Kriewaldt, AJ Krikke, G Krishna, AJ Krizovsky, BC Kroemer, L Krois, NR Kroll, DW Krollig, WMJ Kromwyk, FA Krook, GM Kroon, LB Kropinyeri, TE Kropp, MP Krstic, SL Kruck, AJ Kruger, MC Kruger, PR Kruger, SJ Kruger, WK Kruger, FS Kruimink, JH Kruisdyk, CP Krupowicz, NW Kruse, GB Krushka, M Kryntjes, AP Kryzius, HA Krzemien, M Krzeszkowski, T Krzywokulski, RG Krzyzanski, AR Kube, DHD Kube, P Kubernat, AL Kubiak, MJ Kuchel, CC Kuchenmeister, RW Kucinskas, LA Kucks, LP Kucks, T Kuczborski, J Kuczma, JJ Kuczynski, WJ Kuczynski, FM Kudnig, RP Kudnig, KG Kuehlmann, HHJ Kuessner, J Kuffner, DR Kugler, DJ Kuhl, BA Kuhn, CF Kuhn, K Kuhnert, AL Kuijpers, JM Kuijpers, D Kuiper, J Kuiper, JD Kuipers, MWH Kuit, RW Kukulka, F Kukwa, HP Kummerlowe, HF Kumpel, AW Kunde, S Kunigiskis, GW Kunkel, AJ Kunning, S Kupniewski, RJ Kupsch, TJ Kupsch, ER Kurauskas, WJ Kurcz, JP Kuret, E Kuriata, IA Kuring, B Kurkowski, W Kurtz, LW Kurylowicz, RE Kuschert, FJ Kuslan, NJ Kussrow, MJ Kusternig, I Kustreba, S Kusturin, F Kuzba, S Kuzio, AJ Kuzmanich, H Kvjatkovskis, B Kwas, LJ Kwaterski, JB Kyne, E Kyriazis, S Kyritsis, RK Kyte, R Kyte-Powell, CJ Kyval, PJ La Forest, WA La Galle, H La Housse, MJ Laarhoven, VR Labutis, JP Lacava, MA Lace, AJC Lacey, DJ Lacey, RA Lacey, TW Lacey, WJ Lacey, WW Lachs, IW Lack, PG Lackey, PJ Lackey, CRJ Lackmann, BJ Lacy, EW Lacy, RV Lacy, M Ladbrook, IE Lade, WG Lade, NP Ladhams, MD Ladlow, JF Ladmore, BD Ladyman, RP Ladyman, PJ Laenen, J Laferton, KG Laffer, MB Lafferty, PJ Lafferty, JP Laffey, T Laforest, R Lagana, VJ Lagettie, JR Lah, DJ Lahore, PJ Lahtevanoja, AW Laidlaw, PFJ Laidlaw, RL Laidlaw, AW Laing, B Laing, GM Laing, HG Laing, JA Laing, JW Laing, KG Laing, RA Laing, RJ Laing, RS Laing, W Laing, AJ Laird, DA Laird, DJ Laird, DM Laird, GW Laird, KD Laird, MB Laird, RJ Laird, RW Laird, TA Laird, WR Laird, BW Lake, GJ Lake, JJ Lake, JW Lake, NG Lake, RF Lake, RJ Lake, WJ Lake, AW Laker, GW Lakey, JJ Lakey, KT Lakey, LC Lakey, SA Lakin, JT Lalor, RGJ Lalor, RR Lalor, V Lamanna, AC Lamb, AM Lamb, BJ Lamb, CA Lamb, DF Lamb, FB Lamb, J Lamb, MB Lamb, P Lamb, REM Lamb, SN Lamb, WT Lamb, AH Lambert, AW Lambert, CG Lambert, D Lambert, DW Lambert, G Lambert, GE Lambert, JG Lambert, KR Lambert, LB Lambert, LJ Lambert, LW Lambert, PA Lambert, PW Lambert, RA Lambert, RF Lambert, RH Lambert, RV Lambert, RW Lambert, WD Lambert, WM Lambert, CA Lamberth, EL Lambie, J Lambie, DB Lambley, M Lambley, WS Lambley, MJ Lamborn, MW Lamborn, LA Lambourn, RD Lambshead, RL Lamming, PE Lamond, PR Lamond, RM Lamond, BJ Lamont, IF Lamont, RA Lamont, RW Lamont, AV Lamotte, CW Lamotte, L Lamotte, MG Lamotte, KC Lampard, LM Lampard, DJ Lampert, CR Lampre, DR Lampre, RL Lamprell, GR Lamshed, P Lancashire, AW Lancaster, EF Lancaster, GE Lancaster, GR Lancaster, JW Lancaster, RA Lancaster, RJ Lancaster, BT Lanchester, BF Land, PJ Land, DFE Lander, FL Lander, GW Lander, HM Lander, JA Lander, PJ Landers, PG Landwehr, GD Landy, TM Landy, AD Lane, AJ Lane, AW Lane, BE Lane, CW Lane, DG Lane, DR Lane, EA Lane, GE Lane, GJ Lane, GM Lane, GR Lane, JA Lane, JF Lane, JG Lane, KL Lane, MA Lane, NR Lane, P Lane, RD Lane, RM Lane, RT Lane, WJ Lane, L Lanera, AC Lang, AJ Lang, BW Lang, DR Lang, EW Lang, JA Lang, KB Lang, PJ Lang, RC Lang, RJ Lang, RL Lang, RT Lang, TD Lang, LW Langabeer, MD Langan, LJ Langbein, OM Langburne, DJ Langdon, RJ Langdon, A Lange, BD Lange, GM Lange, JA Lange, JL Lange, RG Lange, RJ Lange, FP Langford, GL Langford, PJ Langford, RJ Langford, TJ Langford, TW Langford, WE Langford, WJ Langford, DA Langham, ER Langham, JE Langham, RA Langham, TJ Langhorn, GD Langlands, IA Langlands, TE Langlands, JB Langler, JW Langler, DP Langley, GR Langley, JR Langley, MG Langley, ML Langley, MS Langley, R Langley, RJ Langley, LJ Langmaid, PA Langman, RB Langman, BA Langridge, CW Langridge, IJ Langridge, ST Langridge, AL Langslow, JR Langston, CC Langton, JG Langton, RJ Lanham, GC Lanigan, MD Lanigan, ID Lankester, DJ Lannigan, B Lans, DH Lansbury, BJ Lansdown, GJ Lansdown, AG Lansdowne, I Lanskis, DK Lansley, RI Lansom, DL Lanthois, MJ Lantry, K Lapeta, NJ Lapham, P Lapko, KJ Lappin, MH Lappin, WJ Lapthorne, WT Laracy, LH Larcombe, RB Larcombe, SL Larfield, BJ Large, CW Large, PA Large, BA Lark, AJ Larkin, BA Larkin, DF Larkin, JR Larkin, MF Larkin, PJ Larkin, RJ Larkin, DL Larking, WJP Larkings, CE Larment, WF Larmour, AW Larnach-Jones, BH Larner, F Larosa, VJ Larracy, KW Larratt, AW Larsen, CA Larsen, DJ Larsen, E Larsen, HA Larsen, RC Larsen, RG Larsen, RR Larsen, AJ Larson, G Larson, RJ Larson, LF Larsson, SG Larsson, DE Larter, G Larter, LW Larter, P Larter, JGA Las, RW Lashbrook, MB Lashman, R Laskowski, T Laskowski, BJ Lassen, WC Lassey, CJ Last, KJ Last, KW Latchford, CR Latemore, NJ Latemore, A Lateo, CL Latham, JK Latham, KG Latham, PJR Latham, RW Latham, GJ Lather, P Lathrope, K Latimer, MH Latimer, HC Latrobe, GJ Latta, RK Latta, AW Latter, WA Lauber, BA Lauder, GP Lauder, IR Lauder, PJ Lauder, IR Laufer, GK Laughlin, HC Laughlin, WF Laughlin, KC Laughton, KL Laughton, DS Launder, GH Launder, RJ Laurence, BR Laurenceson, MS Laurens, G Laurenson, NP Laurent, RD Laurent, FH Laurentsch, GS Laurie, IA Laurie, JP Laurie, WJ Lauriston, AJ Lavell, RG Lavell, RA Lavelle, CB Lavender, TJ Lavender, BJ Laver, DS Laver, IM Laverie, BJ Laverty, DT Laverty, G Laverty, SB Laverty, TE Laverty, GF Lavery, JB Lavery, MF Lavery, RS Lavery, TA Lavery, AJ Lavis, DJ Lavis, GM Lavis, AA Law, BN Law, CM Law, DC Law, EJ Law, GW Law, J Law, KF Law, PJ Law, SW Law, TJ Law, LJ Lawer, AJ Lawler, AL Lawler, CW Lawler, F Lawler, JF Lawler, KJ Lawler, KM Lawler, PJ Lawler, RA Lawler, RF Lawler, RT Lawler, VP Lawler, AJ Lawlor, EJ Lawlor, RD Lawlor, RS Lawlor, GW Lawman, WL Lawn, AS Lawrance, BR Lawrance, FW Lawrance, GD Lawrance, IR Lawrance, JF Lawrance, CC Lawrence, DB Lawrence, DE Lawrence, DG Lawrence, DP Lawrence, DR Lawrence, EW Lawrence, FR Lawrence, FW Lawrence, GB Lawrence, GD Lawrence, GH Lawrence, GJ Lawrence, IR Lawrence, JE Lawrence, JF Lawrence, KE Lawrence, MJ Lawrence, PC Lawrence, PG Lawrence, RC Lawrence, RG Lawrence, RJ Lawrence, TG Lawrence, TJ Lawrence, WJ Lawrence, WJW Lawrence, ID Lawrey, JA Lawrie, WK Lawrie, D Lawrinson, KR Lawry, AJ Laws, GN Laws, PJ Laws, AG Lawson, BT Lawson, CFW Lawson, DE Lawson, DJ Lawson, DW Lawson, F Lawson, FJ Lawson, G Lawson, GM Lawson, IJ Lawson, JA Lawson, JP Lawson, JW Lawson, KE Lawson, KJ Lawson, MJ Lawson, PB Lawson, R Lawson, RA Lawson, RB Lawson, RD Lawson, RH Lawson, RJ Lawson, RO Lawson, C Lawsonbaker, AR Lawton, DK Lawton, JM Lawton, HS Laxton, CA Laybutt, SC Laycock, WA Laycock, WJ Laycock, NR Layt, RL Layt, CG Layton, DJ Layton, J Layton, NK Layton, RA Layton, PR Lazarevic, J Lazaroff, A Lazarou, M Lazarus, RW Lazell, WM Lazic, JF Lazzaro, MF Le Bars, NW Le Bherz, MJ Le Breton, PJ Le Breton, AJ Le Busque, KR Le Clos, BG Le Dan, RH Le Froy, MD Le Gay Brereton, KJ Le Jeune, KJ Le Nepveu, BL Le Sueur, GT Lea, GW Lea, JD Lea, TH Lea, GE Leach, GJC Leach, GR Leach, GW Leach, IC Leach, ID Leach, KB Leach, MM Leach, RJ Leach, RR Leach, SW Leach, WA Leach, PJ Leacy, WK Leadbeater, K Leadbetter, AW Leaf, RS Leaf, D Leafe, BP Leahy, DA Leahy, GPJ Leahy, JJ Leahy, MF Leahy, PL Leahy, PM Leahy, TJ Leahy, WP Leahy, SJ Leak, JF Leal, SV Leale, DC Leaman, JB Leaman, RJ Leaman, DA Lean, DV Lean, RC Lean, JA Leane, DG Leaney, EJ Leaney, CJ Lear, RJ Lear, SH Lear, DJ Learhinan, DC Leary, GJ Leary, EJ Leask, JN Leask, MJ Leask, JA Lea-Smith, LC Leaver, DT Leay, CA Leayr, HA Lebediuks, RJ Leberfinger, FG Lebler, HA Lebusque, F Leca, H Lechner, JH Lechte, K Leckenby, DJ Leckie, JG Leckie, RJ Leckie, PR Lecornu, JR Lecussan, CC Ledden, PD Leddy, KF Leder, DK Ledgard, BJ Ledger, JC Ledlin, WR Ledo, AJ Lee, AL Lee, BG Lee, BJ Lee, CA Lee, CN Lee, DG Lee, E Lee, EJ Lee, G Lee, GA Lee, GH Lee, GJ Lee, GW Lee, HL Lee, I Lee, IL Lee, JH Lee, JW Lee, KG Lee, MDN Lee, MG Lee, MJ Lee, ML Lee, MS Lee, NJ Lee, NT Lee, P Lee, PJ Lee, PL Lee, PR Lee, R Lee, RD Lee, RH Lee, RK Lee, RN Lee, RW Lee, S Lee, TD Lee, TE Lee, TW Lee, WF Lee, WJ Lee, WW Lee, WH Leebody, BR Leech, GR Leech, JL Leech, AJ Leeder, RJ Leedow, J Leeds, E Leeflang, AD Leefson, JC Leeman, RL Leeman, S Leeman, PH Leembruggen, HJ Leerentveld, CA Leermakers, FJ Lees, GJ Lees, MJ Lees, NM Lees, RD Lees, RE Lees, RL Lees, RV Lees, TR Lees, DW Leeson, P Leeson, PM Leeson, BJ Leesue, RN Leesye, GR Leetet, RW Leevers, JM Lefel, B Legarde, JC Legg, OJ Legg, CJ Legge, ET Legge, GE Legge, JD Legge, LH Legge, CE Leggett, D Leggett, GJ Leggett, JA Leggett, JK Leggett, KH Leggett, KR Leggett, RA Leggo, MG Legrand, RL Leguier, ND Lehfeldt, FC Lehman, JL Lehman, AW Lehmann, GN Lehmann, PA Lehmann, TC Lehmann, RD Lehn, AM Leigh, TB Leigh, CJ Leighton, GTS Leighton, HA Leighton, CR Leihy, BR Leiper, IF Leis, JW Leis, KH Leis, IR Leishman, J Leishman, AJ Leitch, GD Leitch, R Leitch, TR Leitch, JK Leith, PJ Leith, K Leithhead, AH Leivers, MG Lemaistre, TB Lemcke, RJP Lemercier, KJ Lemesurier, RJ Lemm, RD Lemmich, PA Lemmo, MJ Lemon, N Lemon, H Lempa, TC Lempriere, A Lenarcic, HR Lenard, RA Lenard, GN Lendich, RC Lengnick, RF Lennen, HW Lennis, BB Lennon, F Lennon, FN Lennon, GF Lennon, JA Lennon, JF Lennon, MJ Lennon, P Lennon, PA Lennon, R Lennon, WD Lennon, WW Lennon, A Lennox, AJ Lennox, AM Lennox, DT Lennox, RI Lennox, NB Lenoy, E Lensing, GR Lenz, JW Lenz, CJ Leo, FW Leo, TM Leo, BJ Leonard, CB Leonard, CR Leonard, GJ Leonard, GP Leonard, IC Leonard, JF Leonard, KJH Leonard, MA Leonard, PJ Leonard, R Leonard, W Leonard, LH Leopold, P Lep, JL L'epagniol, GJ Leplaw, JD Lepoidevin, E Lepore, A Leray, PA Leriche, JV Lerickman, RJ Leroy, N Lesina, RJ Lesinski, DJ Leske, A Leslie, AF Leslie, AJ Leslie,

BJ Leslie, DH Leslie, DR Leslie, GBJ Leslie, IJ Leslie, JW Leslie, PG Leslie, RG Leslie, RJ Leslie, F Lesnik, C Lessells, WD Lessels, GJ Lesslie, BJ Lester, BR Lester, DJ Lester, GB Lester, GF Lester, KC Lester, RC Lester, BE L'estrange, RD Lestrange, RJ Lestrange, A Letford, CB Lethbridge, DR Lethbridge, PA Lethbridge, DP Lethem, MJ Lethlean, AD Lette, BJ Letts, RD Letts, VV Letwinski, TS Levander, JD Levens, PJ Levens, D Levenspiel, DC Lever, GK Lever, IC Lever, KH Lever, RW Lever, RJ Leverton, AW Levey, GR Levey, KJ Levi, GT Levick, MF Levin, JE Levitzke, DL Levy, ES Levy, IM Levy, JA Levy, PM Levy, BT Lew, LP Lewandowski, PJ Lewer, KM Lewicki, DG Lewien, AE Lewin, JE Lewin, K Lewin, CET Lewington, G Lewington, A Lewis, AM Lewis, AW Lewis, B Lewis, BC Lewis, BH Lewis, BJ Lewis, BP Lewis, BT Lewis, BW Lewis, CC Lewis, CJ Lewis, CR Lewis, DC Lewis, DE Lewis, DG Lewis, DJ Lewis, DM Lewis, DR Lewis, DV Lewis, ED Lewis, EG Lewis, EJ Lewis, EL Lewis, ES Lewis, FI Lewis, GJ Lewis, GL Lewis, GP Lewis, GW Lewis, I Lewis, IJ Lewis, IR Lewis, IW Lewis, J Lewis, JA Lewis, JAS Lewis, JC Lewis, JE Lewis, JH Lewis, KD Lewis, KH Lewis, KJ Lewis, KT Lewis, LC Lewis, LJ Lewis, LR Lewis, LV Lewis, MA Lewis, MC Lewis, MI Lewis, MJ Lewis, N Lewis, NF Lewis, PC Lewis, PD Lewis, PE Lewis, PH Lewis, PJ Lewis, RB Lewis, RC Lewis, RD Lewis, RG Lewis, RJ Lewis, RM Lewis, RP Lewis, RT Lewis, SC Lewis, SH Lewis, T Lewis, TA Lewis, TE Lewis, TF Lewis, TG Lewis, TW Lewis, VJ Lewis, WF Lewis, WK Lewis, WM Lewis, WW Lewis, RK Lewisdriver, DW Leworthy, MI Ley, PD Ley, W Leyden, AJ Leyland, GF Leys, JG Librizzi, EI Liddell, I Liddell, JC Liddell, KC Liddell, KM Liddell, KR Liddell, N Liddell, PJ Liddell, WC Liddell, DS Liddelow, KJ Lidden, LA Liddington, HL Liddle, P Liddle, RP Liddy, WR Lidgerwood, PA Lidster, WH Lidster, G Lieben, GR Liebenau, UD Liebich, P Liefman, S Liefting, GP Liersch, NH Liesegang, RJ Lieven, D Liggett, EG Lightbody, AJJ Lightfoot, RJ Lightfoot, CJ Lill, WA Lillebo, AD Lillehagen, HF Lillewhyte, EA Lilley, GP Lilley, LW Lilley, IAG Lillie, DJ Lillis, J Lillis, MF Lilly, GJ Lillyst, RJ Lillywhite, MJ Limb, S Limb, P Limberis, CD Limbrick, T Limburg, AG Limn, DG Limn, RJ Limond, DJ Limpus, BE Linaker, DW Linaker, F Linck, LH Lincoln, MA Lincoln, P Lincoln, TF Lincoln, A Lind, DI Lind, JA Lind, JW Lind, KN Lind, NB Lind, OS Lind, GR Linde, HD Lindel, DG Lindeman, RJ Lindeman, N Lindemeier, JP Linden, MW Linden, DC Lindenberg, HUG Lindfors, DB Lindgren, DE Lindgren, EE Lindgren, IP Lindley, AR Lindmark, NJ Lindroos, A Lindsay, AS Lindsay, AW Lindsay, BDV Lindsay, CB Lindsay, DR Lindsay, F Lindsay, G Lindsay, GA Lindsay, IG Lindsay, J Lindsay, JB Lindsay, LTE Lindsay, MK Lindsay, N Lindsay, NR Lindsay, R Lindsay, RD Lindsay, RJ Lindsay, JR Lindsey, PF Lindwall, DJ Lineham, BD Linehan, BW Lines, DR Lines, MC Lines, TR Lines, AP Ling, GH Ling, JA Ling, RG Ling, TT Ling, J Lingard, LG Lingard, RC Lingard, BJ Lingham, BA Lingwoodock, LR Lingwoodock, GA Linke, H Linke, KA Linke, MT Linke, NJ Linnell, AR Linney, MK Linsell, A Linton, MP Linton, AB Linwood, GR Linwood, LW Linwood, TG Linz, G Lipa, S Lipinski, R Lippett, GJ Lipscombe, P Lipscombe, PD Lipscombe, T Lisiecki, A Lisle, GD Lisle, S Lisowski, DP List, RL List, DR Lister, GK Lister, JNS Lister, RG Lister, RP Lister, JW Listerbest, FJ Liston, GN Liston, JA Liston, RL Lisztes, AD Litchfield, JW Litchfield, L Litchfield, TM Litchfield, RJ Litfin, CT Lithgow, A Little, AJ Little, AL Little, AR Little, BW Little, EJ Little, FG Little, GR Little, HE Little, HJ Little, HP Little, JA Little, JS Little, LG Little, NK Little, PAE Little, PJ Little, PR Little, PT Little, RC Little, TR Little, WA Little, WR Little, LG Littlechild, RH Littlefair, RJ Littlefield, AE Littlehales, AD Littlejohn, GLJ Littlejohn, PD Littler, PJ Littler, PR Littler, RI Littlewood, GR Litzow, PF Livermore, BT Livett, BN Livingston, DA Livingston, FG Livingston, MR Livingston, GJ Livingstone, MR Livingstone, RM Livingstone, RW Livingstone, EC Livock, EA Lizars, LGW Lizier, GG Ljepojevic, IH Llanwarne, DR Llewellyn, I Llewellyn, IR Llewellyn, SJ Llewellyn, ED Llewelyn, PH Llewelyn, A Lloyd, AE Lloyd, BK Lloyd, BL Lloyd, BM Lloyd, D Lloyd, DC Lloyd, DF Lloyd, EM Lloyd, GA Lloyd, GG Lloyd, J Lloyd, JD Lloyd, JEH Lloyd, JJ Lloyd, JW Lloyd, LM Lloyd, MT Lloyd, MW Lloyd, P Lloyd, PJ Lloyd, PR Lloyd, PW Lloyd, RDF Lloyd, RE Lloyd, RI Lloyd, RJ Lloyd, RS Lloyd, SO Lloyd, TR Lloyd, TW Lloyd, WJ Lloyd, NJ Lloyd-Jones, KGR Lloyd-Thomas, NDE Lloyd-Thomas, JD Loader, RB Loader, SR Loader, GF Loadsman, JK Loadsman, MG Loan, IA Loaney, KH Loaring, KS Loas, GH Lobb, GR Lobb, JW Lobb, RW Lobb, JE Lobley, JT Loch, RJ Lochowicz, PJ Lochrie, SR Lochrie, AR Lock, BV Lock, DR Lock, EH Lock, GW Lock, MJ Lock, NG Lock, RN Lock, TD Lock, TK Lock, WR Lock, AR Lockart, AJ Locke, CJ Locke, GJ Locke, GR Locke, KW Locke, LW Locke, PG Locke, RJ Locke, WA Locke, WJB Locke, R Lockeridge, AJ Lockett, CJ Lockhart, GL Lockhart, JD Lockhart, R Lockhart, RN Lockhart, RT Lockhart, JP Lockie, P Lockie, DH Lockley, PR Lockley, KJ Lockman, CG Lockrey, AA Lockwood, DG Lockwood, DL Lockwood, DW Lockwood, GK Lockwood, KR Lockwood, NA Lockwood, GA Lockyer, GWH Lockyer, PD Lockyer, RJ Lodding, AH Lodge, GJ Lodge, IW Lodge, RJ Lodge, WN Lodge, JL Loe, JW Lofdahl, PS Lofdahl, JV Lofthouse, PR Lofthouse, IG Lofts, LD Lofts, WA Lofts, ET Loftus, RD Loftus, TB Loftus, BA Logan, BJ Logan, BR Logan, CT Logan, DR Logan, E Logan, GM Logan, JM Logan, K Logan, KB Logan, KH Logan, L Logan, MW Logan, NR Logan, SW Logan, TE Logan, P Logins, V Logins, PR Logos, P Loguancio, KS Logue, RJ Logue, MJ Lohmann, PG Lohmann, AK Lohrisch, N Lojkin, M Lomax, AJ Lombardo, EB Lombardo, V Lombardo, MV Loncaric, BK London, JL London, LJ London, RV London, GJ Londos, MJ Loneragan, AF Lonergan, JW Lonergan, PG Lonergan, TF Lonergan, AW Long, BG Long, BR Long, CE Long, DW Long, FK Long, GN Long, JC Long, JE Long, KC Long, ME Long, MR Long, PE Long, PH Long, PJ Long, PT Long, RA Long, RC Long, RD Long, RJ Long, RW Long, TJ Long, PG Longbottom, NA Longfield, RW Longfield, GC Longford, GW Longford, NP Longhorn, JA Longhurst, GN Longland, M Longley, TJ Longley, TH Longmire, RC Longobardi, AV Longson, BG Longue, RH Longworth, RJ Longyear, RM Lonie, DB Lons, AS Lonsdale, GL Lonsdale, JE Lonsdale, T Loo, AJ Loomes, AG Loorham, FW Loos, PJ Loosmore, GA Lopez, DJ Loran, B Lorback, AJ Lord, B Lord, DH Lord, EC Lord, GJ Lord, GL Lord, GT Lord, L Lord, PR Lord, RJ Lorimer, DH Lorman, JF Lorraine, TJ Lorraine, D Losberg, J Losiak, GF Loth, LF Lothianblack, WA Lotocki, R Lotstra, JT Lott, LJ Loudon, CR Loughhead, BP Loughlin, M Loughlin, M Loughman, RJ Loughnan, TM Loughnan, TR Loughridge, GJ Loughton, ED Lound, EP Lourens, AJ Lourensen, RF Lourie, GD Lourigan, M Lourigan, RC Lousick, E Loustos, WS Louvel, MW Lovatt, BF Love, DA Love, DD Love, E Love, G Love, GM Love, JR Love, K Love, MD Love, MF Love, P Love, RH Love, W Love, WB Love, CA Loveday, DJ Loveday, EG Lovegrove, GA Lovegrove, GR Lovegrove, RC Lovegrove, DW Lovejoy, EC Loveland, RT Loveless, BJ Lovell, DG Lovell, DJ Lovell, GW Lovell, RJ Lovell, SE Lovell, BJ Lovelock, HD Lovelock, KT Lovelock, RG Lovelock, BC Loveridge, DW Loveridge, GA Loveridge, JJ Loveridge, DC Lovett, GS Lovett, HJ Lovett, HR Lovett, WK Lovett, CN Lovi, VV Lovison, BK Low, DB Low, ER Low, GR Low, RC Low, RJ Low, DG Lowder, JK Lowdon, A Lowe, AB Lowe, AF Lowe, AW Lowe, BK Lowe, D Lowe, G Lowe, GR Lowe, HS Lowe, JS Lowe, ME Lowe, MJ Lowe, MS Lowe, PFJ Lowe, PW Lowe, RE Lowe, RW Lowe, TK Lowe, TT Lowe, WL Lowe, WR Lowe, LR Lowerson, RJ Lowerson, KL Lowery, N Lowes, DA Lowick, RL Lowick, JW Lowis, MJ Lowman, GE Lowrey, VR Lowrey, H Lowrie, CW Lowry, DM Lowry, JF Lowry, MJ Lowry, RW Lowry, DM Lowson, JFL Lowther, MJ Loxley, AR Loxton, DW Loxton, RH Loxton, PC Loy, RJ Lubcke, RO Lubcke, NF Lubeck, JJ Lucaci, BJ Lucas, CJ Lucas, CW Lucas, CWV Lucas, DW Lucas, FJ Lucas, GJ Lucas, JF Lucas, JP Lucas, KF Lucas, LR Lucas, MJ Lucas, NB Lucas, NK Lucas, PJ Lucas, PM Lucas, PR Lucas, RG Lucas, RM Lucas, RW Lucas, TD Lucas, TJ Lucas, AEP Lucca, CJ Lucey, GJ Lucey, AJ Luchetta, CR Lucht, EC Lucht, MW Lucht, TJ Luchterhand, AG Luck, GD Luck, PJ Luck, JW Lucke, FC Luckett, KJ Luckey, JY Luckham, RA Luckman, JR Lucy, HS Luczka, WL Ludbey, AJ Ludington, AL Ludlow, RF Ludlow, IR Ludwell, WP Ludzik, DF Luelf, RB Luelf, DC Luff, K Luff, MG Luff, NF Luff, NJ Luff, PR Luffman, PW Luffman, WG Lugg, JS Lugowski, W Lugowski, DJ Luhrman, RG Luhrs, G Lukacz, S Lukas, H Lukasik, MKA Lukasyewicz, BJ Luke, DG Luke, MA Luke, RA Luke, TJ Luke, PW Lukeis, RJ Luker, SV Luker, IF Lukomski, CR Lukowski, RF Lumb, DJ Lumby, MC Lumley, KW Lummis, ID Lumsdale, CM Lumsden, IM Lumsden, BJ Lund, JE Lund, TE Lund, EP Lundberg, MG Lundy, WN Lunn, JB Lunney, N Lunney, KW Lunny, RA Lunny, RW Lunt, PN Lupton, TWJ Lupton, LG Lupuljev, MD Luschwitz, AP Luscombe, GW Luscombe, JH Luscombe, P Lusk, M Lusso, EJ Lute, WT Luther, PD Lutley, DJR Lutton, DR Luttrell, K Luttrell, DP Lutvey, BJ Lutwyche, DG Lutz, JR Lutz, AG Luxford, NS Luxford, LR Luxmoore, JR Luxton, MC Luxton, GA Lyall, JA Lyall, PD Lyall, RJ Lyall, JW Lyddiard, T Lyddieth, CW Lydeamore, JA Lydeamore, AL Lydiate, GC Lydom, JF Lydon, RJ Lyell, IF Lygoe, J Lygoe, JA Lyle, NJ Lymbery, RM Lymburn, GR Lyme, HG Lynam, AR Lynch, B Lynch, BB Lynch, BJ Lynch, D Lynch, DE Lynch, DJ Lynch, G Lynch, GD Lynch, GM Lynch, HJ Lynch, JA Lynch, JH Lynch, JJ Lynch, JM Lynch, JS Lynch, KB Lynch, KJ Lynch, MG Lynch, MJ Lynch, MW Lynch, PB Lynch, PJ Lynch, PW Lynch, R Lynch, RF Lynch, RJ Lynch, RW Lynch, TJ Lynch, TM Lynch, TW Lynch, WB Lynch, BJ Lyne, EJ Lyneham, ET Lynes, HA Lyness, AV Lynn, E Lynn, JS Lynn, D Lyon, EJ Lyon, GW Lyon, JB Lyon, MP Lyon, TE Lyon, DA Lyons, JC Lyons, JW Lyons, KJ Lyons, KJJ Lyons, MC Lyons, MJ Lyons, MW Lyons, NV Lyons, P Lyons, PC Lyons, PJ Lyons, PT Lyons, R Lyons, RA Lyons, RE Lyons, RH Lyons, RJ Lyons, RT Lyons, TV Lyons, WD Lyons, BA Lyttle, GT Lyttle, WJ Lyttle, JE Lyytikainen, H Maalste, JM Maas, KG Maas, AB Maat, CA Mabbott, R Mabbott, JW Maber, WJ MacAlister, MS Macanas, IF MacArthur, RJ MacArthur, NG MacArthur-Onslow, JH Macartney, MC Macartney, DR Macaulay, ED Macaulay, GJ Macaulay, BM Macauley, IE Macauley, DJ MacBride, JAD Maccioni, D MacColl, PJ MacCullagh, MP MacCuspie, PF MacDermott, AC MacDonald, AJ MacDonald, AL MacDonald, AR MacDonald, AW MacDonald, B MacDonald, BD MacDonald, BH MacDonald, CR MacDonald, D MacDonald, DI MacDonald, DM MacDonald, DR MacDonald, E MacDonald, FB MacDonald, GK MacDonald, GW MacDonald, HV MacDonald, IA MacDonald, ID MacDonald, IM MacDonald, JA MacDonald, JD MacDonald, JML MacDonald, JP MacDonald, KB MacDonald, LR MacDonald, MG MacDonald, MH MacDonald, NI MacDonald, NM MacDonald, PJ MacDonald, PW MacDonald, RA MacDonald, RB MacDonald, RG MacDonald, RM MacDonald, VR MacDonald, WH MacDonald, RA MacDonell, AB MacDougal, RN MacDougall, WR MacDougall, JRK MacDowell, IA Mace, RC Mace, DA MacEwan, RC Macey, PR MacFadyen, JJ MacFarlane, RD MacFarlane, SK MacFarlane, AH MacGregor, CI MacGregor, DH MacGregor, ET MacGregor, GA MacGregor, JW MacGregor, RK MacGregor, G Mach, JM Machell, RW Machen, B Machin, LA Machin, JZ Maciaszek, R Maciejewski, IGA Macinnis, RD Macintosh, AJ Macintyre, J Macintyre, CA Mack, DB Mack, HC Mack, IS Mack, JJ Mack, JND Mack, LA Mack, TH Mack, TJ Mackaay, JH Mackaway, A Mackay, AR Mackay, DJ Mackay, GS Mackay, IB Mackay, ID Mackay, IR Mackay, JH Mackay, K Mackay, R Mackay, RH Mackay, RJ Mackay, RS Mackay, TM Mackay, VJ Mackay, R MacKellar, R Mackelmann, JM Mackenroth, AJ Mackenzie, AW Mackenzie, DR Mackenzie, EG Mackenzie, ER Mackenzie, GP Mackenzie, IM Mackenzie, KA Mackenzie, KF Mackenzie, KW Mackenzie, L Mackenzie, LJ Mackenzie, MJ Mackenzie, RA Mackenzie, RG Mackenzie, RH Mackenzie, RJ Mackenzie, RN Mackenzie, RP Mackenzie, RS Mackenzie, W Mackenzie, WJ Mackenzie, DRK Mackeson, DJ Mackey, NJ Mackey, PT Mackian, GC Mackie, GM Mackie, PA Mackie, PD Mackie, PJ Mackie, RB Mackie, RJ Mackie, SF Mackie, SIM Mackie, J Mackin, JP Mackin, GA Mackinlay, MA Mackinlay, RL Mackinlay, AC Mackinnon, AM Mackinnon, JG Mackinnon, PM Mackinnon, CN Mackintosh, LW Mackintosh, RF Mackley, RG Mackrill, RW Mackrill, DJ Mackworth, IB MacLachlan, WC MacLachlan, TR Maclaine, A Maclean, DJ Maclean, I Maclean, IH Maclean, IMR Maclean, L Maclean, DG Maclennan, LJ Maclennan, A Macleod, GA Macleod, J Macleod, JBF Macleod, RHA Macleod, PN MacMichael, DW Macmillan, MJ Macmillan, IC MacNamara, PS MacNamara, MM MacNaught, CN MacNeill, WJ Maconachie, L MacPanas, D MacPhail, PF Macphee, G Macpherson, GT Macpherson, JL Macpherson, KJ Macpherson, KL Macpherson, RJ Macpherson,

ID Macqueen, WKR Macrae, MW Macreadie, PA MacWilliam, GJ Maczkowiack, JWS Maddams, CJ Madden, EJ Madden, JE Madden, JJ Madden, KR Madden, MJ Madden, MP Madden, MR Madden, NR Madden, NT Madden, PE Madden, RJ Madden, WG Madden, WJ Madden, WS Madden, CW Maddern, JL Maddern, RV Maddern, AL Maddison, DR Maddison, JB Maddock, KA Maddock, RC Maddock, DN Maddocks, JS Maddocks, RG Maddocks, WG Maddocks, DC Maddox, TW Maddy, JE Madeley, LJ Madeley, TJ Madeley, LW Mader, JR Madex, D Madge, G Madge, RE Madgwick, BT Madigan, ED Madigan, GN Madigan, HJ Madigan, JG Madigan, PJ Madigan, PW Madigan, RT Madigan, TJ Madigan, JF Madsen, EJ Madson, SB Madson, PE Maeder, NS Mafodda, W Magalas, BW Magann, PC Magann, AA Magee, DC Magee, DOA Magee, HR Magee, OL Magee, RB Magee, SJ Magee, K Maggs, PL Maggs, BE Magill, MF Magill, MJ Magill, TJ Magill, CG Maginnity, LJ Magnabosco, A Magnanini, B Magnay, KJ Magnay, BE Magnussen, RH Magnusson, CE Magor, LR Magowan, NE Magrath, T Magrath, M Magro, B Maguire, BP Maguire, JRH Maguire, JV Maguire, KA Maguire, KJ Maguire, PJ Maguire, RD Maguire, RG Maguire, RJ Maguire, TJ Maguire, RJ Mahaffey, AD Mahar, DJJ Mahar, NF Mahar, BA Maher, BF Maher, BJ Maher, BL Maher, DJ Maher, EA Maher, IP Maher, JWC Maher, LE Maher, LT Maher, MA Maher, MG Maher, MR Maher, PF Maher, PJ Maher, PM Maher, PR Maher, RB Maher, RE Maher, RF Maher, SM Maher, SR Maher, TJ Maher, TL Maher, WJ Maher, EG Mahlstedt, PJ Mahney, A Mahomet, AJ Mahoney, BV Mahoney, GE Mahoney, JL Mahoney, JT Mahoney, PA Mahoney, PJ Mahoney, PR Mahoney, RW Mahoney, SJT Mahoney, B Mahony, DJ Mahony, JB Mahony, JJ Mahony, SA Mahony, AG Mai, KJ Maiden, FR Maidment, E Maierhofer, AR Main, GT Main, J Maine, GP Mainke, AJ Mainstone, PD Mainwaring, GJ Mair, LR Mair, RB Mair, WW Mair, CCF Maisey, RG Maisey, GL Maitland, WJ Maitland, J Maiurano, SJ Maizey, B Majba, R Majewski, P Majkowycz, GV Major, GW Major, JA Major, RD Major, RJ Major, RK Major, TA Major, DH Majury, AS Makedonez, KR Maker, RS Maker, NJ Makin, RB Makin, TG Makinson, E Makowiecki, JP Makowski, J Maksymec, DJ Malam, JB Malaquin, W Malar, E Malatynski, EJ Malcolm, G Malcolm, GR Malcolm, J Malcolm, RG Malcolm, BT Malcomson, AD Male, IH Male, KJ Male, RT Male, CG Maley, GJ Malherbe, PF Malherbe, EZ Malicki, SJ Malicki, G Maliganis, AJ Malinowski, JR Maliphant, F Malisani, R Mallam, FJ Mallan, AS Mallard, FC Mallard, FFB Mallee, DR Mallett, EJ Mallett, BL Malley, J Malley, LG Malley, GA Malliaros, JW Mallice, BA Malligan, KG Mallinson, G Mallison, RG Mallison, DB Mallon, PJ Mallon, NJ Mallory, DJ Malloy, AJ Malone, BJ Malone, C Malone, E Malone, J Malone, JT Malone, MJ Malone, PA Malone, RF Malone, RR Malone, TF Malone, FR Maloney, J Maloney, JJ Maloney, JM Maloney, JP Maloney, PW Maloney, RK Maloney, WJ Maloney, JR Maloy, DA Malpas, LP Malseed, HD Maltby, NJ Maltby, WB Maltby, AD Manahan, PA Manassa, DJ Mancer, RJ Manchester, AM Mander, MJ Mander, JS Manderson, JT Manderson, MA Manelski, DM Manfield, RE Mangan, WV Mangan, R Mangano, NW Mangels, JA Mangini, PJ Mangioni, DC Manhood, WJ Mani, JG Manicola, LD Mankey, CP Manktelow, JR Manley, Q Manley, RD Manley, BR Manly, AS Mann, BW Mann, DJ Mann, DR Mann, GE Mann, GJ Mann, GW Mann, IE Mann, JE Mann, JH Mann, JW Mann, KF Mann, LR Mann, M Mann, ME Mann, NJ Mann, P Mann, PJ Mann, PR Mann, RA Mann, RV Mann, SF Mann, SP Mann, TW Mann, WA Mann, WP Mann, LC Manna, D Manneke-Jones, DJ Mannell, HT Mannell, HV Mannell, DJ Mannett, BE Manning, BH Manning, DA Manning, DF Manning, DJA Manning, GJ Manning, GR Manning, HB Manning, K Manning, KB Manning, MF Manning, MG Manning, P Manning, PA Manning, PB Manning, PG Manning, RC Manning, RL Manning, RW Manning, JD Mannion, JF Mannion, LS Mannion, BT Mannix, CS Mannix, JF Mannix, FF Manno, G Manno, KW Manny, PG Manoel, K Manoiloff, PI Mansbridge, AR Mansell, CJ Mansell, DW Mansell, JG Mansell, PJ Mansell, WR Manser, BJ Mansfield, DC Mansfield, HW Mansfield, PA Mansfield, GL Mansford, DN Manski, G Manson, IA Manson, JV Manson, TH Manson, W Manson, BK Mantach, DT Mantach, GL Manteit, TI Manteufel, KG Manton, PJ Manton, P Manucci, RI Manuel, TL Manuel, PK Manwaring, G Maple, PW Maplesden, TI Maplesden, DC Mapley, DM Mapp, RL Mapp, BE Mapperson, PJ Mapperson, GJ Mapson, NP Maraldo, VJ Marangoni, M Marazes, RA Marceau, PR Marcelino, AJ Marcer, EW March, IR March, CM Marchant, H Marchant, KV Marchant, SR Marchant, GL Marchesi, RW Marchesi, HC Marchment, JM Marcus, RI Marcus, R Marczak, EA Mardigian, RL Marek, JF Marett, BM Marfleet, JP Margerison, EF Margetts, PN Margetts, RJ Margetts, JB Margison, T Margrain, GK Marheine, MH Marie, RK Marie, J Marine, DJ Marinich, G Marino, JK Mark, FJ Markcrow, RF Markey, CJ Markham, FW Markham, M Markham, NJ Markham, RS Markham, IJ Marki, R Marklew, MV Markovic, R Markovic, S Markovic, DH Marks, GB Marks, GJ Marks, JK Marks, PJ Marks, RB Marks, RT Marks, SJ Marks, WB Marks, WP Marks, PR Marks-Chapman, WJ Markus, A Markwell, FB Markwick, AJ Marlborough, BM Marles, DJ Marley, MA Marlow, WE Marlow, R Marney, RJ Marney, DC Maroney, GF Maroney, PA Maroney, A Marotta, WN Maroulis, RA Marozin, EH Marques, WJ Marquet, GE Marquett, AG Marr, GR Marr, RJ Marr, AP Marriott, GL Marriott, JJ Marriott, RJ Marriott, RL Marriott, TJ Marriott, EF Marron, KF Marron, PK Marrow, DJ Marrs, RF Marsani, HO Marschall, AR Marsden, GD Marsden, GH Marsden, JC Marsden, KL Marsden, RN Marsden, BR Marsh, CB Marsh, DJ Marsh, EW Marsh, GD Marsh, IL Marsh, JG Marsh, JH Marsh, JT Marsh, KJ Marsh, NK Marsh, NL Marsh, PJ Marsh, RG Marsh, RH Marsh, RW Marsh, SG Marsh, TJ Marsh, AA Marshall, AH Marshall, AJ Marshall, AJR Marshall, AL Marshall, AP Marshall, BA Marshall, BH Marshall, BJ Marshall, BW Marshall, CD Marshall, CJ Marshall, DF Marshall, DJ Marshall, ES Marshall, ET Marshall, FR Marshall, GJ Marshall, GR Marshall, GS Marshall, HL Marshall, HR Marshall, IC Marshall, IG Marshall, IK Marshall, IR Marshall, JB Marshall, JL Marshall, JW Marshall, KC Marshall, KR Marshall, LE Marshall, LG Marshall, LH Marshall, MC Marshall, MR Marshall, NH Marshall, PA Marshall, PR Marshall, PS Marshall, R Marshall, RJ Marshall, TG Marshall, W Marshall, WB Marshall, WF Marshall, WJ Marshall, WP Marshall, GP Marshall-Cormack, GW Marshallsea, RG Marshman, TJ Marslen, EP Marson, RJ Marston, RA Martain, HR Marten, BF Martens, TW Marthick, A Martin, AD Martin, AE Martin, AJ Martin, AR Martin, AT Martin, BF Martin, BJ Martin, CA Martin, CD Martin, CJ Martin, CL Martin, CR Martin, CW Martin, DA Martin, DC Martin, DG Martin, DJ Martin, DL Martin, DM Martin, DO Martin, EH Martin, ES Martin, FJ Martin, FM Martin, G Martin, GA Martin, GC Martin, GD Martin, GJ Martin, GL Martin, GN Martin, GR Martin, H Martin, HJ Martin, HM Martin, HR Martin, J Martin, JC Martin, JD Martin, JE Martin, JH Martin, JL Martin, K Martin, KJ Martin, KR Martin, KW Martin, LC Martin, LJ Martin, LL Martin, MB Martin, ME Martin, MG Martin, MJ Martin, NA Martin, NG Martin, P Martin, PG Martin, PJ Martin, PR Martin, PT Martin, R Martin, RA Martin, RC Martin, RE Martin, RF Martin, RG Martin, RI Martin, RJ Martin, RJS Martin, RLJ Martin, RT Martin, RW Martin, SJ Martin, ST Martin, TP Martin, VWT Martin, W Martin, WB Martin, WH Martin, WJ Martin, D Martinez, RAJ Martini, F Martino, PK Martino, HLC Martins, LJ Martinsen, O Martinson, RA Martlew, JC Martorana, L Martyniuk, HA Marum, B Marwick, RJ Marx, JKN Marychurch, WE Maschette, BP Mascord, J Mashford, RL Mashford, MG Mashman, GW Maskell, DJ Maskill, DL Maslen, GH Maslen, MM Masliczek, BR Maslin, AF Mason, AJ Mason, AR Mason, BE Mason, C Mason, CG Mason, CJ Mason, CV Mason, DP Mason, FP Mason, G Mason, GD Mason, GJ Mason, GW Mason, HA Mason, J Mason, JA Mason, JD Mason, JG Mason, JM Mason, JP Mason, JR Mason, KJ Mason, LA Mason, LR Mason, MG Mason, MS Mason, NR Mason, PJ Mason, RD Mason, RE Mason, RF Mason, RG Mason, RL Mason, RM Mason, SA Mason, TC Mason, TG Mason, WJ Mason, WL Mason, WR Mason, N Masonjones, SW Masowita, JT Massam, AJ Massey, GJ Massey, GR Massie, MG Massie, AC Massingham, KD Masson, BJ Masters, DG Masters, GJ Masters, LJ Masters, MJ Masters, RH Masters, RW Masters, A Masterson, KJ Masterson, L Mastop, ZM Masuk, RT Maszak, PJ Maszniew, WJ Matchett, SJ Mate, WA Mate, BJ Mateer, GF Mateer, H Mateja, RJ Materna, KA Materne, GJ Mather, JD Mather, RA Mather, BG Mathers, DB Mathers, IG Mathers, JM Mathers, AJ Matheson, BR Matheson, CS Matheson, DJ Matheson, HM Matheson, JA Matheson, M Matheson, R Matheson, RT Matheson, WJ Matheson, PJ Mathew, B Mathews, BD Mathews, GF Mathews, GK Mathews, HC Mathews, JN Mathews, NF Mathews, PC Mathews, PR Mathews, TW Mathews, VJ Mathews, WJ Mathews, JM Mathewson, PB Mathie, CC Mathieson, DJ Mathieson, GF Mathieson, ID Mathieson, KF Mathieson, RG Mathieson, RL Mathieson, JMG Mathieu, I Mathison, JD Mathwin, AJ Matley, DJ Matley, CF Matons, RD Matson, AIJ Mattay, JW Matten, WG Mattey, RL Matthew, RM Matthewman, A Matthews, AB Matthews, AL Matthews, AM Matthews, AN Matthews, AT Matthews, AV Matthews, BJ Matthews, BR Matthews, BT Matthews, CD Matthews, DG Matthews, DJ Matthews, DW Matthews, ED Matthews, EH Matthews, FA Matthews, GA Matthews, GD Matthews, GR Matthews, GS Matthews, GW Matthews, J Matthews, JA Matthews, JC Matthews, JE Matthews, JJ Matthews, KE Matthews, KJ Matthews, LD Matthews, LJ Matthews, LO Matthews, NA Matthews, NDJ Matthews, PA Matthews, PJ Matthews, RC Matthews, RJ Matthews, RO Matthews, RP Matthews, RR Matthews, RS Matthews, RT Matthews, TF Matthews, TG Matthews, TK Matthews, KW Matthewson, VC Matthies, BR Mattingley, RA Mattingley, RW Mattinson, RE Mattiske, MD Mattner, KD Mattson, DG Matulick, DJ Matulick, RG Matulick, WL Matusch, PJ Matuschka, K Matuszczak, ML Matysiak, ML Mau, RJ Maud, WN Maudsley, BC Mauger, GS Mauger, FA Maughan, GA Maughan, GR Maughan, JA Maughan, WD Maumill, JR Maunder, T Maunder, PW Maunsell, BF Maurer, MM Maurovic, KH Mavin, EA Mavrick, MJ Mavromatis, GR Mawer, RP Mawer, G Mawkes, J Mawkes, FJ Mawson, HG Mawson, KW Mawson, PW Mawson, WR Mawson, RD Maxted, RW Maxted, BJ Maxwell, BR Maxwell, DC Maxwell, EO Maxwell, FC Maxwell, G Maxwell, GJ Maxwell, GR Maxwell, JA Maxwell, JM Maxwell, KJ Maxwell, RA Maxwell, RJ Maxwell, RP Maxwell, TJ Maxwell, TR Maxwell, AJ May, AN May, AS May, BA May, BE May, DD May, DG May, DJ May, DP May, ER May, EW May, FK May, GA May, GJ May, IL May, J May, JF May, JW May, KA May, KE May, KJ May, LK May, LW May, PK May, RC May, RF May, RJ May, RN May, RW May, TG May, TJU May, WC May, WJ May, RV Mayberry, RJ Maybery, BF Maybury, G Maycock, GR Mayer, M Mayer, RG Mayes, AW Mayfield, DJ Mayfield, JA Mayfield, CJ Mayhew, BA Maynard, CJ Maynard, CP Maynard, FM Maynard, GJ Maynard, JH Maynard, KJ Maynard, LH Maynard, LR Maynard, PS Mayne, GG Maynes, BD Mayo, DB Mayo, PJ Mayo, NAH Mays, PR Mays, WA Maythers, TL Maytom, KD Maywald, RW Maywald, RN Maza, MP Mazengarb, P Mazengarb, JJ Mazey, RM Mazoudier, F Mazurek, RJM Mazurek, R Mazurkiewicz, NJ Mazzarol, H Mazzoni, JC McAdam, RG McAdam, RT McAdoo, TK McAlary, KW McAlear, JJ McAleer, MJ McAliece, PJO McAlinden, GJ McAlister, I McAlister, JP McAlister, KH McAlister, RC McAlister, DS McAllan, GE McAllister, JB McAllister, JS McAllister, TN McAllister, JK McAlonan, JD McAloney, PS McAloney, GW McAlpine, SW McAlpine, CJ McAnally, FW McAnally, KH McAndrew, KS McAndrew, JAM McArdle, JP McArdle, RE McArdle, SM McArdle, BP McArthur, DP McArthur, LT McArthur, MC McArthur, NA McArthur, RM McArthur, SR McArthur, TN McArthur, BJ McAteer, AHD McAulay, DA McAulay, MP McAulay, AJ McAuley, CB McAuley, I McAuley, PJ McAuley, EJ McAuliffe, JA McAuliffe, MT McAuliffe, PJ McAuliffe, PW McAuliffe, RB McAuliffe, WJ McAuliffe, KH McAvaney, MN McAvaney, IR McBain, PJ McBain, BW McBaron, PJ McBaron, RJ McBean, RB McBeath, PL McBow, BA McBride, JR McBride, MH McBride, MJ McBride, RA McBride, WA McBurney, RL McCabbin, AB McCabe, AG McCabe, AR McCabe, BB McCabe, BT McCabe, JE McCabe, JS McCabe, RA McCabe, RL McCabe, RW McCabe, DH McCaffery, MB McCaffery, JP McCahill, JK McCaig, GG McCall, IJ McCall, RD McCall, RL McCall, S McCalliom, DA McCallum, DR McCallum, IM McCallum, JWC McCallum, KG McCallum, LJ McCallum, MC McCallum, MP McCallum, NJ McCallum, OJ McCallum, PH McCallum, RA McCallum, RP McCallum, WR McCallum, GD McCalman, RB McCalman, RN McCalman, EC McCamish, CA McCamley, AC McCann, AF McCann, AJ McCann, C McCann, CJ McCann, CR McCann, DM McCann,

DR McCann, FW McCann, GM McCann, JA McCann,
JR McCann, KJ McCann, L McCann, PB McCann,
PJ McCann, PM McCann, RJ McCann, RL McCann,
RP McCann, TL McCann, GA McCarron, EF McCart,
AE McCarthy, AJ McCarthy, DE McCarthy, DW McCarthy,
G McCarthy, GC McCarthy, GE McCarthy, GH McCarthy,
JA McCarthy, JCA McCarthy, JL McCarthy, JN McCarthy,
JP McCarthy, JR McCarthy, KG McCarthy, KK McCarthy,
LC McCarthy, MF McCarthy, MT McCarthy, MV McCarthy,
PJ McCarthy, PM McCarthy, PR McCarthy, PT McCarthy,
PW McCarthy, RB McCarthy, RF McCarthy, RJ McCarthy,
RR McCarthy, TG McCarthy, TJ McCarthy, WF McCarthy,
BJ McCartin, BJ McCartney, HC McCartney, IL McCartney,
IB McCarty, JM McCaskill, T McCaughan, GC McCaughey,
WB McCaughey, DC McCauley, DG McCauley,
EJ McCauley, JR McCauley, PC McCauley, PJ McCauley,
SE McCauley, TO McCauley, WC McCausland,
WJ McCausland, NM McClaren, AA McClean, IS McCleary,
TW McCleary, DJ McClelland, MD McClelland,
MW McClelland, BM McClenaghan, RJ McClennan,
GW McClintock, HJ McClintock, RJ McClintock,
AB McCloskey, DJ McCloskey, CM McCloud,
JG McCloughan, DKR McCloy, JT McCloy, BR McClure,
JR McClure, TJ McClure, WE McClurkin, PP McCluskey,
WL McCluskey, DA McClymans, BS McClymont,
GJ McClymont, JR McClymont, JS McClymont,
MT McClymont, RG McClymont, PJ McCole, CR McColl,
DJ McColl, DW McColl, JC McColl, GR McColley,
A McColm, DJ McCombe, TH McCombe, MR McConachy,
JA McConaghy, JC McCone, BR McConkey,
AH McConnell, BJ McConnell, J McConnell,
JSR McConnell, RF McConnell, SG McConnell,
HS McConville, LM McConville, MJ McCooke,
PJ McCoola, EL McCoombe, RW McCormac,
AF McCormack, AM McCormack, BD McCormack,
BJ McCormack, DJ McCormack, DW McCormack,
G McCormack, GM McCormack, GR McCormack,
JD McCormack, JE McCormack, JW McCormack,
MJ McCormack, R McCormack, RB McCormack,
RO McCormack, RS McCormack, T McCormack,
WE McCormack, WJ McCormack, AP McCormick,
CJ McCormick, DA McCormick, JB McCormick,
JR McCormick, KJ McCormick, MI McCormick,
PJ McCormick, TJ McCormick, K McCosh, BD McCosker,
BJ McCosker, LR McCosker, T McCoubrey,
KL McCoughtry, JS McCourt, KA McCowan,
WJ McCowen, MJ McCoy, MP McCoy, P McCoy,
TJ McCoy, GD McCracken, BJ McCrae, GL McCray,
RA McCrea, GK McCreadie, L McCreath, N McCredden,
ID McCredie, WG McCreeth, DP McCrohan, FE McCrohan,
PD McCrohan, MW McCrone, IM McCudden, TJ McCue,
AR McCullagh, DJ McCullagh, WB McCullagh,
C McCulley, AB McCulloch, GD McCulloch, GJ McCulloch,
JP McCulloch, JS McCulloch, KP McCulloch,
LP McCulloch, M McCulloch, MV McCullough,
NH McCullough, RL McCullough, WJ McCullough,
GA McCullum, RJ McCully, DA McCune, RJ McCurdy,
CJ McCurley, G McCurrach, MG McCurrach,
WR McCutchen, DN McDaniel, GJ McDaniel,
A McDermott, BJ McDermott, EJ McDermott,
GA McDermott, JR McDermott, MJ McDermott,
MK McDermott, N McDermott, RA McDermott,
D McDiarmid, CLT McDonagh, JF McDonagh,
AE McDonald, AJ McDonald, AM McDonald,
AW McDonald, B McDonald, BA McDonald, BJ McDonald,
BM McDonald, BT McDonald, CD McDonald,
CG McDonald, CH McDonald, CJ McDonald,
DF McDonald, DH McDonald, DJ McDonald,
DL McDonald, DM McDonald, DP McDonald,
DW McDonald, GA McDonald, GD McDonald,
GL McDonald, GM McDonald, GT McDonald,
GW McDonald, HJC McDonald, IER McDonald,
IK McDonald, IR McDonald, J McDonald, JA McDonald,
JL McDonald, JM McDonald, JS McDonald, K McDonald,
KF McDonald, KM McDonald, KR McDonald,
LJ McDonald, LL McDonald, M McDonald, MJ McDonald,
MR McDonald, MS McDonald, N McDonald, P McDonald,
PD McDonald, PJ McDonald, PK McDonald, R McDonald,
RA McDonald, RJ McDonald, RL McDonald,
RM McDonald, RN McDonald, RW McDonald,
SC McDonald, SJ McDonald, SM McDonald, T McDonald,
TD McDonald, TF McDonald, TK McDonald,
TR McDonald, VL McDonald, W McDonald,

WC McDonald, WJ McDonald, WL McDonald,
WR McDonald, WW McDonald, JR McDonell,
PE McDonell, AJ McDonnell, BP McDonnell,
GEJ McDonnell, JE McDonnell, LC McDonnell,
ME McDonnell, MJ McDonnell, RB McDonnell,
RG McDonnell, RH McDonnell, SJ McDonnell,
TJ McDonnell, WH McDonnell, EJ McDonough,
JW McDonough, KC McDonough, KJ McDonough,
PJ McDonough, RJ McDonough, EL McDorman,
JC McDougal, D McDougall, DAA McDougall,
DG McDougall, DK McDougall, GJ McDougall,
IA McDougall, JB McDougall, K McDougall, LP McDougall,
PD McDougall, PJ McDougall, PM McDougall,
RA McDougall, RJ McDougall, BE McDowall,
DP McDowall, BE McDowell, BJ McDowell, DJ McDowell,
DW McDowell, IR McDowell, RG McDowell, RP McDowell,
BJ McDuff, PE McDuff, PE McDuffie, NR McDuffie,
DC McEachern, RN McEachern, TR McEffer, J McElhinney,
TL McElligott, JW McElveney, RT McElwaine,
JW McEnerny, RA McEnnulty, RB McErlain, CN McEvoy,
JH McEvoy, JN McEvoy, L McEvoy, MJ McEvoy, RV McEvoy,
IG McEwan, J McEwan, JT McEwan, JW McEwan,
RG McEwan, J McEwan-Ferguson, HJ McEwen, JB McEwen,
MW McEwen, JA McFadden, LE McFadden, MJ McFadden,
WM McFadden, KC McFadyen, RE McFadyen,
JH McFadzean, GL McFadzen, IT McFadzen, LG McFadzen,
JB McFallan, KD McFarland, B McFarlane, BH McFarlane,
BJ McFarlane, BP McFarlane, BW McFarlane, DJ McFarlane,
GF McFarlane, ID McFarlane, J McFarlane, KD McFarlane,
MC McFarlane, NG McFarlane, P McFarlane, PR McFarlane,
RC McFarlane, RH McFarlane, RP McFarlane, DG McFerran,
KP McGahan, RV McGahan, LM McGann, PJ McGann,
CE McGarry, JJ McGarry, LG McGarry, PS McGarry,
RC McGarry, TP McGarry, MR McGarvey, PG McGauchie,
DA McGaughey, BE McGavigan, AG McGavin,
CE McGavisk, NH McGavock, TJ McGaw, RB McGeachie,
AG McGee, AJ McGee, GF McGee, JA McGee, MT McGee,
PN McGee, TM McGee, WH McGee, ML McGeechan,
R McGeoch, AE McGeown, JB McGettigan, M McGettigan,
D McGhee, KJ McGhee, LJ McGhee, JJ McGhie, LW McGie,
B McGill, JC McGill, RA McGill, JM McGillion,
R McGillivray, W McGillivray, JW McGilp, RM McGimpsey,
EH McGinn, AD McGinty, PJ McGirr, BJ McGlashan,
L McGlashan, RN McGlinchey, DJ McGlinn, G McGlinn,
R McGlinn, BJ McGlone, GJ McGlone, GM McGlone,
KB McGlynn, RJ McGlynn, LS McGoldrick, W McGoldrick,
RT McGorey, RJ McGorm, KR McGorman, RW McGovan,
BJ McGovern, GJ McGovern, J McGovern, T McGovern,
DA McGowan, GJ McGowan, J McGowan, JF McGowan,
KN McGowan, RI McGowan, BF McGrath, CE McGrath,
D McGrath, DJ McGrath, DR McGrath, DW McGrath,
IE McGrath, IJ McGrath, JE McGrath, JF McGrath,
LJ McGrath, LW McGrath, M McGrath, MA McGrath,
NM McGrath, PC McGrath, PD McGrath, PJ McGrath,
PN McGrath, RT McGrath, WH McGrath, AL McGrath-
Kerr, AJ McGregor, BD McGregor, BM McGregor,
CR McGregor, CW McGregor, D McGregor, DJ McGregor,
DM McGregor, G McGregor, GW McGregor, JD McGregor,
JH McGregor, JT McGregor, R McGregor, RA McGregor,
RG McGregor, RJ McGregor, RL McGregor, TR McGregor,
GW McGregor-Edwards, P McGregorjones, PB McGrellis,
RJ McGrice, JA McGrigor, RD McGrouther, KFM McGuane,
AF McGuckin, JG McGuffog, PR McGuigan, D McGuiggan,
AE McGuiness, JR McGuiness, D McGuinness,
GJP McGuinness, PEM McGuinness, PJ McGuinness,
PL McGuinness, MT McGuinness, WG McGuinness,
AL McGuire, AP McGuire, GD McGuire, KR McGuire,
MJ McGuire, NJ McGuire, RA McGuire, RJ McGuire,
K McGuirk, BF McGurgan, B McGurk, CB McGurk,
KG McHale, MG McHatton, SA McHenry, AS McHoul,
AJ McHugh, LH McHugh, P McHugh, PR McHugh,
RG McHugh, TA McHutchison, DE McIllree, DW McIlroy,
TI McIlroy, GG McIlvanie, GM McIlvenna, RR McIlwaine,
B McIlwraith, H McInally, JS McInally, JF McInerney,
NA McInerney, RJ McInerney, RM McInerney,
TP McInerney, WJ McInerney, BM McInneny, AD McInnes,
BA McInnes, BC McInnes, BP McInnes, CA McInnes,
DJ McInnes, DP McInnes, GJ McInnes, GW McInnes,
JA McInnes, MW McInnes, P McInnes, SP McInnes,
TF McInnes, DW McInness, RF McInnis, AC McIntosh,
AJ McIntosh, AM McIntosh, DC McIntosh, DR McIntosh,
IG McIntosh, J McIntosh, J McIntosh, JA McIntosh,
JD McIntosh, JJ McIntosh, JT McIntosh, L McIntosh,

LF McIntosh, MJ McIntosh, MW McIntosh, OW McIntosh,
P McIntosh, RJ McIntosh, RL McIntosh, RR McIntosh,
RW McIntosh, SG McIntosh, WA McIntosh, A McIntyre,
AJ McIntyre, CJ McIntyre, D McIntyre, DJ McIntyre,
DR McIntyre, DS McIntyre, ED McIntyre, EJ McIntyre,
FD McIntyre, GJ McIntyre, GM McIntyre, IT McIntyre,
J McIntyre, JA McIntyre, JR McIntyre, KW McIntyre,
MN McIntyre, NA McIntyre, RA McIntyre, RG McIntyre,
RP McIntyre, T McIntyre, TJ McIntyre, WAR McIntyre,
WJ McIntyre, WK McIntyre, WR McIntyre, DR McIver,
GD McIver, KG McIver, WFG McIver, AJ McIvor, GJ McIvor,
K McIvor, AR McKay, BC McKay, C McKay, CH McKay,
DJ McKay, GJ McKay, GR McKay, GW McKay, J McKay,
JD McKay, JH McKay, KL McKay, RJ McKay, RS McKay,
RW McKay, SA McKay, SD McKay, AD McKean,
JB McKean, KRT McKean, PG McKean, RT McKeand,
J McKechnie, JL McKechnie, RM McKechnie,
TR McKechnie, DP McKee, RW McKee, WG McKee,
SDJ McKeever, D McKellar, DGM McKellar, IJ McKellar,
JL McKellar, JM McKelligott, NL McKelvie, PR McKendrick,
RG McKendrick, RJ McKendrick, CJ McKendry,
RF McKendry, AR McKenna, BD McKenna, GA McKenna,
J McKenna, DJ McKenna, PT McKenna, RJ McKenna,
TF McKenna, JF McKenner, JR McKenner, R McKenny,
TJ McKenny, AD McKenzie, AK McKenzie, AR McKenzie,
BA McKenzie, BC McKenzie, BF McKenzie, BG McKenzie,
CJ McKenzie, CR McKenzie, D McKenzie, DA McKenzie,
DD McKenzie, DF McKenzie, DI McKenzie, DS McKenzie,
DW McKenzie, EL McKenzie, GA McKenzie, GC McKenzie,
GJ McKenzie, GL McKenzie, IB McKenzie, IC McKenzie,
IJ McKenzie, JA McKenzie, JD McKenzie, JE McKenzie,
JG McKenzie, JH McKenzie, JK McKenzie, JN McKenzie,
KA McKenzie, KG McKenzie, KJ McKenzie, KS McKenzie,
LD McKenzie, LG McKenzie, MJ McKenzie, ND McKenzie,
PJ McKenzie, RG McKenzie, RK McKenzie, RN McKenzie,
TE McKenzie, BA McKeon, KJ McKeon, BW McKeown,
D McKeown, IG McKeown, JW McKeown, MJ McKeown,
RC McKeown, RE McKeown, ST McKeown, WA McKeown,
D McKerlie, EJ McKerrow, PR McKewin, KM McKie,
PJ McKie, R McKie, JC McKiernan, J McKillop,
JH McKillop, MR McKillop, RF McKimmin,
JRW McKimmon, BD McKinlay, BW McKinlay,
IC McKinlay, JS McKinlay, DR McKinley, JE McKinley,
DA McKinnell, AD McKinnon, AJ McKinnon,
BW McKinnon, DJ McKinnon, GP McKinnon,
IR McKinnon, LW McKinnon, NA McKinnon,
PR McKinnon, RA McKinnon, RJ McKinnon, S McKinnon,
RS McKiterick, PJ McKittrick, IW McKnight, R McKnight,
RS McKnight, JH McKone, RJB McKoy, CW McLachlan,
DJ McLachlan, EK McLachlan, GN McLachlan,
IR McLachlan, LM McLachlan, PR McLachlan,
WT McLachlan, T McLanders, BW McLaren, I McLaren,
J McLaren, RG McLaren, RK McLaren, SM McLaren,
DR McLauchlan, J McLauchlan, AND McLaughlin,
BS McLaughlin, GM McLaughlin, GO McLaughlin,
LD McLaughlin, N McLaughlin, PB McLaughlin,
PJ McLaughlin, RO McLaughlin, SJ McLaughlin,
TM McLaughlin, WM McLaughlin, BH McLay, PR McLay,
A McLean, AB McLean, AC McLean, AJ McLean,
AT McLean, BC McLean, BR McLean, DA McLean,
DI McLean, DJ McLean, DL McLean, DR McLean,
FV McLean, GB McLean, GC McLean, GL McLean,
GW McLean, HW McLean, IB McLean, IC McLean,
IJ McLean, JB McLean, JD McLean, JG McLean, JM McLean,
JS McLean, KJ McLean, LR McLean, LW McLean,
M McLean, MD McLean, MN McLean, NP McLean,
PJ McLean, PN McLean, R McLean, RA McLean,
RC McLean, RG McLean, RK McLean, RM McLean,
RW McLean, SC McLean, TA McLean, W McLean,
WJ McLean, WS McLean, HI McLean-Williams,
GW McLeary, RM McLeay, AG McLellan, BJ McLellan,
FP McLellan, TA McLellan, WN McLellan, WW McLellan,
AD McLennan, BA McLennan, DW McLennan,
GM McLennan, JL McLennan, JN McLennan,
JW McLennan, KN McLennan, NC McLennan,
RC McLennan, RJ McLennan, WE McLennan, AB McLeod,
BF McLeod, CR McLeod, CS McLeod, DG McLeod,
DIW McLeod, DJ McLeod, DR McLeod, DW McLeod,
ER McLeod, GH McLeod, GR McLeod, I McLeod,
IC McLeod, ICW McLeod, JT McLeod, KJ McLeod,
ML McLeod, NR McLeod, NV McLeod, PJ McLeod,
RC McLeod, RD McLeod, RH McLeod, RJ McLeod,
RV McLeod, SA McLeod, WD McLeod, WI McLeod,

A McLeod-Lee, GH McLerie, PH McLernon, J McLevey, CP McLindin, NG McLintock, DA McLoughlin, RP McLoughlin, TJ McLoughlin, JW McLure, P McLure, PJ McLure, AD McMah, BW McMahon, CR McMahon, D McMahon, GA McMahon, GJ McMahon, GS McMahon, JA McMahon, JB McMahon, JF McMahon, JP McMahon, JW McMahon, KA McMahon, KB McMahon, LK McMahon, M McMahon, MJ McMahon, MW McMahon, PE McMahon, PJ McMahon, PR McMahon, RA McMahon, TJ McMahon, WJ McMahon, WV McMahon, CR McManimm, MJ McManimm, TW McManis, AT McManus, DP McManus, E McManus, GM McManus, NRK McManus, LR McMartin, AR McMaster, BA McMaster, CR McMaster, DI McMaster, GA McMaster, GK McMaster, GM McMaster, JG McMaster, KD McMaster, R McMaster, RF McMaster, BJ McMastersmith, BN McMaugh, EL McMaugh, A McMillan, AG McMillan, AS McMillan, B McMillan, D McMillan, ER McMillan, IA McMillan, JA McMillan, JC McMillan, JD McMillan, KR McMillan, MW McMillan, PF McMillan, R McMillan, RA McMillan, RB McMillan, RC McMillan, RE McMillan, RG McMillan, RI McMillan, RL McMillan, WG McMillan, WW McMillan, LT McMillin, HFN McMinn, FT McMonagle, IA McMonigle, A McMullan, AD McMullan, BH McMullan, GB McMullen, RG McMullen, RJ McMullen, JC McMullin, LW McMullin, K McMurray, R McMurray, PL McMurrich, RB McMurrich, D McNab, RA McNab, RL McNab, WJD McNab, GE McNabb, GF McNabb, JA McNabb, N McNae, RJ McNae, D McNair, DI McNair, P McNair, RJ McNair, AR McNally, JM McNally, AT McNamara, BJ McNamara, CT McNamara, EG McNamara, EJ McNamara, GJ McNamara, JC McNamara, JD McNamara, JM McNamara, JP McNamara, JV McNamara, KF McNamara, LJ McNamara, PJ McNamara, PS McNamara, RG McNamara, RGP McNamara, RK McNamara, SA McNamara, PR McNamee, DR McNaught, A McNaughton, IT McNaughton, RD McNaughton, E McNee, GJ McNee, HD McNee, ID McNee, RD McNee, RJ McNee, T McNee, GA McNees, DG McNeil, DL McNeil, DR McNeil, FA McNeil, JL McNeil, PG McNeil, AJ McNeilage, ARJ McNeill, B McNeill, GG McNeill, IG McNeill, JJ McNeill, JM McNeill, K McNeill, LB McNeill, RT McNeill, RD McNeilly, RJ McNellee, GC McNevin, GR McNevin, BJ McNicol, BN McNicol, D McNicol, DI McNicol, LJ McNicol, PA McNicol, JP McNiven, AB McNulty, RJ McOmish, JJ McPadden, NR McParland, CD McPhail, HA McPhail, HJ McPhail, IS McPhail, J McPhail, RS McPhail, D McPhedran, AJ McPhee, DM McPhee, LJ McPhee, MD McPhee, RM McPhee, A McPherson, AC McPherson, AG McPherson, AM McPherson, DB McPherson, DC McPherson, DG McPherson, DL McPherson, DW McPherson, FA McPherson, GH McPherson, IW McPherson, JG McPherson, JN McPherson, JR McPherson, KC McPherson, KL McPherson, LH McPherson, M McPherson, MD McPherson, MF McPherson, MI McPherson, NC McPherson, RD McPherson, RF McPherson, RJ McPherson, WG McPherson, RA McPhie, JA McPoland, BJ McQuade, J McQuade, TG McQuade, RD McQuaid, MB McQualter, JL McQuat, JF McQueen, JL McQueen, K McQueen, LG McQueen, PA McQueen, DK McQuiggan, NJ McQuilkin, CH McQuillan, GW McQuillan, VH McQuillan, BJ McQuilty, WT McQuilty, IW McQuire, DJ McQuoid, AR McRae, BS McRae, GR McRae, IR McRae, JA McRae, MS McRae, RJ McRae, TD McRae, BP McRobert, W McRobert, DR McRoberts, KJ McRostie, KP McRostie, BJ McShane, CJ McShane, GG McSolvin, BF McSweeney, KJ McTaggart, LA McTeer, PL McTiernan, A McTighe, GJ McVeigh, RJ McVey, GD McVie, IR McVie, NW McVilly, B McVinish, NR McWaters, WC McWha, J McWhinney, DM McWhirter, WR McWhirter, A McWilliam, L McWilliam, LJ McWilliam, PR McWilliam, SE McWilliam, AK Mead, AR Mead, CH Mead, DJ Mead, IK Mead, LM Mead, PD Mead, RK Mead, BJ Meade, CJ Meade, DJ Meade, RP Meade, BJ Meadows, JJ Meadows, MB Meadows, WJ Meadows, RB Meager, RW Meager, BR Meakins, JR Meakins, DJ Mealey, LA Mealin, MJ Mealing, CA Mealy, EP Mealy, BM Meaney, DP Meaney, GT Meaney, PJ Meaney, TJ Meany, GE Meares, RL Mearns, AC Mears, AJ Mears, MJ Mears, WR Mears, D Measures, DC Mecham, L Mechtler, BL Meckenstock, PE Meckenstock, BE Medcraft, TJ Medcraft, RH Meddens, A Medelis, DB Medhurst, GJ Medhurst, RE Medhurst, TJ Medhurst, PG Medina, B Medland, RJ Medley, BAR Medlin, KR Medlow, DR Medson, H Mee, RV Meech, WH Meech, BM Meehan, BW Meehan, D Meehan, GA Meehan, JA Meehan, JW Meehan, LR Meehan, MJ Meehan, ML Meehan, RJ Meehan, RL Meehan, DJ Meek, FP Meek, GS Meek, RJ Meeke, WC Meeke, RJ Meeks, HW Meermanvanderhorst, GD Meers, RJ Meffert, WK Meffert, AT Megay, TJ Meggatt, N Megrath, SP Meharg, JL Meharry, WJ Mehegan, IJ Meibusch, JR Meier, LE Meier, DJ Meiers, MB Meiers, FJ Meigan, AG Meiklejohn, RH Meiklejohn, SS Meiklejohn, WC Meilak, JW Meilland, RF Meisenhelter, A Meisinger, JJ Melandri, JA Melberzs, TJ Melbin, GR Melbourne, LG Melbourne, VBE Melbourne, A Meldrum, BJ Meldrum, JF Meldrum, MJ Meldrum, RG Meldrum, WG Meldrum, LJ Meline, A Melki, JH Melksham, MG Melkus, DJ Mell, RG Mell, J Mellema, BC Meller, GW Mellett, RC Mellier, PB Mellifont, RC Melling, JT Mellington, MW Mellington, JR Mellor, KBJ Mellor, M Mellor, WJ Mellords, AW Mellowship, DG Mellowship, KE Mellowship, JR Mellusco, N Melnyczenko, OJ Meloury, D Melrose, I Melrose, JJ Melton, BJ Melville, GR Melville, PC Melville, BR Melvin, GJ Melvin, T Melvin, RJ Membrey, EW Membry, PJ Menagh, PA Mench, NR Mende, RD Mende, M Mendyk, JT Menelaws, AS Menere, LR Mengel, RH Menhennett, RJ Menhennett, CJ Menkins, PR Menner, GR Mennie, BV Mensforth, AT Mensinger, C Mentis, UR Mentlein, JL Menz, MJ Menz, RT Menz, TG Menzel, BW Menzies, DW Menzies, GJ Menzies, ID Menzies, IG Menzies, JB Menzies, MF Menzies, F Mepham, RS Meppom, AG Mercer, BG Mercer, BM Mercer, ED Mercer, RD Mercer, WB Mercer, BN Merchant, JC Merchant, TD Merchant, BJ Mercieca, V Mercieca, V Mercuri, FJ Meredith, FL Meredith, GD Meredith, GG Meredith, JW Meredith, KA Meredith, KJ Meredith, LA Meredith, PJ Meredith, RC Meredith, RJ Meredith, RL Meredith, RW Meredith, TD Meredith, TF Meredith, TP Merenda, WL Mergard, GJ Merkel, RF Merrell, TL Merrell, DR Merrett, JD Merrett, JJ Merrick, MR Merrick, JR Merrifield, MR Merrifield, BW Merrigan, IM Merrilees, P Merrill, DM Merriman, JV Merrin, KS Merrion, EC Merritt, JA Merritt, KW Merritt, RG Merritt, SR Merritt, RJ Merryfull, RA Merson, JH Mertens, TJ Mertens, GD Merton, R Mertyn, GW Mervyn, RB Messent, GR Messer, NG Messer, JA Messina, K Metcalf, LP Metcalf, WJ Metcalf, BR Metcalfe, DG Metcalfe, DR Metcalfe, RJ Metcalfe, TG Metcalfe, WA Metcalfe, PJ Metelmann, G Meter, PJ Metham, MS Metherall, R Methorst, JD Methven, WJ Methven, RW Mettam, RF Metz, VF Metzroth, RA Meuron, DJ Mewburn, DF Meyer, PA Meyer, R Meyer, RH Meyer, WE Meyer, BD Meyers, DJ Meynell, F Meyza, G Mialkowski, WD Micah, LJ Micallef, S Micallef, B Michael, CG Michael, EN Michael, IJ Michael, RJ Michael, WH Michael, IG Michail, C Michalek, J Michalis, R Michalowski, LS Michalowsky, V Michalsky, GD Michel, W Michelic, GF Michell, MD Michell, DK Michelmore, LM Michels, PJ Michelson, DJ Michie, RRH Michod, DC Mickan, G Mickan, GA Mickan, RJ Mickelberg, FD Midavaine, BJ Middis, WT Middlemis, SJ Middlemo, B Middleton, G Middleton, GC Middleton, IS Middleton, JC Middleton, JR Middleton, M Middleton, PC Middleton, RJ Middleton, SW Middleton, WR Middleton, A Midgley, AH Midgley, BW Midson, KA Midson, SC Mieczkowski, T Miekus, JW Mielnikowski, DR Miels, RJ Miels, DG Miers, G Mietto, RW Miffling, CP Mifsud, JF Mifsud, PA Mifsud, PM Mifsud, JM Mihailovic, J Mihal, M Mihelcic, JE Miinchow, RLR Mika, AI Mikelsons, CE Mikkelsen, GJ Mikkelsen, DG Milan, TA Milan, AN Milburn, CR Milburn, I Milburn, BT Milde, DA Milde, GR Mildern, GB Mildwaters, A Miles, B Miles, CO Miles, D Miles, DJ Miles, DV Miles, EC Miles, GE Miles, GL Miles, GW Miles, JR Miles, KJ Miles, MJ Miles, NC Miles, PF Miles, RG Miles, WJ Miles, WT Miles, DG Milford, JEG Milford, TJ Milfull, FJ Milham, RJ Milham, RK Milham, M Milicevic, LG Milich, T Milics, NF Milikins, G Milivojevic, P Milke, TJ Mill, R Millan, TJ Millane, AE Millar, BM Millar, BW Millar, CJ Millar, EM Millar, GA Millar, GJ Millar, GW Millar, J Millar, JC Millar, JP Millar, LJ Millar, M Millar, PM Millar, RG Millar, RJ Millar, RM Millar, VW Millar, WD Millar, CB Millard, DJ Millard, ER Millard, KE Millard, PJ Millard, RD Millard, SR Milledge, AW Millen, CC Millen, AF Miller, AJ Miller, AR Miller, B Miller, BA Miller, BAG Miller, BJ Miller, BM Miller, CA Miller, CJ Miller, CR Miller, D Miller, DA Miller, DI Miller, DJ Miller, DJM Miller, DK Miller, DL Miller, DMB Miller, DT Miller, EC Miller, EF Miller, EM Miller, GI Miller, GM Miller, GP Miller, GR Miller, GW Miller, I Miller, IC Miller, IS Miller, JA Miller, JB Miller, JC Miller, JF Miller, JL Miller, JM Miller, JN Miller, JR Miller, JS Miller, KB Miller, KD Miller, KF Miller, KN Miller, KT Miller, KW Miller, LJ Miller, LP Miller, LW Miller, MD Miller, MR Miller, NA Miller, PA Miller, PF Miller, PG Miller, PJ Miller, PK Miller, RF Miller, RJ Miller, RK Miller, RM Miller, RT Miller, RU Miller, RW Miller, S Miller, VC Miller, WH Miller, WHT Miller, WJ Miller, BJ Millett, LG Millett, PJ Millett, DJ Millhouse, JR Millhouse, RR Millhouse, CV Millican, RD Millican, DR Millie, BC Milligan, GJ Milligan, GW Milligan, NL Milligan, RB Milligan, RD Milliken, AJ Millington, EW Millington, GL Millington, NA Millington, LG Milliss, E Millman, WR Millman, A Mills, AJ Mills, BJ Mills, BW Mills, CC Mills, CJ Mills, CM Mills, DC Mills, DJ Mills, DJB Mills, DL Mills, GG Mills, GR Mills, GS Mills, HL Mills, IA Mills, IT Mills, JAB Mills, JD Mills, JM Mills, JR Mills, K Mills, KJ Mills, KR Mills, LL Mills, LN Mills, MJ Mills, NL Mills, NRJ Mills, PH Mills, PP Mills, PR Mills, RE Mills, RJ Mills, RRE Mills, RT Mills, SJ Mills, TV Mills, WA Mills, WG Mills, DG Millson, JP Millsteed, RJ Millsteed, RJ Millwood, DE Milmlow, A Milne, CR Milne, D Milne, DJ Milne, DR Milne, KC Milne, P Milne, RJ Milne, WL Milne, AJ Milner, AR Milner, BJ Milner, CRK Milner, JS Milner, M Milner, GR Milnes, GS Milnes, IC Milnes, FJ Milroy, BJ Milsom, RD Milsom, A Milton, D Milton, TJ Milton, HG Mimi, JF Minagall, GW Mincherton, RS Minchin, PL Minchinton, KR Minehan, PR Minehan, MW Minell, IM Miners, JW Mines, CH Mingay, AR Minifie, BJ Mining, RF Minn, EN Minner, GEP Minner, WJ Minnett, JP Minney, PJ Minniecon, SJ Minniecon, RN Minnikin, ME Minns, RA Minns, TR Minns, NW Minon, AJ Minos, BE Minster, ND Minter, WJ Minter, GD Mintern, CA Minto, EJ Minton, RD Minton, NF Mintorn, LP Mion, BG Mionnet, DN Mionnet, JW Miosge, AE Miranda, RA Mirrielees, JA Mischke, KH Mischke, DF Misfeld, JS Misiaszek, E Miskiewicz, EE Miskin, WF Miskin, BW Mison, G Missingham, BA Misson, IW Misson, OE Misson, SO Misson, JS Misztal, A Mitchell, AE Mitchell, AJ Mitchell, AL Mitchell, B Mitchell, BD Mitchell, BH Mitchell, BJ Mitchell, BL Mitchell, BM Mitchell, BN Mitchell, BR Mitchell, BS Mitchell, C Mitchell, CL Mitchell, D Mitchell, DE Mitchell, DG Mitchell, DI Mitchell, DJ Mitchell, DL Mitchell, DMJ Mitchell, DV Mitchell, ED Mitchell, FH Mitchell, FJ Mitchell, FS Mitchell, G Mitchell, GA Mitchell, GB Mitchell, GD Mitchell, GH Mitchell, GT Mitchell, GW Mitchell, HW Mitchell, JA Mitchell, JB Mitchell, JC Mitchell, JF Mitchell, JH Mitchell, JL Mitchell, JR Mitchell, JT Mitchell, KA Mitchell, KB Mitchell, KG Mitchell, KJM Mitchell, KN Mitchell, KW Mitchell, LC Mitchell, LH Mitchell, LJ Mitchell, LW Mitchell, MC Mitchell, MJ Mitchell, PA Mitchell, PE Mitchell, PF Mitchell, PH Mitchell, PJ Mitchell, PT Mitchell, PV Mitchell, R Mitchell, RA Mitchell, RB Mitchell, RF Mitchell, RH Mitchell, RJ Mitchell, RL Mitchell, RS Mitchell, RW Mitchell, SJ Mitchell, TJ Mitchell, TR Mitchell, TRA Mitchell, VW Mitchell, W Mitchell, WD Mitchell, WW Mitchell, RJ Mitchelson, FC Mitchener, KC Mitchener, RJ Mitcherson, JR Mitchinson, KL Mitchinson, J Mitka, VP Mitrevics, T Mitt, DG Mitton, JA Mitton, JM Mittra, JF Mizzi, H Moase, BT Mobbs, KW Mobbs, NL Mobbs, J Modlinski, JF Modlinski, S Modlinski, RK Modra, J Modrich, S Modrich, NJ Modystack, RG Modystack, LN Moebus, FJ Moelands, JR Moen, RP Moeser, HM Moffat, KA Moffat, PS Moffat, RA Moffat, RH Moffat, WS Moffat, BS Moffatt, DL Moffatt, GP Moffatt, GD Moffett, DE Moffitt, FM Moffitt, CJ Mogan, JF Mogensen, DR Mogg, AJ Mogridge, J Mogyorossy, AJ Mohr, RF Mohr, RW Moika, RC Moiler, CJ Moir, WD Moir, EJ Mok, U Moldre, BJ Mole, JV Mole, J Molenkamp, GD Moles, JW Moles, KG Moles, LF Molinaro, GW Molineaux, WD Moll, TC Mollard, KJ Mollenhagen, DL Moller, GR Moller, JI Moller, RA Molles, CS Mollison, ET Molloy, JA Molloy, JK Molloy, KT Molloy, KV Molloy, LR Molloy, PJ Molloy, RJ Molloy, WJ Molloy, A Molnar, B Molnar, AP Moloney, BR Moloney, CJ Moloney, DR Moloney, IM Moloney, JB Moloney, JCF Moloney, JJ Moloney, KJ Moloney, M Moloney, MA Moloney, MJ Moloney, PJ Moloney, RJ Moloney, RL Moloney, CR Molony, JP Molony, MP Molony,

RA Molony, MA Moltedo, DW Molyneux, JD Molyneux, K Molyneux, AF Monaghan, BJ Monaghan, D Monaghan, DP Monaghan, DR Monaghan, DS Monaghan, H Monaghan, JG Monaghan, LP Monaghan, PG Monaghan, PJ Monaghan, RS Monaghan, TP Monaghan, WB Monaghan, DR Moncrieff, GC Moncrieff, LFM Mondon, RG Monery, BJ Money, NG Money, LH Mongan, RK Monger, KW Monichon, JR Monico, AP Monin, D Monjean, LR Monjean, BJ Monk, BK Monk, CW Monk, GL Monk, GR Monk, HC Monk, JC Monk, SP Monk, TK Monk, RS Monkcom, RA Monkhouse, SJ Monkley, AN Monks, AR Monks, WJ Monks, IJ Monro, PH Monro, HN Monroe, DW Montague, KJ Montague, JP Monteath, SW Montefiore, GD Monteith, RE Monteith, S Montesalvo, LR Montesini, CJ Montford, CE Montfort, RB Montgomerie, CL Montgomery, DB Montgomery, DH Montgomery, HT Montgomery, J Montgomery, PR Montgomery, RW Montgomery, S Montgomery, KR Moodie, NE Moodie, RG Moodie, AJ Moody, DB Moody, FG Moody, GW Moody, JB Moody, JC Moody, JL Moody, KA Moody, MA Moody, NP Moody, PG Moody, RC Moody, RW Moody, WB Moody, F Mooibroek, BF Moon, EJ Moon, GC Moon, GJ Moon, KJ Moon, LJ Moon, MJ Moon, OC Moon, PJ Moon, RH Moon, BH Mooney, CT Mooney, EE Mooney, JJ Mooney, KJ Mooney, KJA Mooney, MK Mooney, NJ Mooney, PR Mooney, R Mooney, RA Mooney, TB Mooney, PR Moor, BK Moorcroft, GR Moorcroft, AE Moore, AG Moore, AJ Moore, AR Moore, AW Moore, B Moore, BC Moore, BG Moore, BJ Moore, BP Moore, BVJ Moore, CW Moore, DD Moore, DE Moore, DH Moore, DJ Moore, DP Moore, DW Moore, FL Moore, GI Moore, GK Moore, GR Moore, GT Moore, I Moore, IC Moore, JC Moore, JD Moore, JH Moore, JJ Moore, JP Moore, JW Moore, KA Moore, KD Moore, KE Moore, KF Moore, KH Moore, KJ Moore, LJ Moore, LW Moore, MJ Moore, ML Moore, PA Moore, PB Moore, PG Moore, PGS Moore, PJ Moore, PM Moore, R Moore, RD Moore, RF Moore, RG Moore, RJ Moore, RM Moore, RT Moore, SC Moore, SJ Moore, SR Moore, ST Moore, TE Moore, TW Moore, W Moore, WG Moore, WJ Moore, WP Moore, WR Moore, TC Moores, JR Moorhead, R Moorhouse, A Mooy, GF Moraday, JO Morahan, RG Morahan, BJ Moran, CG Moran, K Moran, KJ Moran, LW Moran, RJ Moran, RJ Moranhilford, MJ Morath, PF Moravec, I Moravski, AF Morcom, GT Morcom, R Morcom, AC Morcomb, JL Mordike, GW More, RW More, VA Moreau, KP Morel, JR Morell, E Morello, JE Moremon, MJ Morero, J Moreton, RR Moreton, EA Moretti, JL Morey, RJ Morey, AC Morgan, B Morgan, B Morgan, BA Morgan, BD Morgan, BJ Morgan, CA Morgan, CR Morgan, DJ Morgan, DM Morgan, DN Morgan, DO Morgan, DW Morgan, EA Morgan, EI Morgan, ER Morgan, FJ Morgan, GA Morgan, GH Morgan, GJ Morgan, GL Morgan, GP Morgan, GR Morgan, HJ Morgan, I Morgan, IB Morgan, IM Morgan, J Morgan, JA Morgan, JL Morgan, KA Morgan, KC Morgan, KG Morgan, KM Morgan, KR Morgan, MTS Morgan, NA Morgan, NT Morgan, P Morgan, PE Morgan, PG Morgan, PJ Morgan, PR Morgan, PS Morgan, PW Morgan, RF Morgan, RJ Morgan, RM Morgan, RT Morgan, RW Morgan, TF Morgan, TR Morgan, VA Morgan, W Morgan, WS Morgan, V Morgans, JM Moriarty, DJ Morice, PW Morish, DE Morison, DP Morison, LJ Morison, R Morison, RF Morison, BK Morisset, KE Morisset, PT Moritz, AW Morley, BMH Morley, EA Morley, IC Morley, KF Morley, RW Morley, SM Morley, WE Morley, CP Moroney, DM Moroney, FG Moroney, MJ Moroney, TJ Moroney, TP Morony, E Morosin, AB Morosoli, JW Morphett, LJ Morrall, SK Morrant, CJ Morrell-Porter, SR Morrice, A Morris, AB Morris, AC Morris, AH Morris, AJ Morris, AP Morris, AR Morris, BC Morris, BE Morris, BJ Morris, BN Morris, CA Morris, CJ Morris, DL Morris, DM Morris, DR Morris, DT Morris, E Morris, EB Morris, EJ Morris, FJ Morris, GA Morris, GAN Morris, GG Morris, GR Morris, IF Morris, IR Morris, J Morris, JA Morris, JAJ Morris, JG Morris, JH Morris, JT Morris, KA Morris, KH Morris, KJ Morris, L Morris, LA Morris, LC Morris, LE Morris, NF Morris, NR Morris, PG Morris, PN Morris, RG Morris, RI Morris, RJ Morris, RW Morris, SC Morris, SG Morris, SJ Morris, SK Morris, SP Morris, TD Morris, TJ Morris, TK Morris, WA Morris, WB Morris, WG Morris, WH Morris, WJ Morris, WL Morris, PK Morrisby, A Morrison, AJ Morrison, AL Morrison, AN Morrison,

BR Morrison, DG Morrison, DJ Morrison, DW Morrison, EJ Morrison, FL Morrison, IJ Morrison, IL Morrison, IW Morrison, JD Morrison, JT Morrison, KD Morrison, KG Morrison, KH Morrison, KJ Morrison, LA Morrison, LI Morrison, MC Morrison, ML Morrison, PF Morrison, R Morrison, RA Morrison, RN Morrison, RP Morrison, WC Morrison, BM Morrissey, C Morrissey, DJ Morrissey, GC Morrissey, JP Morrissey, BK Morris-Shaoul, R Morritt, B Morrow, BJ Morrow, CA Morrow, CB Morrow, CD Morrow, DJ Morrow, GJ Morrow, KM Morrow, ML Morrow, NB Morrow, RF Morrow, RJ Morrow, WG Morrow, WH Morrow, WJ Morrow, CM Morse, FT Morse, RD Morse, RJ Morse, PJ Mortell, AW Mortensen, PF Mortenson, BE Mortimer, CR Mortimer, JC Mortimer, MB Mortimer, RD Mortimer, WA Mortimer, GS Mortimore, DM Mortlock, KF Mortlock, AD Morton, AJ Morton, D Morton, DR Morton, DW Morton, EL Morton, G Morton, GW Morton, IK Morton, JW Morton, KD Morton, LC Morton, LR Morton, PJ Morton, PW Morton, R Morton, RD Morton, RW Morton, SG Morton, RW Mosbergen, PG Moscatt, HG Moschetti, R Moschione, PD Mosel, GG Moseley, PM Moseley, RP Moseley, B Moser, IH Moses, RC Moses, GW Mosey, V Moshonkin, J Moskwiak, K Mosley, MC Mosley, PP Mosman, AB Moss, CG Moss, CK Moss, DR Moss, DW Moss, EJW Moss, EL Moss, GJ Moss, GL Moss, JW Moss, KJ Moss, RC Moss, RG Moss, RH Moss, RP Moss, TE Moss, TWE Moss, B Mossman, RWF Mossman, LE Mossop, MJ Mossop, C Mostaard, LJ Mosterd, GR Mostyn, J Mostyn, WD Mostyn, VC Motbey, B Motley, CR Mott, FJ Mott, GJ Mott, RA Mott, RJ Mott, GR Mottershead, JC Mottershead, RJ Motton, C Mottram, PD Mottram, RG Mottram, AJ Mould, JL Mould, GL Moulday, GC Moulds, PE Moulds, AJ Moule, CA Moule, RA Moule, GA Moulton, JG Mounsey, RM Mounsey, PJM Mount, RL Mountain, DM Mountford, KW Mountford, DL Mountney, JL Mountney, W Mountseer, JW Mouthaan, BO Mouton, ML Mouy, BG Mowbray, PH Moxey, R Moxey, EJ Moyers, SW Moyes, TR Moyes, AG Moylan, JN Moylan, LF Moylan, MF Moylan, BJ Moyle, CG Moyle, EC Moyle, HJ Moyle, JA Moyle, LJ Moyle, PA Moyle, RA Moyle, RJ Moyle, S Moyle, TR Moyle, WG Moyle, L Moynham, MB Moynihan, MT Moynihan, M Muc, KG Mucjanko, JC Mucklestone, IG Muckray, LSK Mudaliar, PD Mudd, GF Mudge, GR Mudge, DN Mudie, AT Mudiman, DM Mueller, FF Mueller, DR Muffet, DR Mugeli, TL Muggleton, CL Mugridge, PJ Muhlberg, MS Muhling, AB Muir, AT Muir, BI Muir, BS Muir, DC Muir, DL Muir, DM Muir, GG Muir, GJ Muir, GP Muir, ID Muir, IW Muir, JA Muir, JD Muir, JI Muir, JW Muir, L Muir, LM Muir, MR Muir, P Muir, PA Muir, PAJ Muir, PD Muir, RM Muir, RW Muir, SJ Muir, TP Muir, WF Muir, JT Mulby, BL Mulcahy, JF Mulcahy, IS Mulcaster, GW Mulder, CJ Muldoon, JB Muldoon, JS Muldoon, MJ Muldoon, SD Muldoon, MC Mules, PW Mules, AJ Mulgrew, PA Mulgrew, AJ Mulhall, DP Mulhall, PK Mulhall, IM Mulholland, JA Mulholland, NG Mulholland, RJ Mulholland, PJ Mullan, DV Mullane, AJ Mullavey, GL Mullavey, JD Mullavey, CW Mullen, DJ Mullen, JF Mullen, PJJ Mullens, CF Muller, CL Muller, DM Muller, GW Muller, HL Muller, LR Muller, RJ Muller, RL Muller, SH Muller, WR Muller, JC Mulley, K Mulley, TB Mulley, AN Mulligan, BP Mulligan, JE Mulligan, KW Mulligan, RM Mulligan, SJ Mulligan, ML Mullin, RK Mullings, IR Mullins, JN Mullins, RL Mullins, RT Mullins, SA Mullins, TP Mullins, VW Mullins, J Mulloy, AJJ Mulquiney, DM Mulquiney, GR Mulready, RM Mulree, D Mulvany, G Mulvihill, RP Mulvihill, JCR Mulville, RW Mulville, WE Mulvogue, SA Mumberson, DJ Mumford, KJ Mumford, RE Mumme, MJ Mummery, SR Mummery, BJ Munari, LA Muncaster, CR Muncey, LS Munchow, JC Munckton, BJ Munday, BR Munday, DM Munday, GR Munday, JT Munday, RM Munday, RP Munday, BP Mundy, DF Mundy, PW Mundy, RF Mundy, RJ Mundy, RK Mundy, GT Mungean, JA Mungean, JD Mungoven, AG Munn, MR Munn, RC Munnery, NH Munnoch, AR Munro, BD Munro, BR Munro, DI Munro, GE Munro, GG Munro, GJ Munro, IA Munro, ID Munro, IJ Munro, IR Munro, JE Munro, JEA Munro, KA Munro, MC Munro, NC Munro, PG Munro, PR Munro, RG Munro, RW Munro, TD Munro, W Munro, WA Munro, WR Munro, GR Munsell, HK Munsie, PG Munson, AR Munster, GS Munt, LJ Munt, PE Munt, PS Munyard, GC Munz, GJ Munzer, E Murans,

AC Murchison, RG Murchison, HJ Murcott, K Murdey, CT Murdoch, EB Murdoch, JW Murdoch, RJ Murdoch, RK Murdoch, TJ Murdoch, V Murdoch, WR Murdoch, RE Murie, IG Murley, JE Murley, K Murley, RJ Murn, CJ Murnane, PD Murnane, PM Murnane, TM Murnane, AA Murphy, AJ Murphy, AM Murphy, AS Murphy, AT Murphy, B Murphy, BAJ Murphy, BJ Murphy, BN Murphy, BW Murphy, DJ Murphy, DR Murphy, E Murphy, GA Murphy, GD Murphy, GJ Murphy, IN Murphy, JF Murphy, JG Murphy, JL Murphy, JM Murphy, JP Murphy, JV Murphy, JW Murphy, KA Murphy, KB Murphy, KE Murphy, KJ Murphy, KP Murphy, KT Murphy, LR Murphy, MF Murphy, MJ Murphy, NW Murphy, P Murphy, PC Murphy, PE Murphy, PG Murphy, PJ Murphy, PN Murphy, RJ Murphy, RT Murphy, SP Murphy, TJ Murphy, VM Murphy, VN Murphy, WA Murphy, WF Murphy, WG Murphy, WJ Murphy, WR Murphy, WT Murphy, WTA Murphy, P Murrant, A Murray, AC Murray, AI Murray, AN Murray, AR Murray, BA Murray, DB Murray, DJ Murray, DM Murray, G Murray, GC Murray, GD Murray, GJ Murray, GO Murray, GR Murray, GW Murray, HL Murray, JA Murray, JB Murray, JM Murray, JR Murray, JW Murray, KC Murray, KR Murray, LM Murray, LR Murray, MGW Murray, MJ Murray, NJ Murray, NR Murray, P Murray, PE Murray, PH Murray, PJ Murray, PR Murray, PT Murray, R Murray, RC Murray, RD Murray, RE Murray, RF Murray, RH Murray, RJ Murray, RN Murray, SR Murray, TG Murray, TJ Murray, WA Murray, WB Murray, WJ Murray, WP Murray, G Murray-Wilcox, GE Murrell, J Murrell, JT Murrell, LT Murrell, ML Murrell, RG Murrell, RL Murrell, TB Murrell, JP Murrihy, RG Murry, BN Murtagh, KW Murtagh, KR Murton, LJ Murton, WA Mus, J Muscat, PR Muscat, T Muscat, DN Muscroft, AS Musgrave, MJ Musgrave, R Musgrave, RA Musgrave, WJ Musgrave, DR Musgrove, GJ Musgrove, RC Musgrove, RV Musgrove, BT Musial, AL Musicka, HR Musicka, LE Mussared, TJ Mussared, K Musson, PJ Musson, EJ Mustafa, MS Mustchin, KW Mustey, AR Muston, RJ Mutch, GL Mutton, KB Mutton, BC Myall, SC Myatt, DG Myers, GM Myers, GV Myers, J Myers, JD Myers, JW Myers, KJ Myers, KN Myers, KW Myers, LD Myers, LG Myers, LR Myers, MD Myers, PJ Myers, RWA Myers, SC Myers, SP Myers, TW Myers, WT Myers, CF Myhill, NR Myler, PT Myler, IT Myles, JF Myles, JK Myles, MJ Mylne, PG Mylne, PJ Mylne, JC Mynhart, DG Mynott, MJ Nabbs, DW Nadge, W Nadrez, AWS Nadudvary, BV Nagle, DE Nagle, EJ Nagle, G Nagle, WL Nagle, I Nagy, J Nagy, JE Nailon, TE Nailon, DJ Nairn, EA Nairn, MD Nairn, WJ Nairn, SR Naish, RA Naismith, RH Naismith, WL Nalder, AJ Nall, J Nally, GG Nancarrow, RD Nancarrow, WF Nancarrow, JC Nangle, VN Nani, CR Nankervis, WM Nankervis, KD Nankivell, RH Nankivell, RH Nankiville, RP Nanson, DM Napier, GR Napier, JAK Napier, JC Napier, R Napier, MD Napper, SW Napper, WJ Napthali, MW Narramore, M Naseef, DC Nash, GJ Nash, GR Nash, GW Nash, JL Nash, KJ Nash, LW Nash, P Nash, PF Nash, PJ Nash, R Nash, RB Nash, RC Nash, RJ Nash, WR Nash, CR Nasmyth, RA Nason, DI Nasser, N Natalie, R Nathan, CG Nation, NC Nation, PG Nation, PJ Nation, RJ Nation, MC Natt, L Naudi, BC Naughton, EH Naughton, MA Naughton, PJ Naughton, RV Naughton, RW Naumann, PJ Navarre, GG Navas, BJ Navin, AJ Nayda, CT Nayda, CD Nayler, KD Naylor, P Naylor, PA Naylor, DR Naysmith, GI Neagle, RA Neagle, BP Neal, BW Neal, DW Neal, FJ Neal, I Neal, RE Neal, RJ Neal, TG Neal, CC Neale, GA Neale, JA Neale, MT Neale, PF Neale, RL Neale, VP Neale, DH Nean, MC Nearmy, VM Neary, JD Neate, PA Neate, CD Neave, DE Neave, DL Neave, DJ Nebe, RJ Neboraczek, H Neczas, GP Needham, R Needham, H Needs, JD Needs, PR Needs, M Neels, BA Neely, GC Neenan, JM Neenan, MJ Neenan, JB Neervoort, HT Neesham, W Neeson, DJ Negline, DG Negus, GN Negus, VJ Nehow, IW Nehring, AE Neighman, HLJ Neihoff, DO Neil, DS Neil, M Neil, MJ Neil, PW Neil, RJ Neil, WF Neil, EJ Neill, GW Neill, MR Neill, AC Neilson, FJ Neilson, JH Neilson, JT Neilson, KB Neilson, RP Neilson, RT Neilson, VT Neimanis, TJ Neinert, GC Neitz, WG Nellems, KJ Neller, RJ Nelligan, AD Nelson, AF Nelson, AWL Nelson, BM Nelson, BR Nelson, CJ Nelson, D Nelson, DE Nelson, DJ Nelson, DR Nelson, EA Nelson, GK Nelson, HE Nelson, JA Nelson, JD Nelson, JF Nelson, JG Nelson, JL Nelson, JP Nelson, KJ Nelson, MG Nelson, PG Nelson, RA Nelson, RB Nelson, RC Nelson, RG Nelson, RJ Nelson, RK Nelson, RV Nelson,

SL Nelson, TS Nelson, VW Nelson, WJ Nelson, C Nemeth,
BM Nesbit, GA Nesbit, WA Nesbit, AG Nesbitt, GM Nesbitt,
JC Nesbitt, BS Ness, RJ Ness, PG Nestor, L Netherclift,
WP Nethercote, KF Netting, RN Nettle, RT Nettlefold,
BE Nettleton, MG Nettleton, GC Neubecker, DJ Neuendorff,
CM Neuenkirchen, CA Neumann, PH Neus, BH Neve,
RG Neve, GJ Nevill, BJ Neville, CJ Neville, DJ Neville,
JW Neville, KJ Neville, LW Neville, MC Neville, MJ Neville,
NJ Neville, PA Neville, RB Neville, WF Neville, BT Nevin,
DB Nevins, MT Nevins, EK New, RAL New, T Newall,
DJ Newberry, RL Newberry, GH Newbery, HJ Newbery,
EG Newbold, RW Newbould, JR Newburn, SO Newburn,
F Newby, BA Newcombe, JS Newell, K Newell, LJ Newell,
MF Newell, NJ Newell, RJ Newell, TA Newell, WJ Newell,
DJ Newey, IA Newey, RJL Newham, RK Newham,
AE Newington, DG Newland, PJ Newland, PR Newland,
TJ Newland, TC Newley, CJ Newlyn, AJ Newman,
BM Newman, DC Newman, DCW Newman, GD Newman,
GM Newman, GR Newman, HG Newman, IJ Newman,
J Newman, JG Newman, K Newman, KC Newman,
KE Newman, LE Newman, OS Newman, RAR Newman,
RC Newman, RM Newman, RT Newman, T Newman,
TP Newman, VW Newman, WE Newman, WF Newman,
GW Newnham, L Newnham, MJ Newnham, P Newport,
TR Newport, DJ Newsham, DG Newsome, RE Newsome,
TJ Newsome, BR Newson, GH Newstead, GJ Newstead,
GW Newstead, AM Newton, AP Newton, BJ Newton,
C Newton, DM Newton, EJ Newton, ER Newton,
GA Newton, GAE Newton, GD Newton, GE Newton,
GJ Newton, JE Newton, KGR Newton, KR Newton,
KW Newton, L Newton, LG Newton, MD Newton,
MJ Newton, NG Newton, PJ Newton, RG Newton,
TJ Newton, WJ Newton, RJ Ney, MR Neyland, RJ Neyland,
KD Neylon, GW Nibbs, RJ Niblett, GR Niblock, H Nichol,
RD Nichol, RJ Nichol, EA Nicholas, GR Nicholas,
HJ Nicholas, JD Nicholas, LA Nicholas, MF Nicholas,
RR Nicholas, BJ Nicholls, DE Nicholls, DF Nicholls,
DK Nicholls, DM Nicholls, GJ Nicholls, GT Nicholls,
HJE Nicholls, IR Nicholls, JL Nicholls, JT Nicholls,
LC Nicholls, MG Nicholls, RJ Nicholls, DM Nichols,
DR Nichols, GK Nichols, GP Nichols, GPJ Nichols,
HJ Nichols, HJA Nichols, IP Nichols, K Nichols,
LW Nichols, MJ Nichols, NP Nichols, PJ Nichols,
RA Nichols, RF Nichols, RK Nichols, RM Nichols,
TG Nichols, AG Nicholson, BG Nicholson, CG Nicholson,
DA Nicholson, DG Nicholson, DJ Nicholson,
EHJ Nicholson, GE Nicholson, GF Nicholson, IR Nicholson,
J Nicholson, JA Nicholson, JR Nicholson, KR Nicholson,
LE Nicholson, LJ Nicholson, LP Nicholson, NA Nicholson,
NW Nicholson, P Nicholson, RA Nicholson, RC Nicholson,
RG Nicholson, RH Nicholson, RK Nicholson, RP Nicholson,
TJ Nicholson, WJ Nicholson, GL Niciauskas, UE Nickel,
GD Nicklin, DJ Nickols, JA Nickols, DR Nicks, BO Nicol,
CT Nicol, DR Nicol, GD Nicol, IT Nicol, RG Nicol,
TD Nicol, CB Nicolaou, BB Nicoll, BG Nicoll, JM Nicoll,
P Nicoll, JG Nicolson, ML Nicolson, EH Niddrie, AJ Nie,
SN Niebling, JB Niejalke, RJ Nield, AM Nielsen, D Nielsen,
GW Nielsen, ND Nielsen, DJ Nielson, GL Nielson,
RJ Nielson, PB Niesler, J Nieuwendaal, A Nieuwenhout,
B Niezabitowski, JA Nightingale, JM Nightingale,
N Nightingale, BF Nihill, PJ Nihill, E Nikolajenko,
J Nikolajew, P Nikolic, GJ Nilan, CD Nilon, LM Nilon,
AN Nilsen, EH Nilsen, KJ Nilsen, R Nilsen, PW Nilsson,
MT Ninness, KF Nipperess, KA Niquet, BR Nisbet,
CR Nisbet, PE Nisbet, WF Nisbett, RF Nissen, VR Nissen,
HK Nitarski, AW Nitschke, GA Nitschke, MR Nitschke,
NW Nitschke, RG Nitschke, JA Niukkanen, JR Niven,
RG Niven, WL Niven, GP Nix, LM Nix, AB Nixon,
GG Nixon, IJ Nixon, J Nixon, JW Nixon, KRW Nixon,
KT Nixon, JD Nixon-Smith, EW Noack, RJ Noack,
JA Noade, LD Noakes, NJ Noakes, CA Nobelius, B Nobilia,
BR Noble, DA Noble, DJ Noble, JW Noble, PJ Noble,
PW Noble, RB Noble, RG Noble, RM Noble, RW Noble,
SJ Noble, WJ Noble, GW Noblet, RJ Nock, HF Nockolds,
PJ Nodin, DJ Noe, BR Noel, BS Noel, GP Noferi, AA Nolan,
AJ Nolan, BF Nolan, DC Nolan, DG Nolan, FAP Nolan,
GA Nolan, GN Nolan, HJ Nolan, ID Nolan, JE Nolan,
JJ Nolan, MA Nolan, ML Nolan, PA Nolan, PG Nolan,
RJ Nolan, TJ Nolan, TL Nolan, TM Nolan, VJ Nolan,
BH Nolen, DC Nolte, PH Noom, BB Noonan, BL Noonan,
CD Noonan, CL Noonan, FB Noonan, GA Noonan,
GV Noonan, JR Noonan, LA Noonan, LJ Noonan,
M Noonan, MD Noonan, MJ Noonan, PJ Noonan,
RA Noonan, RE Noonan, RF Noonan, WG Noone,
IJ Noormets, AC Norcott, PE Norcott, CJ Nord,
BC Nordeck, RA Norden, RL Norden, GN Nordstrom,
DH Nordsvan, LS Norgren, GL Norley, KT Norley,
AJ Norman, AR Norman, B Norman, CG Norman,
DC Norman, DR Norman, GR Norman, JG Norman,
JW Norman, LJ Norman, PL Norman, PR Norman,
RA Norman, RG Norman, RK Norman, RM Normington,
EM Norquay, HE Norrie, JW Norrie, AP Norris, CF Norris,
CJ Norris, E Norris, GA Norris, GB Norris, IA Norris,
JA Norris, JD Norris, JL Norris, JN Norris, JR Norris,
JW Norris, MTJ Norris, PC Norris, ST Norris,
AA Norsgaard, AC North, AR North, GE North, JA North,
KM North, LA North, MP North, PC North, RJ North,
EE Northard, RLJ Northcott, LR Northey, RJ Northey,
KJ Northfield, GV Northover, HT Northwood,
PJ Northwood, BC Norton, BJ Norton, DA Norton,
FO Norton, NA Norton, PJ Norton, PN Norton, SF Norton,
SJ Norton, WA Norton, WJO Norton, RB Norton-Baker,
RT Norwell, JH Norwood, DT Nossack, AA Notaras,
GO Nothdurft, CR Nott, DJ Nottage, GT Nottage,
TA Nottle, KD Noud, RA Noud, PL Nourse, J Novello,
RC Novice, MF Nowak, W Nowak, JZ Nowakowski,
FJ Nowell, LA Nowicki, MR Nowill, GH Nowlan,
HE Nowlan, RV Nowlan, RG Nowland, OK Nowotny,
RH Nowrojee, DJ Noy, RH Noy, CL Noyeaux, A Nucifora,
LW Nuffer, JA Nugara, BA Nugent, BE Nugent, JP Nugent,
LP Nugent, RC Nugent, RS Nugent, RTB Nugent,
SM Nugent, VE Nugent, JW Nulty, PJ Nummy, DJ Nunan,
JH Nunan, BG Nunn, BJ Nunn, CJ Nunn, GJ Nunn,
GR Nunn, LR Nunn, PJ Nunn, RJ Nunn, MR Nurse,
JW Nuss, SC Nuss, CR Nutt, RC Nutt, D Nuttall, K Nuttall,
GC Nybo, JG Nyhuis, BL Nykiel, L Nykke, BL Nyman,
L Nyman, CF Oakden, KJ Oakes, PF Oakes, RH Oakes,
RJ Oakes, PK Oakford, DJ Oakley, DW Oakley, JR Oakley,
RF Oakley, RJE Oakley, CJ Oakman, EHB Oakman,
LM Oakman, RC Oakman, JF Oaten, EA Oates, EW Oates,
GD Oates, RB Oates, TJ Oates, WJ Oates, BJ Oatway,
PJ O'Beirne, TB O'Bre, TW O'Bree, AJ O'Brien, B O'Brien,
BJ O'Brien, BP O'Brien, C O'Brien, CC O'Brien,
DA O'Brien, DJ O'Brien, DR O'Brien, DT O'Brien,
DW O'Brien, FEG O'Brien, FK O'Brien, FL O'Brien,
GAJ O'Brien, GJ O'Brien, GP O'Brien, HJ O'Brien,
J O'Brien, JA O'Brien, JD O'Brien, JF O'Brien, JG O'Brien,
JH O'Brien, JJ O'Brien, KJ O'Brien, LC O'Brien, LG O'Brien,
LK O'Brien, LP O'Brien, MF O'Brien, MJ O'Brien,
MPJ O'Brien, NF O'Brien, NT O'Brien, OJ O'Brien,
P O'Brien, PA O'Brien, PAA O'Brien, PJ O'Brien,
PK O'Brien, PM O'Brien, PW O'Brien, R O'Brien,
RA O'Brien, RC O'Brien, RG O'Brien, RJ O'Brien,
RK O'Brien, RP O'Brien, RW O'Brien, SA O'Brien,
SC O'Brien, SF O'Brien, TB O'Brien, TDA O'Brien,
TP O'Brien, TW O'Brien, WE O'Brien, WJ O'Brien,
WT O'Brien, DJ O'Bryan, KFR O'Bryan, PF O'Bryan,
MG O'Byrne, JP O'Callaghan, KJ O'Callaghan,
KL O'Callaghan, MJ O'Callaghan, RG O'Callaghan,
TJ O'Callaghan, TP O'Callaghan, MW O'Callahan,
AGS Ochiltree, RP Ockenden, SC Ockendon, JT Ockwell,
LW Ockwell, DJ O'Connell, DW O'Connell, JP O'Connell,
JR O'Connell, KW O'Connell, M O'Connell, TC O'Connell,
TJ O'Connell, TW O'Connell, AD O'Connor,
AE O'Connor, B O'Connor, BL O'Connor, CM O'Connor,
DJ O'Connor, DP O'Connor, GM O'Connor, JA O'Connor,
JM O'Connor, JW O'Connor, KR O'Connor, LM O'Connor,
MK O'Connor, MKV O'Connor, MN O'Connor,
MS O'Connor, MT O'Connor, NJ O'Connor, PK O'Connor,
PS O'Connor, RA O'Connor, RC O'Connor, RJ O'Connor,
RL O'Connor, RT O'Connor, DF Octigan, JH Odal,
SJ O'Dal, D O'Dare, GO O'Day, MR Oddy, BJ O'Dea,
GA O'Dea, JP O'Dea, L O'Dea, MCJ O'Dea, MG O'Dea,
RJ O'Dea, P O'Dell, K O'Dempsey, RB Odendahl,
PT Odermatt, CE Odgers, NG Odmark, KT O'Doherty,
BL O'Donnell, CD O'Donnell, EJ O'Donnell,
GR O'Donnell, JF O'Donnell, JH O'Donnell, JM O'Donnell,
JP O'Donnell, KW O'Donnell, LG O'Donnell, M O'Donnell,
MJ O'Donnell, MP O'Donnell, MR O'Donnell,
MT O'Donnell, NJ O'Donnell, PA O'Donnell,
PE O'Donnell, PL O'Donnell, PR O'Donnell,
RD O'Donnell, TA O'Donnell, TG O'Donnell,
TP O'Donnell, W O'Donnell, WJ O'Donnell,
WP O'Donnell, DP O'Donoghue, JJ O'Donoghue,
MP O'Donoghue, BM O'Donohue, BT O'Donohue,
JF O'Donohue, TJ O'Donohue, TV O'Donohue,
DA O'Donovan, GR O'Donovan, AP O'Dowd, BS O'Dowd,
JK O'Dowd, DA O'Driscoll, KB O'Dwyer, LJ O'Dwyer,
RM O'Dwyer, SJ O'Dwyer, TH Oehlschlager, HG Oetjen,
PJ O'Farrell, T O'Farrell, RA Offer, JH Offermans,
HJ O'Flynn, BP O'Garey, DL Ogden, GM Ogden, J Ogden,
JJ Ogden, KW Ogden, NS Ogden, RJ Ogden, RL Ogden,
RJ Ogilvie, NP O'Gorman, JD O'Gradey, A O'Grady,
CB O'Grady, CE O'Grady, MJ O'Grady, WJ O'Grady,
WS Ogrodniczek, CL O'Haire, MJ O'Haire, JP O'Halloran,
KF O'Halloran, MJ O'Halloran, NJ O'Halloran,
PF O'Halloran, PJ O'Halloran, RJ O'Halloran,
RM O'Halloran, SJ O'Halloran, TP O'Halloran,
TH O'Hanlon, BJ O'Hara, CD O'Hara, CT O'Hara,
GM O'Hara, GV O'Hara, JL O'Hara, L O'Hara, MR O'Hara,
PE O'Hara, PH O'Hara, PV O'Hara, RA O'Hara, RJ O'Hara,
MP O'Hare, GM O'Hearn, MJ O'Hearn, BG O'Hehir,
RP O'Hehir, AS Ohlback, WA Ohlmus, BR Ohlsen,
KA Okane, GD Oke, DC O'Kearney, BG O'Keefe,
E O'Keefe, EJ O'Keefe, GK O'Keefe, GR O'Keefe,
GT O'Keefe, JA O'Keefe, JF O'Keefe, JP O'Keefe,
KJ O'Keefe, LG O'Keefe, LJ O'Keefe, MF O'Keefe,
MJ O'Keefe, SJ O'Keefe, TP O'Keefe, DR O'Keeffe,
KJ O'Keeffe, RB O'Keeffe, T O'Keeffe, DK O'Kelly,
MR O'Kelly, DF Okely, JR Okley, GJ Old, JH Oldaker,
G Olde, PM Olde, EJ Oldfield, GP Oldfield, JE Oldfield,
KH Oldfield, KW Oldfield, AT Oldham, AR Olding,
EJ Olding, RJ Oldman, LJ Oldmeadow, DL Oldroyd,
BJ O'leary, DJ O'leary, GH O'leary, J O'leary, JD O'leary,
JT O'leary, KJ O'leary, KR O'leary, MJ O'leary, P O'leary,
PJ O'leary, RI O'leary, RJ O'leary, RP O'leary, TMP O'leary,
KG Oleinik, VP Olejniczak, SJ Olek, JF Oleson, S Olinski,
RH Oliphant, TA Oliphant, DA Olive, JRD Olive, KF Olive,
KJ Olive, LJ Olive, CM Oliver, CR Oliver, DJ Oliver,
GJ Oliver, GR Oliver, JR Oliver, JW Oliver, KA Oliver,
KG Oliver, LJ Oliver, MD Oliver, MH Oliver, MJ Oliver,
ONB Oliver, PA Oliver, RI Oliver, RN Oliver, VP Olivieri,
GA Olley, NJ Ollington, GC Olney, JE Olney, KJ Olney,
BK O'loughlin, MA O'loughlin, NW O'loughlin,
P O'loughlin, PJ O'loughlin, RM Olree, BA Olsen, JC Olsen,
JF Olsen, NL Olsen, PC Olsen, RK Olsen, TD Olsen,
AA Olson, DR Olson, JE Olson, RJ Olson, RG Olsson,
KW Olver, HH Omachen, E O'Malley, JM O'Malley,
MF O'Malley, ND O'Malley, R O'Malley, MA O'Mallon,
AJ O'Mara, DP O'Mara, EJ O'Mara, SL O'Mara,
TM O'Mara, TV O'Mara, WO O'Mara, JD O'Meara,
PW O'Meara, DM Omond, DJ O'Moore, C O'Neil,
D O'Neil, AL O'Neill, BD O'Neill, BG O'Neill, BJ O'Neill,
CE O'Neill, CRJ O'Neill, CW O'Neill, DJ O'Neill,
DK O'Neill, ET O'Neill, FJ O'Neill, GA O'Neill, GG O'Neill,
GT O'Neill, J O'Neill, JB O'Neill, JD O'Neill, JM O'Neill,
KF O'Neill, KJ O'Neill, KL O'Neill, KW O'Neill,
LD O'Neill, LF O'Neill, MD O'Neill, PD O'Neill,
PG O'Neill, PR O'Neill, RJ O'Neill, TA O'Neill, TH O'Neill,
TJ O'Neill, VJ O'Neill, VR O'Neill, GP Ongheen,
JW Ongley, BR Onley, KG Onley, MA Onn, PD Onoprienko,
JP Onrust, KW Onslow, R Oonk, A Oost, J Opdam,
ALD Opie, JP Opie, LM Opie, RM Opie, JD Opray,
PR Opray, SG Opray, BJ Oram, AG Orchard, GJ Orchard,
RL Orchard, NG Ordner, A Oredat, JAW O'Regan,
MB O'Regan, RS O'Regan, BR O'Reilly, DL O'Reilly,
DM O'Reilly, E O'Reilly, GJ O'Reilly, JA O'Reilly,
JP O'Reilly, JPM O'Reilly, JT O'Reilly, MF O'Reilly,
MH O'Reilly, MP O'Reilly, MW O'Reilly, NJ O'Reilly,
TM O'Reilly, WJ O'Reilly, WL O'Reilly, G Orel, GA Orford,
JP Orford, RG Orford, AW Organ, R Organ, OM O'Rielley,
PS O'Riley, CA Oriti, PW Orlinski, PK Orlowski,
DM Orman, GJ Ormandy, BE Ormiston, CTL Ormond,
FG Ormond, AJ Ormston, B Ornowski, BD O'Rourke,
BJ O'Rourke, CE O'Rourke, CJ O'Rourke, JW O'Rourke,
LJ O'Rourke, MGE O'Rourke, PH O'Rourke, PJ O'Rourke,
WJ O'Rourke, BA Orphin, AJ Orr, AP Orr, DC Orr,
DFJ Orr, GR Orr, J Orr, JR Orr, JV Orr, KA Orr, RH Orr,
EP Orreal, LL Orreal, RK Orreal, IS Orrell, KE Orriss,
KL Orrock, LP Orsborn, WR Orthman, K Ortlipp,
AD Orton, DE Orwin, JJ O'Ryan, BV Osborn, IR Osborn,
LD Osborn, PD Osborn, RB Osborn, RF Osborn,
RG Osborn, WL Osborn, AF Osborne, BJ Osborne,
BL Osborne, BR Osborne, DB Osborne, GA Osborne,
JF Osborne, JH Osborne, KL Osborne, LC Osborne,
LW Osborne, MW Osborne, RA Osborne, RJ Osborne,
WB Osborne, RK Osburn, A Oschmannz, BP O'Shanassy,
DJ O'Shannessy, JM O'Shannessy, JW O'Shaughnessy,
RJ O'Shaughnessy, BP O'Shea, CT O'Shea, DM O'Shea,

G O'Shea, JD O'Shea, JJ O'Shea, JW O'Shea, LJ O'Shea, MJ O'Shea, NR O'Shea, PJ O'Shea, RC O'Shea, WL O'Shea, WM O'Shea, FDR Osler, RN Osler, E Osman, B Osmond, BJ Osmond, EC Osmond, KJ Osmond, TJ Osmond, WCN Osmond, EB Ostara, EW Ostler, AW O'Sullivan, B O'Sullivan, BD O'Sullivan, CP O'Sullivan, DM O'Sullivan, DR O'Sullivan, GF O'Sullivan, KS O'Sullivan, LV O'Sullivan, MD O'Sullivan, MF O'Sullivan, MJ O'Sullivan, PD O'Sullivan, PS O'Sullivan, TS O'Sullivan, DM Oswald, GN Oswald, J Oswald, PJ Oswin, TW Oswin, AL O'Toole, BW O'Toole, CJ O'Toole, GE O'Toole, RJ O'Toole, VP O'Toole, G Ots, LA Ott, IL Ottaway, GP Otte, RJ Ottery, KG Ottewill, RH Otto de Grancy, GD Otto, AK Otton, AC Ottway, BA Otway, LF Otway, VK Otway, DJ Ouchirenko, P Oudyn, RT Ousby, LE Outen, SH Outhred, G Outram, KP Outridge, D Ovans, GJ Ovenden, MG Ovenden, RE Ovenden, RJ Ovens, TG Ovens, HD Over, AJW Overall, MJ Overend, DR Overstead, DL Overton, JR Overton, KL Overton, DC Owen, DL Owen, DM Owen, DW Owen, FJ Owen, GA Owen, GR Owen, J Owen, JE Owen, JV Owen, KF Owen, LC Owen, M Owen, MJ Owen, PD Owen, PG Owen, RD Owen, RJ Owen, AR Owens, FJ Owens, G Owens, GA Owens, GC Owens, GV Owens, JA Owens, JW Owens, LA Owens, MP Owens, NA Owens, P Owens, PG Owens, RA Owens, RJ Owens, RK Owens, RL Owens, JF Oxenham, JM Oxenham, SM Oxenham, RE Oxer, TD Oxford, PHG Oxley, RW Oxley, AL Oxnam, TR Oxnam, H Ozga, U Ozolins, YR Ozolins, U Pabriks, IF Pacey, RJ Pacey, RM Pack, RL Packenham, AL Packer, CA Packham, G Packham, JR Packington, BJ Paddick, TA Paddison, NR Paddle, RB Paddon, RG Paddon, RL Paddon-Jones, KR Padey, DR Padley, DJ Padovan, KW Paech, RE Paech, AC Page, AJ Page, BE Page, BW Page, CO Page, DB Page, DC Page, DJ Page, DR Page, EJ Page, FEK Page, GAG Page, IL Page, JN Page, KM Page, MA Page, MR Page, OG Page, OH Page, PF Page, PJ Page, RI Page, RJ Page, RR Page, RS Page, RW Page, SB Page, TE Page, TJ Page, VJ Page, WJ Page, JRP Paget, LK Paget, TJ Paget, G Paiano, RG Paice, AJ Paillas, WA Pain, DW Paine, ML Paine, NR Paine, RJ Paine, J Painter, MJ Painter, RJ Painter, VW Painting, BW Paisley, NA Paisley, DB Paix, R Paix, RG Pajuk, DE Pakes, RF Palachicky, JP Palermo, EJ Paleske, IC Palfery, BJ Palfrey, RH Palin, RJ Pallane, PE Pallant, FR Pallas, AT Pallett, GS Palling, BM Palm, GE Palm, KD Palm, RP Palm, KW Palmen, AB Palmer, AW Palmer, BW Palmer, CB Palmer, CV Palmer, DE Palmer, DG Palmer, DJ Palmer, DM Palmer, DS Palmer, EE Palmer, EK Palmer, EW Palmer, FE Palmer, FR Palmer, GR Palmer, I Palmer, IC Palmer, IJ Palmer, JD Palmer, KJ Palmer, KR Palmer, LJ Palmer, MA Palmer, NG Palmer, NP Palmer, RH Palmer, RJ Palmer, RL Palmer, SE Palmer, W Palmer, WG Palmer, WT Palmer, EM Palozzo, GF Paltridge, DM Pammenter, H Pamula, S Pamula, J Panagaris, S Panarello, J Pandel, A Pandeli, MS Pandelus, J Panetta, MI Pang, B Panic, IG Pankhurst, RJ Pankhurst, SA Pankowski, DD Pannach, BW Pannell, RM Pannell, M Pannowitz, EJ Pannuzzo, H Panossian, DV Panozzo, DR Pantall, WJ Pantall, L Pantalone, AGG Pante, BS Panting, JM Panton, P Paola, J Papadopoulos, JC Papandreas, C Papasergio, RM Papps, BW Papworth, FD Papworth, GS Papworth, RL Paramor, JH Parcell, BD Parchert, KJP Pardella, AE Parfitt, CE Parfitt, LL Parfitt, MA Parfrey, MH Paris, GC Parish, KD Parish, FJ Parisio, RM Parison, DR Park, GW Park, KE Park, MH Park, MW Park, AC Parke, GH Parke, LA Parke, AE Parker, AH Parker, AJ Parker, AN Parker, AR Parker, AT Parker, AW Parker, BA Parker, BE Parker, BL Parker, C Parker, CN Parker, CR Parker, DF Parker, DG Parker, EA Parker, FE Parker, FG Parker, FM Parker, FWC Parker, GA Parker, GB Parker, GE Parker, GJ Parker, GM Parker, GR Parker, GT Parker, GW Parker, IG Parker, IH Parker, JC Parker, JD Parker, JV Parker, KJ Parker, LE Parker, LJ Parker, LS Parker, M Parker, N Parker, NJ Parker, NR Parker, PF Parker, R Parker, RA Parker, RH Parker, RHJ Parker, RJ Parker, RK Parker, RM Parker, RTR Parker, RW Parker, SJ Parker, TJ Parker, VW Parker, WE Parker, WF Parker, WJ Parker, WL Parker, WR Parker, AT Parkes, IW Parkes, JP Parkes, KB Parkes, KR Parkes, NS Parkes, WJ Parkes, CF Parkey, WA Parkey, BR Parkin, CL Parkin, V Parkin, WR Parkin, JH Parkins, DR Parkinson, E Parkinson, F Parkinson, J Parkinson, JD Parkinson, JS Parkinson, KT Parkinson, RD Parkinson, GR Parks, LD Parks, GR Parkyn, RC Parkyns, JA Parlett, RW Parlor, JA Parmenter, LJ Parmenter, MA Parmenter, GA Parnaby, BJ Parnell, LR Parnell, AJ Parr, AL Parr, JA Parr, RG Parr, BS Parratt, AR Parrelli, A Parrello, JT Parrington, PJ Parrish, DN Parrot, CA Parrott, KH Parrott, TC Parrott, TH Parrott, AR Parry, EE Parry, JD Parry, RJ Parry, RN Parry, SJ Parry, WO Parry, ERC Parsell, RS Parsissons, BE Parslow, LJ Parslow, T Parslow, PC Parsonage, BW Parsons, CL Parsons, EJ Parsons, G Parsons, GJ Parsons, GL Parsons, IJ Parsons, JC Parsons, JD Parsons, JF Parsons, JG Parsons, JK Parsons, KA Parsons, KP Parsons, LJ Parsons, M Parsons, RD Parsons, RG Parsons, RL Parsons, RW Parsons, W Parth, AJ Partington, CJC Partington, RJ Partis, GR Parton, AK Partridge, BJ Partridge, BV Partridge, CJ Partridge, DJ Partridge, E Partridge, LW Partridge, MH Partridge, MW Partridge, TB Partridge, TR Partridge, HJ Parusel, T Parvin, JA Paschali, AJ Pascoe, FA Pascoe, IKM Pascoe, JL Pascoe, JR Pascoe, JW Pascoe, KW Pascoe, MJ Pascoe, MW Pascoe, NR Pascoe, PJ Pascoe, PR Pascoe, RG Pascoe, RJ Pascoe, RN Pascoe, JE Pashen, GD Pashley, RC Pashley, L Pasini, RJ Pask, JC Paskulich, AJ Pass, J Pass, J Passant, B Passarelli, B Passey, KD Passlow, A Passmore, FD Passmore, G Passmore, JD Passmore, WJ Passmore, JG Pasterczyk, KJ Pata, DF Patch, HE Patch, RC Patch, DW Patchett, JW Patchett, RA Patching, AJ Paten, CJ Patena, AR Paterson, D Paterson, DE Paterson, GJ Paterson, GP Paterson, I Paterson, ID Paterson, JD Paterson, JJ Paterson, JWO Paterson, KA Paterson, LJ Paterson, RC Paterson, RJ Paterson, SF Paterson, WH Paterson, RJ Patison, PR Patmore, TC Patmore, BW Paton, E Paton, GI Paton, GP Paton, IH Paton, JR Paton, MJ Paton, RD Paton, R Patray, DR Patrick, GC Patrick, JW Patrick, NW Patrick, GW Patroney, RB Patten, BJ Patterson, D Patterson, DD Patterson, DM Patterson, ER Patterson, G Patterson, GR Patterson, HP Patterson, IJ Patterson, IR Patterson, IS Patterson, JP Patterson, JP Patterson, JT Patterson, KA Patterson, KJ Patterson, KR Patterson, LA Patterson, M Patterson, MJ Patterson, RL Patterson, RS Patterson, RW Patterson, SE Patterson, SJ Patterson, WD Patterson, AD Pattinson, NE Pattinson, AG Pattison, BJ Pattison, DJ Pattison, PA Pattison, RR Pattison, RS Pattison, DR Pattle, GA Pattle, KA Pattle, LJ Pattle, RN Patton, RW Patton, RW Pattrick, VP Patty, GB Patzel, AW Paul, DBC Paul, DF Paul, JM Paul, KJ Paul, MR Paul, OJ Paul, RB Paul, RL Paul, VG Paul, VJ Paul, WA Paul, W Paulette, EJ Paulin, RA Pauline, IC Paull, JG Paull, JR Paull, KF Paull, KH Paull, KM Paull, MAF Paull, KR Paulsen, WO Paulsen, KW Pauly, P Paunovic, DJ Pausic, RG Pauwels, I Pauza, LJ Pavan, E Pavey, L Pavich, PJ Pavlenko, A Pavlovich, A Pavone, H Pawczynski, BI Pawley, A Pawloff, G Pawloff, M Pawluk, RF Pawson, BJ Paxton, CD Paxton, DJ Paxton, GE Paxton, NI Paxton, RJ Paxton, BC Payne, BH Payne, BK Payne, DJ Payne, DJL Payne, GD Payne, GR Payne, IG Payne, JG Payne, JJ Payne, JR Payne, K Payne, KJ Payne, L Payne, LM Payne, MC Payne, MG Payne, NJ Payne, PL Payne, PT Payne, RB Payne, RC Payne, RF Payne, RLC Payne, RR Payne, RW Payne, SH Payne, TJ Payne, TM Payne, TR Payne, WD Payne, WF Payne, AR Paynter, EJ Paynter, ID Paynter, JA Paynting, GA Payze, J Pazzan, GW Peace, FS Peach, IA Peach, JA Peach, RW Peach, ID Peachey, J Peachey, PJ Peachey, BC Peacock, CJG Peacock, FR Peacock, GR Peacock, JW Peacock, KL Peacock, LAC Peacock, MJ Peacock, NJ Peacock, NS Peacock, R Peacock, RM Peacock, TA Peacock, BS Peak, DJ Peak, GJ Peake, G Peaker, AB Pearce, AJ Pearce, AK Pearce, AW Pearce, BD Pearce, BP Pearce, BW Pearce, CB Pearce, CJ Pearce, CN Pearce, D Pearce, DA Pearce, DG Pearce, DJ Pearce, FW Pearce, GB Pearce, GC Pearce, GG Pearce, GN Pearce, J Pearce, JC Pearce, JD Pearce, JGS Pearce, JN Pearce, JW Pearce, KL Pearce, LB Pearce, LJ Pearce, M Pearce, ME Pearce, MJ Pearce, MM Pearce, P Pearce, PC Pearce, RC Pearce, RF Pearce, RJ Pearce, RR Pearce, RW Pearce, SB Pearce, SH Pearce, TJ Pearce, TM Pearce, TN Pearce, WJ Pearce, WR Pearce, CE Pearcey, MK Peard, AJ Pearman, RJ Pearman, SR Pearman, JH Pearn, CJ Pearsall, SJ Pearsall, AK Pearse, BW Pearse, DG Pearse, JW Pearse, RT Pearse, AM Pearson, BG Pearson, CG Pearson, CMI Pearson, DA Pearson, EC Pearson, EG Pearson, FR Pearson, G Pearson, GH Pearson, HJ Pearson, JA Pearson, JE Pearson, JH Pearson, JR Pearson, K Pearson, KF Pearson, LE Pearson, MC Pearson, PJ Pearson, R Pearson, RC Pearson, RE Pearson, RF Pearson, RJ Pearson, RK Pearson, RL Pearson, SK Pearson, TJ Pearson, W Pearson, WE Pearson, WF Pearson, WG Pearson, WJ Pearson, WJ Pearton, RR Pease, WF Peasey, AM Peat, J Peat, NC Peate, RB Peate, J Peatfield, KW Peatling, NB Peatling, AS Peattie, GA Peattie, JD Peattie, PM Pecic, AP Peck, GD Peck, GK Peck, JS Peck, MC Peck, NJ Peck, RW Peck, SE Peck, B Peckitt, RR Peckman, RL Peddell, AL Pedder, JF Pedder, MJ Pedder, PB Peddie, PJ Peddie, DA Peden, T Peden, JF Pedersen, JK Pedersen, NEA Pedersen, GT Pederson, MJ Pederson, JT Pedler, NJ Pedler, RG Pedler, LJ Pedrana, BJ Pedrazzoli, CR Pedron, JC Peebles, RH Peebles, JD Peek, KM Peek, DR Peel, DW Peel, ER Peel, GA Peel, JR Peel, LM Peel, RD Peele, AJ Peers, WF Peet, WJ Peeters, RC Pefferini, DI Pegg, JG Pegg, RJ Pegg, PB Pegler, JR Peile, BJ Peillon, NS Peirce, PC Peirce, A Peisley, DW Peisley, KJ Peisley, SJ Pelchen, CN Pelham, DP Pelham, RW Pelham, G Pelich, RF Pell, RM Pell, TS Pell, NB Pelling, WR Pelling, DJ Pelly, GH Pember, KR Pember, KS Pember, BM Pemberton, SA Pemberton, BG Pender, CW Pender, FP Pendergast, JH Pendergast, TPP Pendergast, ER Pendergrast, GD Pendle, LA Pendlebury, AE Penfold, AR Penfold, FW Penfold, JC Penfold, GN Pengelly, BM Pengilly, CB Pengilly, RL Pengilly, JD Penglase, SN Penhaligon, RR Penhall, RJ Penington, JW Peninton, DW Penley, D Penman, DJ Penman, GF Penman, RJ Penman, AJ Penn, DH Penn, R Penna, DW Pennay, MG Pennay, AR Pennell, VJ Pennell, BL Penney, PL Penneyston, BA Pennicott, JE Penning, HAJ Pennings, AV Pennington, PJ Penno, BG Penny, BL Penny, RJ Penny, SB Penny, SJ Penny, RG Pennycook, TK Penrose, IR Pentecost, EL Pentony, CR Penver, RM Peoples, CB Pepper, DN Pepper, FG Pepper, JA Pepper, JE Pepper, JM Pepperdine, KC Perandis, RV Perandis, FJ Perceval, KR Perceval, R Perceval, LA Percey, BEH Percival, CR Percival, DH Percival, HN Percival, RD Percival, WB Percival, AR Percsi, CE Percy, KJ Percy, RT Percy, KJ Pereira, AG Perejuan, RH Perfect, RA Perfrement, DW Perger, J Perger, FJ Pergunas, DK Perham, EC Perham, FA Perina, RE Perkin, BR Perkins, D Perkins, DA Perkins, DC Perkins, DH Perkins, GC Perkins, GT Perkins, JE Perkins, JR Perkins, KC Perkins, NC Perkins, PA Perkins, R Perkins, RE Perkins, TG Perkins, TW Perkins, BL Perks, GB Perks, RG Perks, TJ Perks, PL Perman, V Perna, PJ Pernarowski, RG Peronchik, BR Perosin, GA Perren, TL Perren, DP Perrett, JE Perrett, PJ Perrett, RJ Perrett, V Perri, AB Perriman, KJ Perriman, CR Perrin, GD Perrin, GR Perrin, NC Perrin, PM Perrin, RG Perrin, TW Perrin, RF Perring, G Perrins, WH Perro, KW Perrow, AC Perry, CR Perry, DI Perry, DJ Perry, DL Perry, DS Perry, F Perry, FJ Perry, GC Perry, GDH Perry, GF Perry, I Perry, JA Perry, JD Perry, K Perry, KA Perry, KC Perry, KTN Perry, KW Perry, NH Perry, NJ Perry, NR Perry, PA Perry, PR Perry, PW Perry, RD Perry, RG Perry, RJ Perry, RR Perry, RW Perry, SJ Perry, SL Perry, AM Person, RR Pert, JP Pertini, AJ Perussich, W Pervan, CR Pervical, HA Peschke, PW Pescud, TI Pescud, V Pesic, TE Pesonen, RK Petch, HI Petchell, A Peters, AV Peters, BJ Peters, BL Peters, CC Peters, CM Peters, DF Peters, DJ Peters, GE Peters, GM Peters, HF Peters, JA Peters, JC Peters, JD Peters, JE Peters, JR Peters, LG Peters, LJ Peters, LO Peters, ML Peters, NG Peters, NM Peters, NR Peters, PF Peters, RW Peters, TA Peters, TJ Peters, WH Peters, WK Peters, AB Petersen, AC Petersen, AJ Petersen, AT Petersen, BH Petersen, BO Petersen, CJ Petersen, DA Petersen, DJ Petersen, FJ Petersen, GL Petersen, GR Petersen, GW Petersen, JC Petersen, KG Petersen, KJ Petersen, P Petersen, RB Petersen, VN Petersen, U Petersohn, BJ Peterson, CE Peterson, CR Peterson, FJ Peterson, GH Peterson, JA Peterson, L Peterson, PJ Peterson, RJ Peterson, RK Peterswald, GW Petfield, KD Petfield, IJ Petherick, PJ Petherick, BK Petherick-Collins, MDK Petherick-Collins, DH Petkovich, PP Petraitis, WD Petrass, GA Petrie, JD Petrie, KA Petrie, RL Petrie, TJ Petrie, PJ Petrovic, S Petrovic, A Petrovich, JF Petteit, KA Petteit, KW Pettersen, DB Petterwood, RA Pettet, DJ Pettifer, CJ Pettifor, PH Pettiford, JM Pettigrove, MG Pettingill, OR Pettingill, RK Pettingill, J Pettit, JG Pettit, LJ Pettit, RG Pettit, RK Pettit, GW Pettitt, NC Pettitt, AJ Pettman, MJ Petty, RA Petty, RL Petty, IGM Peut, NJ Peut, N Peverett, P Pezet, V Pezzano, H Pfaller, PA Pfeffer, AE Pfeiffer, EP Pfeiffer, RM Pfeiffer, MR Pfennig, CH Pfitzner, EF Pfitzner, BG Pflugradt, DN Pfundt, GR Phair, R Phair, GD Phegan, BV Phelan, GT Phelan, KJ Phelan, NJ Phelan, PA Phelan, PW Phelan, B Phelps, IK Phelps, LD Phelps, TL Phelps, AK Phenna, WD Phie, ER Philip, J Philip, KD Philip, RJ Philip, SJ Philip, P Philippou, MJ Philipps, JW Philipson, SR Philipson, Z Phillip, A Phillips, AC Phillips, AEM Phillips, AG Phillips, AJ Phillips, AS Phillips, AT Phillips, BJ Phillips,

BM Phillips, CA Phillips, CR Phillips, CW Phillips, D Phillips, DB Phillips, DJ Phillips, DL Phillips, DN Phillips, DS Phillips, DW Phillips, E Phillips, EL Phillips, FA Phillips, FW Phillips, GC Phillips, GD Phillips, GJ Phillips, GL Phillips, GM Phillips, GP Phillips, GR Phillips, GS Phillips, IC Phillips, IW Phillips, J Phillips, JA Phillips, JD Phillips, JG Phillips, JH Phillips, JJ Phillips, JLL Phillips, JM Phillips, JR Phillips, JW Phillips, KR Phillips, LC Phillips, LG Phillips, LR Phillips, LU Phillips, LW Phillips, M Phillips, MJ Phillips, ML Phillips, NA Phillips, NG Phillips, NR Phillips, PJ Phillips, PM Phillips, PR Phillips, RA Phillips, RD Phillips, RDP Phillips, RG Phillips, RJ Phillips, RK Phillips, RL Phillips, RM Phillips, SA Phillips, SG Phillips, SJ Phillips, TD Phillips, TJ Phillips, TP Phillips, TR Phillips, WG Phillips, WM Phillips, JL Phillis, M Phillis, CT Phillmore, PH Phillpotts, AJ Philp, BJ Philp, BN Philp, DA Philp, GJ Philp, JC Philp, JE Philp, KD Philp, MR Philp, RG Philp, BE Philpot, D Philpott, PHC Philpott, RG Philps, RT Philps, KR Phipps, JG Phoenix, MJ Phoenix, CA Physick, CV Piazza, V Pica, JI Pick, RA Pick, DR Pickard, BS Picken, GH Picken, BH Picker, AB Pickering, AF Pickering, CD Pickering, CF Pickering, DW Pickering, GA Pickering, GC Pickering, GW Pickering, IG Pickering, JE Pickering, JEG Pickering, LG Pickering, MA Pickering, MJ Pickering, HR Pickers, C Pickett, JC Pickett, LW Pickette, WJ Pickford, D Pickstock, H Pickvance, D Picone, JR Picton, DJ Pidgeon, JC Pidgeon, RJ Pidgeon, DM Pie, E Pieber, R Piefke, J Piening, GJ Pieper, GJ Pierce, KR Pierce, PG Pierce, RJ Pierce, RW Pierce, SN Pierce, RJ Piercey, D Piercy, WL Piercy, RE Pierse, RD Pierssene, U Pierucci, J Pietruszka, JA Pietzner, TH Pietzner, CD Piffero, GW Pigdon, RW Pigdon, DC Piggott, DR Piggott, IJ Pignat, MV Pignatelli, JE Pigott, EJ Pigram, KJ Pigram, WR Pigram, AW Pike, GA Pike, GRB Pike, IR Pike, RA Pike, WA Pike, B Pilat, BK Pilbeam, JF Pilbeam, VJ Pilch, JC Pilcher, JD Pilcher, TC Pilcher, AK Pile, GG Pile, JD Pile, DM Pilgrim, FD Pilkington, J Pilkington, JP Pilkington, JV Pilkington, KA Pilkington, R Pilkington, WJ Pilkington, LE Pill, AB Pilling, E Pilling, T Pilmore, R Pilon, DW Piltz, GC Piltz, DL Pimm, LR Pinch, NA Pinch, WE Pinch, BJ Pinchin, RP Pincott, CP Pinder, JN Pine, MF Pine, PD Pine, EF Pines, BW Ping Kee, DP Pini, RJ Pink, MJ Pinkard, IR Pinker, FV Pinkerton, RG Pinkerton, RJ Pinkerton, NR Pinkham, GJ Pinkus, MD Pinkus, V Pinnell, BJ Pinner, SL Pinney, CR Pinnington, RG Pinnington, RB Pinnow, NW Pinnuck, EP Pinoli, DW Pinson, TM Pinter, SG Pinwill, JP Pioli, AT Piorkowski, P Pioro, FT Piotrowski, A Piper, BC Piper, GD Piper, GE Piper, GW Piper, J Piper, M Piper, RH Piper, RK Piper, RP Piper, WA Piper, BJ Pippen, MG Pippet, EJ Pirani, GM Pires, DG Pirie, P Piromanski, JJ Pirt, G Pisani, J Piscopo, V Pistilli, JR Pitcher, MW Pitcher, WC Pitcher, PW Pitchers, G Pitchford, IC Pitchford, TD Pitham, CM Pitkin, PR Pitkin, RA Pitman, W Pitman, DJ Pitstock, PW Pitstock, AL Pitt, BG Pitt, BK Pitt, CN Pitt, GN Pitt, IS Pitt, RD Pitt, SJ Pitt, AM Pittendreigh, H Pittendreigh, RL Pittman, FP Pittorino, KW Pitts, OM Pitts, RJ Pitts, VG Pitts, PJ Pizimolas, IR Pizzey, RJ Pizzoni, DN Place, EL Place, IG Place, G Placek, H Plachenczenko, DB Plain, RCG Plain, R Plaizier, BJ Plane, AC Plant, AJ Plant, BW Plant, JR Plant, TJ Plant, JN Plapp, SE Plater, AJ Platt, DB Platt, EG Platt, KJ Platt, BD Platts, RR Player, BA Playford, TD Pleace, JJ Pleasance, RJ Pleash, JW Plenty, LR Plester, A Plevier, KD Plew, B Plichota, LO Plim, WG Plint, AD Ploenges, JN Ploenges, JW Ploenges, R Ploszczynski, GC Plowes, G Plowman, J Plowman, LR Plowright, KH Pluck, CR Plumb, KT Plumb, LR Plumb, BF Plummer, CHD Plummer, KA Plummer, RJ Plummer, E Plumridge, GM Plumridge, JD Plumridge, AP Plunkett, CBE Plunkett, GR Plunkett, LB Plunkett, MO Plunkett, PA Pobar, DW Pobje, RM Pobke, WE Pockett, F Poczyhajlo, V Podesta, B Podgorski, DL Podlich, EJ Podlich, KG Podolski, RW Podstawka, GL Pohlner, JB Poiesz, RJ Pointon, BJ Poirrier, RF Poirrier, DA Poke, DR Poke, RB Poke, PJ Pola, RR Polack, JA Poland, DH Polden, RW Poldoja, JC Pole, JW Poletti, RG Poletti, JI Polfanders, GR Polglase, PWJ Polglase, HP Polis, ND Politsch, GM Polkinghorne, JK Polkinghorne, KB Polkinghorne, MT Polkinghorne, PW Polkinghorne, WE Pollack, AB Pollard, BJ Pollard, CG Pollard, CTW Pollard, DW Pollard, GM Pollard, JJ Pollard, LJ Pollard, ME Pollard, MJ Pollard, RJ Pollard, RL Pollard, TR Pollard, WJ Pollard, F Poller, RJ Pollett, KH Polley, RG Polley, JT Pollitt, AJ Pollock, BJ Pollock, BL Pollock, DL Pollock, G Pollock, GD Pollock, JG Pollock, JM Pollock, LR Pollock, RG Pollock, SM Pollock, W Pollock, AK Polotnianka, GA Polson, HA Polson, SJ Polucha, CR Polzin, LM Pomeroy, RW Pomeroy, D Pomery, M Pomfret, VI Pomroy, RJ Pond, TJ Pond, PR Pono, BA Ponsford, P Pont, H Pontaks, GG Pontin, BJ Ponting, DL Ponting, FW Ponting, RJ Ponting, T Ponton, AC Pool, ML Pool, PJ Pool, AJ Poole, BG Poole, BJ Poole, BL Poole, D Poole, DI Poole, FS Poole, GH Poole, MD Poole, MJ Poole, PH Poole, RJ Poole, SG Poole, SK Poole, AS Poolericketts, KG Pooles, DJ Poolier, KW Poore, AA Pope, AE Pope, BB Pope, BJ Pope, CA Pope, CT Pope, DK Pope, E Pope, EE Pope, GS Pope, GW Pope, H Pope, IS Pope, JK Pope, ND Pope, RA Pope, RJ Pope, RL Pope, TN Pope, P Popovic, UB Popovic, MJ Popp, WT Poppell, RJ Popperwell, RA Popple, J Popplewell, DI Porch, S Pors, PJ Porta, RJ Portbury, PJL Portell, J Portelli, DC Porteous, IG Porteous, IM Porteous, A Porter, BK Porter, BL Porter, BS Porter, EJ Porter, GJ Porter, IC Porter, JA Porter, JE Porter, JW Porter, LE Porter, LW Porter, MF Porter, MR Porter, NW Porter, RA Porter, RH Porter, RJ Porter, RK Porter, RT Porter, RV Porter, SM Porter, TC Porter, TH Porter, TJ Porter, WJ Porter, BL Portlock, R Portlock, RE Portlock, GA Portolesi, J Porublev, PR Posener, PB Post, RM Post, RP Post, TS Post, J Postema, MJ Postle, BJ Postlethwaite, JP Postol, MH Potbury, RC Pothof, RO Potiuch, P Potocnik, D Potonides, AE Pott, A Potter, AD Potter, BJ Potter, C Potter, DB Potter, DR Potter, ER Potter, JA Potter, JE Potter, JJ Potter, LG Potter, LR Potter, NJ Potter, PC Potter, PJ Potter, RF Potter, TD Potter, DM Potts, GA Potts, GD Potts, GJ Potts, LD Potts, LK Potts, B Poucki, PA Poulsom, D Poulson, GV Poulson, RH Poulson, BE Poulter, JN Poulter, SN Poulter, EW Poultney, AB Poulton, AG Poulton, CS Poulton, DJ Poulton, PJ Poulton, TW Poulton, GG Pound, AR Pounds, DA Pounsett, KR Pountney, MJ Poustie, RJ Poustie, AM Pout, T Poutakidis, A Povey, DK Povey, LT Povey, TM Pow, PD Powditch, JH Powe, AE Powell, AN Powell, DG Powell, DJ Powell, DT Powell, EA Powell, GE Powell, GT Powell, JA Powell, JE Powell, JF Powell, JG Powell, JR Powell, LJ Powell, MJ Powell, MR Powell, NS Powell, PR Powell, RJ Powell, RL Powell, RMB Powell, RN Powell, SC Powell, TE Powell, VC Powell, ANW Power, AW Power, BJ Power, BW Power, DA Power, DJ Power, EC Power, GG Power, GJ Power, HV Power, IS Power, JC Power, JD Power, JK Power, JP Power, KR Power, LA Power, LJ Power, LJH Power, PA Power, PF Power, RA Power, RE Power, RF Power, RG Power, RL Power, RN Power, RW Power, SH Power, VJ Power, WJ Power, EA Powers, JE Powers, M Powers, K Powick, LF Powning, AJ Powter, DR Powter, BD Poyner, DR Poyner, RA Poynting, AD Poynton, DM Poynton, CL Poyser, M Pozzuto, NA Pracy, HC Prager, RR Prager, AV Pragnell, JH Prance, JP Pranevicius, JO Prasser, SJ Prasser, JP Prat, R Prater, AP Pratt, AW Pratt, GA Pratt, GJ Pratt, GR Pratt, GS Pratt, KA Pratt, KL Pratt, MC Pratt, PJ Pratt, R Pratt, RA Pratt, RD Pratt, RJ Pratt, RW Pratt, JW Pratten, TA Prattis, JS Prebble, GL Precians, RH Preddice, AV Preece, RF Preece, GW Prendergast, LG Prendergast, LJ Prendergast, MN Prendergast, P Prendergast, S Prendergast, WD Prenter, AJ Prentice, JA Prentice, RA Prentice, B Presbury, KA Presbury, NR Presbury, RG Presbury, LM Prescott, AD Presgrave, DC Presgrave, JF Press, RW Presswell, RD Prestage, B Prestidge, AT Preston, BC Preston, DC Preston, DK Preston, EJ Preston, G Preston, JE Preston, LJ Preston, PA Preston, PJ Preston, PW Preston, RA Preston, RR Preston, SC Prestwidge, GJ Pretty, WJ Pretty, KJ Prevost, IC Prewett, PJC Prewett, AA Price, AG Price, AR Price, BC Price, BF Price, BW Price, C Price, CA Price, DC Price, DJ Price, DR Price, FC Price, FJF Price, GR Price, HTS Price, IS Price, JR Price, KN Price, MJ Price, NT Price, PJ Price, PM Price, RD Price, RF Price, RJ Price, CR Prickett, MD Prickett, MJ Priday, RG Pride, RE Prideaux, GR Prider, BJ Pridgeon, DC Pridmore, ESD Pridmore, RW Pridmore, DH Priebbenow, P Priede, LA Priems, PJ Priems, AM Priest, BD Priest, CR Priest, ER Priest, FG Priest, L Priest, ME Priest, MJ Priest, RG Priest, TJ Priest, JC Priestland, WT Priestland, DJ Priestley, EL Priestley, JH Priestley, RC Priestley, GW Priestly, RF Prigg, R Prime, EK Prince, FA Prince, JA Prince, JC Prince, JR Prince, SJ Prince, AJ Prindable, DC Pring, BE Pringle, DW Pringle, BW Printer, JD Printz, BA Prior, BJ Prior, CR Prior, KJ Prior, MJ Prior, ML Prior, MT Prior, PW Prior, RA Prior, RE Prior, RG Prior, RJ Prior, SR Prior, WW Prior, DA Pritchard, FW Pritchard, JC Pritchard, JH Pritchard, JW Pritchard, KJ Pritchard, MA Pritchard, NA Pritchard, PHB Pritchard, RE Pritchard, RG Pritchard, RM Pritchard, T Pritchard, GR Privett, DJ Prizeman, AF Probert, JK Probert, RT Probert, D Probst, V Procko, DS Procopis, BG Proctor, C Proctor, DE Proctor, JR Proctor, JW Proctor, R Proctor, G Proellocks, DL Proh, JW Pronk, TJ Properjohn, N Proskurin, BM Prosper, HL Prosser, MB Prosser, MC Prosser, PJ Prosser, RF Prosser, RT Prosser, TE Prosser, AJ Proud, DL Proud, KR Proud, L Proud, WJ Proud, TJ Proudfoot, WJ Proudfoot, BJ Proudlove, R Prouse, RL Prout, TR Provis, GJ Prowd, IR Prowse, JM Prowse, L Prowse, PR Prowse, R Prowse, TA Prowse, WR Prowse, A Pruckner, RJ Pryce, MB Pryce-Jones, AE Pryde, HD Pryde, J Pryde, KD Pryde, TW Pryer, RA Pryke, AJ Pryor, RK Pryor, GJ Prys, Z Przedworski, EA Przeradzki, RE Przewloka, N Psomadellis, HS Puckeridge, MR Puckey, RA Puddy, B Pudney, TW Pudney, C Pugh, KG Pugh, LB Pugh, OJ Puie, LS Pukallus, GC Pulford, AJ Puli, J Pulis, PAJ Pulis, NA Pullan, DC Pullar, GD Pullar, RJ Pullar, AR Pullen, LE Pullen, PH Pullen, RJ Pullen, WD Pullen, GW Pullin, RC Pullinger, TJ Pullinger, RG Pullman, GN Pumpa, AL Punch, MD Punch, LM Punshon, S Pupillo, AT Purcell, CJ Purcell, CW Purcell, DN Purcell, JD Purcell, LJ Purcell, MW Purcell, NR Purcell, PFJ Purcell, RE Purcell, RF Purcell, AG Purchase, WA Purchase, AM Purdie, BJ Purdie, KG Purdie, LG Purdie, SW Purdie, JB Purdon, KF Purdon, PL Purdon, TG Purdue, JM Purkis, NE Purkis, R Purnell, GA Pursell, RJ Pursell, BN Purser, JT Purser, EJ Purtell, LW Purton, RA Purton, VH Purton, CG Purvey, AJ Purvis, DW Purvis, JAF Purvis, M Pustelnik, FJ Putland, LR Putt, NW Puttick, CA Puttman, WA Pybus, BI Pye, DE Pye, DI Pye, DJ Pye, DT Pye, JA Pye, JC Pye, JR Pye, NGH Pye, RL Pye, TK Pye, TM Pye, G Pyerin, JK Pyers, EJ Pyke, PK Pyke, AD Pyle, GW Pyle, AR Pym, DA Pym, LR Pyne, RR Pyne, PG Pynn, GA Quail, DH Quaile, X Quain, IH Quake, JH Quane, JR Quantrill, PD Quarmby, BE Quarrell, NH Quarrell, RG Quarrell, GS Quarry, BG Quartermaine, EL Quartermaine, ES Quartermaine, WG Quass, EJ Quatermass, AF Quattromani, A Quayle, GI Quayle, LJ Queale, MV Quealy, BM Quee, GL Quelch, WA Quenault, DC Quick, DH Quick, DR Quick, JH Quick, KL Quick, IR Quigg, RL Quigg, SV Quigg, AV Quigley, D Quigley, NJ Quigley, JR Quilford, GM Quilkey, KR Quilkey, JA Quilty, AW Quin, BA Quin, NK Quince, JH Quincey, GR Quinlan, MJ Quinlan, PJ Quinlan, AD Quinn, AM Quinn, BC Quinn, CJ Quinn, D Quinn, DJ Quinn, DN Quinn, GM Quinn, GP Quinn, JA Quinn, JJ Quinn, KA Quinn, M Quinn, PD Quinn, PF Quinn, PJ Quinn, PM Quinn, RG Quinn, SR Quinn, TB Quinn, VS Quinn, KP Quinnell, GN Quint, DM Quinto, GM Quinton, A Quintrell, DA Quirk, RD Quirk, TW Quirk, WG Quirk, KE Quirke, AM Raabe, J Raasch, DA Rabbitt, RA Rabbitt, JC Raby, ME Raby, AR Racca, SM Rackley, TE Rackley, RA Rackliff, K Racman, GE Radburn, AD Radcliffe, PR Radcliffe, R Radcliffe, RJ Raddatz, FR Radford, IA Radford, JM Radford, LT Radford, PD Radford, PJ Radford, RD Radford, RF Radford, RG Radford, RM Radford, OW Radke, EJ Radley, P Radmilowich, SE Radomi, SN Radovich, MJ Radtke, ZI Radvanyi, MJ Radwell, APP Rae, BA Rae, BW Rae, DL Rae, GW Rae, IL Rae, PJ Rae, RG Rae, SE Rae, T Rae, PJ Raffan, FL Raffen, H Rafferty, IM Rafferty, JR Raftery, LJ Raftery, TM Raftery, AG Ragg, MVJ Ragg, WV Raggatt, W Rahe, RBJ Railton, GD Rainbird, PC Raine, RD Raine, DC Rainer, R Raines, BF Rainey, BJ Rainey, GD Rainey, MR Rainey, NG Rains, PG Rainsbury, BG Rainsford, KC Raison, LR Raison, J Raistrick, JG Raitt, J Rak, LJ Rake, EJ Rakowski, BP Raleigh, AJ Ralph, BE Ralph, DF Ralph, GJ Ralph, LD Ralph, M Ralph, MJP Ralph, T Ralph, EH Ralphs, GR Ralston, IR Ramadge, J Ramadon, SA Ramage, HG Ramalli, GL Ramm, G Ramma, MA Ramplin, HAF Ramsauer, BJ Ramsay, DJ Ramsay, DS Ramsay, IR Ramsay, JS Ramsay, KM Ramsay, KS Ramsay, MR Ramsay, NR Ramsay, PG Ramsay, RG Ramsay, RK Ramsay, RN Ramsay, RV Ramsay, TB Ramsay, WJ Ramsay, DS Ramsdale, KG Ramsdale, KW Ramsdale, EC Ramsden, GJ Ramsden, JR Ramsden, RE Ramsey, FT Rana, RL Rand, AD Randall, CJ Randall, DJ Randall, GJ Randall, JC Randall, MGP Randall, NR Randall, PR Randall, RF Randall, RJ Randall, SJ Randall, DG Randall-Smith, AJ Randell, DE Randell, RW Randell, DA Randle, RW Randle, PJ Randolph, JM Rands,

DC Ranford, PM Ranford, DJ Range, GR Ranger, JC Ranger, WT Ranger, K Ranginui, BT Rankin, JF Rankin, NJ Rankin, NW Rankin, TJ Rankin, WW Rankin, D Rankine, BG Ranking, T Rankovic, GR Ransom, PJ Ransom, AJ Ransome, GN Ransome, LA Ransome, BF Ranson, CA Ranson, GH Ranson, JE Ranson, N Rant, AF Rantall, AR Ranyard, RB Raper, BD Rapley, KG Rapley, RC Rapley, JR Rapp, EC Rashleigh, ET Rashleigh, GV Rashleigh, E Rasmussen, IT Rasmussen, JT Rasmussen, MJ Rasmussen, S Rasmussen, V Raspanti, PN Rastall, O Ratajczek, DJ Ratcliff, PS Ratcliff, FJ Ratcliffe, JA Ratcliffe, KA Ratcliffe, RJ Rathjen, MJ Rathmell, GA Ratjens, SR Rattery, PA Rattley, DJ Rattray, PJ Rattray, P Ravelje, AB Raven, GG Ravenscroft, HB Ravenscroft, RB Ravenscroft, RG Ravensdale, PD Rawling, WJ Rawling, GJ Rawlings, HD Rawlings, D Rawlins, JB Rawlins, LJ Rawlins, SH Rawlins, GD Rawlinson, K Rawnsley, LA Rawnsley, JH Rawson, AJ Ray, GA Ray, IC Ray, IP Ray, PE Ray, PJ Ray, CJ Rayfield, G Rayfield, NW Rayfield, PR Rayfield, TF Rayfield, MJ Rayment, PS Rayment, BG Raymond, DA Raymond, DP Raymond, DW Raymond, MLJ Raymond, N Raymond, NSJ Raymond, RK Raymond, AMJ Rayner, BA Rayner, BE Rayner, CW Rayner, DE Rayner, DL Rayner, E Rayner, EJL Rayner, GE Rayner, GP Rayner, JW Rayner, KE Rayner, LP Rayner, MB Rayner, PJ Rayner, PW Rayner, RK Rayner, AJ Raynor, KW Rays, RJ Rayward, DA Rea, NH Rea, RA Rea, BC Read, BD Read, BGP Read, BK Read, BPR Read, CD Read, CS Read, DC Read, DG Read, DJ Read, DT Read, G Read, GC Read, JD Read, LM Read, NF Read, PA Read, R Read, RR Read, WG Read, JR Readdy, GS Reading, JF Reading, LL Reading, NG Reading, RG Reading, VE Reading, IM Ready, KJ Reale, AC Reardon, BT Reardon, DA Reardon, DR Reardon, G Reardon, MJ Reardon, MS Reardon, RE Reardon, RJ Reardon, TS Reason, RG Reay, GJ Reberger, CW Rebetzke, L Rechsteiner, LA Reck, CE Reddacliff, WL Reddick, KL Reddicliffe, ID Reddie, WD Reddin, AN Redding, AP Redding, GK Redding, GR Redding, RG Redding, WG Reddrop, GJ Reddy, MS Reddy, F Redenbach, EJ Redfern, JP Redfern, MJ Redfern, K Redford, DG Redgrove, E Redhead, R Redhead, TJ Redhead, JE Redman, JW Redman, KJ Redman, RW Redman, GLD Redmond, GR Redmond, WA Redsell, GR Redshaw, WJ Redshaw, AF Reece, DT Reece, L Reece, AA Reed, AJ Reed, BD Reed, CD Reed, CN Reed, DP Reed, GT Reed, HJ Reed, JG Reed, JP Reed, JV Reed, KBK Reed, PR Reed, R Reed, RC Reed, RW Reed, WD Reed, WT Reed, LE Reeder, B Reeds, AC Reeks, BJ Reeks, GJ Reeman, LG Reeman, MD Reeman, A Rees, AC Rees, BH Rees, DC Rees, DM Rees, EA Rees, HN Rees, JE Rees, KJ Rees, PJ Rees, TR Rees, WAJ Rees, AJ Reeson, GA Reeve, LA Reeve, MJ Reeve, N Reeve, AD Reeves, AF Reeves, AW Reeves, BA Reeves, BG Reeves, CJ Reeves, DA Reeves, JR Reeves, JW Reeves, L Reeves, LS Reeves, NL Reeves, PJ Reeves, RJ Reeves, RT Reeves, RW Reeves, TE Reeves, B Regan, JJ Regan, KM Regan, RT Regan, RV Regan, BJ Regent, P Regent, AL Regnart, WJ Regtop, AJ Rehder, CR Rehn, HH Rehorn, ND Reich, LF Reichle, GC Reichstein, AB Reid, AL Reid, B Reid, BM Reid, BT Reid, C Reid, CD Reid, CS Reid, DJ Reid, DL Reid, DM Reid, DR Reid, FA Reid, GE Reid, GRA Reid, GT Reid, GW Reid, IA Reid, IV Reid, JA Reid, JD Reid, JF Reid, JH Reid, JL Reid, JT Reid, KJ Reid, KL Reid, KS Reid, MJ Reid, ML Reid, NJ Reid, PE Reid, PF Reid, PJ Reid, PM Reid, RF Reid, RJ Reid, RP Reid, RW Reid, SF Reid, SG Reid, TD Reid, TH Reid, TW Reid, WJ Reid, WN Reid, PF Reidy, TG Reidy, WV Reifschneider, AL Reig, BJ Reilly, BR Reilly, DE Reilly, DK Reilly, JR Reilly, JW Reilly, KJ Reilly, KW Reilly, M Reilly, RJ Reilly, EJ Reily, HE Reiman, RK Reimer, WR Reimer, JM Reimers, RW Reimers, TE Reimers, E Reinders, J Reinders, CG Reinertsen, VP Reinhard, DR Reinke, JR Reinke, AJ Reinmuth, TM Reinmuth, GCA Reissig, J Reister, LP Reiter, RM Reith, RN Reith, IB Reither, GJ Rejnowicz, BF Remeeus, A Remeljej, S Remete, SA Remfry, RV Remigio, MW Remin, J Remynse, PH Remynse, JR Renaud, RL Rencher, PL Rendall, JG Rendalls, LC Rendalls, BJ Rendell, GA Rendell, K Rendell, RE Rendell, CF Renehan, AG Renfrey, RM Renfrey, BI Rennard, JR Rennex, B Rennie, DT Rennie, RE Rennie, WK Rennie, DJ Rennison, JA Renowden, MW Renshaw, PM Renshaw, TJ Renshaw, G Rentmeester, BR Renton, DK Renton, JS Renton, LW Renton, RC Renton, RD Renton, K Rentoul, PJ Renwick, PG Renz, BJ Reschke, IB Reschke, PL Reschke, RK Reside, VJ Restuccia, MR Rethamel, RW Retrot, JW Retschlag, DM Rettig, NJ Reus, PA Reus, GD Reuter, AW Revell, JO Revington, CG Rewell, KR Rexter, FK Reynders, AE Reynolds, AH Reynolds, BJ Reynolds, CA Reynolds, CF Reynolds, CJ Reynolds, GC Reynolds, GT Reynolds, J Reynolds, JA Reynolds, JC Reynolds, JR Reynolds, JT Reynolds, KH Reynolds, KR Reynolds, KS Reynolds, L Reynolds, LA Reynolds, LW Reynolds, MC Reynolds, NC Reynolds, NW Reynolds, OC Reynolds, PB Reynolds, PE Reynolds, RK Reynolds, RM Reynolds, SJ Reynolds, TC Reynolds, TM Reynolds, WJ Reynolds, WL Reynolds, WS Reynolds, P Rezek, R Rezek, CR Rhead, JG Rhoden, BJ Rhodes, I Rhodes, JC Rhodes, LJ Rhodes, ML Rhodes, MP Rhodes, NT Rhodes, PG Rhodes, RJ Rhodes, V Rhodes, WM Rhodes, CC Rhook, E Riajansky, BJ Rial, R Ribic, JV Ricardo, AA Rice, BA Rice, CK Rice, DA Rice, DC Rice, DW Rice, JB Rice, JJ Rice, KL Rice, KP Rice, MR Rice, MS Rice, RE Rice, RK Rice, WL Rice, AW Rich, EA Rich, RA Rich, RS Rich, TB Rich, RA Richard, DK Richard-Preston, AE Richards, BJ Richards, BR Richards, BW Richards, CA Richards, CF Richards, CN Richards, DJ Richards, DP Richards, EG Richards, EI Richards, FH Richards, FW Richards, GA Richards, GJ Richards, GK Richards, JC Richards, JR Richards, KA Richards, KJ Richards, KT Richards, KW Richards, LG Richards, LJ Richards, M Richards, MJ Richards, MM Richards, MR Richards, NW Richards, OI Richards, PG Richards, PJ Richards, PM Richards, PV Richards, RC Richards, RE Richards, RF Richards, RJ Richards, RN Richards, TE Richards, TJ Richards, TM Richards, WJ Richards, WW Richards, AJ Richardson, AR Richardson, AW Richardson, BCF Richardson, BD Richardson, BR Richardson, CDA Richardson, CJ Richardson, CN Richardson, DF Richardson, DG Richardson, DJ Richardson, DR Richardson, E Richardson, EA Richardson, EJ Richardson, GA Richardson, GFT Richardson, GK Richardson, GR Richardson, GW Richardson, HA Richardson, HD Richardson, I Richardson, IF Richardson, IT Richardson, J Richardson, JT Richardson, KJ Richardson, KM Richardson, N Richardson, NE Richardson, NJ Richardson, NT Richardson, P Richardson, PA Richardson, PM Richardson, PR Richardson, PW Richardson, R Richardson, RA Richardson, RD Richardson, RI Richardson, RK Richardson, RW Richardson, SJ Richardson, TA Richardson, TC Richardson, TJ Richardson, TR Richardson, WJ Richardson, J Richards-Pugh, GP Riches, LD Riches, P Riches, GJ Richey, RW Richings, CE Richmond, GF Richmond, GR Richmond, HC Richmond, JP Richmond, AG Richter, GW Richter, PM Richter, TD Richter, WC Richter, GA Richters, B Rickaby, A Rickard, BE Rickard, RH Rickard, RW Rickard, EL Rickards, GFB Rickards, IVO Rickerby, RJ Rickert, BC Ricketts, RG Ricketts, RS Ricketts, RW Ricketts, D Rickinson, GV Riddell, WJ Riddell, PJ Riddett, RR Riddett, ER Riddle, JB Riddle, PS Riddle, RJA Riddle, KJ Riddler, NJ Riddock, KW Rideout, RA Rideout, GS Rider, ML Rider, RV Rider, GW Ridge, WF Ridge, KD Ridgeway, NJ Ridgewell, RT Ridgley, JT Ridgway, MW Ridgway, NJ Ridgway, NW Ridgway, RG Ridgway, RV Ridgwell, BA Ridland, BN Ridley, JH Ridley, IW Rieck, AE Riedel, LE Riedlinger, PA Riedlinger, H Riedstra, HW Riemersma, GD Rieper, AJ Ries, SF Ries, J Riesinger, VP Rigano, BM Rigby, CJ Rigby, GW Rigby, JF Rigby, MG Rigby, PG Rigby, B Rigelsford, JW Riggs, D Riha, DG Riik, TDB Rikken, JG Rikkerink, T Rikus, A Riley, AP Riley, BK Riley, BS Riley, CL Riley, DE Riley, DJ Riley, FW Riley, GC Riley, GG Riley, GK Riley, GW Riley, IC Riley, JD Riley, JE Riley, JH Riley, JR Riley, JT Riley, JV Riley, KG Riley, KM Riley, KV Riley, LJ Riley, NJ Riley, P Riley, PG Riley, PJ Riley, R Riley, RE Riley, RL Riley, SA Riley, SW Riley, WM Riley, JD Rimmer, R Rimmrodt, FN Rinaldi, RA Rindfleish, RS Rindzevicius, DC Ring, JF Ring, JM Ring, LR Ring, RD Ring, KP Rinkin, LA Rinkin, JM Rinses, CB Rintoul, BJ Ripper, TR Rippey, JD Rippin, GC Rippingale, JE Risby, CJ Riseley, PJ Riseley, PO Riseley, PC Rishman, PF Risinger, BC Rissel, B Ristic, WJ Ritchens, ADG Ritchie, BG Ritchie, BJ Ritchie, DB Ritchie, DR Ritchie, FW Ritchie, G Ritchie, GC Ritchie, HHM Ritchie, JA Ritchie, LJ Ritchie, RDA Ritchie, RW Ritchie, TG Ritchie, WA Ritchie, WW Ritchie-Robins, JA Riters, SB Ritter, WW Rittson, JW Rivers, DL Rivett, JC Rivett, RF Rix, RO Rix, GJ Rixon, JC Rixon, MG Rixon, PK Rixon, AJ Roach, BDA Roach, CR Roach, DA Roach, GF Roach, GW Roach, JF Roach, LJ Roach, MJ Roach, RW Roach, KG Roads, LN Roband, RJ Robards, KF Robarts, TJ Robarts, AW Robartson, CW Robartson, AE Robb, AM Robb, GO Robb, NT Robb, WE Robb, DF Robbins, JC Robbins, JH Robbins, NJ Robbins, P Robbins, RJ Robbins, SK Robbins, KG Robbs, GC Robert, AF Roberton, HR Roberton, JJ Roberton, AF Roberts, AG Roberts, AJ Roberts, AR Roberts, AT Roberts, AW Roberts, BA Roberts, BC Roberts, BD Roberts, BE Roberts, BG Roberts, BH Roberts, BL Roberts, BR Roberts, CAM Roberts, CD Roberts, D Roberts, DB Roberts, DJ Roberts, DM Roberts, DR Roberts, DS Roberts, DW Roberts, EM Roberts, FA Roberts, FAR Roberts, FH Roberts, FJ Roberts, G Roberts, GA Roberts, GC Roberts, GJ Roberts, GP Roberts, GR Roberts, GS Roberts, GV Roberts, GW Roberts, H Roberts, HE Roberts, I Roberts, ID Roberts, J Roberts, JL Roberts, JR Roberts, JS Roberts, JT Roberts, JV Roberts, K Roberts, KJ Roberts, KWH Roberts, LD Roberts, LE Roberts, LJ Roberts, LK Roberts, MA Roberts, MC Roberts, MH Roberts, MJ Roberts, MK Roberts, MP Roberts, MR Roberts, MT Roberts, NJ Roberts, NL Roberts, NR Roberts, PD Roberts, PE Roberts, PH Roberts, PJ Roberts, PL Roberts, R Roberts, RA Roberts, RC Roberts, RJ Roberts, RJP Roberts, RK Roberts, SP Roberts, T Roberts, TG Roberts, TM Roberts, VL Roberts, W Roberts, WA Roberts, WG Roberts, WJ Roberts, RT Robertsen, I Robertshaw, AJ Robertson, AL Robertson, AS Robertson, BAJ Robertson, BED Robertson, BJ Robertson, CH Robertson, DG Robertson, DI Robertson, DL Robertson, DM Robertson, DS Robertson, DW Robertson, FA Robertson, G Robertson, GA Robertson, GC Robertson, GG Robertson, GR Robertson, H Robertson, HC Robertson, I Robertson, IN Robertson, IW Robertson, J Robertson, JA Robertson, JD Robertson, JE Robertson, JT Robertson, JW Robertson, KD Robertson, KW Robertson, LJ Robertson, MD Robertson, MH Robertson, MJ Robertson, MR Robertson, NJ Robertson, NM Robertson, PD Robertson, PJ Robertson, PK Robertson, PR Robertson, RA Robertson, RAP Robertson, RE Robertson, RJ Robertson, RW Robertson, RWG Robertson, SC Robertson, T Robertson, TA Robertson, TJ Robertson, WA Robertson, WI Robertson, WJ Robertson, J Robilotta, II Robin, AJ Robins, BJ Robins, DJF Robins, JL Robins, K Robins, KJ Robins, NH Robins, R Robins, RJ Robins, WJ Robins, A Robinson, AB Robinson, AD Robinson, AG Robinson, AJ Robinson, AL Robinson, AM Robinson, AO Robinson, BA Robinson, BG Robinson, BJ Robinson, BL Robinson, CA Robinson, CJ Robinson, CR Robinson, D Robinson, DL Robinson, DN Robinson, DP Robinson, DW Robinson, E Robinson, ER Robinson, EW Robinson, FA Robinson, GA Robinson, GC Robinson, GH Robinson, GJ Robinson, GM Robinson, GR Robinson, GT Robinson, GV Robinson, ID Robinson, IJ Robinson, IK Robinson, IM Robinson, J Robinson, JA Robinson, JB Robinson, JC Robinson, JE Robinson, JM Robinson, JR Robinson, KA Robinson, KE Robinson, KG Robinson, KJ Robinson, KL Robinson, KM Robinson, KO Robinson, KW Robinson, LJ Robinson, LW Robinson, M Robinson, MA Robinson, MB Robinson, MC Robinson, ME Robinson, ML Robinson, MW Robinson, NEC Robinson, NJ Robinson, NL Robinson, OA Robinson, PA Robinson, PF Robinson, PH Robinson, PJ Robinson, PL Robinson, PM Robinson, PR Robinson, PS Robinson, RC Robinson, RE Robinson, RG Robinson, RHJ Robinson, RJ Robinson, RK Robinson, RM Robinson, RT Robinson, RW Robinson, SH Robinson, SN Robinson, SR Robinson, T Robinson, TE Robinson, TW Robinson, VJ Robinson, W Robinson, WR Robinson, WW Robinson, JE Robison, CPD Robley, AD Robotham, MA Robotham, A Robson, AF Robson, B Robson, CC Robson, DA Robson, DR Robson, KO Robson, TA Robson, UD Robson, JN Roby, PH Roby, FR Roca, B Rocchi, I Roccisano, DJ Roche, JF Roche, JJ Roche, NO Roche, PG Roche, TE Roche, WA Roche, ERC Rochester, TCA Rochester, PJ Rock, MD Rockett, RJ Rockliffe, JP Rockstroh, HA Rodd, WJ Roddy, GB Roden, TC Roden, AV Roderick, CR Roderick, TW Roderick, MG Rodger, BL Rodgers, DG Rodgers, DM Rodgers, G Rodgers, GJ Rodgers, IJ Rodgers, IL Rodgers, JA Rodgers, JP Rodgers, RP Rodgers, SW Rodgers, TH Rodgers, WO Rodgers, GA Rodie, D Rodway, AM Roe, BE Roe, IW Roe, JF Roe, MJ Roe, P Roe, RJ Roe, TA Roe, PT Roebig,

HP Roeder, GJ Roese, BG Roesler, AWF Rofe, JL Roffey, KW Roffey, LW Roffey, MF Roffey, MW Roffey, AH Rogalsky, GF Rogan, PB Rogan, LB Rogasch, AC Rogers, AL Rogers, BA Rogers, BD Rogers, BM Rogers, BR Rogers, DA Rogers, DR Rogers, DS Rogers, ER Rogers, G Rogers, GE Rogers, GF Rogers, GL Rogers, GS Rogers, J Rogers, JD Rogers, JI Rogers, JL Rogers, JM Rogers, JP Rogers, JW Rogers, K Rogers, KA Rogers, KG Rogers, KL Rogers, KM Rogers, KR Rogers, MB Rogers, MP Rogers, MR Rogers, N Rogers, NA Rogers, NH Rogers, NJ Rogers, NP Rogers, PB Rogers, PG Rogers, PHD Rogers, PJ Rogers, R Rogers, RC Rogers, RJ Rogers, RW Rogers, SL Rogers, WB Rogers, WE Rogers, DA Rogerson, NJ Rogerson, RS Rogerson, DE Roggenkamp, RR Rohan, P Rohanek, AR Rohde, GJ Rohde, MJ Rohde, GB Rohead, E Rohleder, CI Rohlf, PJ Rohrsheim, PE Rohwer, G Rojahn, S Rojek, R Rok, PL Rokay, AJ Rokesky, AJ Rolfe, DS Rolfe, JW Rolfe, RH Rolfe, RJ Rolfe, WD Rolfe, AD Rolff, BD Rollason, WA Rollason, RA Rolleston, G Rolley, KWG Rollings, ED Rollins, PJ Rollinson, HK Rolls, DM Rollston, RH Rollston, D Rolph, L Rolph, AP Romano, BJ Romeo, S Romeo, KH Romich, JF Romig, TJ Ronald, GC Ronalds, SW Ronalds, JT Ronaldson, FJ Ronan, JJ Ronan, RP Ronan, G Roney, RV Roney, WH Roods, D Rook, GS Rook, MK Rook, JR Rooke, ME Rooke, NF Rooke, RA Rooks, RE Rooks, VE Rooks, FE Roome, JG Rooney, KM Rooney, MJ Rooney, PS Rooney, RE Rooney, RJ Rooney, L Roosendaal, CW Roost, WJ Rootham, ML Roots, DL Roper, PK Roper, BJ Rosborough, J Rosborough, R Rosborough, LG Roscarel, DJ Roscoe, AB Rose, BD Rose, D Rose, DD Rose, DG Rose, DJ Rose, GR Rose, GW Rose, JB Rose, JC Rose, JD Rose, JK Rose, JV Rose, MAG Rose, PR Rose, RC Rose, RF Rose, RG Rose, RJ Rose, SI Rose, SR Rose, WJ Rose, JE Roseberry, PW Rosemond, B Rosenberg, KJ Rosenberg, SD Rosenberg, NH Rosenblatt, DN Rosengren, KR Rosenlund, RK Rosenow, HW Rosens, BA Rosenthal, MG Rosentreter, DL Rosenzweig, IT Rosenzweig, AW Roser, JR Roser, CM Rosetto, KG Rosewarne, PT Rosewarne, TW Rosewarne, LN Rosewell, NB Rosie, RJ Rosier, A Ross, AB Ross, AJ Ross, B Ross, BJ Ross, BW Ross, CJ Ross, D Ross, DA Ross, DJ Ross, DM Ross, DS Ross, DW Ross, EM Ross, GF Ross, GH Ross, GM Ross, GS Ross, IG Ross, IM Ross, IP Ross, IS Ross, J Ross, JA Ross, JG Ross, JG Ross, JJ Ross, JK Ross, JR Ross, JS Ross, JW Ross, KC Ross, KJ Ross, LH Ross, LJ Ross, LM Ross, LO Ross, ME Ross, NP Ross, PF Ross, PG Ross, RJ Ross, RKS Ross, RM Ross, RS Ross, SA Ross, SG Ross, T Ross, TJ Ross, TL Ross, WA Ross, WB Ross, WE Ross, WG Ross, WJ Ross, WL Ross, WW Ross, AR Rosser, KJ Rosser, MG Rosser, RR Rosser, DG Rossi, KV Rossi, AG Rossiter, DW Rossiter, GW Rossiter, NHJ Rossiter, P Rossiter, PE Rossiter, FP Rossl, E Ross-Smith, I Rostoks, MJ Rostron, RJ Rostron, KJT Roth, RE Rothall, RJ Rothall, RB Rothe, LC Rotherham, DR Rothero, RM Rothero, RD Rothfield, AW Rothwell, D Rothwell, R Rothwell, DJ Roubin, L Roubin, HC Rough, ME Rough, WF Roughan, JW Roughley, KJ Roughley, RJ Rouhan, LJ Roulston, LD Round, MJ Round, LR Rounds, DP Rourke, DL Rouse, VJ Rouse, GH Rousell, L Roussos, SC Rout, JW Routledge, LH Routley, CJ Roverts, LF Row, CP Rowan, JE Rowan, LR Rowan, PG Rowan, JE Rowbotham, C Rowcliffe, LJ Rowcliffe, AD Rowe, B Rowe, BE Rowe, DEJ Rowe, DJF Rowe, DM Rowe, GE Rowe, GH Rowe, GR Rowe, IG Rowe, IW Rowe, JE Rowe, JF Rowe, JS Rowe, KJ Rowe, KL Rowe, LE Rowe, MA Rowe, NJ Rowe, PJ Rowe, R Rowe, RA Rowe, RB Rowe, RP Rowe, RR Rowe, SW Rowe, T Rowe, VW Rowe, WC Rowe, WEJ Rowe, WG Rowe, NJ Rowell, PF Rowell, AW Rowen, ID Rowland, K Rowland, NW Rowland, RW Rowland, TR Rowland, AR Rowlands, DW Rowlands, MR Rowlands, RH Rowlands, EK Rowles, LE Rowles, C Rowley, EP Rowley, GT Rowley, RL Rowley, ID Rowling, KA Rowney, BJ Rowse, PW Rowse, EJ Rowsell, BE Roy, BR Roy, JD Roy, JL Roy, NF Roy, SA Roy, T Roy, DF Royal, LN Royal, RV Royal, PL Royce, GF Royes, DJ Roylance, RJ Royston, J Rozentals, RJW Ruck, KW Rucker, AG Rudd, BJ Rudd, IW Rudd, KJ Rudd, MJ Rudd, MW Rudd, VV Ruddick, FM Ruddle, WJ Ruddle, GR Ruddock, JN Ruddock, BHJ Rudduck, J Ruddy, MO Rudelbach, MJ Rudge, R Rudowski, A Ruduss, ALJ Rudzinski, F Ruediger, KJ Ruff, AJ Ruffin, MJ Ruffin, CJ Ruge, P Ruger, JP Ruggero, JP Ruig, F Ruiz, BR Rule, CL Rule, DG Rule, ED Rule, JC Rule, JE Rule, JR Rule, L Rule, PJ Rule, RA Rule, DP Rumble, GR Ruming,

GD Rummer, DC Rummery, CT Rump, NS Rumsey, PR Rumsey, GN Runciman, KE Rundell, TL Rundell, JA Rundle, RF Rundle, RD Runge, LL Rupe, PAJ Rusack, M Rusden, RG Ruse, BJ Rush, EJ Rush, KC Rush, WG Rush, D Rushan, RG Rushbrook, CB Rushby, WW Rushby, A Rushton, IJ Rushton, LC Rushton, P Rushton, E Ruska, DJ Ruskin, AJ Russ, BA Russ, JW Russack, AF Russell, AJ Russell, AK Russell, BB Russell, BT Russell, BW Russell, CR Russell, CW Russell, DA Russell, DJ Russell, DR Russell, DW Russell, G Russell, GBL Russell, GI Russell, GJ Russell, GM Russell, GR Russell, GW Russell, HC Russell, IM Russell, J Russell, JC Russell, JE Russell, JJ Russell, JL Russell, JW Russell, KA Russell, LE Russell, MD Russell, R Russell, RC Russell, RD Russell, RF Russell, RJ Russell, RL Russell, RW Russell, SG Russell, TG Russell, WJ Russell, WMP Russell, M Russellgreen, KW Russell-Smith, A Russo, A Russo Facciazza, J Russo, BJ Rust, PJ Rust, AR Rustichelli, DJ Ruston, LH Rutgers, RM Ruth, AF Rutherford, CA Rutherford, DJ Rutherford, FAP Rutherford, GS Rutherford, PD Rutherford, RBD Rutherford, RJ Rutherford, J Rutkowski, Z Rutkowski, JD Rutland, BG Rutledge, BJ Rutledge, GFM Rutten, JH Rutten, KG Rutter, BD Ruttle, WL Ruttledge, DW Ruttley, J Ruttley, DJW Ruxton, RH Ruygrok, RE Ryall, RJ Ryall, A Ryan, AE Ryan, AJ Ryan, AL Ryan, AN Ryan, AP Ryan, BA Ryan, BJ Ryan, BM Ryan, BR Ryan, CL Ryan, CP Ryan, D Ryan, DC Ryan, DJ Ryan, DR Ryan, EC Ryan, EJ Ryan, FJ Ryan, FP Ryan, FX Ryan, GM Ryan, GP Ryan, GR Ryan, GT Ryan, GV Ryan, IA Ryan, ID Ryan, IL Ryan, J Ryan, JB Ryan, JC Ryan, JF Ryan, JO Ryan, JP Ryan, JT Ryan, JW Ryan, KA Ryan, KD Ryan, KJ Ryan, KL Ryan, KR Ryan, KRE Ryan, LF Ryan, LJ Ryan, LK Ryan, LN Ryan, LR Ryan, LW Ryan, MB Ryan, MJ Ryan, MP Ryan, MT Ryan, NM Ryan, NP Ryan, PA Ryan, PA Ryan, PCJ Ryan, PD Ryan, PJ Ryan, PW Ryan, R Ryan, RA Ryan, RD Ryan, RE Ryan, RF Ryan, RK Ryan, RP Ryan, RR Ryan, RS Ryan, RV Ryan, TA Ryan, TC Ryan, TJ Ryan, TL Ryan, TM Ryan, TP Ryan, VC Ryan, VR Ryan, WF Ryan, WJ Ryan, WL Ryan, W Ryba, H Rybicki, CA Rychlewski, RJ Rycroft, AG Ryder, D Ryder, FA Ryder, JA Ryder, KG Ryder, LJ Ryder, GR Rye, PA Rye, PR Rye, RW Rye, RS Rygucki, RG Rylah, GD Ryland, CW Ryles, KR Ryley, JH Ryman, MJ Rynne, P Ryrie, Z Rys, DF Ryschka, PR Rzeskowski, BM Saal, DR Sabben, ET Sabel, C Sabell, HL Sabin, KD Sabolic, IC Sach, RA Sachs, DR Sachse, EF Sachse, NJ Sachse, RH Sadauskas, JD Saddington, TW Saddington, GE Saddler, ER Sadleir, DS Sadler, MJ Sadler, P Sadler, PS Sadler, RJ Sadowski, Z Sady, PG Safe, A Saffin, WW Sahajdak, HJ Sahariv, DJ Saidey, D Saillard, RA Saillard, JH Sainsbury, MJ Sainsbury, PJ Sainsbury, SA Sainsbury, PR Saint, BG Sainty, BR Sajatovic, N Sajtinac, SW Sak, RG Salas, JM Salau, PJ Salecich, G Salerno, JRD Sales, P Sali, M Salienko, I Salinovich, VW Salis, WL Salisbury, P Salkowski, LB Sallaway, PF Salm, AL Salmon, DM Salmon, GD Salmon, GT Salmon, JR Salmon, LP Salmon, RJ Salmon, TA Salmon, VT Salmon, J Salmond, JA Salmond, GM Salom, KJ Saloway, AM Salter, CG Salter, DS Salter, GS Salter, J Salter, JJ Salter, JN Salter, JP Salter, R Salter, WP Salter, HJ Saltmarsh, DJ Salveron, RJ Salzmann, RW Salzmann, W Samakowidic, JP Sambrook, RD Sambrooks, EC Samin, AG Samiotis, SA Sammartino, VJ Sammon, T Samojlowicz, B Sampson, BW Sampson, ET Sampson, ID Sampson, JM Sampson, MA Sampson, PG Sampson, RW Sampson, VE Sampson, WCK Sampson, LC Sams, PA Sams, AW Samuel, LA Samuels, RJ Samuels, MC Samuelson, JF Sandars, WS Sanday, R Sandell, GW Sander, NH Sander, TJ Sander, R Sandercock, CC Sanders, CJ Sanders, GA Sanders, GC Sanders, GN Sanders, IF Sanders, J Sanders, JE Sanders, JT Sanders, LK Sanders, PM Sanders, RN Sanders, SA Sanders, TL Sanders, TW Sanders, WC Sanders, WR Sanders, C Sanderson, CJJ Sanderson, DH Sanderson, DW Sanderson, G Sanderson, GC Sanderson, JCA Sanderson, JM Sanderson, JW Sanderson, KHS Sanderson, LA Sanderson, LN Sanderson, MW Sanderson, PN Sanderson, S Sanderson, TJ Sanderson, AA Sandery, RT Sandford, GG Sandiford, HP Sandiford, KJ Sandilands, JW Sandison, TK Sando, DJ Sandow, RA Sandow, RW Sandow, MJ Sandry, GH Sands, WR Sands, E Sanelli, DR Sanford, GHW Sangster, K Sankey, SW Sankey, K Sankowsky, RE Sansbury, AB Sansom, KE Sansom, BW Sant, A Santamaria, FS Santich, AF Sara, IR Sarah, ED Sarapuu, HM Sare, IR Sargeant, TC Sargeant, AL Sargent, BC Sargent, FH Sargent, JP Sargent, KA Sargent, RE Sargent, RM Sargent, TC Sargent, TR Sargent, JZ Saric,

PH Sarina, GM Sarteschi, L Sartori, SZ Sashalmi, AC Satchell, JH Satchell, GJ Sattler, CW Saul, RB Saul, AJ Saunders, AR Saunders, AV Saunders, B Saunders, CJ Saunders, CW Saunders, D Saunders, DJ Saunders, EA Saunders, EC Saunders, EH Saunders, FF Saunders, GE Saunders, JC Saunders, JE Saunders, KE Saunders, KJ Saunders, KW Saunders, LH Saunders, LJ Saunders, LW Saunders, M Saunders, MA Saunders, MJ Saunders, NJ Saunders, NR Saunders, PR Saunders, RA Saunders, RJ Saunders, RT Saunders, RW Saunders, SCE Saunders, TF Saunders, TJ Saunders, W Saunders, WL Saunders, WW Saunders, GJ Saunderson, LJ Saunderson, MP Saunderson, B Saunus, LE Saurine, BG Savage, BS Savage, CA Savage, D Savage, DG Savage, DJ Savage, GA Savage, GD Savage, GJ Savage, IC Savage, JCR Savage, JH Savage, JT Savage, ME Savage, PD Savage, R Savage, RH Savage, RJ Savage, RW Savage, DJ Saverin, LH Savidge, BR Savige, LF Savige, LR Savige, RJ Savige, DG Saville, JA Saville, PA Saville, PR Saville, WR Saville, E Savino, C Savoca, RJ Saw, H Sawa, RJ Sawdy, GL Sawers, RWL Sawers, JR Sawka, DN Sawkins, CJ Sawtell, GK Sawtell, JF Sawtell, TJ Sawtell, AF Sawyer, DR Sawyer, EE Sawyer, KR Sawyer, LH Sawyer, LR Sawyer, LT Sawyer, ME Sawyer, PR Sawyer, RL Sawyer, BL Saxby, JL Saxby, KM Saxby, MD Saxby, RA Saxby, TA Saxby, JF Saxe, GT Saxon, KL Saxon, RW Saxon, JE Saxton, PR Saxton, RL Sayce, AM Sayer, GT Sayer, JE Sayer, LR Sayer, NM Sayer, PH Sayer, KJ Sayers, VG Sayers, RB Scaddan, CO Scafe, GW Scafe, JA Scafidi, P Scaife, AW Scales, GJ Scales, J Scales, JF Scales, KB Scales, MJ Scales, RW Scales, TM Scales, N Scalisi, G Scally, JT Scally, DW Scammell, PE Scammell, PJ Scanes, IR Scanlan, JW Scanlan, P Scanlan, PJ Scanlan, TJ Scanlan, AW Scanlin, CM Scanlon, DG Scanlon, EP Scanlon, WH Scanlon, TG Scarborough, GK Scarce, RH Scarfe, SH Scarlett, JL Scarman, T Scarman, PR Scarr, GW Scarterfield, LD Scattini, JMJ Scaysbrook, KW Scaysbrook, KR Sceney, AMJ Scerri, J Scerri, LA Schache, JD Schaeche, RW Schaeche, RA Schaefer, RR Schaefer, RJ Schaeffer, AC Schafer, BJ Schafer, JT Schafer, RN Schafer, RS Schafer, GT Schaffer, WP Schaffer, NF Schafferius, IC Schahinger, BR Schalk, CN Schaper, KW Schaper, PA Schaper, MJ Schar, AL Schaschke, BA Schaumann, DL Schaumberg, DW Scheele, PC Scheinpflug, GW Scheithe, DJ Scheiwe, CF Schelfhout, BR Schell, JWO Schellhorn, JL Schembri, WA Schepis, JF Schepisi, KW Scheuermann, AG Schick, EJ Schick, IJ Schick, DN Schickert, RK Schieb, DC Schiemer, GK Schifcofske, LK Schifcofske, JH Schifferle, AR Schiffmann, JP Schiller, KR Schiller, J Schindlauer, RV Schinkel, CW Schipp, WC Schipp, AB Schirmer, CL Schirmer, DK Schirmer, M Schlatter, GJ Schleehauf, RZ Schlegel, NK Schlein, N Schluter, KR Schlyder, LE Schmeirer, KJ Schmerl, TA Schmerl, HH Schmerlaib, E Schmid, P Schmid, BA Schmidt, DJ Schmidt, EC Schmidt, EM Schmidt, FU Schmidt, HH Schmidt, LG Schmidt, LO Schmidt, OH Schmidt, PE Schmidt, PR Schmidt, RA Schmidt, RE Schmidt, TG Schmidt, WR Schmidt, DB Schmidtchen, JF Schmidtchen, GJ Schmied, RJ Schmiede, JL Schmitt, KF Schmitt, JJM Schmitz, JC Schnaars, HL Schnabl, EJ Schneemilch, A Schneider, CH Schneider, CR Schneider, DE Schneider, GC Schneider, HJ Schneider, JF Schneider, RJ Schneider, RN Schneidewin, RE Schnitzler, DR Schodel, CW Schoemaker, NG Schoemaker, LG Schoenauer, UP Schoenherr, RA Schoevers, CA Schofield, CE Schofield, CR Schofield, DA Schofield, DJ Schofield, HF Schofield, J Schofield, LW Schofield, M Schofield, MW Schofield, R Schofield, RK Schofield, WF Schofield, IE Scholes, EL Scholl, AD Scholtz, JG Scholz, JM Scholz, J Schonkala, GA Schoorl, MW Schopp, B Schossow, J Schotte, JE Schrader, BL Schrapel, GM Schraven, GA Schreck, WD Schreck, PA Schreiber, RA Schreuder, LOA Schreyer, HS Schroder, GN Schroeder, J Schroeder, PG Schroeder, GE Schuberg, DC Schubert, DJ Schubert, JH Schubert, LI Schubert, DH Schuberth, PN Schubinski, EK Schuh, MJM Schuit, OW Schuler, CF Schulte, PC Schulte, AD Schultz, AR Schultz, BJ Schultz, GW Schultz, JW Schultz, LG Schultz, PG Schultz, PK Schultz, TN Schultz, TW Schultz, VM Schultz, BS Schulz, CM Schulz, IL Schulz, LA Schulz, MT Schulz, AK Schulze, DT Schulze, MB Schulze, PG Schulze, PJ Schuman, EJ Schunemann, NH Schurr, K Schuster, GJ Schuts, MJ Schuts, DB Schwab, RD Schwab, RC Schwager, GF Schwan, RH Schwarschnik, DC Schwartz, WN Schwartz, PJ Schwartzkoff, BR Schwarz, GH Schwarz, KG Schwarz, RS Schwarz, JE Schwarze, PB Schwarze, R Schwarzer,

JW Schweitzer, RS Schwer, BM Schwind, KP Schwung, S Sciberras, A Scicluna, DD Scicluna, FS Scicluna, J Scicluna, BM Scobie, RE Scoffell, FE Scofield, FPP Scoglio, GW Scolyer, GW Scorgie, JWM Scorse, A Scott, AB Scott, AD Scott, AG Scott, AJ Scott, AR Scott, BB Scott, BC Scott, BD Scott, BN Scott, BR Scott, BW Scott, CD Scott, CK Scott, CL Scott, CWJ Scott, DA Scott, DB Scott, DC Scott, DI Scott, DJ Scott, DNC Scott, DR Scott, DW Scott, EJ Scott, F Scott, FP Scott, G Scott, GC Scott, GD Scott, GH Scott, GJ Scott, GK Scott, GM Scott, GW Scott, IG Scott, IJ Scott, IN Scott, J Scott, JA Scott, JE Scott, JJ Scott, JM Scott, JS Scott, JT Scott, KG Scott, KR Scott, KW Scott, LC Scott, LJ Scott, LW Scott, MA Scott, ME Scott, MW Scott, NM Scott, PA Scott, PF Scott, PG Scott, PHJ Scott, PR Scott, PW Scott, RA Scott, RF Scott, RG Scott, RJ Scott, RL Scott, RM Scott, RW Scott, TD Scott, TH Scott, TJ Scott, TR Scott, WB Scott, WE Scott, WJ Scott, WT Scott, DJ Scottbranagan, J Scott-Findlay, L Scott-Kemmis, M Scott-Malcolm, PN Scottney-Turbill, AR Scottrees, KJ Scovell, LBC Scowcroft, RC Scowen, CW Scragg, MA Scrase, GE Screaigh, JR Screen, WP Screen, AH Scriber, KR Scrimshaw, RA Scrimshaw, BE Scrivener, LW Scrivener, MC Scrivener, WO Scrivener, BE Scrivenor, TE Scroggie, PJ Scroop, A Scroope, LT Scruse, RG Scruth, JJ Sculley, P Scullin, BF Scully, CH Scully, D Scully, EL Scully, GJ Scully, IJ Scully, JF Scully, JJ Scully, GR Scurrah, RG Scurrell, K Scutt, RGH Scutter, JR Scutts, PR Scutts, SR Scutts, RE Seaborn, CH Seabrook, ID Seabrook, S Seabury, DH Seager, RD Seager, JR Seagg, AJ Seal, CA Seal, J Seal, JL Seal, L Seal, P Seal, PM Seal, MD Sealy, BJ Seaman, LJR Seaman, RR Seaman, GJ Searl, RA Searl, RG Searl, AB Searle, DA Searle, GW Searle, JF Searle, JH Searle, JL Searle, LJ Searle, RC Searle, RD Searle, RE Searle, BA Searles, PW Searles, SF Searles, GA Searson, MP Seary, BB Seater, JTA Seath, DC Seaton, EAC Seaton, MA Seats, PR Seaward, KS Secker, RS Secrett, MG Seddon, PE Seddon, RJ Seddon, AJ Sedgers, KE Sedgmen, CD Sedgwick, RL Sedunary, CH See, GJ See, JC See Kee, DR Seebohm, KJ Seebohm, CB Seeger, UG Seeger, TC Seekamp, BR Seeley, GM Seeley, GW Seers, CH Seery, DJ Seery, RJ Seery, CR Segrott, FP Segui, GC Seibold, DL Seidel, FC Seidenkamp, DM Seiffert, JR Seiler, R Seiler, SF Seinor, RD Seipel, P Selakovic, J Selan, ET Selby, GA Selby, C Self, DJ Self, G Self, PG Selfe, BJ Sell, JE Sell, JM Sell, QL Sell, SA Sell, RT Sellar, GA Selleck, NT Selleck, EG Sellens, G Sellentin, DB Sellers, IR Sellers, AW Sellke, DJ Sellwood, JF Sellwood, J Selmes, JN Selmes, AS Selva, RF Selway, KC Selwood, RH Selwood, RN Selwood, JW Semini, BJ Semler, SR Semmel, LS Sempel, AG Semple, DG Semple, EG Semple, JR Semple, RJ Semple, RW Semple, TH Senden, RA Sendjirdjian, RYA Seneque, TJ Seng, RT Sengstock, TM Sengstock, A Senior, RB Senior, R Serafin, GC Serbutt, PS Serella, MH Sergeant, TR Sergeant, LG Seri, PJ Serle, FP Serong, DM Serradura, GJ Sertori, R Service, RF Setchell, GK Seton, KS Seton, EJ Setter, REJ Settle, W Setzinger, A Severino, DJ Severn, JH Severyn, DW Seward, RG Seward, BA Sewell, DW Sewell, GA Sewell, JS Sewell, PR Sewell, PW Sewell, TH Sewell, AT Sexton, BJ Sexton, DA Sexton, GM Sexton, HE Sexton, JF Sexton, JK Sexton, LF Sexton, PA Sexton, PB Sexton, PF Sexton, RH Sexton, A Seychell, C Seychell, GJ Seymon, CL Seymour, JS Seymour, MG Seymour, RF Seymour, RJ Seymour, RW Seymour, SM Sfiligoj, CJ Shackleton, GW Shadbolt, SD Shaddock, RJ Shadwick, SR Shafto, WH Shakespeare, PR Shalders, PT Shalders, EM Shale, DT Shales, CJ Shallis, WH Shallvey, DJ Shambler, EJ Shambrook, PL Shambrook, RT Shambrook, CJ Shanahan, GC Shanahan, JG Shanahan, JP Shanahan, LJ Shanahan, MJ Shanahan, P Shanahan, PJ Shanahan, PM Shanahan, RP Shanahan, TH Shanahan, PJ Shand, DA Shangie, DL Shanhun, GE Shankland, BI Shanks, IS Shanks, BM Shannon, DG Shannon, GE Shannon, GR Shannon, KJ Shannon, MBR Shannon, MJ Shannon, GF Shard, BK Share, DK Sharkey, MW Sharland, TH Sharland, JF Sharman, JP Sharman, K Sharman, VJ Sharman, DW Sharp, EJ Sharp, GC Sharp, GR Sharp, GW Sharp, J Sharp, JL Sharp, JM Sharp, MR Sharp, PC Sharp, PF Sharp, PG Sharp, PJ Sharp, PK Sharp, R Sharp, RA Sharp, RG Sharp, RJ Sharp, TWL Sharp, CR Sharpe, GR Sharpe, GW Sharpe, KM Sharpe, NW Sharpe, RC Sharpe, RW Sharpe, WA Sharpe, WS Sharpe, MF Sharples, GR Sharrad, DJ Sharrock, JS Sharrock, MJ Shave, A Shaw, AE Shaw, BG Shaw, BJ Shaw, BL Shaw, CE Shaw, CJ Shaw, DR Shaw, DW Shaw, FG Shaw, G Shaw, GJ Shaw, GL Shaw, GW Shaw, JE Shaw, JI Shaw, JL Shaw, K Shaw, KC Shaw, KJ Shaw, KW Shaw, LH Shaw, LK Shaw, MN Shaw, NW Shaw, PJ Shaw, R Shaw, RB Shaw, RC Shaw, RG Shaw, RJ Shaw, TL Shaw, TM Shaw, WA Shaw, WH Shaw, WR Shaw, CB Shawcross, CT Shay, JB Shay, AM Shea, BF Shea, DK Shea, EJ Shea, PR Shea, SRM Shea, PM Shead, LJ Sheahan, MD Sheahan, TJ Sheahan, RG Shean, DH Shearer, NJ Shearer, PR Shearer, RN Shearer, W Shearer, RB Shearing, AD Shearman, AJ Shearman, JR Shears, PJ Shears, PO Shears, RJ Shears, L Shearwin, GB Sheather, GJ Sheather, MC Sheather, RV Sheather, SB Sheaves, B Shedden, K Shedden, JPA Sheddick, GL Sheean, RJ Sheean, WC Sheean, GJ Sheedy, GT Sheedy, JM Sheedy, JMM Sheedy, PA Sheedy, PB Sheedy, BT Sheehan, FA Sheehan, J Sheehan, JF Sheehan, JN Sheehan, MH Sheehan, ML Sheehan, MP Sheehan, MW Sheehan, PD Sheehan, PJ Sheehan, PT Sheehan, RG Sheehan, RW Sheehan, TJ Sheehan, T Sheehy, CJ Sheekey, DS Sheekey, EJ Sheen, VJ Sheen, KL Sheffield, PC Sheffield, WJ Sheffield, RS Shegog, ML Sheils, JL Shekleton, PR Shekleton, J Sheldon, JA Sheldon, AG Sheldrake, JA Sheldrick, GW Shelley, JG Shelley, LC Shelley, MJ Shelley, TF Shelley, WP Shelley, AT Shelton, BM Shelton, IA Shelton, JJ Shelton, RF Shelton, ML Shelverton, RG Shennan, WE Shennan, GM Shephard, J Shephard, WT Shephard, AA Shepherd, AG Shepherd, AJ Shepherd, BE Shepherd, CR Shepherd, EC Shepherd, GJ Shepherd, JL Shepherd, JW Shepherd, KR Shepherd, LJ Shepherd, MJ Shepherd, PF Shepherd, R Shepherd, RA Shepherd, RH Shepherd, RJ Shepherd, RL Shepherd, RS Shepherd, SR Shepherd, TWG Shepherd, VC Shepherd, WG Shepherd, MR Shepherdson, GJ Shepley, A Sheppard, BJ Sheppard, BK Sheppard, BM Sheppard, DC Sheppard, DR Sheppard, DW Sheppard, JM Sheppard, JR Sheppard, KW Sheppard, LR Sheppard, PB Sheppard, RB Sheppard, RG Sheppard, W Sheppard, DW Shepperbottom, GR Shepperd, NL Sherar, LE Sherd, PW Sherer, RG Sherer, DT Shergold, BJ Sheridan, DA Sheridan, WA Sheridan, RF Sheriff, RJ Sheringham, LR Sherlock, MP Sherlock, AE Sherman, J Sherman, RJ Sherman, KW Sherrell, A Sherriff, GW Sherriff, WG Sherriff, CJR Sherrin, ILJ Sherrington, MG Sherrington, N Sherritt, MJ Sherry, PR Sherry, IR Sherwin-White, AL Sherwood, DM Sherwood, JE Sherwood, KJ Sherwood, RM Sherwood, BS Sheumack, DM Shewan, RV Shewring, DF Shield, EF Shield, NF Shield, RN Shield, BK Shields, CC Shields, DI Shields, IC Shields, JE Shields, JF Shields, JL Shields, KA Shields, MS Shields, PA Shields, R Shields, RL Shields, RWP Shields, SR Shields, IM Shiell, MD Shiels, RE Shiels, CH Shier, RJ Shillabeer, AC Shilling, S Shilling, PJ Shilston, WJ Shimmin, DJ Shine, RJ Shine, GJ Shingles, JR Shingles, LG Shingles, LF Shinn, JW Shinnick, TG Shinnick, RJ Shipard, BR Shipp, IL Shipp, IR Shipp, WF Shipp, RC Shipton, GM Shires, JW Shirley, KC Shirvington, JC Shoebridge, RG Shoebridge, RP Shoebridge, G Shoemark, JF Shoesmith, JK Shoesmith, WN Shonk, RW Shoosmith, DC Shoppee, SL Shore, K Shorrock, M Shorrock, AB Short, BG Short, DA Short, DG Short, HJ Short, KE Short, KJ Short, MG Short, PC Short, PJ Short, RJ Short, DA Shorter, GM Shorter, SV Shortis, JP Shortland, KG Shorto, HD Shortt, RJ Shortt, R Shotter, JW Shotton, MR Shoumack, NR Shoveller, RN Showman, AE Shrapnel, JM Shreeve, MG Shreeve, RT Shuard, RN Shuey, JE Shugg, KM Shugg, ME Shultz, BH Shute, GS Shute, AN Shuttleworth, DG Sibbison, B Sibilia, AL Sibley, HF Sibley, NP Sibley, JC Sibly, JD Sibly, PA Sibree, LJ Sibson, SD Siddell, B Siddons, PW Sidebottom, CJ Sidey, WA Sidey, BB Sidor, HP Siegloff, T Sielicki, V Siemionow, DP Siemsen, AT Siepen, JP Sierakowski, WA Siersema, RR Sievers, TL Sievers, KJ Sievewright, PJ Siganto, RF Sigg, AP Siggers, WE Siggins, GJ Sigley, DG Sigston, JA Sigvart, VA Siiankoski, ZT Sikorski, JM Siladi, BG Silcock, GJ Silcock, RM Silcock, BS Silk, RJ Silk, VE Silk, RA Sillar, PW Sillard, JA Sillence, HR Silman, KF Silman, U Silpaps, CG Silver, FE Silver, GG Silver, JA Silver, WM Silverstone, RB Silverwood, MC Silvey, MJ Silvy, AM Sim, BK Sim, RC Sim, JP Simcock, IF Simcox, WA Simeon, DC Simeons, RD Simes, RJA Simes, MD Simic, MB Simkin, MJ Simm, AE Simmonds, GT Simmonds, J Simmonds, RA Simmonds, TR Simmonds, WJ Simmonds, WL Simmonds, WW Simmonds, DV Simmons, EE Simmons, FJ Simmons, KW Simmons, MR Simmons, PJ Simmons, MR Simms, TW Simms, AM Simon, RB Simon, VW Simon, ZAM Simon, CH Simons, KG Simons, RG Simons, RL Simons, RJ Simopoulos, KL Simper, SD Simpkin, DR Simpkins, AM Simpson, AR Simpson, B Simpson, BG Simpson, BO Simpson, C Simpson, CMW Simpson, CP Simpson, DA Simpson, DB Simpson, DBJ Simpson, DH Simpson, DJ Simpson, DP Simpson, DW Simpson, EJ Simpson, ER Simpson, EW Simpson, G Simpson, GA Simpson, GE Simpson, GJ Simpson, GL Simpson, GV Simpson, HM Simpson, IJ Simpson, IM Simpson, JB Simpson, JF Simpson, JH Simpson, JJ Simpson, JR Simpson, KR Simpson, LE Simpson, LJR Simpson, MH Simpson, NB Simpson, NW Simpson, P Simpson, PJ Simpson, PL Simpson, RB Simpson, RD Simpson, RG Simpson, RJ Simpson, RS Simpson, SW Simpson, T Simpson, WT Simpson, DB Sims, DR Sims, GB Sims, GO Sims, KWF Sims, NR Sims, PS Sims, R Sims, RC Sims, RK Sims, WA Sims, JEE Simson, PR Simson, LKB Sinay, A Sinclair, AJM Sinclair, AP Sinclair, BJ Sinclair, CE Sinclair, CN Sinclair, CV Sinclair, CW Sinclair, DJ Sinclair, DR Sinclair, EH Sinclair, FG Sinclair, GR Sinclair, IB Sinclair, IL Sinclair, JS Sinclair, M Sinclair, MO Sinclair, MR Sinclair, NA Sinclair, NC Sinclair, R Sinclair, RF Sinclair, RL Sinclair, SS Sinclair, WE Sinclair, WM Sinclair, WW Sinclair, BJ Sincock, AR Sindell, AG Singer, AW Singh, JR Single, DC Singletary, DR Singleton, G Singleton, JF Singleton, JW Singleton, MJJ Singleton, WE Singleton, MJ Singline, PM Singline, TW Singstock, J Sinhalewycz, MH Sinnema, SL Sinnitt, IR Sinnott, RJ Sinnott, RW Sirett, AR Sisley, I Sist, J Sitarz, M Sitarz, PJ Sivier, HG Siwes, WJ Sizeland, GS Sizer, FR Skalecki, R Skalij, GC Skardon, DL Sked, WR Skeen, NR Skeggs, BJ Skehan, KW Skelding, GP Skell, CJ Skelly, MB Skelly, HA Skelton, HF Skelton, KG Skelton, PD Skelton, PG Skelton, RG Skelton, TW Skelton, JH Skennar, GS Skennerton, ID Skennerton, CE Skerritt, LW Skevington, DK Skewes, PW Skewes, VJ Skewes, KL Skews, GW Skidmore, RW Skidmore, PR Skien, CT Skillen, RW Skillen, LML Skilling, GJ Skilton, A Skinner, AL Skinner, BW Skinner, FWL Skinner, HJ Skinner, IR Skinner, ITF Skinner, JJ Skinner, KJ Skinner, KM Skinner, MJ Skinner, NF Skinner, RF Skinner, TJ Skinner, TO Skinner, TR Skinner, KV Skippen, BA Skipworth, BH Skipworth, RF Skitch, A Skowronski, IM Skreja, JG Skubis, JS Skuce, RJ Skurray, TJ Skurrie, RM Skuse, GRM Skuthorp, J Skyba, L Skybinsky, CA Slack, IJ Slack-Smith, P Slacksmith, DJ Slade, GL Slade, JW Slade, RN Slade, R Slagboom, TD Slaney, A Slann, BP Slape, WJ Slape, JP Slatcher, AG Slater, GL Slater, HL Slater, HW Slater, JC Slater, KS Slater, LW Slater, MJ Slater, OW Slater, R Slater, RA Slater, RE Slater, RK Slater, RW Slater, WT Slater, RW Slatter, AW Slatterie, ND Slatterie, BL Slattery, E Slattery, JF Slattery, JM Slattery, KW Slattery, PA Slattery, PJ Slattery, PL Slattery, TJ Slattery, TL Slattery, PR Slaughter, RN Slaughter, B Slavik, JF Slavin, KJ Slavin, S Slawinski, BC Slee, BJ Slee, BJ Sleeman, KA Sleeman, N Sleeman, RH Sleeman, FW Sleep, KJ Sleep, WJ Slegers, RJ Sleight, MP Slevin, RP Slingsby, PH Slipczenko, EA Sloan, GA Sloan, K Sloan, KD Sloan, MI Sloan, RH Sloan, GM Sloane, LT Sloane, VR Slockie, GT Slockwitch, BP Slocombe, T Slocombe, WJ Slocombe, DE Sloman, AR Sloss, JM Sloss, MT Sloss, M Slot, KJ Slow, GP Sluiter, EE Sly, PG Sly, RJ Sly, JE Smail, GS Smailes, JS Smailes, KJ Smailes, B Smails, L Smale, ML Smale, AL Small, AR Small, AT Small, CJ Small, DJ Small, DW Small, GE Small, GJ Small, GS Small, IH Small, KJ Small, NM Small, PE Small, PG Small, R Small, RA Small, PR Smallacombe, AW Smallbon, SR Smalldon, SN Smalley, GR Smallwood, RC Smallwood, TN Smallwood, G Smart, HS Smart, JA Smart, JW Smart, MJ Smart, TG Smart, FM Smeaton, PC Smeaton, SJ Smeaton, BG Smedley, CL Smedley, RT Smedley, KJ Smee, MT Smeeth, NJ Smerdon, S Smerdon, NR Smethurst, TF Smethurst, R Smidt, JG Smigowski, JA Smiles, G Smiley, LD Smillie, RG Smillie, V Smiltnieks, PMC Smirk, JH Smit, P Smit, A Smith, AA Smith, AB Smith, AC Smith, AE Smith, AG Smith, AH Smith, AJ Smith, AK Smith, AM Smith, AR Smith, ASR Smith, AT Smith, AV Smith, AW Smith, AWP Smith, BA Smith, BC Smith, BD Smith, BE Smith, BF Smith, BG Smith, BH Smith, BI Smith, BJ Smith, BK Smith, BL Smith, BM Smith, BM Smith, BP Smith, BR Smith, BS Smith, BW Smith, C Smith, CA Smith, CB Smith, CC Smith, CD Smith, CE Smith, CEW Smith, CG Smith, CJ Smith, CL Smith, CO Smith, CP Smith, CR Smith, CS Smith, CT Smith, CW Smith, D Smith, DA Smith, DC Smith, DD Smith, DE Smith, DG Smith, DH Smith, DJ Smith, DJN Smith, DK Smith, DL Smith,

DM Smith, DPB Smith, DR Smith, DRL Smith, DT Smith, DV Smith, DW Smith, E Smith, ED Smith, EH Smith, EHF Smith, EJJ Smith, ER Smith, ET Smith, F Smith, FAM Smith, FD Smith, FG Smith, FJ Smith, FR Smith, FS Smith, G Smith, GA Smith, GB Smith, GC Smith, GD Smith, GF Smith, GG Smith, GI Smith, GJ Smith, GJH Smith, GK Smith, GL Smith, GM Smith, GR Smith, GRJ Smith, GS Smith, GT Smith, GW Smith, HA Smith, HE Smith, HG Smith, HK Smith, HL Smith, HR Smith, HW Smith, IB Smith, IC Smith, ID Smith, IF Smith, IL Smith, IM Smith, IP Smith, IR Smith, IV Smith, IW Smith, IWB Smith, J Smith, JA Smith, JAF Smith, JAS Smith, JE Smith, JF Smith, JG Smith, JH Smith, JJ Smith, JL Smith, JP Smith, JPS Smith, JPT Smith, JR Smith, JRS Smith, JS Smith, JW Smith, K Smith, KA Smith, KB Smith, KE Smith, KFB Smith, KG Smith, KGV Smith, KJ Smith, KL Smith, KM Smith, KMG Smith, KO Smith, KR Smith, KS Smith, KW Smith, L Smith, LC Smith, LF Smith, LG Smith, LH Smith, LJ Smith, LK Smith, LM Smith, LP Smith, LR Smith, LRJ Smith, LT Smith, LW Smith, M Smith, MA Smith, MAL Smith, MB Smith, MD Smith, MF Smith, MG Smith, MJ Smith, MJT Smith, MK Smith, MM Smith, MR Smith, MW Smith, N Smith, NA Smith, NB Smith, NC Smith, ND Smith, NG Smith, NH Smith, NI Smith, NJ Smith, NM Smith, NR Smith, OD Smith, OG Smith, P Smith, PA Smith, PB Smith, PC Smith, PD Smith, PE Smith, PF Smith, PG Smith, PI Smith, PJ Smith, PK Smith, PL Smith, PM Smith, PP Smith, PR Smith, PRC Smith, PS Smith, PV Smith, PW Smith, R Smith, RA Smith, RB Smith, RC Smith, RD Smith, RE Smith, RF Smith, RG Smith, RH Smith, RI Smith, RJ Smith, RK Smith, RL Smith, RM Smith, RN Smith, RP Smith, RR Smith, RS Smith, RT Smith, RV Smith, RW Smith, RWJ Smith, SA Smith, SC Smith, SE Smith, SG Smith, SJ Smith, SJJ Smith, SL Smith, SN Smith, T Smith, TA Smith, TB Smith, TD Smith, TE Smith, TG Smith, TJ Smith, TL Smith, TM Smith, TP Smith, TR Smith, TS Smith, TT Smith, TW Smith, VCY Smith, VJ Smith, VR Smith, VW Smith, WA Smith, WC Smith, WG Smith, WH Smith, WJ Smith, WK Smith, WLH Smith, WP Smith, WR Smith, WT Smith, AFP Smitheringale, JA Smitheringale, AN Smithers, CJ Smithers, GR Smithers, JE Smithers, NR Smithers, AH Smithett, LP Smithlester, BJ Smithson, LG Smithson, RP Smithson, BA Smithurst, HN Smithwick, JV Smithwick, MD Smithwick, DA Smits, LJ Smits, DL Smock, JT Smout, EJ Smylie, RP Smylie, T Smylie, DJ Smyth, GB Smyth, HC Smyth, KW Smyth, MG Smyth, RJ Smyth, RN Smyth, AVF Smythe, BJ Smythe, CA Smythe, GT Smythe, J Smythe, PGA Smythe, PV Smythe, VW Smythe, MG Snaith, NG Snape, RB Snape, RJ Snape, WG Snape, JH Snare, WH Snarr, B Snashall, NGL Snashall, RD Snedden, AJ Sneddon, AS Sneddon, IC Sneddon, IR Sneddon, KJ Sneddon, PCE Sneddon, WE Sneddon, GT Sneesby, JH Sneesby, BH Snell, P Snell, PS Snell, DR Snelling, EW Snelling, LJ Snelling, RE Snelling, WE Snelson, BO Snezwell, R Sniegowski, GB Snook, PK Snook, DG Snooks, BF Snow, BJ Snow, DJ Snow, RC Snow, M Snowball, JJ Snowden, PG Snowdon, RM Snowdon, BJ Snoxell, MI Snoxell, RA Snuggs, C Soar, RW Soar, J Sobczyk, W Sobczyk, H Sobczynski, GK Sobey, KW Sobey, A Sobolewsky, PA Sochacki, WD Soden, RJ Soderblom, LR Soderholm, SE Sodervik, HR Soelberg, BN Soeurt, KR Sofield, RG Sojan, RJ Sojan, M Sokil, W Sokoluk, DJ Soley, GC Solly, NF Solly, C Solomon, DF Solomon, GD Solomon, HAH Solomon, JD Solomon, JH Solomon, RA Solomon, RG Solomon, DJ Solomons, MJ Somerfield, SG Somerfield, AJ Somers, BJ Somers, EJ Somers, PJ Somerville, WL Somerville, M Somic, DA Sommer, BW Sommerfeld, FA Sommerton, JM Sonego, RL Sonners, TJ Sonners, MJ Sonneveld, BW Sonter, WR Soorley, GE Soper, GR Soper, OW Soper, S Sorbello, AP Sorensen, DR Sorensen, EC Sorensen, NL Sorensen, VL Sorley, DR Sorrell, GD Sorrensen, JA Sorrensen, KJ Sorrensen, HW Sosenko, WS Sosnowski, PN Sothman, G Sotnikov, CN Soulos, G Soumilas, AM Soutar, H Souter, RJ Souter, M South, RH South, WJ South, BR Southall, DW Southee, JE Southeron, GS Southon, JC Southwell, PJ Southwell, SJ Southwell, TJ Southwell, DL Soutter, RH Soutter, EG Sowden, RC Sowden, J Sowrey, MH Sowsun, DJ Sowton, JJ Soxsmith, GM Spackman, GW Spackman, RE Spackman, WP Spaderna, BD Spain, RA Spain, FE Spalding, A Spann, CS Spann, GS Spannagle, LJ Spanner, V Spano, BW Spargo,

ED Spargo, MJ Spargo, ES Sparham, DE Spark, DW Spark, PJ Spark, TG Spark, RS Sparke, TB Sparke, DJ Sparkes, DW Sparkes, NF Sparkes, PAE Sparkes, RL Sparkes, SJ Sparkes, KJ Sparling, CL Sparrow, CS Sparrow, KR Sparrow, MJ Sparrow, NJ Sparrow, BJ Spash, B Spaulding, LC Spaulding, W Spaven, RG Speakman, MJ Spear, BJ Speck, GM Speck, PA Spedding, JGM Spee, DJ Speechley, S Speechley, AL Speelman, AR Speet, DJ Spehr, ND Speight, JF Spellacy, BA Spelta, DR Spence, II Spence, IW Spence, LWJ Spence, PA Spence, PJ Spence, PM Spence, RJ Spence, SB Spence, WJ Spence, AW Spenceley, AD Spencer, BA Spencer, BR Spencer, CD Spencer, CF Spencer, CR Spencer, DA Spencer, DJ Spencer, EJ Spencer, ER Spencer, G Spencer, GA Spencer, GP Spencer, GR Spencer, IG Spencer, J Spencer, JD Spencer, JEG Spencer, JF Spencer, JN Spencer, JW Spencer, MJ Spencer, MP Spencer, MW Spencer, N Spencer, ND Spencer, NW Spencer, SA Spencer, SB Spencer, TN Sperling, RL Sperring, C Speth, JJ Spiby, DH Spice, EK Spice, MW Spice, DM Spicer, GA Spicer, PD Spicer, TJ Spicer, E Spielman, GA Spiers, GR Spiers, RD Spiers, CB Spies, CR Spies, JP Spillane, MJ Spiller, BF Spilsbury, BW Spilsbury, J Spindler, P Spindler, JA Spinks, LE Spinks, NJ Spinks, RE Spinks, RJ Spinks, GD Spinkston, AA Spinney, WJ Spiteri, JP Spitzers, DJ Spivey, RA Spivey, GBJ Spizzirri, RW Splatt, LR Splite, DD Spokes, FJ Spokes, TG Spokes, B Spollen, G Spooner, PB Spoor, JB Sporle, SW Sporn, HC Spradbrow, EB Spragg, GS Spragg, RE Spragg, PC Spragge, FH Sprague, RT Sprague, WN Sprague, PC Sprake, RC Sprake, CL Spratt, DR Spratt, LR Spratt, PL Spratt, W Spratt, GW Spreadborough, TJ Sprenkeler, JE Sprice, DA Sprigg, RJ Sprigg, MD Spriggs, TJ Spriggs, DE Spring, GL Spring, JA Spring, TL Spring, AE Springall, SJ Springer, MG Springett, RA Springfield, A Sprogis, L Sprogis, N Sproles, GK Sprott, JW Sprott, LC Sproule, LW Sproules, J Spruce, NA Spruce, WJ Spruce, WJ Sprudd, BW Spry, DM Spry, FJ Spry, IC Spry, JL Spry, MB Spry, RJ Spry, RC Spurling, DA Spurr, DC Spurr, RJ Spurr, DP Spurrier, BF Spurway, JD Spurway, EF Spy, AW Squibb, DJ Squibb, F Squillacioti, KD Squire, GG Squires, ID Squires, KT Squires, RD Squires, RJ Squires, CJ St Clair, DG St Leon, RW St Leon, TD StGeorge, PR Staal, DJ Staas, LK Staatz, L Stace, R Stace, DH Stacey, EW Stacey, RG Stacey, S Stacey, TA Stacey, RB Stach, R Stachow, RJ Stack, T Stack, VM Stack, DH Stacy, BH Stadhams, AC Stafford, AJ Stafford, BW Stafford, DA Stafford, GE Stafford, JA Stafford, JW Stafford, KV Stafford, R Stafford, RJ Stafford, JE Stafrace, CK Stagg, MF Staggard, DM Stahl, JJ Stahtoures, DL Stainer, LE Stainer, RF Stainer, PF Stainthorpe, KL Staisch, A Stajkowski, BD Stalder, RJ Staley, SR Stalker, WG Stallan, DC Stallard, RG Stallard, IF Stammers, PG Stammers, CE Stamp, IS Stamp, JH Stamp, JR Stanborough, PJ Stanbridge, IW Stanbury, MT Stanbury, AJ Stancombe, HJ Stanczyk, CHC Standaar, TL Standage, DW Standen, FB Standen, HB Standen, IW Standen, WG Standen, WR Standfast, WR Standing, AR Standish, GB Standish, JE Standish, GG Standley, RJ Standring, PJ Stanfield, AJ Stanford, AR Stanford, BA Stanford, GI Stanford, GS Stanford, JG Stanford, JW Stanford, LB Stanford, LJ Stanford, ME Stanford, P Stanford, RH Stanford, HS Stanhope, DR Staniland, H Stanios, EP Stankowski, J Stankowski, AG Stanley, AK Stanley, GW Stanley, LA Stanley, MK Stanley, PF Stanley, RA Stanley, RE Stanley, RG Stanley, RJ Stanley, RM Stanley, SI Stanley, RE Stanmore, BA Stannard, JR Stannard, TE Stannus, LJ Stansfield, PJ Stansfield, AD Stanton, DR Stanton, EJ Stanton, JL Stanton, LR Stanton, NG Stanton, PM Stanton, RF Stanton, RK Stanton, TH Stanton, TN Stanton, DM Stanway, JP Stanwix, B Staples, MB Staples, PA Staples, BF Stapleton, DJ Stapleton, EJ Stapleton, K Stapleton, PJ Stapleton, RJ Stapleton, BH Stark, BJ Stark, DM Stark, HW Stark, JE Stark, MJ Stark, BC Starkey, LE Starkey, MB Starkey, MN Starkey, SJ Starkey, GS Starks, JFJ Starmans, SP Starostecki, AJ Starr, GA Starr, GR Starr, MT Starr, P Starr, T Starr, WJ Starrenburg, DW Starr-Nolan, BL Start, J Stasiewicz, I Stasyshyn, S Staszko, J Staszynski, RC Statham, JH Statton, PR Statton, AJ Staugaitis, G Staunton, GR Staunton, JB Stauntonlatimer, J Stawyskyj, KJ Stayner, GS Staziker, KJ Stclair, TLG Stdenis, AJ Stead, JR Stead, PJ Stead, PT Stearman, TC Steart, TM Stebbings, SPL Stechwey, V Steciuk, KP Steckelbruck, CJ Steddy, PR Steege, AE Steel, CM Steel, GR Steel, MA Steel, NK Steel, PR Steel, FA Steele, G Steele, GJ Steele, I Steele, IR Steele, JN Steele, KJ Steele, L Steele, MC Steele, NJ Steele, PJ Steele,

RC Steele, RM Steele, WB Steele, WG Steele, WR Steele, WT Steele, AJ Steels, DJ Steen, GT Steen, JH Steen, PN Steen, HY Steep, RS Steeper, DJ Steer, PD Steer, PSA Steer, RJ Steer, T Steer, AP Stefanou, S Stefanowicz, RC Steffan, AA Steffen, JR Steggles, TR Stegman, GH Stehn, MR Steiger, FA Stein, J Stein, JA Stein, JC Stein, JM Stein, JN Stein, PE Stein, PW Stein, R Stein, CJ Steinert, BF Steinhardt, EG Steinhardt, LJ Steinhardt, PG Steinkellner, JR Steley, JB Stella, AJ Stellema, RJ Stelling, AB Steltman, BD Stemp, PB Stenchion, PT Stenchion, ZJ Stengelis, DW Stenner, GA Stenner, MJ Stenning, GV Stenson, DR Stent, PD Stent, GR Stephan, AR Stephen, EL Stephen, R Stephen, WJ Stephen, AM Stephens, BJ Stephens, BL Stephens, CD Stephens, CE Stephens, CJ Stephens, DG Stephens, G Stephens, GR Stephens, HA Stephens, IG Stephens, IH Stephens, J Stephens, JB Stephens, JK Stephens, JM Stephens, K Stephens, KA Stephens, KP Stephens, KR Stephens, L Stephens, LJ Stephens, LP Stephens, LR Stephens, PJ Stephens, RK Stephens, TJ Stephens, WK Stephens, GR Stephensen, RL Stephensen, RM Stephensen, BM Stephenson, GI Stephenson, GT Stephenson, JI Stephenson, JR Stephenson, LM Stephenson, MM Stephenson, MW Stephenson, PT Stephenson, RJ Stephenson, TE Stephenson, WJ Stephenson, C Stepien, J Stepien, AM Stepney, AF Steptoe, GC Sterel, AT Sterland, KJ Sterland, ER Sternbeck, RW Sterrett, G Steven, KS Steven, H Stevenhaagen, AJ Stevens, AR Stevens, BA Stevens, BG Stevens, C Stevens, CP Stevens, FG Stevens, GA Stevens, GC Stevens, GD Stevens, GJ Stevens, GL Stevens, GR Stevens, H Stevens, IJ Stevens, JB Stevens, JC Stevens, JG Stevens, JH Stevens, JM Stevens, JP Stevens, JR Stevens, KA Stevens, KO Stevens, LJ Stevens, MJ Stevens, PA Stevens, PJ Stevens, PN Stevens, R Stevens, RA Stevens, RB Stevens, RC Stevens, RF Stevens, RJ Stevens, RM Stevens, RW Stevens, SK Stevens, SP Stevens, TD Stevens, TJ Stevens, TL Stevens, TM Stevens, WA Stevens, WK Stevens, A Stevenson, BA Stevenson, CR Stevenson, D Stevenson, DD Stevenson, EH Stevenson, EL Stevenson, FDB Stevenson, GD Stevenson, GJ Stevenson, GL Stevenson, HV Stevenson, J Stevenson, JD Stevenson, JL Stevenson, KJ Stevenson, KL Stevenson, LJ Stevenson, LR Stevenson, NA Stevenson, OS Stevenson, R Stevenson, RD Stevenson, RJ Stevenson, RPJ Stevenson, RT Stevenson, SG Stevenson, TG Stevenson, TW Stevenson, WH Stevenson, C Steward, RW Steward, AC Stewart, AF Stewart, AG Stewart, AH Stewart, AJ Stewart, AW Stewart, B Stewart, BF Stewart, BT Stewart, C Stewart, CD Stewart, CR Stewart, D Stewart, DI Stewart, DM Stewart, EP Stewart, FW Stewart, G Stewart, GC Stewart, GE Stewart, GG Stewart, HL Stewart, HS Stewart, IA Stewart, IBK Stewart, IG Stewart, IL Stewart, IT Stewart, JA Stewart, JC Stewart, JD Stewart, JG Stewart, JM Stewart, JR Stewart, JT Stewart, JTD Stewart, JW Stewart, KB Stewart, KC Stewart, KC Stewart, KD Stewart, KJ Stewart, KM Stewart, KR Stewart, LA Stewart, LR Stewart, MJ Stewart, MT Stewart, NJ Stewart, P Stewart, PM Stewart, R Stewart, RA Stewart, RC Stewart, RF Stewart, RG Stewart, RJ Stewart, RN Stewart, RW Stewart, W Stewart, WB Stewart, WE Stewart, WJ Stewart, BL Steyger, RJ Stibbe, ML Sticher, RB Stickells, DJ Stickland, RA Stickman, KE Sticpewich, TC Stidwell, CD Stidworthy, J Stienstra, IW Stiff, DE Stiles, IL Stiles, MJ Stiles, RC Stiles, RG Stiles, RW Stiles, RA Still, RL Still, A Stiller, BD Stillwell, AP Stilo, JW Stimpson, AG Stimson, RN Stimson, PJE Stingemore, WM Stinson, WG Stinton, LWK Stirling, RM Stirling, TM Stirling, AW Stirzaker, AD Stitiford, GD Stitt, GP Stitz, WA Stoate, DJ Stoba, GH Stock, GJ Stock, PX Stock, RT Stock, MJ Stockbridge, EJ Stockdale, KF Stockdale, KR Stockdale, RM Stockdale, EJ Stocker, DN Stockham, BA Stockley, JW Stockley, KD Stockley, LH Stockley, H Stockman, BR Stockmann, JF Stockton, N Stockwell, PT Stockwell, RG Stockwell, TA Stockwell, AJ Stoddart, GR Stoddart, RA Stoddart, RD Stoddart, RF Stoddart, WW Stoddart, PB Stoeckel, RN Stoeckel, KW Stoertebecker, J Stoffels, N Stogianopoulos, KJ Stojko, G Stojkovic, MJ Stokell, GR Stoker, JV Stoker, JW Stoker, JW Stoker, KW Stoker, RA Stoker, AA Stokes, B Stokes, BD Stokes, BHC Stokes, BJ Stokes, BL Stokes, BM Stokes, BR Stokes, EC Stokes, GJ Stokes, JW Stokes, PA Stokes, PJ Stokes, RH Stokes, RJ Stokes, TA Stokes, TL Stokes, KW Stolberg, M Stolk, RL Stolte, F Stolzenberg, A Stoma, AD Stone, AR Stone, AW Stone, CB Stone, CK Stone, CW Stone, D Stone, DC Stone, DF Stone, DL Stone, EM Stone,

FD Stone, GJ Stone, GR Stone, IN Stone, JG Stone, JJ Stone, JM Stone, KG Stone, KR Stone, KV Stone, LJ Stone, LV Stone, MF Stone, MJ Stone, PJ Stone, RB Stone, RH Stone, RJ Stone, RL Stone, TC Stone, TJ Stone, TW Stone, WE Stone, BM Stonehouse, RL Stonehouse, VC Stonehouse, WJ Stonehouse, AW Stoneman, CG Stoner, BR Stones, J Stones, SG Stones, FR Stonham, RRR Stonier, CW Stoodley, JJ Stopford, GC Stopp, LJ Storan, BS Storch, AG Storen, MW Storen, TJ Storen, AT Storer, BJ Storer, DA Storer, F Storer, AD Storey, AF Storey, DA Storey, HL Storey, IG Storey, KD Storey, MC Storey, PJ Storey, WJ Storey, CK Storie, GA Storm, GB Storm, B Storok, M Story, PC Stothers, CC Stott, JM Stott, MJ Stott, ML Stott, MT Stott, P Stott, PE Stott, RB Stott, RM Stott, RP Stott, DF Stout, AM Stove, P Stow, RM Stow, GR Stoward, PH Stoward, KG Stower, WC Stowers, RF Stquintin, P Straatman, DA Strachan, DE Strachan, GW Strachan, JCN Strachan, RH Strachan, RNR Strachan, WG Strachan, CJ Strahan, WB Strahan, A Strain, JHC Strain, J Straka, BM Straker, JA Straker, MH Straker, J Straksye, JE Strandly, TW Strang, ID Strange, KM Strange, LW Strange, TL Strange, TW Strange, WE Strange, WR Stranks, RW Strapps, JJ Strasser, BCA Stratford, HF Stratford, MS Stratford, NB Stratford, GP Strathdee, GJ Stratton, KJ Stratton, M Stratton, RG Stratton, RL Straub, RR Straughair, J Strautins, JB Strawbridge, S Strazdas, RL Strazdins, TJ Stream, TP Streatfield, C Street, DE Street, GJ Street, LR Streeting, W Streltschenko, BP Strempel, JL Stretch, AB Stretton, RC Stretton, AJ Stribling, AJ Strickland, BJ Strickland, DM Strickland, EG Strickland, GKR Strickland, JA Strickland, JW Strickland, KR Strickland, LR Strickland, RE Strickland, CA Strike, HAN Strindberg, DR Stringer, ME Stringer, NA Stringer, RE Stringer, K Stringfellow, DK Stritzke, BA Stroet, PP Stromski, AB Strong, DA Strong, EC Strong, JW Strong, LE Strong, MJ Strong, MR Strong, R Strong, RM Strong, G Stroscio, R Stroszynski, DJ Strother, M Strothers, J Stroud, PP Stroud, EJ Strub, MH Struchlak, CA Strudwick, PF Strudwick, RW Strudwick, PJ Strunks, WG Strutton, JA Strzelczykowski, A Stuart, AN Stuart, BG Stuart, BL Stuart, C Stuart, CG Stuart, IC Stuart, JR Stuart, KJ Stuart, KL Stuart, MB Stuart, RF Stuart, RJ Stuart, TJ Stuart, VP Stuart, WF Stuart, IC Stubbins, BC Stubbs, GD Stubbs, JA Stubbs, JB Stubbs, KR Stubbs, RK Stubbs, RL Stubbs, GM Stuchbery, R Stuckey, JE Studholme, LJ Studley, BG Studman, JS Studman, WJ Studte, JR Stumer, RD Stumer, FM Stummer, H Stumpp, MT Stunell, G Sture, RE Sturges, T Sturges, SC Sturgess, WJ Sturgess, JR Sturla, JW Sturla, DL Sturmer, S Sturniolo, BC Sturrock, TJ Sturrock, GJ Sturzaker, WE Stuth, BJ Stutley, LR Stutley, HJ Stuttard, W Styke, RJ Style, AL Styles, GC Styles, ID Styles, JW Styles, KF Styles, KW Styles, RJ Styles, RL Styles, DHE Styman, RK Styner, M Suba, AG Suckling, PA Suckling, P Suda, P Sugden, J Sugistaff, DJ Suhr, JF Suiker, RE Suiter, WD Suiter, M Sukmanowsky, AE Sukys, JA Sulc, MS Sulley, AD Sullivan, AJ Sullivan, BD Sullivan, BJ Sullivan, BK Sullivan, BR Sullivan, DJ Sullivan, DK Sullivan, DT Sullivan, DW Sullivan, GD Sullivan, GJ Sullivan, GW Sullivan, IL Sullivan, J Sullivan, JA Sullivan, JB Sullivan, JC Sullivan, JE Sullivan, JG Sullivan, JP Sullivan, JW Sullivan, KR Sullivan, LJ Sullivan, M Sullivan, MF Sullivan, MJ Sullivan, NW Sullivan, PC Sullivan, PD Sullivan, PF Sullivan, PJ Sullivan, PL Sullivan, RA Sullivan, RD Sullivan, RF Sullivan, SJ Sullivan, TB Sullivan, TJ Sullivan, TR Sullivan, WE Sullivan, WL Sullivan, RJ Sully, WL Sully, JE Sulman, AR Summerfield, CR Summerfield, LR Summerfield, G Summergreene, WE Summerhayes, M Summerhill, A Summers, BJ Summers, FA Summers, FN Summers, IG Summers, IR Summers, JL Summers, JM Summers, KJ Summers, LR Summers, LW Summers, PM Summers, RJ Summers, RR Summers, TL Summers, KG Summersford, KJ Summerson, HA Summerville, RT Summerville, AB Sumner, DC Sumner, JW Sumner, MW Sumpton, RG Sund, UK Sund, EJ Sungalis, P Sunman, RE Sunner, RJ Sunnucks, J Supple, RW Supple, AV Surman, RJ Surman, HW Surowka, RJ Surridge, DJ Surtees, CD Sutcliffe, GV Sutcliffe, MF Sutcliffe, RJ Sutcliffe, TJ Sutcliffe, W Sutczak, T Suter, A Sutherland, AD Sutherland, AR Sutherland, BW Sutherland, CD Sutherland, D Sutherland, DF Sutherland, GD Sutherland, GJ Sutherland, GM Sutherland, IS Sutherland, JD Sutherland, LC Sutherland, NR Sutherland, SB Sutherland, SM Sutherland, WA Sutherland, WC Sutherland, DG Suthers, GS Suthers, AJ Sutton, AR Sutton, C Sutton, CJA Sutton, CR Sutton, DJ Sutton, ES Sutton, GE Sutton, GJ Sutton, GV Sutton, HJ Sutton, JR Sutton, KJ Sutton, KN Sutton, MS Sutton, NG Sutton, NJ Sutton, NL Sutton, PA Sutton, PF Sutton, R Sutton, RD Sutton, RF Sutton, RG Sutton, RJ Sutton, RK Sutton, RT Sutton, TC Sutton, WJ Sutton, WR Sutton, HE Suttor, VC Svanberg, KC Svenson, J Svoboda, IK Swadling, K Swadling, BJ Swain, CA Swain, DJ Swain, DW Swain, JJ Swain, RJ Swain, GA Swaine, J Swaine, HN Swales, JR Swales, TD Swales, GJ Swalling, MR Swalling, TR Swallow, BG Swan, D Swan, EC Swan, ES Swan, GJ Swan, GS Swan, HPJ Swan, J Swan, JG Swan, PD Swan, RD Swan, RW Swan, WM Swan, SP Swane, WE Swaney, RW Swankie, GJ Swann, GW Swann, JJ Swann, R Swann, CR Swanson, JC Swanson, JR Swanson, PL Swanson, PR Swanson, RG Swanson, RH Swanson, RA Swanston, RJ Swanton, TJ Swanton, LS Swarbrick, RJ Swarbrick, RS Swarbrick, MW Sward, RJ Swartz, MA Swayn, B Swayne, CC Swaysland, DR Sweatman, BJ Sweeney, CJ Sweeney, FJ Sweeney, MR Sweeney, PM Sweeney, PT Sweeney, RH Sweeney, RL Sweeney, SF Sweeney, T Sweeney, TC Sweeney, PJ Sweeny, BW Sweet, GP Sweet, PA Sweet, WA Sweet, AL Sweetman, JR Sweetnam, WF Sweetnam, DA Swensen, RE Swenser, FH Swiderski, AJ Swift, BF Swift, DJ Swift, LB Swifte, CH Swinbourn, AF Swinbourne, ES Swinbourne, GJ Swincer, RL Swincer, EG Swindells, DG Swiney, CT Swinfield, TM Swinkels, BR Swinnerton, PW Swinnerton, WA Swinton, AL Switzer, AJ Sydenham, BS Sydes, KR Sydney, C Sydor, A Sykes, F Sykes, J Sykes, LC Sykes, DS Syme, FK Symes, JA Symes, KF Symes, R Symes, DF Symington, JM Symington, LG Symington, N Symon, RFB Symon, GRJ Symonds, JE Symonds, JJ Symonds, MC Symonds, MD Symonds, PF Symonds, BH Symons, CW Symons, EJ Symons, JW Symons, LR Symons, RG Symons, MJ Synan, JFJ Synnott, M Systermanns, DL Szabo, J Szabo, P Szabo, RJ Szabo, LJ Szafnicki, JD Szajner, LT Szalay, Z Szalek, BA Szapiel, Z Szaraszek, EJ Szczesniak, G Szczurko, J Szczurowski, Z Szczygielski, L Szegedi, RJ Szelag, T Szelest, AW Szepanowski, IO Szeremeta, SC Szigeti, JM Szmiglo, AM Szoeke, MK Szpajchler, RR Szuszkewicz, F Szymanski, WJ Szymanski, J Szymkow, M Szypulski, IR Tabb, AA Taber, G Tabone, AP Tabotta, MS Taeuber, JO Taggart, LA Taggart, R Taggart, L Tagliapietra, KE Taheny, KJ Tainsh, AJB Tait, DM Tait, JW Tait, KJ Tait, LR Tait, RR Tait, RW Tait, CE Talbert, PM Talbert, A Talbot, DJ Talbot, JJ Talbot, MN Talbot, JD Tallack, DW Tallis, BJ Tallon, JJ Talty, WA Talty, NT Tambling, RN Tambousoff, MA Tame, PL Tancred, IB Tandy, IN Tangey, KR Tangney, PJ Tangney, WT Tanks, DA Tanner, DB Tanner, FW Tanner, N Tanner, RB Tanner, RS Tanner, WR Tannock, M Tanovic, EK Tansey, MJ Tansey, JR Tansley, EJ Tanti, P Tanzer, DB Tape, R Tape, IJ Tapley, CL Taplin, GR Taplin, BF Tapp, GE Tapp, PA Tapp, KT Tapper, GF Tapping, RG Tapping, BW Tapps, PA Tapscott, AJ Taranto, GH Tardrew, DS Targett, R Targett, L Tarka, EG Tarleton, RJ Tarman, ZS Tarnawsky, PC Tarr, WG Tarr, BC Tarran, H Tarrant, J Tarres, MJ Tarte, JE Taske, CF Tasker, IR Tasker, J Tassanyi, RL Tassie, N Tatarynowicz, G Tatasciore, CS Tatchell, DM Tate, DW Tate, JR Tate, LEC Tate, SJ Tate, BF Tateson, WE Tatham, PJ Tatler, VW Tatnall, BE Tatrai, JJ Tattam, RJ Tattersall, JR Tattis, NC Taugge, HJ Tauzowski, E Tavani, T Tay, BG Tayler, JR Tayler, AC Taylor, AI Taylor, AJ Taylor, AM Taylor, AT Taylor, AW Taylor, B Taylor, BE Taylor, BJ Taylor, BK Taylor, BR Taylor, D Taylor, DA Taylor, DC Taylor, DG Taylor, DM Taylor, DP Taylor, DR Taylor, DW Taylor, E Taylor, EA Taylor, EF Taylor, EW Taylor, FA Taylor, GA Taylor, GD Taylor, GJ Taylor, GJT Taylor, GK Taylor, GL Taylor, GN Taylor, GP Taylor, GR Taylor, GS Taylor, GT Taylor, H Taylor, HJ Taylor, I Taylor, IA Taylor, IC Taylor, IJ Taylor, IR Taylor, IW Taylor, J Taylor, JA Taylor, JD Taylor, JG Taylor, JH Taylor, JK Taylor, JL Taylor, JM Taylor, JR Taylor, JW Taylor, K Taylor, KA Taylor, KB Taylor, KC Taylor, KE Taylor, KG Taylor, KJ Taylor, KO Taylor, KR Taylor, L Taylor, LA Taylor, LE Taylor, LG Taylor, LH Taylor, LL Taylor, LM Taylor, LO Taylor, LS Taylor, LW Taylor, MB Taylor, MF Taylor, MH Taylor, MJ Taylor, MK Taylor, ML Taylor, MP Taylor, MR Taylor, MS Taylor, NA Taylor, P Taylor, PA Taylor, PB Taylor, PC Taylor, PG Taylor, PJ Taylor, PR Taylor, R Taylor, RA Taylor, RB Taylor, RC Taylor, RF Taylor, RG Taylor, RJ Taylor, RJH Taylor, RL Taylor, RM Taylor, RN Taylor, RN Taylor, RP Taylor, RR Taylor, RS Taylor, RW Taylor, SH Taylor, SN Taylor, SV Taylor, TA Taylor, TE Taylor, TG Taylor, TJ Taylor, TK Taylor, TL Taylor, TV Taylor, VG Taylor, W Taylor, WA Taylor, WG Taylor, WJ Taylor, WS Taylor, PB Te Brinke, IC Teague, LK Teague, PW Teague, BL Teakle, RH Teal, AK Teale, BR Teale, WD Tear, FB Tearle, GL Teasdale, K Teasdale, PJ Teather, DC Tebb, P Tebb, BW Tebbit, PJ Tebbit, KM Tebby, PNO Tedder, CD Tee, KP Teefey, RG Teeling, WE Teeling, RW Teesson, CF Tegan, DC Teichelman, AH Teichmann, JJ Telfer, WJ Telfer, CA Telford, DS Telford, KJ Telford, NR Telford, RM Telford, SJ Telford, WR Telford, MD Telley, B Temby, GW Temby, MA Temby, BE Tempest, JPK Tempest, W Templar, P Temple, WG Temple, WH Temple, RH Templeman, A Templeton, C Templeton, GM Templeton, RJ Templeton, A Ten Hoope, J Tenabel, WD Tennant, KJ Tennent, WH Tennent, T Tenuyl, RD Ter Horst, JM Terhoeve, H Terhorst, V Terpsopulos, C Terranova, G Terranova, AG Terrell, MA Terrell, CD Terrey, AEW Terry, BJ Terry, HG Terry, KB Terry, PW Terry, RJ Terry, RM Teschendorff, AJ Tesler, HR Tessmer, P Tet Fong, RC Tetley, HH Tetlow, RW Tetlow, PAJ Teuma, PJL Teuma, A Teunissen, GE Teusner, R Teusner, RA Tevelen, WM Tewson, MC Teys, AC Thacker, NA Thacker, RV Thacker, AG Thackray, IH Thackray, RL Thallon, DM Thamm, AH Thatcher, B Thatcher, CA Thatcher, JB Thatcher, JM Thatcher, JN Thatcher, RM Thatcher, G Theckston, CJ Thelander, IW Theobald, LJ Theodore, SW Theodore, T Theodorou, EP Thetford, PA Theune, ND Thew, ST Thicknesse, MJ Thiel, PC Thiel, RL Thiele, JH Thiessens, AT Thirkell, B Thirkell, NJ Thirkell, R Thirkell, JA Thirlwall, RSJ Thirlwell, KA Thistlethwaite, TA Thistlethwaite, T Thistleton, FH Thom, HG Thoma, A Thomas, AB Thomas, AE Thomas, AG Thomas, AJ Thomas, AL Thomas, AR Thomas, AW Thomas, B Thomas, BC Thomas, BJ Thomas, BS Thomas, CLN Thomas, CR Thomas, CV Thomas, D Thomas, DA Thomas, DG Thomas, DIK Thomas, DJ Thomas, DS Thomas, DW Thomas, E Thomas, EC Thomas, FC Thomas, FE Thomas, FM Thomas, GA Thomas, GB Thomas, GD Thomas, GF Thomas, GL Thomas, GP Thomas, GR Thomas, HB Thomas, I Thomas, IM Thomas, IS Thomas, JA Thomas, JC Thomas, JF Thomas, JJ Thomas, JL Thomas, JM Thomas, JR Thomas, JW Thomas, K Thomas, KA Thomas, KC Thomas, KE Thomas, KM Thomas, KT Thomas, KW Thomas, LH Thomas, LJ Thomas, LLJ Thomas, LN Thomas, LW Thomas, M Thomas, MD Thomas, MJ Thomas, MV Thomas, NA Thomas, NL Thomas, P Thomas, PC Thomas, PD Thomas, PJ Thomas, PW Thomas, RA Thomas, RD Thomas, RE Thomas, RG Thomas, RH Thomas, RJ Thomas, RP Thomas, RW Thomas, SR Thomas, TC Thomas, WA Thomas, WB Thomas, WD Thomas, WG Thomas, WH Thomas, WJ Thomas, WL Thomas, WM Thomas, WR Thomas, RH Thomason, KH Thomasson, GR Thomasz, A Thompson, A Thompson, AA Thompson, AG Thompson, AH Thompson, AJ Thompson, AK Thompson, AM Thompson, AP Thompson, AR Thompson, ARM Thompson, B Thompson, B Thompson, BA Thompson, BF Thompson, BJ Thompson, BK Thompson, BL Thompson, BP Thompson, BW Thompson, CC Thompson, CCW Thompson, D Thompson, DA Thompson, DC Thompson, DE Thompson, DJ Thompson, DK Thompson, DL Thompson, DW Thompson, EA Thompson, ED Thompson, EN Thompson, ER Thompson, FA Thompson, FJE Thompson, GB Thompson, GD Thompson, GFC Thompson, GJ Thompson, GN Thompson, GO Thompson, GW Thompson, IP Thompson, IS Thompson, JA Thompson, JC Thompson, JD Thompson, JE Thompson, JF Thompson, JM Thompson, K Thompson, KA Thompson, KD Thompson, KJ Thompson, KR Thompson, L Thompson, LB Thompson, LIS Thompson, LJ Thompson, LR Thompson, LW Thompson, MA Thompson, MB Thompson, MJ Thompson, MM Thompson, MV Thompson, NG Thompson, NW Thompson, P Thompson, PC Thompson, PD Thompson, PL Thompson, PN Thompson, QN Thompson, R Thompson, RB Thompson, RC Thompson, RE Thompson, RF Thompson, RG Thompson, RJ Thompson, RL Thompson, RN Thompson, RR Thompson, RT Thompson, SD Thompson, SJ Thompson, TA Thompson, TC Thompson, TJ Thompson, TM Thompson, TR Thompson, TW Thompson, VJ Thompson, W Thompson, WA Thompson, WC Thompson, WH Thompson, WI Thompson, WJ Thompson, WK Thompson, WP Thompson,

WR Thompson, WTC Thompson, DC Thomsen,
TK Thomsen, A Thomson, AJ Thomson, AM Thomson,
B Thomson, BA Thomson, BFL Thomson, BL Thomson,
BM Thomson, CF Thomson, DA Thomson, DC Thomson,
DS Thomson, G Thomson, GB Thomson, GD Thomson,
GG Thomson, IA Thomson, ID Thomson, IG Thomson,
IJ Thomson, IM Thomson, JD Thomson, JDL Thomson,
JE Thomson, JF Thomson, JM Thomson, KJ Thomson,
KM Thomson, L Thomson, LA Thomson, LG Thomson,
LJ Thomson, M Thomson, PR Thomson, RB Thomson,
RC Thomson, RD Thomson, RF Thomson, RG Thomson,
RK Thomson, RL Thomson, RP Thomson, RW Thomson,
TG Thomson, TJ Thomson, WJ Thomson, JA Thorburn,
JLB Thorburn, JR Thorburn, RG Thorburn, DA Thoresen,
IJ Thorley, IW Thorley, NE Thorley, FW Thorn, LN Thorn,
R Thorn, RM Thornbury, MD Thorncraft, R Thorncraft,
KP Thorne, MR Thorne, PA Thorne, PTH Thorne,
RE Thorne, RF Thorne, GW Thornell, JW Thorneycroft,
PJ Thorneycroft, KJ Thornhill, SP Thornhill, RE Thornley,
AJ Thornton, J Thornton, JC Thornton, JD Thornton,
JJ Thornton, KA Thornton, RJ Thornton, RL Thornton,
SD Thornton, SG Thornton, SN Thornton, WC Thornton,
FE Thorogood, AJH Thorp, AL Thorp, AP Thorp, RC Thorp,
AW Thorpe, BC Thorpe, BE Thorpe, BL Thorpe, BR Thorpe,
CA Thorpe, HA Thorpe, J Thorpe, PE Thorpe, PJ Thorpe,
TG Thorpe, WSM Thorpe, VJ Thouard, GM Thow, RM Thoy,
GP Thredgold, B Threlfall, AW Thring, PW Thring, B Thripp,
I Throssell, LK Thrupp, KM Thrush, SJ Thuell,
DB Thumpkins, KJ Thurecht, JD Thurgar, KD Thurgar,
DJ Thurgood, JH Thurgood, JC Thurling, WL Thurling,
GG Thurlow, GJ Thurlow, JR Thurlow, RM Thurn,
BJ Thursby, RG Thursby, JP Thursky, BT Thurston,
CR Thurston, FR Thurston, LN Thurston, NE Thwaite,
GE Thwaites, REJ Thynne, CF Tibballs, PJ Tibbett,
IM Tibbits, IE Tibbles, DG Tibbs, M Tiberi, CW Tichborne,
PJ Tichborne, JE Tick, KG Tickell, DR Tickle, GW Tickle,
JD Tickle, JM Tickle, LE Tickle, PJ Tickle, BJ Ticknell,
ER Tickner, JR Tickner, NW Tickner, RH Tickner,
BW Tideswell, P Tidey, BJ Tidyman, LW Tidyman, RC Tiegs,
DJP Tier, MD Tier, RL Tier, BJ Tiernan, DJ Tiernan,
BW Tierney, FM Tierney, JJ Tierney, K Tierney, MV Tierney,
PJ Tierney, AN Tilbrook, FD Tilbrook, GB Tilbrook,
JD Tilbrook, N Tilbrook, P Tilbrook, RR Tilbury,
BE Tiligadis, A Tiliks, FE Tilke, SG Tiller, WE Tillett,
CJ Tilley, CW Tilley, F Tilley, FC Tilley, JM Tilley,
NR Tilley, PL Tilley, R Tilley, RW Tilley, SG Tilley,
JI Tillman, C Tilmouth, IC Tilmouth, R Tilmouth,
WG Tilse, DJ Tilyard, BD Timberlake, FG Timbrell,
DT Timbs, MA Timewell, H Timmerman, CP Timmins,
JP Timmins, JW Timmins, RG Timmins, RW Timmins,
IA Timms, MJ Timms, G Timonin, MB Timothy,
GS Timson, AM Tincknell, PA Tindal, EN Tindale,
GP Tindale, TR Tindale, WW Tindale, B Tindall,
GG Tindall, RG Tindall, IP Tinetti, AJ Tingiri,
RLM Tingley, B Tingwell, DM Tininczky, DJ Tink,
DG Tinker, JA Tinker, JR Tinkham, BR Tinkler, JF Tinkler,
JH Tinkler, MB Tinkler, A Tinni, NE Tinning, DJ Tinson,
DH Tipper, RK Tippet, BE Tippett, RA Tippett, GJ Tipping,
KG Tippins, RV Tippo, WE Tisdale, PF Titchener, JA Tite,
KJW Titheradge, EW Titley, CN Titmarsh, MG Titmus,
TV Titmuss, JA Tivendale, DC Tiver, LAS Tizard,
SKH Tizzard, PA Tobe, JL Tobiasen, BD Tobin, BM Tobin,
GJ Tobin, KJ Tobin, MF Tobin, NJ Tobin, PJ Tobin,
RM Tobin, TJ Tobin, VJ Tobin, RC Toby, KA Tocock,
MA Tod, BE Todd, BG Todd, BK Todd, GG Todd, GL Todd,
GT Todd, J Todd, JL Todd, JM Todd, ML Todd, NS Todd,
PJ Todd, PR Todd, PWR Todd, R Todd, RG Todd, RJA Todd,
RS Todd, SN Todkill, I Todorovic, L Toff, AC Toghill,
MP Tognolini, JP Tokarczyk, TM Tokarczyk, MV Tola,
AJ Toleman, BW Tolhurst, NW Tolhurst, TJ Tolhurst,
CW Toll, RJ Tolland, M Tollens, B Tolley, BA Tolley,
OG Tolliday, GD Tollis, MS Tollis, MC Tollner, M Tolnay,
SJ Tolsher, MJ Tolson, WW Tom, TJ Toman, M Tomas,
E Tomczak, PM Tome, RR Tomkins, BL Tomkinson,
KW Tomkinson, L Tomkinson, M Tomkowiak, RSA Tomlin,
TJ Tomlins, AG Tomlinson, JM Tomlinson, NJ Tomlinson,
WA Tomlinson, GC Tommasi, TMM Tommasi, AJ Tompkin,
DJ Tompkins, BG Tompson, AS Toms, BJ Toms, GC Toms,
GE Toms, GS Toms, PM Toms, AJ Tonge, RL Tonge,
AP Tonich, PJ Tonkes, FH Tonkies, AC Tonkin, AJ Tonkin,
AN Tonkin, AR Tonkin, BN Tonkin, CS Tonkin, DF Tonkin,
DL Tonkin, EK Tonkin, FJ Tonkin, JF Tonkin, KD Tonkin,
NE Tonkin, WK Tonkin, TJ Tonking, WP Tonkinson,
JW Tonks, MJ Tonks, PM Tonks, PR Tonks, EL Tonna,
T Tonuri, RR Tooby, DS Tooes, BN Toohey, BR Toohey,
JC Toohey, PJ Toohey, RJ Toohey, JT Toohill, RC Toole,
RW Toolin, U Tooming, JE Toonen, JS Tootell, GA Tooth,
GW Tooth, PD Tooth, SC Tooth, MJ Toovey, RW Toovey,
BR Topfer, N Topham, BE Topp, FB Topp, LV Topp,
RP Topp, LR Toppinen, RG Topping, JS Tormey, JR Torney,
JL Torpey, CF Torrens, IG Torrens, MD Torrens, RF Torrens,
RJ Torrens, EE Torresan, RA Torrisi, BJ Tory, R Toscano,
M Tosic, NPA Touchard, R Tough, RH Tough, JD Toulmin,
PF Tournay, WK Tournier, CT Tournoff, VT Tournoff,
AA Toussaint, LH Toussaint, EJ Tovell, WH Tovey,
BA Towart, CR Towe, LJ Towers, MC Towers, RA Towers,
TC Towers, RG Towie, JG Towler, M Towler, GL Towner,
RJ Towner, KF Towning, GE Townley, JA Townley,
JH Townley, DSG Townrow, GJ Towns, M Towns, RA Towns,
AW Townsend, CC Townsend, CM Townsend,
DS Townsend, DW Townsend, EJ Townsend, GH Townsend,
GM Townsend, GN Townsend, GR Townsend,
GW Townsend, HJ Townsend, JG Townsend, JL Townsend,
KBE Townsend, KJ Townsend, LF Townsend, PW Townsend,
RE Townsend, RH Townsend, AM Townson, JR Townson,
DL Toy, IP Toy, MJ Toy, R Toyer, JM Toyne, KK Tozer,
RC Tozer, DJ Tracey, JE Tracey, JS Tracey, LW Tracey,
PD Tracey, WT Tracey, GR Tracy, RJ Tracy, P Trad,
JR Traeger, TJ Traeger, D Trahair, FJ Trail, GA Traill, P Traill,
RS Traill, VR Traill, RJ Train, MW Trainer, CD Trainor,
GL Trainor, TG Trainor, Z Trajdos, PA Tramacchi,
JW Tramby, CH Tranberg, CR Tranby, LL Tranby,
DD Tranter, LJ Tranter, NA Tranter, SJ Trantino, KT Trapp,
AE Trappel, RL Trappel, JA Trappett, AEJ Tratt, IL Traveller,
AJ Travers, DA Travers, DJ Travers, KD Travers, MH Travers,
PB Travers, B Traverse, JL Travis, JW Travis, RJ Travis,
VR Travis, J Trawinski, WL Trayhurn, DL Traynor,
IF Traynor, JJ Traynor, KM Traynor, PJ Traynor,
CB Treadaway, DN Treadgold, DJ Trease, PJ Trease,
CW Treasure, ME Treasure, MJ Treasure, TA Treasure,
JM Trebilco, CF Trebilcock, KJ Trebilcock, DL Treble,
JH Trebley, DW Tredinnick, GD Tredrea, MJ Tredrea,
DA Treen, DJ Treen, GD Treeve, CA Treffers, A Treffry,
B Tregear, TR Tregent, GF Tregenza, IL Tregenza,
JD Tregenza, RL Treherne, PJC Treleaven, A Treloar,
DA Treloar, JCW Treloar, LJ Treloar, MR Treloar, N Tremain,
PR Tremain, TR Tremain, KR Trembath, PJ Trembath,
RT Tremble, AW Tremellen, RB Tremellen, LH Tremenheere,
RA Trenear, JBM Trenerry, JR Trenerry, GJ Trengove,
LA Trengove, PH Trengrove, WL Trenorden, KR Trent,
PG Trent, TR Trent, KA Treschman, WDW Tresise,
KH Trevan, AR Trevarthen, DE Trevarthen, JM Trevellyn,
WA Trevenen, PR Trevillian, RL Trevor, GF Trevor-Hunt,
PE Trew, KN Trewartha, JK Trewern, D Trewick, GD Trewin,
RL Trewin, A Trezise, AM Trezise, DL Trezise, EJ Trezise,
RW Trezise, GE Triantafyllou, DJ Triat, TW Tribe, JW Trice,
P Trichilo, DJ Trick, ES Tricker, BGH Trickett, CJ Trickett,
PT Trickett, KJ Trickey, RF Trickey, BE Tridgell, BN Triffett,
TB Triffett, LJ Triffitt, MJ Triffitt, AR Trigg, NA Trigg,
J Triggell, GR Trigwell, H Trikeriotis, MJ Trim, MV Trim,
BM Trimble, OH Trimmer, MP Trimper, J Trinder,
JW Trinks, CC Trinnick, AW Tripet, IC Triplett, PJ Triplett,
TS Triplett, MT Tripp, RA Tritton, M Troha, KJ Tronc,
RW Tronc, GR Trood, PG Troon, AB Trost, JM Trotman,
DL Trott, GM Trott, HA Trotter, RH Troughear, RV Trout,
WJ Trouten, RJ Trowbridge, RL Trowbridge, SR Trowbridge,
C Trower, JM Trower, BL Trowse, JM Troxell, KJ Troy,
WJ Troy, Y Troynar, GF Truan, JF Truan, RJ Trudgen,
JW Trudgeon, FJ Trudgian, EA True, GW True, H True,
CD Truelove, DR Truelove, J Trueman, PJ Trueman,
NG Truman, AV Trumbull-Ward, LG Trump, GL Truscott,
PG Truscott, GL Trusler, EW Truslove, GR Truss,
GW Trussell, IL Trusz, GC Tryhorn, CJ Trynes, PF Trynes,
PZ Trzecinski, G Tsakisiris, R Tschannen, LW Tscherne,
GE Tschirpig, G Tsoleridis, TO Tubb, TW Tubbs, E Tuchin,
H Tuck, JF Tuck, PL Tuck, RJ Tuck, AH Tucker, AN Tucker,
BL Tucker, CD Tucker, DA Tucker, DE Tucker, GN Tucker,
HM Tucker, JM Tucker, K Tucker, KE Tucker, LR Tucker,
MA Tucker, MF Tucker, NP Tucker, PJ Tucker, R Tucker,
RM Tucker, RV Tucker, RW Tucker, VG Tucker, VL Tucker,
WG Tucker, WM Tucker, MG Tuckett, PJF Tuckett,
AD Tuckfield, ND Tuckwell, RH Tuckwell, DJ Tudman,
BR Tudor, DH Tudor, TJ Tueno, AR Tugwell, J Tuia,
BJ Tulip, IA Tulk, AT Tull, CH Tull, KJ Tull, GA Tulloch,
RA Tulloch, RA Tulloh, AR Tully, BWJ Tully, DJ Tully,
NBJ Tully, PF Tully, PW Tully, RF Tully, RW Tully,
M Tumini, JK Tun Tin, GA Tunbridge, KC Tunbridge,
BE Tunnah, RJ Tunnelljones, DW Tunney, JW Tunney,
NF Tunny, KV Tunstall, MR Tunstall, GC Tunzi, V Turco,
WJ Turczynski, AR Turl, IW Turley, ML Turley, AB Turnbull,
AF Turnbull, AS Turnbull, DR Turnbull, FE Turnbull,
GJ Turnbull, JR Turnbull, KJ Turnbull, KN Turnbull,
NS Turnbull, PB Turnbull, RA Turnbull, RK Turnbull,
RW Turnbull, AB Turner, AC Turner, AE Turner, AF Turner,
AG Turner, AJ Turner, AL Turner, ASM Turner, B Turner,
BA Turner, BE Turner, BP Turner, BT Turner, BV Turner,
BW Turner, CC Turner, CE Turner, CF Turner, CJ Turner,
DFF Turner, DI Turner, DN Turner, DR Turner, GD Turner,
GF Turner, GJ Turner, GL Turner, GM Turner, GT Turner,
GW Turner, HJ Turner, IN Turner, J Turner, JF Turner,
JR Turner, JW Turner, KS Turner, LF Turner, LJ Turner,
LK Turner, LV Turner, M Turner, MI Turner, MJ Turner,
NF Turner, NM Turner, PA Turner, PE Turner, PJ Turner,
PL Turner, PW Turner, RC Turner, RD Turner, RG Turner,
RJ Turner, RS Turner, RW Turner, S Turner, ST Turner,
TAJ Turner, TC Turner, TF Turner, TJ Turner, TO Turner,
TV Turner, WA Turner, WB Turner, WJ Turner, WT Turner,
KN Turnham, MP Turnock, G Turra, DC Turrall,
MT Turrell, BR Turrise, LF Turton, GJ Turvey, JE Tuttle,
MI Tuttle, LP Tuttleby, PA Tuxford, BE Twaddell, AB Twaits,
GB Tweedale, GL Tweedie, CC Twelftree, BJ Twible,
TW Twible, GA Twidale, DE Twigden, DM Twigg, H Twigg,
RJ Twigg, DR Twigg-Patterson, KS Twining, LC Twiss,
RLC Twiss, JJ Twist, BJ Twomey, IA Twomey, JR Twomey,
JW Twomey, N Twyford, AJ Twynam-Perkins, JM Tyack,
WJ Tyacke, CA Tye, DK Tye, JC Tye, GD Tyers, IR Tyers,
JL Tyers, RG Tyers, DH Tyler, GC Tyler, GJ Tyler, JT Tyler,
PJ Tyler, SM Tyler, DW Tylor, M Tylor, KJ Tylutki,
MF Tynan, MW Tynan, RJ Tynan, K Tyndall, MM Tynon,
GE Tyres, DN Tyrrell, JS Tyrrell, RA Tyrrell, RC Tyrrell,
RJ Tyrrell, WE Tyrrell, PJ Tys, AJ Tyson, DG Tyson,
PW Tyson, GS Udvardy, PF Uebergang, LJ Ufer, BJ Ugarte,
IM Uhlmann, JW Uhlmann, RW Uhrhane, SV Uilderks,
R Ulanowicz, AM Ulanowski, WO Ullathorne, RJ Ullrich,
DB Ulyatt, FJ Umecki, PJ Umina, HEM Ummels,
RD Umphelby, NH Underhill, RJ Underhill,
DW Underwood, GL Underwood, JF Underwood,
KM Underwood, NJ Underwood, RJ Underwood,
SJ Underwood, VG Underwood, JF Ungermann, NP Uniacke,
GA Unmack, KW Unmeopa, KF Unthank, A Unwin,
KA Unwin, PJ Unwin, RG Unwin, BR Upjohn,
SC Uppington, TW Upson, CR Upton, JF Upton,
ML Upton, PM Upton, HM Urban, Z Urbancic, B Uren,
BT Uren, DK Uren, RJ Urlich, AG Urquhart, AJ Urquhart,
BJ Urquhart, HA Urquhart, LJ Urquhart, RGL Urquhart,
RWG Urquhart, RG Usback, CC Usher, KJ Usher,
WRA Ussfeller, GK Utschink, MJ Utting, RM Utting, PJ Utz,
UB Vaak, RA Vadeikis, VK Vadiveloo, CR Vagg, B Vahdat,
AR Vahlberg, G Vahlis, AJ Vains, GIF Vaivarinsh, BL Vale,
DT Vale, GD Vale, PD Vale, HO Valentin, AG Valentine,
MB Valentine, J Vallance, RJ Vallance, PF Vallejo,
JT Vallender, JH Valliant, IC Valuks, JJ Valvo, LJ Van de
Kamp, KW Van Kruyssen, A Van Moolenbroek, HJ Van
Rijswijk, HF Van Tongeren, GA Van Aken, RC Van Aken,
GW Van Arkel, MJ Van As, PJ Van As, TPJ Van Bakel,
WF Van Bakel, JBM Van Beek, DG Van Beekhuizen, CJ Van
Bergen, JJ Van Berkel, HMJ Van Dartel, MHA Van de
Nieuwenhof, JP Van de Velde, G Van de Wege, KW Van Den
Belt, H Van Den Boog, FC Van der Kley, JA Van der Klugt,
AR Van der Linden, PA Van der Meeden, PW Van der Meer,
PC Van der Pol, DJ Van der Toorn, RC Van der Veen,
WC Van Diemen, PM Van Doorn, MHM Van Driel, MJ Van
Droffelaar, WM Van Dyk, RG Van Eede, JE Van Eldik, PJ Van
Ewyk, MM Van Gelder, RV Van Gils, PH Van Haeff, BF Van
Ham, GC Van Haren, RC Van Harskamp, JFJ Van Hattem,
PWF Van Heteren, TE Van Heythuysen, GJM Van Hoof,
S Van Kralingen, BA Van Kuyk, AD Van Leeuwen, FWL Van
Leeuwen, GE Van Liessum, JT Van Loon, WFM Van Loon,
FC Van Luyk, DG Van Maanenberg, VVL Van Mosseveld,
J Van Munster, D Van Neuren, MPM Van Nus, JD Van Ooran,
LM Van Oosterwijck, PRP Van Rijsewijk, GJM Van Rysinge,
AW Van Sleeuwen, B Van Tienhoven, A Van Valen, J Van
Wageningen, WH Van Wegberg, AN Van Winden,
C Vanamstel, JW Vananholt, LJ Vanboeckel, M Vance,
JL Vandam, W Vandam, P Vandenberg, PW Vandepeer,
GJ Vander, HC Vander Vinne, CP Vanderaar, N Vanderboon,
J Vanderheide, R Vanderheiden, DR Vanderhoeven,
KH Vanderhorst, GT Vandermaat, WM Vanderschoot,
SE Vandervelden, P Vandervinne, BJ Vandervlag,

JW Vanderwall, PA Vanderwel, JW Vanderzon, C Vandevelde, HJ Vandiemen, FC Vandongen, R Vandongen, JC Vandyke, M Vandyke, RA Vandyke, N Vanegdom, AC Vangeyzel, MS Vanheerde, AJ Vanhulst, PF Vanny, JW Vanpelt, M Vanpoeteren, JH Vanpoppel, JM Vanroosmalen, G Vanrooy, NW Vansleve, DM Vansprang, RD Vanstan, DW Vanstone, PJL Vantongeran, JB Vanvliet, MJ Vanwyck, WJ Vanzetten, JA Vanzwol, GG Vapp, B Vardanega, R Vardanega, KW Vardy, AT Varga, EI Varga, NB Varley, PA Varley, SW Varley, RW Varlow, PJ Varney, P Varricchio, C Vasarelli, RJ Vasey, G Vasiliev, FW Vass, BF Vassella, MS Vassilakos, JT Vat, SR Vatovez, BF Vaughan, CH Vaughan, IT Vaughan, KJ Vaughan, PA Vaughan, JS Vautin, IS Vayro, NG Veal, GJ Veale, MJ Veale, RW Veale, TJ Veale, DR Vealey, JL Veall, RJ Veall, R Vear, RE Vear, AV Vearing, BR Vearing, KW Vears, S Vecchio, HR Veenhuizen, HS Veenstra, W Veenvliet, SL Veitch, TD Veitch, WJ Veivers, GM Veldhuis, WJ Veldkamp, A Vella, KC Vella, VF Vella, HGW Vellacott, RJ Vellacott, PJ Veltmeyer, DR Venables, EM Venables, GH Venables, KJW Venables, BE Venaglia, CF Venema, JCT Veness, RF Veness, GW Vening, AJ Venn, IJ Venning, AW Ventham, HB Ventriss, LR Venz, LR Verco, LS Verco, NM Verco, RC Verco, GS Vercoe, RF Vercoe, FG Verdi, R Vere, JE Verhelst, WP Verhoeven, P Verkuylen, RJ Verkys, HC Vermeeren, RA Vernieux, CG Vernon, RS Vernon, AN Verrall, PG Verrall, MJ Verran, RW Verrender, P Versluys, GEH Vertigan, B Vertzonis, DL Verwoert, WF Vesey, G Veth, J Vezgoff, PJ Vial, RR Vial, GM Vibert, EA Viccars, P Vicino, JR Vickary, AL Vickers, CH Vickers, CR Vickers, MC Vickers, PA Vickers, WC Vickers, BJ Vickery, CC Vickery, IC Vickery, KM Vickery, NA Vickery, RA Vickery, M Vidal, LJ Vidler, N Vidler, R Vidler, RJ Vidler, RT Vidler, SJ Vidler, N Vidot, RSP Vidulich, IJ Viergever, JL Viergever, GM Vigar, CH Vigh, J Viksne, RPM Vikuckis, GL Villalba, RG Villinger, RE Villis, AFG Vinall, JCM Vince, MR Vince, NB Vince, PJ Vince, A Vincent, AL Vincent, AR Vincent, D Vincent, DF Vincent, DL Vincent, EO Vincent, FN Vincent, GW Vincent, JH Vincent, JR Vincent, KT Vincent, LR Vincent, NG Vincent, NJ Vincent, PJ Vincent, PN Vincent, PZ Vincent, RH Vincent, TM Vincent, WM Vincent, LS Vine, RH Vine, RA Vines, RK Vines, WA Vines, G Viney, KD Viney, P Viney, J Vingelis, HJ Vink, JRA Vintner, JRD Vipen, JT Virgin, RJ Virgin, DJ Virgo, WL Virieux, B Virtue, KJ Virtue, TC Virtue, CJ Vis, M Visinko, LA Visser, RA Visser, P Vitale, M Vitasovic, JJ Vitkovsky, KP Vitnell, RC Vitnell, TJ Vize, DM Vizzone, PB Vlachou, OM Vladich, J Vlavianos, EP Vock, MJ Vogt, TB Vogt, KS Voigt, T Vojinov, DJ Vokes, MFJ Volders, PE Volkoff, DW Vollmerhause, RH Volraat, DL Voltz, RE Voltz, AA Von Kurtz, H Von Muenchhausen, DK Vonbertough, JR Vonharten, AAW Vonk, GT Vonstanke, CD Von-Stieglitz, RE Vonthethoff, JB Vonwiller, PJ Vortronald, FH Voss, PJ Voss, RJ Voss, SF Voss, WG Voss, SJ Vosti, J Votta, BP Vowles, GR Voycey, B Voyzey, DJ Voyzey, J Voznaks, J Vranjic, A Vrieling, PI Vuckovich, RP Vuichoud, GD Vulich, CJ Vyner, RW Wachmer, GS Wackett, JD Wackett, DJ Waddell, IR Waddell, JM Waddell, KJ Waddell, DA Waddingham, LB Waddington, MR Waddington, DM Waddle, A Wade, B Wade, BL Wade, DG Wade, DJ Wade, DL Wade, EJ Wade, ER Wade, GA Wade, GD Wade, GL Wade, J Wade, LS Wade, MJ Wade, RB Wade, RJ Wade, SP Wade, V Wade, B Wadeson, BJ Wadie, WA Wadsworth, CH Wadwell, BE Wagenaar, W Wagenknecht, GJ Wager, TA Waghorn, TL Waghorn, CN Wagner, DR Wagner, GL Wagner, K Wagner, RG Wagner, RL Wagner, TJ Wagner, WM Wagner, DW Wagstaff, RT Wagstaff, VN Wagstaff, MW Wahl, RG Wahlheim, TP Wahlin, ATJ Waide, DJ Waight, MJ Waight, JA Wailes, PN Wailes, R Wailes, AA Wain, DF Wain, G Waine, GR Wainwright, RW Wainwright, DR Wait, KH Wait, DK Waite, PJ Waite, JF Waiter, B Waites, GW Waites, SG Waites, PJ Wake, TG Wake, B Wakefield, BA Wakefield, BE Wakefield, DG Wakefield, GN Wakefield, JC Wakefield, RJ Wakefield, L Wakeham, TA Wakeham, JJ Wakelin, ML Wakelin, RH Wakelin, GL Wakeling, RD Wakeling, RJ Wakeling, P Wakely, JF Wakeman, H Walburg, GD Walch, TH Walch, GJ Walcher, H Waldau, PP Waldeck, AR Walden, GA Walden, GF Walden, WE Waldhart, CH Waldhauser, G Waldie, DJ Waldock, TW Waldock, WC Waldock, M Waldon, CD Waldron, M Waldron, EJ Wales, KC Wales, MR Wales, WS Wales, A Walford, NM Walk, PM Walkaden, AB Walker, AC Walker, AG Walker, AH Walker, AJ Walker, AL Walker, AP Walker, AR Walker, BA Walker, BE Walker, BG Walker, BR Walker, BT Walker, BW Walker, CG Walker, CJ Walker, CL Walker, D Walker, DB Walker, DG Walker, DJ Walker, DL Walker, DS Walker, DT Walker, EJ Walker, F Walker, G Walker, GA Walker, GF Walker, GL Walker, HE Walker, HJ Walker, HN Walker, J Walker, JC Walker, JCC Walker, JD Walker, JF Walker, JH Walker, JL Walker, JW Walker, KA Walker, KF Walker, KJH Walker, KM Walker, KR Walker, KW Walker, L Walker, LA Walker, LB Walker, LC Walker, LD Walker, LJ Walker, M Walker, MB Walker, MC Walker, MF Walker, MJ Walker, NJ Walker, NR Walker, OH Walker, OL Walker, P Walker, PA Walker, PR Walker, RA Walker, RAM Walker, RD Walker, RE Walker, RF Walker, RG Walker, RJ Walker, RL Walker, RM Walker, RN Walker, RO Walker, RR Walker, RW Walker, RWR Walker, SJ Walker, SL Walker, TC Walker, TD Walker, TF Walker, TFH Walker, TP Walker, TT Walker, WH Walker, WL Walker, LJ Walker-Smith, TJ Walkinshaw, GI Walkley, J Walkley, BJ Wall, CI Wall, CL Wall, CW Wall, DA Wall, HW Wall, IC Wall, JFH Wall, KN Wall, RD Wall, RE Wall, RH Wall, RJ Wall, SG Wall, WT Wall, AE Wallace, AJ Wallace, BJ Wallace, CA Wallace, CJ Wallace, CW Wallace, DC Wallace, DW Wallace, GB Wallace, GC Wallace, GE Wallace, HA Wallace, IJ Wallace, JD Wallace, KJ Wallace, NL Wallace, PJ Wallace, RB Wallace, RG Wallace, RS Wallace, RW Wallace, SJ Wallace, TA Wallace, WA Wallace, RH Wallbank, DT Wallbridge, GV Wallbridge, PJ Wallbridge, KJ Wallder, MR Wallder, DC Wallent, BD Waller, FT Waller, LJ Waller, OD Waller, PB Waller, RW Waller, AJ Wallis, AM Wallis, AR Wallis, BE Wallis, BG Wallis, BJ Wallis, CM Wallis, DA Wallis, DC Wallis, EL Wallis, GE Wallis, JB Wallis, JF Wallis, KD Wallis, KR Wallis, ME Wallis, PE Wallis, RE Wallis, RK Wallis, RW Wallis, SH Wallis, SM Wallis, NJ Walliss, DJ Wallner, GN Walls, NM Walls, RJ Walls, AJ Walmsley, EH Walmsley, R Walmsley, A Walpole, JD Walpole, LJ Walpole, PA Walpole, TW Walpole, WJ Walpole, AP Walsh, AR Walsh, B Walsh, BM Walsh, D Walsh, DI Walsh, DJ Walsh, DS Walsh, DW Walsh, EM Walsh, FJ Walsh, GF Walsh, JA Walsh, JC Walsh, KE Walsh, KJ Walsh, LM Walsh, LRT Walsh, LW Walsh, MD Walsh, MF Walsh, MJ Walsh, P Walsh, PA Walsh, PJ Walsh, PM Walsh, PV Walsh, R Walsh, RL Walsh, RT Walsh, T Walsh, TA Walsh, TK Walsh, TM Walsh, TW Walsh, AJ Walter, CR Walter, DC Walter, FL Walter, RE Walter, RI Walter, RND Walter, AA Walters, BN Walters, CV Walters, EL Walters, GA Walters, GR Walters, GW Walters, JC Walters, JG Walters, NG Walters, OR Walters, PM Walters, RA Walters, RF Walters, RJ Walters, TJ Walters, WR Walters, KJ Waltham, BJ Walton, BR Walton, DW Walton, GA Walton, GF Walton, GR Walton, KJ Walton, KR Walton, KW Walton, ND Walton, PG Walton, PW Walton, RI Walton, SJ Walton, SL Walton, TJT Walton, TK Walton, TW Walton, CA Walz, NJ Walz, AA Wand, JD Wandless, DJ Wanless, DM Wann, WH Wansley, IG Wanstall, PH Wapshott, LJ Warbrook, GFA Warburton, IE Warburton, K Warburton, TC Warburton, LJ Warby, AH Ward, AL Ward, BF Ward, BK Ward, CA Ward, CJ Ward, DA Ward, DH Ward, DHV Ward, DJ Ward, DK Ward, DL Ward, DS Ward, GA Ward, GD Ward, GE Ward, GJ Ward, GL Ward, GR Ward, GX Ward, HH Ward, ID Ward, IL Ward, IW Ward, J Ward, JE Ward, JG Ward, JJ Ward, JL Ward, JN Ward, JPF Ward, JR Ward, JW Ward, K Ward, KC Ward, KW Ward, L Ward, LP Ward, MJ Ward, MS Ward, PA Ward, PD Ward, PJ Ward, PL Ward, R Ward, RA Ward, RE Ward, RG Ward, RH Ward, RJ Ward, RM Ward, RT Ward, RW Ward, SC Ward, SL Ward, TD Ward, TJ Ward, WDT Ward, WT Ward, DA Wardell, DJ Warden, GR Warden, JO Wardlaw, CW Wardle, DJ Wardle, EH Wardle, AB Wardley, VW Wardrop, PG Wardrope, TJ Wardrope, CR Ware, RA Ware, RC Ware, VI Wareham, R Wareing, BG Warendorp, JA Wares, MJ Wargent, RW Warhurst, AEL Waring, L Waring, CC Wark, IM Wark, TF Wark, KD Warke, GP Warland, IR Warlters, IR Warman, MW Warmbold, B Warn, RF Warn, S Warn, RJ Warncke, DJ Warne, KLG Warne, MR Warne, PM Warne, JP Warneke, AM Warner, CL Warner, DB Warner, DRW Warner, ER Warner, FC Warner, JA Warner, PG Warner, RJ Warner, RM Warner, SM Warner, EJ Warnes, WB Warnes, MR Warnest, BJ Warnock, J Warr, JA Warr, RA Warr, SLE Warr, GC Warrell, AC Warren, AG Warren, AK Warren, AL Warren, BJ Warren, CR Warren, DJ Warren, DK Warren, DM Warren, DP Warren, DR Warren, EJ Warren, I Warren, IH Warren, J Warren, KR Warren, LD Warren, LJ Warren, MA Warren, N Warren, NJ Warren, PM Warren, PR Warren, R Warren, RB Warren, RD Warren, TR Warren, WC Warren, WE Warren, WM Warren, WR Warren, GR Warrener, T Warrington, AJ Warry, R Warsop, IA Warton, BJ Warwick, JVW Warwick, LW Warwick, PC Warwick, JP Waser, WN Washington, SJ Wasiak, M Wasiu, RJ Wason, AD Wass, DL Wass, DP Wass, KJ Wass, MS Wass, TE Wass, KB Waterfall, DC Waterfield, DE Waterford, G Waterman, GR Waterman, PL Waterman, WF Waterman, AR Waters, B Waters, BD Waters, BJ Waters, BN Waters, BT Waters, CD Waters, EJ Waters, GA Waters, GE Waters, GJ Waters, GS Waters, JR Waters, KR Waters, MB Waters, MP Waters, PJ Waters, PV Waters, TM Waters, W Waters, WE Waters, WT Waters, JK Waterson, RG Waterson, BA Waterston, DR Waterston, GJ Watkin, HR Watkin, AW Watkins, CB Watkins, DJ Watkins, E Watkins, FS Watkins, GR Watkins, GW Watkins, IR Watkins, JD Watkins, KL Watkins, MF Watkins, ND Watkins, R Watkins, RG Watkins, RI Watkins, RJ Watkins, BW Watkinson, DR Watling, SH Watling, AJ Watson, AP Watson, BJ Watson, BP Watson, CS Watson, CW Watson, D Watson, DC Watson, DE Watson, DH Watson, DI Watson, DJ Watson, DR Watson, DS Watson, EC Watson, EF Watson, EJ Watson, FW Watson, G Watson, GC Watson, GJ Watson, GT Watson, J Watson, JB Watson, JDJ Watson, JG Watson, JR Watson, JT Watson, K Watson, KG Watson, KM Watson, KR Watson, LE Watson, M Watson, MP Watson, NA Watson, NR Watson, OJ Watson, P Watson, PA Watson, PC Watson, PJ Watson, PR Watson, PW Watson, RA Watson, RCA Watson, RE Watson, RJ Watson, RP Watson, RS Watson, RT Watson, SA Watson, TE Watson, TJ Watson, TO Watson, TR Watson, WC Watson, WF Watson, WJ Watson, WM Watson, AC Watt, B Watt, BG Watt, BJ Watt, DH Watt, DL Watt, IM Watt, ME Watt, NW Watt, RD Watt, RK Watt, RL Watt, RM Watt, RR Watt, S Watt, WB Watt, WM Watt, KG Watters, RJ Watters, PA Watterson, JM Watton, AJ Watts, BK Watts, BS Watts, BT Watts, DE Watts, DJ Watts, DK Watts, DL Watts, GE Watts, GG Watts, GJ Watts, GL Watts, GP Watts, GR Watts, GT Watts, HR Watts, JD Watts, LJ Watts, ND Watts, P Watts, PG Watts, PH Watts, PJ Watts, RA Watts, RL Watts, RM Watts, RW Watts, TJ Watts, TW Watts, V Watts, VA Watts, WJ Watts, PV Wauchope, TK Wauer, UH Wauer, ER Waugh, PR Waugh, WA Waugh, RV Wawrykiewicz, WM Wawrzycki, DM Way, IR Way, LC Way, RS Way, SA Way, WA Way, EBJ Wayland, H Wayne, WS Wayne, CA Weaire, TW Weakley, GD Weale, RB Wear, RJ Wear, HR Wearing, MT Wearing, GA Wearn, GR Wearne, RM Wearne, WJ Wearne, GE Wease, RG Weatherald, D Weatherall, EJ Weatherall, ER Weatherall, JH Weatherley, AE Weaven, A Weaver, AR Weaver, BM Weaver, CJ Weaver, JR Weaver, JW Weaver, MT Weaver, PJ Weaver, PR Weaver, AV Webb, B Webb, BL Webb, BS Webb, C Webb, CJ Webb, D Webb, DD Webb, DR Webb, EJ Webb, FJ Webb, GB Webb, GE Webb, GF Webb, GR Webb, GS Webb, HA Webb, HJ Webb, HP Webb, IG Webb, JC Webb, JE Webb, JS Webb, JW Webb, K Webb, KF Webb, KG Webb, KR Webb, LM Webb, LR Webb, MC Webb, MD Webb, MJ Webb, MS Webb, N Webb, NA Webb, PW Webb, R Webb, RA Webb, RE Webb, RF Webb, RG Webb, RH Webb, RJ Webb, RL Webb, RP Webb, RW Webb, SE Webb, SM Webb, TA Webb, TF Webb, DE Webbe, JFP Webbe, AH Webber, AJ Webber, BN Webber, DR Webber, G Webber, JF Webber, PFP Webber, PR Webber, RC Webber, SJ Webber, WA Webber, CD Weber, HR Weber, I Weber, PL Weber, SL Weber, AC Webster, AJ Webster, BG Webster, BT Webster, CF Webster, CJ Webster, CW Webster, DA Webster, DAW Webster, DE Webster, DJ Webster, DR Webster, EJ Webster, FI Webster, GJ Webster, GLJ Webster, GT Webster, GW Webster, IA Webster, JC Webster, JF Webster, LA Webster, LG Webster, MC Webster, MN Webster, MW Webster, NJ Webster, PD Webster, PJ Webster, RB Webster, RJ Webster, RS Webster, SM Webster, TE Webster, TJ Webster, CA Wecker, GA Weda, RE Wedding, HD Wedemeyer, AB Wedgwood, IW Wedlock, JN Wedmaier, R Weed, GR Weeden, JE Weeden, RS Weeding, PF Weedman, GM Weekes, NH Weekes, TJ Weekes, DA Weekley, JH Weekley, TM Weekley, EC Weeks, GT Weeks, IW Weeks, JE Weeks, KG Weeks, J Weers, AR Weertman, DW Wegener, J Wegman, LJ Wegmann, BA Wehr, DA Wehrman, TJ Wehrmann, LJ Weidenhofer, DR Weigall, CR Weigand, HF Weight, KM Weightman, ML Weightman, CR Weiley, DP Weinert, PL Weingott,

NC Weinheimer, FE Weinman, AM Weir, CG Weir, DD Weir, GS Weir, JC Weir, JR Weir, KM Weir, KW Weir, NJ Weir, RJ Weir, RL Weir, SP Weir, TS Weir, W Weir, WJ Weir, GL Weire, JB Weire, JV Weirick, RL Weirman, PJ Weir-Smith, WS Weis, GE Weise, LJ Weise, GP Weismantel, CE Weiss, KP Weiss, JR Weissel, RH Weitzmann, AP Welbourn, PF Welbourne, AJ Welch, DF Welch, GW Welch, PEH Welch, S Welch, CR Welden, AH Weldon, DT Weldon, J Weldon, TJ Weldon, WA Weldon, RJ Welfare, WK Welfare, RJ Wellard, TJ Wellard, WJ Wellby, AC Weller, BJ Weller, DJ Weller, GR Weller, MF Weller, SL Weller, CH Wellings, AP Wellington, BL Wellington, RR Wellington, TL Wellins, A Wells, AD Wells, AJC Wells, BR Wells, CB Wells, CR Wells, DK Wells, GA Wells, GM Wells, IM Wells, IS Wells, JA Wells, JB Wells, JC Wells, JR Wells, KD Wells, KF Wells, KJ Wells, LJ Wells, M Wells, NT Wells, PA Wells, PI Wells, RJ Wells, RL Wells, RM Wells, RW Wells, SR Wells, TW Wells, WD Wells, WJ Wells, WL Wells, AA Welsh, AJ Welsh, IJ Welsh, JA Welsh, JG Welsh, JR Welsh, LH Welsh, P Welsh, R Welsh, RC Welsh, T Welsh, TL Welsh, L Welyczko, RC Wemm, CR Wemyss, R Wench, BA Wendelgelst, AE Wendell, SD Wendland, KH Wendon, DM Wendt, DR Wendt, GW Wendt, IJ Wendt, KS Wendt, RD Wendt, GR Wenhlowskyj, PR Wenholz, K Wenitong, L Wenitong, LR Wenitong, CS Wennekes, RL Wensley, AJ Went, RL Went, AJ Wenzel, DW Wenzel, EN Werchon, B Weremijenko, YN Werndly, R Werth, EJ Wertheimer, BE Wesener, BW Wesiak, GD Wesley, RJ Wessel, W Wesseler, AP Wessing, F Wessing, DR Wesson, RJ Wesson, AC West, AL West, AR West, ARH West, AS West, BD West, BG West, CP West, CV West, CW West, DH West, DJ West, DN West, E West, EA West, ED West, GJ West, GM West, GW West, HA West, IK West, IL West, JE West, JP West, KR West, KW West, LA West, LJ West, MG West, P West, PH West, PN West, RF West, RG West, RJ West, RJH West, RS West, SA West, SR West, TJ West, CM Westaway, PJ Westbrook, EW Westburgh, TA Westbury, GJ Westcott, AH Westerman, D Western, TH Westerway, RE Westfold, DP Westgate, TW Westhead, DJ Westlake, KR Westlake, AJ Westland, GB Westmore, BG Weston, CB Weston, GA Weston, GN Weston, JH Weston, JN Weston, L Weston, LJ Weston, LS Weston, MK Weston, N Weston, NE Weston, NJ Weston, R Weston, RA Weston, RJ Weston, RL Weston, RM Weston, SH Weston, MR Westphal, JA Westwood, ND Westwood, PC Westwood, LA Westworth, MR Wettenhall, BJ Wetzig, SZ Weusten, WMJ Weyers, AJ Weymouth, PL Weymouth, PM Weymouth, JJ Whaites, JG Whalan, NR Whalan, PA Whalan, RF Whalan, TP Whalan, WO Whalan, PS Whale, JL Whalley, JR Whalley, R Whalley, RM Whalley, T Wharmby, JL Wharton, KJ Wharton, WR Wharton, GJ Whateley, JR Whatling, GE Whatman, LH Whatmore, LJ Whatmore, RG Whatson, DJ Wheare, GL Wheat, GR Wheat, AK Wheatley, EG Wheatley, G Wheatley, GM Wheatley, JA Wheatley, KA Wheatley, KE Wheatley, MS Wheatley, WA Wheatley, IG Wheaton, KA Wheelahan, CD Wheeldon, HR Wheeldon, AJ Wheeler, B Wheeler, BH Wheeler, DF Wheeler, GP Wheeler, JW Wheeler, KE Wheeler, LR Wheeler, LW Wheeler, OG Wheeler, RJ Wheeler, TM Wheeler, EP Whelan, GP Whelan, JJ Whelan, JM Whelan, KW Whelan, LG Whelan, MN Whelan, RC Whelan, RF Whelan, T Whelan, TM Whelan, TP Whelan, GJ Wheldon, DG Whellum, RJ Whellum, DR Whelpton, GD Whennan, DH Wherrett, RB Wherrett, AL Wheway, ER Wheway, JK Whiddon, RV Whiley, RA Whillas, BW Whinfield, RJ Whinnen, LG Whip, AJ Whipp, KJ Whipp, RT Whipp, EU Whippy, BJ Whiston, CJ Whiston, AC Whitaker, GP Whitaker, JJ Whitaker, P Whitaker, PF Whitaker, GK Whitbourne, PG Whitbourne, KB Whitbread, WJ Whitbread, JM Whitburn, DE Whitby, BC Whitcher, JA Whitcombe, A White, AC White, AE White, AG White, AJ White, AN White, ARJ White, AW White, BA White, BM White, BS White, C White, CH White, DJ White, DK White, DN White, DS White, EA White, EC White, ED White, G White, GA White, GG White, GJ White, GL White, GM White, HAD White, HW White, IBN White, IR White, J White, J White, JD White, JED White, JF White, JGW White, JM White, JP White, JPB White, JR White, JW White, KA White, KC White, KE White, KM White, KR White, LA White, LC White, LJ White, LJP White, LL White, LM White, M White, MM White, MP White, MR White, N White, NG White, NH White, NJ White, P White, PA White, PC White, PE White, PF White, PHJ White, PJ White, PL White, PND White, PR White, PSP White, PV White, PW White, QNL White, RA White, RB White, RC White, RD White, RE White, RG White, RJ White, RK White, RM White, RN White, RP White, RS White, RT White, RV White, TC White, TD White, TL White, WH White, WJ White, WR White, WV White, J Whiteaker, LR Whiteaker, BR Whitehead, GR Whitehead, GS Whitehead, JF Whitehead, JR Whitehead, JW Whitehead, MJ Whitehead, MR Whitehead, NP Whitehead, PR Whitehead, RG Whitehead, RH Whitehead, SP Whitehead, WJ Whitehead, RD Whitehill, CA Whitehorn, JM Whitehorn, DR Whitehorne, DM Whitehouse, MH Whitehouse, RW Whitehurst, CW Whitelaw, FT Whitelaw, J Whitelaw, IL Whiteley, PA Whiteley, RM Whiteley, AR Whiteman, DF Whiteman, CJ Whiteside, DJ Whiteside, DP Whiteside, HT Whiteside, AF Whiteway, AT Whitfield, CM Whitfield, GJ Whitfield, RK Whitfield, WA Whitfield, WD Whitfield, KJ Whitford, RB Whitford, SJ Whitford, JW Whithorn, RJ Whiticker, CD Whiting, DJ Whiting, JH Whiting, KD Whiting, NT Whiting, GJ Whitla, MW Whitley, IH Whitman, NS Whitman, PS Whitmee, DE Whitmey, KB Whitmore, L Whitmore, JD Whitney, LE Whitney, MH Whitney, NW Whitney, WH Whitney, J Whittaker, JK Whittaker, JN Whittaker, P Whittaker, PF Whittaker, RJ Whittaker, RV Whittaker, JW Whittam, CD Whitten, CE Whittington, JC Whittington, RL Whittington, KA Whittle, PJ Whittle, RJ Whittle, WJ Whittle, GT Whittley, DK Whitton, GA Whitton, JH Whitton, KEC Whitton, PB Whitton, TR Whitton, MJ Whitty, DJ Whitwam, TJ Whitwam, IR Whitwell, JH Whitworth, MV Wholohan, BL Whybrow, NJ Whybrow, GJ Whykes, HR Whyman, BD Whyte, GJ Whyte, K Whyte, JD Whyte-Southcombe, RD Wibrow, BK Wicke, RN Wickenden, BH Wickens, RC Wicker, RTF Wickes, BK Wickham, EC Wickham, JE Wickham, RJ Wickham, TR Wickham, AJ Wicks, BJ Wicks, DC Wicks, GA Wicks, JA Wicks, KE Wicks, LA Wicks, MGA Wicks, RB Wicks, RD Wicks, RT Wicks, MF Wickstein, EA Widders, GB Widdison, PE Widerberg, EF Widermanski, HB Widermanski, BW Wieben, PR Wieden, JE Wieland, LJ Wieland, MJ Wiering, JE Wieringa, MFM Wiezel, DF Wigg, JW Wigg, KJ Wigg, MT Wiggin, ER Wiggins, KA Wiggins, LA Wiggins, RC Wiggins, TR Wiggins, PJ Wight, WS Wight, MJ Wighton, WJ Wigmore, CW Wignell, DR Wignell, RA Wigney, TJ Wilbow, BA Wilby, JH Wilby, EWB Wilcox, GT Wilcox, H Wilcox, WR Wilcox, T Wilczek, JD Wild, RE Wild, HC Wilde, RN Wilde, RW Wilde, W Wilde, LJ Wildeboer, AL Wilden, PL Wildes, B Wilding, R Wildschut, AJ Wiles, CE Wiles, NE Wilesmith, WA Wilesmith, CJ Wiley, RF Wilhelm, S Wilinski, AA Wilkes, AB Wilkes, AL Wilkes, KC Wilkes, PD Wilkes, D Wilkie, GM Wilkie, GR Wilkie, JA Wilkie, JG Wilkie, PA Wilkie, RJ Wilkie, CK Wilkin, PE Wilkin, AA Wilkins, BH Wilkins, DS Wilkins, GJ Wilkins, JA Wilkins, KA Wilkins, M Wilkins, ML Wilkins, PA Wilkins, PG Wilkins, PL Wilkins, PW Wilkins, RJ Wilkins, WJ Wilkins, ACF Wilkinson, AG Wilkinson, AJ Wilkinson, D Wilkinson, DC Wilkinson, DJ Wilkinson, DR Wilkinson, E Wilkinson, FJ Wilkinson, GE Wilkinson, GJ Wilkinson, GW Wilkinson, JW Wilkinson, K Wilkinson, KF Wilkinson, KR Wilkinson, LA Wilkinson, LJ Wilkinson, LW Wilkinson, MTR Wilkinson, PM Wilkinson, R Wilkinson, RA Wilkinson, T Wilkinson, TJ Wilkinson, VB Wilkinson, WG Wilkinson, LJ Wilks, RA Wilks, AG Will, DF Will, JA Will, JH Willbery, BS Willcock, AF Willcocks, RG Willcocks, BE Willcott, AJ Willcox, DA Willcox, PR Willcox, A Willemsen, LR Willet, BR Willett, FJ Willett, JG Willett, D Willetts, LF Willey, PJ Willey, R Willey, RG Willey, AC Williams, AF Williams, AJ Williams, AL Williams, AM Williams, AP Williams, AR Williams, AS Williams, AT Williams, AW Williams, B Williams, BA Williams, BB Williams, BC Williams, BF Williams, BG Williams, BH Williams, BJ Williams, BK Williams, BM Williams, BR Williams, BS Williams, CB Williams, CD Williams, CF Williams, CJ Williams, COG Williams, D Williams, DA Williams, DF Williams, DG Williams, DH Williams, DJ Williams, DP Williams, DR Williams, EC Williams, EDR Williams, EG Williams, EJ Williams, EL Williams, EM Williams, EP Williams, ER Williams, EW Williams, F Williams, G Williams, GA Williams, GB Williams, GC Williams, GE Williams, GJ Williams, GR Williams, GV Williams, IC Williams, IM Williams, IN Williams, J Williams, JA Williams, JAE Williams, JC Williams, JD Williams, JE Williams, JF Williams, JH Williams, JJ Williams, JL Williams, JM Williams, JP Williams, JR Williams, JV Williams, JW Williams, KA Williams, KB Williams, KE Williams, KJ Williams, KR Williams, KW Williams, L Williams, LA Williams, LJ Williams, LR Williams, LS Williams, LT Williams, M Williams, M Williams, MBP Williams, MD Williams, ME Williams, MG Williams, MH Williams, MJ Williams, N Williams, NTJ Williams, NW Williams, P Williams, PA Williams, PC Williams, PF Williams, PG Williams, PH Williams, PJ Williams, PK Williams, PR Williams, PW Williams, R Williams, RA Williams, RC Williams, RD Williams, RE Williams, RG Williams, RJ Williams, RK Williams, RL Williams, RM Williams, RN Williams, RP Williams, RR Williams, RV Williams, RW Williams, SE Williams, SR Williams, TA Williams, TE Williams, TG Williams, TJ Williams, TP Williams, TR Williams, VR Williams, W Williams, WA Williams, WC Williams, WD Williams, WG Williams, WJ Williams, WR Williams, WS Williams, AC Williamson, AM Williamson, BG Williamson, CJ Williamson, DJ Williamson, EA Williamson, EJ Williamson, FJ Williamson, G Williamson, GG Williamson, GV Williamson, ID Williamson, IE Williamson, IN Williamson, J Williamson, JI Williamson, JR Williamson, KJ Williamson, LB Williamson, LE Williamson, N Williamson, R Williamson, RF Williamson, RJ Williamson, RN Williamson, TA Williamson, TJ Williamson, WT Williamson, CD Williamson-Cameron, WT Willicombe, BW Willing, EJ Willingham, NE Willingham, PR Willington, B Willis, BR Willis, D Willis, DB Willis, DL Willis, GLG Willis, GTK Willis, HR Willis, J Willis, KC Willis, MF Willis, MW Willis, NF Willis, PR Willis, RA Willis, SA Willis, SVL Willis, TJ Willis, WG Willis, BP Willison, GJ Willits, GK Willmann, JW Willmington, AB Willmot, DC Willmot, MA Willmot, AP Willmott, TJ Willmott, DJ Willoughby, FJ Willoughby, GI Willoughby, GJ Willoughby, IR Willoughby, TJ Willoughby, KA Willox, DJ Wills, GR Wills, IR Wills, NE Wills, RG Wills, WT Wills, JB Willshire, AL Willson, HJ Willson, JC Willson, RJ Willson, LW Wilmen, Q Wilmer, DJ Wilmore, GE Wilmot, KG Wilmot, NP Wilmot, RP Wilsen, RG Wilshier, RL Wilshier, RN Wilshier, PR Wilshire, A Wilson, AD Wilson, AG Wilson, AJ Wilson, AM Wilson, AR Wilson, AW Wilson, BA Wilson, BD Wilson, BFE Wilson, BG Wilson, BH Wilson, BJ Wilson, BK Wilson, BL Wilson, BP Wilson, BR Wilson, BS Wilson, BT Wilson, BW Wilson, C Wilson, CB Wilson, CD Wilson, CE Wilson, CG Wilson, CM Wilson, DA Wilson, DB Wilson, DC Wilson, DE Wilson, DF Wilson, DG Wilson, DJ Wilson, DL Wilson, DM Wilson, DR Wilson, DS Wilson, DW Wilson, EJ Wilson, ELG Wilson, ER Wilson, FN Wilson, G Wilson, GA Wilson, GB Wilson, GC Wilson, GD Wilson, GF Wilson, GI Wilson, GJ Wilson, GL Wilson, GS Wilson, H Wilson, HC Wilson, HR Wilson, IA Wilson, IC Wilson, ID Wilson, IGJ Wilson, IK Wilson, J Wilson, JA Wilson, JB Wilson, JC Wilson, JCT Wilson, JD Wilson, JE Wilson, JF Wilson, JK Wilson, JR Wilson, JS Wilson, JT Wilson, JW Wilson, K Wilson, KG Wilson, KJ Wilson, KL Wilson, KP Wilson, KR Wilson, LC Wilson, LD Wilson, LHC Wilson, LJ Wilson, LNG Wilson, LR Wilson, LS Wilson, M Wilson, MA Wilson, MAF Wilson, MH Wilson, MJ Wilson, MM Wilson, MR Wilson, MW Wilson, NC Wilson, ND Wilson, NJ Wilson, NM Wilson, P Wilson, PJ Wilson, PS Wilson, PT Wilson, RA Wilson, RB Wilson, RC Wilson, RG Wilson, RH Wilson, RJ Wilson, RK Wilson, RL Wilson, RR Wilson, RS Wilson, RT Wilson, RV Wilson, RW Wilson, SA Wilson, SAM Wilson, SE Wilson, SP Wilson, ST Wilson, T Wilson, TC Wilson, TG Wilson, TJ Wilson, TP Wilson, TW Wilson, WC Wilson, WJ Wilson, WN Wilson, WP Wilson, WT Wilson, AP Wilson-Brown, T Wilsonsmith, IJ Wilton, JGN Wilton, PF Wilton, PW Wilton, BL Wiltshire, MS Wiltshire, RJ Wiltshire, TJ Wiltshire, KO Winbank, DE Winch, DL Winch, GJ Winchester, RJ Winchester, W Windberg, KC Windebank, AJJ Windle, DN Window, GJ Window, BG Windred, JK Windred, KC Windred, AJ Windsor, AR Windsor, BR Windsor, GR Windsor, AC Wine, PJ Wines, K Winfield, AL Wing, RA Wingard, RG Wingett, RG Wingrove, R Winiarski, WC Winkel,

AL Winkleman, R Winkler, V Winkler, KE Winkley, KJ Winkworth, WV Winlaw, JR Winn, KE Winn, RW Winn, BO Winner, RE Winnett, AR Winney, PJ Winney, IH Winning, NJ Winning, RV Winroe, AE Winship, BJ Winsor, KR Winsor, WA Winsor, RL Winstanley, JD Winstone, EJ Winter, JE Winter, JM Winter, JRD Winter, M Winter, OC Winter, PJ Winter, PM Winter, RA Winter, RL Winter, WA Winter, DR Winterbotham, RA Winterfield, WJ Winterford, FP Winters, KD Winters, PD Winters, WN Winters, TA Winterton, OA Wintle, LF Winton, MK Winwood, RJ Winwood, GV Winzar, KJ Winzer, RS Wirth, IEK Wischusen, DE Wise, GG Wise, IR Wise, JM Wise, JP Wise, KW Wise, SJ Wise, TJ Wise, DN Wiseman, GR Wiseman, GW Wiseman, JP Wiseman, JS Wiseman, JW Wiseman, LA Wiseman, PR Wiseman, RJ Wiseman, BI Wishart, LA Wiskar, M Wisman, GR Wisniewski, ZSZ Wisniewski, GFL Wissink, GR Witchard, JC Witcombe, B Witford, MG Withall, JK Wither, T Witheridge, KJ Witherow, DE Withers, JG Withers, JW Withers, MJ Withers, WL Withers, RJ Withington, SD Witjas, FS Witkowski, DJ Witt, GC Witt, RH Witten, PJ Wittig, F Wittmer, DM Wittner, SR Witzerman, A Wodianicky, JC Woganbrowne, CP Woithe, WJ Wojciechowski, H Wojtowicz, S Wojtowicz, FG Wolber, GP Wolf, DR Wolfe, ED Wolfe, NH Wolfe, LC Wolfel, NJ Wolfenden, RJ Wolfenden, TJ Wolff, U Wolk, DB Wollage, HA Wollaston, RD Wollaston, SP Wollaston, AJ Wollen, DD Wollner, SD Wollstein, DJ Wolsey, IS Wolter, LF Wolters, A Wolyniec, NJ Womal, JB Wombell, DG Woo, AE Wood, AG Wood, AW Wood, B Wood, BA Wood, BC Wood, BJ Wood, BT Wood, CA Wood, DC Wood, DF Wood, DJ Wood, DK Wood, FV Wood, GA Wood, GC Wood, GP Wood, GS Wood, HY Wood, IM Wood, JF Wood, JH Wood, JL Wood, JS Wood, JW Wood, K Wood, KG Wood, KJ Wood, KL Wood, LG Wood, LH Wood, LI Wood, LN Wood, LR Wood, LT Wood, M Wood, ME Wood, MJ Wood, MP Wood, MS Wood, MT Wood, NC Wood, OD Wood, PC Wood, PG Wood, PM Wood, PS Wood, R Wood, RE Wood, RG Wood, RJ Wood, RS Wood, RW Wood, S Wood, SC Wood, SJ Wood, SR Wood, TJ Wood, V Wood, WD Wood, WE Wood, WK Wood, WT Wood, G Woodall, CW Woodard, NM Woodberry, KO Woodbine, KJ Woodbridge, KW Woodbridge, RV Woodbridge, DP Woodbury, RA Woodbury, RJ Woodbury, DR Woodcock, J Woodcock, PA Woodcock, GW Woodcroft, PA Wooden, GM Woodfield, AJ Woodford, FB Woodford, ND Woodford, CG Woodforde, DJR Woodforde, RJ Woodforde, LK Woodforth, RJ Woodforth, MJ Woodhams, A Woodhouse, AT Woodhouse, BJ Woodhouse, CC Woodhouse, CG Woodhouse, DR Woodhouse, E Woodhouse, FR Woodhouse, H Woodhouse, JW Woodhouse, MA Woodhouse, RD Woodhouse, RH Woodhouse, RL Woodhouse, CFJ Woodland, DT Woodland, KJ Woodlands, LR Woodlands, JW Woodley, NS Woodley, TR Woodley, AJ Woodman, DT Woodman, GA Woodman, GW Woodroff, KC Woodroffe, RW Woodroffe, DR Woodrow, GD Woodrow, RM Woodrow, GW Woodruff, BL Woods, BP Woods, BR Woods, BW Woods, CK Woods, CM Woods, DG Woods, DP Woods, EJ Woods, HW Woods, I Woods, J Woods, JE Woods, KJ Woods, LW Woods, MF Woods, MG Woods, ML Woods, MP Woods, NH Woods, NR Woods, RB Woods, RC Woods, RD Woods, RJ Woods, RW Woods, SJ Woods, TK Woods, WT Woods, AR Woodward, CH Woodward, G Woodward, GB Woodward, GJ Woodward, J Woodward, JH Woodward, KL Woodward, NA Woodward, PJ Woodward, RC Woodward, RF Woodward, RG Woodward, TF Woodward, TM Woodward, R Woolan, PG Woolaston, SJ Woolcock, AE Wooldridge, R Wooldridge, GE Wooler, RA Woolfe, K Woolfenden, DF Woolford, GP Woolford, JA Woolford, LJ Woolford, RM Woolford, CJ Woolhouse, JA Woolhouse, RP Woollard, AJ Woolley, BS Woolley, DB Woolley, DL Woolley, DP Woolley, DR Woolley, PE Woolley, RF Woolley, RG Woolley, RW Woolley, SEK Woolley, SR Woolley, TG Woolley, DR Woolmer, PC Woolmer, TK Woolmer, JR Woolnough, SA Wools-Cobb, WA Woolston, MF Woosnam, DE Wooster, SJ Wooster, RH Wootton, AJ Worboys, NB Worboys, PG Worboys, PG Wordsworth, LJ Workman, NB Workman, EG Worland, GJ Worland, JT Worle, AW Worling, RG Worlley, DC Wormald, JB Wormald, KH Wormald, RC Wormald, RJ Wornes, WP Wornes, W Worontschak, JD Worrad, GW Worrall, IJ Worsley, PG Worsley, LJ Worsteling, BW Worth, GP Worth, BM Worthing, DB Worthington, NC Wortlehock, DF Wotherspoon, LB Wotherspoon, NA Wotherspoon, KJ Wotton, HJ Wouters, MV Wozniak, GH Wragg, DC Wraight, FA Wraight, PF Wraith, FJ Wrathmall, BCT Wratten, JT Wray, PA Wreford, CB Wregg, CC Wren, DS Wride, KM Wriedt, AB Wright, AC Wright, AD Wright, AJ Wright, AK Wright, B Wright, BA Wright, BJ Wright, BJ Wright, BP Wright, BR Wright, CG Wright, CJ Wright, CM Wright, CR Wright, CW Wright, DA Wright, DH Wright, DL Wright, DW Wright, EA Wright, ED Wright, EJ Wright, EW Wright, FP Wright, G Wright, GA Wright, GC Wright, GH Wright, GI Wright, GJ Wright, GW Wright, HC Wright, HF Wright, HJ Wright, IM Wright, IW Wright, JA Wright, JD Wright, JK Wright, JL Wright, JS Wright, JT Wright, JW Wright, JWB Wright, KJ Wright, KR Wright, LA Wright, LT Wright, M Wright, MA Wright, MEG Wright, MM Wright, MR Wright, MW Wright, ND Wright, NG Wright, NS Wright, P Wright, PG Wright, PJ Wright, RA Wright, RC Wright, RJ Wright, RW Wright, SG Wright, SJ Wright, SL Wright, T Wright, TG Wright, TRK Wright, WC Wright, WF Wright, WH Wright, WJ Wright, WL Wright, WR Wright, WS Wright, WT Wright, BJ Wrigley, JB Wrigley, LJ Wrobel, RA Wroe, BW Wruck, LR Wruck, RT Wu, BS Wuillemin, GL Wunderer, MP Wunderlich, DF Wust, DJ Wust, LG Wust, WS Wust, M Wuttke, MJ Wuttke, NC Wuttke, GF Wyatt, RJ Wyatt, TDT Wyatt, DJ Wyborn, JD Wyborn, KE Wyer, RE Wyer, MJ Wyeth, TJ Wyeth, GE Wykes, KD Wykes, MB Wykes, NA Wykes, AD Wyles, BA Wylie, BR Wylie, D Wylie, DG Wylie, EA Wylie, KJ Wylie, RA Wylie, VJJ Wynands, AJ Wynd, BN Wynd, GA Wynd, LR Wynd, PL Wynd, JH Wyndham, WG Wyndham, JB Wynen, DW Wyness, GJ Wynn, AJ Wynne, BA Wynne, CG Wynne, DR Wynne, PR Wynne, RW Wynne, RL Wyse, EA Wyszynski, NB Wyvill, G Xanthopoulos, GA Xuereb, JE Yabsley, CP Yacopetti, AK Yacoubian, RJ Yallop, NB Yandle, CG Yannopoulos, WK Yarde, PJ Yardley, IG Yarrow, CJ Yates, D Yates, DC Yates, DV Yates, FJ Yates, GA Yates, LJ Yates, PL Yates, R Yates, RJ Yates, RM Yates, S Yates, TJ Yates, DP Yau, PF Yeates, DH Yeats, GF Yeats, J Yelland, JR Yelland, LD Yelland, TG Yellow, DG Yench, GH Yench, K Yeo, RG Yeo, TR Yeo, CH Yeoman, BB Yeomans, GF Yeomans, IM Yerbury, KJ Yesberg, RJ Yewen, RA Yielding, DL Yole, MC Yon, PD Yonge, HA Yopp, CH York, GK York, PG York, W York, PH Yorke, KE You, GA Youd, KA Youd, MF Youd, PW Youde, ME Youl, NJ Youlden, AJ Youles, GB Youlten, RT Youman, AA Young, AFS Young, AH Young, AW Young, BA Young, BG Young, BJ Young, BL Young, BT Young, CA Young, CB Young, CJ Young, CO Young, CW Young, D Young, DA Young, DB Young, DG Young, DJ Young, DM Young, DR Young, FA Young, FR Young, GC Young, GH Young, GI Young, GJ Young, GK Young, GL Young, GN Young, GR Young, H Young, HD Young, IL Young, IW Young, JD Young, JE Young, JF Young, JP Young, JR Young, K Young, KG Young, KJ Young, KW Young, LJ Young, MA Young, MC Young, MJ Young, MM Young, NA Young, OG Young, P Young, PA Young, PB Young, PC Young, PE Young, PF Young, PJ Young, PR Young, PT Young, PW Young, R Young, RA Young, RE Young, RG Young, RJ Young, RJB Young, RK Young, RL Young, RM Young, RN Young, RP Young, RS Young, RT Young, RW Young, SJ Young, TC Young, TD Young, TF Young, TW Young, WD Young, WL Young, WT Young, FW Youngberg, CJ Youngberry, CFA Younger, CJ Younger, TN Youngman, WK Youngson, GL Young-Western, AG Younie, BJ Yovkoff, SJ Yow Yeh, RT Yow Yeh, P Yuille, MM Yukich, JR Yule, JW Yule, RJ Yule, JE Yurisich, R Yuswak, PHB Zaat, J Zabaznow, V Zabenko, CS Zabielo, J Zaboj, M Zacharko, HG Zaffino, G Zaffiris, AS Zagame, S Zagon, V Zahra, TR Zajer, Z Zalewski, A Zammit, AM Zammit, JA Zammit, S Zammit, T Zammit, LR Zanchetta, PH Zandbergs, GJ Zander, N Zander, FV Zanier, GN Zanker, PV Zannino, RV Zanoni, JE Zanotti, JJ Zaplatynskyj, ZK Zapletal, PH Zapolskis, GH Zappala, M Zarew, JZ Zarewicz, BI Zavattaro, CM Zavattaro, ZJ Zawada, B Zazoniuk, GJ Zbierski, WJ Zealley, T Zeckomski, JM Zegenhagen, JC Zeilstra, CE Zeitinger, HG Zeller, JE Zeller, KWJ Zeller, AJ Zerafa, F Zerafa, HP Zerbes, DJ Zerner, MF Zeugofsge, PL Zeuschner, VV Zhukov, FA Ziccone, S Zielezna, EJ Zielinski, SC Zielke, KF Ziems, RA Ziemski, GB Zikking, J Zilm, JG Zima, SC Zimmerman, CK Zimmermann, HH Zinke, HG Zinner, E Ziogas, RD Zions, P Zissis, R Zitzelsberger, J Zmijewski, S Zoina, D Zollo, RC Zomer, V Zorich, BM Zotti, B Zoubakin, A Zsolt, PP Zuccato, EA Zuch, M Zukowski, A Zulian, SA Zuliani, BH Zunneberg, RJ Zunneberg, F Zuppar, HP Zurakowski, K Zurawel, D Zwart, J Zyla, E Zylstra, PM Zyrucha.

Royal Australian Air Force

ALH Abbott, J Abela, R Abercrombie, RJ Ablett, JK Ablong, SC Abrahamson, RN Absell, ADR Aburn, RJ Acheson, KW Achilles, CL Ackland, RK Adair, RW Adam, AG Adams, BJ Adams, CC Adams, DC Adams, HC Adams, HJ Adams, J Adams, JI Adams, KJ Adams, LJ Adams, RE Adams, SR Adams, AB Adamson, CA Adamson, RG Adamson, LR Addison, RJ Addison, A Adler, IC Affleck, TF Agnew, MJ Ahern, BC Ahrens, AD Aiken, BM Aisthorpe, JM Aitken, RW Aitken, GH Aizlewood, J Akaczonek, RJ Aked, JW Akker, JR Alberdi, DJ Alchin, AT Alcock, W Alderson, LA Alderton, NS Aldridge, GM Aleckson, BI Alexander, JR Alexander, LD Alexander, MM Alexander, N Alexander, PL Alexander, RJ Alexander, AV Allan, M Allan, PK Allan, RL Allchin, CA Allen, EG Allen, JM Allen, GW Allsopp, AC Allum, BC Allwright, GAF Altmann, E Alves-Veira, PR Amos, CE Andersen, DR Andersen, NCW Andersen, NJ Andersen, AK Anderson, AR Anderson, AW Anderson, BGM Anderson, BWJ Anderson, D Anderson, GPL Anderson, H Anderson, MA Anderson, MC Anderson, R Anderson, RG Anderson, RL Anderson, RM Anderson, TR Anderson, WA Anderson, RD Anderssen, GH Andrew, BF Andrews, CG Andrews, GA Andrews, GLE Andrews, JM Andrews, KW Andrews, MJ Andrews, PJ Andrews, R Andrews, LC Anesbury, DJ Angus, CM Anson, MJ Antaw, GB Apperley, CRA Appleby, KB Appleby, RJ Appleford, TM Appleton, VJ Archie, RJ Arlott, A Armitage, DJ Armour, DM Armstrong, ECC Armstrong, IK Armstrong, PB Armstrong, PJ Armstrong, PR Armstrong, WE Armstrong, RB Aronsen, DC Ashe, PW Ashley, NR Ashman, RW Ashton, GG Ashworth, CJ Asimus, PE Asker, A Atherton, JA Athorn, DCD Atikinson, RA Atkinson, RG Atkinson, RK Aubrey, LJ Auger, JC Auld, RA Auld, RW Auld, RJ Aulick, RJ Aust, N Austin, B Avery, RE Axelsen, KE Ayers, JE Bach, BD Bachovzeff, LJH Backers, RM Backhouse, GT Bacon, WJ Bacon, MS Badcoe, RF Badenoch, GM Badgery, KC Baff, GJ Baggaley, WD Baggett, GA Baggs, CJ Bailey, GJ Bailey, IL Bailey, JW Bailey, P Bailey, WC Baillie, G Bainrot, CG Baker, DJ Baker, GC Baker, J Baker, JP Baker, JSG Baker, KO Baker, LW Baker, PV Baker, TK Baker, VL Baker, J Balawejder, BA Balding, IM Baldwin, JP Baldwin, LY Baldwin, E Ball, FAE Ball, TR Ball, JM Ballantyne, RJ Ballard, RTA Ballinger, MV Balstad, GA Banfield, LB Banham, Z Banhidi, KR Bankin, AW Banks, PA Banks, IE Bannerman, C Bannister, MK Bannister, SR Bannister, WD Bannister, CJ Bansemer, Z Barbadyn, F Barber, CM Barbour, JM Barbour, RE Barcham, WD Barclay, AW Barker, GR Barker, LR Barker, RK Barker, TM Barker, DR Barling, HC Barlow, E Barnard, RG Barnard, A Barnes, EW Barnes, KG Barnes, MJ Barnes, PR Barnes, GT Barnett, DJ Barnicoat, JE Barnie, CP Barr, KI Barr, DA Barratt, AG Barrett, JP Barrett, KC Barrett, LE Barrett, JC Barrington, JL Barry, RJ Barry, BC Barter, DJ Bartlett, JF Bartlett, KD Bartlett, KR Bartlett, RW Bartlett, T Bartlett, TH Bartlett, RL Barton, DW Bastick, GV Bastin, RA Bastock, NJ Batcheldor, BEW Bates, JR Bates, MD Bates, NO Bates, PG Bates, WJ Bates, RE Bateson, RW Batey, WJ Bath, PA Batterham, RJ Bauer, T Baumback, GA Bausch, BJ Bawcombe, MJ Baxter, RJE Baxter, JJ Bayly, NJ Beach, R Beagle, BH Bean, GD Bean, H Bean, RA Bean, PA Beard, DR Beardmore, G Beasley, PJ Beath, HO Beattie, JR Beattie, CA Beatty, CG Beatty, AE Beaumont, JE Beaumont, RA Beaven, RT Beaven, CJ Beazley, NL Bebbington, DH Bechly, GJJ Beck, JRP Beckman, KJ Beckwith, PJ Beckwith, KR Beddoes, RJ Bedson, AJ Beeby, AM Beech, AF Beehag, NG Beeson, NA Beeston, AR Begg, WH Beggs, GP Behan, AHW Bell, HT Bell, JE Bell, JRO Bell, KIA Bell, PM Bell, RG Bell, JA Bellamy, JN Bellamy, N Bellas, PG Benfield, GW Bennett, JE Bennett, JS Bennett, JW Bennett, MM Bennett,

NB Bennett, R Bennett, RC Bennett, KM Bennetts, TW Benneworth, G Bensi, CE Benson, L Benson, GW Bentley, MA Bergin, RA Bergman, RK Berrell, WR Berriman, GE Berry, GEM Berry, MI Berry, MWB Berry, WGH Berry, MJ Berryman, BT Bertram, RM Bertram, GF Besley, RJ Bessen, CJ Betar, HR Betar, KJ Betts, RW Betts, TH Bevan, R Beveridge, T Beveridge, TG Bibo, AEC Bicker, GM Bickle, RL Biddell, CJ Biddle, NV Biddle, WD Biddle, AG Bielby, AJ Biggins, NW Biggs, PJ Biglands, KH Bilboe, IF Bill, KN Biltoft, GD Binder, R Bingley, BJ Binney, HH Birch, JW Birch, PA Birch, BK Bircham, AJ Bird, JW Bird, MB Birks, TG Birks, BM Birrell, JA Birrell, RI Birtles-Crute, KN Bischof, AR Bishop, RD Bishop, JW Black, RAL Black, RS Black, WG Black, EJ Blackburn, TRR Blackburn, PD Blacker, RJ Blackman, RA Blackshaw, RR Blackstock, GB Blackwood, PM Bladen, PR Blair-Hickman, GS Blake, GV Blake, AP Blakeney, HW Blakey, RI Blanch, DN Bland, RG Blatchford, MJ Blayney, LD Bleakley, DG Bliss, JB Block, PA Bloom, KJ Blowers, AC Bloxsom, LT Bloxsom, JE Blundell, MA Blunsdon, AT Blyth, JR Boast, HH Bock, LJ Bock, KH Bodel, RH Boerth, CJ Bohr, LJ Boileau, M Bojko, RD Bold, HD Bolden, RG Boldery, GJ Boler, CP Bolger, EBJ Bolger, RE Bolton, J Bolvig, GG Bond, MJ Bond, RE Bond, RG Bond, WP Bondfield, EM Bone, AC Boness, SH Bonett, J Bonner, FJC Bonnor, DJ Booth, EA Booth, GJ Booth, GJ Borbas, RA Borysewicz, CJ Boshammer, KJ Bosley, GD Boss, NR Boss, VEE Botha, RA Bottles, GL Bottrill, NJ Boulton, TW Bourbon, FG Bourke, TD Bourke, TL Bourke, RS Bournes, T Bousfield, JE Bovell, KH Bowden, WL Bowen, DH Bower, LT Bower, NA Bowers, GL Bowes, JL Bowes, DF Bowie, LJ Bowles, AJ Bowman, ET Bowman, PL Bowyer-Johnson, GW Boxall, IF Boxall, EJ Boyd, PJ Boyd, AC Boyden, CW Boye, MF Boyle, RL Boyle, PG Boyling, JF Boyne, PA Boys, KF Brace, RJ Brackin, JH Bradbery, HC Bradford, IG Bradford, PR Bradford, RW Bradford, SJ Bradley, EJ Bradshaw, JW Brady, RE Brady, RE Bragge, JM Brame, LE Bramich, PR Brammer, CJ Bramwell, GL Brand, JD Branson, SW Brash, SA Brauer, DL Bray, HF Bray, JR Bray, PDJ Bray, GW Brazel, AR Brazil, RW Breakspear, SA Breasley, MJ Brennan, PD Brennan, VF Brennan, KJ Brent, RG Brice, AG Bridges, HR Bridgett, RL Brien, BN Brierley, JR Brighton, GA Brindley, NW Brindley, WS Brisbane, KJ Bristow-Stagg, ID Britton, NS Britton, GA Broadbent, JR Broadbent, JD Brodie, MT Brodie, RWE Bromley, EG Brooker, MEM Brooker, VC Brooker, WL Brooker, DA Brooks, GP Brooks, HR Brooks, R Brooks, G Brosnan, JR Brosnan, JI Brough, AG Brown, BA Brown, BI Brown, CF Brown, DG Brown, DJ Brown, FB Brown, FED Brown, FG Brown, FL Brown, GB Brown, GS Brown, JBH Brown, JC Brown, JK Brown, JW Brown, LC Brown, LD Brown, ML Brown, NJ Brown, NP Brown, P Brown, PR Brown, RF Brown, RG Brown, RJ Brown, RK Brown, RNC Brown, RW Brown, SJ Brown, TW Brown, RC Browne, RJ Browning, AR Bruce, CH Bruce, RA Bruce, RD Bruce, T Bruce, GD Brumfield, NR Brunne, CJ Bryant, GJ Bryant, H Bryant, IM Bryant, L Bryant, VC Bryant, SA Bryce, DM Bryson, MJ Bryson, RJ Bubeck, CI Buchanan, EJ Buchanan, MW Buchanan, SN Bucholtz, NJ Bucholz, RJ Buck, GV Buckby, S Buckham, NV Buckler, CE Buckley, G Buckley, N Buckley, BA Bucktin, RA Budd, RR Budd, PC Budick, BD Bugden, JE Bugg, JA Buise, J Bulinski, RG Bull, JAW Bulloch, AJ Bullock, EH Bullock, JW Bullough, DW Bunker, LF Bunter, RJ Burans, TJ Burden, RB Burford, AM Burgers, AR Burgess, CJ Burgess, CW Burgess, ER Burgess, JA Burgess, NEE Burgess, PJ Burgess, T Burgess, VJ Burgess, PJ Burgin, BE Burke, PA Burkett, AC Burling, DJ Burling, R Burnell, A Burns, AR Burns, MJ Burns, CG Burris, AF Burt, PJ Burt, RP Burtenshaw, GA Burton, JF Burton, KT Burton, NJ Burton, FE Burtt, A Busby, AG Bush, NJ Bush, GJ Bushell, JA Bushell, EA Busuttil, MB Butcher, JH Butler, JW Butler, RJ Butler, T Butler, WS Butler, GF Buttler, GD Buttriss, GD Bydder, TP Byfield, MT Byrne, PF Byrne, JF Byrnes, KF Byrnes, KW Byrnes, MJ Byron, WB Byron, NC Bywaters, GGJ Cabral, AT Cadd, DJ Caesar, DR Cain, AG Cairns, IH Cairns, RJ Caldow, RW Caldwell, SR Callaghan, IJ Callander, GRG Calliess, MHJ Calliess, MS Calvert, AD Cameron, IC Cameron, JTR Cameron, L Cameron, PJ Cameron, RJ Cameron, A Camilleri, RG Camons, BH Campbell, DB Campbell, GD Campbell, JB Campbell, JC Campbell, JG Campbell, JL Campbell, LR Campbell, MJ Campbell, ML Campbell, RJ Campbell, RJC Campbell, RL Campbell, RN Campbell, RR Campbell, JPG Campigli, BH Candy, IR Canham, GK Canning, JD Canning, EJ Cannons, GL Cansick, KB Cantle, CS Cantor, AJ Capell, SR Caporn, WF Cappa, WA Capper, VD Carbone, RA Carey, TJ Carey, DS Carlos, RJ Carlson, AC Carlyon, PN Carmichael, DR Carmody, KJ Carmody, BG Carney, GE Carney, BJ Carpenter, LS Carpenter, RF Carpenter, RR Carpenter, GA Carr, PH Carr, RD Carr, RG Carrier, GV Carrol, AL Carroll, BAF Carroll, DP Carroll, GJ Carroll, AKS Carruthers, SG Carseldine, WJ Carson, KW Carswell, WL Carswell, BR Carter, DAB Carter, DF Carter, DM Carter, GL Carter, JB Carter, JT Carter, KF Carter, PF Carter, VB Carter, WEL Carter, WM Carter, RC Carver, CD Case, A Caselli, DJ Casey, MJ Casey, AJ Cash, RE Cashin, RR Cassell, CNM Cassels, LGF Cassidy, HF Castle, MA Castle, MF Castles, RG Cave, M Cavell, A Cavuoto, IR Cawse, MC Chalk, JE Chalker, BJ Challans, BR Challenor, GP Chalmers, JA Chamberlain, GJ Chambers, DH Champion, RJ Champion, AW Chandler, BJ Chandler, ER Chandler, JA Chandler, RC Chandler, GR Chaplin, AC Chapman, CP Chapman, F Chapman, GR Chapman, LV Chapman, MA Chapman, RJ Chappel, NR Chappell, TW Chappell, WKL Chappell, LI Chapple, BC Charles, E Charles, HJ Charles, ACR Charlesworth, GA Charlton, IS Charlton, WL Charlton, LJ Chatenay, CR Chatham, WD Chesher, JM Chesterfield, TL Childs, WL Childs, AB Chiles, JT Chiller, MJ Chipchase, LG Chisnall, RW Chittenden, WC Chitty, GH Christian, OT Christie, RA Christie, RJ Christie, RM Christie, TL Christie, CK Christoffersen, NC Church, AE Churches, WM Churchin, BK Chynoweth, HM Cichowski, RP Cicolini, AJ Clancy, LR Clancy, A Clark, B Clark, DR Clark, EG Clark, EJ Clark, GJ Clark, GT Clark, JE Clark, JW Clark, KD Clark, KR Clark, RJ Clark, S Clark, TP Clark, WE Clark, WJ Clark, AW Clarke, AW Clarke, B Clarke, LJ Clarke, NA Clarke, RD Clarke, RJ Clarke, DA Clarkson, JW Clarkson, GW Clavan, AC Clay, JM Clay, BC Clayton, RC Clayton, RW Clayton, WD Clayton, HA Cleary, J Cleary, HMA Clegg, VJM Cleland, PW Clemmens, AR Clifford, RK Clinch, RJ Clive, FL Clough, RA Cluff, NC Clunne, AS Coad, MD Coate, FA Coborn, S Cocks, EG Coffee, JH Coffey, RJ Cogan, NB Cogger, DL Cole, JW Cole, CP Coleman, GN Coleman, GR Coleman, MJP Coleman, NLB Coleman, GW Coles, RS Coles, WT Colgrave, MR Collard, EN Collas, AJ Collett, CE Collett, JM Collier, PJ Collier, TJ Collier, DJ Collins, JH Collins, JM Collins, KA Collins, ME Collins, ML Collins, RG Collins, RJ Collins, TM Collins, TL Collis, HA Collits, J Colman, WHS Colman, DE Colthup, LJ Colthup, GA Colyer, EJ Comber, TA Combes, MJ Commerford, NH Compassi, KM Condon, PD Condon, FJ Coningham, JS Conlon, MI Conlon, JT Connell, PF Connell, DP Connelly, EF Connelly, JA Conner, KA Conner, GJ Connolly, OE Connolly, AA Connor, DA Connor, RJ Connor, BD Connors, KJ Connors, P Conroy, WA Conroy, GL Consadine, JR Constable, WR Convery, JE Conway, MJ Conway, RJ Conway, CM Cook, DA Cook, HG Cook, KH Cook, LP Cook, MW Cook, RA Cook, GR Cooke, OP Cooke, OV Cooke, PK Cooke, DH Cool, DK Coomber, DR Coomber, TO Coombs, JS Coomer, AB Cooper, AJ Cooper, BG Cooper, DM Cooper, EA Cooper, GG Cooper, HJ Cooper, IB Cooper, MC Cooper, NMC Cooper, RWJ Cooper, SD Cooper, WJ Cooper, GJ Cootes, J Cope, JM Copeland, BJ Copley, JS Corbett, JL Corcoran, B Corkill, EG Cornell, G Corner, KW Corney, RL Cornwell, MJ Corrie, TA Corti, JM Cosgrove, RE Cosgrove, A Costello, MJ Cottee, CF Cotter, PA Cotter, R Cotterill, M Cottrell, RJ Cottrell, WL Cottrell, JD Coughlan, EL Coughlin, BPG Coull, FC Coulthard, RA Couper, TN Coventry, PM Covington, A Cowan, DJ Cowan, JM Cowan, VH Cowdroy, VJ Cowen, AR Cox, AT Cox, DH Cox, EC Cox, FD Cox, ID Cox, J Cox, JH Cox, RL Coxon, WS Coxon, PLH Coy, WJ Coyer, I Crabbe, GH Cragg, NT Cram, GM Cramer, KR Cramer, NI Cramer, GT Crane, TJ Cranswick, KF Craven, GN Crawfoot, AW Crawford, CB Crawford, RG Crawford, GA Crawley, DB Cremin, PD Cremin, GA Creswell, JJ Cridland, BA Crimeen, RJ Crimmins, LG Crisp, PO Crisp, AE Crispe, AMA Croaker, B Crockett, CJ Croker, GR Crombie, JFD Crook, RE Crooks, IA Crosbie, VW Crosby, SS Crosling, EJ Cross, NJL Cross, LJ Crossley, RK Crossley, WJ Crouch, AL Crowe, V Crowle, HR Crowther, RD Crump, I Crutchley, MC Cryer, GA Cubit, NC Cuell, KN Culey, LR Cullen, R Cullen, GK Cumes, AM Cummins, EJ Cunningham, J Cunningham, KJ Cupitt, E Curchin, J Cureton, MJ Curgenven, GR Curnow, RR Curnow, AJ Curr, DPD Currie, GJ Currie, HT Currie, JH Curry, AJ Curtis, PE Curtis, WJ Curtis, MP Cuthbert, RM Cutlack, FC Cutler, AWK Cutmore, RJ Cuttriss, MJ Cuy, RO D'Abreu, KW Dadge, SP Daetz, TG Daff, JH Dahlitz, IA Dainer, JJ Dainer, RG Dakin, DG Dale, NLH Dale, MJ Daley, RM Daley, DJ Dalgleish, PR Dalgleish, SW Dalgleish, RB Dallman, WP Dalmeida, O Dalmolen, DJ Dalton, MJ Dalton, KJ Daly, PF Daly, TK Daly, DI Darby, DA Darcey, BL Darch, BL D'Arcy, FA Darcy, PJ Darcy, WD Darcy, AS Dare, ND Darr, RH Dash, RE Dauth, PJ Davern, BJ Davey, MJ Davey, JW Davidson, PA Davidson, SL Davidson, BE Davie, B Davies, BR Davies, CT Davies, ER Davies, JA Davies, JB Davies, JD Davies, JW Davies, KA Davies, OT Davies, PW Davies, WEH Davies, BO Davis, DJ Davis, DO Davis, EN Davis, G Davis, GE Davis, GR Davis, HT Davis, KC Davis, MJ Davis, NG Davis, RC Davis, RT Davis, TJ Davis, PH Davison, PT Davison, AR Dawe, BJ Dawkins, DJ Dawson, EL Dawson, JK Dawson, RF Dawson, RJ Dawson, RJ Dawson, RP Dawson, TY Dawson, CJ Day, DG Day, EJ Day, NG Day, RV Dayas, D De Boer, GJ De Courcey, RJ De Friskbom, P De Jonge, FS De Landelles, NJ De Le Torre, AW De Longville, BD De Loub, AF De Luca, GJ De Silva, RN De Vene, BJ Deadman, EJ Deakin, BJ Dean, DR Dean, ML Dean, SK Dean, RH Deane, GC Dearden, AJ Dearman, SRC Deaves, KJ Dedman, ML Deecke, GJ Deede, PR Degotardi, EFW Delaney, RJ Delaney, AP Delatorre, DW Del-Fabbro, MR Demery, RJ Dempsey, G Denford, LJ Denison, BP Dennes, RJ Denning, KL Dennis, RJ Dennis, TJ Dennis, WK Dennis, PC Dent, RJ Denton, R Dernedde, DM Derrick, RG Des-Jardins, BJ Desmond, IH Devantier, JW Devenish, IE Devereux, HE Devery, KJ Devine, PF Devine, RJ Devlin, RP Dewar, IG Dewbery, RJ Dexter, CA Di Giacomo, DR Dick, PG Dickens, IA Dickie, PE Dickie, KW Dickinson, M Dickinson, JR Dickson, WE Dickson, WM Dickson, FA Diehm, DJ Dillon, EJ Dilworth, DF Dimmock, PJ Dinneen, GR Dinte, BLJ Dirou, P Disher, SW Distant, B Ditchburn, KR Dixon, NF Dixon, NJ Dixon, PH Dixon, RF Dixon, RW Dixon, WG Dixon, WJ Dixon, ME Djula, FG Doak, MJ Doak, WC Docherty, BB Docker, NR Docksey, GB Dodd, MJ Dodd, RE Dodd, RE Dodds, JRP Dods, DR Doherty, JP Doherty, MW Doherty, CM Dohle, JEJ Dolling, LD Donald, AK Donaldson, HD Donaldson, MG Donaldson, NR Donaldson, PD Donaldson, JE Doney, D Donlan, JA Donlan, DW Donnelly, JA Donohoe, RB Donohoe, JRS Donohue, GC Donovan, RJ Doonan, C Dor, PJ Dorman, JJ Dorrell, GG Dorward, RL Doudle, DF Dougall, CW Douglas, PJA Douglas, RN Douglas, RJ Douglass, K Douran, NJ Dow, DJ Dowling, EMR Dowling, HG Dowling, J Dowling, GK Downer, CJ Downes, JM Downes, RB Downes, TR Downey, JA Downie, FJL Downing, BS Downs, GJ Downs, HN Dowse, KJ Doyle, KP Doyle, PJ Doyle, R Doyle, RA Doyle, RPP Doyle, WA Doyle, K Dransfield, HA Dreimanis, WJ Dreise, IJ Drenan, RJ Drever, JA Drew, K Drew, GJ Drinkwater, J Drinkwater, MS Drinkwater, BF Driscoll, JH Driver, MHJ Driver, RES Drought, V Drummond, AR Drury, KW Drury, PW Drury, BH Druwitt, GS Drysdale, DJ Dubber, AJM Duddington, BS Duddington, PE Dudley, WL Duff, CR Duffield, CW Duffield, AT Duggan, ES Duggan, AJ Dunbar, EGW Dunbar, GE Dunbar, JS Dunbar, IJ Duncan, JC Duncan, JE Duncan, L Duncan, RA Duncan, GA Duncombe, WT Dundas, JC Dunn, JE Dunn, JH Dunn, LD Dunn, LNC Dunn, MJ Dunn, J Dunne, JE Dunne, JE Dunne, MSA Dunne, WJ Dunne, BE Dunsdon, DL Dunstan, GW Dunstan, BT Dunston, JP Durkin, TN Dutschke, GL Dutton, LB Dutton, NL Duus, JR Dwyer, ML Dwyer, MN Dwyer, PJ Dwyer, GK Dyce, AR Dyer, BA Dyer, H Dyer, G Dyke, KP East, EC Easterbrook, BR Easton, B Eastwood, BT Eastwood, WJ Eather, JL Eaton, P Eaton, RE Eaton, AE Eaves, NL Ebsworth, RC Eccles, DJ Eddy, PA Edgar, BDT Edge, MJ Edie, S Edlund, MB Edmonds, DC Edmunds, J Edmunds, AB Edwards, AJ Edwards, DB Edwards, DC Edwards, DG Edwards, DH Edwards, GA Edwards, GC Edwards, GS Edwards, JG Edwards, JJ Edwards, JL Edwards, KJ Edwards, KM Edwards, KW Edwards, L Edwards, LA Edwards, LS Edwards, RCL Edwards, RJ Edwards, TT Edwards, JK Egan, JT Egan, LJ Egan, PD Egan, MR Eggins,

RA Egginton, JO Eggleton, R Egle, JL Egoroff, KA Einam, RW Eivers, FJ Element, KW Element, RM Eley, DM Ellacott, AR Ellem, ED Ellem, AJ Ellems, A Elliott, AD Elliott, AH Elliott, BC Elliott, GT Elliott, JA Elliott, K Elliott, PB Elliott, RD Elliott, WM Elliott, BJ Ellis, CR Ellis, DI Ellis, EST Ellis, JL Ellis, MJ Ellis, BJ Ellison, BJ Ellison, AW Ely, GM Ely, WJ Emery, PF England, AF Englander, GJ Ennis, CA Ephraums, ER Erhardt, H Erskine, KF Erwin, TW Esbensen, MD Eschbach, BJ Espeland, JD Espie, AH Essam, A Essery, RF Ethell, CT Etherden, TR Etheridge, AK Evans, CEH Evans, CS Evans, DC Evans, ER Evans, JC Evans, LA Evans, RE Evans, RJ Evans, RK Evans, SD Evans, AM Everett, KR Every, BT Ewers, KW Ewin, RP Ewing, RK Eyears, GR Eyre, DG Eyres, WH Fagan, PG Fairbrother, RC Fairhall, JR Fallows, R Falls, JM Falvey, JM Fanderlinden, LW Fankhauser, CG Farley, HJ Farmer, SJ Farmer, RA Farnham, JR Farquhar, RD Farquhar, TL Farquharson, TB Farr, MS Farrar, BJ Farrell, GR Farrell, JM Farrell, RW Farrell, NA Fatin, BW Faulkner, FB Faulkner, PL Faulkner, JC Faux, JS Favell, I Favilla, WM Fawkner, BN Fay, F Fearnley, KM Feather, KM Featherston, KJ Feeney, LB Feige, AG Fellowes, PR Felsman, EJ Felton, PF Feneley, RG Fennell, WJ Fennell, RE Fenton, SJ Fenton, HH Fenwick, MJ Fenwick, DR Ferguson, IR Ferguson, JC Ferguson, NO Fernance, RC Fernance, RG Ferry, JE Feutrill, NH Fewkes, A Fickler, AF Field, DR Field, FJ Field, LK Field, RS Field, TL Field, DM Fielding, KJ Fietz, AN Filkin, I Findlay, GD Fing, EC Finlay, MJ Finn, BJ Fish, WL Fish, GD Fisher, GF Fisher, KD Fisher, PL Fisher, R Fisher, RA Fisher, WR Fisher, EK Fisk, AJ Fittler, BW Fitzell, CW Fitzgerald, DG Fitzgerald, GJ Fitzgerald, M Fitzgerald, WJ Fitzgerald, HG Fitzgerrald, GB Fitzgibbon, RS Fitzhenry, BF Fitzpatrick, J Fitzpatrick, J Fitzpatrick, JE Fitzpatrick, JF Fitzpatrick, SB Fixter, RW Flack, BA Flanagan, EL Fleming, KC Fleming, KJ Fleming, TF Fleming, JH Flemming, BC Fletcher, BL Fletcher, BT Fletcher, HE Fletcher, N Fletcher, CJ Flinn, JJ Flis, JA Florence, RW Florence, FJ Flowers, BF Flux, BF Flynn, J Flynn, PE Flynn, RG Flynn, SM Flynn, TJ Flynn, ID Fogarty, JH Fogarty, HG Foks, RFS Folan, C Foley, D Foley, FA Foley, JW Foley, PR Foley, GJ Follett, KJ Folley, AJ Fookes, BH Fooks, DE Foote, DV Foote, GP Forbes, IC Forbes, AP Ford, B Ford, KR Ford, NP Ford, SB Ford, SR Ford, BF Fordham, J Fordyce, WD Fordyce, RH Foreman, KT Forman, AG Forrest, RA Forrester, CA Forsyth, GA Forsyth, FL Fortescue, R Forth, RA Forward, GW Foskett, GT Foster, KH Foster, IGA Fothergill, CJ Fowler, AF Fox, SJ Foxwell, IS Frame, GI Frampton, FE Francis, GM Francis, RC Francis, RS Francis, AP Franks, RR Frasa, AJ Fraser, CS Fraser, GT Fraser, IK Fraser, ML Frazer, DC Freedman, DJ Freeman, GC French, LG French, RJ French, WM Frew, GD Fridd, AL Friske, F Frith, BJ Frost, RR Frost, AW Fry, FR Fry, JW Fry, LG Fry, GR Fryer, D Fuchs, HJH Fuhrmann, DD Fuller, KA Fuller, LS Fuller, TH Fuller, LA Fulloon, KW Fulton, MT Fulton, PW Fulton, PA Furbank, CR Furlonger, DM Furner, PM Furniss, JM Furse, MM Furze, RJS Furze, R Fyfield, JA Gable, AN Gadsby, SW Gainsford, AD Gale, BL Gale, GF Gale, MV Gale, AM Gall, GC Gall, KM Gallagher, P Gallagher, PP Gallagher, GB Gallard, DE Gallet, GA Gamble, JA Gamble, RP Gamble, N Gannaway, TG Ganzer, GW Garbutt, RW Garbutt, RD Garcia, CI Gardiner, DJ Gardiner, FL Gardiner, WL Gardiner, CJ Gardner, RJ Gardner, BHJ Garland, BT Garland, JA Garland, JW Garland, LF Garland, WL Garland, CP Garnett, EAH Garrard, TG Garrard, NJ Garrett, RJ Garrett, CE Garton, DF Garvie, JP Gaskell, CF Gauci, DAM Gauld, WM Gavin, RL Gay, JG Gazley, NJ Gear, KG Gearside, V Geddes, RF Gee, KJ Gehrig, PW Geissmann, LG Gentle, AH George, K George, MA George, DA Georgeson, CJ Geraghty, J Gersbach, PR Gerstle, CN Geschke, IL Getley, MJ Gibb, TO Gibbs, GS Gibson, JW Gibson, RJ Gibson, JC Giddey, RM Giddings, DH Giesecke, GC Giffin, J Gilbert, NG Gilbert, RG Gilbert, TC Gilbert, WR Gilbey, P Gilchrist, JG Gill, WA Gill, GI Gillett, LK Gillies, RK Gillies, ES Gilligan, DJK Gilliland, BF Gillis, BR Gillson, MJ Gilmore, RL Gilmore, TG Gilmour, AE Giltrap, EG Gimm, P Ginman, P Gippel, RE Gittus, RB Gladwell, M Glajnaric, JF Glasgow, BR Glasson, GA Glasson, RH Glassop, BAW Glatte, GDE Gleeson, L Gleeson, RT Glew, NH Glore, AT Glover, JC Glover, S Glover, BE Gluyas, RH Goad, JJ Gobbie, PAJ Godby, GN Goddard, MB Goddard, DJH Godfrey, G Godfrey, CM Godwin, DW Goggin, F Golder, GA Goldie, RP Goleby, GJ Golley, RD Golley, M Gooch, GM Good, NM Goodall, KG Goodchild, LD Goode, C Goodrum, MJ Goodsell, R Goodship, IM Goodson, JR Goodwin, PW Goodwin, RS Goosey, AE Gordon, GW Gordon, HS Gordon, IR Gordon, JP Gordon, KR Gordon, R Gordon, FG Gosbee, JR Gosper, AB Gosselink, KT Gossner, PD Gough, RH Gough, WG Gould, KW Goulds, RM Govan, RP Gower, MW Gowty, KJ Grace, J Gracey, BT Gracie, RHW Gracie, AJ Graham, D Graham, DJ Graham, JH Graham, RA Graham, RI Graham, T Graham, WJ Graham, WJ Graham, DI Grainger, SJ Grainger, RG Grandin, JE Grannall, AR Grant, HR Grant, I Grant, JA Grant, CJ Gray, CLH Gray, EE Gray, HGL Gray, I Gray, IA Gray, K Gray, LA Gray, LD Gray, RI Gray, JR Grayson, WD Grealy, AG Greatorex, AE Greaves, B Grebert, AJ Green, AP Green, AR Green, AW Green, BJ Green, JD Green, JW Green, RA Green, IH Greenacre, PL Greenaway, NJ Greene, JA Greenshields, RE Greenwood, RM Greenwood, T Greenwood, PM Greer, RA Gregg, PG Greggor, J Gregor, RB Gregory, WC Gregory, AH Greig, HC Greig, M Gretton, SJ Gribbin, BD Gribble, RF Grieff, SR Grieff, JD Grierson, DC Grieve, TI Grieves, DL Griffin, KV Griffin, JL Griffith, KH Griffith, BG Griffiths, BW Griffiths, JC Griffiths, JM Griffiths, LK Griffiths, PJ Griffiths, CS Grigg, FR Grigg, DW Griggs, TG Grigson, IW Grimes, C Grindley, PM Grindon-Ekins, LJ Grinham, AR Grinter, RJ Grocke, CE Grogan, PD Groom, AW Grossel, JB Grosvenor, IL Grove, MB Grove, DR Grover, PW Growder, J Gryga, ME Guest, PA Guest, AK Gummow, EN Gunn, ID Gunton, RN Gurevitch, KW Gurney, PA Gustafson, FL Guthrie, KL Guthrie, VD Guthrie, KJ Guy, WE Guy, M Guzelian, RT Gwilliam, DM Gwin, RJ Haack, NL Hackett, PJ Hackett, MJ Haddock, DE Hadfield, MJ Hague, AWC Haimes, JW Haines, KC Haines, AE Hains, AJ Hair, P Hajduk, PGA Halasz, W Haldane, GL Hale, CA Haley, T Halicki, LM Haling, AJ Hall, BA Hall, D Hall, G Hall, GI Hall, GR Hall, GW Hall, GW Hall, JN Hall, PB Hall, PJ Hall, R Hall, W Hall, WF Hall, BJ Hallett, JD Halliday, MAL Halliday, WJ Halliday, RW Halling, C Halsey, LAR Halvorson, LJ Halvorson, BA Hamdorf, TL Hamill, DA Hamilton, GC Hamilton, GHJ Hamilton, SWJ Hamilton, BG Hammond, ME Hampshire, MD Hampson, RJ Hampson, BA Hancock, CJ Hancock, RS Hancock, WN Hancock, GAJ Handford, JJ Handley, WKG Handover, LS Handsaker, GA Handyside, JF Hanigan, CJ Hanks, RJ Hanlon, RL Hannah, AJ Hannam, PW Hanrahan, GJ Hansberry, B Hansen, JD Hansen, JM Hansen, KJ Hansen, KS Hansen, NW Hanson, RD Hardcastle, DV Harding, J Harding, PE Harding, RA Harding, SL Harding, B Hardingham, FJ Hardwick, DJ Hardy, HT Hardy, RW Hardy, BD Hare, TF Hargraves, J Harker, AGH Harlow, GSN Harmer, MR Harness, KJ Harnetty, DF Harper, PJ Harradine, WR Harrington, AJ Harris, BD Harris, BR Harris, DJ Harris, F Harris, HB Harris, ILA Harris, JM Harris, LW Harris, MO Harris, NR Harris, RB Harris, RB Harris, SW Harris, TM Harris, DJ Harrison, E Harrison, GA Harrison, JJ Harrison, JM Harrison, RT Harrison, JG Harrod-Eagles, P Harrold, GL Harrop, JC Harry, RT Harrys, RJ Hart, WH Hart, RA Hartfield, BG Hartigan, JM Hartigan, SJ Hartigan, GJ Hartley, RO Hartley, JWG Hartshorn, M Hartwell, DC Harvey, IG Harvey, JW Harvey, P Harvey, RH Harvey, W Harvey-Smith, AK Harwood, TW Harwood, WJ Haskew, BN Haskins, MJ Hatcher, RK Hateley, AJ Hatten, GT Hauck, MR Hauser, JE Hausler, PM Haviland, JF Hawkes, LB Hawkes, RA Hawkins, KWH Hawley, M Hawryluk, G Hawthorne, DJ Hawtin, GC Hawtin, MJ Haxell, PF Hay, R Hay, WJ Hay, BW Hayden, JP Hayden, CB Haydon, AP Hayes, BJF Hayes, DJ Hayes, JF Hayes, JMI Hayes, JS Hayes, KS Hayes, ML Hayes, RM Hayes, RN Hayes, RP Hayes, BG Haylock, RK Hayman, AJ Hayne, I Hayne, LJ Hayne, DT Haynes, PR Hays, PW Hays, EC Hayward, GW Hayward, HF Hayward, KR Hayward, RH Haywood, WJ Hazel, JW Hazelton, JF Hazelwood, JP Head, WA Head, HE Headon, JW Heagney, BJ Healey, EJ Healey, RK Healey, RV Healy, RC Heaslip, DJ Hebiton, JM Heck, W Hecker, WA Hector, DJ Hedges, RJ Heffernan, RE Hegarty, BAL Heiman, AL Heiner, DJ Helman, GA Hemy, AG Henderson, BC Henderson, DW Henderson, KB Henderson, NM Hendrix, HG Hendry, CR Hendy, BJ Henley, JH Hennessy, JP Hennessy, NM Hennessy, RP Hennings, DP Henny, CD Henry, DA Henry, ER Henry, RB Henry, JA Hensby, RD Henseleit, JA Henson, MD Hentschke, SR Hepburn, RE Hepe, RJ Heptinstall, MPJ Herbert, PLC Herbert, WR Herbert, JF Herbertson, WCS Herbison, NF Herfort, R Herrington, JI Herriot, AW Herron, HE Hersant, DC Hersey, HV Hesterman, FW Heuke, AE Hewby, PW Hewett, GE Hewitt, RD Hewitt, KR Hey, KG Heyer, ID Heylen, JF Heyward, RW Hibben, PS Hick, MJ Hickey, WJ Hickey, BS Hicks, GB Hicks, IS Hicks, SL Hicks, TE Hickton, LCD Higgerson, AJ Higginbottom, RA Higgins, LR Highfield, HK Hildebrandt, AC Hill, BB Hill, CJ Hill, CS Hill, DC Hill, FV Hill, HJ Hill, KD Hill, ME Hill, NC Hill, R Hill, RN Hill, TA Hill, VJ Hill, WP Hill, DB Hillebrand, TH Hillhouse, CA Hillis, WF Hills, WH Hilton, AJ Hind, AF Hinder, LO Hindley, MH Hinds, TP Hinsby, JF Hirst, PT Hirvonen, M Hislop, MB Hitchens, DW Hitchins, RJ Hitchman, MJ Hoare, AE Hoath, GR Hobbs, NW Hobson, RA Hobson, RJ Hockham, RD Hocking, D Hodge, JW Hodge, PH Hodge, DB Hodgen, GD Hodgen, CA Hodges, DAN Hodges, E Hodges, FR Hodges, JR Hodges, PJ Hodgson, RB Hodgson, RP Hodgson, KP Hodson, J Hoey, IC Hoffman, BJ Hogan, DB Hogan, JF Hogan, MR Hogan, R Hogan, DW Hogben, GE Hogbin, DK Holbourn, RE Holdcroft, DW Holden, AG Holland, GJ Holland, ML Holland, DH Holley, K Holley, PR Hollingworth, JE Hollis, RW Hollis, WA Hollis, GC Holman, RR Holmes, HH Holsken, RT Holsken, AA Holt, DM Holt, HR Holt, JF Holt, LR Holt, MT Holt, TP Holt, W Holt, FT Holtmann, RJ Holtsbaum, JM Holze, GN Hombsch, GHG Homer, RTG Homewood, WR Honey, CL Honisett, H Hood, HHJ Hoogland, EA Hooke, BE Hooker, DF Hoolahan, A Hooton, DW Hooworth, RB Hope, VJ Hopewell, PV Hopgood, EJ Hopper, BR Hopson, RE Horder, E Hore, DM Horgan, FA Horne, KW Horne, TM Horne, EJ Horner, KP Horton, JC Horwood, RW Horwood, TJ Hoskins, CL Host, JR Hotchin, H Houghton, AR Howard, C Howard, JW Howard, KL Howard, KR Howard, RA Howard, MJ Howden, RP Howe, RW Howe, TJ Howe, HFB Howell, JR Howell, AG Howes, RD Howes, JR Howie, AH Hoy, LR Hoy, L Hubbard, PS Hubbard, JW Hubble, WB Huber, CG Hudnott, AR Hudson, JR Hudson, JW Hudson, MJ Hudson, RL Hudson, BA Huey, JR Huggett, GB Hughes, HA Hughes, C Hulcombe, AF Hull, D Hull, SA Hull, RE Humble, CE Humfrey, DJ Humphrey, PA Humphrey, RC Humphrey, RW Humphrey, BL Humphreys, MC Humphreys, EWT Humphry, LJ Humphrys, JL Hunt, TB Hunt, WR Hunt, AR Hunter, R Hunter, SA Huntley, H Hurkens, BM Hurley, BJ Hurlock, KH Hurman, JW Hurn, DJ Hurst, DP Hurst, WTC Hurst, JT Hussey, PJ Hussin, TJ Hutchins, M Hwozdeckyj, DR Hyde, PJ Hyland, SG Hyland, GH Hynes, KC Hynson, HJ Igras, RA Iliffe, KR Illman, D Ingall, BT Ingate, JE Ingham, CJ Inglis, GJ Ingram, RI Ingram, D Innes, JB Ireland, OD Ireland, PD Ireland, GM Irvin, JM Irvine, NW Irvine, N Irving, DC Irwin, R Irwin, GM Ivers, GS Ivory, B Jabour, LR Jack, PJ Jackman, AV Jackson, BR Jackson, GA Jackson, GC Jackson, GH Jackson, PR Jackson, RCG Jackson, RH Jackson, TD Jackson, WG Jacob, KM Jacobs, RH Jacobs, IG Jacobsen, JB Jacobsen, RT Jacobsen, LM Jaeger, FFG Jago, GWA Jago, JB Jagoe, AB James, AF James, AHL James, D James, FA James, GE James, RE James, RN James, SW James, BD Jamieson, K Jamieson, E Jansons, LR Jaques, LW Jaques, BV Jarasius, DW Jarmyn, SJ Jarosinski, MJ Jarrett, FH Jarvis, GR Jarvis, GW Jarvis, WH Jarvis, M Jasny, DE Jasper, BK Javens, AF Javes, PB Jay, VR Jefferies, AM Jeffery, DC Jeffery, JR Jefferys, GR Jeffree, H Jeffries, NF Jelfs, J Jellicoe, RM Jenkin, FW Jenkings, DJ Jenkins, F Jenkins, GT Jenkins, IRP Jenkins, JM Jenkins, RT Jenkins, RN Jennings, DG Jenson, S Jerga, MA Jesinowski, K Jifkins, RJ Jiggins, LG Johansen, BA Johnson, BE Johnson, DM Johnson, EL Johnson, FH Johnson, GH Johnson, GT Johnson, JD Johnson, JM Johnson, KA Johnson, LN Johnson, MA Johnson, MD Johnson, NWE Johnson, PI Johnson, PL Johnson, WM Johnson, ATI Johnston, DA Johnston, GP Johnston, IR Johnston, JA Johnston, LF Johnston, TR Johnston, WB Johnston, WL Johnston, WSM Johnston, IC Johnstone, JH Johnstone, S Johnstone, RW Jolley, PL Jolly, NF Jonasson, A Jones, AA Jones, AH Jones, AN Jones, AO Jones, BK Jones, DA Jones, DW Jones, EA Jones, FA Jones, FK Jones, GL Jones, HL Jones, JA Jones, JB Jones, JI Jones, KG Jones, KG Jones, LJ Jones, MP Jones, P Jones, PR Jones, RA Jones, RF Jones, RJ Jones, RK Jones, RLC Jones, RW Jones, SF Jones, WJ Jones,

PJ Jongkryg, JD Jordan, LC Jordan, RW Jordan, RL Jorgensen, AC Jory, MJ Joyce, RB Joyce, RE Joyner, JW Jude, PJ Judges, R Judson, TE Jukes, DW Juleff, ML Julienne, HE Kaiser, S Kaluza, KE Kane, DE Kaney, DE Karoll, A Karpys, A Kastropil, HW Kaufman, JI Kaulins, BL Kavanagh, IR Kay, RN Kay, A Kaye, D Kaye, KJ Keane, BJ Keast, GD Keating, RL Keeley, EG Keenan, WJ Keep, PR Keeshan, T Kehoe, JR Keighran, NJ Keilar, AS Keller, RN Kelloway, M Kells, A Kelly, AJ Kelly, BD Kelly, EB Kelly, JC Kelly, JWF Kelly, KJ Kelly, RG Kelly, RH Kelly, PJ Kemp, KG Kenafacke, GA Kendall, RG Kendall, RAC Kendell, JJ Kenna, AMS Kennedy, AV Kennedy, BD Kennedy, CF Kennedy, DJ Kennedy, JM Kennedy, KS Kennedy, PW Kennedy, R Kennedy, RM Kennedy, BF Kennett, DWH Kennett, BM Kenny, JR Kenny, RJ Kenworthy, AH Kenyon, J Kenyon, GA Keppler, RD Ker, JM Kerins, WC Keritz, KJ Kerle, KD Kerr, LRC Kerr, RJ Kerr, K Kershaw, LG Kershler, KJ Kersnovske, RA Kersten, LJ Kevan, JC Kichenside, VS Kicinski, DJ Kidd, ER Kidd, HN Kidd, RL Kidd, B Kiernan, JJ Kiewiet, RA Kilah, J Kilby, CT Kilian, IP Killeen, RJ Kilpatrick, CG Kilsby, GD Kimber, VJ Kimber, GJ Kimberley, RJ Kime, DH Kinch, KA Kinch, C King, CR King, GR King, JL King, JWH King, NW King, RJ King, RP King, JF Kingdom, BL Kingston, GG Kingston, BN Kingswood, RJ Kinnane, BE Kinsela, CP Kinsella, AD Kirby, BR Kirby, JS Kirby, ET Kirk, JE Kirk, NC Kirkby, GM Kirke, JL Kirkwood, JD Kirwan, BH Kirwin, KA Kitson, LR Klaffer, L Klooger, EJ Kluukeri, JJ Kluver, AH Knight, CS Knight, IB Knight, JS Knight, KW Knight, LA Knight, LD Knight, PE Knight, PR Knight, WN Knight, DJ Knights, KE Knott, GC Knowles, KC Knowles, WM Knox, CM Knudsen, FO Knudsen, NC Knudsen, HJ Koers, RP Koger, WF Koller, E Konashenko, W Konemann, F Korbl, GG Koudelka, T Kovacs, PJ Koy, CB Kraft, KE Kranenburg, PWH Kranenburg, JD Krebs, AJ Kretschmann, PJM Kropman, BD Krosch, RJ Kruckow, NR Kruse, LA Kuchel, BG Kucks, FA Kuhn, WK Kuiler, HJ Kuipers, RV Kunde, WWW Kuster, G La Grasta, PR La'brooy, BT Ladd, TF Laffer, RJ Laing, RJ Laing, WG Laing, CJ Lake, AM Lamb, DG Lamb, KR Lamb, D Lambert, RG Lamond, GN Lamont, RH Lamont, JW Lamprecht, DJ Lancaster, EM Lance, GW Land, WA Land, JA Landale, AR Lane, BB Lane, BI Lane, KJ Lane, MG Lane, WG Lane, WJ Lane, B Lang, DA Lang, NR Lang, KM Langdon, AE Lange, GR Lange, JL Lange, RH Langham, FG Langridge, AS Langton, CS Langton, DJ Langton, PB Lannen, JM Lanning, AJ Lanza, A Lapins, PG Larard, CA Large, KG Large, DL Larkin, WK Larnach, LE Larney, EW Larsen, PJ Larter, FA Latham, PG Latimer, JJ Latto, RB Lauder, SR Laughlin, AM Laurence, BW Law, GE Law, BJ Lawler, NH Lawless, BTK Lawrence, JJE Lawrence, KG Lawson, BC Lawton, IC Lay, P Le Brink, AM Lea, DJ Leach, J Leach, RH Leach, VB Leach, SE Leader, JB Leahey, RA Leahy, LW Leaman, BF Lean, GJ Learhinan, JE Leaver, AP Lee, C Lee, DY Lee, E Lee, EF Lee, EJ Lee, FC Lee, I Lee, PM Lee, RA Lee, TW Lee, WM Lee, WR Lee, WT Lee, C Leedham, R Leek, DB Leembruggen, EW Leembruggen, AB Lees, LJ Lees, S Leggatt, JF Legge, JA Leifels, TM Lemke, PJ Lennon, JA Lennox, DE Lenox, TG Lenton, DC Leonard, FC Lepinath, GJ Lepp, N Leray-Meyer, HR Leslie, IJ Leslie, PF Leslie, DW Lester, R Lever, PGL Levick, CJE Levien, HO Levien, DC Lewin, MR Lewino, AE Lewis, CE Lewis, JA Lewis, MA Lewis, MJ Lewis, RG Lewis, TV Lewis, WJ Lewis, RD Leys, PR Libbis, KD Liddiard, IG Liddicoat, B Liekefett, BJ Lightfoot, GHG Lilley, JA Linabury, MF Linden, JE Lindner, MA Lindsay, RL Linsket, IJ List, WF Little, K Littlefair, MAE Littleford, FC Littlejohn, BD Livings, J Livingstone, JA Livingstone, EK Lloyd, IA Lloyd, JH Lloyd, RHG Lloyd, VT Loader, KR Lock, DW Locke, AR Lockett, MA Lockett, WA Lockhart, RT Lockitt, HM Loeckenhoff, D Lofts, R Loftus, RV Logan, TA Logan, WM Logan, NG Loggie, J Lohf, AJ Lollback, DW Lomas, RW Lomas, NH Lonergan, DC Long, DM Long, PH Long, RJ Long, KA Longbottom, MR Longhurst, ML Longland, P Longwill, FR Lonie, RG Lord, RJ Lord, BR Loseby, PA Loudon, CW Loughlin, DCA Louis, MAP Lourensz, GS Love, WHH Love, JF Lovegrove, BM Lovell, D Lovell, EJ Lovell, KJ Lovell, KN Lovell, C Lovett, DR Lovett, R Lovett, FV Low, GR Low, R Low, GN Lowe, J Lowe, JAT Lowe, PW Lowe, VA Lowe, WL Lowe, CM Lucas, GJ Lucas, WG Lucas, WJ Lucas, LJ Luckman, JA Luder, JW Ludwig, W Lukan, JC Luker, D Lumsden, GI Lumsden, JAR Lumsden, EE Lundberg, JW Lunn, NW Lupton, JF Lush, TJC Lusink, LW Luskey, D Luttrell, LGA Lutz, BL Lynch, DJ Lynch, J Lynch, L Lynch, ML Lynch, NV Lynch, TJ Lynch, JT Lyndon, RA Lynn, MT Lyon, RW Lyon, A Lyons, RJ Lyons, WJ Lyons, RT Maas, IR Mac Gillivray, DW Macarty, DG MacDonald, JF MacDonald, KL MacDonald, RC MacDonald, REF MacDonald, WB MacDonald, PR MacDougall, J MacGowan, N MacGregor, EJ MacGuffie, RA Macintosh, DR Mack, AR Mackay, DW Mackay, P Mackay, RH Mackay, MJC Mackenzie, LS Mackie, E Mackinnon, MJ Macklin, NT Mackrill, RJ Maclean, PF MacManus, TJ MacNamara, DP MacNeall, WA Maconachie, NF Macpherson, DM Macrae, A Madden, JR Madden, A Maddock, CC Maddock, TS Maddock, EW Madgwick, SG Magann, JC Magee, RC Maggs, RP Magill, WJ Magnay, JN Maguire, PM Maguire, ALP Maher, GJ Maher, GR Maher, LA Maher, N Maher, PL Maher, BR Mahoney, GH Mahony, PW Mahood, B Main, JWA Main, A Maiolo, JFJ Mair, RL Maisey, ACG Maitland, P Makarov, KL Makkink, IB Malcolm, RJ Malcolm, T Malcolm, KT Maley, NJ Mallett, TJ Malligan, P Mallon, GT Malone, J Malone, BTC Maloney, D Maloney, TB Maloney, TJ Maloney, K Manion, GA Manktelow, DR Mann, JA Manning, KD Manning, TC Manning, RC Mannion, TJ Mansbridge, JA Manser, N Mansfield, DJ Manson, GC Manton, GRJ Mapstone, AE March, KM March, RE Marchant, A Marinac, PJF Marinich, JA Marion, KW Marks, KO Markwell, LT Markwort, DW Marland, JP Marlow, RP Marman, CWE Marney, LG Marr, DP Marriott, RC Marschke, AP Marsh, HD Marsh, HJ Marsh, LJ Marsh, MH Marsh, CA Marshall, EL Marshall, N Marshall, TH Marshall, BK Martin, D Martin, DK Martin, FB Martin, FD Martin, GA Martin, JA Martin, JF Martin, JWT Martin, K Martin, KA Martin, KG Martin, MC Martin, MJ Martin, MR Martin, NC Martin, OA Martin, PJ Martin, RH Martin, RJ Martin, RL Martin, TE Martin, TR Martin, AF Martini, NF Marxsen, LA Maschette, FAJ Mascord, LJ Maslen, BA Mason, EDH Mason, ERG Mason, GG Mason, JE Mason, NG Mason, EU Massie, AW Masters, LD Masters, GW Matheson, J Mathews, TRW Mathews, RL Mathieson, DJ Mathlin, AS Matters, WR Mattes, RL Matthes, AE Matthews, GE Matthews, JC Matthews, KR Matthews, MG Matthews, NB Matthews, RJ Matthews, WJ Matthews, PF Matthiesson, RJ Mattiazzi, RL Mattiazzi, EE Matuschka, DR Mauger, IB Maurice, TR Maw, EG Maxwell, JH Maxwell, KE Maxwell, MC May, RA May, TA May, TB May, BHS Mayfield, KJ Mayfield, KV Mayfield, HG Mayhew, RC McAleer, RG McAlister, WS McAlister, J McAllister, WM McAlpine, WK McAndrew, DMC McArdle, PL McArthur, G McAulay, GP McAuliffe, IC McBryde, RB McBurney, DA McBurnie, MWJ McCain, GJ McCallum, ND McCallum, EW McCarthy, FT McCarthy, G McCarthy, JP McCarthy, WI McCarthy, EJ McCartney, KA McCleay, GK McCleery, PK McClenaghan, JT McClenahan, BW McColm, JV McConville, EJ McCormack, JR McCormack, ML McCormack, TD McCormack, B McCormick, G McCormick, HB McCormick, PJ McCormick, W McCreadie, JG McCredie, CR McCubbin, PH McCullagh, RW McCullum, BR McCutcheon, QA McCutcheon, DR McDermott, KR McDiarmid, AA McDonald, BF McDonald, CR McDonald, DO McDonald, JA McDonald, K McDonald, ME McDonald, NA McDonald, RA McDonald, RJ McDonald, RN McDonald, JT McDonnell, GG McDougall, JW McDougall, RO McDougall, DK McDowall, RJ McDowall, GJ McEniery, EG McEvoy, MJ McEvoy, W McEwan, IF McFadyen, GJ McFarlane, AR McGaw, WJ McGennity, JSP McGhie, JM McGill, KJ McGinley, RA McGoogan, V McGough, JA McGowan, DJ McGrath, LJ McGrath, LP McGrath, M McGrath, MJ McGrath, MR McGregor, RJ McGregor, TE McGregor, FG McGuiness, KB McGuiness, PJ McGuinness, PGL McHugh, DH McHutchison, HS McIndoe, KV McInerney, RM McInnes, WG McIntosh, JG McIntyre, LP McIntyre, PJ McIntyre, SR McIntyre, FJ McIver, MDJ McIver, A McKay, BJ McKay, GA McKay, I McKay, MF McKay, VWD McKean, RL McKee, SP McKeig, RC McKellar, K McKenna, RJ McKenna, BJ McKenny, BN McKenzie, DK McKenzie, JJ McKenzie, NH McKenzie, RP McKenzie, WJ McKenzie, SV McKenzie-Trout, MP McKeon, GL McKeown, JW McKeown, LH McKeown, PWJ McKern, RA McKernan, EJ McKewin, GA McKie, RJ McKimm, AT McKinnon, ME McKinnon, RM McKinnon, RJ McKlaren, AL McKnight, DG McLaren, JA McLaren, RM McLaren, BD McLean, GC McLean, JRW McLean, LJ McLean, PN McLean, JR McLennan, GC McLeod, GH McLeod, JI McLeod, KJ McLeod, JS McLoughlin, NJ McLoughlin, RT McLucas, C McMahon, LJ McMahon, MA McMahon, DL McManus, A McMichael, CN McMillan, VA McMinn, RN McMullen, DG McNair, JA McNally, NP McNamara, RN McNamara, TJ McNamara, JA McNaught, IK McNaughton, RS McNeill, WD McNeven, WA McPhail, CC McPhee, GC McPhee, DG McPherson, G McPherson, H McPherson, J McQueen, DW McRae, TJ McSweeney, JB McTaggart, RA McWhinney, MW Meacham, GF Mead, TJ Meagher, JC Meakin, KL Meares, RF Meares, ME Mears, RM Mech, MJ Mecham, WF Mecham, R Medana, TR Medhurst, L Medlen, TD Meehan, BJ Meekings, BS Meekings, KJ Megaw, DGJ Mehegan, IG Meier, CJ Melchert, M Mellenfield, PA Mellies, SD Mellow, DM Melville, RE Melville, EL Membrey, PD Menear, JC Mennen, D Menzies, DJ Mepham, A Mercer, CE Mercer, JC Mercer, JC Mercieca, AR Meredith, KB Merrigan, BR Merry, R Messenger, BR Messer, GK Metcalfe, RN Metcalfe, NG Meteyard, MH Mewett, DP Meyer, RF Meyer, LJ Micallef, W Middlemiss, AA Middleton, D Middleton, PM Middleton, WJ Mignot, J Migus, AA Miles, CP Miles, JD Miles, PW Miles, W Miles, TS Milham, AE Millar, AL Millar, BG Millar, JT Millar, NE Millar, TM Millar, KP Millard, B Miller, BR Miller, CH Miller, DLR Miller, GJ Miller, JGN Miller, JM Miller, JS Miller, KA Miller, MD Miller, N Miller, RD Miller, CHB Millers, G Millett, JL Millhouse, DS Milligan, RK Milligan, WAK Milligan, AJ Millin, LAJ Mills, NJ Mills, PG Mills, RG Mills, TC Mills, J Millsom, AG Milne, LG Milne, BJ Milner, RM Milner, LR Milsom, SG Milsted, OR Milton, RG Milton, EL Minahan, BE Minchin, DR Minon, TR Minter, CB Mirow, RP Mischlewski, E Misztal, BK Mitchell, JF Mitchell, JW Mitchell, JW Mitchell, KJ Mitchell, RD Mitchell, RJ Mitchell, SCK Mitchell, CB Moffat, DR Moffat, N Moffat, HG Moffatt, MJ Moffitt, PA Mogridge, R Mohr, PF Mole, DT Moles, BC Moloney, RJ Molony, TJ Monahan, C Monk, JA Montgomery, N Montgomery, RJ Montgomery, RA Moodie, MD Moon, AA Moorcroft, BE Moore, DG Moore, EE Moore, HT Moore, JD Moore, JJ Moore, JS Moore, LR Moore, MD Moore, MM Moore, PG Moore, RA Moore, RD Moore, RD Moore, RJ Moore, RW Moore, TR Moore, WD Moore, WR Moore, A Moran, PF Moran, RM Morcom, NR Moreton, A Morgan, BL Morgan, CD Morgan, FH Morgan, JR Morgan, NB Morgan, TJ Morgan, MP Moroney, ED Morris, L Morris, LW Morris, EM Morrison, GF Morrison, GJ Morrison, RA Morrison, FA Morrissey, MT Morrissey, PJ Morrissey, MD Morrissy, TM Morrissy, GD Morrow, R Morrow, RSJ Morrow, GE Morthorpe, DO Mortimer, AJ Morton, JA Morton, GL Moscrop, HLJ Mosler, MFG Moss, SL Moss, J Mosur, BJ Mouatt, GJ Mounsey, EJ Mowat, JR Mowbray, FJ Moylan, NB Moyle, RD Moyle, RL Moyle, LF Muhleisen, PJ Mulcahy, KW Muldowney, GT Mulholland, GJ Mullaly, EE Mullens, JR Mullens, CW Muller, EJ Muller, FE Muller, KC Muller, WJ Muller, GA Mullins, HM Mullins, JH Mullins, JW Mullins, DT Mumford, TJ Munce, EF Munday, KJ Munns, GWE Munrowd, PR Munson, NL Munster, BJ Murphy, DJP Murphy, FA Murphy, HM Murphy, JD Murphy, JF Murphy, MJ Murphy, MS Murphy, NJ Murphy, PV Murphy, RD Murphy, RG Murphy, RWJ Murphy, WF Murphy, A Murray, AG Murray, AR Murray, BJ Murray, EJ Murray, GD Murray, GF Murray, JEF Murray, JK Murray, KJ Murray, ME Murray, NB Murray, NS Murray, RE Murray, VW Murray, WM Murray, M Murray-Alston, DT Murrell, OC Murrell, TR Murry, J Muscat, PV Musk, GJA Mussig, JJ Mustard, MP Mutton, KJP Myers, C Nafpliotis, JG Nagel, RE Naggs, WS Nan, KJ Napier, DE Napper, BR Nash, JF Nash, J Nast, DS Naylor, JA Naylor, LA Naylor, LW Naylor, JR Neale, J Neatherway, AJ Neave, JS Neave, JD Nebauer, JC Nebe, RK Neems, PO Neesham, KLH Neeves, JW Neighbour, DC Neil, GW Neil, GE Neill, KF Neilsen, RJ Neilson, TE Neilson, BM Nelson, GC Nelson, GD Nelson, W Nelson, DW Neumann, DF Neville, PJ Newark, JT Newcombe, RL Newcombe, WR Newell, PR Newey, RB Newlands, MC Newman, MD Newman, WR Newman, OJ Newson, GT Newstead, AE Newton, MT Newton, AJ Nibbs, LJ Nice, JR Nichol, GR Nicholas, DO Nicholls, DR Nicholls, GP Nicholls, JE Nicholls, MJ Nicholls, PC Nicholls,

GC Nichols, I Nichols, RJ Nichols, GA Nicholson, JJ Nicholson, HG Nicoll, BFS Nicolls, J Nicolson, AN Nielsen, GB Nielsen, NE Nielsen, WM Nielsen, JA Nightingale, KS Ninness, GW Nixon, EG Noble, WN Noble, TA Noblet, PE Nolan, BJ Noonan, CG Noonan, LJ Norgaard, CC Norris, GH Norris, JV North, WF North, FJ North-Coombes, TJ Northcott, CI Norton, WTM Nott, JE Noyce, TF Nugent, PR Nuske, TA Nye, CS O'Brien, D O'Brien, GT O'Brien, JP O'Brien, KI O'Brien, MB O'Brien, MS O'Brien, RF O'Brien, RF O'Brien, TG O'Brien, WK O'Brien, WW O'Brien, AJ O'Bryan, PG O'Byrne, CA O'Connor, RW O'Connor, PR O'Davis, RO Odell, JC O'Dempsey, GJ Odgers, RJ O'Doherty, EJ O'Donnell, JM O'Donnell, MJ O'Donnell, TW O'Donohoe, WH O'Farrell, WJ O'Farrell, RE O'Ferrall, JN Ogden, LB Ogle, BG O'Gorman, LT O'Gorman, RM O'Hanlon, RA O'Hara, KL O'Keefe, TE O'Keeffe, GS Old, WA Oldfield, BJ Olive, D Oliver, RA Oliver, PD Ollett, HJ Olliver, DF Olsen, FW Olsen, GJ Olsen, RJ O'Malley, JC O'Meagher, K O'Neil, J O'Neill, JG O'Neill, LR O'Neill, MK O'Neill, MP O'Neill, R O'Neill, JG Ooms, JR Oostenbroek, JE Opie, RC Orchard, ZMJ Ord, WBC Ormsby, CL O'Rourke, JJ O'Rourke, PJ O'Rourke, WW O'Rourke, MRD Orr, BJ Osborne, RN Osborne, BE O'Shea, LW Osmond, RM O'Sullivan, AS Oswell, ME Otago, TJ Otley, B O'Toole, GN Ott, BW Overall, RC Oversby, SC Overy, BL Owens, DW Owens, JJ Owens, A Owston, DG Oxenham, DE Ozanne, REK Paddon, KWG Padgett, AA Page, HE Page, J Page, KR Page, MG Page, VJ Page, TB Paget, AM Pahl, AW Pahl, MJ Pahl, EJ Paine, JC Paine, OH Paine, TJ Paine, BR Palmer, DK Palmer, GJ Palmer, KJ Palmer, LH Palmer, RJ Palmer, PF Pannowitz, CC Parcell, LK Parchert, G Paris, KE Paris, KJ Park, MA Park, PJ Park, FJ Parker, GW Parker, HK Parker, RL Parker, GG Parkes, BJ Parks, Z Parnell, KM Parry, MG Parry, JH Parsons, PJ Parsons, RJ Parsons, RJ Parsons, WD Parsons, WF Parsons, LS Pascoe, JE Pasmore, BJ Passfield, B Patchett, GL Patchett, JD Pateman, KJ Paterson, KL Paterson, RA Paterson, J Paton, BD Patrick, RV Patrick, B Patten, RJ Patten, DS Patterson, RJ Patterson, W Patterson, NL Pattison, PDC Pattison, DR Paul, JA Paule, J Paulga, JW Paulin, AL Payne, CF Payne, DE Payne, JS Payne, JT Payne, JW Payne, PR Payne, WE Payne, WWB Peace, DW Peacock, IM Peacock, NH Peacock, RW Peacock, DW Peak, DW Pearce, RJ Pearce, RN Pearce, AT Pearson, BR Pearson, NP Pearson, RK Peasley, BS Peck, TJ Pedelty, CJ Pedersen, WT Pedersen, BJ Pedrana, JA Pedrina, RA Peiniger, AG Pellizzer, J Pemberton, DJM Pendergast, KWA Pendergast, IC Pengilley, J Penn, DM Penny, WER Penrose, GT Penwarn, GV Perazic, DK Percy, DP Perkins, RA Perkins, ML Perrett, PNM Perrow, AJ Perry, BJ Perry, EP Perry, ET Perry, RL Perry, CF Pershouse, DP Peters, EH Peters, ND Peters, WJ Peters, WS Peters, CJ Peterson, TG Petith, BO Petriw, LC Pettet, MDA Pettigrew, JE Pettit, BJ Pettitt, RP Pfoeffer, MB Phelan, RG Phelps, LJ Phibbs, JDF Philip, RJP Philips, CA Phillips, CA Phillips, CJ Phillips, DT Phillips, HG Phillips, KA Phillips, KJ Phillips, PC Phillips, PN Phillips, RD Phillips, RH Phillips, RJ Phillips, SJ Phillips, WFJ Phillips, BT Phipps, RL Pick, CJ Pickering, DW Pickering, HAH Pickering, RR Pickering, JA Pickett, GS Piddington, DR Piggott, KA Piggott, RG Piggott, CE Pike, FW Pike, GJ Pike, WJ Pike, AJ Pinches, TJ Pinkerton, ID Pinkus, A Pitt, LJ Pittman, M Plate, SW Platt, JG Pleass, N Plowright, RW Plowright, AW Pluck, RJ Pluis, DF Plummer, DL Politch, TC Politch, GI Pollard, WJ Pollard, MA Pollington, BN Pollock, DT Pollock, BA Pomroy, FH Pope, MW Pope, DH Porter, GF Porter, A Portlock, DA Potter, J Potter, DN Potts, RF Potts, JN Poulish, WL Poustie, P Powe, A Powell, AJ Powell, AW Powell, PG Powell, GA Power, J Power, JA Power, NE Power, CK Powles, TW Pracy, CJ Pratt, JDA Pratt, KA Pratt, NR Pratt, TJ Pratt, TJ Pratt, DE Prattey, OJ Preece, RJ Preece, RE Prefke, JP Presdee, DJ Presnell, EH Preston, GA Preston, MJ Preston, EG Prevett, BJ Prewett, KM Price, RJ Price, DW Priday, LA Priest, GR Priestley, JF Prince, JT Pringle, DT Pritchard, JAM Pritchard, KC Pritchatt, SJ Proh, RW Properjohn, JS Prosper, D Prosser, M Provost, GJ Prowd, JG Prowse, RJ Prowse, DF Pryce, GD Pryke, PG Puck, ER Pugh, GN Pugh, JS Puleston-Jones, TA Pullar, CM Pullen, BM Purcell, WA Purdie, CM Purdon, JT Purkiss, JH Purnell, GF Purves, RRJ Pyers, RR Pym, M Quibell, MP Quigley, FDI Quiller, JF Quinlan, JM Quinn, JT Quinn, OM Quinn, KJ Quintal, SA Raabe, BM Raby, RA Raby, BFN Rachinger, JA Radbone, DW Radburn, JA Radford, KG Radford, AD Rae, JJ Rae, JS Rae, J Raichert, RM Rainbow, DW Ralph, FC Ralph, RS Ralph, D Ramm, CD Rampant, CV Ramsay, DR Ramsay, EI Ramsay, LR Ramsay, RD Ramsay, RH Ramsay, TJ Ramsay, RS Ramsey, SJ Rancic, AT Randall, GC Randall, N Randall, D Rands, RJ Ranger, B Rankin, DJ Rankine, RG Ranney, RT Raph, LJ Rappo, RL Raston, GE Ratchford, AD Ratcliffe, LE Raue, JRP Raven, PF Raw, MJ Rawlinson, PF Raymant, GM Raymond, RG Raymond, DG Rayner, WR Rayner, FG Rayner-Sharpe, AJ Read, DJ Read, EFN Read, JB Reader, RJA Reading, JS Reale, JF Reardon, PM Reardon, RS Reardon, RWG Reardon, DF Reber, RW Reddacliff, TJ Reddacliff, SG Redden, IB Redfern, RL Redman, DW Redmond, J Redmond, KR Redpath, B Redshaw, RP Redway, AR Reed, GA Reed, PJ Reed, TL Reed, GG Reeds, AG Reeks, HS Rees, IC Rees, JA Rees, JE Rees, MM Rees, TR Rees, CH Reeve, FT Reeves, WW Reeves, R Reher, BE Reichardt, J Reichvalds, EJ Reid, GJ Reid, IF Reid, JM Reid, M Reid, NH Reid, RJ Reid, RP Reid, CW Reif, JE Reilly, KJ Reilly, ID Reinke, JF Reis, GJ Relf, WA Remes, AR Renfree, JS Renfrew, AM Rennick, RC Rennie, PR Renshaw, E Resetar, DR Retallack, K Revill, EP Reville, AJ Reynolds, DCH Reynolds, DW Reynolds, GBW Reynolds, TD Reynolds, AM Reynolds-Huntley, RD Rhoades, DA Rhodes, R Rhodes, RJ Rhodes, WJ Rhone, LJ Rice, GD Rich, GP Rich, B Richards, BF Richards, CJ Richards, CS Richards, J Richards, JD Richards, JP Richards, P Richards, R Richards, RK Richards, SWG Richards, AO Richardson, BR Richardson, DS Richardson, GSW Richardson, PB Richardson, RL Richardson, RV Richardson, WE Richardson, WGM Richardson, JD Riches, JE Riches, JE Riches, KW Riches, DT Ridding, AD Riddock, RJ Rider, G Ridgers, BW Ridgewell, DJS Riding, JW Ridout, EJ Riebeling, HK Rieck, JRK Rielly, JT Riemann, RF Rigby, JFH Rigg, MB Rigg, WT Riggs, DB Riley, DW Riley, FP Riley, G Riley, GN Riley, IW Riley, K Riley, PJ Riley, SW Riley, EN Rinaldi, FW Rinaldi, PF Rinehart, CP Ring, DJ Ringe, C Ringshaw, TJ Riordan, HK Riseley, RH Riseley, FP Rishworth, HA Ritchie, HR Ritchie, S Ritchie, CM Robb, JG Robb, PB Robb, DL Robbie, JF Robbins, BM Roberts, BV Roberts, CA Roberts, GC Roberts, KW Roberts, RJ Roberts, TW Roberts, A Robertson, AO Robertson, AR Robertson, HJ Robertson, MR Robertson, RA Robertson, THM Robertson, VG Robertson, WN Robertson, FS Robey, MJ Robin, CI Robins, RJB Robins, CH Robinson, FC Robinson, FW Robinson, LP Robinson, M Robinson, PL Robinson, PM Robinson, RG Robinson, RJ Robinson, RJ Robinson, RM Robinson, AJ Robson, DP Robson, J Robson, JL Robson, LG Robson, A Roche, JH Roche, JA Rochford, WW Rock, RW Rockliff, VR Rodda, JF Roddy, RR Roddy, KM Rodgers, TL Rodgers, DH Roe, CJ Roese, NCO Roeszler, CJ Roffe, AC Rogers, AW Rogers, AWJ Rogers, DJ Rogers, DM Rogers, IH Rogers, JL Rogers, JW Rogers, LS Rogers, MA Rogers, NJ Rogers, WG Rogers, P Roggenkamp, DJ Roles, BK Rolfe, DD Rolph, CJ Romeo, F Romeyn, JT Ronan, RJ Ronan, AE Ronke, SF Roodhouse, AC Rooney, AW Rooney, BJ Rose, DFF Rose, GN Rose, HO Rose, JK Rose, MR Rose, RW Rose, JD Rosendale, HJF Roser, HC Rosielle, AJ Ross, JK Ross, PL Ross, WA Ross, FJ Rossello, A Rossetto, CI Rossington, JV Rossiter, A Roth, JM Rough, KF Routledge, LW Routledge, KL Row, HJ Rowatt, WL Rowbottom, AJ Rowe, AW Rowe, FW Rowe, GH Rowe, GL Rowe, J Rowe, RA Rowe, RW Rowe, CE Rowland, EA Rowland, BH Rowley, RW Rowley, WG Rowley, GC Roxburgh, RS Royston, GH Ruck, AW Rudd, D Rudkin, DL Ruggero, DWM Rule, FH Rule, MT Rumpf, AR Rundle, MJ Rush, RB Rush, SF Russ, AD Russell, BE Russell, CR Russell, FG Russell, LA Russell, LC Russell, NJ Russell, RKW Russell, SS Russell, VJ Russell, PV Rust, PS Ruston, HG Rutherford, NP Rutherford, J Rutland, RA Rutter, AJ Ryan, E Ryan, FP Ryan, GF Ryan, HA Ryan, M Ryan, MR Ryan, NJ Ryan, NW Ryan, PC Ryan, RD Ryan, SE Ryan, VJ Ryan, RS Ryding, JW Rydstrom, MJ Ryle, K Saal, BJ Sadler, SJB Sainsbury, RJ Sallaway, RH Sallway, MG Salmon, AR Salter, RC Salter, PT Salvair, WF Salzmann, JT Sambrooks, JR Sampson, RW Sampson, VC Sams, JH Sandercott, BR Sanders, DR Sanders, AI Sanderson, RK Sanderson, CJ Sandford, J Sargent, IF Satrapa, R Sauer, C Saunders, CSG Saunders, GD Saunders, GJ Saunders, IR Saunders, JC Saunders, RJ Saunders, DJ Savage, RG Saville, WS Sawdy, AL Sawtell, ME Sayer, MI Sayers, WK Scanlin, LR Schafer, IB Schafferius, WD Scheer, A Schekahn, A Scherini, DL Schier, CF Schiller, KH Schirrmeyer, WF Schleiger, DA Schmidt, JA Schmidt, JEM Schmidt, JH Schmidt, AG Schmitt, L Schneider, PG Scholz, PAJ Schoutens, RJ Schreiber, NC Schroeter, GA Schubert, GW Schubert, RB Schultz, BM Schulz, PAM Schumann, CR Schwerin, DAW Sciortino, PJ Sciortino, GS Scobie, JC Scotland, DC Scott, DG Scott, GR Scott, GRJ Scott, IK Scott, JA Scott, JA Scott, KJ Scott, NL Scott, PA Scott, RA Scott, SR Scott, WA Scott, WR Scott, RE Scovell, LJ Scrase, GF Scully, JLE Scully, PJ Scully, GF Scurr, JG Seage, RJ Seager, BD Searle, LJ Searle, JG Sebastian, KT Seckington, BW Seedsman, TA Seedsman, JL Seibel, B Selge, GR Sellar, CW Selman, KI Semmler, I Senini, LD Senior, RB Setchfield, AP Sewell, JJ Sewell, JP Seymour, RE Shade, TRC Shanahan, DT Shanley, GJ Shanley, MT Shanley, JD Sharley, BA Sharman, GR Sharp, RG Sharp, CAM Sharpe, HR Sharpe, KC Sharpe, BW Sharper, KJ Sharpley, AE Shaw, GL Shaw, MF Shaw, PS Shaw, BC Shearer, JR Shearer, WJ Shee, AT Sheean, MT Sheean, GE Sheehan, MW Shelley, RKW Shepherd, WJ Shepherd, AM Shepley, EA Sheppard, J Sheppard, JM Sheppard, NJ Sheppard, PJ Sheriff, RC Sheriff, WG Sherman, JA Sherren, RR Sherrin, BJ Shewan, GJ Shiel, HK Shields, GR Shiels, FV Shilton, PW Shiner, AL Shipard, KC Shipard, DJ Shipp, KJ Shipp, ID Shore, GM Shores, BH Short, HA Shortridge, JC Shumack, R Shuttleworth, AC Sibthorpe, CF Sievier, JG Siffer, GM Silcock, FJ Silver, JA Silver, DH Sim, DK Simmons, JH Simmons, NC Simmons, KJ Simons, A Simpson, JF Simpson, KIP Simpson, L Simpson, LJ Simpson, PW Simpson, RN Simpson, RS Simpson, HA Sims, WA Sims, PJ Sinclair, FD Singleton, DJ Sinkinson, NB Sinkinson, NEJ Sinnott, P Sinnott, RT Sivyer, W Skeaf, JB Skewis, TM Skinner, NF Skoglund, MJ Slack, GO Slade, WJ Slag, F Slater, RA Slater, PA Sloane, A Slootjes, RF Sloper, N Slyney, RJ Smalley, NJ Smallwood, DB Smedley, J Smigiel, AB Smith, AD Smith, AE Smith, AJ Smith, APS Smith, AT Smith, AW Smith, BJ Smith, BS Smith, CJ Smith, CR Smith, CV Smith, D Smith, DA Smith, DJ Smith, DR Smith, E Smith, EMG Smith, FK Smith, GD Smith, GJ Smith, GK Smith, GT Smith, GW Smith, ID Smith, IMS Smith, IR Smith, J Smith, JC Smith, JD Smith, JD Smith, JE Smith, JR Smith, K Smith, KC Smith, KJ Smith, KP Smith, LH Smith, LJ Smith, NB Smith, NH Smith, PC Smith, PG Smith, PJ Smith, PS Smith, RJ Smith, RL Smith, RM Smith, RW Smith, SB Smith, SG Smith, T Smith, TN Smith, TP Smith, VRM Smith, WJ Smith, DGS Smithers, CDF Smithies, AC Smithson, BF Smooker, RE Smoothy, AK Smorti, D Smyth, CE Smythe, RH Smythe, RF Snedden, SJ Snodgrass, EJ Soanes, HW Solomons, LA Solomons, HF Somers, AC Sommer, AW Sommer, DJ Sonntag, A Soos, S Sorahan, RG Sorby, TR Sorenson, SJ Sounness, CF South, HCW Spackman, PM Spackman, DR Spalding, EB Spanner, J Spark, L Sparkman, GB Spaulding, DA Speis, MT Spence, JN Spencer, KM Spendlove, AL Spillane, BAJ Spillane, SG Spinks, AJ Spooner, NH Spradau, VP Sprague, CL Spratt, IJ Springfield, CE Sproul, CH Spurgeon, JO Spurgeon, PC Spurgin, RCH Spurr, RJ Squiers, B Squires, BD Squires, PC St John, RP St John, J Staal, GR Stacey, WN Stallebrass, ML Stanborough, AG Stanbridge, HB Stanbrook, DK Staniforth, VV Stankevicius, RJ Stanley, RL Stanley, AJD Stanton, RG Stanton, KR Stapleton, NJ Stark, PL Stark, RT Starkie, BM Starkoff, IK Starr, RJ Stebbings, R Steel, WR Steel, KL Stegelman, LD Stein, PH Steiner, LA Steinhardt, RA Stemp, DG Stenhouse, SJ Stenner, AW Stephens, DJ Stephens, HH Stephens, JJ Stephens, RA Stephens, BC Stephenson, EH Stephenson, JF Stephenson, JS Stephenson, P Stephenson, RE Stephenson, GE Stevens, GK Stevens, JT Stevens, KVN Stevens, AJ Stevenson, GW Stevenson, RA Steward, BT Stewart, CT Stewart, DC Stewart, DL Stewart, DP Stewart, GB Stewart, GD Stewart, GI Stewart, IR Stewart, JE Stewart, RV Stewart, A Stickland, DH Stidston, JG Stirling, MD Stockton, RJ Stokes, SJ Stokes, GE Stolberg, AD Stollery, DR Stone, JM Stone, KJ Stone, RL Stone, WJ Stone, JR Storer, J Storrie, RZ Storta, GL Story, DK Stott, WT Stott, RO Stoy, RJ Stoyles, G Strachan, RJ Straney, LC Stratford, GT Stratton, T Straub, DK Streatfeild, JB Street, AA Streeter, MK Streitberg, CR Strickland, BJ Stringfellow, DG Stringfellow, AE Stripe, PL Strong, WM Strong, RG Strudwick, EA Strugnell, G Strutt, JS Stryker, BT Stuart,

RA Stuart, CA Stubbs, KD Stutz, TL Sugars, CJ Sugden, BC Sullivan, BF Sullivan, DD Sullivan, DP Sullivan, FJ Sullivan, WG Sullivan, GI Summerfield, RCH Sund, GJ Sundberg, GM Sunderland, LI Suosaari, IG Surawski, MR Susans, PR Sutcliffe, BM Sutherland, DB Sutherland, DJ Sutherland, KD Sutherland, WA Sutherland, JA Suthers, AN Sutton, CH Sutton, DR Sutton, GJH Sutton, MN Sutton, RV Svensen, MR Swain, MS Swain, G Swan, JH Swan, ML Swanson, ND Swanson, RR Swanson, BT Sweeney, WAE Sweeney, MJ Sweetman, NH Swenson, WJ Swinton, MW Sycz, SG Symonds, RL Symons, GA Szczecinski, R Szmelter, D Taffe, PR Tainton, KM Tait, RE Tait, VR Tame, G Tanner, KF Tanswell, ND Tanswell, BW Tanzer, JH Tapp, MR Tardent, BC Tarr, RT Tarrant, S Tarrier, FR Tate, AG Taylor, AJ Taylor, AR Taylor, B Taylor, BR Taylor, BV Taylor, DJ Taylor, DJ Taylor, ER Taylor, F Taylor, I Taylor, JA Taylor, KAG Taylor, KJ Taylor, NB Taylor, NL Taylor, PJN Taylor, PW Taylor, R Taylor, RL Taylor, RM Taylor, WNE Taylor, JM Teague, GR Teakle, RJL Tebbutt, PJ Tedge, NF Tegge, WJ Tejcek, BN Tennant, JA Tennent, WC Tennick, W Tersic, BG Tesch, KJ Thackeray, DA Thatcher, LE Thatcher, WP Theilemann, DA Theodore, WJ Therkelsen, MA Thiele, OC Thiele, PS Thom, A Thomas, BM Thomas, CG Thomas, EAP Thomas, EJ Thomas, HRT Thomas, I Thomas, JE Thomas, JFK Thomas, KB Thomas, KH Thomas, RC Thomas, RJ Thomas, RM Thomas, RS Thomas, TD Thomas, WAV Thomas, A Thompson, AJ Thompson, BB Thompson, CJ Thompson, CO Thompson, DB Thompson, G Thompson, GA Thompson, IR Thompson, KA Thompson, LRE Thompson, RB Thompson, RC Thompson, RE Thompson, R Thompson, RJ Thompson, RP Thompson, GA Thoms, DG Thomson, DN Thomson, GD Thomson, JI Thomson, LJ Thomson, RJ Thomson, R Thorley, KE Thorn, WJ Thorn, BR Thornton, JO Thornton, DL Thorogood, RW Thorp, GP Thorpe, MF Thorpe, TH Thorpe, KR Throup, HWC Thwaites, JG Thyer, JD Thynne, DR Tibbey, PW Tickner, DAE Tidd, RG Tidd, ST Tideswell, CL Tidswell, GT Tierney, JH Tierney, CC Tigwell, GJ Tillack, G Tilley, RA Tilley, RE Tilley, SR Tilley, NM Timson, FH Tindall, G Tindall, BV Tipping, KFJ Tipping, TH Tite, RL Tobias, DB Tobin, MJ Tobin, AD Todd, SN Todhunter, IJ Tolj, PC Tollemache, RW Tolman, PM Toman, CB Tomlinson, MB Tomlinson, JG Toner, EW Tonkin, BW Tonks, H Tonner, T Topping, G Toscan, DJ Tottenham, JA Towill, GW Townend, TC Townley, BC Townsend, RH Townsend, AH Trafford, JP Trappett, WA Trattles, DR Travers, HP Travers, TC Travers, MK Traves, RJ Trease, DP Treasure, KP Treasure, AL Tregea, AJ Tregilgas, JJ Tregillgas, BW Treller, KJ Treloar, RB Treloar, APE Tremain, GT Tremethick, RJ Trenholme, B Trenning, WR Trevethan, WA Trewartha, KA Triffitt, BR Triggs, WA Triggs, KD Trim, KR Trimmer, JPH Trinder, A Trinks, LR Triplett, MG Trrgilgas, RR Truntic, SP Tsicalas, T Tsikleas, PA Tuck, RG Tuck, JE Tucker, LG Tucker, LS Tucker, MC Tucker, NP Tucker, RH Tucker, EJ Tuckfield, AN Tudehope, GA Tulk, M Tulk, DS Tully, AM Turnbull, DJ Turnbull, K Turnbull, T Turnbull, AC Turner, BW Turner, DJ Turner, J Turner, JA Turner, JW Turner, LJ Turner, MG Turner, P Turner, TA Turner, WG Turner, WJ Turner, G Turpin, MER Tutte, WR Tutty, BLA Twomey, PW Twomey, AH Tye, DA Tyers, CJ Tyler, K Tyler, KR Tyndall, NR Tyne, JV Tyrrell, GJ Underhill, GE Unicomb, EEJ Unwin, R Upham, RM Uprichard, T Vale, JD Valentine, PW Vallely, JA Van der Harst, B Van der Maat, WJ Van der Ryken, HG Van der Woude, JC Van Deventer, T Van Dyken, E Van Gilst, DP Van Kessel, RF Van Leuven, FAM Van Look, JW Van Rooy, H Van Straten, JB Vanden Bosch, WB Vanderheld, JB Vanderkyl, J Vandersteege, JJ Vandervegt, S Van-Stam, MF Vaughan, MC Veach, JE Veitch, BJ Vellacott, JP Vellacott, JA Venn, BKJ Verity, RL Vernon, JM Versluis, BD Vertigan, RW Verzelberg, BH Vest, JR Vicary, KJ Vicary, DJ Vickers, P Vidler, N Viereckel, AA Vilcins, VB Villa, G Vince, EG Vincent, AF Viney, RG Viney, MB Vink, FWJ Vizzard, G Volker, WF Voltz, RI Waddy, RN Wade, WR Wade, MJ Wadley, KS Wadling, DK Waghorn, NW Wagner, BR Wakefield, DC Wakefield, DF Wakelin, GW Walden, CW Walford, AT Walker, CM Walker, EH Walker, GL Walker, HJ Walker, JA Walker, JF Walker, LE Walker, LF Walker, LR Walker, MJM Walker, NH Walker, NRF Walker, RJ Walker, BA Wallace, BK Wallace, BL Wallace, FJ Wallace, GB Wallace, I Wallace, R Wallace, W Wallace, RW Waller, BD Wallis, GH Wallis, NC Wallis, RD Wallis, AJ Walsh, GM Walsh, LN Walsh, LR Walsh, PR Walsh, TC Walsh, CJ Walters, DJ Walters, JL Walters, TP Walters, WF Walters, GC Walton, GJM Walton, BW Wanstall, JH Warbrick, JR Warbrook, BTB Ward, C Ward, GS Ward, J Ward, RJ Ward, RT Ward, T Ward, TP Ward, J Wardle, DJ Ware, EE Ware, PJ Ware, RJ Waring, FA Wark, RM Wark, LR Warn, BK Warnock, HG Warr, EG Warren, ME Warren, RA Warren, CE Warthold, KD Warton, V Wasiljew, M Waterman, BM Waters, DH Waters, MR Waters, PJ Waters, AGD Waterton, SR Watherston, JW Watkins, NJG Watling, CJ Watson, DC Watson, DJ Watson, G Watson, HG Watson, MS Watson, NJ Watson, PJ Watson, PL Watson, R Watson, WT Watson, GG Watt, TN Watt, NF Watterson, PB Wattie, AW Watts, JG Watts, LC Watts, RE Watts, RJ Watts, GF Way, GR Waycott, RV Waycott, CH Wayth, RJ Wearne, CJ Weatherall, DE Webb, FMW Webb, JW Webb, K Webb-Wagg, JA Weber, BC Webster, JN Webster, LL Webster, PJ Webster, TJ Webster, TJ Wedding, GD Weekes, DR Weeks, DM Weir, DW Weir, R Weir, GJ Welch, GN Welch, EM Weller, EP Weller, RC Wellings, EBW Wells, LJC Wells, MP Wells, RL Wells, TA Wells, JM Wellsmore, CW Welsby, JV Welsh, SS Welsh, VM Welsh, KB Wendt, JC Wenman, IR Wescombe, JE Wesley, JR West, RK West, SD West, WA West, GW Westbury, AD Westland, CR Westland, RB Weston, LB Weymouth, A Whalley, EL Whalley, RP Wharton, DBM Whately, JA Wheal, IL Wheat, T Wheatland, HD Wheatley, AE Wheeler, JM Wheeler, WT Wheeler, HM Whelan, GW Wheldon, AJ Whish-Wilson, IH Whisker, LN Whitby, AW Whitchurch, AJ White, AN White, AR White, C White, DC White, G White, GL White, J White, JC White, JE White, JJ White, JR White, K White, KA White, PA White, SE White, SR White, ST White, TA White, JA Whitehead, WB Whiteman, W Whitley, JJ Whittaker, J Whitton, NW Whyburn, EH Whytcross, AM Whyte, KR Whyte, EC Wickers, D Wickham, TJ Wicking, ST Wicks, RE Widdowson, PS Widgery, BV Wiggins, NR Wiggins, AE Wilcox, AR Wilcox, RJ Wilde, A Wildeboer, AH Wilkie, RN Wilkie, AR Wilkinson, D Wilkinson, IE Wilkinson, JJ Wilkinson, WR Wilkinson, CJ Wilks, GP Willans, MJ Willcocks, AC Williams, AD Williams, AH Williams, BF Williams, DJ Williams, EK Williams, GJ Williams, HR Williams, IT Williams, JP Williams, JR Williams, JSM Williams, JT Williams, KC Williams, KJ Williams, LJ Williams, LJ Williams, NB Williams, PC Williams, PH Williams, RB Williams, RE Williams, RJ Williams, RL Williams, SD Williams, SW Williams, TL Williams, TM Williams, TR Williams, VE Williams, WJE Williams, BES Williamson, DJ Williamson, JN Williamson, JR Williamson, JW Williamson, RL Williamson, BH Willis, KM Willis, OH Willis, AJ Willmett, H Willmore, JR Willoughby, KM Willoughby, JA Wills, RN Wills, FAM Wilmink, WE Wilmot, D Wilmott, PG Wilms, AR Wilson, BA Wilson, BM Wilson, CA Wilson, DB Wilson, DF Wilson, DO Wilson, EJ Wilson, G Wilson, GJ Wilson, HA Wilson, HG Wilson, J Wilson, JA Wilson, JF Wilson, JJ Wilson, JM Wilson, JR Wilson, KJ Wilson, KR Wilson, KW Wilson, L Wilson, MG Wilson, NJ Wilson, R Wilson, RA Wilson, RA Wilson, RT Wilson, SJ Wilson, SW Wilson, TCA Wilson, JV Wilton, AG Wiltshire, DH Wiltshire, WH Wiltshire, RG Winbank, RC Winckel, AD Window, DK Window, GE Window, RM Window, R Windsor, DM Winfield, ADM Winkelmann, RF Winkleman, LT Winn, NF Winnett, KD Winning, JO Winter, AN Winton, AO Winton, DR Winyard, JM Wishart, BE Witenden, RW Wittman, EJH Wittup, RJ Wockner, AF Wode, WG Wolrige, A Wood, BR Wood, D Wood, EJ Wood, GG Wood, GH Wood, HA Wood, HGA Wood, J Wood, KC Wood, KW Wood, PC Wood, RJ Wood, RW Wood, AK Woodall, WR Woodburgess, AH Woodcock, P Woodford, ST Woodger, RJ Woodrow, EJ Woods, MJ Woods, RH Woods, DN Woodward, SJ Woolcock, GE Wooldridge, MK Woolf, IA Woolley, AW Woolston, JC Woolston, JL Wootton, RS Workman, DC Worner, HJ Worner, PG Worsley, GB Worth, MTA Worth, RL Worthey, BJ Worthington, KJ Worthington, CR Wotton, RH Wotton, AG Wray, DJB Wray, NJ Wren, DR Wright, EF Wright, J Wright, JS Wright, MJG Wright, MK Wright, RL Wright, RW Wright, SN Wright, TD Wright, IB Wrigley, BW Writer, MJ Wruck, PL Wundenberg, RM Wundenberg, WW Wurm, KW Wyatt, RF Wyatt, WCA Wyatt, AK Wylie, DC Wynn, STW Wynn, TE Yanner, C Yates, P Yates, DL Yeates, RN Yee, JG Yorke, P Youd, A Young, BG Young, CL Young, DW Young, EJ Young, GJ Young, NJ Young, RA Young, RJR Young, SJ Young, J Younger, JH Youngman, APJ Zammit-Ross, JA Zammit-Ross, DR Zanker, JR Zarb, WJ Zietek, MC Zigenbine, D Zingelmann, EW Zinnecker.

ACKNOWLEDGEMENTS

The Age 177,178,180,183,184,191; Army Public Relations 23,27,29,82,86,87,89,93,96,98,102,105,107,109,119,126,127; Australian Associated Press 31,113,116, 132; Australian News and Information Bureau 144; Australian Overseas Information Service 63,65,66,73,142,143,145 below, 147,166,171, 216 (Mike Jensen), 218 (John Crowther), 226 (M. Lindsay), 227, 228 (Patrick McArdell) 230; Australian War Memorial (file numbers included) FAI/70/23/VN 2, CUN/72/VN 14, BUL/69/27/VN 17, ERR/68/842/VN 20, P145/11/03 21, BRO/70/627/VN 26, COL/67/208/VN 38, CUN/66/552/VN 42, CUN/66/703/VN 45, SHA/66/5/VN 49, SHA/65/205/VN 52, COA/66/877/VN 54, FOR/66/661/VN 55, MISC/67/41/VN 56, MISC/67/11/VN 58, CUN/67/31/VN 59, (Ron Ryan) 61, BEL/69/858/VN 85, BEL/69/395/VN 91, BEL/69/372/VN 92, COM /69/48/VN 99, COM /69/738/VN 100, FAI/70/590/VN 101 above, PJE/71/109/ VN 101 below, LES/69/637/ VN 111, COM/69/250/VN 120, FAI /70/404/ VN 124, P671/14/01 155, ERR/68/716/VN 164, ERR / 68 / 708/ VN 173; *The Boarder Morning Mail* 189 below; John Fairfax and Sons Ltd 71; Frank Frost 1 (18; Elizabeth Gilliam 195, 197, 211, 221, 222; Mr and Mrs Gordon Granl 189 above; Mirror Australian Telegraph Publications 77 above and below, 79, 145 above, 214, 217, 219 (W. Harrison); National Library of Australia 11, 19, 46, 47, 48, 50–51, 94, 139, 152, 157, 161; Jane Ross 194, 208; Semper Floreal 154, 156, 158; The Stale Library of Victoria 186, 190. 225; *Sun Herald* 150.

Facing pages are listed. Unless otherwise stated, photographs were supplied by the Australian War Memorial, whose file numbers are quoted. EKN / 67 /150 / VN 16 EKN / 67 /130 / VN 17 CT / WAR / 70 / 52F / VN 32 above. EKN/67/138/VN32 below EKT/68/83/VN33 above CN7JON/70/438/VN33 below EKT/69/5/VN48 EKN/69/23/VN49EKT/69/21/VN64 above EKN / 69/140/VN 64 below EKN/69/120/VN 65 above EKN/66/CUN/65/VN65 below CN/JON/70/463/VN above EKN/68/18/VN below EKN/67/COL/85/VN97 above CT/CN/MISC/71/720/VN97 below EKT/COL/67/42/VNU2 above EKN/ 68 /162 / VN 112 below EKN / 69 / 135 / VN 113 above EKN / 69 / 96 / VN 113 below EKN / 67 /145 / VN 144 EKN/ 69 /144 / VN between 144 4 145 above left National Library of Australia between 144 4 145 below left EKT / 67/47/VN between 144 & 145 right EKN/68/138/VN 145 above EKT/COL/67/56/VN 145 below EKN / 69 / 67 / VN 160 EKT / 69 / 57 / VN between 160 & 161 left EKT / 67/MISC/14/VN between 160 & 161 above right KN / 69 /164 / VN between 160 4 161 below right EKN / 68 / 153 / VN 161 above EKN / 68 / 144 / VN 161 below; Jack Thurgar and Charles Wright 192; *The Bulletin* 193 above; EKN / 69 / 81 / VN 193 below; Rob McIntyre 208, 209; Sipa-Press 216, between 216 & 217 left; Australian Overseas Information Service between 216 4 217 right, 217 above and below.

LYRICS
Part of the lyrics of 'Almost Cut My Hair' by D. Crosby, reprinted by kind permission of Polygram Records 172.
Lyrics of 'I Was Only Nineteen' reproduced by permission of John Schumann and the publishers, MCA Music Chris Gilbey Pty Ltd 196.

MAPS
Allen and Unwin 90, Stan Lamond 12.

PRINTED MATTER
Details concerning previously published material are to be found in the Notes relating to each essay. Allen and Unwin 173; Angus and Robertson/Collins 123; *The Advertiser* 130; *The Age* 128,135; Bodley Head 12, 24: *The Courier Mail* 128, 134, 135; *The Daily Bulletin* 192; *The Daily Mirror* 130; *The Daily Telegraph* 136; *Debrief* 193, 200; Department of the Parliamentary Library 118; Harper and Row 181; William Heinemann Australia 179; A.D. Hope c/- Curtis Brown (Aust) Pty Ltd Sydney 169; Denis Kevans 175; *The Sunday Telegraph* 174; *The Sydney Morning Herald* 129, 134, 210; V.I.E.W. World 182; *The West Australian* 128.

THE AUTHORS

Gregory Pemberton, of the Australian War Memorial, the editor of this volume, has published on the diplomatic and strategic policies which led Australia into the Vietnam War. He is co-author of the political and diplomatic volumes of the official history of *Australia in the Southeast Asian Conflicts*.

Greg Lockhart, of the Australian National University, is an internationally recognised historian of the military conflict in Vietnam.

Ann Mari Jordens has published widely on the political and social impact of the Vietnam War in Australia. She is co-author of the political and social volumes of The Australian War Memorial's Official History of Australia's involvement in the Vietnam war.

Frank Frost, of the Parliamentary Research Service in Canberra, is an acknowledged authority on Australia's military involvement in Vietnam.

Rodney Tiffen, of the University of Sydney, has taught and published extensively on the media and politics in Australia. He is the author of *News and Power* and co-editor of *Australia's Gulf War*.

Ann Curthoys, Professor of History at the Australian National University, is an historian who has spent many years investigating Australian attitudes to the war in Vietnam.

Peter Cochrane teaches history at Sydney University and is a freelance writer. He has a particular interest in myths and legends and their relationships to national culture as well as a general interest in social change in Australian society.

Jane Ross has published work on the Australian army in the world wars and in Vietnam, and is working on an oral history of soldiers' experiences of the Vietnam war. She is currently working as an Equity Officer at Charles Sturt University.

Nancy Viviani, of Griffith University, Queensland, is Professor of International Politics, and has made several studies of Vietnamese migration and settlement in Australia.

New Holland Publishers

Level 1, 178 Fox Valley Road, Wahroonga, NSW 2076, Australia

newhollandpublishers.com

First published in 1990 by Kevin Weldon & Associates Pty Ltd
Reprinted 1991
Reprinted in 1993 and 1996 (limp) by Landsdowne Publishing Pty Ltd
Reprinted in 2002 by New Holland Publishers
Updated edition published in 2009 and re-printed in 2017
This edition published in 2024 by New Holland Publishers

Copyright © 1990 New Holland Publishers

A record of this book is held at the National Library of Australia.

ISBN: 9781760796020

Managing Director: Fiona Schultz
Designer: Andrew Davies
Production Director: Arlene Gippert
Printed in China

All rights reserved. No part of this publication may be reproduced, stored in a retrieval system or transmitted, in any form or by any means, electronic, mechanical, photocopying, recording or otherwise, without the prior written permission of the publishers and copyright holders.

The publisher acknowledges the role of Professor Kenneth Maddock in drawing up the initial outline for this book.

Keep up with New Holland Publishers:
NewHollandPublishers
@newhollandpublishers